# An Introduction to Investment Banks, Hedge Funds, and Private Equity

## The New Paradigm

# Companion Web Site

Ancillary materials are available online at:
www.elsevierdirect.com/companions/9780123745033

# An Introduction to Investment Banks, Hedge Funds, and Private Equity
## The New Paradigm

David P. Stowell
Kellogg School of Management
Northwestern University

AMSTERDAM • BOSTON • HEIDELBERG • LONDON
NEW YORK • OXFORD • PARIS • SAN DIEGO
SAN FRANCISCO • SINGAPORE • SYDNEY • TOKYO
Academic Press is an imprint of Elsevier

Academic Press is an imprint of Elsevier
30 Corporate Drive, Suite 400, Burlington, MA 01803, USA
525 B Street, Suite 1900, San Diego, California 92101–4495, USA
84 Theobald's Road, London WC1X 8RR, UK

**Library of Congress Cataloging-in-Publication Data**
Stowell, David.
    An introduction to investment banks, hedge funds, and
private equity : the new paradigm / David Stowell.
        p. cm.
    Includes bibliographical references and index.
    ISBN 978-0-12-374503-3 (casebound : alk. paper)
1. Investment banking. 2. Hedge funds. 3. Private equity.
4. Finance–History–21st century. I. Title.
    HG4534.S76 2010
    332.66–dc22
                                    2009050831

**British Library Cataloguing-in-Publication Data**
A catalogue record for this book is available from the British Library.

ISBN: 978-0-12-374503-3

For information on all Academic Press publications
visit our Web site at www.elsevierdirect.com

Printed in the United States of America
10   11   12   9   8   7   6   5   4   3   2   1

For Janet, Paul, Lauren, Audrey, Julia and Peter

# Contents

# Preface

The world of finance has experienced a paradigm shift following the global financial meltdown of 2007–2009. Market participants have been significantly impacted and attitudes about risk, transparency, regulation and compensation have changed. Investment banks, hedge funds and private equity firms are at the epicenter of a transformed financial landscape, forging new roles and seeking new ways to create value in an environment of lower risk and greater regulation. This book provides an overview of investment banks, hedge funds and private equity firms and describes the relationships between these organizations: how they simultaneously compete with and provide important services to each other, and the significant impact they have on corporations, governments, institutional investors and individuals. Together, they have reshaped global financing and investing patterns, attracting envy and awe but also criticism and concern. They dominate the headlines of the financial press and create wealth for many of their managers and investing clients. This book enables readers to better understand these heavily interconnected organizations, their impact on the global financial market, principal activities, regulatory environment, historical development, and risks and opportunities in the post-crisis world.

Ultimately, the objective of this book is to demystify investment banks, hedge funds and private equity firms, revealing their key functions, compensation systems, unique role in wealth creation and risk management and their epic battle for investor funds and corporate influence. After reading this book, the reader should better understand financial press headlines that herald massive corporate takeovers, corporate shareholder activism, large capital market financings and the myriad strategies, risks, and conflicts in the financial market landscape. The inclusion of case studies and spreadsheet models provides an analytical framework that allows the reader to apply the book's lessons to real-world financing, investing and advisory activities.

## Target Audience

The target audience for this book includes MBA, MSF and Executive MBA students, and upper-level undergraduates who are focused on finance and investments. Investment banking classes can use this book as a primary text and corporate finance and investments classes can use the book either as a secondary text or as a principal text to focus on hedge funds and private equity. In addition, professionals working at investment banks, hedge funds and private equity firms can use the book to broaden understanding of their industry and competitors. Finally, professionals at law firms, accounting firms and other firms that advise investment banks, hedge funds and private equity firms should find this book useful as a resource to better understand and assist their clients.

## Distinguishing Features

This book is unique for two reasons. First, it is the product of a long career working for and with investment banks, hedge funds, and private equity firms, combined with five years in classrooms teaching students about these institutions. Second, by addressing investment banks, hedge funds, and private equity firms in the same book, and focusing on their simultaneous competition and cooperation the book provides a more holistic view of the changing boundaries and real-world impact of these institutions than has previously been available.

I wrote this book following a twenty year career as an investment banker at Goldman Sachs, JP Morgan and UBS, and an additional four years at O'Connor & Associates, a large hedge fund that is now part of UBS. As an investment banker, in addition to completing numerous M&A, debt and equity financing, equity derivative, and convertible transactions with corporate clients, I worked with private equity firms (financial sponsors) as they acquired companies and pursued exit strategies through recapitalizations, M&A sales and IPOs. Since 2005, I have been a professor of finance at Northwestern University's Kellogg School of Management, where I have had the privilege of teaching what I learned during my pre-academic career, while completing ongoing research into the ever-changing landscape of investment banks, hedge funds and private equity. The opportunity to teach bright students at a first class business school has provided great feedback and a forum to refine concepts and make them more relevant to students. This book is therefore a product of both real world and academic experience, creating a new educational offering that more fully opens the door to understanding the key participants in the global financial and advisory markets.

## Cases

The inclusion of ten cases facilitates greater understanding of the concepts described in the chapters. These cases focus on recent actual financial and advisory transactions and include a summary of risks, rewards, political considerations, impact on corporations and investors, competition, regulatory hurdles and other subjects that are linked to chapter topics. The cases include questions for students and case notes and teaching suggestions for instructors. In addition, several cases include spreadsheet models that allow readers to create an analytical framework for considering choices, opportunities and risks that are described in the cases. The cases are assembled together at the end of the book, but are all linked to preceding chapters. As a result, cases are designed to be used in conjunction with chapter reading to reinforce concepts and enhance learning.

## The World Has Changed

During 2008, Bear Stearns collapsed into a fire-sale to JP Morgan, Lehman Brothers declared bankruptcy, Fannie Mae and Freddie Mac were placed into U.S. government conservatorship, the U.S. government assumed majority control over AIG after injecting over $100 billion to keep it afloat, under duress, Countrywide and Merrill Lynch both sold themselves to Bank of America, Wells Fargo bought Wachovia at the brink of bankruptcy, Washington Mutual went into receivership with its branches absorbed by JP Morgan, Goldman Sachs and Morgan Stanley became bank holding companies, and banks all over the world had to be rescued by their respective governments. In the United States, this included the rapid provision to banks of over $200 billion of equity capital by the U.S. Treasury as part of a larger $700 billion rescue program, guarantees of debt and asset pools by the FDIC totaling many hundreds of billions of dollars, and an unprecedented expansion of the Federal Reserve's balance sheet by trillions of dollars as it provided credit based on almost any type of collateral.

All of this occurred as the world experienced the most significant, globalized downturn since the Great Depression of the 1930s.

The investment banking business, in many ways, will never be the same. Leverage has been reduced, some structured financial products have ceased to exist, and regulation has increased. However, the fundamental business remains unchanged: advising corporations and investors; raising and investing capital; executing trades as an intermediary and principal; providing research; making markets; and providing ideas and capital directly to clients. As investment banks reinvent some aspects of their business and learn to live in a world of decreased leverage and increased regulation, new opportunities loom large, while issues such as public perception, compensation, and risk management must be carefully worked through.

Hedge funds and private equity funds suffered significant reversals during 2008, with hedge funds recording investment losses of over 19% on average and private equity firms acknowledging similar potential losses to their investors. Although these results were undesirable and caused some investors to abandon funds, the global equity markets fared even worse, with the major U.S. stock market indices dropping by more than 38% and other equity and non-government debt indices throughout the world posting similar, or greater, losses. Hedge funds and private equity have had to adjust to a changing landscape and re-explain their value proposition while contending with downsizing in the number of funds, assets under management and return expectations. Reinvention and patience were the watchwords during the global financial crisis as these funds fought to hold on to as many limited partners as they could while considering new investment strategies for a credit-deficient world. During 2009, many hedge funds and private equity firms bounced back, with positive returns for most hedge funds and a refocus on smaller and less leveraged investments the hallmark of private equity investment activity.

Investment banks, hedge funds and private equity firms have redefined their roles and developed new processes and business plans designed to maintain historical positions of power and influence. The world has changed, but these institutions will continue to have a significant impact on global capital markets and M&A transactions. This book projects how they will achieve this, and the resultant impact on corporations, governments, institutional investors and individuals.

# Structure of the Book

The book is divided into three sections. The first section is comprised of ten chapters that focus on investment banks. The second section includes five chapters that discuss hedge funds and five chapters that review the activities of private equity firms. The third section of the book includes ten cases that focus on recent transactions and developments in the financial markets. These cases are cross-referenced in the preceding chapters and are used to illustrate concepts that benefit from more rigorous analysis.

# Section One: Investment Banking

This section includes ten chapters that provide an overview of the industry and the three principal divisions of most large investment banks, including descriptions of the M&A and financing activities of the banking division; the intermediation and market-making, as well as principal (proprietary) activities of the trading division; and the investment gathering and money management activities of the asset management division. In addition, the other businesses of large investment banks and the activities of boutique investment banks are reviewed. Other chapters focus in more detail on financings, including the activities of capital markets groups and the underwriting function, and discussion of IPOs, follow-on equity offerings, convertibles and debt transactions. The role of credit rating agencies, prime brokerage groups, structured credit, derivatives and exchanges is also explored. Finally, regulations, leverage, risk management, clearing and settlement, international investment banking, career opportunities and the interrelationship between investment banks, hedge funds and private equity is discussed. The capstone chapters in this section of the book drill deeply into M&A, convertible securities and investment bank innovation.

Section One is designed to be used as the text for a full course on investment banking. It should be used in conjunction with cases in Section Three that are specifically referenced in Section One chapters. Section Two's hedge fund and private equity chapters may be used as supplemental material.

## Section Two: Hedge Funds and Private Equity

The **first** five chapters of Section Two focus on hedge funds, including an overview of the industry; a focus on selected hedge fund investment strategies; shareholder activism and impact of hedge fund activists on corporations; risk, regulation and organizational structure of hedge funds; and a review of performance, risks, threats and opportunities, as well as the changing value proposition offered by hedge funds to their limited investor partners. Finally, hedge fund competition with investment banks and private equity is reviewed, as well as the symbiotic relationship between all three parties.

The **second** five chapters of Section Two examine private equity from the perspective of those firms that principally focus on leveraged buyouts (LBOs) and other equity investments in mature companies. These chapters provide an overview of private equity; an explanation of an LBO model and how it drives decision-making; private equity impact on corporations, including a case history of more than a dozen LBO transactions; a description of organization, compensation, regulation and limited partner relationships; and a discussion of private equity issues and opportunities, diversification efforts, IPOs, historical performance and relationships with hedge funds and investment banks.

Section Two is designed to be used as the text for a full course that focuses on Hedge Funds and Private Equity. It should be used in conjunction with cases in Part Three that are specifically referenced in Section Two chapters. Section One's investment banking chapters may also be used as supplemental material.

## Section Three: Cases

This section contains ten cases that are referenced in different chapters in Sections One and Two. The cases enable students to drill deeper into the subject matter of the chapters and apply concepts in the framework of real transactions and developments. Case questions and teaching notes for each case are provided, as well as several spreadsheet models that enable students to manipulate data. The cases focus on the following: the dramatic change in the global investment banking landscape that occurred during the 2008 financial crisis; the use of equity derivatives by Porsche and CSX as these two corporations interacted with investment banks and hedge funds in effecting significant corporate change; Cerberus's investments in Chrysler and GMAC (GM's captive finance subsidiary); the divergent CDO investment strategies of two hedge funds, which, in the first case, resulted in excellent returns, and in the second case, caused bankruptcy; Freeport McMoRan's acquisition of Phelps Dodge, which focuses on M&A, risk taking and financing activities; the acquisition through a bankruptcy court process and management of Kmart and Sears by ESL, one of the world's largest hedge funds; Procter & Gamble's acquisition of Gillette, including the advisory role of investment bankers and discussion of corporate governance and regulatory issues; the LBO of Toys R Us, focusing on the role of private equity funds and investment banks; and activist hedge fund investor Pershing Square's impact on the capital and organizational structure of McDonald's Corporation.

# Acknowledgments

I am very grateful to many who have contributed to this publication. My wife, Janet, and children (Paul, Lauren, Audrey, Julia and Peter) have been patient and supportive during the more than two year process of researching and writing this book. When I decided to become an academic, they assumed that my investment banker work-week would drop from 70+ hours to less than half that amount. This has not been the case, as I learned that academics work long hours too, and the book added many hours to my schedule. My oldest son, Paul, is a banker, derivatives structurer, and former convertibles trader, and I relied on and appreciated his wisdom in thinking through the organization of the book and benefited from technical suggestions he made. I wish to thank Xiaowei Zhang, who worked in my team at JP Morgan, for her very diligent and efficient contributions as my principal assistant during the editing and model production stage of this project. I was very fortunate to be able to rely on her many talents during an interlude in her investment banking career.

As I transitioned from practitioner to academic over past 5 years, many finance department colleagues and administrators at Northwestern University's Kellogg School of Management offered support for this project and me. Special thanks to Kathleen Haggerty for her assistance from the Office of the Dean and to senior finance department faculty members Robert Korajczyk, Robert McDonald and Mitchell Petersen for providing valuable suggestions regarding the content of the book.

I am indebted to the following colleagues and friends from investment banks who provided excellent input to selected chapters:

John Gilbertson, Managing Director, Goldman Sachs
Mark Goldstein, Managing Director, Deutsche Bank
Cary Kochman, Managing Director, UBS
David Topper, Managing Director, JP Morgan
Jeffrey Vergamini, Executive Director, Morgan Stanley
Jeffrey Zajkowski, Managing Director, JP Morgan
Xiaoyin Zhang, Managing Director, Goldman Sachs

The following professionals provided greatly appreciated information regarding hedge funds and private equity firms, as well as suggestions regarding legal, regulatory and tax topics in the book:

Bryan Bloom, Principal, W.R. Huff Asset Management Co.
Deirdre Connell, Partner, Jenner & Block
Thomas Formolo, Partner, Code Hennessy & Simmons
Margaret Gibson, Partner, Kirkland & Ellis
Jason Krejci, Vice President, Standard & Poor's
Anna Pinedo, Partner, Morrison & Foerster
James Neary, Managing Director, Warburg Pincus
Joel Press, Managing Director, Morgan Stanley
James Rickards, Senior Managing Director, Omnis

Chirag Saraiya, Principal, Training the Street
Phillip Torres, Portfolio Manager, ForeSix Asset Management
Catherine Vaughn, Managing Director, Highbridge Capital Management
Julie Winkler, Managing Director, CME Group
Elaine Wolff, Partner, Jenner & Block

I express appreciation to Kellogg PhD candidates Fritz Burkhardt and Jonathan Brogaard and Northwestern undergraduate research assistants Esther Lee, Tom Hughes, Anya Hayden and Ashley Heyer for their work on this book. Finally, I appreciate the patience and guidance extended to me by my contacts at Elsevier, especially Scott Bentley, Executive Editor and Kathleen Paoni, Development Editor.

# Investment Banking

# Overview of Investment Banking

The material in this chapter should be cross-referenced with **Case Study 1, "Investment Banking in 2008 (A),"** and **Case Study 2, "Investment Banking in 2008 (B)."**

Investment banking changed dramatically during the 20-year period preceding the global financial crisis that started in mid 2007 as market forces pushed banks from their traditional low-risk role of advising and intermediating to a position of taking considerable risk for their own account and on behalf of clients. This high level of risk-taking, combined with high leverage, transformed the industry during 2008, when several major firms failed, huge trading losses were recorded, and many firms were forced to reorganize their business.

Risk-taking activities of investment banks were reduced following large losses that stemmed primarily from mortgage-related assets, bad loans, and an overall reduction in revenues due to the financial crisis. This led to an industry-wide effort to reduce leverage and a string of new equity capital issuances. By the end of 2008, five *pure-play* investment banks headquartered in the United States that did not operate deposit-taking businesses (unlike large *universal* banks such as J.P. Morgan, which operated a large investment bank, a deposit-taking business, and other businesses) had undergone significant transformations: Goldman Sachs and Morgan Stanley converted into bank holding companies; the U.S. Federal Reserve (Fed) pushed Bear Stearns into the arms of J.P. Morgan to avoid a bankruptcy; Lehman Brothers filed for bankruptcy protection after the Fed and Treasury Department ignored its pleas for government support; and Merrill Lynch, presumably to avoid a similar bankruptcy filing, agreed to sell their firm to Bank of America (see Exhibit 1.1).

Historically through 1999, U.S. banks with deposit-taking businesses (commercial banks) were barred from operating investment banking businesses. This rule was created by the

---

**Transformation of Pure-Play/Non-Deposit Taking Investment Banks**

- Bear Stearns: sold to J.P. Morgan on March 16, 2008[1]
- Lehman Brothers: filed for bankruptcy protection on September 14, 2008
    - Sold U.S. operations to Barclays on September 16, 2008
    - Sold part of European and Asian operations to Nomura on September 22, 2008
- Merrill Lynch: sold to Bank of America on September 14, 2008[2]
- Goldman Sachs: converted to bank holding company on September 21, 2008
- Morgan Stanley: converted to bank holding company on September 21, 2008

Note 1: Initial price of sale at $2 per share was increased to $10 under a revised agreement on March 24, 2008.
Note 2: Date of announcement; deal completed on January 1, 2009.

**EXHIBIT 1.1**

Glass-Steagall Banking Act of 1933, which was enacted after the stock market crash of 1929 to protect depositors' assets. In 1999, the Gramm-Leach-Bliley Act overturned the requirement to keep investment banks and commercial banks separate, and led to the formation of U.S.-headquartered universal investment banks, including J.P. Morgan, Citigroup, and Bank of America. Two of the main arguments for rejoining these two kinds of businesses were (1) to provide for a more stable and countercyclical business model for these banks, and (2) to allow U.S. banks to better compete with international counterparts (e.g., UBS, Credit Suisse, and Deutsche Bank) that were less encumbered by the Glass-Steagall Act. As a result, Citigroup, which was created through the 1998 merger of Citicorp and Travelers Group (which owned the investment bank Salomon Brothers), did not have to divest Salomon Brothers in order to comply with federal regulations. J.P. Morgan and Bank of America followed the lead of Citigroup in combining businesses to create universal investment banks. These banks rapidly developed a broad-based investment banking business, hiring many professionals from pure-play investment banks and strategically using their significant lending capability as a platform from which they were able to capture investment banking market share.

## Post-Crisis Global Investment Banking Firms

As of 2009, the surviving nine key global firms that encompass both investment banking and deposit-taking businesses and operate throughout the world included J.P. Morgan, Bank of America, Citigroup, Credit Suisse, UBS, Deutsche Bank, Barclays, Goldman Sachs, and Morgan Stanley. See Exhibits 1.2, 1.3, 1.4, and 1.5 for a summary of financial results, financial measures, and market capitalization for these nine firms.

**Financial Results**

| Firm | 2008 Net Revenues (in millions) | 2008 Net Earnings (in millions)[1] | 2008 Return on Equity (ROE)[2] | 2008 Price/Book Value[3] | Mid-2009 Net Earnings |
|---|---|---|---|---|---|
| Bank of America | $72,782 | $4,008 | 1.80% | 1.4 | $7,471 |
| Barclays[4] | $42,420 | $9,703 | 12.00% | 1.1 | $3,481 |
| Citigroup | $52,793 | ($32,094) | -47.70% | 1.2 | $6,081 |
| Credit Suisse[5] | $10,009 | ($7,118) | -24.00% | 1.5 | $3,184 |
| Deutsche Bank[6] | $19,830 | ($5,637) | -12.50% | 1.0 | $3,006 |
| Goldman Sachs | $22,222 | $2,322 | 4.30% | 1.0 | $5,249 |
| JPMorgan Chase | $67,252 | $3,699 | 2.20% | 1.6 | $4,862 |
| Morgan Stanley | $24,739 | $1,807 | 5.30% | 0.6 | ($345) |
| UBS[5] | $4,096 | ($19,372) | -64.30% | 1.5 | ($2,627) |

Note 1: Earnings exclude discontinued operations and extraordinary gains.
Note 2: Return on common equity computed by dividing net earnings to common shareholders from continuing operations by common shareholders' equity. Excludes extraordinary gains.
Note 3: Book value of common shareholders' equity adjusting for goodwill and intangible assets. Market capitalization as of December 31, 2008.
Note 4: Calculated at 2008 average GBP/USD rate of 1.84 and 1H-2009 average GBP/USD rate of 1.49.
Note 5: Calculated at 2008 average CHF/USD rate of 0.93 and 1H-2009 average CHF/USD rate of 0.89.
Note 6: Calculated at 2008 average EUR/USD rate of 1.47 and 1H-2009 average of EUR/USD rate of 1.33.
Source: Respective 2008 10-K and 1H-2009 10-Q filings

EXHIBIT 1.2

**Financial Measures**

| Firm | Credit Ratings[1] | 2008 Total Assets (in millions) | Average 2008 Daily VaR (in millions)[2] | Number of Employees |
|---|---|---|---|---|
| Bank of America | AA- | $1,817,943 | $111 | 243,000 |
| Barclays[3] | AA- | $2,971,027 | $798 | 156,000 |
| Citigroup | A | $1,938,470 | $292 | 326,900 |
| Credit Suisse[4] | A | $1,108,181 | $163 | 47,800 |
| Deutsche Bank[5] | A+ | $3,104,190 | $179 | 80,456 |
| Goldman Sachs | A | $884,547 | $180 | 30,067 |
| JPMorgan Chase | A+ | $2,175,052 | $202 | 228,452 |
| Morgan Stanley | A | $658,812 | $135 | 46,964 |
| UBS[4] | A+ | $1,907,788 | $347 | 77,783 |

Note 1: S&P rating for long-term debt in respective 2008 annual reports.

Note 2: Barclays, Goldman Sachs and Morgan Stanley's average daily value-at-risk (VaR's) are calculated based on a 95% confidence level. All others are based on a 99% confidence level.

Note 3: Assets calculated at GBP/USD rate of 1.45 on December 31, 2008; VaR calculated at average GBP/USD rate of 1.84.

Note 4: Assets calculated at CHF/USD rate of 0.95 on December 31, 2008; VaR calculated at average CFH/USD rate of 0.92.

Note 5: Assets calculated at EUR/USD rate of 1.41 on December 31, 2008; VaR calculated at average EUR/USD rate of 1.46.

Source: Respective 2008 10-K filings

**EXHIBIT 1.3**

**Leverage and Average ROE**

| Firm | Leverage (Assets / Equity) | | | | Avg. ROE[1] |
|---|---|---|---|---|---|
| | YE-06 | YE-07 | YE-08 | Mid-09 | 2004-2008 |
| Bank of America | 10.8 | 11.7 | 10.3 | 10.0 | 13.2% |
| Barclays[2] | 39.2 | 41.4 | 49.8 | 41.0 | 17.6% |
| Citigroup | 15.7 | 19.3 | 13.7 | 12.1 | 3.8% |
| Credit Suisse | 28.8 | 31.5 | 36.2 | 30.1 | 12.6% |
| Deutsche Bank[2] | 34.3 | 50.8 | 71.7 | 50.5 | 9.7% |
| Goldman Sachs | 23.4 | 26.2 | 13.7 | 14.2 | 21.9% |
| JPMorgan Chase | 11.7 | 12.7 | 13.0 | 13.1 | 8.3% |
| Morgan Stanley | 31.7 | 33.4 | 13.0 | 14.5 | 13.8% |
| UBS[2] | 48.2 | 61.7 | 61.9 | 47.7 | -1.1% |

Note 1: ROE calculated based on net income from continuing operations available to common equity holders divided by average common shareholders equity.

Note 2: Barclays, Deutsche Bank and UBS financials are presented under IFRS standards. All other banks are presented according to U.S. GAAP. A major difference between IFRS and U.S. GAAP is the accounting for derivatives, non-derivative trading assets, and reverse repos/borrowed securities. The former shows gross exposures while the latter shows values on a net basis. For example, after taking into consideration the netting impact of U.S. GAAP accounting, Deutsche Bank's total assets at year-end 2008 drops from EUR 2,202 billion to EUR 1,030 billion. According to Deutsche Bank's targeted leverage ratio definition, which adjusts for U.S. GAAP netting rules (and some additional minor adjustments), its adjusted assets / adjusted equity ratio was 28 at December 31, 2008.

Source: Respective 10-K and 10-Q filings; Deutsche Bank roadshow presentation from February 19 – 20, 2009

**EXHIBIT 1.4**

**Share Price and Market Capitalization**

| Bank | Mid-2007 Share Price[1] | End of 2008 Share Price[2] | % Change | Mid-2009 Share Price[3] | Mid-2009 Market Cap |
|------|------------------------:|---------------------------:|---------:|------------------------:|--------------------:|
| Bank of America | $ 48.89 | $ 14.08 | -71% | $ 13.20 | $ 114,200 |
| Barclays | $ 55.79 | $ 9.80 | -82% | $ 18.44 | $ 50,839 |
| Citigroup | $ 51.29 | $ 6.71 | -87% | $ 2.97 | $ 16,358 |
| Credit Suisse | $ 70.96 | $ 28.26 | -60% | $ 45.73 | $ 54,181 |
| Deutsche Bank | $ 144.74 | $ 40.69 | -72% | $ 61.00 | $ 37,704 |
| Goldman Sachs[4] | $ 216.75 | $ 84.39 | -61% | $ 147.44 | $ 77,391 |
| J.P. Morgan | $ 48.45 | $ 31.53 | -35% | $ 34.11 | $ 133,851 |
| Morgan Stanley[4] | $ 69.37 | $ 16.04 | -77% | $ 28.51 | $ 38,751 |
| UBS | $ 60.01 | $ 14.30 | -76% | $ 12.21 | $ 39,492 |

Note 1: Closing price as of June 29, 2007.
Note 2: Closing price as of December 31, 2008.
Note 3: Closing price as of June 30, 2009.
Note 4: Morgan Stanley and Goldman Sachs were formerly pure-play investment banks, but are now considered universal investment banks since they converted to bank holding companies.
Source: Respective 1H-2009 10-Q filings; share price data provided by Commodity Systems Inc.

**EXHIBIT 1.5**

## Other Investment Banking Firms

In addition to these nine key global investment banks, other large banks compete effectively in regional markets worldwide and, in some countries, have a larger market share for investment banking business than the nine designated global banks. Examples of banks in the category of large regional investment banks include HSBC, Société Générale, BNP Paribas, CIBC, MUFG, Sumitomo Mitsui, Mizuho, Nomura, and Macquarie. Other firms that engage in investment banking business on a more limited scale are called *boutique banks*. Boutique banks principally focus on merger and acquisition (M&A)–related activity, although some participate in other businesses such as financial restructuring, money management, or proprietary investments. Retail brokerage firms are securities firms that narrowly compete with large investment banks in relation to retail client investments in stocks and bonds. They generally do not conduct a full investment banking business. See Exhibit 1.6 for a sampling of banks that compete in each of these areas.

## Investment Banking Businesses

Although each investment bank takes a somewhat different approach, the principal businesses of most large investment banks include an (a) investment banking business managed by the Investment Banking Division, which focuses on capital raising and M&A transactions for corporate clients and capital raising for government clients; (b) sales and trading business managed by the Trading Division, which provides investing, intermediating, and risk-management services to institutional investor clients, performs research, and also participates in nonclient-related investing activities; and (c) asset management business managed by the Asset Management Division, which is responsible for managing money for individual and institutional investing clients (see Exhibit 1.7).

Within the nine large global investment banks, Goldman Sachs and Morgan Stanley are examples of more narrowly focused investment banks. They operate each of the businesses

## Investment Banking Firms

| Global Investment Banks | Large Regional Investment Banks | Boutique Investment Banks | Retail Brokerage Firms[1] |
|---|---|---|---|
| • Bank of America<br>• Barclays<br>• Citigroup<br>• Credit Suisse<br>• Deutsche Bank<br>• Goldman Sachs<br>• J.P. Morgan<br>• Morgan Stanley<br>• UBS | • BNP Paribas<br>• CIBC<br>• HSBC<br>• Macquarie<br>• Mizuho<br>• MUFG<br>• Nomura<br>• Royal Bank of Canada<br>• Royal Bank of Scotland<br>• Société Générale<br>• Standard Chartered Bank<br>• Sumitomo Mitsui<br>• Wells Fargo | • Broadpoint Gleacher<br>• Evercore Partners<br>• Greenhill & Co.<br>• Houlihan Lokey<br>• Jefferies & Co.<br>• Keefe, Bruyette & Woods<br>• Lazard<br>• Moelis & Co.<br>• Perella Weinberg Partners<br>• Rothschild<br>• William Blair | • Charles Schwab<br>• Commonwealth Financial Network<br>• E*Trade<br>• Edward Jones<br>• LPL Financial<br>• Royal Alliance<br>• Scottrade<br>• TD Ameritrade |

Note 1: Retail brokerage firms generally do not provide a full range of investment banking products and services.

**EXHIBIT 1.6**

## Principal Businesses of Investment Banks

### Investment Banking Business
- Arranges financings for corporation and governments
  - Debt
  - Equity
  - Convertibles
- Advises on mergers and acquisitions (M&A) transactions

### Trading Business
- Client Trading
  - Sells and trades securities and other financial assets as an intermediary on behalf of investing clients
  - Operates in two business units: (1) Equity and (2) Fixed Income, Currency & Commodities (FICC) [1]
  - Research is provided to investing clients
- Proprietary Trading and Principal Investing[2]
  - Investment activity by the firm that affects the firm's accounts, but does not involve investing clients
  - Focused on investments in equity (public and private), bonds, convertibles and derivatives in a manner similar to the investment activities of hedge funds and private equity funds

### Asset Management Business
- Offers equity, fixed income, alternative investments, and money market investment products and services to individual and institutional clients
- For alternative investment products, the firm co-invests with clients in hedge fund, private equity and real estate funds

Note 1: Fixed income refers to an investment such as a bond that yields a regular (or fixed) periodic return; currency refers to foreign exchange (FX); commodities refers principally to energy and metals based commodities.

Note 2: At some firms, Principal Investing is included within the Investment Banking Business.

**EXHIBIT 1.7**

described above and recently added deposit-taking as a new business, following their transformation to bank holding companies. However, they do not participate in most non-investment banking businesses that the other global firms conduct. J.P. Morgan and Barclays are examples of more broadly focused financial organizations that operate a large investment banking business, but also conduct large non-investment banking businesses. See Exhibits 1.8 and 1.9 for an overview of the principal businesses of Goldman Sachs and J.P. Morgan, respectively.

## Investment Banking Division

The Investment Banking Division of an investment bank is responsible for working with corporations that seek to raise capital through public or private capital markets, risk-manage their existing capital, or complete an M&A-related transaction. In addition, at some firms, this division has increasingly provided financing through direct investments in corporate equity and debt securities, and provided loans to corporate clients. Finally, this division helps government-related entities raise funds and manage risk. Individuals who work in the Investment Banking Division are called *bankers* and are assigned to work in either a product group or a client coverage group (see Exhibit 1.10). The two key product groups are M&A and Capital Markets. In the M&A product group, bankers typically specialize by industry (and at some investment banks, they work within the industry coverage group). In the Capital Markets Group, bankers specialize by working in either debt capital markets or equity capital markets. Client coverage bankers are usually organized into industry groups, which typically focus on the following industries: healthcare,

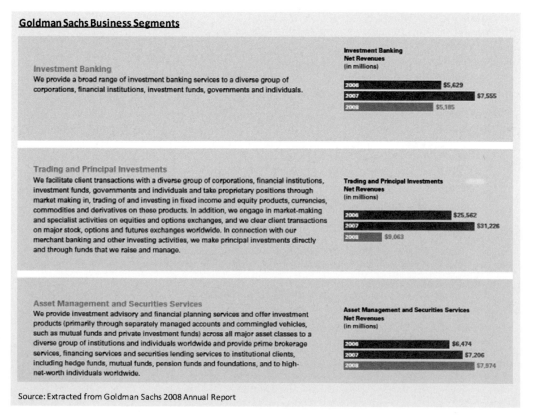

Source: Extracted from Goldman Sachs 2008 Annual Report

**EXHIBIT 1.8**

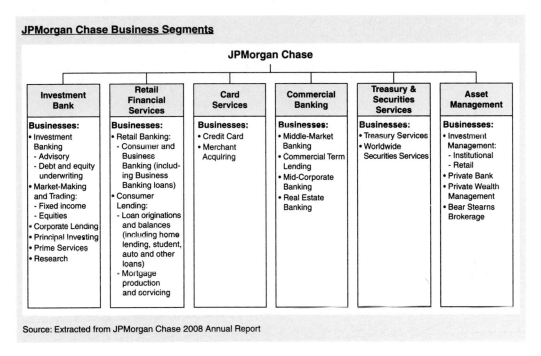

**EXHIBIT 1.9**

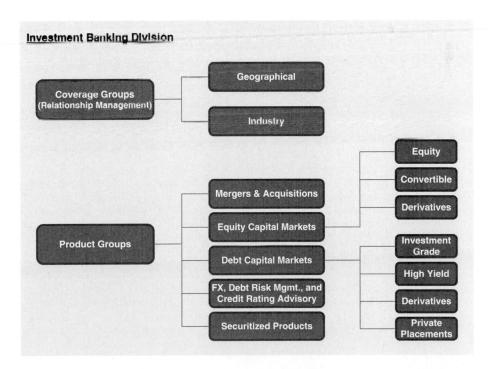

**EXHIBIT 1.10**

consumer, industrials, retail, energy, chemicals, financial institutions, real estate, financial sponsors, media and telecom, technology, and public finance, among others (see Exhibit 1.11). Exhibit 1.12 provides a summary of the product groups in Morgan Stanley's Investment Banking Division.

## Morgan Stanley Industry Coverage

| | |
|---|---|
| Basic Materials | Industrials |
| Consumer Products | Power and Utilities |
| Communications | Real Estate |
| Energy | Retail |
| Financial Institutions | Technology |
| Financial Sponsors | Transportation |
| Healthcare | |

Source: *Industry and Regional Coverage*. Morgan Stanley.  Web. 25 Aug. 2009.

**EXHIBIT 1.11**

## Morgan Stanley Product Groups

### Mergers and Acquisitions

Morgan Stanley's Mergers and Acquisitions (M&A) department devises and executes innovative, customized solutions to our clients' most challenging issues. The M&A team excels in domestic and international transactions including acquisitions, divestitures, mergers, joint ventures, corporate restructurings, recapitalizations, spin-offs, exchange offers, leveraged buyouts and takeover defenses as well as shareholder relations. Morgan Stanley applies its extensive experience with global industries, regions and banking products to meet our clients' short- and long-term strategic objectives.

### Global Capital Markets

Morgan Stanley's Global Capital Markets (GCM) group responds with market judgments and ingenuity to clients' needs for capital. Whether executing an IPO, a debt offering or a leveraged buyout, GCM integrates our expertise in Sales and Trading and in Investment Banking to offer clients seamless advice and sophisticated solutions. We originate, structure and execute public and private placement of a variety of securities: equities, investment-grade and non-investment-grade debt and related products. With fresh ideas and distribution capabilities in every major market, GCM works to help clients get the most value from each stage of a transaction. GCM also is continually developing capital market solutions to enable clients to mitigate strategic, operational, credit and market risks.

### Securitized Products Group

The Securitized Products Group (SPG) engages in a wide array of activities that include structuring, underwriting, and trading collateralized securities across the globe. SPG makes active markets and takes proprietary positions in the full range of asset-backed, residential mortgage-backed, commercial-backed and collateralized debt obligation securities in both the cash and synthetic markets. In addition, SPG originates commercial mortgage and single-family loans through conduit and loan purchase activities, and advises clients on securitization opportunities. Bringing together Morgan Stanley's Fixed Income and Investment Banking divisions, SPG draws on their expertise in finance, capital markets, trading and research to give clients the best of securitization finance.

Source: *Product Overview Services*. Morgan Stanley.  Web. 25 Aug. 2009.

**EXHIBIT 1.12**

## Client Coverage Bankers

Bankers assigned to industry teams are required to become global experts in the industry and understand the strategic and financing objectives of their assigned companies. They help CEOs and CFOs focus on corporate strategic issues such as how to enhance shareholder value. This sometimes leads to an M&A transaction in which clients sell the company or buy another company. These bankers also assist companies to achieve an optimal capital structure, with the appropriate amount of cash, equity, and debt on their balance sheet. This often leads to a capital markets transaction in which the company issues equity or debt, or repurchases outstanding securities. In short, client coverage bankers develop an in-depth understanding of a company's financial problems and objectives (within the context of its industry) and deliver the full resources of the investment bank in an effort to assist their clients. They are the key relationship managers and provide a centralized point of contact for corporate clients of the investment bank.

A financing or M&A assignment usually results in a partnership between client coverage bankers and product bankers to execute the transaction for a corporate client. Other investment banking services can also be introduced by the client coverage banker to the company, including risk management and hedging advice in relation to interest rate, energy, or foreign exchange risks; credit rating advice; and corporate restructuring advice. There are product bankers who are responsible for each of these product areas (which are a much smaller source of revenue compared to the capital markets and M&A product areas). Sometimes the role of the client coverage banker is to encourage a corporate client to *not* complete a transaction if it is not in the best interests of that client. The banker's mission is to become a trusted advisor to clients as they complete appropriate transactions that maximize shareholder value and minimize corporate risk.

In order for client coverage bankers to be helpful to their clients, bankers must first develop strong relationships with CEOs and CFOs, and subsequently with corporate development and treasury groups. The corporate development group usually reports to the CFO but sometimes directly to the CEO. Their role is to identify, analyze, and execute strategic transactions such as mergers, acquisitions, or divestitures. The treasury group reports to the CFO and focuses on acquiring and maintaining appropriate cash balances, achieving an optimal capital structure for the company, and risk managing the company's balance sheet. This group also manages the company's relationship with credit rating agencies. See Exhibit 1.13, which summarizes a client coverage banker's template for providing investment banking products and services to corporate clients.

Sometimes clients of the Investment Banking Division prefer being covered by bankers who work in geographical proximity to the client. As a result, some client coverage bankers may be assigned to cover clients based on a geographic coverage model rather than an industry coverage model. Each investment bank attempts to coordinate the activities of industry coverage and geographic coverage bankers in an effort to meet client preferences and achieve operating efficiency for the bank.

## Capital Markets Group

The Capital Markets Group is comprised of bankers who focus on either equity capital markets or debt capital markets.[1] At some investment banks, these two groups coordinate their activities and report to the same person, who oversees all capital markets transactions. At other banks, the

---

[1]Banks may subdivide the Capital Markets Group even further, for instance, by having a leveraged finance group that is separate from debt capital markets.

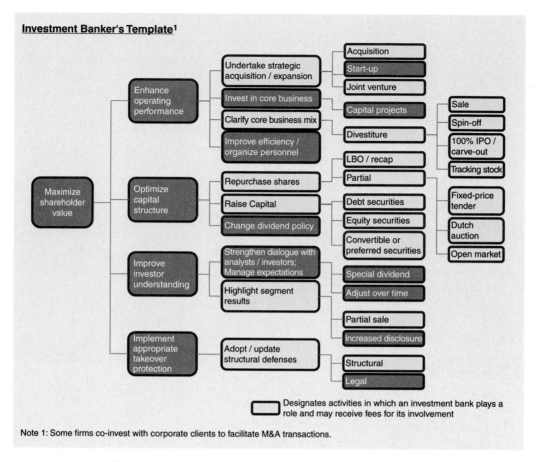

**EXHIBIT 1.13**

two groups report to different individuals and remain fairly autonomous. The Capital Markets Group operates either as a joint venture between the Investment Banking Division and the Trading Division, or is included solely within the Investment Banking Division. When issuers need to raise capital they work with a team comprised of a client coverage banker and a capital markets banker. The capital markets banker *executes* the capital raising by determining pricing, timing, size, and other aspects of the transaction in conjunction with sales professionals and traders in the Trading Division, who are responsible for creating investment products that meet the needs of their investing clients (see Exhibit 1.14).

### Equity Capital Markets

The Equity Capital Markets (ECM) business is comprised of bankers who specialize in common stock issuance, convertible security issuance, and equity derivatives. Common stock issuance includes initial public offerings (IPOs); follow-on offerings for companies that return to the capital markets for common stock offerings subsequent to issuing an IPO; secondary offerings for major shareholders of a company who wish to sell large *blocks* of common shares for which the proceeds are received by the selling shareholders and not by the company; and private placements, which do not require registration with a regulator. Convertible security issuance (see Chapters 3 and 9) usually takes the form of a bond or preferred share offering that is converted

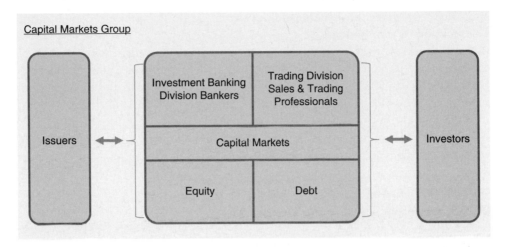

Capital Markets Group

| | | |
|---|---|---|
| Issuers ⟷ | Investment Banking Division Bankers | Trading Division Sales & Trading Professionals |
| | Capital Markets | |
| | Equity | Debt | ⟷ Investors |

**EXHIBIT 1.14**

(either by mandate or at the investor's option) into a predetermined number of the issuer's common shares. Equity derivatives enable companies to raise or retire equity capital, or hedge equity risks, through the use of options and forward contracts.

Bankers in ECM work closely with client coverage bankers to determine suitable corporate targets for equity-related products. If a company decides to complete an equity financing, ECM assumes primary responsibility for executing the transaction. This involves close coordination with sales and trading professionals in the Trading Division to determine the investment appetite of their clients. In essence, ECM intermediates between the Investment Banking Division's issuing clients, who want to sell securities at the highest possible price, and the Trading Division's investing clients, who want to buy securities at the lowest possible price. This poses a challenge that requires considerable dexterity to balance competing interests and structure an optimal equity-related security.

ECM and client coverage bankers must consider many issues with their corporate clients before initiating a transaction, including credit rating impact and whether the offering will be "bought" by the investment bank (with the resale price risk borne by the bank), or sold through a "book-building" process (with the price risk borne by the issuer). In addition, they focus on capital structure impact (including cost of capital considerations); earnings per share dilution; likely share price impact; shareholder perceptions; use of proceeds; and, if it is a *public offering* by a U.S. company, filing requirements with the SEC (Securities and Exchange Commission); as well as other issues. This process can take several weeks to several months to complete, depending on the vagaries of the market and potential issues raised by regulators.

## Debt Capital Markets

Bankers in Debt Capital Markets (DCM) focus principally on debt financings for corporate and government clients. Their clients can be grouped into two major categories: investment-grade and non-investment-grade issuers. Investment-grade issuers have a high credit rating from at least one of the major credit rating agencies (Baa or stronger from Moody's; BBB- or stronger from Standard & Poor's). Non-investment-grade issuers have lower ratings, and their debt offerings are sometimes called *junk bonds,* or *high-yield bonds.*

DCM bankers stand between corporate or government issuers (with whom relationships are maintained by client coverage bankers in the Investment Banking Division) and investors (covered by sales professionals in the Trading Division). Their role is to find a balance between the competing price objectives of issuers and investors, while facilitating communication and providing execution of transactions.

Bankers in DCM work closely with client coverage bankers to determine suitable corporate and government issuer targets and to help clients decide timing, maturity, size, covenants, call features, and other aspects of a debt financing. Of critical importance is the determination of the likely impact that a new debt offering will have on the company's credit ratings, and investor reaction to a potential offering.

In the U.S., DCM bankers help clients raise debt in the public capital markets through SEC-registered bond offerings or through privately placed 144A transactions (investors limited to qualified institutional investors). They also serve as the conduit through which a bank loan can be secured and provide debt risk management services (using derivatives) and advice regarding the potential credit rating impact of a debt issuance.

## M&A Group

At some investment banks, the M&A Group is an independent group from the client coverage group, although at other banks the two are blended. Regardless, most bankers specialize in one or more industries. Unlike the Capital Markets Group, which at some firms is a joint venture between the Investment Banking Division and the Trading Division, the M&A Group always falls under the sole responsibility of the Investment Banking Division.

The principal products of the M&A Group include: (a) *sell-side* transactions, which involve the sale or merger of an entire company or disposition of a division (or assets) of a company; (b) *buy-side* transactions, which involve the purchase of an entire company or a division (or assets) of a company; (c) restructurings or reorganizations that focus on either carving out businesses from a company to enhance shareholder value or dramatically changing a company's capital structure either to avoid bankruptcy or to facilitate a sell-side transaction; and (d) hostile acquisition defense advisory services (see Exhibit 1.15).

### Merger & Acquisition Products

| | |
|---|---|
| Sell Side assignment | • Involves the sale, merger, or disposition of a company<br>• Highest priority since higher probability of completion |
| Buy Side assignment | • Involves the purchase of a company<br>• Lower priority since lower probability of completion |
| Merger of Equals (MOE) | • The merger of two companies of equal assets that have comparable market value |
| Joint Venture | • Two companies contribute assets and form a new entity to undertake economic activity together |
| Public Market Separation | • Includes carve-out, spin-off, and tracking stock<br>• Completed in coordination with equity capital markets group |
| Hostile Defense | • Raid defense: defense against a specific take-over proposal<br>• Anti-raid preparation: work to deter future unsolicited take-over activity<br>• Advice to hostile bidders: strategic and tactical advice on initiating an unsolicited take-over |

See Chapter 4 for a detailed description of these products.

**EXHIBIT 1.15**

M&A bankers develop strong valuation analysis and negotiation skills, and they usually work directly with a company's CEO, CFO, and corporate development team. Fees are typically paid to M&A bankers only upon successful completion of a transaction (although in the case of buy-side, restructuring, and defense advisory services, a nominal retainer fee may be charged during the period of the engagement).

# Trading Division

The Trading Division is responsible for (a) all investment-related transactions with institutional investors, including financial institutions, investment funds, and the cash management arms of governments and corporations; (b) taking proprietary positions in fixed income and equity products, currencies, commodities, and derivatives; (c) market-making and clearing activities on exchanges; and (d) principal investments made both directly and through managed funds. This division typically operates in three different business areas: Fixed Income, Currencies, and Commodities; Equities; and Principal Investments. At some investment banks, Principal Investments activity is conducted from a different division. Research on economics, fixed income, commodities, and equities is also provided by the Trading Division to investing clients (see Chapter 6 for more information on the research function and its regulatory history).

## Fixed Income, Currencies, and Commodities (FICC)

FICC makes markets and trades in government bonds, corporate bonds, mortgage-related securities, asset-backed securities, currencies, and commodities (as well as derivatives on all of these products). At some firms, FICC is also involved in the provision of loans to certain corporate and government borrowing clients (in coordination with the Investment Banking Division). The business also engages in proprietary (non-client-related) transactions in the same product areas. Individuals who work in the client-related area of FICC are either traders, who price these products and hold them in inventory as a risk position, or sales professionals, who market trade ideas and bring prices from the traders to investors to facilitate purchases and sales of the products.

## Equities

Equities makes markets in and trades equities, equity-related products, and derivatives in relation to the bank's client-related activities. The business generates commissions from executing and clearing client transactions on global stock, option, and futures exchanges. Equities also engages in proprietary (non-client-related) transactions in the same product areas. As is the case in FICC, individuals who work in the client-related area of Equities are either traders or sales professionals.

Investment banks typically have a Prime Brokerage business that provides bundled services such as securities borrowing and lending, financing (to facilitate leverage), asset custody, and clearing and settlement of trades to hedge fund clients and other fund managers. Prime brokers provide fund managers with a centralized location for the clearing of securities, reporting, and financing, while also allowing them to trade with other firms. Although initially an equity-centric business, Prime Brokerage has expanded its capabilities to many other asset classes (in step with the diversification of strategies employed by hedge funds). A large part of Prime Brokerage–related revenue comes from commissions from executing and clearing client trades by sales and trading professionals. Other revenue sources include earning spreads on financing and lending activities. Refer to Chapter 5 for a more detailed discussion of Prime Brokerage and its services.

# Non-Client-Related Trading and Investing

## Principal Investing

Although an important role of large investment banks is to act as intermediaries to investing clients, they also invest in securities and real estate for their own account. For example, the Principal Investments division within Goldman Sachs invests directly in public and private companies in the same way that KKR, a large private equity firm, invests. This frequently involves purchasing public companies using equity provided by Goldman Sachs (and its investing partners) and debt provided through loans (from Goldman Sachs or other banks) or bonds underwritten by Goldman Sachs in the capital markets. This process is called a *leveraged buyout* (LBO), or *taking a company private* in the case of a publicly traded target. In addition to control investments, Goldman Sachs also purchases minority positions in companies. For example, the firm owned common shares of Industrial and Commercial Bank of China Ltd. (one of China's largest banks), which has been valued in excess of $5 billion, and preferred shares of Sumitomo Mitsui Financial Group (one of Japan's largest banks), which has been valued in excess of $1 billion. The fair market value of equity securities and real estate owned by the Principal Investments area of Goldman Sachs exceeded $21.7 billion at the end of fiscal year 2008. See Exhibit 1.16 for a summary of Goldman Sachs' Principal Investments positions.

---

**Goldman Sachs Principal Investments**
As of November 2008

| (in millions) | Financial Instruments Owned, at Fair Value |
|---|---|
| ICBC | $5,496 |
| SMFG | 1,135 |
| Other principal investments | 15,126 |
| **Principal Investments** | **$21,757** |

1) Includes interests of $3.48 billion and $4.30 billion as of November 2008 held by investment funds managed by Goldman Sachs. The fair value of our investment in the ordinary shares of ICBC, which trade on The Stock Exchange of Hong Kong, includes the effect of foreign exchange revaluation for which we maintain an economic currency hedge.

2) The following table sets forth the principal investments (in addition to our investments in ICBC and Sumitomo Mitsui Financial Group, Inc. (SMFG) included within the Principal Investments component of our Trading and Principal Investments segment:

| (in millions) | Corporate | Real Estate | Total |
|---|---|---|---|
| Private | $10,726 | $2,935 | $13,661 |
| Public | 1,436 | 29 | 1,465 |
| Total | $12,162 | $2,964 | $15,126 |

Source: Goldman Sachs 2008 Annual Report

**EXHIBIT 1.16**

## Proprietary Trading

In addition to making long-term, non-client-related principal investments as described above, most major investment banks make short-term, non-client-related investments in securities, commodities, and derivatives for their own account. This *proprietary* investment activity is similar to the investment activities of hedge funds. Indeed, investment banks' proprietary investing activity competes directly with hedge funds for investing and hedging opportunities worldwide.

During 2005 and 2006, investment banks' proprietary investing contributed in a significant way to robust Trading Division earnings. During 2007 and 2008, however, this same proprietary trading activity contributed to very large losses at some banks: Deutsche Bank, for example, reported $1 billion in proprietary credit-related losses and another $500 million in proprietary equities-related losses during the fourth quarter of 2008. Other investment banks, including UBS, Citigroup and Merrill Lynch, reported even larger losses. As a result of significant losses experienced by most investment banks' proprietary trading desks during 2007 and 2008, banks scaled back these trading operations. However, during 2009, there was some recovery in proprietary trading activities.

Depending on each bank's compliance policy, proprietary traders at investment banks can sometimes be clients of their own firm's client-related trading business. These traders have the opportunity, but not the obligation, to trade with the firm's internal sales professionals. Covered by salespersons at other firms as well, these traders often deal with competitor firms in order to achieve the best prices and execution. Proprietary traders must be dealt with on an arm's length basis by internal salespeople, and confidentiality is paramount. There are strict compliance guidelines that *wall off* proprietary traders from certain information that is available to the client-related areas of the firm. Some firms go even further and completely wall off proprietary traders from any interaction with client-related sales and trading persons within their firm.

Sometimes, outside clients of the firm are concerned about the effectiveness of the wall and potential conflicts of interest, since the "best investment ideas" cannot always be shared with all investing clients without introducing excessive competition. Investment banks carefully monitor this situation and attempt to comply with all laws and internal policies, while finding a balance between the interests of external and internal clients.

At some investment banks, proprietary investment activity can be a very meaningful source of revenue and earnings. At other firms, this activity is considerably smaller. See Chapter 5 for a more complete description of specific proprietary investment activity and corresponding opportunities and threats.

# Asset Management Division

The Asset Management business offers equity, fixed income, alternative investments (such as private equity, hedge funds, real estate, currencies, and commodities), and money market investment products and services to individuals and institutions. Investments are offered in the form of mutual funds, private investment funds, or separately managed accounts, and are sometimes co-mingled with the bank's own investments. Revenues are created principally based on fees that are paid by investors as a percentage of assets under management (AUM), which varies depending on the asset class. At times, investors pay an incentive fee to the investment bank when returns exceed a predetermined benchmark. Most firms have a private wealth management business organized alongside the asset management business, reporting to the same division head (see Exhibit 1.17). The professionals in the private wealth management business act as advisors to

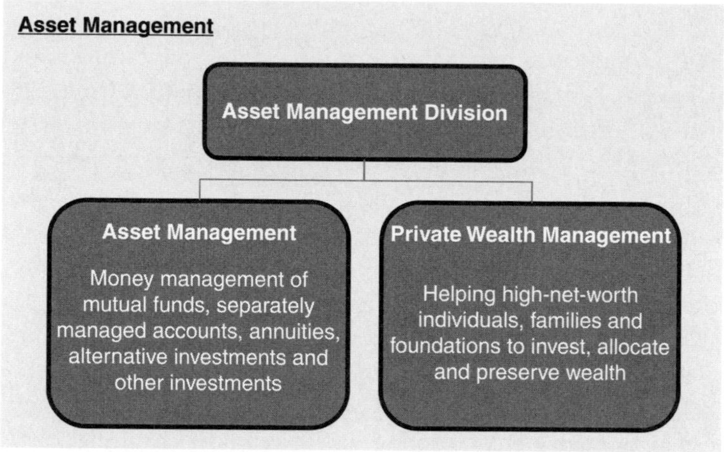

**Asset Management**

Asset Management Division

**Asset Management**

Money management of
mutual funds, separately
managed accounts, annuities,
alternative investments and
other investments

**Private Wealth Management**

Helping high-net-worth
individuals, families and
foundations to invest, allocate
and preserve wealth

**EXHIBIT 1.17**

investors, helping them decide how to invest their cash resources. In most cases (but not all), investors will be encouraged to invest in funds managed by the firm's asset management teams. However, advisors have a fiduciary obligation to direct investments into the funds (internal or external) that best meet the risk and return objectives of investors. Chapter 6 provides a more detailed discussion of the asset management business.

## Co-Investments in Asset Management Division Funds

Investment banks sometimes make direct investments in funds managed by their Asset Management Division that focus on: (1) private equity (LBOs and other equity control investments); (2) hedge-fund-type investments; and (3) real estate. Investment banks typically invest their own capital alongside the capital of their high net-worth individual and institutional clients in these funds (and they charge investing clients both management fees and performance fees based on the clients' AUM). This has become a very large business for some investment banks. For example, as of January 1, 2009, two of the largest hedge funds in the world were managed by the Asset Management Divisions of J.P. Morgan and Goldman Sachs (see Exhibit 1.18).

**Hedge Fund Ranking, January 2009**

| Firm | Region | AUM ($bln) |
|---|---|---|
| Bridgewater Associates | US | 38.6 |
| J.P. Morgan | US | 32.9 |
| Paulson & Co. | US | 29.0 |
| D.E. Shaw Group | US | 28.6 |
| Brevan Howard[1] | Europe | 26.8 |
| Och-Ziff Capital Management | US | 22.1 |
| Man AHL[1] | Europe | 22.0 |
| Soros Fund Management | US | 21.0 |
| Goldman Sachs Asset Management[1] | US | 20.6 |
| Farallon Capital Management[2] | US | 20.0 |
| Renaissance Technologies[2] | US | 20.0 |

Note 1: As of December 31, 2008. All other figures as of January 1, 2009.
Note 2: Tied for 10th place.
Source: Absolute Return Billion Dollar Club, March 2009 rankings

EXHIBIT 1.18

## Questions

1. Looking at the leverage ratios of former pure-play investment banks GS and MS in Exhibit 1.4, why were these banks able to operate at higher leverage ratios as investment banks, compared to as bank holding companies?

2. U.S. companies currently report their financials based on U.S. GAAP (Generally Accepted Accounting Principles) rules. Many companies in Europe report according to IFRS (International Financial Reporting Standards) rules. There has been a movement for all companies to shift to an IFRS basis globally. When this occurs, what may happen to the leverage ratios of U.S. banks?

3. Why might a universal bank be better able to compete against a pure-play investment bank for M&A and other investment banking engagements?

4. Investment bank clients can be categorized into two broad groups of issuers and investors. These two groups often have competing objectives (issue equity at highest possible price vs. acquire stock in companies at lowest possible price). Who within the investment bank is responsible for balancing these competing interests?

5. What is a key consideration in determining the cost and other parameters of a corporate debt offering, and why is it important?

6. Why might an investment bank place higher priority on sell-side M&A engagements over buy-side engagements?

7. Many investment banks have a principal investment group that invests directly in public and private companies. What conflicts of interest might arise from operating this type of business?

8. What conflicts might exist between the proprietary trading division and the rest of the investment bank?

9. What conflicts might exist as a result of having both an Asset Management (AM) business and a Private Wealth (PW) Management business?

# Regulation of the Securities Industry

## Introduction

Activities of investment banks impact the global economy and are very important to the smooth functioning of capital markets. Given their significance, it is no surprise that the business of investment banking has been subject to a great deal of government regulation. This chapter discusses the regulatory environment of investment banking. In the first section, the U.S. history of investment banking and regulation is discussed. The second section looks at more recent events and regulations. The third section summarizes the regulatory environment in the United Kingdom, Japan, and China.

## U.S. History and Regulations

### Early Investment Banking

The essence of what an investment bank does in its underwriting business is to act as an intermediary between issuers and investors so that one party can gain access to capital, while the other party can preserve and grow wealth. These underwriting services were essential to the foundation and development of the United States. George Washington, the first president, took office in 1789. At this time the federal government had already incurred $27 million of debt, and the states had debts totaling $25 million. Alexander Hamilton, the first U.S. Treasury secretary, persuaded Congress and President Washington to assume the state debt and issue bonds to finance this obligation, in spite of strong opposition from Thomas Jefferson. Investment bankers played a role in negotiating the terms and conditions of these bonds.

The firms conducting these premodern investment banking activities were referred to as *loan contractors*. Their services were to guarantee issuers' security offerings and sell them to investors, hopefully at a profit. The loan contractors' business was performed by speculators, merchants, and by some commercial banks. In addition, professional auctioneers were often intermediaries in the sale of investment products, taking bids and selling securities to the highest bidder. Finally, there were private bankers and stockbrokers who also performed the functions of modern-day investment banks.

As the new country began to spread over a vast continent, technological innovation fed into the industrial revolution. The benefits from increased economies of scale made large projects essential and profitable. Large-scale implementation of new technologies allowed for the extraction of natural resources, which created a need for trains to transport people and resources between cities. This and many other activities required capital that no individual or firm could afford alone. As a result, a more formal version of investment banking developed to intermediate between firms needing capital and individuals desiring to build wealth. By underwriting securities, investment banks made it possible for many investors to pool together their wealth to meet the great capital needs of a growing nation.

Industrial growth created a new class of wealthy industrialists and bankers who helped finance their empires. During this period, investment bankers operated in a regulatory vacuum and were largely free to respond as they saw fit to changing market forces. The practices they developed brought them power and influence. From 1879 to 1893, the mileage of railroads in the United States tripled, and investments in railroad bonds and stocks rose from $4.8 billion to $9.9 billion, keeping investment bankers busy underwriting these new issues. At the same time, other industrial growth was emerging that required family-owned businesses with limited resources to incorporate in order to raise more capital than could otherwise be obtained. This led to the use of investment banking services by an ever-increasing number of companies. The demand for capital had grown, as had the supply of capital, including capital provided by foreigners, which doubled from $1.4 billion to $3.3 billion between 1870 and 1890.

## The Growth of Investment Banking

Investment banking practices expanded further between 1890 and 1925. During this period, banks were highly concentrated and the industry was largely run by an oligopoly, which included J.P. Morgan & Co.; Kuhn, Loeb & Co.; Brown Brothers; and Kidder, Peabody & Co. The United States did not require separation between commercial and investment banks, which meant deposits from the commercial banking side of the business often provided an in-house supply of capital to deploy in the bank's underwriting projects.

From 1926 to 1929 equity issuance jumped from $0.6 billion to $4.4 billion while bond issuance decreased, as companies increasingly took advantage of a seemingly unstoppable rise in the stock market by preferring equity issuance to debt.

## Limited Regulation

During the investment environment of the first three decades of the 20th century, the lack of regulation, strong demand for securities, and fierce competition resulted in weak internal controls within banks. Despite their previous attempts at self-regulation, banks could not prevent scandals. In response to growing criticism and societal desire for industry regulation, the banking industry formed the Investment Bankers Association of America (IBAA) in 1912 as a splinter group of the American Bankers Association. One of the ideas established by the IBAA was the concept of non-price discrimination in the sale of securities, regardless of the investor and transaction size.

Although there was limited federal regulation of investment banks before the Great Depression started in 1929, banks had to adhere to state securities laws, or *Blue Sky* laws. The first Blue Sky law was enacted in Kansas in 1911. Among other features, it required that no security issued in the state could be offered without previously obtaining a permit from the state's Bank Commissioner. Between 1911 and 1933, 47 states enacted similar state laws regulating the issuance of new securities (all of the existing states at the time except Nevada). As federal regulations were enacted in the 1930s and 1940s, the state laws remained on the books while the federal laws mostly duplicated and extended the Blue Sky laws. The passage of the National Securities Markets Improvement Act by Congress in 1996 effectively removed states from securities regulation of investment banks, except for antifraud matters.

On October 28, 1929, the day referred to as Black Monday, a precipitous fall in the stock market began. In spite of the 1929 crash and the ensuing economic malaise, President Herbert

Hoover did not promote any meaningful new regulation of the financial markets. In contrast, Franklin Roosevelt, who became president in 1933, took an active approach to the economic difficulties and instituted a variety of regulations that shaped the financial sector, and investment banks in particular, for the remainder of the century. At Roosevelt's urging, Congress passed seven pieces of legislation that significantly impacted the business of investment banking.

Three of these laws, the 1933 Securities Act, the 1933 Glass-Steagall Act, and the 1934 Securities Exchange Act, drastically altered the business environment in which investment banks practiced. The following discussion will detail the regulatory requirements found in these three pieces of legislation. The other four legislative acts that impacted investment banking to a lesser extent will also be covered briefly.

## The Securities Act of 1933

The Securities Act of 1933 was meant to bring stability to capital markets and stop manipulative and deceptive practices in the sale or distribution of financial securities. The Securities and Exchange Commission (SEC) states that the 1933 Act had two purposes: "[to] require that investors receive financial and other significant information concerning securities being offered for public sale; and prohibit deceit, misrepresentations, and other fraud in the sale of securities."[1] To fulfill these objectives, the 1933 Act required investment banks that participated in the distribution of securities to disclose a significant amount of relevant and important details regarding securities and the firms they represented. Prior to the enactment of this law, few investors received basic information regarding their investments. The new law set a minimal requirement for providing information and ensured that all potential investors could access relevant issuer records.

The 1933 Act has four main sections of regulation that impact investment banks. The relevant sections relate to (1) submitting a registration statement to the SEC; (2) providing an investment prospectus to potential investors; (3) assuming civil and criminal liability for disclosure; and (4) having a post-filing waiting period before selling issues to the public.

### The Registration Statement

Before a security can be sold in the United States, certain information regarding the issuer and the securities being issued must be provided to regulators and prospective investors through a filing with the SEC. Exhibit 2.1 is an abridged list of information regarding the issuer and the issuance that must be included in the registration statement.

There are certain exceptions or exclusions from the registration requirements of the 1933 Act. These include when the issuance will only be offered intrastate, making it solely the jurisdiction of state laws; when the issuance of securities is by a municipality, a state, or the federal government; when the offering is below a certain value cutoff; and when the offering is made privately or is made to a small number of investors. Generally, the 1933 Act provides for certain exceptions based on the type of security that is offered (security-based exceptions) and for certain exceptions based on the type of offering (transaction-based exceptions).

### The Investment Prospectus

Companies are also required to provide investors with a prospectus, which contains certain elements of the information included in the registration statement. The securities cannot be distributed until after the issue has been registered with the SEC. Any known misstatement or

---

[1] www.sec.gov

<u>**Information Required in the Registration by the 1933 Act**</u>

- Summary information, risk factors and ratio of earnings to fixed charges
- Use of proceeds
- Dilution
- Selling security holders (if any)
- Plan of distribution
- Description of securities to be registered
- Interests of named experts and counsel
- Information with respect to the registrant
    - Description of business
    - Audited financial information
    - Description of property
    - Legal proceedings
    - Market price of and dividends on the registrant's common equity and related stockholder matters
    - Management's discussion and analysis of financial condition and results of operations
    - Changes in and disagreements with accountants on accounting and financial disclosure
    - Quantitative and qualitative disclosures about market risk
    - Directors and executive officers
    - Executive compensation
    - Corporate governance
    - Security ownership of certain beneficial owners and management
    - Transactions with related persons, promoters and certain control persons
- Material changes
- Disclosure of commission position on indemnification for securities act liabilities

Source: U.S. Securities and Exchange Commission

**EXHIBIT 2.1**

omission of material information from the registration statement is a criminal offense and can leave the issuer and underwriter liable to investor lawsuits.

### New Liabilities

Before the 1933 Act, there were no special laws assigning liability to investment bankers beyond those that applied to the activities of all citizens. After the 1933 Act was enacted, investment bankers became liable for securities law violation if *material facts* are omitted from the registration statement and investors suffer a loss that is attributable to that omission. If this occurs, investors can sue the banks to repurchase their shares at the original price and rescind the transaction. Underwriters' liabilities have been broadly defined since, as intermediates between issuers and investors, banks have more information than do investors regarding a company. To mitigate their liability, bankers seek to be indemnified by the issuers for any losses (including any costs associated with litigation) arising from material misstatements or omissions, resulting in a shared responsibility to provide accurate and complete information to purchasers of securities. See Exhibit 2.2 for sample indemnification language found in underwriting agreements.

**Sample Indemnification Section from Underwriting Agreements**

*Indemnification*

The Company agrees to indemnify and hold harmless the Underwriters and each person, if any, who controls the Underwriters within the meaning of Section 15 of the Securities Act or Section 20(a) of the Exchange Act against any and all losses, liabilities, claims, damages and expenses as incurred (including but not limited to reasonable attorneys' fees and any and all reasonable expenses incurred in investigating, preparing or defending against any litigation, commenced or threatened, or any claim, and subject to subsection [ ] of this Section, any and all amounts paid in settlement of any claim or litigation), joint or several, to which they or any of them may become subject under the Securities Act, the Exchange Act or any other federal or state statutory law or regulation, at common law or otherwise, insofar as such losses, liabilities, claims, damages or expenses (or actions in respect thereof) arise out of or are based upon any untrue statement or alleged untrue statement of a material fact contained in the Prospectus, or any amendment or supplement thereto, or arise out of or are based upon the omission or alleged omission to state therein a material fact required to be stated therein or necessary to make the statements therein not misleading; provided, however that the Issuers will not be liable in any such case to the extent but only to the extent that any such loss, liability, claim, damage or expense arises out of or is based upon any such untrue statement or alleged untrue statement or omission or alleged omission made therein in reliance upon and in conformity with written Information furnished to the Issuers relating to the Underwriters by the Underwriters expressly for use therein. This indemnity agreement will be in addition to any liability which the Issuers may otherwise have including under this Agreement.

Source: Jenner & Block LLP

**EXHIBIT 2.2**

One impact of the law has been a greater distinction between underwriters and dealers or selling group members. In general, an underwriter refers to the party that works directly with an issuer and agrees to purchase a new securities issue. A dealer is the party that works with the end investors and sells securities that are on an underwriter's books. These functions were originally intertwined, but because dealers are not liable under the 1933 Act, to some extent, the two functions have separated in order to limit further the entities exposed to liabilities and to reduce the likelihood for a civil liability suit.

## Due Diligence

Due diligence is the practice of reviewing information about an issuer in an effort to mitigate risk. Due diligence is conducted in connection with most securities offerings, with most acquisitions, and with many other transactions. In order to avoid being held liable for false or misleading disclosure in a registration statement, an underwriter must conduct an investigation "reasonably calculated to reveal all those facts [that] would be of interest to a reasonably prudent investor."[2] What is appropriate will be determined based on the facts and circumstances of each offering and then only in hindsight. Exhibit 2.3 summarizes six proposed practices to be included in an underwriter's due diligence effort. Exhibit 2.4 summarizes factors considered by courts when they review an underwriter's due diligence activity.

---

[2]www.sec.gov

**Six Proposed Practices to be Included in an Underwriter's Due Diligence Effort**

- Whether the underwriter received the registration statement and conducted a reasonable inquiry into any fact or circumstance that would cause a reasonable person to question whether the registration statement contains an untrue statement of a material fact or omits to state a material fact required to be stated therein or necessary to make the statements therein not misleading;
- Whether the underwriter has discussed the information contained in the registration statement with the relevant executive officers of the registrant (including, at minimum, the CFO or Chief Accounting Officer) and the CFO (or his/her designee) has certified that s/he has examined the registration statement and that, to the best of his/her knowledge, it does not contain any untrue statement of a material fact or omit to state a material fact required to be stated therein or necessary to make the statements therein not misleading;
- Whether the underwriter has received a SAS 100 comfort letter from the issuer's auditors;
- Whether the underwriter received a 10b-5 negative assurance from issuer's counsel;
- Whether the underwriter employed counsel that, after reviewing the issuer's registration statement, Exchange Act filings and other information, provided a 10b-5 negative assurance; and
- Whether the underwriter employed and consulted a research analyst that:
  - Has followed the issuer or the issuer's industry on an ongoing basis for at least 6 months immediately before the commencement of the offering; and
  - Has issued a report on the issuer or its industry within the 12 months immediately before the commencement of the offering.

Source: Morrison & Foerster LLP

**EXHIBIT 2.3**

**Factors Considered by Courts When Reviewing an Underwriter's Due Diligence Activity**

- Reasonable reliance on expertised portions of a registration statement (like certified financial statements)
- Investigation in response to a "red flag," including independent verification (management interviews; site visits; customer calls; receipt of written verification from the issuer, issuer's counsel, underwriter's counsel and the auditors; familiarity with the issuer's industry; a review of the issuer's internal documents; and an interview with independent auditors)
- Updating information through the offering date, including updating information contained in the issuer's Exchange Act reports (bring-down diligence)
- Documentation of diligence investigation

Source: Morrison & Foerster LLP

**EXHIBIT 2.4**

## Gun-Jumping Rules

Securities offerings can be divided into three stages under the 1933 Act:

1. The *pre-filing period* begins with the decision to proceed with an offering and ends with the filing of the registration statement.
2. The *waiting period* is the period between the filing and effectiveness of the registration statement.

3. The *post-effective period* is the period after the registration statement has been declared effective by the SEC (sales of securities can be made during this period).

Prior to reforms promulgated during 2005, during the waiting period (which is also called the *quiet period*) oral or written offers but not sales could be made, and any offers made in writing could only be made by means of a prospectus that conformed to the requirements of the 1933 Act. This prospectus is typically called a *red herring* prospectus (because of the red legend on the first page that reminds investors that the information contained in the prospectus is "preliminary"). Violations of these basic restrictions are referred to as *gun-jumping* and may result in an SEC-imposed "cooling-off" period, rescission rights to purchasers in the public offering, and class action or other litigation.

The securities offerings reforms enacted in 2005 provide safe harbors for communications made more than 30 days before filing a registration statement that do not reference a securities offering, for the regular release of "factual business information," and, in the case of reporting issuers, for certain "forward-looking information." For certain large issuers that meet minimum size standards and are followed by sophisticated investors and research analysts (called Well-Known Seasoned Issuers, or WKSIs), unrestricted oral or written offers are permitted before a registration statement is filed without violating gun-jumping provisions. For all issuers, the use of *free writing prospectuses* following the filing of a registration statement, which may include information that goes beyond (but may not be inconsistent with) the information in the prospectus, is permitted. This avoids the need to file a more formal and time-consuming prospectus supplement or amendment to the registration statement when new information needs to be disclosed.

In summary, with the exception of the favorable treatment given to WKSIs, the regime governing dissemination of information during the offering process remains largely unchanged since 1933, although simplified to reflect technological advances and changes in the capital markets, and issuers must be careful how they communicate before and during the offering process to avoid actions that could be deemed as conditioning the market. (See Exhibit 2.5 for a summary of the 1933 Act.)

## The Glass-Steagall Act

Another legislative response to the stock market crash of 1929 and the collapse of numerous banks thereafter was passage of the Glass-Steagall Act, which was signed into law on June 16, 1933. The Glass-Steagall Act was a large piece of regulation that, among other things, separated commercial and investment banks and created the Federal Deposit Insurance Corporation (FDIC), which insured depositors' assets in the event of a bank's default (originally for up to $2,500; today it is for up to $250,000). This Act had a significant effect on investment banking since it required the industry to alter its operations and the structure of its firms, changed the process for distribution and underwriting of securities, and cut off a key source of capital for new security underwriting.

During the Great Depression, over 11,000 banks closed or merged: one out of every four banks that existed in 1929 was no longer operating by 1934. Before the Glass-Steagall Act, there was no required separation between underwriting, investment, and depository banking services. A bank could (and did) take in deposits from checking account holders and use that money to invest in securities it was underwriting for its own in-house investment activities. Given this situation, the safety of a depositor's assets was in doubt, especially since there was no FDIC insurance to guarantee repayment. The Glass-Steagall Act was a response to this unstable environment.

## Securities Act of 1933

Often referred to as the "truth in securities" law, the Securities Act of 1933 has two basic objectives:
- Require that investors receive financial and other significant information concerning securities being offered for public sale; and
- Prohibit deceit, misrepresentations, and other fraud in the sale of securities.

**Purpose of Registration:**
- A primary means of accomplishing these goals is the disclosure of important financial information through the registration of securities. This information enables investors, not the government, to make informed judgments about whether to purchase a company's securities. While the SEC requires that the information provided be accurate, it does not guarantee the accuracy of the information. Investors who purchase securities and suffer losses have important recovery rights if they can prove that there was incomplete or inaccurate disclosure of important information.

**The Registration Process:**
- In general, securities sold in the U.S. must be registered. The registration forms that companies file provide essential facts while minimizing the burden and expense of complying with the law. In general, registration forms call for:
  - a description of the company's properties and business;
  - a description of the security to be offered for sale;
  - information about the management of the company; and
  - financial statements certified by independent accountants.
- Registration statements and prospectuses become public shortly after filing with the SEC. If filed by U.S. domestic companies, the statements are available on the EDGAR database accessible at www.sec.gov. Registration statements are subject to examination for compliance with disclosure requirements. Not all offerings of securities must be registered with the SEC. Some exemptions from the registration requirement include:
  - private offerings to a limited number of persons or institutions;
  - offerings of limited size;
  - intrastate offerings; and
  - securities of municipal, state, and federal governments.

Source: U.S. Securities and Exchange Commission

**EXHIBIT 2.5**

## Separation of Private Banks into Deposit and Investment Banks

Private banks were able to both accept deposits and perform the functions of an investment bank prior to the Glass-Steagall Act. The Act required private banks to choose to be either a private depository bank or an investment bank.

## Separation of Commercial and Investment Banks

Commercial banks, like private banks, were both accepting deposits and engaging in the functions of investment banking. After the Glass-Steagall Act was passed, investment banking functions that a commercial bank could perform were substantially reduced and their underwriting capacity was severely limited. They were only allowed to underwrite bonds or to "agent" offerings for municipal, state, and federal government bodies. Those banks that chose commercial banking over investment banking either spun off their investment banking business (e.g., J.P. Morgan & Co. decided to operate as a commercial bank and spun off its investment banking arm to form Morgan Stanley in 1935), or drastically cut staff. In addition, commercial banks were limited to earning no more than

10% of total income from securities transactions, not including an exemption for the underwriting of government-issued bonds.

### Separation of Directors and Officers from Commercial Banks and Security Firms

Partners and officials of firms associated with security investments were restricted from serving as directors or officers of commercial banks.

All of these changes had the same goal: to ensure that resources from depositors were protected from being unknowingly put at risk. However, the Glass-Steagall Act was overturned by the Gramm-Leach-Bliley Act in 1999, which once again allowed banks to conduct both investment banking and commercial banking activities, if these activities operated under a holding company structure.

## Securities Exchange Act of 1934

The Securities Exchange Act of 1934, a supplement to the Securities Act of 1933, was the third and final expansive law passed during the Roosevelt presidency that reshaped the investment banking industry. This Act is sometimes referred to as the Exchange Act. Passed on June 6, 1934, the new law dealt primarily with the supervision of new security offerings, ongoing reporting requirements for these offerings, and the conduct of exchanges. The law also significantly changed the secondary market for securities by requiring minimal reporting standards and codifying rules for transactions. In addition, it required that exchanges be governed by self-regulatory organizations (SROs). NYSE Euronext and NASDAQ, the two largest U.S. exchanges, are self-regulated SROs.

The Exchange Act also created the Securities and Exchange Commission (SEC), which took over responsibility of supervising the capital markets, including the supervision of investment banks. To carry out its mission, the SEC was provided with broad powers to enact and enforce new regulations on exchanges, investment banks, broker/dealers, and traders in order to protect the safety and soundness of the securities business. The SEC is responsible for carrying out and enforcing the Securities Act of 1933; it regulates activities on the exchanges and adopts rules and procedures for its members to follow, and it prohibits manipulative practices like wash sales and matched orders, while setting strict standards for short selling and stop-loss orders. The role of the SEC in capital markets cannot be overstated. It continually makes adjustments to prior rules and regulations to minimize the potential for unfair undertakings while promoting the efficiency of the capital markets. In addition, the SEC maintains flexibility in order to keep up with the regulation of new types of securities and financial products (e.g., the trading of Collateralized Debt Obligations) and investment practices (such as the change from a fractional system of reporting stock prices to a decimal system). See Exhibit 2.6 for a summary of the Exchange Act.

The four laws reviewed in the following sections were passed between 1935 and 1940. These laws are less influential than the three laws just discussed, but nonetheless imposed certain restrictions on investment banks.

## Public Utility Holding Company Act

Passed in 1935, the Public Utility Holding Company Act (PUHCA) allowed the SEC to supervise the relationship between utility holding companies and investment banks. PUHCA restricted investment banks from owning these utility companies based on the belief that the banks would limit competition and engage in monopolistic behavior. The Act was replaced in 2005 by the Energy Policy Act, which

**Securities Exchange Act of 1934**

With this Act, Congress created the Securities and Exchange Commission (SEC). The Act empowers the SEC with broad authority over all aspects of the securities industry. This includes the power to register, regulate, and oversee brokerage firms, transfer agents, and clearing agencies as well as the nation's self regulatory organizations (SROs), including securities exchanges such as NYSE Euronext and NASDAQ.

The Act also identifies and prohibits certain types of conduct in the markets and provides the SEC with disciplinary powers over regulated entities and persons associated with them.

The Act also empowers the SEC to require periodic reporting of information by companies with publicly traded securities.

**Corporate Reporting:**
Companies with more than $10 million in assets whose securities are held by more than 500 owners must file annual and other periodic reports. These reports are available to the public through the SEC's EDGAR database. Other companies that are not required to file may voluntarily choose to do so.

**Proxy Solicitations:**
The Securities Exchange Act also governs the disclosure in materials used to solicit shareholder votes in annual or special meetings held for the election of directors and the approval of other corporate actions. This information, contained in proxy materials, must be filed with the SEC in advance of any solicitation to ensure compliance with the disclosure rules. Solicitations, whether by management or shareholder groups, must disclose all important facts concerning the issues on which holders are asked to vote.

**Significant Ownership Stakes and Tender Offers:**
The Securities Exchange Act requires disclosure of important information by anyone seeking to acquire more than 5 percent of a company's securities by direct purchase or tender offer. Such an offer often is extended in an effort to gain control of the company. As with the proxy rules, this allows shareholders to make informed decisions on these critical corporate events. The Act also requires holders of a significant amount of a public security to file certain regular reports in order to inform non-affiliated shareholders about potential ownership changes.

**Insider Trading:**
The securities laws broadly prohibit fraudulent activities of any kind in connection with the offer, purchase, or sale of securities. These provisions are the basis for many types of disciplinary actions, including actions against fraudulent insider trading. Insider trading is illegal when a person trades a security while in possession of material nonpublic information in violation of a duty to withhold the information or refrain from trading.

Source: U.S. Securities and Exchange Commission

**EXHIBIT 2.6**

transferred regulatory power over utility companies from the SEC to the Federal Energy Regulatory Commission (FERC) and relaxed restrictions on the M&A activity of utility holding companies.

## Chandler Act

The Chandler Act, passed in June 1938, added Chapter X bankruptcies to the National Bankruptcy Act. Prior to this time corporate bankruptcies had limited government involvement and were greatly influenced by private firms, which typically led to bankruptcy proceedings that discriminated against smaller investors. The passage of this Act gave the SEC the authority to be a party to all corporate restructuring activity. With the inclusion of the SEC in the reorganization, investors received additional protection against inequitable restructuring plans. The Chandler Act also explicitly restricted the role of investment banks in the restructuring of bankrupt public firms. Before this Act was passed, there was suspicion that banks were not "disinterested parties" and were obtaining excessive profits from their involvement at the expense of investors. The rule separating investment banks from bankruptcy proceedings was replaced by the Bankruptcy Abuse

Prevention and Consumer Protection Act of 2005 (BAPCPA). Under the BAPCPA, investment banks are no longer automatically disqualified as disinterested parties in the restructuring process. As a result, subject to their meeting the criteria provided in Exhibit 2.7, investment banks are now allowed to participate in a bankruptcy process.

## Maloney Act

The second relevant legislation to be passed in 1938 was the Maloney Act, which continued the practice of self-regulation. The Maloney Act established that members who voluntarily joined self-regulated associations would receive preferential business advantages. In addition, it forced all over-the-counter (OTC) brokers and dealers to register with the SEC. This transformed the Investment Bankers Conference into the National Association of Securities Dealers (NASD). The NASD became the self-regulator of the securities market, overseeing the OTC markets, creating professional practice standards, and applying fair trading rules. All trading of equities, corporate bonds, securities futures, and options are regulated by the NASD. The NASD licenses individuals who engage in the securities industry, creates rules that govern their behavior, and reviews member firms for regulatory compliance. It also has enforcement jurisdiction, as authorized by the SEC, to discipline registered representatives and member firms that violate federal securities laws and NASD rules and regulations. In 2007, the NASD merged with the enforcement arm of the New York Stock Exchange. The combined entity assumed the new name of Financial Industry Regulatory Authority (FINRA).

### Investment Company Act of 1940

The Investment Company Act of 1940 describes what constitutes an investment company (including its best-known form, a mutual fund) and separates the functions of investment banks and investment companies. This Act sets out restrictions on the number of investment bankers who can serve as directors of an investment company, and restricts business transactions between investment banks and investment companies. See Exhibit 2.8 for a summary.

## Recent Developments in Securities Regulations

After 1940, little happened with regard to major legislation impacting investment banks in the United States for almost 60 years. This section discusses recent changes in regulation, including the Gramm-Leach-Bliley Act, the Sarbanes-Oxley Act, and the regulatory handling of the Bear Stearns breakdown.

---

**Revised Definition of "Disinterested Person" as per BAPCPA**

Section 101 (14):'disinterested person' means a person that -

(A) is not a creditor, an equity security holder, or an insider;

(B) is not and was not, within 2 years before the date of the filing of the petition, a director, officer or employee of the debtor; and

(C) does not have an interest materially adverse to the interest of the estate or of any class of creditors or equity security holders, by reason of any direct or indirect relationship to, connection with, or interest in, the debtor, or for any other reason.

Source: Bankruptcy Abuse Prevention & Consumer Protection Act of 2005

**EXHIBIT 2.7**

**Investment Company Act of 1940**

This Act regulates the organization of companies, including mutual funds, that engage primarily in investing, reinvesting, and trading in securities, and whose own securities are offered to the investing public. The regulation is designed to minimize conflicts of interest that arise in these complex operations. The Act requires these companies to disclose their financial condition and investment policies to investors when stock is initially sold and, subsequently, on a regular basis. The focus of this Act is on disclosure to the investing public of information about the fund and its investment objectives, as well as on investment company structure and operations. It is important to remember that the Act does not permit the SEC to directly supervise the investment decisions or activities of these companies or judge the merits of their investments.

Source: U.S. Securities and Exchange Commission

**EXHIBIT 2.8**

## The Gramm-Leach-Bliley Act

On November 12, 1999, the U.S. Congress passed the Gramm-Leach-Bliley Act, which overturned the mandatory separation of commercial banks and investment banks required by the Glass-Steagall Act of 1933. The Gramm-Leach-Bliley legislation is also referred to as the Financial Services Modernization Act. The original reason for the separation was the concern that depositors' holdings would be used aggressively in risky endeavors by the investment banking side of the firms. The argument for joining the two types of firms is that it would provide a more stable business model irrespective of the economic environment. In poor economic environments, people tend to hold on to cash, which drives up commercial banking deposit revenues, thereby providing a balance to a slow new securities issuance market. On the other hand, in a booming economy, cash deposits are low but new issuance activity is high.

Another argument for rejoining investment banks and commercial banks was that non-U.S.-headquartered universal banks, such as Deutsche Bank, UBS, and Credit Suisse, were not encumbered by the Glass-Steagall Act. These banks had a competitive advantage over U.S.-headquartered commercial banks, such as Citigroup, JPMorgan, and Bank of America, and stand-alone investment banks, such as Goldman Sachs and Morgan Stanley, because the non-U.S.-headquartered banks could participate in both commercial banking and investment banking activities.

The separation of commercial and investment banks had already been gradually weakened over the years, and the Gramm-Leach-Bliley Act was the final step. As early as 1986, the Federal Reserve allowed bank holding companies to participate in the underwriting of corporate issues, whereas they were previously restricted to only government debt underwriting. The Fed required that this non-government underwriting activity could represent no more than 10% of a commercial bank's total revenues. In 1996 this was further weakened by increasing the revenue limit from 10% to 25%. Finally, in 1999 the remaining restrictions were relaxed through passage of the Gramm-Leach-Bliley Act. This Act allowed Citigroup, formed through the merger of Citicorp and Travelers Group in 1998, to keep the investment banking business that was a part of Travelers Group. It also enabled J.P. Morgan and other large commercial banks to substantially expand their investment banking business.

The regulatory environment of banks also changed with this Act. Commercial banks were already regulated by the Federal Reserve (among other regulators, depending on the specific type of commercial bank). The Act, however, failed to give the SEC (or any other agency) direct authority to regulate large investment bank holding companies. Without explicit statutory authority over these institutions, the SEC created the Consolidated Supervised Entities (CSE) program in 2004, pursuant to which investment bank holding companies were subject to voluntary regulation by the SEC, as an attempt to fill this regulatory gap. As a result of the financial crises that led to the conversion of the remaining U.S. investment banks (Goldman Sachs and Morgan Stanley) into bank holding companies during the fall of 2008, the CSE program was no longer necessary and was, therefore, ended in September 2008. The previous regulatory gap was automatically filled by virtue of the adoption of bank holding company status by the remaining investment banks. The Federal Reserve now shares with the SEC principal regulatory oversight of all investment banking activities in the United States.

## The Sarbanes-Oxley Act

The Sarbanes-Oxley Act of 2002 produced a sweeping change in regulation that impacted corporate governance, disclosure, and conflicts of interests. Although this bill was expansive, its impact on investment banking was less significant than its impact on auditors and public companies and their boards of directors.

The principal impact of this Act on investment banking related to research and due diligence. The Act required the SEC to adopt rules to minimize the risk of investment bankers influencing equity analysts' research reports by separating stock analysis from underwriting activities. For example, analysts' compensation could no longer be based on investment banking underwriting revenues, and analysts who provided a negative report of a company were protected from retaliation by bankers who are responsible for underwriting activities.

The Sarbanes-Oxley Act had several other broad implications that impacted the regulatory environment of securities markets. It created the Public Company Accounting Oversight Board to set accounting rules and standards and also reduced the influence of auditors on corporate decision making. Outside auditors' independence was more carefully defined to avoid conflicts of interest. Top executives of the corporations were required to certify personally that information made available to investors was accurate by signing a statement accompanying quarterly and annual filings. Loans to insiders (employees or others with close ties to the firm) were restricted, and additional disclosures were required by issuers, including off balance-sheet transactions. In addition, the Act criminalized certain activities and created more responsibilities for the audit committee of the board, while imposing a significant new layer of costs to enable compliance. See Exhibit 2.9 for a summary of the Sarbanes-Oxley Act.

## Regulation Analyst Certification

The SEC adopted new legislation in 2003 to bring more accountability to research analysts. Regulation Analyst Certification (Regulation AC) requires research analysts to "certify the truthfulness of the views they express in research reports and public appearances, and disclose whether they have received any compensation related to the specific recommendations or views expressed in those reports and appearances," for both equity and debt securities.[3] For research reports distributed to U.S. residents, the analyst must certify that (1) the views expressed in the research report accurately reflect the research analyst's personal views about the subject securities and issuers; and (2) either (a) no part of the analyst's compensation was, is, or will be directly or indirectly related to the specific recommendations or views contained in the research report, or (b) part or all of the analyst's compensation was, is, or will be directly or indirectly related to the specific recommendations or views contained in the research report. If the latter, the certification statement must then

---

[3] www.sec.gov

## Summary of the Sarbanes-Oxley Act of 2002

**Restoring Confidence in the Accounting Profession**
- The Act established the Public Company Accounting Oversight Board
- Section 108(b) - The SEC recognized the Financial Accounting Standards Board (FASB) as the accounting standard setter.
- Title II - The SEC adopted rules improving the independence of outside auditors.
- Section 303 - The SEC adopted rules forbidding the improper influence on outside auditors.

**Improving the "Tone at the Top"**
- Section 302 - The SEC adopted rules requiring CEOs and CFOs to certify financial and other information in their companies' quarterly and annual reports.
- Section 306 - The SEC adopted rules prohibiting company officers from trading during pension fund blackout periods.
- Section 402 - This section prohibits companies from making loans to insiders
- Section 406 - The SEC adopted rules requiring companies to disclose whether they have a code of ethics for their CEO, CFO and senior accounting personnel.

**Improving Disclosure and Financial Reporting**
- Section 401(a) - The SEC adopted rules requiring disclosure of all material off-balance sheet transactions.
- Section 401(b) - The SEC adopted Regulation G, governing the use of non-GAAP financial measures, including disclosure and reconciliation requirements.
- Section 404 - The SEC adopted rules requiring an annual management report on and auditor attestation of a company's internal controls over financial reporting.

**Improving the Performance of "Gatekeepers"**
- Section 407 - The SEC adopted rules requiring the disclosure about financial experts on audit committees.
- Section 501 - The SEC approved new SRO rules governing research analyst conflicts of interest.

**Enhancing Enforcement Tools**
- Section 305 - This section sets standards for imposing officer and director bars and penalties.
- Section 704 - The SEC issued a study of enforcement actions involving violations of reporting requirements and restatements.
- Section 1105 - This section gives the SEC the authority in administrative proceedings to prohibit persons from serving as officers or directors.

Source: U.S. Securities and Exchange Commission

**EXHIBIT 2.9**

include the source, amount, and purpose of such compensation, and include cautionary language that it may influence the analyst's recommendation in the research report.

## Global Research Settlement

On April 28, 2003, the SEC and other regulators (Regulators) announced enforcement actions against the 10 largest investment banking firms (Investment Banks). Regulators charged that the Investment Banking Division of Investment Banks had undue influence over equity research analysts, thereby affecting the objectivity of their investment opinions. In addition, Regulators charged that these conflicts of interest were not adequately managed or disclosed to investors.

The Investment Banks, who did not admit to or deny the charges brought against them, agreed to settle with the Regulators for approximately $1.4 billion. In addition to agreeing to pay this amount, the Investment Banks agreed to a number of reforms:

1. Structural reforms: the Investment Banks would comply with significant restrictions relating to interaction between the Investment Banking Division and the equity research department.

2. Enhanced disclosures: additional disclosures would be made to recipients of research reports regarding (among other things) potential conflicts of interest resulting from investment banking activities.
3. Independent research: the Investment Banks would contract with independent, third-party research firms to make available to U.S. customers these independent research firms' reports.

Finally, outside of research, the Investment Banks also voluntarily agreed to restrict allocations of securities in "hot" IPOs (offerings that begin trading in the secondary market at a premium) to certain company executive officers and directors, a practice known as *spinning*. See Chapter 6 for further discussion regarding this enforcement action and the role of equity research.

## Bear Stearns Collapse

On March 14, 2008, Bear Stearns, one of the oldest and most prominent investment banks based in the United States, collapsed. The crisis occurred abruptly over a matter of days as investors, lenders, and other counterparties rapidly withdrew funds. The bank encountered a liquidity (cash) crunch: its liquid assets were less than its short-term liabilities. At the time, Bear Stearns had over $2.5 trillion in outstanding contracts with other institutions.

Bear Stearns was integrated throughout the global markets, and regulators concluded that a Bear Stearns failure would have dramatic consequences for the financial system. To avert disaster, the Federal Reserve took an unprecedented action by brokering the sale of Bear Stearns to J.P. Morgan. In addition, to facilitate the orderly unwinding of Bear Stearns' assets deemed too risky by J.P. Morgan to assume on its balance sheet, the Fed set up a separate entity (Maiden Lane LLC) to buy those assets, funded by a $1 billion loan from J.P. Morgan and a $29 billion loan from the Fed. Collateralized by the assets, the loans were to be repaid as the assets were unwound over time. In theory, the Fed (and ultimately U.S. taxpayers) had up to a $29 billion exposure from this agreement. As of April 1, 2009, the Fed reported that the fair value of the Maiden Lane portfolio was $26.3 billion, implying a book loss of over $2 billion for the Fed. During this crisis, the Federal Reserve opened up its lending window (discount window) for the first time to investment banks that were not part of bank holding companies, which created new risks for the Fed. As a result, the Fed placed examiners in the banks to review trades, asset positions, leverage levels, and capital reserves, providing the Fed with greater visibility and the ability to impose controls that supplemented the regulatory controls exercised by the SEC.

On July 7, 2008, in response to the stress experienced by the financial markets and also in recognition of the continued merging of functions between commercial and investment banks, the Fed and the SEC entered a Memorandum of Understanding in which they agreed to openly share information with each other regarding financial concerns relating to investment banking organizations, regardless of who the primary regulator was.

On September 26, 2008, in response to further changes in the investment banking landscape, the SEC announced that it was ending its Consolidated Supervised Entities program (as discussed earlier in the section on the Gramm-Leach-Bliley Act) that oversaw investment banks, because the remaining major players (Goldman Sachs and Morgan Stanley) were converted to bank holding companies.

Additional understandings and new regulations continued to develop following the collapse of Lehman Brothers during September 2008, including efforts to achieve better coordination between different regulators and minimize systemic risk. See Exhibit 2.10 for a summary of the major legislation that has shaped the investment banking industry as well as additional reforms being considered in the wake of the financial crisis of 2007–2008.

---

**Summary of Key U.S. Laws and Agreements That Impact Investment Banks**

The Securities Act of 1933

- Often referred to as the "truth in securities" law, the Securities Act of 1933 has two main objectives: to require that investors receive financial and other significant information concerning securities being offered for public sale; and to prohibit deceit, misrepresentations, and other fraud in the sale of securities.
- In general, securities sold in the U.S. must be registered with the SEC (unless qualified for certain exemptions) and must provide a minimum required amount of information regarding the security. After a registration statement is filed with the SEC, investment prospectuses must also be provided to potential investors.

Glass-Steagall Act (1933)

- This Act separated commercial and investment banks and limited the underwriting capabilities of commercial banks. Partners and officials of firms associated with security investments were restricted from serving as directors or officers of commercial banks.
- The Federal Deposit Insurance Corporation (FDIC) was founded by this Act to insure bank deposits.

Securities Exchange Act of 1934

- This Act deals primarily with the supervision of new security offerings, ongoing reporting requirements for these offerings and the conduct of exchanges. Companies with >$10 million in assets and >500 owners must file annual and other periodic reports that need to be available to the public through the SEC's EDGAR database. Proxy solicitations and the acquisition of significant ownership stakes (>5%) are subject to filing requirements as well.
- The Act required that exchanges be governed by self-regulatory organizations (SROs).
- This Act created the SEC, which took over the responsibility of supervising the capital markets, including the supervision and regulation of investment banks, exchanges, broker/dealers and traders.
- Insider trading is prohibited by this Act.

Gramm-Leach-Bliley Act (1999)

- Also known as the Financial Services Modernization Act, this Act overturned the mandatory separation of commercial and investment banks, as originally required by the Glass-Steagall Act.

Global Research Settlement (2003)

- Investment Banks have to comply with significant restrictions relating to interaction between the Investment Banking Division and equity research department. Disclosures must be made to recipients of research reports regarding (among other things) potential conflicts of interest resulting from investment banking activities.
- The practice of "spinning" hot IPOs is restricted.

Financial Crisis Regulatory Reform (2009)

- In the wake of the financial crisis of 2007-2008, a number of reforms impacting the banking industry are being considered, including: the role of the Federal Reserve, the supervision of banks and bank holding companies, bank capital guidelines, consumer protection, global accounting standards and the "harmonization" of OTC derivatives regulation.

**EXHIBIT 2.10**

# Securities Regulations in Other Countries

The following discussion provides a broad overview of the regulatory environment in Japan, the United Kingdom, and China.

## Japan

The current Japanese system of regulation has some similarities with the U.S. regulatory system. After World War II, the United States directed the rebuilding of Japan, which led to many Japanese regulatory organizations initially resembling U.S. regulatory organizations. As discussed earlier in this chapter, the most influential regulations for investment banks in the United States were contained in the 1933 Securities Act, the 1934 Securities Exchange Act, and the Glass-Steagall Act of 1933. These codes were transferred almost wholly to the Japanese system in 1948 when the Japanese Diet passed the Securities and Exchange Law. Even so, given the differences between the countries, Japan's system has evolved into a somewhat different regulatory environment.

Japan's regulations differed in the distinction of bank types and the ownership structure of businesses. Similar to the U.S. Glass-Steagall Act, Japanese regulators distinguished banks based on their business activities. Commercial banks, also known as *City Banks,* were restricted from underwriting securities until 1999 (banks that accepted consumer deposits and distributed loans were restricted from underwriting securities, with the exception of government bonds or government-guaranteed bonds). Pre-WWII Japanese banks were often controlled by a *Zaibatsu,* a large conglomerate of businesses owned by a single holding company. Although the Zaibatsu were banned after WWII, they were later allowed to reintegrate (through share purchases in each other) in order to expedite the rebuilding of Japan's economy. A Zaibatsu that is formed around a bank is called a *Keiretsu* and has a similar structure as a Zaibatsu, but with many owners. Several different banks are owners in a Keiretsu, since banks are not allowed to own more than 5% of equity in companies to which they lend. The City Banks have maintained an influential role in Japan's financial and industrial activities through the Keiretsu. Correspondingly, however, the securities market has grown slowly in Japan because of the City Banks' underwriting restrictions. As a result, most companies finance their business through short- and medium-term loans instead of through the securities market.

The Japanese regulatory environment has gone through three significant periods since the U.S.-assisted restructuring: 1947–1992, 1992–1998, and 1998–present.

### 1947–1992

Established in 1947, the Ministry of Finance (MOF) is in charge of regulating the Japanese financial system. It has a large mandate, including the supervision of banks, and shares responsibility for fiscal and monetary policy with the Bank of Japan. Before 1971, foreign securities firms were banned from operating in Japan. The Law Concerning Foreign Securities Firms that was passed in 1971 allowed foreign firms to enter the market for investment banking services.

### 1992–1998

As in the United States, Japan also eliminated the separation of investment banking and commercial banking. This process started in 1992 with the Financial Institution Reform Act, which allowed commercial banks, investment banks, and insurance companies to engage in each other's business through subsidiaries. This Act also established the Securities Exchange and Surveillance Commission (SESC), which assumed many of the regulatory responsibilities of the MOF.

### 1998–Present

Starting in 1998, Japan initiated the "Big Bang" and began to deregulate the financial industry. A key part of the Big Bang was the separation of the SESC from the MOF, and the creation of the Financial Supervisory Agency (which in 2000 turned into the Financial Services Agency), which is the current regulator of Japan's securities industry. During 1999, the Financial System Reform Law allowed commercial banks to own brokerage firms that underwrite equity and debt securities. In addition, a new securities law was passed, called the Law Concerning the Sale of Financial Products, which governs underwriter practices.

In 2006, the Financial Instruments and Exchange Law passed and became the main statute codifying securities law and regulating securities companies in Japan. The law provides for registration and regulation of broker-dealers; disclosure obligations applicable to public companies; tender offer rules; disclosure obligations applicable to large shareholders in public companies;

and internal controls in public companies (similar to the controls imposed in the United States by the Sarbanes-Oxley Act).

## United Kingdom

Founded in 1694, the Bank of England was the principal regulator in the United Kingdom for over 300 years until 1997. As in Japan, the evolution of the regulatory system can be separated into three periods: pre-1986, 1986–1997, and 1997–present.

### Pre-1986

Until 1986, self-regulation (e.g., by members of the London Stock Exchange) prevailed. In 1986 there was a "Big Bang" in the U.K. financial industry, which placed the self-regulatory system into a statutory framework. This was the precursor to the Japanese Big Bang: both were meant to shake up the regulatory system.

### 1986–1997

Sweeping reform in the regulation of the U.K. investment industry started with the Financial Services Act of 1986, which created a comprehensive government regulator called the Securities and Investment Board (SIB). A financial firm had to register with the SIB, unless it was a member of an SRO. The SROs were given enforcement powers (fines, censures, and bans) at this time. Under the Financial Services Act of 1986, undertaking any investment business without authorization by the SIB was a criminal offense.

### 1997–Present

In 1997 an overhaul of the financial regulatory system was announced and the SIB changed its name to the Financial Services Authority (FSA). The FSA consolidated the powers of nine regulatory agencies into a single regulator for the entire industry and removed the influence of SROs. In the process, the FSA also took over responsibility for regulating banks from the Bank of England. This contrasts with the United States, which has several different financial regulators. The FSA has the power to create rules by its mandate, and like the SEC, the FSA rules are binding without any parliamentary action. In 2001, the Financial Services and Markets Act 2000 replaced the Financial Services Act 1986.

Following the outbreak of the global financial crisis in 2007, the FSA worked with the Bank of England and the U.K. Treasury (together called the *Tripartite Authorities*) to reform and strengthen the existing U.K. regulatory framework.

### Effect of EU Legislation

As a member state of the European Union (EU), the United Kingdom is also subject to a number of EU banking and securities legislation that seeks to impose a level playing field in relation to the regulation of financial markets across the EU, particularly for wholesale markets. The FSA acts as the United Kingdom's authority responsible for implementing and performing applicable regulatory functions.

## China

Although Hong Kong is now under Chinese rule, it differs significantly from the rest of the country in its investment banking regulation standards because it operated under English control until 1997. This discussion will exclude Hong Kong and focus strictly on the mainland Chinese financial regulatory environment. The Chinese financial regulatory system for investment banking only recently modernized to resemble more closely the standards found in other countries with developed financial systems. The regulatory system can be separated into four periods: pre-1992, 1992–1998, 1998–2005, and 2005–present.

### Pre-1992
Prior to 1992, China was essentially closed to investment banking. However, economic reforms initiated under Deng Xiaoping's administration set the stage for a market-based economy that opened the doors for foreign trade and investments.

### 1992–1998
In 1992, the Chinese government implemented two commissions: the State Council Securities Commission (SCSC) and the China Securities Regulatory Commission (CSRC). The SCSC deals with centralized market regulation, whereas the CSRC is the enforcement arm of the SCSC and supervises the securities markets. In 1995, Morgan Stanley became the first and only global investment bank to operate inside of China.

### 1998–2005
In 1998, the Securities Law of the People's Republic of China was created as the main statute regulating investment banks. The SCSC was merged into the CSRC to form a single government body. The new CSRC was a direct government entity of the State Council, the head council of the Central People's Government of China. Under the Securities Law, there was a separation of banks engaging in deposit taking and securities activities.

### 2005–Present
In 2005 the Securities Law of the People's Republic of China and the Company Law of the People's Republic of China underwent revisions. The changes in law were extensive: over 40% of the articles were amended, 53 provisions were added, and 27 were deleted. After the 2005 Securities Law update, the restriction on banks and their affiliates engaging in securities activities was relaxed. It also allowed for the creation of derivative markets, whereas previously China restricted the financial markets to only cash markets. In addition, the updated Securities Law took further actions to protect investors dealing with new security issuance. Article 5, for example, states that "[the] issuance and transaction of securities shall observe laws and administrative regulations. No fraud, insider trading, or manipulation of the securities market may be permitted."[4] Finally, the new Law provided securities regulators with additional powers to investigate and gather information, and to control a securities firm's assets if necessary.

## Questions

1. Following the 1929 stock market crash, Congress passed a series of Acts to regulate the securities industries. Name four of these Acts and briefly describe their purpose.
2. A goal of many parts of U.S. regulatory legislation has been to eliminate or minimize conflicts of interest between issuers, investment banks, and investors. Provide examples

---

[4]Article 5 of the Securities Law of the People's Republic of China

of conflicts of interest in the U.S. investment banking industry and the corresponding regulations that attempted to resolve those issues.

3. Disclosure of information to investors is another recurring theme in U.S. regulation of the securities industry. Provide examples of disclosure required by U.S. regulations.

4. What is the role of U.S. states in regulating investment banks?

5. What types of U.S. securities offerings do not need to be registered with the SEC?

6. What is a *red herring*?

7. Widgets Inc. is a publicly traded company with approximately $300 million in market capitalization. The company filed a registration statement for a follow-on offering in May of this year, but began selectively speaking to investors about the issue in March. Its offering is now being delayed by the SEC. What is the likely reason for the delay?

8. What are the *risk factors* in a prospectus? Why are they important to the issuer and to the investor?

9. What is the significance of the Gramm-Leach-Bliley Act of 1999 in relation to the securities industry?

10. What are some securities regulations in place in the United Kingdom, Japan, and China that mirror U.S. regulations?

11. What are some major differences between the regulatory frameworks of the four countries covered in this chapter?

12. Compare the regulatory bodies of the four countries covered in this chapter.

# Financings

The material in this chapter should be cross-referenced with **Case Study 3, "Freeport-McMoRan: Financing an Acquisition."**

This chapter focuses on financings for corporate and government clients, one of the two key businesses conducted by the Investment Banking Division of an investment bank.

## Capital Markets Financings

A capital markets financing is a long-term funding obtained through the issuance of a security in a regulated market. A security is a fungible, negotiable instrument representing financial value. The security can be debt (bonds, debentures, or notes), equity (common stock), or a hybrid (a security with both debt-like and equity-like characteristics, such as preferred shares or convertibles). A capital markets financing is usually underwritten by investment banks, meaning that the banks take on risk when purchasing securities from an issuer and then reselling those securities to investors. This financing process is governed by securities laws that determine disclosure, marketing limitations, and underwriter compensation, among other things. A capital markets offering where investment banks purchase securities at a discount from issuers and then resell them to investors is called a *primary offering*. The sale of securities by a major shareholder through a capital markets offering where the proceeds do not go to the issuer of the security, but to the current holder, is referred to as a *secondary offering*.

After securities are sold in the capital markets through either a primary or secondary market offering, subsequent trades are called *secondary market trades*, which take place on an exchange or in the over-the-counter (OTC) market. In a secondary market trade, cash is received by a seller, the buyer receives the purchased security, and the original issuer of the security does not receive any cash proceeds or issue a new security.

In the United States, a primary market securities offering must either be registered with the Securities and Exchange Commission (SEC) through a registration statement (a portion of which is called a *prospectus*), or sold pursuant to an exemption from this registration requirement. The most frequently used exemption is Rule 144A, which allows for the immediate resale of restricted securities among qualified institutional buyers. These institutions, often referred to as *QIBs*, manage $100 million or more in discretionary investable assets. The majority of debt offerings and a large portion of convertible offerings in the United States are now completed on a 144A basis. Transactions in securities that are exempt from registration because the securities were not offered or sold in a public offering are called *private placements*, and investors in private placements must be contacted without the use of a general solicitation or advertising process. A primary market offering that is registered with the SEC is called a *public offering* (see Exhibit 3.1).

When a company sells stock to the public for the first time in an SEC-registered offering, this is an Initial Public Offering (IPO). Subsequent sales of stock to the public by the company are called *follow-on offerings*. If major shareholders of a company wish to sell their shares,

**Private Placements**

Private placements of bonds (that are not of the same class as an exchange-listed security) may be exempt from registration with the SEC when both initial sale (to an underwriter) and subsequent sales are limited to sophisticated investors who are qualified institutional buyers (QIBs). The terms for private placements are often either more restrictive or more expensive for the borrower because of illiquidity: investors are restricted when reselling the bonds to other QIBs, which usually results in a lower resale price compared to a public market security that has a much broader investor base to tap into.  Most bond and convertible transactions (other than mandatory convertibles) are completed without registration with the SEC based on a Rule 144A exemption.

**EXHIBIT 3.1**

subject to the company's agreement, the shares can be sold using the company's registration statement, enabling a broad selling effort. This is called a *selling shareholder offering* (or a *secondary offering,* as described earlier), and the agreement to use the company's registration statement is called a *registration rights agreement.*

Most public market securities offerings are underwritten by investment banks, where the bank buys the entire issue at a discount and attempts to resell it at a higher price. The difference between the purchase and sale price is called the *gross spread* and represents compensation for the bank for undertaking a distribution effort and certain legal risks. Subject to agreement between the issuer and the bank (called an *underwriting agreement*), the underwriting can be completed either on a best-efforts basis, in which the issuer bears security price risk, or on a firm-commitment basis (bought deal), in which the bank bears security price risk. In either scenario, the investment bank still bears closing and settlement risks.

Typically, a group or *syndicate* of investment banks underwrites a securities offering. In this case, the issuer must decide which banks will act as the *lead bookrunners* of the transaction. The lead bookrunners have responsibility for determining the marketing method and pricing for the transaction and, therefore, receive the highest underwriting allocation and a proportionately higher percentage of the gross spread. Sometimes, one bank will be the dominant bookrunner, and in other cases, the bookrunners operate on an equal basis. Other banks that participate in the syndicate, called *co-managers,* take on smaller underwriting allocations. They may provide minor input to the bookrunner(s) on marketing and pricing issues, but they do not control this process, and have less risk and less work to do. As a result, they receive lower compensation. There can be between one and seven co-managers in an underwriting syndicate. In some securities offerings, there may be another group of investment banks that participate in the *selling group* for the offering. These banks don't take any financial risk and receive even lower compensation.

The investment banking industry keeps track of underwriting participations by all banks, and this becomes a basis for comparing banks' underwriting capabilities. This record is called a *league table,* and every different type of security (and geographic region) has its own league table. The most important league table is the one that keeps track of a bank's bookrunning underwriting activity. In this table, the bookrunners receive full credit for the entire proceeds of the offering (with the proceeds divided by the number of bookrunners), irrespective of the percentage actually underwritten by the bookrunning banks. (See Exhibits 3.2 and 3.3, for equity and debt league tables, respectively.)

## Global Equity League Tables, 2008 and 1H-2009

### 2008 Total Equity

| Rank | Bookrunner Parents | Value $bn | No. | % share |
|---|---|---|---|---|
| 1 | Bank of America Merrill Lynch | 80.7 | 189 | 12.7 |
| 2 | J.P. Morgan | 73.6 | 179 | 11.6 |
| 3 | Goldman Sachs | 61.2 | 126 | 9.6 |
| 4 | Citi | 49.7 | 149 | 7.8 |
| 5 | Morgan Stanley | 47.1 | 134 | 7.4 |
| 6 | UBS | 40.3 | 163 | 6.3 |
| 7 | Credit Suisse | 32.1 | 117 | 5.1 |
| 8 | Deutsche Bank | 25.7 | 108 | 4.1 |
| 9 | Barclays Capital | 25.1 | 52 | 3.9 |
| 10 | RBS | 16.9 | 55 | 2.7 |
| | Subtotal | 452.3 | 810 | 71.2 |
| | Total | 635.4 | 3,025 | 100.0 |

### 2008 IPO

| Rank | Bookrunner Parents | Value $bn | No. | % share |
|---|---|---|---|---|
| 1 | Bank of America Merrill Lynch | 9.3 | 27 | 11.2 |
| 2 | Citi | 8.0 | 24 | 9.6 |
| 3 | UBS | 7.6 | 25 | 9.2 |
| 4 | J.P. Morgan | 6.8 | 15 | 8.2 |
| 5 | Morgan Stanley | 5.0 | 22 | 6.0 |
| 6 | Goldman Sachs | 5.0 | 11 | 6.0 |
| 7 | Deutsche Bank | 4.4 | 15 | 5.3 |
| 8 | Credit Suisse | 4.2 | 20 | 5.0 |
| 9 | HSBC | 4.1 | 10 | 4.9 |
| 10 | Wells - Wachovia Securities | 2.6 | 3 | 3.2 |
| | Subtotal | 56.8 | 102 | 68.7 |
| | Total | 82.8 | 696 | 100.0 |

### 2008 Stock (Follow-On + IPO)

| Rank | Bookrunner Parents | Value $bn | No. | % share |
|---|---|---|---|---|
| 1 | Bank of America Merrill Lynch | 64.5 | 141 | 12.2 |
| 2 | J.P. Morgan | 59.4 | 133 | 11.2 |
| 3 | Goldman Sachs | 48.9 | 95 | 9.2 |
| 4 | Morgan Stanley | 38.7 | 104 | 7.3 |
| 5 | Citi | 37.6 | 115 | 7.1 |
| 6 | UBS | 36.3 | 138 | 6.9 |
| 7 | Credit Suisse | 28.3 | 96 | 5.3 |
| 8 | Deutsche Bank | 21.1 | 86 | 4.0 |
| 9 | RBS | 16.3 | 50 | 3.1 |
| 10 | Barclays Capital | 15.0 | 36 | 2.8 |
| | Subtotal | 366.2 | 658 | 69.1 |
| | Total | 530.0 | 2,737 | 100.0 |

### 2008 Convertibles

| Rank | Bookrunner Parents | Value $bn | No. | % share |
|---|---|---|---|---|
| 1 | Bank of America Merrill Lynch | 16.2 | 48 | 15.3 |
| 2 | J.P. Morgan | 14.1 | 46 | 13.4 |
| 3 | Goldman Sachs | 12.3 | 31 | 11.7 |
| 4 | Citi | 12.1 | 34 | 11.5 |
| 5 | Barclays Capital | 10.1 | 16 | 9.6 |
| 6 | Morgan Stanley | 8.4 | 30 | 7.9 |
| 7 | Deutsche Bank | 4.6 | 22 | 4.4 |
| 8 | UBS | 4.0 | 25 | 3.8 |
| 9 | Credit Suisse | 3.8 | 21 | 3.6 |
| 10 | Nomura | 2.8 | 6 | 2.6 |
| | Subtotal | 88.3 | 155 | 83.8 |
| | Total | 105.4 | 288 | 100.0 |

### 1H-2009 Total Equity

| Rank | Bookrunner Parents | Value $bn | No. | % share |
|---|---|---|---|---|
| 1 | J.P. Morgan | 58.4 | 180 | 16.7 |
| 2 | Goldman Sachs | 39.5 | 104 | 11.3 |
| 3 | Morgan Stanley | 34.4 | 139 | 9.8 |
| 4 | UBS | 26.2 | 119 | 7.5 |
| 5 | Bank of America Merrill Lynch | 22.9 | 139 | 6.5 |
| 6 | Citi | 19.0 | 116 | 5.4 |
| 7 | Credit Suisse | 17.9 | 88 | 5.1 |
| 8 | Deutsche Bank | 16.2 | 76 | 4.6 |
| 9 | Nomura | 10.0 | 23 | 2.9 |
| 10 | HSBC | 9.4 | 18 | 2.7 |
| | Subtotal | 253.8 | 601 | 72.5 |
| | Total | 350.2 | 1,874 | 100.0 |

### 1H-2009 IPO

| Rank | Bookrunner Parents | Value $bn | No. | % share |
|---|---|---|---|---|
| 1 | J.P. Morgan | 1.6 | 7 | 12.1 |
| 2 | UBS | 1.4 | 4 | 10.6 |
| 3 | Goldman Sachs | 1.3 | 4 | 9.3 |
| 4 | Morgan Stanley | 1.1 | 9 | 7.9 |
| 5 | Banco do Brasil SA | 0.7 | 1 | 5.3 |
| 6 | Banco Santander SA | 0.7 | 1 | 5.3 |
| 7 | Banco Bradesco SA | 0.7 | 1 | 5.3 |
| 8 | Bank of America Merrill Lynch | 0.6 | 5 | 4.8 |
| 9 | HSBC | 0.6 | 3 | 4.6 |
| 10 | Credit Suisse | 0.5 | 7 | 4.1 |
| | Subtotal | 9.3 | 25 | 69.1 |
| | Total | 13.5 | 145 | 100.0 |

### 1H-2009 Stock (Follow-On + IPO)

| Rank | Bookrunner Parents | Value $bn | No. | % share |
|---|---|---|---|---|
| 1 | J.P. Morgan | 52.1 | 144 | 16.7 |
| 2 | Goldman Sachs | 36.1 | 84 | 11.5 |
| 3 | Morgan Stanley | 29.7 | 115 | 9.5 |
| 4 | UBS | 25.7 | 114 | 8.2 |
| 5 | Bank of America Merrill Lynch | 20.1 | 115 | 6.4 |
| 6 | Credit Suisse | 15.9 | 72 | 5.1 |
| 7 | Citi | 15.7 | 93 | 5.0 |
| 8 | Deutsche Bank | 14.4 | 62 | 4.6 |
| 9 | Nomura | 9.5 | 20 | 3.0 |
| 10 | HSBC | 9.1 | 16 | 2.9 |
| | Subtotal | 228.2 | 518 | 72.9 |
| | Total | 313.1 | 1,708 | 100.0 |

### 1H-2009 Convertibles

| Rank | Bookrunner Parents | Value $bn | No. | % share |
|---|---|---|---|---|
| 1 | J.P. Morgan | 6.3 | 36 | 17.0 |
| 2 | Morgan Stanley | 4.6 | 24 | 12.5 |
| 3 | Goldman Sachs | 3.4 | 20 | 9.2 |
| 4 | Citi | 3.2 | 23 | 8.7 |
| 5 | Bank of America Merrill Lynch | 2.8 | 24 | 7.5 |
| 6 | Calyon | 2.2 | 7 | 5.8 |
| 7 | Credit Suisse | 2.0 | 16 | 5.4 |
| 8 | SG Corporate & Invst. Banking | 1.9 | 6 | 5.1 |
| 9 | Deutsche Bank | 1.9 | 14 | 5.0 |
| 10 | BNP Paribas | 1.7 | 7 | 4.5 |
| | Subtotal | 30.0 | 87 | 80.9 |
| | Total | 37.1 | 166 | 100.0 |

Note: Subtotal under deal count column does not foot to summation of top 10 bookrunners as some deals have multiple bookrunners. Values are apportioned among the bookrunners and each receives one credit under deal count.

Source: Dealogic

**EXHIBIT 3.2**

## Global Debt League Tables, 2008 and 1H-2009

| 2008 Total Debt | | | |
|---|---|---|---|
| Rank | Bookrunner Parents | Value $bn | No. | % share |
| 1 | Bank of America Merrill Lynch | 398.0 | 2,580 | 9.0 |
| 2 | Barclays Capital | 370.5 | 1,497 | 8.4 |
| 3 | J.P. Morgan | 352.7 | 1,200 | 8.0 |
| 4 | Deutsche Bank | 253.4 | 830 | 5.7 |
| 5 | Citi | 252.9 | 940 | 5.7 |
| 6 | RBS | 211.5 | 807 | 4.8 |
| 7 | UBS | 203.1 | 1,096 | 4.6 |
| 8 | Goldman Sachs | 187.0 | 543 | 4.2 |
| 9 | Credit Suisse | 180.8 | 678 | 4.1 |
| 10 | Morgan Stanley | 169.4 | 713 | 3.8 |
| | Subtotal | 2,579.2 | 8,618 | 58.2 |
| | Total | 4,433.6 | 18,157 | 100.0 |

| 2008 Investment Grade | | | |
|---|---|---|---|
| Rank | Bookrunner Parents | Value $bn | No. | % share |
| 1 | J.P. Morgan | 151.5 | 358 | 7.9 |
| 2 | Bank of America Merrill Lynch | 148.7 | 344 | 7.8 |
| 3 | Barclays Capital | 132.1 | 298 | 6.9 |
| 4 | Citi | 127.6 | 354 | 6.7 |
| 5 | RBS | 101.6 | 252 | 5.3 |
| 6 | Deutsche Bank | 100.0 | 230 | 5.2 |
| 7 | Goldman Sachs | 89.1 | 180 | 4.7 |
| 8 | UBS | 82.2 | 242 | 4.3 |
| 9 | HSBC | 80.3 | 226 | 4.2 |
| 10 | Morgan Stanley | 79.3 | 185 | 4.1 |
| | Subtotal | 1,092.1 | 1,557 | 57.0 |
| | Total | 1,916.5 | 3,745 | 100.0 |

| 2008 High Yield | | | |
|---|---|---|---|
| Rank | Bookrunner Parents | Value $bn | No. | % share |
| 1 | Bank of America Merrill Lynch | 11.9 | 53 | 10.7 |
| 2 | J.P. Morgan | 9.2 | 45 | 8.3 |
| 3 | Credit Suisse | 8.0 | 33 | 7.2 |
| 4 | Citi | 6.4 | 38 | 5.8 |
| 5 | Morgan Stanley | 5.6 | 25 | 5.0 |
| 6 | Deutsche Bank | 3.7 | 25 | 3.3 |
| 7 | RBS | 3.7 | 19 | 3.3 |
| 8 | UBS | 3.5 | 23 | 3.2 |
| 9 | Goldman Sachs | 3.5 | 22 | 3.1 |
| 10 | Barclays Capital | 2.7 | 19 | 2.4 |
| | Subtotal | 58.1 | 161 | 52.3 |
| | Total | 111.2 | 766 | 100.0 |

| 2008 Structured Finance (ABS & MBS) | | | |
|---|---|---|---|
| Rank | Bookrunner Parents | Value $bn | No. | % share |
| 1 | Bank of America Merrill Lynch | 76.0 | 154 | 17.0 |
| 2 | Barclays Capital | 49.4 | 117 | 11.1 |
| 3 | J.P. Morgan | 44.9 | 101 | 10.1 |
| 4 | RBS | 35.5 | 111 | 7.9 |
| 5 | Citi | 34.8 | 96 | 7.8 |
| 6 | Credit Suisse | 30.0 | 83 | 6.7 |
| 7 | Deutsche Bank | 29.2 | 87 | 6.5 |
| 8 | Goldman Sachs | 16.4 | 48 | 3.7 |
| 9 | Morgan Stanley | 14.1 | 34 | 3.2 |
| 10 | UBS | 13.2 | 33 | 3.0 |
| | Subtotal | 343.6 | 652 | 76.9 |
| | Total | 446.8 | 1,069 | 100.0 |

| 1H-2009 Total Debt | | | |
|---|---|---|---|
| Rank | Bookrunner Parents | Value $bn | No. | % share |
| 1 | J.P. Morgan | 303.9 | 808 | 8.8 |
| 2 | Barclays Capital | 251.0 | 752 | 7.3 |
| 3 | Citi | 231.8 | 693 | 6.7 |
| 4 | Bank of America Merrill Lynch | 208.5 | 682 | 6.1 |
| 5 | Deutsche Bank | 175.3 | 569 | 5.1 |
| 6 | HSBC | 172.7 | 591 | 5.0 |
| 7 | Goldman Sachs | 168.9 | 400 | 4.9 |
| 8 | RBS | 159.3 | 507 | 4.6 |
| 9 | Morgan Stanley | 152.4 | 454 | 4.4 |
| 10 | BNP Paribas | 143.4 | 418 | 4.2 |
| | Subtotal | 1,967.2 | 3,922 | 57.2 |
| | Total | 3,441.3 | 9,288 | 100.0 |

| 1H-2009 Investment Grade | | | |
|---|---|---|---|
| Rank | Bookrunner Parents | Value $bn | No. | % share |
| 1 | J.P. Morgan | 132.0 | 294 | 7.9 |
| 2 | Citi | 131.7 | 283 | 7.9 |
| 3 | Barclays Capital | 107.1 | 246 | 6.4 |
| 4 | Bank of America Merrill Lynch | 100.4 | 240 | 6.0 |
| 5 | RBS | 90.2 | 204 | 5.4 |
| 6 | HSBC | 83.9 | 229 | 5.0 |
| 7 | Morgan Stanley | 82.2 | 171 | 4.9 |
| 8 | BNP Paribas | 77.8 | 214 | 4.7 |
| 9 | Deutsche Bank | 72.7 | 201 | 4.4 |
| 10 | Goldman Sachs | 70.9 | 157 | 4.3 |
| | Subtotal | 948.8 | 1,093 | 57.0 |
| | Total | 1,663.8 | 2,389 | 100.0 |

| 1H-2009 High Yield | | | |
|---|---|---|---|
| Rank | Bookrunner Parents | Value $bn | No. | % share |
| 1 | Bank of America Merrill Lynch | 12.0 | 73 | 12.9 |
| 2 | J.P. Morgan | 10.4 | 65 | 11.1 |
| 3 | Citi | 8.7 | 56 | 9.3 |
| 4 | Deutsche Bank | 6.8 | 43 | 7.2 |
| 5 | Morgan Stanley | 5.6 | 27 | 6.0 |
| 6 | Goldman Sachs | 4.6 | 29 | 5.0 |
| 7 | BTA Bank | 4.3 | 2 | 4.6 |
| 8 | Credit Suisse | 4.2 | 33 | 4.5 |
| 9 | Wells Fargo Securities | 3.7 | 32 | 4.0 |
| 10 | RBS | 2.0 | 16 | 2.2 |
| | Subtotal | 62.3 | 152 | 66.7 |
| | Total | 93.4 | 410 | 100.0 |

| 1H-2009 Structured Finance (ABS & MBS) | | | |
|---|---|---|---|
| Rank | Bookrunner Parents | Value $bn | No. | % share |
| 1 | Bank of America Merrill Lynch | 36.7 | 59 | 16.7 |
| 2 | J.P. Morgan | 27.2 | 48 | 12.4 |
| 3 | Barclays Capital | 23.8 | 40 | 10.9 |
| 4 | Goldman Sachs | 21.3 | 28 | 9.7 |
| 5 | RBS | 18.0 | 43 | 8.2 |
| 6 | Citi | 17.8 | 34 | 8.1 |
| 7 | Credit Suisse | 16.1 | 37 | 7.3 |
| 8 | Deutsche Bank | 12.8 | 40 | 5.8 |
| 9 | Rabobank | 3.4 | 2 | 1.5 |
| 10 | Amherst Securities Group Inc | 3.1 | 8 | 1.4 |
| | Subtotal | 180.2 | 257 | 82.1 |
| | Total | 219.4 | 421 | 100.0 |

Note: Subtotal under deal count column does not foot to summation of top 10 bookrunners as some deals have multiple bookrunners. Values are apportioned among the bookrunners and each receives one credit under deal count.

Source: Dealogic

EXHIBIT 3.3

The capital markets groups at investment banks are principally responsible for originating and executing capital markets transactions. In this role, they coordinate with client coverage bankers to target likely issuers and, with professionals from the syndicate desk, determine appropriate potential pricing. In conjunction with the client coverage banker, the capital markets group enters into an intensely competitive process to receive a *mandate* from an issuer for a financing. Competitive pressures sometimes compel investment banks to undertake considerable risks, such as agreeing to a bought deal: buying an entire transaction at a specified price from the issuer and attempting to resell the security at a higher price to investors. Another risk that investment banks sometimes assume involves providing a large loan to a client as a *bridge* financing (to support an M&A transaction) prior to a subsequent *take-out* financing underwritten by the bank in the capital markets. If markets do not permit a take-out financing on reasonable terms, the bank is required to fund the loan for the client.

## Financing Considerations

When investment bankers advise issuers regarding potential financing transactions, the bankers typically focus on liquidity (cash balances, marketable securities, and available lines of credit), cash flow multiples, debt/earnings multiples, cost of capital, and rating agency considerations before recommending whether a client should raise financing, and, if so, whether it should be in the form of debt, equity, or a hybrid security like a convertible. Bankers also analyze the company's liquidity as a percentage of market capitalization, total debt, annual interest payment obligations, and other balance sheet and income statement metrics. These metrics are then compared with results from other companies in the same industry to determine whether the client has relatively more or less liquidity than its competitors. This analysis provides a foundation for discussing whether a company needs to increase or decrease liquidity (see Exhibit 3.4). If it is determined that a company needs to increase liquidity, bankers will discuss a range of financing alternatives, as described in Exhibit 3.5.

### Corporate Capital Structure

Companies focus on raising cash or reducing cash:

| Raise Cash Through: | Reduce Cash Through: |
|---|---|
| Debt issuance: | Share repurchases: |
| • public or private bonds, loans or securitization | • open market, auctions, or derivatives |
| Equity-related issuance: | Asset acquisitions: |
| • public or private share issuance, convertibles or preferred shares | • M&A |
| | Retire debt, convertibles, or preferred shares |
| Selling assets: | Increase capital expenditures |
| • M&A | Dividend payments: |
| Decrease capital expenditures | • quarterly small payments or one time large special dividend |
| Cut dividends or eliminate share repurchases | |

Key areas of focus that relate to capital structure include EPS, credit ratings, financial flexibility, hedging assets and liabilities, tax implications and maintaining capital structure parity with principal competitors.

**EXHIBIT 3.4**

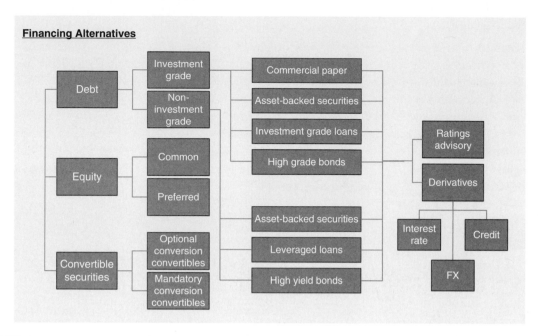

**EXHIBIT 3.5**

After a company and its banker agree on the need for new financing, they must, in the first case, decide whether to offer debt securities or equity securities. An equity offering generally has a higher cost of capital than a debt financing and will likely cause a drop in earnings per share (EPS) for the issuer, which may negatively impact the company's share price. However, equity will strengthen the company's balance sheet and may lead to a higher bond rating from a credit rating agency, which may result in lower future bond financing costs and higher long-term value. A debt offering usually has a lower cost of capital, but may weaken the company's balance sheet and reduce financial flexibility. As a result, the company and its banker must consider the risk-adjusted cost of debt when comparing this form of financing with an equity financing. Before issuing new debt, bankers and their clients must consider both the impact of debt on cash flow multiples (to determine if additional interest charges can be adequately covered by cash flow), and the likely impact on credit ratings. They also must decide whether management has the requisite skills to manage a more leveraged company. In the final analysis, risk-adjusted cost of capital, credit ratings, comparisons with peer companies, equity and debt analyst views, and management comfort with the resultant balance sheet are among the many considerations that determine whether a company raises financing from debt, equity, or convertible markets.

## Financing Alternatives

After making a decision regarding the type of financing (debt, equity, or hybrid), the client and the banker consider an array of financing alternatives to determine the optimal financing product.

## Debt Financing

If a company decides to issue debt that will be rated by credit rating agencies, the debt offering will be classified as either investment-grade debt or non-investment-grade debt. Investment-grade debt has bond ratings of BBB- or higher from Standard & Poor's (S&P) or Fitch, and/or Baa3 or higher from Moody's (see Exhibit 3.6). Investment grade ratings suggest stronger balance sheets and greater ability to withstand large demands on cash balances. Non-investment-grade ratings start at BB+ or Ba1 and decline based on the relative weakness of the debt issuer. Debt financing alternatives include investment-grade (high-grade) bonds, non-investment-grade (high-yield or *junk*) bonds, investment-grade loans, low-grade (leveraged) loans, asset-backed securities, and commercial paper (see Exhibit 3.6).

### Credit Ratings

| Investment Grade | | Below Investment Grade | |
|---|---|---|---|
| Moody's | S&P and Fitch | Moody's | S&P and Fitch |
| Aaa | AAA | Ba1 | BB+ |
| Aa1 | AA+ | Ba2 | BB |
| Aa2 | AA | Ba3 | BB- |
| Aa3 | AA- | B1 | B+ |
| A1 | A+ | B2 | B |
| A2 | A | B3 | B- |
| A3 | A- | Caa | CCC |
| Baa1 | BBB+ | | |
| Baa2 | BBB | | |
| Baa3 | BBB- | | |

Source: Standard & Poor's, Moody's and Fitch

**EXHIBIT 3.6**

### Bonds

A bond is debt in the form of a security, issued as a long-term obligation of a borrower with a specific maturity and coupon. The debt capital markets group at an investment bank underwrites a bond offering by purchasing the security from the issuer and reselling it to institutional investors or individual investors through a registered public offering or through a 144A offering. The underwriting could be in the form of a best-efforts underwriting (issuer bears price risk), a bought deal underwriting (investment bank bears price risk), or a backstop commitment (investment bank commits to a worst-case price). See Exhibit 3.7 for a description of these types of bond underwritings. Investment-grade bonds and junk bonds are originated through two different teams within the debt capital markets group of an investment bank.

### Loans

Loans are not securities from a U.S. regulatory perspective, and therefore there is no registration process with the SEC. The banks and other sophisticated lenders who provide loans require more onerous restrictions (covenants) on the borrower compared to the restrictions imposed by a bond. See Exhibit 3.8 for a description of the principal differences between loans and bonds.

**Types of Bond Underwritings**

| **Best Efforts** | |
|---|---|
| • Comprises a majority of transactions<br>• Issuer of bond bears price risk | • Least expensive<br>• Market deal |
| **Bought Deal** | |
| • Investment bank buys the bond at a certain rate<br>• Generally seen in competitive markets | • Investment bank bears the price risk |
| **Backstop Commitments** | |
| • Rate is "backstopped" or committed to, but issuer will get the lower rate if it clears the market | • Investment bank commits to a worst case price |

EXHIBIT 3.7

**How Do Companies Choose Between Loans and Bonds?**

- Prepayable vs. non-prepayable debt
  - ○ Loans are generally prepayable at anytime at par
  - ○ Bonds are non-callable for some period of time, usually 4 to 5 years
- Bonds usually have no covenants
  - ○ Incurrence covenants vs. maintenance covenants
  - ○ Usually less restrictive on incurring more debt
- Loans require amortization
- Bond investors generally accept more risk and therefore receive higher returns
- Bonds have longer maturities
- Bonds are generally more expensive

EXHIBIT 3.8

## Asset-Backed Securities

Asset-backed securities are debt securities that have interest, and principal payments that are backed by underlying cash flows from other assets such as first mortgage loans, home equity loans, auto loans, credit card receivables, student loans, or equipment leases. Investment banks create asset-backed securities by either selecting a pool of assets to sell directly to investors or by acquiring collateralized debt and selling the cash-flow-producing debt to specially created third parties called special-purpose vehicles (SPVs). An SPV is designed to insulate investors from the credit risk of the originating financial institution. The SPV sells pooled loans to a trust, which issues interest-bearing securities that can achieve an independent credit rating based solely on the cash flows created by the assets. (See **Case Study 5, "A Tale of Two Hedge Funds: Magnetar and Peloton,"** for further discussion of asset-backed securities.)

Collateralized Debt Obligations (CDOs) are a type of asset-backed security that divides assets into different tranches: senior tranches (rated AAA), mezzanine tranches (AA to BB), and equity tranches (unrated). Losses are applied in reverse order of seniority, so lower-rated tranches offer higher coupons to compensate for higher default risk. The coupons on each tranche are slightly higher than the coupons on correspondingly rated corporate debt. This *yield pick-up* is a principal reason why CDO issuance grew rapidly from 2000 to 2007, creating significant profits for investment bank underwriters. Collateralized Loan Obligations (CLOs) are CDOs that are backed by leveraged loans. Collateralized Bond Obligations (CBOs) are CDOs that are backed by high-yield bonds. The credit crunch that started during mid-2007 dramatically decreased CDO issuance (see Exhibit 3.9) and created huge losses at investment banks that held large CDO underwriting-related and investment inventory. The International Monetary Fund has estimated that all CDO-related losses suffered by global financial firms between mid-2007 and the end of 2008 may have been up to $1 trillion.

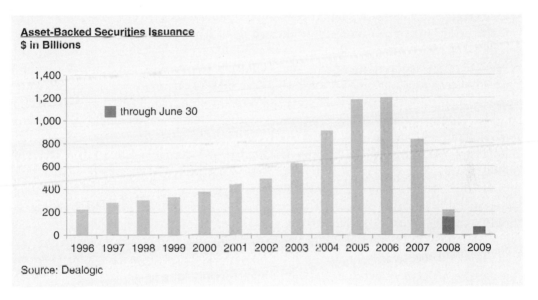

**EXHIBIT 3.9**

## Commercial Paper
Commercial paper is a short-term U.S. promissory note with a maturity that does not exceed 270 days. Financial companies comprise approximately three quarters of all commercial paper issuance. Commercial paper is exempt from registration with the SEC, widely marketed, subject to market conditions and represents a very low-cost vehicle for raising short-term financing.

## Equity Financing

### Initial Public Offerings (IPOs)
An investment bank's equity capital markets group helps private companies determine if an initial public offering of stock is a logical decision based on an analysis of benefits and disadvantages (see below). The bank then determines if there is sufficient investor demand to purchase new equity securities offered by the company. Assuming sufficient interest, the investment bank

determines the expected value of the company based on comparisons with publicly traded comparable companies or values derived through other methods (including discounted cash flow [DCF] analyses). This is an imperfect process that requires analysis of both historical operating earnings and revenues, and forecasts for future earnings and revenues. Because it is sometimes difficult to find good comparable companies, and forecasts can be problematic, the valuation process for some prospective IPO candidates can be more art than science. The discussion of Comparable Company Analysis in Chapter 4 provides some insight into this valuation process.

Principal benefits of going public include:

1. Access to public market funding: for a U.S. offering, registration with the SEC enables the broadest exposure to investors, not only for the initial public offering but also for subsequent follow-on offerings. This allows the company to have a broad, diverse ownership structure (including retail and institutional ownership) that could help stabilize share prices during market downcycles. The rigorous disclosures required by the SEC create investor confidence and, potentially, a stronger demand for shares.

2. Enhanced profile and marketing benefits: public companies receive more attention from the public media, which can result in heightened interest in company products and increased market share.

3. Creation of an acquisition currency and compensation vehicle: public stock can be used instead of cash for future acquisitions, which can be very important for companies with high growth opportunities. In addition, stock and stock options can be used as employee incentives and compensation vehicles. This preserves cash, creates greater employee commitment, and facilitates recruiting.

4. Liquidity for shareholders: an IPO allows founders to reduce exposure to their company by selling shares. However, sales by founders and other key employees (selling shareholders) are usually no more than 25% of the IPO offering in order to maintain a significant risk position (although this percentage can be higher, depending on how long selling shareholders have held the stock and the total size of the offering). This provides IPO purchasers with confidence that founders and managers will remain economically motivated to increase shareholder value. In addition, the need for primary capital in order to operate and grow the business is a key consideration in determining the mix of primary and secondary shares offered in an IPO.

Principal disadvantages of going public include:

1. Reporting requirements: an SEC registration requires not only upfront accounting and other reporting that conforms to SEC requirements, but also quarterly, annual, and other event-related reporting through filing of 10-Ks, 10-Qs, and 8-Ks. In addition, proxy statements and individual reporting for officers, directors, and principal shareholders are required. Equally important are the compliance requirements for public companies that were created by the Sarbanes-Oxley Act of 2002 (SOX), which imposes a vast array of time-consuming reporting and procedural obligations on a public company and its officers.

2. Costs: these ongoing reporting requirements create significant annual costs, including legal, accounting, and tax reporting costs (which substantially increased post-SOX). Most companies also have to replace or significantly upgrade their corporate information systems, which is very expensive as well. In addition, the upfront costs for an IPO are considerable. For example, up to 7% (this percentage may decrease as the deal size increases) of the IPO proceeds go to investment bankers as a gross spread (fee), and approximately 3% of IPO

proceeds pay for legal, printing, accounting, and other costs, depending on the size of the transaction. As a result, often less than 90% of the IPO proceeds are kept by the issuer. Finally, a cost should be assigned to management time spent launching an IPO. Management will be required to allocate a large amount of time reviewing documents to be filed with the SEC and then traveling to multiple cities to meet with prospective institutional investors during the *road show.*

3.  Disclosure: the SEC requires companies to share an extensive amount of information in the registration process, and some of this may be potentially sensitive information that could benefit competitors.

4.  Short-term management focus: the requirement to provide quarterly information to investors through 10-Q filings often diverts management's attention from managing a business that creates long-term value to managing a business that achieves quarterly results expected by the market. Shareholders usually expect steady growth in quarterly earnings, and if this is not achieved, the company's share price may decline. This can create pressure to manage the company for the short-term, at the expense of creating long-term value.

The IPO process starts with a selection by the company of the investment banks they will work with as the lead bookrunners. The selected banks will develop a valuation model to determine the share price range for the offering and recommend the number of shares to be offered. The company also selects other investment banks to act as co-managers of the offering, determines the use of proceeds, and chooses the exchange on which to list its shares. The company then works with its auditing firm to create financial statements that are consistent with SEC requirements. The company's and the investment banks' legal counsels prepare filing documents with the SEC (usually an "S-1" filing) in conjunction with the bankers and company officers. This filing is referred to as the *registration statement,* of which a portion is called the *prospectus.* The filing notifies the public regarding the potential IPO and provides considerable information regarding the issuer. The registration statement is subsequently amended one or more times based on comments received from the SEC. After all changes requested by the SEC are incorporated, and the lead bookrunners and company agree on a share price range (which is usually based principally on either a comparable company valuation, or DCF valuation completed by the lead bookrunners), the registration statement is amended for the last time to include the price range.

The company and lead bookrunners then decide on a schedule for a road show, which could take up to two weeks and starts after a *teach-in* at each of the investment banks participating in the underwriting. The teach-in is an opportunity for research analysts at each bank to provide their views on the company to sales people in the bank's Trading Division. The equity capital markets and sales teams from the lead bookrunners, together with company management, will then talk with prospective investors during the road show, using a *red herring* prospectus, which is taken from the most recently amended S-1 registration statement filed with the SEC.

Road show discussions focus on the current health of the company, management's plans for the company going forward, comparisons with other companies, and investor reactions to the share price range and expected size of the offering (which is generally less than 25% of shares privately held, although this can vary, depending on the cash needs of the business). During the road show, investors provide the lead bookrunners with indications of interest, or specific prices at which they may buy a designated number of shares. Once the *book* is built and the lead bookrunners believe that they have a strong deal to price, the company asks the SEC to get ready to declare their registration statement "effective," and then the deal is priced (typically within the most recent price range, although approximately a quarter of IPOs end up pricing out of range). At this point, the SEC declares the registration effective and the lead bookrunners "allocate" shares to investors (see a sample IPO timeline in Exhibit 3.10).

The period between the beginning of the registration process (which starts when an issuer files the original S-1 prospectus with the SEC) until the SEC declares a registration effective has historically been called the *quiet period*. During the quiet period, the SEC allows a company to disclose their interest in offering IPO shares to investors only by means of a preliminary, red herring prospectus (so called because of a red legend on the cover page that states the preliminary nature of the information provided). In 2005, as a result of reforms enacted by the SEC, the company may also provide free-writing prospectuses (written offers to sell or solicit to buy securities) to investors after filing the registration statement, as long as a copy of the prospectus precedes or accompanies the free-writing prospectus. Further, if the free-writing prospectus is in electronic format, the issuer only needs to provide a hyperlink to the statutory prospectus. Other than this, "offers to sell" are not allowed during the quiet period, and publicity initiated by the company that has the effect of "conditioning the market" or arousing public interest in the issuer or its securities is also forbidden. Failure to abide by these rules may result in a *gun-jumping* violation, and the SEC may require the issuer to withdraw its filing. An example of a gun-jumping problem experienced by Google during 2004 in its "Dutch Auction" IPO is described in Exhibit 3.11. See Chapter 2 for a more detailed explanation of gun-jumping and other SEC issues associated with an IPO offering.

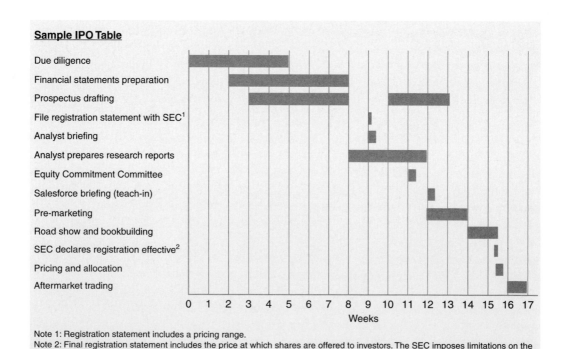

Note 1: Registration statement includes a pricing range.
Note 2: Final registration statement includes the price at which shares are offered to investors. The SEC imposes limitations on the issuer's communications during the "quiet period" that begins when a company files a registration statement with the SEC and ends when the final registration is declared effective.
Source: Morgan Stanley

**EXHIBIT 3.10**

## Google's Initial Public Offering

| Deal size: $1.7 billion | Date announced: April 29, 2004 | Date completed: August 18, 2004 |
| --- | --- | --- |

When Google set out to choose the bankers for its IPO, the company organized a working team that was charged with identifying qualified investment banks. The group initially selected 20 firms, requiring them all to sign confidentiality agreements before proceeding. Each firm was then sent a 21-point questionnaire, asking for its credentials and thoughts on the best way Google could approach its offering.

Google started holding in-person interviews with individuals from 12 firms. But instead of allowing bankers to make their traditional pitches, Google conducted the meetings as question-and-answer sessions, judging each firm's response to their plan to hold a modified Dutch auction for the company's IPO. By using an auction, Google hoped to ensure the greatest distribution possible to retail investors. Following the interviews, the company chose Credit Suisse First Boston and Morgan Stanley as joint-bookrunners.

Many investment banks tried to persuade Google to pursue a traditional "book-building" IPO based on a road show that enables bankers to obtain pricing input from large institutional investors. They reasoned that a Dutch auction would alienate these investors since it disenfranchises their pricing input and removes the opportunity to receive a large allocation directed by the bookrunner. However, Google persevered because they wanted a more egalitarian process. They also wanted to avoid some of the excesses that can occur in large IPOs, particularly the large first-day pop in a stock's price.

In a Dutch-auction system, investors weigh in with bids, listing the number of shares they want and how much they're willing to pay for them. Bids are stacked with the highest price at the top. Starting at the top of the stack and going down, a final market price is established at which all shares available for sale can be sold. All bidders get the selected lowest price offered. The system, heavily dependent on participation from retail investors, is not popular on Wall Street.

The Google IPO was a conundrum for investment bankers. Their firms wanted the cachet that would come with underwriting the highest-profile offering ever, but they were put off by the auction process and the lower-than-average fees Google was paying.

Banks typically earn commissions as high as 7 percent of the value of traditional IPOs they help to sell. That arrangement would have netted about $250 million for Google's banks. Instead, the company was offering to pay $97.8 million in commissions and underwriting discounts, or 2.7 percent of the $3.6 billion it was aiming to raise in its IPO.

When the SEC declared Google's registration effective in early August, bankers found themselves faced with the prospect of not only pricing the offering in a month that is traditionally slow for new issuance, but also with the Nasdaq index near a low for the year. Most issuers were pricing their deals below their target range, if not withdrawing their offerings altogether. But unwilling to postpone the deal, Google decided to go ahead, agreeing to cut the target price range to $85 – $95 per share, from the initial hopes of $108 – $135 per share. The company also cut the number of shares it would offer to 19.6 million, from 25.7 million.

In the weeks leading up to the pricing, Google faced another obstacle. First off, its efforts to level the playing field between institutional and retail investors were put under the microscope as Google refused to provide institutional investors with the same sort of in-depth financial guidance about its business that most issuers do.

All this secrecy, along with a unique, very short lockup structure that would allow Google employees to sell shares only 15 days following the IPO, spooked institutions. Then a Playboy magazine interview with Google's founders riled the SEC, leading to speculation that the deal would be pulled for possible quiet-period violations.

Google's management and bankers agreed to push forward, ultimately pricing the deal at $85 per share, with its electronic auction proving enough of a success that investors who placed bids at or above that price were granted at least 74% of their orders. And, despite all the criticism, Google's stock quickly proved a success. Shares closed at $100.34 at the end of the first day of trading. At the end of 2004, it closed at 192.79, a 127% increase over the offering price.

Note: This transaction did not fully meet Google's objectives because there was almost no retail participation (since Google did not allow a selling concession to retail brokers), and the price jumped 18% during the first day of trading, invalidating the principal purpose of the Dutch Auction (by leaving money on the table).

Source: Tunick, Britt Erica. "Google Goes Its Own Way: Novel Dutch auction had twists and turns all the way to IPO." IDD. 17 Jan. 2005.

EXHIBIT 3.11

## *Follow-on Offerings*

After an IPO is completed, subsequent SEC-registered equity offerings by a public company are called follow-on offerings. For these financings, an investment bank underwriting group is formed, with one or more lead bookrunners and a number of co-managers selected by the issuer.

For a U.S. follow-on offering, the company files an S-3 registration statement with the SEC (subject to their meeting the requirements to do so, among which is the requirement that the company must have been public for at least 1 year at the time of the filing), which enables, as is the case with an IPO, a broad-based marketing effort using a red herring prospectus during a road show (if conducted). A final prospectus that has been declared effective by the SEC is then used as the basis for confirming orders from investors. Unlike an IPO, however, a follow-on offering does not include a price range, since shares are priced in relation to the market price of the issuer's shares at the exchange on which they are listed. As a result, for follow-on transactions, investment bankers do not go through a valuation process with the company to establish a price range. Instead, they focus on, among other things, the most effective marketing plan for the offering, including the appropriate size, targeted investor base, and the appropriate price to set in relation to the price of outstanding shares at the time of the offering.

The size of a follow-on offering is important, because new shares cause dilution to current shareholders in terms of earnings per share (EPS). EPS concerns are mitigated if the company forecasts that future earnings will grow fast enough to offset the dilution associated with issuance of additional shares. If the offering size is too large relative to the growth in projected earnings, declining EPS may negatively impact the company's share price (subject to the use of proceeds and other considerations). Therefore, bankers and their issuing clients must be careful to properly size a follow-on offering. It is unusual for the proceeds of a follow-on offering to be in excess of 25% of the then-current stock market value (market capitalization) of the issuing company.

Good targets for follow-on offerings include companies that demonstrate the characteristics indicated in Exhibit 3.12. These companies must always consider the cost of capital associated with an equity offering. For most companies, an equity issuance will have a higher cost of capital compared to the issuance of debt. Consequently, many companies are reluctant to complete follow-on offerings, unless the proceeds of the offering can be used to create significant growth opportunities that will, over time, result in an increase in EPS (accretion) as opposed to EPS dilution. However, even in the case of dilution, some companies will still proceed with a follow-on offering if they determine that a financing is essential and that a debt offering would significantly weaken their balance sheet. Too much debt in a company's capital structure may cause rating agencies to reduce their credit ratings, which will likely increase the cost of debt financing. The focus of both the company and its investment bankers, therefore, is on striking a balance between

**Characteristics of Prospective Equity Issuers**

- Strong stock performance or supportive equity research
- Large insider holdings or small float/illiquid trading
- Overly leveraged capital structure
- Strategic event: finance acquisition or large capital expenditure
- Sum of the parts analysis indicates hidden value
    - Carve-out
    - Spin-off
    - Tracking stock
- Investor focus
    - Road show focuses investors on misunderstood value
    - Brings additional equity research

EXHIBIT 3.12

the amount of debt and equity in the company's capital structure. Frequently, bankers advise companies on the likely credit rating that will result from both debt and equity financing alternatives and build models to guide optimal financing decisions.

## Convertible Securities

A convertible security is a type of equity offering, even though most convertibles are originally issued in the form of a bond or preferred shares. Most convertible bonds or convertible preferred shares are convertible anytime, at the option of the investor, into a predetermined number of common shares of the issuer. This is called an *optionally converting convertible*. The other type of a convertible is a *mandatorily converting convertible,* where the investor must receive a variable number of common shares (based on a floating conversion price) at maturity (a mandatory receipt rather than an option to receive).

The issuer's preference regarding equity content of the convertible determines whether the convertible will be issued as an optionally converting convertible or a mandatorily converting convertible. From the perspective of a credit rating agency, an optionally converting bond is considered to have bond-type characteristics, since there is no assurance that the bond will convert into common shares and there is a fixed coupon payment obligation. As a result, when originally issued, an optionally converting bond weakens a company's balance sheet in almost the same way that a straight bond of the same size and maturity would, although the company's balance sheet will subsequently be strengthened if the convertible bond eventually converts into common shares. By contrast, mandatorily converting convertibles (mandatory convertible), from a credit rating agency perspective, are considered to have equity-type characteristics. This is because there is certainty regarding conversion into common stock, and therefore no cash repayment obligation at maturity in the event of nonconversion. In addition, most mandatory convertibles are issued in the form of preferred stock and there is no contractual issuer obligation to pay dividends on preferred shares, compared to a contractual obligation to pay interest coupons for a convertible bond. Therefore, mandatory convertibles strengthen a company's balance sheet in almost the same way that a common share offering of the same size would. Depending on the structure of the mandatory convertible, credit rating agencies generally assign between 50% and 100% equity content to this security.

### Rationale for Issuing Optionally Converting Convertible Bonds

If a company wants to issue debt, they might consider a convertible bond rather than a straight bond in order to reduce the coupon associated with debt issuance. For example, if a company could issue a $100 million bond with a 7-year maturity and a coupon of 6%, that same company might be able to issue a convertible bond for the same amount and maturity but with a coupon of 3%. The reason convertible bond investors might accept a coupon that is 3% lower than a straight bond coupon is because the convertible bond gives them the option to receive a predetermined number of common shares of the issuer's stock in lieu of receiving cash repayment. This option is valuable to investors because the future value of the stock might be considerably higher than the $100 million cash repayment value of the convertible bond. Basically, a convertible bond has an embedded call option on the issuer's common stock, and the investor "pays" for this option by accepting a lower coupon.

If the value of the common shares that convertible bond investors have the right to receive does not exceed $100 million during the life of the convertible, they will generally not elect to convert the bond into shares and will therefore receive $100 million in cash at maturity in 7 years. If the value of the shares exceeds $100 million on or any time before maturity, investors may elect to convert the bond and receive shares. See Exhibit 3.13 to determine the break-even future share price for the investor to be economically indifferent between purchasing a convertible compared to purchasing a bond issued by the same company.

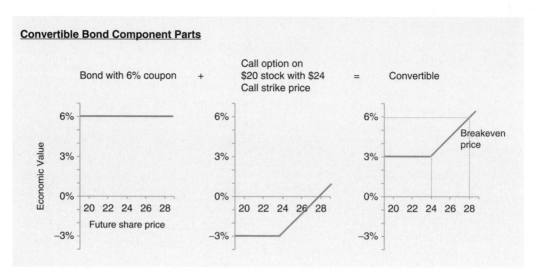

**EXHIBIT 3.13**

Convertible Bond Example

A company issues a $100 million convertible with a 7-year maturity and a 3% annual coupon. Investors are given the right to receive either $100 million repayment at maturity or, at their option, give up receipt of this cash amount in exchange for receiving a predetermined number of shares of the issuer's common stock. On the date of convertible issuance, the company's stock price is trading at $25, and the company agrees to a *conversion price* for the convertible of $31.25, which is 25% above $25. This percentage is called the *conversion premium,* because the conversion price is set at a premium (in this case, a 25% premium) to the company's share price on the date of convertible issuance. The conversion price determines the number of shares that the investor has the right to convert into. This determination is made by dividing the total proceeds of the offering by the conversion price. The result, in this example, is $100 million / $31.25 = 3.2 million shares. Convertible investors, therefore, have a choice to make: either take $100 million in cash at maturity, or give up the cash right in exchange for receiving 3.2 million shares any time at or before maturity. If, for example, the issuer's share price increases to $45 at maturity in 7 years, convertible investors might elect to give up the right to receive $100 million in cash in exchange for 3.2 million shares because the value of these shares would be 3.2 million × $45 = $144 million. In practice, most investors wait until maturity to make the conversion decision due to the value of the options embedded in the convertible, but they have the right to convert earlier.

Convertible Market

With the exception of the second half of 2008, the global convertible market has historically been a robust market, with proceeds raised typically equal to 20% to 70% of proceeds raised through follow-on common stock issuance (see Exhibit 3.14). During September of 2008, the SEC instituted a ban on short selling U.S. listed financial stocks. Because major investors in convertible bonds include convertible arbitrage hedge funds that short the underlying stock to hedge their long position in the convertible security, the short-sale ban effectively made this strategy impossible. As a result of this and the severe dislocation experienced by the credit markets following Lehman Brothers' bankruptcy, a large portion of the convertible bond market was essentially shutdown during the second half of 2008 and partway into 2009.

**Convertible Issuance vs. Follow-On Common Stock Issuance**

|  | #of Deals in 2008 | Total Proceeds in 2008 | #of Deals In 1H-2009 | Total Proceeds in 1H-2009 |
|---|---|---|---|---|
| Convertible Issuance | 288 | $105 billion | 166 | $37 billion |
| Follow-On Common Stock Issuance | 2,041 | $447 billion | 1,563 | $300 billion |

The second half of 2008 saw convertible issuance drop significantly to below historical norms, in part due to the temporary short sale ban instated by the SEC in September and October. Hedge funds, traditionally a major investor group in convertible securities (for their convertible arbitrage strategy funds), would not be able to hedge their long positions in the convertibles. With little demand, convertible issuance was notably anemic during the second half of 2008.

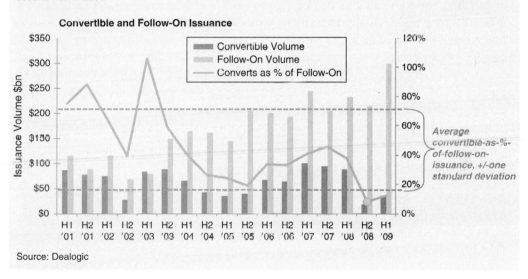

**EXHIBIT 3.14**

The two main types of convertible investors are *outright buyers* and *arbitrage buyers*. Outright buyers purchase convertibles with the expectation that the company's share price will exceed the conversion price (by an amount in excess of the break-even amount illustrated in Exhibit 3.13). Arbitrage buyers are focused on hedging share price risk and creating profits in excess of the coupon through *delta hedging* their position. This is described in more detail in Chapter 9. Arbitrage buyers principally consist of hedge funds that leverage their investment by using the convertibles they purchase as collateral for borrowing a significant portion of the purchase price of the convertibles. Historically, more than 70% of all convertibles have been purchased by hedge funds.

## Fees to Bankers

Investment banks that underwrite capital markets transactions are paid fees in the form of a gross spread (the difference between total proceeds of the offering and cash that the company receives, before paying legal, accounting, printing, and other offering expenses). This fee is broken into three parts:

1. Management fee (typically 20% of the total fee): This compensates the managers of the financing for their role in preparing the offering. The lead bookrunners receive a disproportionate amount of this fee.
2. Underwriting fee (typically 20% of the total fee): This compensates for underwriting risk. The fee is divided proportionally among underwriters based on the actual amount each firm underwrites.
3. Selling concession (typically 60% of the total fee): Usually apportioned based on each firm's underwriting commitment, this compensates underwriters for their selling efforts. Sometimes (although less common now), there is a *jump ball* selling structure in which the selling concession allocations are decided by investors.

See Exhibit 3.15 for a summary of global fees for equity underwriting.

The fees associated with convertible financing depend on the type of convertible security (i.e., convertible bond, convertible preferred shares, or mandatory convertible), the maturity, and structural issues. Generally in the United States, convertible financing fees range from 1.5% of proceeds for convertible bonds to 3% of proceeds for mandatory convertibles. Mandatory convertible fees are much higher than convertible bond fees because mandatory convertibles are similar to common stock from the perspective of investor share price exposure and are generally more complicated securities than convertible bonds. By comparison, bond fees range from 0.5% to 0.875% for high-grade bonds and 1.5% to 2.0% for high-yield (junk) bonds, and equity fees range from 2% to 6% for follow-on equity offerings and 3% to 7% for IPOs. For equity deals, the fee percentage is mostly an inverse function of the offering size. Fees for convertibles, IPOs, follow-on offerings, and bonds are somewhat lower outside of the United States.

**Equity Underwriting Gross Spreads (Fees), 2008 and 1H-2009**

|  | 2008 Total Global Volume | 2008 Total Global Fees | 1H-2009 Total Global Volume | 1H-2009 Total Global Fees |
|---|---|---|---|---|
| IPOs | $82.8 billion | $2,461.6 million | $13.5 billion | $495.7 million |
| Follow-On's | $447.2 billion | $9,646.7 million | $299.6 billion | $7,978.8 million |
| Convertibles | $105.4 billion | $2,121.5 million | $37.1 billion | $780.3 million |

Source: Dealogic

**EXHIBIT 3.15**

## Distribution Alternatives

A company and its investment bank must decide on how to distribute a capital markets offering. Historically, investment banks have conducted a 3- to 5-day road show for follow-on offerings (in comparison to a 7- to 10-day period for an IPO), since the market is already familiar with a company that initiates a follow-on offering. However, the road show period has recently been shortened to limit issuer price risk. The company's share price is subject to change during the road show for a follow-on offering, so if the share price drops, the company will receive lower proceeds than they would have if the offering had been completed immediately, without a road show. Sometimes, issuers mitigate this share price risk either by completing an accelerated offering with a shorter road show period of 1 or 2 days, or by carrying out a block trade, in which the investment bank buys the securities without a road show and bears full price risk (see Exhibit 3.16).

**Historical Distribution Alternatives**

| | |
|---|---|
| **Fully Marketed** | • Issuer bears share price risk<br>• 3-5 day management roadshow<br>• Red herring prospectus delivered<br>• Accesses widest pool of investor demand |
| **Accelerated** | • Issuer bears smaller share price risk<br>• 1-2 day management roadshow<br>• Red herring prospectus delivered<br>• Narrower access to investor demand |
| **Block Trade** | • Investment bank bears share price risk<br>• Marketing limited to sales calls to potential investors during the evening, with purchase commitment from bank before market opens the next morning<br>• No red herring prospectus<br>• Eliminates market risk for issuer<br>• Requires a discount to market price to accommodate risk taken by the bank |

Note 1: Recently, almost all distributions have been completed on an accelerated basis.

Note 2: Regardless of the distribution alternative, investment banks bear the risk of settlement: if an investor changes his mind the morning after a verbal commitment to purchase is made, the investment bank must purchase the securities at the offered price.

**EXHIBIT 3.16**

Because of the increased market volatility associated with the credit crisis of 2007–2008, the marketing timeline for follow-on offerings decreased significantly in an attempt to help issuers minimize pricing risk. Fully marketed deals are now completed in 1 to 2 days, and some offerings are conducted exclusively over the phone. One recent innovation is an *over the wall* deal, in which select institutional investors are approached on a confidential basis by investment bankers about a yet-to-be-named issuer. Interested parties are brought *over the wall* and provided with confidential information about the issuer (after which they can no longer trade the company's stock until the deal is completed, regardless of whether they decided to purchase shares from the offering).

## Shelf-Registration Statements

Many large companies that engage in regular U.S. public capital markets financings, such as equity offerings, debt, and convertible securities, file a shelf registration statement (an "S-3" filing) with the SEC at some point (at least 1 year) after completing their IPO. A shelf registration enables a company to file one registration statement that covers multiple issues of different types of securities (under Rule 415). Once made effective by the SEC, this registration, which provides much of the same accounting, disclosure, and descriptive information found in an IPO filing, allows multiple offerings of several types of securities over a 3-year period, as long as the company updates the registration with quarterly financial statements and other related required updates. This enables a company to use the registration opportunistically, without having to file separately for each financing and wait for SEC clearance each time. A financing using a shelf registration statement is called a *shelf take-down*.

In 2005, the SEC created new rules for *Well-Known Seasoned Issuers* (WKSI filers), which allows companies that satisfy a number of requirements (among which is a minimum market capitalization of $700 million) to file a shelf registration and have it become immediately effective and useable for offerings, without SEC review. For this reason, the practice of filing a shelf "just in case" is no longer widely used by WKSIs.

## *Green Shoe* Overallotment Option

A *Green Shoe* is an *overallotment* option that gives an investment bank the right to sell short a number of securities equal to 15% of an offering the bank is underwriting for a corporate client. The term overallotment is used because the investment bank allocates 115% of the base deal to investors and only takes delivery from the issuer of 100% of the base deal, thus creating a "naked" short position. An investment bank will need to buy shares after the initial offering equal to the 15% overallotment. To do this, the bank either buys shares from the issuer at the offering price (if the share price increases over the coming days or weeks), or buys shares in the market at the prevailing market price in order to generate demand and support the stock (if the share price decreases during this period). The SEC permits this activity to enable investment banks to stabilize the price of an equity offering following its initial placement. The objective is to mitigate downside share price movement in the secondary market (trades between investors after the

---

**Green Shoe Option (Over-Allotment Option)**

In order to mitigate downside share price risk in an SEC registered securities offering and to meet potential investor demand for more securities, an investment bank and the issuer are able to enter into an over-allotment option prior to the offering. The over-allotment option allows an investment bank to sell short securities that are equal to 15% of the securities sold in a public offering by a company at the time of the offering. The following example shows the outcome of this activity for both the company and the investment bank. Assume that the company agrees to (a) sell 100 shares of common stock through the investment bank at a price of $100 per share, (b) a 15% overallotment option and (c) pay the investment bank a 2% fee (gross spread) on issuance proceeds.

**Outcome**

The investment bank sells on behalf of the company 100 shares long @ $100/share = $10,000 proceeds.

The investment bank simultaneously sells short 15 of the company's shares @ $100/share = $1,500 proceeds.

If the company's share price increases after the offering, the investment bank buys 15 shares from the company at $100/share and delivers these shares to the initial short sale buyers. In this case, the company receives total proceeds of $11,500 and issues 115 shares. Investor demand has been met for 115, instead of 100 shares and the company receives more money than they would have if only 100 shares had been issued. The investment bank's short position has been hedged (resulting in no gain or loss) and it receives a fee of 2% of $11,500 = $230.

If the company's share price decreases after the offering, the investment bank buys 15 shares from the market, at, say $99/share (paying $99 x 15 = $1,485) and delivers these shares to the initial short sale buyers. In this case, the company receives total proceeds of only $10,000 and issues only 100 shares. The investment bank's short position has created a profit for the bank of $1,500 - $1,485 = $15. The bank's purchase of 15 shares in the market mitigates downside pressure on the company's stock (without this purchase, the stock may have dropped to, say $95, which would make both the company and investors unhappy). The investment bank receives a fee of 2% of $10,000 = $200. As a result, the bank is better off if the company's share price increases because they earn more ($230 fee is better than $200 fee plus $15 short position profit).

The company, investment bank, and investors all hope the company's share price increases after the equity offering. However, this means that the company must have board approval for issuing a range of shares between 100 and 115 shares (accepting the negative earnings per share consequences of issuing more shares). The quid pro quo for the earnings per share risk is the stabilizing benefit of the investment bank's purchase of shares from the market if the company's share price decreases after the offering.

Note: The investment bank may purchase less than 15 shares in this example if there is only a modest drop in the company's share price.

**EXHIBIT 3.17**

initial sale from the issuer) by allowing the underwriting banks to cover their short position by buying shares in the open market if the issuer's share price drops after issuance. This benefits the shareholders, the company, and the investment bank underwriters, because it increases demand for the shares in the secondary market if the issuer's share price is falling after the offering is launched, reducing the perception of an unstable or undesirable offering (which can lead to further share price declines). Because of the benefits to the issuer, most companies decide to include a Green Shoe option in their securities offerings. Exhibit 3.17 describes in detail how the Green Shoe option works.

The term *Green Shoe* comes from a company founded in 1919 called Green Shoe Manufacturing Company (now known as Collective Brands), which was the first company allowed to use this option in an equity offering during 1971.

## Questions

1. What type of securities offerings do not need to be registered with the SEC?
2. List the three types of bank participants in an underwriting syndicate and their core responsibilities, in order of compensation received, from high to low.
3. What are league tables, and why are league tables important in investment banking?
4. Describe the function of the equity capital markets group, including the two major divisions they directly work with and the two types of clients they indirectly work with.
5. Describe the unique process utilized by Google in its IPO, including its intended advantages and potential disadvantages.
6. What is a shelf registration statement, and what securities can be included in it?
7. Why might a younger high-tech company select equity over debt when raising capital?
8. A BBB-/Baa3 rated company is looking at acquiring a smaller (but sizeable) competitor. Discuss considerations the company should take into account when deciding whether to fund the acquisition with new debt, equity, or convertible securities.
9. Suppose a company issues a $180 million convertible bond when its stock is trading at $30. Assuming it is convertible into 5 million shares, what is the conversion premium of the convertible?
10. How many shares will be issued by a convertible issuer if conversion occurs for a $200 million convertible with a conversion premium of 20%, which is issued when the issuer's stock price is $25? (Show your calculation.)
11. Why did the SEC delay declaring Google's IPO registration effective?
12. Provide reasons that an investment bank might give to support their advice that a private company should "go public."
13. List six characteristics of companies that are good targets for an equity issuance.
14. How does a negotiated (best efforts) transaction differ from a "bought deal"?
15. What are some methods used by investment banks to help equity issuers mitigate price risk during the marketing process?
16. Explain what a *green shoe* is.
17. When a company has agreed to a green shoe, who does the underwriter buy shares from if the share price drops? Who do they buy shares from if the share price increases?
18. Calculate the investment bank's fees and profit for a 5 million share equity offering at $40/share, with a 15% green shoe option (fully exercised) assuming a 2% gross spread, assuming the issuer's share price decreases to $38/share after the offering.
19. What is the tradeoff for having a stabilizing green shoe option in a common equity offering?

# Mergers and Acquisitions

The material in this chapter should be cross-referenced with **Case Study 4, "The Best Deal Gillette Could Get? Procter & Gamble's Acquisition of Gillette."**

Corporate change of ownership transactions or combinations such as mergers, acquisitions, divestitures, and joint ventures (collectively, *M&A*) are important strategic considerations for companies that are contemplating ways to enhance shareholder value or reduce shareholder risk. Investment bankers play a key role in initiating, valuing, and executing M&A transactions. This activity accounts for a substantial portion of revenue generated by the Investment Banking Division within large investment banks and represents most of the revenue at certain boutique investment banks.

M&A is a global business, with less than half of all transactions completed inside the United States (see Exhibit 4.1). Virtually no major company or industry across the globe is unaffected by M&A transactions.

## The Core of M&A

At the core of M&A is the buying and selling of corporate assets in order to achieve one or more strategic objectives. Before entering into an acquisition, companies typically compare the costs, risks, and benefits of an acquisition with their organic opportunity (often referred to as a *Greenfield analysis*). This buy versus build analysis is an important departure point for a company as it begins to think about an acquisition. Is it better to build a brand, geographic coverage, distribution network, installed base of products or services, and relationships? Or is it better to acquire them? Obviously, time, expense, and assessment of risk play a key role in this decision-making process.

The analysis is never static. Strategic decisions must be reevaluated in light of new circumstances. The success or failure of competitors, the changing costs of capital and pricing of public assets all come into play and constantly alter the equations.

The inverse decision—whether to sell—is an analysis that asks whether the benefits of continuing to operate an asset (for oneself or as the fiduciary of shareholders) is a better risk-adjusted option than monetizing the asset for cash or other considerations such as stock of the acquirer. Often, boards refer to the sale of a company for cash at a premium as a *de-risking* of the investment for the benefit of shareholders.

The critical component that enables this decision making begins with a thorough understanding of the asset (for sale or to be acquired). The development of a base operating plan is the starting point. Investment bankers must review past management forecasts in order to gain a sense of management's predictive ability, and then help management make an honest assessment of the value of the asset.

## Mergers and Acquisitions League Tables, 2008 and 1H-2009

### 2008 Global Completed M&A

| Rank | Advisor | Value $bn | Deals |
|---|---|---|---|
| 1 | J.P. Morgan | 916.2 | 372 |
| 2 | Goldman Sachs | 801.5 | 326 |
| 3 | Bank of America Merrill Lynch | 746.8 | 378 |
| 4 | UBS | 610.5 | 333 |
| 5 | Morgan Stanley | 600.7 | 304 |
| 6 | Citi | 593.0 | 314 |
| 7 | Credit Suisse | 559.5 | 314 |
| 8 | Deutsche Bank | 544.3 | 296 |
| 9 | Lazard | 324.3 | 218 |
| 10 | Rothschild | 277.3 | 268 |

### 2008 European[1] Completed M&A

| Rank | Advisor | Value $bn | Deals |
|---|---|---|---|
| 1 | J.P. Morgan | 493.5 | 182 |
| 2 | Bank of America Merrill Lynch | 491.7 | 170 |
| 3 | UBS | 432.7 | 172 |
| 4 | Morgan Stanley | 387.7 | 145 |
| 5 | Goldman Sachs | 379.8 | 138 |
| 6 | Deutsche Bank | 311.8 | 195 |
| 7 | Citi | 271.1 | 109 |
| 8 | Lazard | 243.4 | 138 |
| 9 | Credit Suisse | 241.2 | 153 |
| 10 | Rothschild | 230.7 | 206 |

### 2008 US[1] Completed M&A

| Rank | Advisor | Value $bn | Deals |
|---|---|---|---|
| 1 | Goldman Sachs | 525.7 | 201 |
| 2 | J.P. Morgan | 487.6 | 192 |
| 3 | Citi | 360.2 | 118 |
| 4 | Bank of America Merrill Lynch | 307.8 | 204 |
| 5 | Deutsche Bank | 305.9 | 96 |
| 6 | Credit Suisse | 294.1 | 153 |
| 7 | Barclays Capital | 249.8 | 95 |
| 8 | Morgan Stanley | 232.4 | 144 |
| 9 | UBS | 220.1 | 127 |
| 10 | Centerview Partners | 177.3 | 11 |

### 2008 Asia Pacific[1] Completed M&A

| Rank | Advisor | Value $bn | Deals |
|---|---|---|---|
| 1 | Morgan Stanley | 82.8 | 84 |
| 2 | UBS | 82.6 | 84 |
| 3 | J.P. Morgan | 80.9 | 71 |
| 4 | Bank of America Merrill Lynch | 79.5 | 72 |
| 5 | Nomura | 73.8 | 133 |
| 6 | Citi | 72.6 | 135 |
| 7 | Credit Suisse | 63.5 | 61 |
| 8 | Goldman Sachs | 62.2 | 78 |
| 9 | China Int'l Capital Corp Ltd | 42.4 | 13 |
| 10 | Macquarie Group | 39.2 | 93 |

### 1H-2009 Global Completed M&A

| Rank | Advisor | Value $bn | Deals |
|---|---|---|---|
| 1 | Citi | 300.2 | 101 |
| 2 | Goldman Sachs | 298.0 | 107 |
| 3 | Morgan Stanley | 265.6 | 111 |
| 4 | Bank of America Merrill Lynch | 232.6 | 88 |
| 5 | J.P. Morgan | 216.9 | 118 |
| 6 | UBS | 216.1 | 117 |
| 7 | Deutsche Bank | 154.8 | 82 |
| 8 | BNP Paribas | 153.2 | 43 |
| 9 | Lazard | 145.4 | 100 |
| 10 | Credit Suisse | 116.8 | 82 |

### 1H-2009 European[1] Completed M&A

| Rank | Advisor | Value $bn | Deals |
|---|---|---|---|
| 1 | J.P. Morgan | 185.0 | 73 |
| 2 | Goldman Sachs | 179.1 | 54 |
| 3 | Citi | 174.5 | 39 |
| 4 | UBS | 166.2 | 70 |
| 5 | Bank of America Merrill Lynch | 142.1 | 44 |
| 6 | Lazard | 129.6 | 67 |
| 7 | Morgan Stanley | 118.0 | 45 |
| 8 | BNP Paribas | 116.4 | 39 |
| 9 | Deutsche Bank | 111.2 | 41 |
| 10 | Commerzbank Group | 97.4 | 16 |

### 1H-2009 US[1] Completed M&A

| Rank | Advisor | Value $bn | Deals |
|---|---|---|---|
| 1 | Goldman Sachs | 169.8 | 48 |
| 2 | Morgan Stanley | 129.1 | 47 |
| 3 | Citi | 117.2 | 36 |
| 4 | Bank of America Merrill Lynch | 102.1 | 47 |
| 5 | Greenhill & Co | 65.5 | 8 |
| 6 | UBS | 45.4 | 45 |
| 7 | Deutsche Bank | 43.5 | 23 |
| 8 | Barclays Capital | 39.6 | 21 |
| 9 | J.P. Morgan | 38.9 | 42 |
| 10 | BNP Paribas | 37.3 | 8 |

### 1H-2009 Asia Pacific[1] Completed M&A

| Rank | Advisor | Value $bn | Deals |
|---|---|---|---|
| 1 | Morgan Stanley | 15.7 | 29 |
| 2 | UBS | 13.4 | 28 |
| 3 | Nomura | 12.8 | 59 |
| 4 | Goldman Sachs | 12.0 | 25 |
| 5 | Credit Suisse | 11.0 | 17 |
| 6 | Mizuho | 9.6 | 47 |
| 7 | J.P. Morgan | 9.4 | 22 |
| 8 | Citi | 9.1 | 38 |
| 9 | Daiwa Securities SMBC Co Ltd | 7.2 | 36 |
| 10 | Rothschild | 6.8 | 13 |

Note 1: Includes any region involvement (i.e.: acquiror, target or divestor).
Source: Dealogic

**EXHIBIT 4.1**

# Creating Value

The global capital markets are significantly impacted by the thousands of M&A-related financings that are completed each year. Investment banks, lawyers, accountants, management consultants, public relations firms, economic consultants, and deal magazines are all important participants in this business. However, there is an ongoing debate about whether M&A is benefi-cial to shareholders. Furthermore, even if a transaction benefits shareholders, there are questions about the potential resulting harm to consumers (if a monopolistic business is created), employees (if they lose their jobs), and communities (if their tax base is impaired).

In determining after the fact whether an M&A transaction was beneficial to shareholders, it is important to consider the change in value following completion of an acquisition compared to share prices of other companies in the same industry over the same interval of time. For example, America Online announced its agreement to acquire Time Warner for about $182 billion in stock and debt during January of 2000. With dominating positions in the music, publishing, news, entertainment, cable, and Internet industries, the combined company, called AOL Time Warner, boasted unrivaled assets among media and online companies. This was the largest M&A transac-tion in history at the time, and some analysts heralded it as a "great transaction," an "unprece-dented powerhouse," and an "unbeatable alliance." The new company was owned 55% by AOL shareholders and 45% by Time Warner shareholders. However, 2 years later following the bursting of the technology bubble, the company's share price had dropped over 55%, and some of the same analysts who called the transaction an unprecedented powerhouse were calling it an unprecedented failure.

Although AOL Time Warner's share price drop was indeed remarkable and discouraging to shareholders, a determination of whether this transaction enhanced or destroyed value should be made in the context of comparable company share price movement during the same time period. For example, during this same two-year period, News Corp, a major competitor, saw a drop in its share price of over 50%. Moreover, many pure-technology companies during this period suffered share price drops that were even larger.

## Strategic Rationale

A company must have a strategic rationale for completing an M&A transaction. This includes a desire to achieve cost savings through economies of scale that come from sharing central services such as legal, accounting, finance, and executive management, as well as through reducing real estate holdings, corporate jets, and other redundant assets. An investment banker works closely with the company's senior management to create a strategic rationale for an M&A transaction and develop a list of acquisition targets or, in the case of a sale, target buyers. Ultimately, the goal of an M&A transaction should be to drive either an immediate or a near-term increase in shareholder value. To determine if this can be accomplished, a banker, together with the client, attempts to project an M&A transaction's impact on EPS, post-transaction cost of capital, return on equity (ROE), return on invested capital (ROIC), and trading multiple expansion or contraction.

## Synergies and Control Premium

A key component in determining whether or not an M&A transaction is strategically justifiable is the analysis of projected synergies that should be created by the transaction. Synergies in this con-text refers to expected reduced costs or increased revenues. Cost synergies are most important, and they arise through efficiencies created from elimination of redundant activities, improved operating practices, and economies of scale. Revenue synergies, which are usually given less weight, come from the ability to create greater revenue through a combined company than the sum of the independent companies' revenues. Companies should develop a thorough, realistic process for forecasting synergies by bringing representatives from both companies together to define what needs to be done to capture synergies and the value derived from this capturing process.

Cost synergies can be identified in the following general areas: Administration (exploiting economies of scale in central and back office functions); Manufacturing (eliminating overcapacity); Procurement (purchasing power benefits through pooled purchasing); Marketing and Distribution (cross-selling and using common sales channels and consolidated warehousing); and R&D (eliminating R&D overlap in personnel and projects). Investment bankers are responsible for making sure that forecasted synergies are realistic and a credible total cost savings amount is included in post-transaction valuation calculations. Revenue synergies should be, in many cases, discounted from management's projections since they are very difficult to capture. According to research by McKinsey, 88% of acquirers were able to capture at least 70% of estimated cost savings, while only half of acquirers were able to capture at least 70% of estimated revenue synergies.

A control premium relates to the price that an acquiring company is willing to pay to purchase control over a target company's decision-making and cash flow. This premium equals the difference between a control-based purchase and a minority (non-control) purchase of shares. In many acquisitions, the acquirer is willing to pay a higher price than the current market price for a public company based on consideration of both expected synergies and a control premium.

## Credit Ratings and Acquisition Currency

Companies must consider the credit rating impact of an M&A transaction: a transaction can result in a ratings upgrade, downgrade, or no rating change. A downgrade may lead to a risk-adjusted higher cost of capital, which impacts the benefits of the transaction as well as the company's operating model going forward. As a result, companies and their investment bankers sometimes have confidential discussions with rating agencies before transactions are consummated to determine the probable rating impact of a transaction. This, in turn, can affect the decision regarding whether to use shares or cash as an acquisition currency. Share-based acquisitions have a more salutary effect on the acquirer's balance sheet, so ratings may not be negatively impacted.

When considering the acquisition currency, acquiring companies should also focus on the transaction's impact on their EPS, balance sheet, cash flow, financial flexibility, and taxes. Although using shares as the acquisition currency can mitigate credit rating concerns, it can also have a negative impact on EPS relative to a cash-based acquisition. In addition, if more than 20% of the outstanding shares of a U.S. public company are to be issued in an acquisition, a shareholder vote is required to support the issuance. Higher P/E (price to earnings) companies use stock as consideration more frequently than lower P/E companies do. However, the cost of issuing equity should always be compared to the cost of debt when determining whether to use cash or shares as the acquisition currency. If a target firm prefers receiving the acquiring company's shares because it is more tax-effective for selling shareholders (capital gains taxes are deferred until the shares received from the acquisition are sold), the acquirer may need to consider shares as the acquisition currency. In addition, target shareholders might prefer receiving shares to enable their participation in the future share appreciation potential of the post-acquisition company. See **Case Study 4, "The Best Deal Gillette Could Get? Procter & Gamble's Acquisition of Gillette,"** to review acquisition currency considerations.

When using shares as the acquisition currency, the acquirer and seller must consider share price risk associated with this payment method. Because there is a meaningful time lag from the announcement of the transaction to the actual closing (typically 3 to 9 months), there is the potential for significant share price movement during this period. Therefore, if shares are to be delivered in an acquisition, a decision must be made to structure the transaction either with a fixed share exchange ratio and floating economic value, or with a floating share exchange ratio with a fixed economic value. The exchange ratio is the number of acquiring company shares to be exchanged for each target company share, calculated as follows: offer price for target / acquiring company's closing share price on the last trading day before the deal is announced = exchange ratio. For example, in an all-stock acquisition, if the exchange ratio is 2.0×, at closing (which could be 3 to 9 months after the deal is announced) the acquiring company will deliver to target company shareholders 2.0 acquiring company shares for every outstanding target company share. This is a fixed exchange ratio transaction, creating the potential for changing economic value, depending on changes in the acquiring company stock price. In a floating exchange ratio transaction, the exchange ratio moves up or down during the period from announcement to closing, depending on the acquiring company's stock price. This arrangement creates the same economic outcome (from a cash equivalence perspective) regardless of whether the acquirer's share price increases or decreases.

A common adjustment to a fixed exchange ratio is to impose a collar around the ratio that provides for an increase in the exchange ratio if the acquiring company's share price drops below a predetermined floor price, and a reduction in the exchange ratio if the acquiring company's share price increases above a predetermined cap price. This collar arrangement creates a cash equivalent economic outcome at closing that has boundaries that, for example, might be 10% above and below the value of the transaction based on the exchange ratio on the date the transaction was announced.

## Regulatory Considerations

Companies, and their legal and investment banking advisors, must analyze the regulatory approvals that are necessary to complete an M&A transaction, focusing on local, regional, national, and international regulators. Approvals required to close a transaction depend on the size of the deal, the location of major businesses, the industry and the industry regulatory body, if one exists. In the United States, most public M&A transactions require a Hart-Scott-Rodino (HSR) filing with the Federal Trade Commission (FTC) and the Department of Justice (DOJ). Upon filing, there is a 30-day waiting period during which the FTC and the DOJ may request further information. If there are international operations, the companies might also need to file with the European Commission (EC) or with antitrust regulators in other relevant countries. Other U.S. regulatory considerations include filing a merger proxy or a financing registration statement with the SEC, determining whether a report should be filed with the Pension Benefit Guaranty Corporation (if the transaction impacts company pension plans), and, potentially, filing with tax agencies such as the IRS.

## Social and Constituent Considerations

There are numerous social considerations in any potential M&A transaction. For example, what is the quality of the target company's management team, and should they be retained or asked to leave? Can two different management teams be combined without unduly disrupting the overall business? How many and who will be on the board of directors? Are there golden parachutes (severance packages payable upon termination) that must be accounted for? Will there be large job losses? Are there environmental or political issues that must be addressed? Will the tax base of the communities in which the company operates be affected? Are there significant relocation issues? These social issues are particularly important in stock-for-stock combinations.

The principal constituents that must be considered in any potential transaction include:

1. Shareholders, who are concerned about valuation, control, risk, and tax issues.
2. Employees, who focus on compensation, termination risk, and employee benefits.
3. Regulators, who must be persuaded that antitrust, tax, and securities laws are adhered to.
4. Union leaders, who worry about job retention and seniority issues.
5. Credit rating agencies, who focus on credit quality issues.
6. Equity research analysts, who focus on growth, margins, market share, and EPS, among other things.
7. Debt holders, who consider whether debt will be increased, retired, or if there is potential for changing debt values.

Each of these constituents' concerns must be considered, but since there are many competing concerns, more often than not every constituent (other than regulators) will not be satisfied.

It is imperative that, as constituent priorities are considered, the companies involved in the M&A transaction and their advisors determine the potential reaction of politicians and the media. Not anticipating criticism from these sectors can imperil a deal. Considering criticism in advance and developing strategies for dealing with it is an increasingly important part of the M&A landscape (see **Case Study 4, "The Best Deal Gillette Could Get? Procter & Gamble's Acquisition of Gillette"**).

## Role of Investment Bankers

Investment bankers identify potential companies or divisions to be bought, sold, merged, or joint ventured. They create scenarios for successful transactions, including pro-forma projections and analysis of benefits and disadvantages. When a client agrees to proceed with a transaction, investment bankers provide extensive financial analysis, deal structure recommendations, tactical advice, and sometimes financing—that they provide themselves, or arrange through the capital markets. Bankers work with a company's corporate development group to manage all phases of the transaction and, with attorneys, assist senior management in negotiating the terms of the transaction and documentation. In most cases, an investment bank also delivers a fairness opinion (to be discussed shortly) at the time of transaction closing.

Bankers are paid different fees for advising on the transaction and for providing a fairness opinion. The bulk of an advisory fee is usually only paid if the transaction is successfully closed. The fee is normally calculated as a percentage of total consideration, and may vary from 2% for a relatively small transaction ($100 million) to a fraction of 1% for a very large transaction ($10 billion or greater). Transactions may have much higher or lower fees, depending on the type and complexity of the transaction.

# Other M&A Participants

In addition to investment bankers, there are many other key participants in an M&A transaction. The senior management of the company determines strategy, selects advisors, and makes key deal decisions. The company's corporate development group brings the best ideas presented by investment bankers (or through their own initiatives) to senior management and works on all aspects of deal execution. The board of directors is in charge of either recommending or rejecting proposed transactions, and must act under the Business Judgment Rule, a legal standard that requires the transaction to be in the best interests of shareholders. They must also perform their Revlon Duties (another legal convention) that, if triggered, requires that the highest possible reasonable value be obtained through a market test or an auction. Other key participants include business unit heads, who participate in due diligence, integration planning, and synergy discussions; internal and external legal counsel; internal and external investor relations people; human resources people; and accountants. Each of these participants plays a role in identifying, analyzing, and advancing an M&A transaction.

# Fairness Opinion

Investment bankers are usually asked to render a fairness opinion to the respective boards of companies involved in an M&A transaction (see Exhibit 4.2). The opinion is made publicly available and states, among other things, that the transaction is "fair from a financial point of view." A fairness opinion is not an evaluation of the business rationale for the transaction, a legal opinion, or a recommendation to the board to approve the transaction. The fairness opinion includes a summary of the valuation analysis conducted by the investment bank to show the basis on which the opinion is offered.

A typical fee paid for a fairness opinion in a large M&A transaction is around $1 million, although this amount can vary, depending on the size and complexity of the transaction. This fee is paid separately from the M&A advisory fee, which is paid only if the deal is consummated. A fairness opinion is not a guarantee that a deal is fair, or even good. It is simply a document that reviews a deal's valuation based on standard valuation processes, including comparison of similar deals, and states that it falls within the parameters of the analysis. Boards of directors use fairness opinions as a data point in deciding whether to vote for or against a transaction and to create evidence that they have fulfilled their fiduciary duty in the event that they need to defend against any lawsuit relating to the M&A transaction.

There is division about whether it makes sense for the same investment bank that provides the fairness opinion to also act as the M&A advisor, since the advisory fee will only be paid if the

---

**Origins of the Fairness Opinion**

Fairness opinions are an outgrowth of a court case that involved the 1981 acquisition of TransUnion by Marmon Group. Defendant Jerome Van Gorkom, who was TransUnion's Chairman and CEO, chose a proposed price of $55 per share without consultation with outside financial experts. He only consulted with the firm's CFO and did not determine an actual total value for the company. A Delaware court was highly critical of his decision, writing that "the record is devoid of any competent evidence that $55 represented the per share intrinsic value of the Company." The court found that the company's directors were grossly negligent, because they quickly approved the merger without substantial inquiry or any expert advice. For this reason, the board of directors breached the duty of care that it owed to the corporation's shareholders. As such, the protection of the Business Judgment Rule was unavailable. Ever since, most public company boards have decided it is best to obtain a fairness opinion for any material M&A transactions.

**EXHIBIT 4.2**

transaction is completed, and it will not be completed unless, among other things, the board is advised that the purchase price is fair. Sometimes, to mitigate this concern, companies employ one investment bank to render the fairness opinion and a different bank to provide M&A advice. Alternatively, consulting firms or accounting firms can be hired to provide the fairness opinion. Bringing in a third party to perform the fairness opinion is not without its issues, however. Although independent, a third party will not understand as much about the deal as the party who negotiated it. As a result, it can be a problematic decision to divide up the advisory and fairness opinion roles: there are good arguments for and against both positions.

# Acquisitions

A publicly traded company can be acquired through either (1) a merger; (2) an acquisition of stock directly from the target company shareholders using a tender offer, followed by a merger to acquire any remaining untendered shares; or (3) an acquisition of the target company assets and a distribution of the proceeds to the target company shareholders. The third acquisition method is rarely used since it is usually tax inefficient, so only the first two methods are summarized here.

## Merger

A merger is the most common way to acquire a company. It involves the legal combination of two companies based on either a stock swap or cash payment to the target company shareholders. In order for a merger to proceed, there must be a shareholder vote that favors the merger by more than 50% (or an even higher percentage, depending on the corporate articles and the state of incorporation). Typically, the acquiring firm has principal control of the board and senior management positions. A merger of equals (MOE) is a combination of two companies with approximately equal assets. There is a less obvious designated buyer or seller, and the control premium is either nonexistent or negligible, because, in theory, value created through synergies are shared approximately equally by shareholders of both companies. For example, when Daimler-Benz and Chrysler merged, this was an MOE and a new company, DaimlerChrysler, was formed, and a new stock was issued for it. Although, in theory, an MOE results in equal representation on the board of directors and within senior management ranks, this seldom occurs. Usually one side or the other is subtly dominant.

## Tender Offer

Another way to acquire a company is to purchase stock directly from shareholders, without requiring a shareholder vote, which is easiest if there is a single majority shareholder, or a small group of like-minded shareholders who together hold a majority position. If it is difficult to obtain the shares through private negotiations, or if the board is not supportive, a tender offer can be initiated. A tender offer is a public offer by an acquirer to all shareholders of a target company to tender their stock for sale at a specified price during a specified period of time. If less than 100% of shareholders accept the tender offer, a second step is required to gain control of the non-tendered shares through a merger. If 90% or more of the shares are tendered, the merger can be effected through a short-form merger process, which allows the acquirer to "squeeze out" the non-tendered shares, requiring that they be sold without a shareholder vote. Typically a tender offer is initiated if the target company's board is not supportive of the acquisition. However, even with board support, a tender offer is sometimes initiated rather than a merger, because without the need for a shareholder vote, the tender offer can be completed faster than a merger. Tender offers in the United States are governed by the Williams Act, which requires that bidders include all details of their offer in a filing with the SEC. Interpretations of the Williams Act have become more difficult with the increasing use of derivative instruments employed by activist hedge funds in their acquisition efforts (see Exhibit 4.3 and Chapter 13).

### Proxy Contest

A proxy contest is an indirect method of acquisition, since it is designed to gain minority representation on or control of a board of directors. This strategy is often initiated by a financial agitator, but can also be used by a strategic acquirer to put pressure on senior management and existing board members. If successful, the proxy contest may change the composition of a board.

## Due Diligence and Documentation

To enhance the chances of a successful acquisition, the buyer must carefully review a full range of issues regarding the target company. Every M&A transaction requires a due diligence process that investigates a company's business in detail by reviewing publicly available information and, subject to agreement by the parties, non-public information, after signing a confidentiality agreement. For a private sale of a division it is customary to include in due diligence a tour of major facilities, discussion with management regarding their business, an extensive "data room" review (physical or electronic) of confidential documents, discussions with selected customers or suppliers, and a follow-up session to ask questions that develop during data analysis. In a U.S. public company takeover, there is less due diligence because of SEC disclosure that already exists.

Documents that are used in an M&A transaction include either a Merger Agreement, if an acquiring company directly purchases the stock of a target company, or a Stock Purchase

---

**CSX and TCI**

During June, 2008, New York District Judge Lewis Kaplan found that two hedge funds had used derivatives as a vehicle to deliberately avoid U.S. securities laws that require investors owning more than 5% of a company's voting shares to disclose their holdings at the end of every quarter. The two hedge funds, Children's Investment Fund Management (TCI) and 3G Capital Partners (3G) were found to be illegally plotting a bid for control of railroad company CSX Corporation without disclosing their intentions.

Although Judge Kaplan's decision provided legitimacy to CSX as it waged a proxy fight against 3G and TCI, it was not a total victory with CSX. The judge stated that it was too late to reverse the actions of the hedge funds, and that he was legally prevented from defusing or "sterilizing" their votes when shareholders choose a board of directors. The funds, however, were prohibited from making future violations of this nature.

Hedge funds watched the outcome of this case carefully, and many were fearful that Judge Kaplan would outlaw derivatives that funds sometimes use to acquire large stakes of companies. They were especially worried about how he viewed swaps, which allow shareholders to create synthetic stock through private contracts with large Wall Street firms. These synthetic shares may be traded in tandem with a company's real shares, but they do not afford their holders voting rights. This allows hedge funds to post economic gains without filing share-ownership and, as Judge Kaplan believed, to control voting rights indirectly by potentially influencing the investment banking counterparties that own the shares as a hedge to their swap position.

In response to this case, the Securities and Exchange Commission (SEC) mentioned that it did not have any problems with swaps, as long as they were not used to disguise takeover intentions. Judge Kaplan, however, found that TCI and 3G used swaps in a way that allowed them to build a position for takeover without disclosing it to the market.

Rather than defining an owner as a person who has the right to vote, buy or sell the securities, many companies pushed the SEC to expand the definition to include anyone who owns derivatives or synthetic arrangements.

Source: Slater, Dan. "Judge Kaplan Reprimands Hedge Funds in Takeover Battle with CSX". The Wall Street Journal. 12 Jun. 2008

**EXHIBIT 4.3**

Agreement, if an acquiring company purchases stock but does not want to complete a merger filing. Mergers involve the legal combination of two companies, are governed by state statutes, and require an affirmative vote of either a majority or a super-majority of the target company shareholders for approval, depending on the company's charter or bylaws (or by state laws if the company's charter or bylaws are silent on this point). If an acquiring company issues more than 20% of its pre-transaction shares in a share for share merger, then the acquiring company shareholders also must vote in favor of the transaction. With a Stock Purchase Agreement, rather than merging two companies, an acquiring company can acquire stock directly from majority shareholder(s) in privately negotiated agreements, or through a tender offer, which does not require a shareholder vote if all shareholders sell. If not all shareholders agree to sell, then a merger is required as a second step to gain control of non-tendered shares. If only assets are purchased, and not the entire company, an Asset Purchase Agreement is used.

An important provision in M&A documents is the *material adverse change clause* (MAC). A MAC is an event that materially changes the economic substance of the transaction after signing but before closing. If a MAC clause is triggered, the transaction may be terminated. MAC clauses are carefully negotiated, with a particular focus on what constitutes materiality. This clause, in turn, impacts any payments that may be owed under deal protection provisions, including a breakup fee. Another key provision in documents relates to whether the target company is allowed to "shop" its deal with an acquiring company to other prospective buyers. If so, there is a "go shop" provision; if precluded, there is a "no shop" provision.

## Breakup Fee

A breakup fee is paid if a transaction is not completed because a target company walks away from the transaction after a Merger Agreement or Stock Purchase Agreement is signed. This fee is designed to discourage other firms from making bids for the target company since they would, in effect, end up paying the breakup fee if successful in their bid. A reverse breakup fee is paid if the acquiring company walks away from a transaction after signing the agreement. These fees are usually set at 2–4% of the target company's equity value, but this is the subject of considerable negotiation during the documentation process. In some instances there is no breakup fee but rather language enabling "specific performance," whereby a court can compel the deal to close.

## Alternative Sale Processes

Investment banks generally give priority to solicitation of M&A assignments that allow them to help sell a company or a division of a company. This is because there is a higher likelihood that a *sell-side* deal will be completed than for a *buy-side* deal. Sell-side processes are somewhat different, depending on the industry; the type of asset being sold; timing, acquisition currency, and tax concerns; impact on the company's business; and employee and confidentiality concerns. However, there are four general ways in which a sell-side assignment can be approached:

### Preemptive

Bankers screen and identify the single most likely buyer and contact that buyer only. This process maximizes confidentiality (disclosing confidential selling company information to only one buyer) and speed, but it may reduce the potential for price maximization.

## Targeted Solicitation

Bankers identify and contact two to five most likely buyers. By avoiding public disclosure of the sale effort, this process may eliminate a perception that the deal is being shopped (unless there is an inadvertent disclosure). This process allows for reasonable speed and maintains control over confidentiality, while improving the potential for price maximization.

## Controlled/Limited Auction

Bankers approach a subset of buyers (perhaps 6 to 20 potential buyers) who have been prescreened to be the most logical buyers. This process is slower and quickly becomes known in the market, which sometimes creates undesirable share price pressure. Although confidentiality agreements will be signed with any potential buyer that the seller and investment bankers are comfortable with, there are a significant number of parties that obtain confidential selling company information (hence, greater business risk). The payoff for this risk is a higher potential for price maximization.

## Public Auction

The company publicly announces the sales process and invites all interested parties to participate. This creates potentially significant disruptions in the company's business, since there are more moving parts and even greater confidentiality concerns, compared to a controlled auction. In addition, the process may take more time. The benefit of a public auction is that it may result in finding "hidden" buyers, creating the greatest potential for price maximization. See Exhibit 4.4 for a summary of these four alternative sale processes.

**Alternative Sell-Side Processes**

| Divestiture Strategy | Description | # of Buyers | Advantages | Disadvantages | Circumstances |
|---|---|---|---|---|---|
| Preemptive | • Screen and identify most likely buyer | 1 | • Efforts focused on one buyer<br>• Maximum confidentiality<br>• Speed of execution<br>• Minimum business disruption | • Unlikely to maximize value<br>• Tied to result of one negotiation | • Have very clear sense of most logical buyer<br>• High risk of damage from business disruptions<br>• Have strong negotiating position |
| Targeted Solicitation | • High-level approach to selected potential buyers<br>• Customized executive summary-type presentation<br>• No pre-established guidelines or formal process<br>• No public disclosure | 2 to 5 | • Speed of execution<br>• Confidentiality maintained<br>• Limited business disruption<br>• Sense of competition enabled | • Requires substantial top-level management time commitment<br>• Risks missing interested buyers<br>• May not maximize value | • Have limited group of logical buyers<br>• Have key objectives of confidentiality and limiting any business disruption |
| Controlled Auction | • Limited range of logical potential buyers contacted<br>• Requires formal guidelines on sale process<br>• No public disclosure | 6 to 20 | • Reasonably accurate test of market price<br>• High degree of control over process<br>• Creates strong sense of competition | • Lack of confidentiality<br>• May "turn off" logical buyers<br>• Potential for disruption due to rumors | • Seek good balance between confidentiality and value |
| Public Auction | • Public disclosure made<br>• Preliminary materials distributed to wide range of potential buyers | N/A | • Most likely to obtain highest offer<br>• Finds "hidden" buyers | • May limit subsequent options if process fails<br>• Highest risk of business disruption | • Believe business is unlikely to be damaged by public process<br>• Have difficulty identifying potential buyers |

**EXHIBIT 4.4**

## Cross-Border Transactions

A large number of M&A transactions are completed between companies that are based in two different countries. These transactions are almost always more complicated, since there are multiple regulators (focusing principally on antitrust and securities law matters), complex accounting and disclosure considerations, and especially difficult tax matters to resolve. For example, in a transaction where a non-U.S. company acquires a U.S. company in a stock-for-stock arrangement, American Depositary Receipts (ADRs) may need to be used, since most U.S.-based shareholders want an acquisition currency that is freely monetized in the United States, and some institutional investors are not allowed to own foreign stocks (see Chapter 8 for an explanation of ADRs). If an ADR program doesn't already exist for the acquirer's stock, it may need to be organized. In a stock-for-stock transaction where a U.S. company acquires a non-U.S. company, some non-U.S. shareholders may feel compelled to sell their shares immediately because they don't want foreign exchange risk, or are uncomfortable holding a foreign stock. In this case, there may be large amounts of the U.S. company's stock being sold, which puts downward pressure on the stock (see Exhibit 4.5). This phenomenon is called *flow-back*.

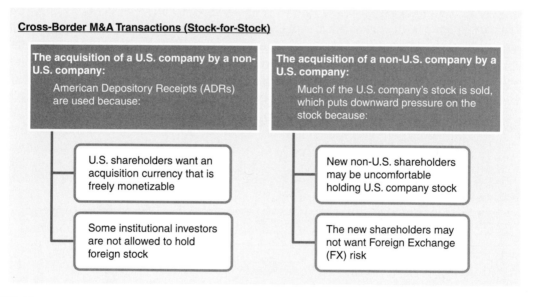

**EXHIBIT 4.5**

## Tax-Free Reorganizations

M&A transactions, if structured properly, may be characterized as tax-free reorganizations. In the United States, the Internal Revenue Code provides a tax exemption for the exchange of shares (in a stock-for-stock transaction) that has the objective of reorganizing or rearranging the company. The objective of the parties involved is to qualify the transaction as a tax-free reorganization that results in no corporate-level or shareholder-level taxes. However, this does not mean that taxes will never be paid. This designation simply delays the taxable event until the target company's shareholders sell the acquirer shares received from the transaction. When target company shareholders receive acquiring company shares, the original basis in the target company shares is passed on to the new shareholding. Whenever the shares are sold, a tax will be paid based on the gain between the basis and the sales price of the shares. In addition, a substantial part of the consideration must consist of stock—at least 40%, or more, depending on the structure of the transaction—which will result in tax-free treatment of the portion of the consideration paid in shares (the cash portion will still be taxable). Finally, the acquiring company must continue to operate or use a significant part of the target company's business or assets.

# Corporate Restructurings

Corporate restructurings involve either bankruptcy-related concerns or strategic opportunities. This section focuses on the latter: creating strategic opportunities that unlock shareholder value through the separation of a subsidiary from a parent company. Senior management and boards of directors must constantly analyze new opportunities to maximize shareholder value. From a strategic opportunity standpoint, this includes determining whether it is possible to create a new publicly traded company from one or more of the parent company's businesses. Sometimes, separating a non-core business from a company's other businesses can create greater clarity in the market and unlock value, if the separated business participates in a higher growth industry. In addition, separating a business can improve operating performance, reduce risk profiles (including credit risk), and provide more efficient access to public capital markets. A separation event can either be completed in the private or public market. A private market event involves selling a subsidiary to private investors or to another company. A public market event involves selling or separating part of or the entire subsidiary in a public market transaction such as an IPO, carve-out, spin-off, split-off, or tracking stock transaction.

## IPO

A subsidiary IPO is the sale of all shares of a subsidiary to new public market shareholders in exchange for cash. This creates a new company with a new stock that trades independently from the former parent company stock. If the cash received by the parent is in excess of the parent's tax basis, then the IPO is a taxable event for the parent.

## Carve-Out

The sale through an IPO of a portion of the shares of a subsidiary to new public market shareholders in exchange for cash is called a *carve-out*. This type of transaction leaves the parent with ongoing ownership in a portion of the former subsidiary. In practice, since a large sale might flood the market with too many shares, thereby depressing the share price, usually less than 20% of the subsidiary is sold in a carve-out. Selling a minority position of the subsidiary also enables the parent to continue having control over the business and, importantly, makes it possible to complete a potentially tax-free transaction if less than 20% of the shares are sold. (See **Case Study 4, "McDonald's, Wendy's, and Hedge Funds: Hamburger Hedging?"** for a description of McDonald's carve-out of Chipotle.) One consideration of a carve-out is the potential conflict of interest between the parent and the separated company. For example, if the separated company is vertically integrated with the parent company (i.e., a supplier), potential conflicts may arise if the former subsidiary pursues business with the parent company's competitors.

## Spin-Off

In a spin-off, the parent gives up control over the subsidiary by distributing subsidiary shares to parent company shareholders on a pro-rata basis. This full separation avoids conflicts of interest between the parent and the separated company (unlike in a carve-out). No cash is received by the parent company, since a spin-off is essentially redistributing assets owned by parent company shareholders to those same shareholders. A spin-off may be accomplished in a two-step process. First, a carve-out is completed on a fraction of the shares to minimize downside pressure on the stock. It also allows the subsidiary to pick up equity research coverage and market making in the stock prior to delivery of the remaining shares to the original parent company shareholders. The carve-out sale is usually on less than 20% of the subsidiary's shares in order to preserve tax benefits. A spin-off provides the new company with its own acquisition currency, enables the new company management to receive incentive compensation, and unlocks the value of the business if comparable companies trade at higher multiples than the parent company multiple. Negatives include potentially higher borrowing costs and takeover vulnerability.

## Split-Off

In a split-off, the parent company delivers shares of the subsidiary to only those parent shareholders who are willing to exchange their parent company shares for the shares of the subsidiary. This leaves the original parent company shareholders with either subsidiary shares (and no parent company shares) or parent company shares (and no subsidiary shares). A split-off is preferred to a spin-off when a portion of parent company shareholders prefers to own only the subsidiary's shares and not the parent company's shares. A split-off can be structured as a tax-free event if an initial carve-out of less than 20% of the subsidiary is followed with a split-off transaction. Since a split-off requires parent company shareholders to choose between keeping parent company stock and exchanging this stock for subsidiary stock, to achieve complete separation, sometimes a premium must be offered for the exchange (providing more shares of the subsidiary than a valuation analysis without incentives would suggest). A split-off transaction is much less common than a spin-off transaction.

## Tracking Stock

In a tracking stock transaction, a separate class of parent company shares is distributed to existing shareholders of the parent company either through a spin-off or through a sale to new shareholders in a carve-out. Although a tracking stock offers the parent company the advantage of maintaining control over a separated subsidiary, it complicates corporate governance because there is no formal legal separation and a single board of directors continues to operate for both businesses. In addition, both entities are liable for each other's debt obligations, so in a bankruptcy scenario it is unclear how the assets will be split up. As a result, this is a potentially confusing form of separation, and the logic of this transaction is frequently debated.

# Takeover Defenses

Companies that either have received or expect to receive a hostile takeover bid often retain investment bankers to assist them. This effort is designed to either fight off the bid and remain independent or to negotiate a transaction that maximizes shareholder value. A takeover defense strategy is critically dependent on the specific laws that govern attempts to acquire a company. In the

United States, the SEC governs all tender offers, but companies are incorporated based on state laws, and most states have adopted anti-takeover statutes as part of their state corporation laws. Delaware has a separate court system for corporate law called the Delaware Chancery Court, which has been a leader in the development of corporate law. Many large U.S. corporations are incorporated in Delaware because of the perceived benefits received from the state's clarity on corporate law matters.

Various defense strategies can be deployed by corporations, based on the advice of their investment bankers and legal counsel. The most actively utilized defense strategy is a shareholder rights plan.

## Shareholder Rights Plan

A shareholder rights plan usually does not require a shareholder vote and often has a 10-year maturity. The key feature of this plan involves implementation of a *poison pill*, which gives non-hostile shareholders a right to purchase additional shares in the company at a substantial discount (usually 50%). The result of the exercise of this right is that hostile shareholder ownership percentage declines as "friendly" shareholder ownership increases. This dilution of hostile ownership economically compels the hostile party to give up, negotiate a higher price, or launch a proxy contest to gain control of the target company's board and then rescind the poison pill. Poison pills have been a very effective deterrent to hostile takeover attempts for several decades, but since 2001 the number of companies that implemented (or renewed) this defense provision has declined in the face of shareholder activism. Some shareholders believe that a poison pill entrenches ineffective management and boards, resulting in a failure to maximize shareholder value. Following the stock market fall off during 2008, the adoption of rights plans reversed course and became more popular.

# Risk Arbitrage

In a stock-for-stock acquisition, some traders will buy the target company's stock and simultaneously short the acquiring company's stock. The purchase is motivated by the fact that after announcement of a pending acquisition, the target company's share price typically trades at a lower price in the market compared to the price reflected by the Exchange Ratio that will apply at the time of closing. Traders who expect that the closing will eventually occur can make trading profits by buying the target company's stock and then receiving the acquiring company's stock at closing, creating value in excess of their purchase cost. To hedge against a potential drop in value of the acquiring company's stock, the trader sells short the same number of shares to be received at closing in the acquiring company's stock based on the Exchange Ratio. The participation of these traders (called *risk arbitrageurs* or *risk arbs*) is an important consideration in stock-for-stock acquisitions, since their trading puts downward pressure on the acquiring company's stock and upward pressure on the selling company's stock.

For example, if an acquiring company agrees to purchase a target company's stock at an Exchange Ratio of 1.5×, then at closing the acquirer will deliver 1.5 shares for every share of the target's stock. Assume that just prior to when the transaction is announced, the target's stock price is $25, the acquirer's stock is $20, and it will be 6 months until the transaction closes. Since 1.5 acquirer shares will be delivered, the value to be received by target company shareholders is $30 per share. However, because there is some probability that the acquisition will not close in 6 months, the target company stock will likely trade below $30 until the date of closing. If the target stock trades at, for example, $28 after announcement, for every share of target stock that risk arbs purchase at $28, they will simultaneously short 1.5 shares of the acquirer's stock. This trade enables risk arbs to profit from the probable increase in the target's share price up to $30, assuming the closing takes place, while hedging its position (i.e., the shares received by risk arbs at closing will be delivered to the parties that originally lent shares to them). The objective for risk arbs is to capture the spread between the target company's share price after announcement of the deal and the offer price for the target company, as established by the Exchange Ratio, without exposure to a potential drop in the acquirer's share price. However, if the transaction doesn't close or the terms change, the risk arbs' position becomes problematic and presents either a diminution in profit or a potential loss. Investment bankers keep close track of risk arb activity throughout the transaction period, since the prices of both the acquirer and target stocks can be significantly impacted by risk arb trading.

## Valuation

In determining the appropriate value for a public company that is the subject of a potential acquisition or sale, the starting point is consideration of the company's current share price. This price may represent the best indicator of fair value for a large public company without a control shareholder. To reflect the appropriate value for control of the company, this price must be adjusted upward. In other words, when purchasing a small fraction of the company, the closing market price is the best barometer of value, but if a majority of the company is purchased, there generally should be a control premium added to this closing market price.

There are four basic valuation methods that guide investment bankers (and others) in determining the appropriate price for the purchase of a controlling interest in a company: comparable company analysis, comparable transaction analysis, leverage buyout (LBO) analysis, and discounted cash flow (DCF) analysis. In addition, a sum-of-the-parts analysis is often useful if a company has many different (and disparate) businesses and there is the possibility that individual businesses, if sold independently, could create value in excess of the company's value. For certain industries, other valuation approaches may also be appropriate. For a private company, all or some of these valuation methods may be applicable in determining the appropriate value for an acquisition. The key to selecting the best valuation methodologies for public and private companies (or divisions of companies) is to determine the methods based on the industry, available information, and market precedent.

Comparable company analysis and comparable transactions analysis are multiples-based methods for determining value in relation to a set of peers. This means that a company's value is calculated as a multiple of a metric such as earnings or, more importantly in most cases, earnings before interest, taxes, depreciation, and amortization (EBITDA). EBITDA is a proxy for cash flow, but the two are not identical. In multiples valuation, EBITDA is generally used because it can be calculated using only the income statement, whereas cash flow also requires information from the balance sheet. The most common multiples are enterprise value to EBITDA (EV/EBITDA); price to earnings (P/E); and price to book (P/B).

To obtain meaningful information from a multiples analysis it is essential to select a peer group of public companies that have the most similar characteristics to the company being valued. This usually means analyzing companies in the same industry by using Standard Industrial Classification (SIC) codes, or by using the North American Industry Classification System (NAICS), or a database such as Thompson Financial or Dealogic. However, sometimes a company should be excluded from a comparable peer group if the company competes in the same product area, but also has other large businesses that are unrelated to the key products of the company being valued. For example, General Electric produces GE lanterns, which directly competes with Coleman lanterns, but GE and Coleman should not be in the same peer group when determining comparable multiples since GE's business activities extend far beyond the activities of Coleman. Size of comparable companies is also important. A company that has a market capitalization of $50 billion may not be a good comparable to a company that has a market capitalization of $500 million. Also, a thinly traded company that has limited analyst coverage may be removed from a peer group of comparable companies that have robust trading volume and active analyst coverage, because its fundamental value may not be fully reflected in its share price. These and many other factors must be considered when determining the best comparables. Coming up with the ideal list of comparables is challenging, and if the wrong companies are included, valuation conclusions may be incorrect. Finally, in addition to selecting the right peers, it is also important to normalize the financials of the peer companies to exclude any extraordinary items, nonrecurring charges, and restructuring charges. This ensures that the comparison across peers is on an apples-to-apples basis.

DCF analysis and LBO analysis are cash-flow-based methods of valuation. Both require projected future cash flows, which are discounted by a company's cost of capital. A DCF analysis attempts to determine the intrinsic value of a company based on future cash flow projections. An LBO analysis attempts to determine an internal rate of return (IRR) for a private equity firm acquirer based on future cash flow projections. The challenge for both DCF and LBO analysis is developing accurate projections, since up to 10 years of cash flow is industry convention for this valuation method. As an incentive to accurately project future cash flow, the future compensation and career track of managers who provide forecasts (and are tasked with managing the business going forward) can be linked to these projections. Another challenge is determining the most accurate discount rate, which varies considerably between companies and between industries.

## Comparable Company Analysis

A comparable company analysis provides a helpful reference point, but it is not used as a principal basis for determining the value for an acquisition target since it does not incorporate a control premium. It is a useful exercise to look at companies in the same industry, or companies that have similar business characteristics in terms of growth, profitability, and risk. This analysis relies on the assumption that markets are efficient and current trading values are an accurate reflection of current industry trends, business risks, growth prospects, and so forth. A multiples range can be developed for comparable companies, and then this range can be applied to the company being valued to determine implied valuation, which doesn't include a control premium. The derived value for the company can then be compared with the company's stock price, which is always the best barometer of value for a company in an efficient market. Discrepancies between the company's stock price and implied value range from this analysis can provide insights into unique challenges or prospects faced by the company. This is a starting point in a valuation analysis, but it is not relevant without utilizing other valuation processes that include a control premium.

Comparable companies in many cases can be analyzed based on their P/E multiple, which is calculated by dividing the current stock price by the annual earnings per share. The P/E multiple is usually calculated based on both the latest 12-month (LTM) EPS as well as using forecasted EPS for the next fiscal year. EPS is calculated by dividing net income for a period by the weighted average shares outstanding for the period. When the P/E multiple range has been determined for comparable companies, this range should be applied to the company being valued by multiplying the company's earnings by this multiple range to arrive at a valuation of the company's equity.

Comparable companies should also be analyzed based on their enterprise value (EV), which represents the total cost of acquiring a company. Enterprise value is equal to the current market value of equity plus net debt (and minority interests, if they exist). Net debt is comprised of short-term debt + long-term debt + capitalized leases + preferred stock − cash and cash equivalents. Net debt is included in EV because the acquirer of a company's stock has the eventual obligation to pay off debt (and related obligations) and assumes cash on hand will be used in the first case to retire debt, leaving net debt as an addition to equity market value. Because EV takes into consideration the value of equity and net debt, it provides a better comparison across companies with differing capital structures, thereby making the EV/EBITDA multiple a key basis for valuation. When an EV/EBITDA multiple range has been determined for comparable companies, this multiple range can be applied to the company being valued by multiplying the company's EBITDA by this multiple range.

## Comparable Transactions Analysis

A comparable transaction analysis focuses on M&A transactions in which comparable companies were acquired. A comparable transaction analysis is similar to a comparable company analysis in relation to using multiples. However, comparable transactions include control premiums (and expected synergies) and so the multiples will generally be higher than for comparable companies and more reflective of a reasonable price to be paid for the acquisition of a target company. In this analysis, as with the previous analysis, it is important to compare only companies in the same industry, or companies that exhibit the same business characteristics.

The company being analyzed for a potential takeover should be valued at approximately the same relative value as the comparable transaction companies, if the peer group is appropriately developed. In other words, if the comparable companies that completed transactions in the same industry sold for an EV/EBITDA multiple of $10\times$ to $11\times$, then this multiple range should be applied to the EBITDA of the target company being considered for an acquisition. If the target company's EBITDA is, for example, $100 million, the logical EV range for the target company is $1.0 billion to $1.1 billion ($100 million $\times$ 10 to 11). The equity value of the company would be based on the following formula: Equity Value = EV − net debt. If the target has total debt of $300 million, cash of $100 million, and no preferred shares, capitalized leases, or minority interests, the company's equity value is $1.0 billion to $1.1 billion − ($300 million − $100 million) = $800 million to $900 million. If the target company has 20 million shares, the value range per share for an acquisition is $40 to $45 ($800 million to $900 million / 20 million shares).

Comparable transactions are typically drawn from the previous 5- to 10-year period, although the most recent transactions are generally considered the most representative. It is essential to use the relevant financials for the completed acquisitions based on the year of completion and to use both historical and forecasted EPS and EBITDA multiples from the announcement date. If done properly, a comparable transactions analysis can be very helpful in determining a potential range of prices to offer when purchasing a company, since the multiples for comparable transactions include control premiums and synergies. By looking at similar transactions over a historical period, this analysis is also useful in identifying industry trends such as consolidations, foreign investments, and active financial buyers. After establishing the value of the target company using a comparable transaction analysis, it is important, when possible, to complete at least two other valuation processes and then attempt to triangulate the best price to offer for an acquisition based on multiple reference points. A subset of a comparable transaction analysis is a premium paid analysis, which compares the acquisition premium being considered to the premium paid in previous comparable transactions.

## Discounted Cash Flow Analysis

A discounted cash flow (DCF) analysis is considered an essential valuation methodology, since it attempts to determine the intrinsic value of a company. This valuation, when it employs a perpetuity method, does not involve selection of comparable companies and so is immune to the inherent problems in creating a comparable company list. DCF relies on the projected cash flows of the company. A DCF analysis assumes that the value of a company (the enterprise value) is equal to the value of its future cash flows discounted by the time value of money and the riskiness of those cash flows. The company's value is calculated in two parts in a DCF analysis: (1) the sum of the cash flows during the projection period; and (2) the terminal value, or the estimated value of the business at the end of the projection period. Both parts are discounted using the company's weighted average cost of capital (WACC). The end result is determination of the net present value (NPV) of the company's operating assets. The cash flows used are unlevered, which means that they do not include financing costs (e.g., interest on debt or dividends on stock). Because EV is the value to all capital providers of the company (debt and equity), unlevered cash flows represent the cash available to each of these providers. After establishing the EV of a company, the equity value can be determined by subtracting net debt from EV.

In a DCF analysis, future projections can incorporate changes in a company's long-term strategic plan. As a result, a DCF analysis is flexible enough to incorporate changing assumptions about growth rates and operating margins, while allowing for adjustments for nonoperating items. However, a DCF valuation also has limitations. For example, it is critically dependent on accurate projections, and the longer the projected period of time is, the less confident one should be in its accuracy. Senior management's projections can be tested or sensitized by the investment banker. In addition, a DCF analysis utilizes WACC, which can be the subject of a wide range of costs estimates. Calculation of the cost of equity requires a number of variable inputs, such as the levered beta of the company (which itself is the subject of numerous variables) and the market risk premium (which may also include a size discount or premium). Finally, it is important in a DCF analysis to project cash flows through the period of time covered by a full operating cycle so that cash flows at the end of the projection period are "normalized." The end of this projection period is often called the *termination value date,* which is typically up to 10 years in the future. The terminal value (TV) of a company should be determined as of the termination value date. TV is the present value (for the period into perpetuity that starts as of the termination value date) of all future cash flows, assuming a stable growth rate forever. There are two methods of projecting TV: (1) terminal multiple method, which applies a multiple such as EV/EBITDA to projected EBITDA at the termination value date; or (2) perpetuity growth rate method, which is determined based on the following formula: $TV = FCF \times (1 + g)/(r - g)$, where FCF is free cash flow projected as of the terminal valuation date, r is equal to WACC, and g is the perpetual growth rate (equal to the expected rate of inflation + the long-term real growth in GDP). So, for example, if FCF is $100 million as of the terminal valuation date, g is 5% and WACC is 11%, $TV = \$100$ million $\times (1.05)/(.11 - .05) = \$1.75$ billion. It is important to note that because TV represents a significant portion of EV, overall value becomes highly sensitive to TV calculation assumptions.

The three steps that are necessary to complete a DCF valuation are as follows:

1. Determine unlevered free cash flows for an up-to-10-year period, such that the end of this period represents a steady-state condition for the company.
2. Estimate the terminal value of the company at the time when the company has reached a steady state, which coincides with the end of the cash flow forecast period, and continuing into perpetuity.
3. Determine WACC, which is the blended cost of debt and equity for the company, and then discount the unlevered free cash flows and the terminal value by WACC to create a present value (enterprise value) of the company.

A DCF analysis can be completed without inclusion of any synergies (Standalone DCF), but a typical DCF analysis usually is sensitized to show the impact of net synergies related to cost savings (Standalone plus cost savings DCF) and, sometimes, inclusion of total synergies, including revenue synergies (Standalone plus total synergies DCF).

## Leveraged Buyout Analysis

A leveraged buyout (LBO) analysis is a relevant acquisition analysis when there is the possibility of a financial sponsor buyer. Financial sponsors are private equity firms that purchase companies using equity they have raised in a private investment fund combined with new debt raised to facilitate the purchase. Compared to corporate buyers (strategic buyers), private equity firms (financial buyers) include higher amounts of debt to fund their acquisition. Financial buyers usually include senior secured debt provided by banks, subordinated unsecured debt, and sometimes mezzanine capital in their financing package. Management of the newly acquired company, which can be either the pre-acquisition team, or a new team brought in by the financial buyers, usually makes an equity investment in the company alongside the private equity firm. See Chapters 16 and 17 for a more complete overview of private equity and LBO transactions.

Targets for private equity firms are typically companies in mature industries that have stable and growing cash flow in order to service large debt obligations and, potentially, to pay dividends to the financial buyers. In addition, targets usually have low capital expenditures, low existing leverage, and assets that can be sold. Financial buyers generally expect an exit event within 3 to 7 years, which is usually accomplished through either an IPO or M&A sale to a strategic buyer or, sometimes, to another financial buyer. Financial buyers usually target an IRR on their investments of more than 20%, although this target can move down depending on the overall economic climate and financing environment.

An LBO analysis includes cash flow projections, terminal value projections (the price at which a financial buyer thinks the company can be sold in 3 to 7 years), and present value determination (the price that a financial buyer will pay for a company today). The analysis solves for the IRR of the investment, which is the discount rate that results in the cash flow and terminal value of the investment equaling the initial equity investment. If the resulting IRR is below their targeted IRR, the financial buyer will lower the purchase price. Investment bankers run LBO models and assume a minimum IRR required by financial buyers based on risks associated with the investment and market conditions. They can then solve for the purchase price that creates this targeted IRR. If the purchase price is above the current market value of the company, the company may be an economically viable investment for a financial buyer. In this case, investment bankers will include an LBO analysis as one of several valuation methods they use to determine the appropriate value for a target company, and financial buyers will be included in addition to strategic buyers in the list of potential acquirers.

An LBO analysis is similar to a DCF analysis in relation to use of projected cash flows, terminal value, present value, and discount rate. The difference is that a DCF analysis solves for the present value (enterprise value), while the LBO analysis solves for the discount rate (IRR). Once the IRR is determined in the LBO analysis, the purchase price may need to increase or decrease in order to align with the targeted IRR (see Exhibit 4.6).

In addition to focusing on IRR, the LBO analysis considers whether there is enough projected cash flow to operate the company and also pay down debt principal and cover interest payments. The analysis also determines if there is sufficient cash flow to pay dividends at some point to the private equity investor. The ability to retire debt and pay dividends results in a higher IRR. Subject to consideration of financial risk, financial buyers will often raise the highest amount of debt that providers of debt will allow in order to minimize their equity contribution, which, in turn, maximizes the IRR.

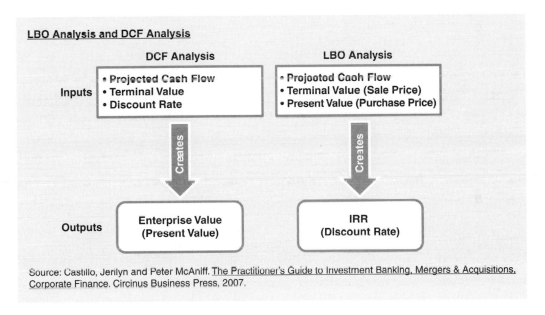

Source: Castillo, Jerilyn and Peter McAniff. The Practitioner's Guide to Investment Banking, Mergers & Acquisitions, Corporate Finance. Circinus Business Press, 2007.

**EXHIBIT 4.6**

## Sum-of-the-Parts Analysis

A break-up analysis is a useful additional valuation tool when a company has many different businesses that, when analyzed separately, are worth more than the value of the company as a whole. If the sum of the parts of a company is greater than the current market value of the company, then there may be an opportunity to break up the company and sell it to different buyers, creating incremental value in the sale process. Investment bankers who are on the sell side might employ a sum-of-the-parts analysis that focuses on EV/EBITDA multiples for each separate business and then add all EVs together to create a case for a higher sale price for the company. Bankers who are on the buy side might focus on a sum-of-the-parts analysis to determine certain businesses that their client might want to sell post-acquisition if those businesses do not fit in well with the acquiring company's existing businesses. In this case, bankers will need to determine business unit values separately and then adjust values based on allocation of assets and liabilities and consideration of tax issues. Bankers need to determine whether unwanted businesses are best sold in an IPO, carve-out, or spin-off (in which case a comparable company analysis is helpful), sold to another company (in which case a comparable transaction analysis and DCF plus synergies analysis is most helpful), or sold to a private equity fund (in which case an LBO analysis is appropriate). See Exhibit 4.7 for a summary of the different valuation methods described in this section.

**Summary of Valuation Methods**

| Publicly Traded Comparable Companies Analysis | Comparable Transactions Analysis | Discounted Cash Flow Analysis | Leveraged Buyout Analysis | Other |
|---|---|---|---|---|
| **Description** | | | | |
| • "Public Market Valuation"<br>• Value based on market trading multiples of comparable companies<br>• Applied using historical and projected multiples<br>• Does not include a control premium | • "Private Market Valuation"<br>• Value based on multiples paid for comparable companies in sale transactions<br>• Includes control premium | • "Intrinsic" value of business<br>• Present value of projected free cash flows<br>• Incorporates both short and long-term expected performance<br>• Risk in cash flows and capital structure captured in discount rate | • Value to a financial buyer<br>• Value based on debt repayment and return on equity investment | • Sum-of-the-parts analysis<br>• Liquidation analysis<br>• Break-up or net asset value analysis<br>• Historical trading performance<br>• Discounted future share price<br>• Dividend discount model |
| **Comments** | | | | |
| • Similarity of companies (size, growth prospects, product mix)<br>• Placement within peer group<br>• Underlying market / sector trading fluctuations<br>• Market may view firm's outlook differently<br>• Valuing synergies, tax benefits problematic | • Limited number of truly comparable transactions<br>• Dated information due to changes in market<br>• Data missing or hard to find (earnings often unavailable on subsidiary transactions) | • The preferred valuation technique when credible cash flows can be projected and confident in WACC determination<br>• Sensitive to terminal value assumptions | • Usually represents a floor bid because of lack of synergies and high cost of capital and high required return (IRR)<br>• Requires various assumptions on capital structure<br>• May not be a viable option due to size or type of business | • May be more situational and not as relevant as a broad-based valuation technique<br>• Near-term EPS impact may not reflect true value |

**EXHIBIT 4.7**

## Valuation Summary

After completing all appropriate valuation methodologies, investment bankers summarize the result by creating what is called a *football field* that shows the valuation ranges for each methodology. This summary, in turn, enables bankers to establish a valuation range for a company that is the subject of an M&A transaction. Normally, a football field will show a comparable company range that is lower than a comparable transaction range, because a control premium is included in the comparable transaction analysis. A DCF analysis generally creates a valuation range that is similar to the range for a comparable company analysis, although there are examples where this is not the case. Typically, a company's current acquisition value falls above the overlapping ranges provided by the comparable company analysis and the DCF analysis, although again, there are examples where this is not the case. This is because an acquirer should pay a control premium, which is not included in either of these valuation methodologies. An LBO analysis usually provides a *floor value* for a company, since it represents a price that a financial buyer would be willing to pay, based on achievement of their required IRR. Generally speaking, strategic buyers are able to pay more than financial buyers, since they can take advantage of synergies with their own company. However, if the market allows especially high leverage (as was the case from 2006 to mid-2007), which drives higher IRRs, or if there are unique operating strategies that a financial buyer brings to the transaction, then it is possible for financial buyers to outbid strategic buyers, notwithstanding the lack of synergy benefits. If there are multiple major lines of businesses within a company, then a break-up analysis may be included in the football field. Depending on the company and industry, other valuation methodologies may also be included in the summary.

An example of a football field is included in Exhibit 4.8. Looking at this football field, assuming a company's current share price is $40, a typical comparable company analysis might show a valuation range of $36 to $44, which is lower than a comparable transaction valuation range of $42 to $51, based on the control premium inherent in the comparable transaction analysis. A DCF analysis might show a valuation range of $38 to $45, unless synergies are added, in which case the range might increase to $43 to $50, assuming cost synergies of $5. In this football field, it has been determined that financial buyers might be interested in the target company based on the company's strong cash flow, low leverage, and small capital expenditure requirements, and so an LBO valuation was completed, which shows a valuation range of $39 to $45, based on an assumed 20% IRR requirement. A break-up analysis was completed, because there are several different business lines run by the company, and the valuation range based on this analysis is $41 to $51, which is the widest range due to uncertainty regarding different business line values after allocating debt and considering tax issues. Based on this football field, investment bankers might determine that the appropriate triangulated value for the target company is $50 (which might be expressed as a range of $48 to $52), which represents a 25% premium to the current share price of $40. However, $50 could be adjusted up or down based on the acquisition consideration (shares or cash), probability of completion, and other factors.

A case is provided in Exhibit 4.9 that summarizes the strategic considerations of a public company that is feeling pressure from some key investors regarding the need to take actions that will enhance shareholder value. In the case, the company asks for advice from an investment bank regarding a range of strategic issues and a valuation analysis to help determine if a sale of the company is the optimal way to enhance shareholder value.

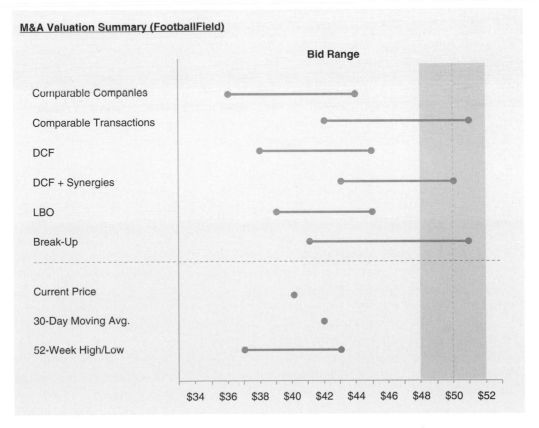

EXHIBIT 4.8

# Service Company Case

## Case Focus

This case simulates the experience of an investment banking firm advising a publidy traded client on evaluating strategic alternatives at a time when the client's operating and stock price performance have been stagnant and the management team and Board of Directors are getting pressure from certain shareholders, notably hedge funds, to take action that will enhance near-term shareholder value. It requires the reader to determine the value of the Company under a number of strategic alternatives available using traditional valuation techniques including comparable company trading analysis, comparable transactions analysis, discounted cash flow analysis, and leveraged buyout analysis.

## The Assignment

Service Company ("ServiceCo" or the "Company"), a publicly traded company, provides services including lawn care, janitorial and maintenance service, and building repair to the consumer and commercial markets. It is October 2007 and hedge funds have recently started building positions in the Company's stock, attracted by the Company's strong and stable cash flows, relatively low valuation, and stagnant stock performance. You are a Managing Director in your firm's investment banking department. Given your firm's history of advising the Company on past acquisitions and capital market decisions, the Company's Board of Directors has asked your team to evaluate strategic alternatives for the Company.

The first step in evaluating strategic alternatives is to determine valuation under the following scenarios:

- Continue running the Company as is
- Change the capital structure
- Sell the Company to a strategic buyer
- Sell the Company to a financial buyer

Due to the management team's lack of experience in operating a company with significant leverage, the Board of Directors is not willing to significantly change the capital structure unless the Company is sold.

You have a meeting next week where you will be presenting your preliminary valuation and recommendations to the Board of Directors, including whether to pursue a broad or targeted sale process.

- Broad "Auction" Process
  - Likely to achieve the highest price
  - Sale process more likely to become public, leading to greater customer and employee disruption
  - Greater drain on company resources (both management's time and expense)
  - Harder to control dissemination of competitive information (detailed financials, customer lists, organizational charts, etc.)
  - Likely will take longer for process to be completed
  - Less likely to trigger a shareholder lawsuit
- Targeted Process

  - More difficult to achieve the highest price
  - Sale process less likely to become public, leading to less customer and employee disruption

- Lesser drain on company resources
- Easier to control dissemination of competitive information
- Can be a faster process
- More likely to trigger a shareholder lawsuit
- Requires company and advisors to select the "right" group of buyers

Your task is to recommend a potential sale process to ServiceCo's Board of Directors assuming the following for ServiceCo:

- Hedge funds are advocating a sale at the highest value possible
- Key employees may defect if the process takes a long time and becomes public
- Top management is very concerned about dissemination of competitive information
- Top managers are significant holders of the Company's stock
- Company employees are spending a large portion of their time focused on the Company's turnaround plan

Use the provided ServiceCo operating projections (see Figure I) to compare ServiceCo's operating performance to the operating statistics of ServiceCo's publicly traded comparable companies and companies that have been acquired in precedent transactions that have taken place in the industry to determine a public trading valuation range and change of control valuation range, respectively, for ServiceCo. In addition, use the provided ServiceCo operating projections and return on equity, average borrowing rate and tax rate statistics to determine the intrinsic value of ServiceCo using a DCF analysis. Finally, use the provided ServiceCo operating projections, debt structure, and interest rate assumptions and LBO model to determine a purchase price range for ServiceCo assuming a private equity firm will take the Company private.

Your presentation should include the following:

- Preliminary Valuation Summary ("Football Field"): see Figure V

  - This is a summary of the results of the various valuation techniques and provides a good illustrative summary slide from which to communicate your conclusions to the Board of Directors
  - Depending on the results, conclusions drawn, and audience, this slide could come before all of the summary slides for the respective analyses performed
  - Assume the Company has 250 million shares outstanding, $800 million of debt and $200 million of cash

- Comparable Company Trading Analysis: see Figures II and III

  - This analysis provides an indication of the potential implied value of the Company *excluding* a change of control premium by comparing ServiceCo to similar selected publicly traded comparable companies
  - Use the provided list of publicly traded comparable companies to ServiceCo and their respective comparable operating performance and trading valuation multiples to develop a view on the appropriate 2007 and 2008 P/E and enterprise value / EBITDA multiples to be used to value ServiceCo
    - This can be accomplished by taking the ratio of (1) enterprise value, defined as the sum of market capitalization and total debt minus cash and cash equivalents, often referred to as net debt, to (2) EBITDA, defined as estimated earnings before interest, taxes, depreciation, and amortization, for calendar years 2007 and 2008; and

(Continued)

- ▪ The ratio of share price to estimated earnings per share ("EPS") for calendar years 2007 and 2008
  - – Based on the analysis of the relevant financial multiples and ratios for each of the comparable companies, select representative ranges of financial multiples for the companies and apply these ranges of multiples to the corresponding ServiceCo financial statistics
  - – For this exercise, account for how "comparable" the companies are to ServiceCo based on relative size, growth expectations, and profitability margins. Assume (just for the purposes of this analysis) all of the companies compete in the same end markets as ServiceCo
  - – Assume ServiceCo's 2007 and 2008 EPS are $1.46 and $1.50, respectively

- • Precedent Transactions Analysis: see Figure IV

  - – This analysis provides an indication of the potential value of the Company *including* a change of control premium by reviewing the publicly available financial terms of precedent transactions that share certain characteristics with ServiceCo
  - – Use the provided list of precedent transactions and compare their respective size and operating performance metrics (profitability margins) and transaction valuation multiples to develop a view on the appropriate transaction enterprise value to 2007 EBITDA and EBIT multiples to be used to value ServiceCo
  - – Assume this is the best list of representative precedent transactions; however, account for how "comparable" the transactions are to the potential ServiceCo transaction based on the relative size and profitability margins of the respective target companies in the data set

- • Discounted Cash Flow ("DCF") Analysis: see DCF Valuation Model in publisher's website

  - – This analysis enables you to determine the long-term intrinsic standalone value of the Company
  - – Use the provided ServiceCo operating projections to determine DCF value of the Company
  - – Use the enterprise value / EBITDA multiple method to calculate your terminal value; use the comparable company operating and trading statistics to determine an appropriate terminal multiple range
  - – To determine the appropriate discount rates, assume the following information:
    - ▪ 10-year U.S. Treasury Rate of 4.47%
    - ▪ Unlevered forward predicted Beta of 1.254
    - ▪ Equity market risk premium of 4–6%
    - ▪ Debt / Equity Ratio of 0.43
    - ▪ Cost of debt is 8%
    - ▪ Implied tax rate of 39%
  - – Determine whether the discount rate assumption or the exit multiple assumption has a larger impact on the DCF valuation
  - – Determine the additional potential value that the Company may be worth for a strategic buyer using the synergy assumptions outlined below:
  - – Synergies – ServiceCo has identified a broad range of potential synergies that could be available to a strategic buyer, resulting in an increase in EBITDA if those synergies are realized:
    - ▪ Cost Synergies – potential total EBITDA increase of $50–100 million
      Consolidate headquarters
      Consolidate purchasing of raw materials
      Consolidate back-office functions
      Leverage increased marketing and advertising purchasing power
    - ▪ Revenue synergies – potential total EBITDA increase of $200–300 million (in addition to potential cost synergies)

Cross-sell ServiceCo products to the customer base of the Buyer
Cross-sell Buyer products to the ServiceCo customer base
Bundle multiple services to increase customer loyalty
Increase advertising spend effectiveness by lowering the cost of advertising and co-advertising brands and services
- Evaluate the potential valuation impact of the identified synergies
- Apply your assumed 2007 EBITDA multiple to the synergy value that you believe that a strategic buyer will conservatively include in their valuation considerations
- Briefly explain why you believe that a strategic buyer would pay for the synergies you identified
- Add this "synergy" value to the DCF value to estimate the potential value of the Company for a strategic buyer

• Leveraged Buyout ("LBO") Analysis: see LBO Valuation Model in publisher's website

- This analysis enables you to determine what a financial sponsor (private equity firm) could potentially pay for the Company and still achieve its targeted return thresholds
- Use the provided ServiceCo operating projections to build an LBO model with an expected exit in year 5 (2012)
- The leveraged finance group at your firm has provided you with the following debt structure and rate assumptions:
  - Bank debt maximum of 2.5 × 2007 EBITDA at LIBOR + 250 basis points
  - Total debt maximum of 5.5 × 2007 EBITDA with the remainder of the debt in bonds at 10.0%
- For the LBO analysis, you will need to calculate the incremental transaction amortization from the purchase accounting adjustment made at the closing of the transaction. The incremental transaction amortization (which is not tax deductible) is calculated as follows:
  - Implied equity purchase price plus transaction fees and expenses (which changes based on the purchase price: 1% of new bank debt + 2% of all other new debt) less tangible book value of – $800 million (shareholder's book equity less existing goodwill and intangibles)
    - Assume 25% of new goodwill can be amortized
    - Assume amortization period of 20 years
- Given the operating projections, leverage and rate assumptions, determine the maximum that a financial sponsor could pay per share and still achieve 15–20% returns in 5 years
  - Use the comparable company operating and trading multiple statistics and precedent transaction operating and valuation multiple statistics to determine an appropriate exit multiple range for the potential financial sponsor to appropriately exit the ServiceCo LBO investment through either an initial public offering ("IPO") or a sale to a strategic buyer or another financial sponsor; justify the exit multiples you choose to use
  - Using ServiceCo management's financial forecasts for fiscal years 2007 to 2013, assume that the potential financial sponsor would value its ServiceCo investment in calendar year 2012 at an aggregate value range that represented your chosen exit multiples for calendar year 2013 EBITDA. Then calculate ServiceCo's calendar year-end 2012 equity value range by adding ServiceCo's forecasted calendar year end 2012 cash balance and subtracting ServiceCo's forecasted debt outstanding at calendar year-end 2012. Based on your calendar year-end 2012 equity value range for ServiceCo, assume that the financial sponsor would likely target 5-year internal rates of return ("IRR") ranging from

approximately 15% to 20%. Based on this, derive estimated implied values per share that the financial sponsor might be willing to pay to acquire ServiceCo
- Please note that your exit multiple assumption should not be higher than the entry multiple assumption and could be lower; discuss why this is relevant
  - "Credit Crunch" Analysis
    - ServiceCo's Board is particularly concerned about a downturn in the credit markets
    - The leveraged finance group at your firm suggests that a credit market downturn would result in the following structure and rates:
      - Bank debt maximum of 2.0 × 2007 EBITDA at LIBOR + 350 basis points
      - Total debt maximum of 4.5 × 2007 EBITDA with the remainder of the debt in bonds at 12.0%
    - Discuss whether the decrease in leverage or increase in rates has a larger impact on ServiceCo's valuation

- Conclusions

  - Provide clear conclusions on the best strategic option and suggested next steps for the Company
  - Recommend a targeted process or a broad auction and justify your choice
  - You are being paid to give advice, not calculate numbers!

## Overview of ServiceCo

ServiceCo is a national company serving both residential and commercial customers. Its services include lawn care, landscape maintenance, termite and pest control, home warranty, disaster response and reconstruction, cleaning and disaster restoration, house cleaning, furniture repair, and home inspection. As of December 31, 2006, ServiceCo provided these services through a network of approximately 5,500 company-owned locations and franchise licenses operating under a number of leading brands. Incorporated in Delaware in 1995, ServiceCo is the successor to various entities dating back to 1940. ServiceCo is organized into five principal operating segments: LawnCare, LandCare, Exterminator, Home Protection, and Other Operations and Corporate.

The following table shows the percentage of ServiceCo's consolidated revenue from continuing operations derived from each of ServiceCo's reportable segments in the years indicated:

| Segment | 2006 | 2005 | 2004 |
| --- | --- | --- | --- |
| LawnCare | 31% | 32% | 32% |
| LandCare | 13% | 14% | 14% |
| Exterminator | 31% | 33% | 33% |
| Home Protection | 16% | 16% | 16% |
| Other Operations and Corporate | 9% | 5% | 5% |

### ServiceCo LawnCare Segment

The LawnCare segment provides lawn care services primarily under the ServiceCo LawnCare brand name. Revenues derived from the LawnCare segment constituted 31%, 32%, and 32% of the revenue from continuing operations of the consolidated ServiceCo enterprise in 2006, 2005, and 2004, respectively. The ServiceCo LawnCare business is seasonal in nature. Weather conditions, such as a drought, or snow in the late spring or fall, can affect the demand for lawn care services. These conditions may result in a decrease in revenues or an increase in costs.

ServiceCo LawnCare is the leading provider of lawn care services in the United States serving both residential and commercial customers. As of December 31, 2006, ServiceCo LawnCare provided these services in 45 states and the District of Columbia through 225 company-owned locations and 45 franchised locations.

## ServiceCo LandCare Segment

The ServiceCo LandCare segment provides landscape maintenance services primarily under the ServiceCo LandCare brand name. Revenues derived from the ServiceCo LandCare segment constituted 13%, 14%, and 14% of the revenue from continuing operations of the consolidated ServiceCo enterprise in 2006, 2005, and 2004, respectively. The ServiceCo LandCare business is seasonal in nature. Weather conditions such as a drought can affect the demand for landscape maintenance services, or declines in the volume of snowfall can affect the level of snow removal services and may result in a decrease in revenues or an increase in costs.

ServiceCo LandCare is a leading provider of landscape maintenance services in the United States serving primarily commercial customers. As of December 31, 2006, ServiceCo LandCare provided these services in 43 states and the District of Columbia through 102 company-owned locations and had no international operations.

## Exterminator Segment

The Exterminator segment provides termite and pest control services primarily under the Exterminator brand name. Revenues derived from the Exterminator segment constituted 31%, 33%, and 33% of the revenue from continuing operations of the consolidated ServiceCo enterprise in 2006, 2005, and 2004, respectively. The Exterminator business is seasonal in nature. The termite swarm season, which generally occurs in early spring but varies by region depending on climate, leads to the highest demand for termite control services and therefore the highest level of revenues. Similarly, increased pest activity in the warmer months leads to the highest demand for pest control services and, therefore, the highest level of revenues.

Exterminator is the leading provider of termite and pest control services in the United States serving both residential and commercial customers. As of December 31, 2006, Exterminator provided these services in 45 states and the District of Columbia through 380 company-owned locations and 127 franchised locations.

## Home Protection Segment

The Home Protection segment provides home warranty contracts for systems and appliances primarily under the Home Protection brand name and home inspection services primarily under the Home Inspection brand name. Revenues derived from the Home Protection segment constituted 16%, 16%, and 16% of the revenue from continuing operations of the consolidated ServiceCo enterprise in 2006, 2005, and 2004, respectively. The Home Protection and Home Inspection businesses are seasonal in nature. Sales volume in the Home Protection segment depends, in part, on the number of home resale closings, which historically has been highest in the spring and summer months. Home Protection's costs related to service call volume are highest in the summer months, especially during periods of unseasonably warm temperatures.

## Other Operations and Corporate Segment

The Other Operations and Corporate segment provides disaster response and reconstruction services, residential and commercial disaster restoration and cleaning services primarily

(Continued)

domestic house cleaning services and on-site furniture repair and restoration services primarily under the Furniture Medic brand name. In addition, the Other Operations and Corporate segment includes ServiceCo's headquarters functions. Revenues derived from the Other Operations and Corporate segment constituted 9%, 5%, and 5% of the revenue from continuing operations of the consolidated ServiceCo enterprise in 2006, 2005, and 2004, respectively.

## Franchises

Franchises are important to ServiceCo. Total franchise fees (initial and recurring) represented 3.5%, 3.4%, and 3.3% of consolidated revenue in 2006, 2005, and 2004, respectively. Related franchise operating expenses were 2.2%, 2.1%, and 2.1% of consolidated operating expenses in 2006, 2005, and 2004, respectively. Total franchise-related profits comprised 11.3%, 10.5%, and 10.3% of consolidated operating income before headquarters overhead and restructuring charges in 2006, 2005 and 2004, respectively. Franchise agreements made in the course of these businesses are generally for a term of 5 to 10 years. The majority of these franchise agreements are renewed prior to expiration.

## Competition

ServiceCo competes with many other companies in the sale of its services, franchises, and products. The principal methods of competition in ServiceCo's businesses include quality and speed of service, name recognition and reputation, pricing and promotions, customer satisfaction, brand awareness, professional sales forces, and reputation/referrals. Competition in all of the Company's markets is strong.

- Lawn Care Services. Competition in the market for lawn care services comes mainly from local, independently owned firms and from homeowners who care for their own lawns. ServiceCo continues to expand toward a more national footprint.
- Landscape Maintenance Services. Competition in the market for commercial landscape maintenance services comes mainly from small owner-operated companies operating in a limited geographic market and, to a lesser degree, from a few large companies operating in multiple markets and from property owners who perform their own landscaping services.
- Termite and Pest Control Services. Competition in the market for termite and pest control services comes mainly from thousands of regional and local, independently owned firms, from homeowners who treat their own termite and pest control problems and from Orkin, Inc., a subsidiary of Rollins, Inc., which operates on a national basis. Ecolab competes nationally in the commercial pest control segment.
- Home Warranty Contracts for Systems and Appliances. Competition in the market for home warranty contracts for systems and appliances comes mainly from regional providers of home warranties. Several competitors are initiating expansion efforts into additional states.
- Home Inspection Services. Competition in the market for home inspection services comes mainly from regional and local, independently owned firms.
- Residential & Commercial Disaster Restoration and Cleaning Services. Competition in the market for disaster restoration and cleaning services comes mainly from local, independently owned firms and a few national professional cleaning companies.
- House Cleaning Services. Competition in the market for house cleaning services comes mainly from local, independently owned firms and a few national companies.

- Furniture Repair Services. Competition in the market for furniture repair services comes mainly from local, independent contractors.

## Major Customers

ServiceCo has no single customer that accounts for more than 10% of its consolidated operating revenue. Additionally, no operating segment has a single customer that accounts for more than 10% of its operating revenue. None of ServiceCo's operating segments is dependent on a single customer or a few customers where the loss of which would have a material adverse effect on the segment.

**ServiceCo Projections**
Management Case - January 2008
$MM

| | Actual 2007 | 2008 | 2009 | 2010 | 2011 | 2012 | 2013 | 2014 | 2015 | 2016 | 2017 |
|---|---|---|---|---|---|---|---|---|---|---|---|
| **Key Operating Statistics** | | | | | | | | | | | |
| Net Sales | 6,400 | 6,600 | 6,800 | 7,050 | 7,300 | 7,600 | 7,904 | 8,220 | 8,549 | 8,891 | 9,247 |
| % Growth | – | 3.1% | 3.0% | 3.7% | 3.5% | 4.1% | 4.0% | 4.0% | 4.0% | 4.0% | 4.0% |
| EBITDA | 800 | 825 | 884 | 917 | 949 | 988 | 1,028 | 1,069 | 1,111 | 1,156 | 1,202 |
| % Margin | 12.5% | 12.5% | 13.0% | 13.0% | 13.0% | 13.0% | 13.0% | 13.0% | 13.0% | 13.0% | 13.0% |
| EBIT | 750 | 765 | 814 | 827 | 839 | 858 | 892 | 928 | 965 | 1,004 | 1,044 |
| % Margin | 11.7% | 11.6% | 12.0% | 11.7% | 11.5% | 11.3% | 11.3% | 11.3% | 11.3% | 11.3% | 11.3% |
| Investment in Non-Cash Working Capital | (30) | (5) | (7) | (10) | (12) | (14) | (15) | (16) | (16) | (17) | (10) |
| % as Change in Net Sales | – | 2.5% | 3.5% | 4.0% | 4.6% | 4.7% | 5.0% | 5.0% | 5.0% | 5.0% | 5.0% |
| Capital Expenditures | (80) | (100) | (110) | (115) | (120) | (130) | (135) | (141) | (146) | (152) | (158) |
| % of Net Sales | 1.3% | 1.5% | 1.6% | 1.6% | 1.6% | 1.7% | 1.7% | 1.7% | 1.7% | 1.7% | 1.7% |

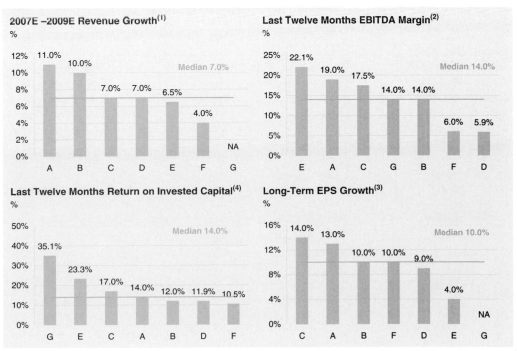

2007E –2009E Revenue Growth[1]

Last Twelve Months EBITDA Margin[2]

Last Twelve Months Return on Invested Capital[4]

Long-Term EPS Growth[3]

(Continued)

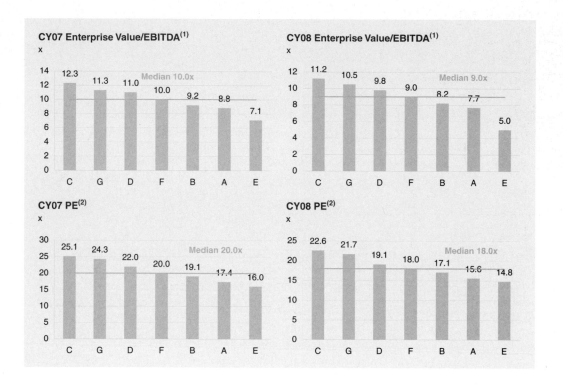

| $MM | | | | EV Multiple (LTM Data) | | | LTM Margin | |
|---|---|---|---|---|---|---|---|---|
| **Date** | **Acquiror** | **Target** | **Transaction Value** | **Revenue** | **EBITDA** | **EBIT** | **EBITDA** | **EBIT** |
| 11/16/06 | Acquiror A | Target A | $897.0 | 1.9 | 11.5 | 19.0 | 16.5% | 10.0% |
| 08/08/06 | Acquiror B | Target B [1] | 8,121.8 | 0.7 | 8.8 | 13.9 | 8.0% | 5.1% |
| 03/01/06 | Acquiror C | Target C | 2,669.4 | 0.8 | 9.5 | 13.5 | 8.3% | 5.8% |
| 01/24/06 | Acquiror D | Target D | 141.8 | 1.1 | NA | NA | NA | NA |
| 03/29/05 | Acquiror E | Target E | 5,147.5 | 0.8 | 10.6 | 14.1 | 7.7% | 5.8% |
| 12/22/04 | Acquiror F | Target F | 113.9 | 0.2 | 14.6 | 49.4 | 1.4% | 0.4% |
| 12/16/04 | Acquiror G | Target G | 1,837.2 | 1.0 | 12.5 | NA | 8.3% | NA |
| 10/01/04 | Acquiror H | Target H | 103.5 | 4.4 | NA | 9.6 | NA | 46.2% |
| 03/08/04 | Acquiror I | Target I | 110.0 | 1.2 | NA | NA | NA | NA |
| 01/05/04 | Acquiror J | Target J | 629.0 | 3.5 | 8.7 | NA | 40.0% | NA |
| 02/12/02 | Acquiror K | Target K | 186.0 | 0.3 | NA | NA | NA | NA |
| 10/05/01 | Acquiror L | Target L | 800.0 | 0.4 | 9.8 | 13.3 | 4.2% | 3.1% |
| 08/07/01 | Acquiror M | Target M | 170.0 | 0.3 | NA | NA | NA | NA |
| 11/03/99 | Acquiror N | Target N | 856.9 | 0.5 | 5.9 | 7.3 | 9.1% | 7.3% |
| 10/27/99 | Acquiror O | Target O | 322.2 | 0.6 | NA | 9.7 | NA | 6.1% |
| 03/23/99 | Acquiror P | Target P | 260.9 | 0.5 | 10.3 | 20.1 | 5.0% | 2.6% |
| 11/02/98 | Acquiror Q | Target Q [2] | 331.0 | 1.1 | NA | 16.6 | NA | 6.6% |
| 08/08/96 | Acquiror R | Target R | 218.5 | 1.1 | 8.6 | 12.4 | 13.4% | 9.3% |
| | | **Mean** | | 1.1 | 10.1 | 16.6 | 11.1% | 9.0% |
| | | **Median** | | 0.8 | 9.8 | 13.7 | 8.3% | 6.0% |

Notes:

1. August 8, 2006 Target B deal represents revised and accepted bid (LTM data as of 6/30/06). Initial proposal dated 5/1/06, based on 3/30/06 data, was valued at 0.7x, 8.6x and 13.2x of revenue, EBITDA and EBIT, respectively

2. EV Multiple based on run-rate volume of $300 million at time of acquisition per Equity Research

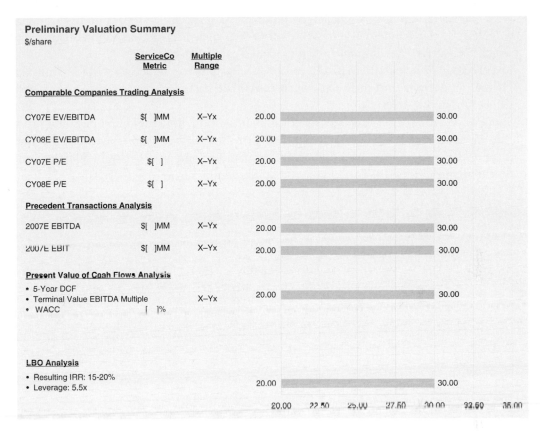

**EXHIBIT 4.9**

# Questions

1. Provide definitions for strategic buyers and financial buyers in a prospective M&A transaction.
2. Why have strategic buyers traditionally been able to out-bid financial buyers in auctions?
3. Why are revenue synergies typically given less weight than cost synergies when evaluating the combination benefits of a transaction?
4. In the United States, if an M&A transaction is relatively large within its industry, what is the name of the regulatory filing that is probably necessary before the transaction can be consummated? Which agency is it filed with? How long is the waiting period after a filing is made? What is the name of the European regulator that may be relevant in an M&A transaction?
5. Assume an acquiring company's P/E is 15× and the target company's P/E is 11×. Is the acquirer more or less likely to use stock as the acquisition currency? Why?
6. What is a potential risk of trying to complete a stock-based acquisition during periods of high market volatility?
7. Assume an investment bank has provided a fairness opinion on a proposed M&A transaction. Does this mean the board should go ahead and approve the transaction?
8. Why might a board want to include a *go-shop* provision in the merger/purchase agreement?
9. When is a break-up fee paid? What is the typical fee charged as a percent of equity value?

10. Of the various methods by which a corporate subsidiary can be separated from the parent company in the public markets (IPO, carve-out, spin-off, split-off, and tracking stock), which ones offer the subsidiary the most and least independence?

11. List the four principal alternative methods for establishing value in an M&A transaction.

12. Of the major valuation methods, which one(s) are based on relative values? on intrinsic values? on ability to pay?

13. Suppose you are the sell-side advisor for a multinational household and personal products manufacturer and marketer that sells primarily to the mass consumer markets. The analyst on your deal team prepares the following comparable companies analysis. Which, if any, of the companies in the list would you potentially remove from the analysis?

**Comparable Companies Analysis**
**$ in billions**

| | Location | Market Cap | Enterprise Value (EV) | LTM Revenue | LTM EBITDA | LTM EBITDA Margin | EV/ Revenue | EV/ EBITDA |
|---|---|---|---|---|---|---|---|---|
| Alberto Culver Co. | U.S. | $2.4 | $2.3 | $1.5 | $0.2 | 11.2% | 1.5x | 13.1x |
| Beiersdorf AG | Germany | $15.9 | $15.1 | $8.0 | $1.2 | 14.6% | 1.9x | 12.9x |
| Chattem Inc. | U.S. | $1.4 | $1.7 | $0.4 | $0.1 | 29.4% | 4.4x | 15.1x |
| Church & Dwight Co. | U.S. | $3.9 | $4.2 | $2.1 | $0.3 | 15.6% | 2.0x | 12.7x |
| Colgate-Palmolive Co. | U.S. | $42.8 | $41.9 | $13.4 | $2.9 | 21.8% | 3.1x | 14.4x |
| Henkel KGaA Nvtg Prf | Germany | $21.6 | $26.2 | $19.3 | $2.5 | 13.0% | 1.4x | 10.5x |
| McBride PLC | U.K. | $0.3 | $0.9 | $1.2 | $0.1 | 8.7% | 0.8x | 9.2x |
| Prestige Brands Holdings Inc. | U.S. | $0.4 | $1.0 | $0.3 | $0.1 | 31.5% | 3.0x | 9.6x |
| Procter & Gamble Co. | U.S. | $232.2 | $268.1 | $77.9 | $18.9 | 24.3% | 3.4x | 14.2x |
| Reckitt Benckiser Group PLC | U.K. | $38.1 | $41.3 | $10.3 | $2.7 | 26.1% | 4.0x | 15.4x |

14. Which valuation method tends to show the lowest valuation range? Why?

15. Which of the following companies would make a better LBO target, and why? (a) A diversified manufacturer of consumer snack products, or (b) a manufacturer of factory automation equipment for car makers, agricultural equipment, and other heavy machinery.

# Trading

The material in this chapter should be cross-referenced with **Case Study 5, "A Tale of Two Hedge Funds: Magnetar and Peloton,"** and **Case Study 6, "Kmart, Sears, and ESL: How a Hedge Fund Became One of the World's Largest Retailers."**

This chapter focuses on the two types of trading conducted by investment banks: Client-Related Trading and Proprietary Trading. The chapter also describes the activities of the two key trading businesses: Equities Trading and Fixed Income, Currencies, and Commodities (FICC) Trading.

## Client-Related Trading

An investment bank's client-related trading business is comprised of traders, sales professionals, and research analysts. Traders are responsible for buying securities from institutional and individual investors and, at some point in the future (minutes, hours, days, or months), reselling those securities at a higher price to other investing clients. The conduct of this risk taking function is affected by multiple inputs, including research, regulators, litigation, public relations, competitors, bankruptcies, credit rating agencies, arbitrageurs, and a myriad number of other variables. A good trader has the ability to keep track of and synthesize a large volume of information so that intelligent decisions can be made rapidly. The consequence of decisions can be a quick gain or loss on a security holding, but sometimes it takes months for the result to be known.

Regardless of the investment timeframe, a trader must keep track of every risk position's value on a daily basis. This is called *marking-to-market*. If a trader holds a public company's stock, the value can be taken from the intraday or closing price as reported by an exchange. If the trader holds a private company's securities for which no exchange or reporting service shows a closing price, the trader will need to determine a mark-to-market value by using comparable securities that trade on an exchange. Alternatively, the trader can determine value based on a model that has been developed to predict the realizable value of the security. Irrespective of the valuation method, a trader must mark-to-market all securities and derivative positions held in inventory each day, which gives rise to a daily profit and loss statement.

A trader must be able to deal analytically and unemotionally with trading losses, since even the best traders usually have a number of losing trades in their portfolio, alongside profitable trades. The key is to have more profitable trades than unprofitable trades, and for the cumulative mark-to-market trading position to be positive over a quarter or calendar year timeframe.

Traders basically buy and sell securities to make profits, but client-related traders also have the additional objective of helping investing clients trade profitably. If a client cannot trade profitably with an investment bank, the client may eventually stop trading with that bank. As a result, sometimes traders decide to accept lower trading margins (and occasional losses) to accommodate client investment objectives and to facilitate greater trading volume.

An Introduction to Investment Banks, Hedge Funds, and Private Equity
Copyright © 2010 by Elsevier Inc. All rights of reproduction in any form reserved.

Trading is a highly analytical position that requires a large number of daily decisions, intensive analysis of public and private data, and quick assimilation of information from multiple sources. Regardless of trading specialization, a strong understanding of global economics, interest rates, currencies, credit risks, valuation techniques, and even politics is important.

Traders divide their focus into two principal areas: (a) supporting primary market transactions, which involves purchasing securities directly from a corporate or government issuer and reselling those securities at a profit (investment bank underwriting); and (b) participating in the secondary market by buying and selling previously issued securities at a profit. Traders work closely with the capital markets group (often a joint venture between the Investment Banking Division and the Trading Division) on pricing for all primary market financing transactions for corporate and government issuers. They also work closely with sales professionals in the Trading Division to sell securities to investing clients, providing those clients with bids and offers on all securities that are underwritten by the investment bank or that the bank chooses to trade in the secondary market. To provide this "market-making" service, the bank keeps an inventory of securities after an offering has been completed, and creates bid/offer spreads for investors that reflect the risk and liquidity of these securities. They also keep other securities in inventory to facilitate their secondary market activities in these securities.

## Pricing Securities Offerings

When the Trading Division and the Capital Markets Group price new securities, they focus on outstanding securities from the same issuer or, if none exist, on outstanding securities from comparable issuers as pricing reference points. Depending on the security, different pricing methods are used:

1. IPOs are principally priced based on a comparable public company valuation methodology, although other methodologies may also be utilized, depending on the industry (see Chapter 3).
2. Follow-on equity and bond offerings use the prevailing public market prices of the company's securities as a starting point to determine the appropriate offering price. In addition, traders determine whether a pricing discount to the public price is necessary based on the size of the offering and market dynamics.
3. Convertible securities are principally priced based on a convertible valuation model that is similar to the model that convertible arbitrageurs utilize.

When traders work with the capital markets desk to discuss pricing prior to launching a public offering, the traders are said to be brought *over-the-wall*. This means that certain traders will become aware of material nonpublic information regarding an upcoming financing, and they must "wall" themselves off from trading outstanding securities of that issuer. As a result, traders are careful in determining who will work with the capital markets desk to finalize pricing. Compliance departments diligently monitor which traders have non-public information and on which companies.

Whenever pricing is committed to an issuer in a capital markets financing, over-the-wall traders must make a risk decision regarding pricing, timing, size, and structure. Sometimes the risk associated with these underwritings is considerable. For example, when a company asks an investment bank to complete a bought deal, the bank buys the entire securities offering without a road show that would have provided investors' views on potential pricing. In this scenario, the bank is exposed to the risk that investors won't purchase the underwritten securities at a price equal to or greater than the price at which the bank purchased the securities from the issuer, creating a potential loss for the bank.

Before an underwriting commitment can be made to any issuing client, an investment bank assembles a *commitments committee* to determine the riskiness of the underwriting and whether to proceed with an underwriting transaction. The over-the-wall traders (usually senior traders who manage other traders more so than trade directly themselves) are a key voice in this committee. If they are convinced that the firm will lose money on the underwriting or expose itself to other significant risks, they will likely oppose the transaction. However, if underwriting fees are large and there is a strong push from the Investment Banking Division to support a key issuing client, traders will sometimes accept an underwriting even when the risks are perceived to be higher than normal.

Regulatory capital must be set aside to mitigate risks associated with underwriting activity. This means that the bank will invest some amount of cash (the amount is determined by regulators depending on the risk characteristics of each firm's underwriting business) in a low return/low risk security (often U.S. Treasuries) to cushion against potential trading losses. Because cash is considered a scarce resource and a low-return investment reduces the bank's return on equity, the commitments committee makes underwriting decisions based on both trading considerations and the amount of regulatory capital needed to support the business.

## Research

Traders conduct extensive research to gain insight into the securities that they trade. They utilize both trading-desk-based research that they initiate, and research provided by others that is publicly available (from both internal and external sources). Research can focus on specific securities, industries, and financial products, or on general economic, political, or regulatory topics. High-quality research is imperative when attempting to profitably manage a portfolio of securities. See Chapter 6 for a more complete description of the research function.

## Sales

Sales professionals cover individual and institutional investing clients. Their role is to bring to clients value-added investing or hedging ideas, as well as pricing from traders. When an investing client wishes to purchase a security, their sales representative will quote an *offer* price. When the client wishes to sell a security, their sales representative will quote a *bid* price. Sales teams have the dual objective of helping both traders and investing clients create profits, but sometimes it is difficult to meet the objectives of both sides. The best sales people are adept at managing both investment earnings expectations and egos. They know the pressure points and priorities of both traders and investors and keep track of wins and losses over an extended period of time. Analytical skills are an essential part of the sales process, but people skills can be equally important.

A sales professional provides investment ideas developed from research and analysis. The provision of research that provides unique insights and solutions in a timely way is an important part of the sales process. This is especially the case with complex investment transactions, where research and analysis is tailored by sales professionals to meet individual client needs.

# Equity Trading

Equity traders trade common shares, derivatives on common shares or equity indexes (options, swaps, and forwards), convertibles, and share-based products, including exchange-traded funds (ETFs). Each of these is a large business area that requires a high degree of specialization. Each trader focuses on a limited number of securities or derivatives. Sometimes this is a global focus, but usually traders concentrate geographically, since each country has its own unique regulatory regime and stock exchange practices. Examples of a trader's focus area include U.S. technology companies, U.S. healthcare companies, emerging market stocks in Asia, and European equity derivatives. There are dozens of other areas of focus for traders, depending on the size of the firm. Generally speaking, each trader has responsibility for 20–50 securities or derivatives.

There are several benefits to being an active trader in a specific stock. When an investment bank solicits underwriting mandates for follow-on equity offerings, Equity Trading may be able to improve the bank's competitive position if it has significant trading activity in the stock of the prospective issuer. Services such as AutEx keep track of trading activity in individual stocks, and the information is carefully monitored and included in banker underwriting pitches when the numbers are favorable. Being active in a stock can also lead to more accurate pricing and higher trading-based revenue. This is because more active traders see more bids and offers, become well versed in the trading characteristics of that stock, and have a deeper understanding of who currently holds the stock, the approximate price at which the stock was acquired, and which investors are willing to sell.

A sales team is aligned with each trading area in an investment bank to facilitate trades with investing clients. Traders also work closely with the Equity Capital Markets Group to price new issue equity and convertibles that are underwritten by the bank.

The relationship between Equity Trading and investing clients is complex. On the bank's side, it involves traders, sales traders, research sales people, and research analysts. On the client side (assuming an institutional client), it involves portfolio managers, institutional traders, and operations people (see Exhibit 5.1). In addition to facilitating investing clients' purchases and sales of securities, Equity Trading provides other services to their clients, including financing, hedging, tax solutions, regulatory solutions, securities lending, and development of trading platforms.

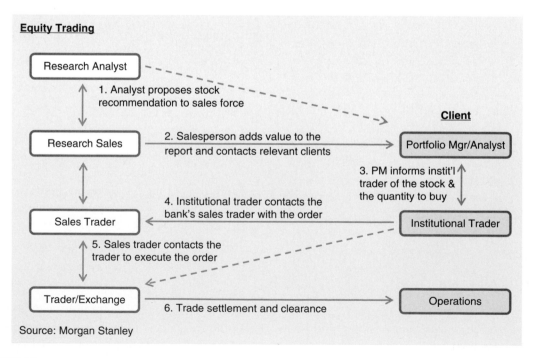

Source: Morgan Stanley

**EXHIBIT 5.1**

## Prime Brokerage

The Prime Brokerage business is housed in the Trading Division and focuses principally on hedge funds and other clients who borrow securities and cash to support their investment business. In addition to lending, other services provided to investing clients include trade clearing, custody and settlement, real estate and computer assistance, performance measurement, and performance reporting. These products and services bring in fees that can be several billion dollars per year at some banks.

Hedge funds sometimes borrow securities to enable them to sell the securities short, that is, selling a borrowed security, with the obligation to return it after repurchasing it in the market in the future. Depending on a hedge fund's strategy, shorting is used to create downside security price protection (a hedge), or to generate a potential gain based on speculation that a security's price will drop. Hedge fund cash borrowings from investment banks (called *margin loans*) require the use of securities as collateral. If the value of the collateral drops over time, banks will exercise margin calls to receive repayment of a portion of the loan. Sometimes this creates a forced sale of securities to raise cash, causing potential losses for the hedge fund. Cash borrowings enable hedge funds to extract higher returns for their investments, if returns are positive. Conversely, if returns are negative, borrowings (leverage) will create incrementally higher losses.

Prime Brokerage is a very profitable business for the largest investment banks, and when combined with the commissions earned from trading with hedge funds, it is clear that hedge funds represent the largest source of client-related revenue within the Trading Division at many large investment banks. Some non-hedge fund institutional investors also borrow securities and cash from the Prime Brokerage arm of investment banks, but in much lesser overall volumes compared to hedge funds.

### Securities Lending

Many large institutional investors own sizeable blocks of stock that they expect to hold for an extended period of time. These investors are often willing to lend their shares to investment banks, who re-lend to other parties for a fee (which is split between the lenders and the bank). Lenders receive cash collateral when they lend shares, and the collateral is adjusted daily, based on a mark-to-market value of the shares lent. Usually the required collateral is 2% to 5% greater than the value of the shares. The lenders will pay interest on the cash collateral at a rate close to or considerably less than the market rate, depending on demand and supply conditions for lending of different stocks. If, for example, a market overnight risk-free interest rate is 4% per annum (p.a.) and there is limited demand for borrowing a particular stock, the lender might pay interest on the collateral to the stock borrower of 3.5% p.a. If, however, demand for the shares exceeds the availability of lendable shares, the interest rate paid might be 2% p.a. The rate of interest paid by lenders to share borrowers is called *rebate*.

As an example, if an investor lent 4,000 shares of IBM stock when the stock traded at $100 (valued at $400,000), the borrower might be required to post $416,000 in cash collateral with the stock lender when the stock was borrowed. If the loan was for one month, the market interest earned on the $416,000 cash collateral at 4% p.a. would be $1,387. Because IBM shares are fairly easy to borrow, the stock lender might pay a rebate to the stock borrower at a rate of 3.5% p.a., or $1,213. The 50-basis-point spread or $174 difference between market rate and the rebate rate paid to the stock borrower, is mostly kept by the stock lender, with a portion paid to the investment bank that facilitated the transaction. The lower the rebate, the higher the effective cost for the borrower.

Shares of stock can be difficult to borrow under certain scenarios, including the following: demand exceeds supply; a large portion of the stock is held by insiders who are restricted from lending it; investors who might normally lend shares decide they want to sell the shares the next day; or investors owning the shares are concerned about potential negative share price consequences if there is excessive shorting in the stock.

Short-selling activity represents an important part of the global capital markets. Hedge funds are the largest participants in short selling and are, accordingly, the most important users of an investment bank's securities lending business. The investment bank sets up stock borrowing arrangements with most of its large institutional investing clients and with some large individual investing clients. The borrowing arrangements are typically based on overnight loans, although the arrangement can be extended for weeks or months based on different rebate rates. Many investors are willing to lend a portion of their securities to obtain income that enhances the returns of their securities holdings. For some large institutional investors this can amount to hundreds of millions of dollars a year.

When shares are loaned, title to the shares is transferred to the party that the borrower sells stock short to. This means that the short buyer receives dividends if title is held on a *record date* and is able to vote if a shareholder election is held. In most cases, the stock loan agreement provides that whenever short buyers receive dividends, the borrower (short seller) must pay to the lender a cash amount that is equal to the dividends received.

By far the largest shorting activity is conducted by investors that want to hedge downside share price risk positions (hedge a long stock position or convertible holding). Another principal reason to short stock is to create a "bearish" position in a company's shares, based on the view that it will be profitable to sell stock short today and then buy stock back in the open market at a lower price if the share price declines. Shares are fungible (completely interchangeable), which enables a borrower of shares to return to the lender different (but equivalent) shares acquired from purchases in the open market.

Sometimes shares are sold short without taking steps to borrow the shares. This is called *naked* shorting. If this shorting activity is done to avoid settlement failure, this is considered legal naked shorting. For example, if an investor agrees to sell stock, but fails to deliver shares to a buyer on the settlement date, the buyer may need to sell stock short to avoid settlement failure (and associated costs and penalties) if the buyer has already resold the stock that should have been received in the original settlement. There has been considerable regulatory analysis of legal naked shorting and non-legal naked shorting (selling stock short without taking steps to borrow it and without legitimate settlement concerns). See Exhibit 5.2 for a discussion of historical issues and regulatory changes to this practice.

Shares that are sold short create *short interest,* as recorded by exchanges. The short interest ratio is the number of shares of a publicly traded company that are sold short divided by the average daily trading volume. Sometimes it is also important to consider shares sold short in relation to free float (shares that are not held by owners of more than 5% of the stock or by senior executives or insiders). A high short interest ratio may imply that the market is bearish on a particular stock. However, this can be misleading since a large portion of the short interest reported for some companies relates to hedge fund purchases of convertible securities. In this scenario, hedge funds short some of the shares that underlie the convertible in order to hedge share price risk. This type of shorting is therefore usually not an expression of a bearish view on a stock. As a result, an accurate interpretation of short interest ratios must factor in convertibles that have been issued. See Chapter 9 for a more detailed overview of convertibles and related shorting activity.

**Short Selling**

In a short sale of stock, a trader borrows stock and sells it. If the stock falls in price, then the short seller can buy the stock in the open market at the lower price, return what was borrowed, and pocket the difference.

Through the years, government authorities have occasionally attempted to restrict short selling. Although short selling is a legitimate trading strategy and helps to prevent "irrational exuberance" and bubbles, the SEC has clamped down on short selling because it was worried that these trades, along with false rumors, negatively impact the financial system.

During September of 2008, the SEC issued an emergency order, which curbed short selling in Fannie Mae and Freddie Mac stocks, as well as 17 other financial firms. They subsequently extended this order to include other financial firm stocks. The order attempted to stop both short selling and "unlawful manipulation through 'naked' short selling." Naked short selling refers to the practice of selling stock short without taking steps to borrow it. Historically, a short seller located shares to borrow and sold the shares short, but was not obligated to enter into a contract with the share lender. Additionally, sometimes more than one trader was able to borrow the same shares, which multiplied the effect of the short position. Under the SEC order, however, a short seller is now required to have entered into a contract to borrow the shares.

During July 2009, the SEC made permanent the emergency order, requiring traders to complete short sales within four days and exchanges to post information regarding short sales, including exact timing and size of short positions, on a one-month delay basis.

EXHIBIT 5.2

## *Margin Financing*

When an investor borrows money to purchase securities, and the securities (or other agreed upon assets) are posted as collateral, an investor is buying on margin. Investment banks arrange margin accounts for their investing clients when investors want to leverage their investments. The value of the securities held as collateral is marked-to-market daily, and the investor must maintain a predetermined loan to value percentage. If the value of the collateral drops, the investor will be required to repay part of the loan or deposit additional collateral. A bank's demand for cash or collateral is called a *margin call*. Margin calls by investment banks against hedge funds were a precipitating factor in the blow-up of several hedge funds during 2006–2008 and created an increased level of volatility in the market as hedge funds were forced to rapidly liquidate part or all of their portfolios. See Exhibit 5.3 for a summary of Peloton, a large hedge fund that shut down following margin calls by investment banks. Also refer to **Case Study 5, "A Tale of Two Hedge Funds: Magnetar and Peloton."**

# Fixed Income, Currencies, and Commodities (FICC) Trading

FICC usually focuses on interest rate products, credit products, and commodities. Traders in these three areas run many different businesses, each of which has its own sales force and research function. Although this has historically been the most profitable division in most of the large investment banks, the business was subjected to very large write-downs during 2007 and 2008.

## Interest Rate Products

At most banks, Interest Rate Products include foreign exchange (since currency exchange rates are inextricably connected to interest rates of different countries), government bond trading in U.S., U.K., German, French, Japanese, and other government and agency bonds and notes, and interest rate derivatives (including swaps, futures, and options).

**Margin Calls by Prime Brokers Against Hedge Funds**

After years of strong growth and outsized returns, during the 2007-2008 credit crunch, hedge funds encountered their worst crisis since the 1998 collapse of Long-Term Capital Management (LTCM). Hedge funds rely on prime brokers at investment banks to clear trades, service assets, and perhaps most important to their portfolio strategy, provide leverage. Hedge funds take on debt to enhance asset returns and to facilitate certain investment strategies.

However, for some hedge funds that owned MBS or CDOs in 2007 and 2008, leverage proved to be the source of their downfall. Sharp declines in housing prices reduced the value of these securities' collateral, leading prime brokers to demand additional collateral. As a result, many funds were forced to offload assets to meet margin calls. Some funds, such as Carlyle Capital and Peloton Partners, were unable to meet requests for additional cash and were forced to unwind their holdings at fire-sale prices.

While massive leverage ratios and untimely bets on the housing market were to blame for most of the hedge fund industry's woes, the large subprime losses experienced by investment banks also played a role in the collapse of several hedge funds. With their profits wiped out by asset writedowns, the prime broker operations within investment banks became more conservative with credit and gave even their best clients little latitude.

Peloton Partners, a London-based hedge fund started in 2005 by two former Goldman Sachs partners, is a striking example of an otherwise successful hedge fund brought down by margin calls from its prime brokers. In 2007, Peloton's fund posted an 87% return by shorting BB-rated tranches of subprime MBS and going long AAA-rated tranches. However, in January 2008, Peloton revised its strategy after determining that there was little additional downside in subprime securities. As the value of subprime mortgages dropped further with higher default rates and declining housing prices, Peloton's losses were great enough to prompt demands for cash from banks. Unable to meet their requests, Peloton shut down its fund and suspended client redemptions, causing losses of several billion dollars. The implosion of one of London's premiere hedge funds underscores how quickly a fund can go under when margin financing from prime brokerage lenders is pulled.

EXHIBIT 5.3

## *Currencies*

Currency trading is the largest and most liquid trading market in the world. It is estimated that in excess of $4 trillion in currencies are traded every day. Currency trading is also commonly referred to as foreign exchange (FX) trading. Each currency has a value relative to other currencies. Currency value fluctuates constantly as money is exchanged into different currencies to facilitate international travelers' purchases abroad, or business purchases and sales of products to meet import and export objectives. Another reason for currency fluctuation relates to speculation. When investors expect certain currencies to strengthen or weaken, they purchase or sell currencies based on these expectations to create trading profits.

The FX market is comprised of spot FX transactions (buying one currency with a different currency for immediate delivery), forward FX transactions (contract between two parties to exchange currencies on a specified date in the future at an agreed-upon price), and FX swap transactions (exchange of one currency for another at a certain price at multiple points over time).

## Credit Products

Credit Products include corporate bonds (investment grade, high yield, and distressed debt securities), mortgage-backed securities, asset-backed securities (credit card receivables, automobile loans, computer leases, trade receivables, equipment leases, etc.), structured credit, and credit derivatives (including swaps, futures, and options).

## Structured Credit

The Structured Credit business is primarily focused on collateralized debt obligations (CDOs) that are linked to bonds (collateralized bond obligations, or CBO) and loans (collateralized loan obligations, or CLO). A CBO is a debt security underwritten by an investment bank that is backed by a pool of non-investment-grade bonds. Because the pool includes a broadly diversified group of assets, credit rating agencies have given an investment grade rating to certain tranches in many of these CBOs. In a CBO, a special purpose trust is formed to purchase non-investment-grade bonds, and then the trust issues three or more tranches of bonds (each with a different credit rating) to investors who purchase these securities as a means to receive slightly higher coupons than similarly rated straight bonds. A CLO is similar to a CBO, except the collateral pool backing this security is comprised of lower-quality loans instead of bonds. Further information on CDOs and yield pick-up for investors is found in Exhibits 5.4 and 5.5.

During 2007 and 2008, investment banks recorded significant losses on their structured credit positions because of the credit crisis that started during the middle of 2007. The effects of diversification on CDO portfolios proved to be much less than estimated by ratings agencies and investors. Losses reported by financial institutions approached $1 trillion in relation to this product area by the end of 2008, based on losses from both commercial and residential mortgage-backed securities.

Mortgage-backed securities (MBS) are debt obligations where the underlying assets (collateral) are mortgage loans. In the case of residential MBS, the loans are purchased from mortgage originators such as banks and mortgage companies and then assembled into pools. Securities are then issued to investors who become claimants to the interest and principal payments made by borrowers in the pools of loans. MBS issuers include U.S. government sponsored entities Fannie Mae (Federal National Mortgage Association) and Freddie Mac (Federal Home Loan Mortgage Corporation), the U.S. government agency Ginnie Mae (Government National Mortgage Association), and some private institutions such as banks and brokerage firms.

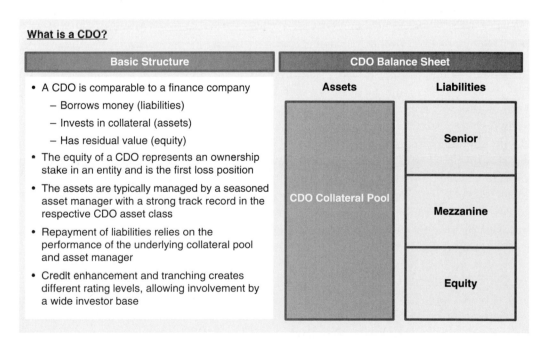

**EXHIBIT 5.4**

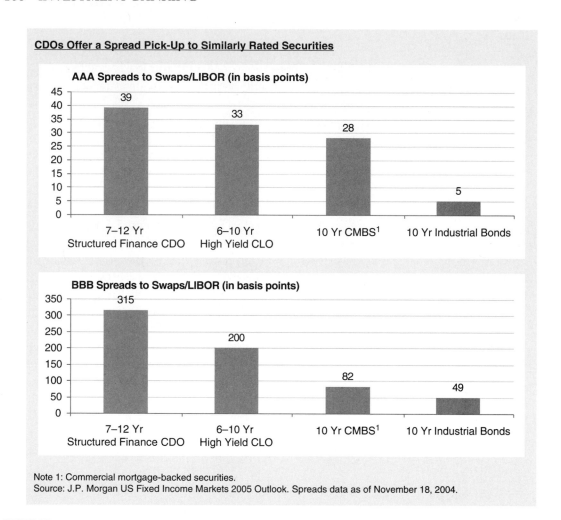

**CDOs Offer a Spread Pick-Up to Similarly Rated Securities**

**AAA Spreads to Swaps/LIBOR (in basis points)**

| | 7–12 Yr Structured Finance CDO | 6–10 Yr High Yield CLO | 10 Yr CMBS[1] | 10 Yr Industrial Bonds |
|---|---|---|---|---|
| | 39 | 33 | 28 | 5 |

**BBB Spreads to Swaps/LIBOR (in basis points)**

| | 7–12 Yr Structured Finance CDO | 6–10 Yr High Yield CLO | 10 Yr CMBS[1] | 10 Yr Industrial Bonds |
|---|---|---|---|---|
| | 315 | 200 | 82 | 49 |

Note 1: Commercial mortgage-backed securities.
Source: J.P. Morgan US Fixed Income Markets 2005 Outlook. Spreads data as of November 18, 2004.

**EXHIBIT 5.5**

Historically, many MBS securities have been used to create CDOs, and many of the buyers (and insurers) of MBS-related CDOs have been financial institutions. They viewed some of these securities as very low risk investments (the senior tranches typically had AAA credit ratings), with a slightly higher yield than straight AAA bonds. Unfortunately, until 2008, most of these institutions underestimated the risk of these securities and ignored the real estate bubble. Many statistical models utilized by issuers, rating agencies, and investors did not incorporate the possibility of a significant decline in housing prices. As a result of large losses stemming from this product area, as well as losses on loans to fund private equity transactions, an unprecedented number of senior executives of investment banks were asked to step down during 2007 and 2008. Exhibit 5.6 summarizes Merrill Lynch's multiyear aggressive build-up of its CDO book, which resulted in huge write-downs and the ultimate sale of the firm to Bank of America.

### Credit Default Swaps

A credit default swap (CDS) is a contract between two counterparties whereby one party makes periodic payments in return for receiving a payoff if an underlying security or loan defaults. For example, if an investor purchased $10 million of a 5-year $100 million bond issued by Company ABC and then decided to protect their investment risk by entering into a CDS on a $10 million

> ### Merrill Lynch
>
> During July 2008 Merrill Lynch agreed to sell more than $30 billion in toxic mortgage-related CDOs at a steep loss, hoping to purge its balance sheet of problems that plagued the brokerage giant. The sale was to Lone Star, an affiliate of a private-equity firm, which paid $6.7 billion, or 22 cents on the dollar. This created a $5.7 billion write-down for Merrill.
>
> Merrill's move was an effort to stem the tide of losses after more than $46 billion in write-downs during the previous 12 months. Faced with this leak in its balance sheet, Merrill sold $8.5 billion in new common stock, diluting existing shareholders by about 38%
>
> Many CDOs held by Merrill were viewed as highly likely to default and lose some or most of their principal value. Of the 30 CDOs totaling $32 billion that Merrill underwrote in 2007, 27 had seen their top triple-A ratings downgraded to "junk."
>
> Merrill had been hit especially hard by the mortgage crisis, largely because of big bets on mortgage-backed securities not long before the market for those securities collapsed. During 2007, Stanley O'Neal, the CEO who oversaw those bets, was forced out and replaced by John Thain, a former Goldman Sachs mortgage trader who later ran the New York Stock Exchange.
>
> Despite installing new risk controls and a new management team, Thain was unable to steer Merrill out of trouble. During September of 2008, these ongoing troubles led to the sale of Merrill Lynch to Bank of America for a price that was less than one-half the value of the firm 15 months earlier.

**EXHIBIT 5.6**

notional amount of the Company ABC bond, they might pay 2% of $10 million annually for 5 years in exchange for the right to deliver defaulted bonds in exchange for $10 million if Company ABC defaults. The party that receives an annual fee is a credit protection seller; the fee payer is a credit protection buyer. None of the cash flows from the CDS directly involves Company ABC, but it is their bond that is the subject of the CDS contract. A CDS is essentially an insurance policy to hedge against default. Because there is no requirement to own the actual underlying security or loan when entering into this type of contract, many CDS credit protection buyers engage in this transaction purely for speculative purposes.

CDS transactions were historically not regulated in the United States, because the SEC determined that a CDS contract was not a security and the Commodities Futures Trading Commission (CFTC) determined that CDS was not a commodity. As a result, there was concern about unregulated CDS risk positions that grew substantially over many years. The total face amount of CDS contracts was estimated to exceed $50 trillion as of the end of 2008 (although most of this amount represented offsetting trades) and these contracts related to bond and loan obligations of more than 3,000 companies worldwide.

The CDS market came under regulatory scrutiny because of its massive size, lack of regulation, and potential to permit insider-trading activity. An example of the last point follows. The cost of CDS sometimes increases considerably in the weeks prior to the announcement of a corporate takeover by a private equity fund. Upon completion of a leveraged buyout, the target company's credit rating generally deteriorates, because the buyout is financed in large part by leveraging the target's balance sheet. Because this increases the riskiness of the company's outstanding bonds, the result is an increase in CDS pricing relative to these bonds. During 2007 and 2008, prior to announcement of a number of acquisitions by private equity funds, CDS pricing for the target company increased substantially, suggesting that CDS credit protection buyers became aware of the acquisition before it was publicly announced. Speculators evidently purchased CDS on private equity target companies before the announcement, and then sold CDS after the announcement, creating a substantial profit. Such insider trading would likely be caught, and prosecuted, in the highly regulated stock market, but the CDS market did not have much regulatory surveillance.

A notable disaster in relation to CDS occurred during late 2008 when AIG, which had previously been one of the world's largest and strongest insurance companies, had to be bailed out by the U.S. government. As a credit protection seller, AIG had approximately $500 billion notional exposure in its CDS positions. After marking-to-market the amount it owed as a credit protection seller on a portfolio of mortgage-backed securities following the collapse of the real estate market, AIG's capital reserves were reduced and, as a result, the company lost its AAA credit rating. Subsequent ratings downgrades triggered requirements to post tens of billions in collateral to AIG's CDS counterparties. Because AIG could not provide the required collateral, rather than allow the insurer to fail, the U.S. government in late 2008 provided an emergency $85 billion loan to the company. By June of 2009, the total amount of bailout funding available to AIG through various programs grew to over $180 billion.

In response to concerns about the impact of an unregulated CDS market, InterContinental Exchange, an operator of electronic exchanges, launched the first CDS central clearinghouse in March 2009. By shifting CDS transactions to centralized clearinghouses, transparency is increased and counterparty risk is reduced.

## Bank Loans

In order to meet the full financing objectives of selected clients, in addition to arranging capital markets financings, investment banks sometimes provide bank loans for strong credit borrowers and leveraged loans for weaker credit borrowers. During 2002–2008, the largest portion of the leveraged loan business involved loans committed for private equity acquisitions. Private equity firms are among the most important clients of the Investment Banking Division, since they bring equity underwriting, debt underwriting, and M&A advisory business to the bank. Based on its experience underwriting, investing in, and trading corporate bonds, the Trading Division collaborates with the Investment Banking Division in providing loans to important clients of the firm when there are other revenue opportunities with the client.

Leveraged buyouts require a substantial amount of debt financing. Investment bankers help private equity firms meet the massive debt requirements of their acquisitions, either through an underwritten bond offering or through a syndicated bank loan in which the investment bank typically tries to sell up to 90% of the loan to other banks, hedge funds, and other investors. Historically, most of these financings involved a "best efforts" commitment from the bank, and not an absolute commitment. Unfortunately for the investment banks, during 2006 and the first half of 2007, banks were persuaded by private equity firms to make binding commitments for large financings whereby the banks provided the full funding if bond market and syndicated loan market participants were unwilling to provide it. This resulted in significant large loan drawdowns from the investment banks when other lenders and investors refused to buy the debt, creating unexpected credit exposures for the banks. Private equity-related bank loans exceeded $400 billion at the end of 2007, and when banks ultimately sold many of these loans to other investors at prices as low as 70 cents on the dollar, the banks recorded very large write-downs.

## Commodities

Contracts on commodities are traded by investment banks principally in the energy (electricity, natural gas, and oil) and metals (precious metals and base metals) sectors. A number of investment banks trade physical commodities as well and even own energy production facilities. Clients buy and sell financial contracts on commodities in order to hedge risk positions arising in the regular course of business (airlines, distributors, industrial companies, producers, refiners, shipping companies, and utility companies) or to invest in or trade them as part of an investment portfolio (funds and high net-worth individuals).

## Market-Making

The client-focused trading activities of large investment banks are often referred to as *market-making*. The meaning is that the bank stands willing to "make a market" any time it is requested by a client. In other words, the bank will quote a client a bid price or an offer price (or often both simultaneously) on many securities or derivatives at any time.

If the client wishes to buy a security or derivative, the bank will sell it to them, and if the client wishes to sell, the bank stands ready to buy. The difference between the price at which the bank is willing to buy (bid price) and the price at which it is willing to sell (ask, or offer price) is referred to as the *bid-ask spread*.

Market-making is the business of "capturing" bid-ask spreads, by continuously buying securities at the bid price, and selling securities at the higher offer price. However, in order to capture bid-ask spreads, market-makers must take risk. The nature of the risk varies greatly, depending on the security or derivative, the length of time the risk position is held, and the liquidity of the security or derivative. In general, bid-ask spreads are narrower in liquid markets and less complex products. See Exhibits 5.7 and 5.8 for examples of the business of market-making.

## Proprietary Trading

Proprietary traders are non-client-related traders who trade solely for the benefit of their firm. They have no responsibility to balance their profitability interests with the interests of clients of the firm and therefore can be considered competitors to these clients. At some investment banks, they are covered by sales professionals within the same firm and are considered one of the most important clients of the sales team. At other firms, internal sales contacts are limited. Even when proprietary traders are allowed to trade with their own firm, they always trade with others as well, including competitor firms, and will execute transactions with whichever firm best enables them to achieve profits and mitigate risks.

Proprietary traders take positions in interest rate and credit products, mortgage-related securities and loan products, and multiple kinds of asset-backed securities. They also take positions in commodities and currencies, as well as in the derivatives of all of these products. In the equity world, they take positions in all forms of equity and equity-related products, including derivatives. Their positions can be long or short and, in many cases, are leveraged by borrowing, using their positions as collateral.

Proprietary traders do their own research and rely on the research of others as well. They build models that track credit markets, regulatory and legal developments, accounting and tax developments, market anomalies, and economic events. Their models attempt to predict mean reversion or a collapse in historical relationships, among other phenomena.

Basically, the proprietary trading business is similar to the business conducted by hedge funds. Accordingly, investment banks have become significant competitors to hedge funds, who are the most important clients of the bank's client-related trading business. This sometimes

**Market-Making Example 1 – The Ideal: Riskless and Unsolicited Transaction**

On the high yield bond trading desk, a salesperson picks up a ringing phone and hears the familiar voice of a pension fund manager. The client says that she wants to sell $10 million face amount of ABC Corp 8% bonds due June 2020. (If there is a good relationship with the client, the salesperson may also be able to get additional information, such as why they are selling, whether this represents their whole position in the bond or just a fraction, and what they think about the company and the sector generally.)

Simultaneously, a bond portfolio manager at an insurance company calls another salesperson on the same desk. He says he is adding to his energy positions and wants to buy $10 million face amount of the same ABC Corp 8% bonds.

Both salespeople tell their clients they will quickly check the price, put them on hold, and yell over to the trader who handles high yield energy bonds. These bonds generally only trade several times a week, making this outcome very unusual. Despite the illiquidity, the trader will have already been following the bonds, tracking any reported trades in the market and adjusting his view of the appropriate bid and ask prices many times each day based on factors such as the current yields of Treasury bonds (which define the risk-free interest rate for various maturities), the price movements of high yield bonds generally on that day, and any sector or company-specific news which has recently come out.

Based on all of this, the trader tells the salespeople to quote the pension fund a bid price of 91.25% of par and quote the insurance company an ask price of 91.75% of par. Both salespeople relay the prices to their clients, and both clients immediately agree to the trade at the price quoted to them.

The desk books a purchase of $10 million bonds at 91.25% and a sale of $10 million bonds at 91.75%. The two salespeople and one trader just earned the desk a $50,000 profit with no residual risk for the bank, and with very little effort.

Three important notes on this example:

1) The transaction which occurred turned out to be riskless, but the bank actually had to take substantial risk in order to get the business. Recall that while the clients had equal, offsetting, simultaneous interest in the bond, unlike the bank, neither of them was obligated to go through with the anticipated transaction. In fact, either of them could have changed their mind after hearing the price, or might have called three other investment banks to ensure they got the best price possible. If the bank in this example was "best bid" of three banks quoted by the pension fund, but was not the "best offer" of the three banks quoted by the insurance company, then it would have purchased $10 million of bonds at a cost of $9.125 million, with no offsetting sale. In this case, no profit has been locked in, and the bank retains the risk of the bonds declining in price before it can sell them to another client, as well as the more drastic possibility of issuer's bankruptcy.

2) A situation like this is very rare. For illiquid securities with bid-ask spreads of 0.50% or higher, the chances of simultaneous unsolicited offsetting orders is very small. Liquid securities with high trading frequency (on which clients with offsetting orders do sometimes send orders in simultaneously) tend to have much lower bid-ask spreads.

3) Clients are sometimes not willing to tell the bank what they are doing. In many cases they will ask to see a "two-sided" market, or both the bid and offer price, and the bank does not know whether the client plans to buy or sell. In that case, the trader would not know whether his worst-case residual risk was being long or short $10 million bonds, or $20 million if both clients turned out to be buyers or sellers.

EXHIBIT 5.7

creates conflict, and some hedge funds have, as a result, limited their trading activity with those investment banks that have the largest proprietary trading businesses.

At Goldman Sachs, proprietary trading was a profitable business within the firm's Trading and Principal Investments Division between 2002 and 2007. Although their financials do not break out revenue for client-related trading and proprietary trading, it is possible that proprietary trading represented larger revenue and earnings than were achieved during 2007 by Och-Ziff, the largest publicly reporting hedge fund in the United States and one of the largest hedge funds in the world (see Exhibit 5.9).

## Market-Making Example 2 – Block Trade of Stock

A trader at a mutual fund calls a salesperson at a bank at 10:45am and says he wants to sell 500,000 shares of XYZ Corp and is asking two banks for an "at risk" price at 11:00am. The salesperson and the client agree that when the price is quoted, the fund will agree within 2 minutes if it wants to proceed.

The salesperson walks over to the trader who is responsible for XYZ shares to consider the situation together. XYZ shares on average trade 1.25 million shares per day, so the sale represents 40% of average daily volume. While mutual funds usually trade in and out of shares gradually, accepting the market price and paying very small commissions, this fund wants to get out of its entire position at a guaranteed price, passing the risk on to the bank.

The stock is currently trading at $60, so 500,000 shares represent $30 million of risk for the bank. The trader and salesperson review a shareholder list, call up internal records of clients that have recently been buying or selling the stock, and ask the other salespeople about qualitative comments clients have made about the stock, and what they think clients' interest may be in buying the stock if it came in large size and at a slight discount to the market price. The team also checks recent sentiment among research analysts who cover the stock. In conjunction with the trading desk head and a market risk controller, they review recent price moves in the stock and what caused them and study the general volatility profile of the stock.

After analyzing all the risks involved, at 10:59 am the trader agrees to bid $59.30 for the 500,000 shares. This represents a 1.17% discount from the current market price of $60.

The salesperson calls the client to commit the price. The client puts him on hold for thirty seconds, then comes back on the line and says, "You're done. I sell 500,000 shares of XYZ to you at $59.30."

The trader and salesperson get the attention of the rest of the salespeople on the desk and tell them about the trade, and the need to sell the shares. Together, they formulate a strategy regarding which clients to call and the price and minimum size to offer. Given the risk position, the sales force might decide to only call a handful of trusted clients to minimize the information flowing into the marketplace.

The salespeople tell investors that they have stock for sale, without mentioning the exact amount, and offer to sell 25,000 shares or more to each investor, at a price of $59.60.

Two investors express interest in 150,000 shares each, so the bank re-sells 300,000 shares at $59.60. The bank has made a profit of $90,000 on these shares.

The trader decides that rather than have the sales force make any further calls to less trusted clients, he will trade out of the remaining 200,000 shares on his own. Using program trading software, he inputs an order for the computer to sell 200,000 shares gradually into the flow of market trading, targeting 25% of total market volume. The software will drop a few hundred shares into the market several times per minute, trying to match the frequency and size of the sales as closely as possible to 25% of volume.

The stock begins to trade down rapidly. By 11:30 am the stock is at $59, where it stays for the rest of the trading day. The trader manages to sell the last shares just before the market close. He calculates that on the 200,000 shares that the desk wasn't able to place with clients, his average sale price was $59.08. This represents a loss of $44,000 on the unplaced shares, making the desk's net profit on the entire trade $46,000.

**EXHIBIT 5.8**

Until the credit crisis that started during the summer of 2007, proprietary trading at many investment banks was a very profitable business. Proprietary traders were often the highest paid people in an investment bank. Their risk positions sometimes gave rise to significant unanticipated profits or losses, especially in periods of high volatility. In many cases, risk positions were significantly leveraged, allowing for greater earnings or losses, depending on whether the positions were on the right or wrong side of the market. As a result of very large trading losses and extreme market turbulence stemming from the credit crisis, there was a decline in proprietary trading at some investment banks as their appetite for risk taking and leverage diminished.

**Goldman Sachs vs. Och-Ziff**
($ in millions)

| | Net Revenues | | Operating Expenses | | Pre-Tax Earnings | |
|---|---|---|---|---|---|---|
| | 2008 | 2007 | 2008 | 2007 | 2008 | 2007 |
| Goldman Sachs Trading & Principal Investments Division | $9,063 | $31,266 | $11,808 | $17,998 | $(2,745) | $13,228 |
| Och-Ziff Funds[1] | $587 | $1,126 | $271 | $307 | $316 | $818 |

Note 1: Economic income figures are shown to present an apples-to-apples comparison of the two years. Och-Ziff significantly reorganized its operations in 2007 such that GAAP financials would not be comparable from 2007 to 2008.
Source: Respective 2008 10-K filings

**EXHIBIT 5.9**

Banks including Morgan Stanley, Credit Suisse, UBS, and Deutsche Bank announced in 2008 that they were reducing or reorganizing their proprietary trading operations. Although proprietary trading continues to be an important business at most large investment banks, overall, risk positions have been reduced and firmwide leverage that supports these positions has declined significantly. As a result, the earnings capacity of this business has been reduced and hedge funds have benefited from somewhat lower competition.

## Risk Monitoring and Control

Investment banks have risk committees that review the activities of trading desks, approve new businesses and products, and approve market risk limits and credit risk limits. There is also a capital committee that reviews and approves transactions involving commitments of the firm's capital to support extensions of credit, bond underwritings, equity underwritings, distressed debt acquisitions, and principal investment activities. In addition, investment banks usually have risk monitoring committees that focus on structured products, new products, operational risk, credit policies, and business practices.

## Value at Risk (VaR)

A key tool in measuring an investment bank's trading risk is VaR (Value at Risk). VaR represents the potential loss in value of trading positions due to adverse market movements over a defined time horizon based on a specified statistical confidence level. Typically, investment banks use a one-day time horizon and a 95% confidence level in reporting VaR. This means that there is a 1 in 20 chance that daily trading net revenues will fall below expected revenues by an amount at least as large as the reported VaR. Stated another way, shortfalls from probable trading net revenues on a single trading day that are greater than the reported VaR would be expected to occur, on average, once a month, assuming 20 trading days in an average month.

Typical implementations of VaR use historical data, with more recent data given greater weight. An inherent limitation of VaR is that the distribution of historical changes in market risk factors may not produce an accurate prediction of future market risk. In addition, VaR calculated over a one-day time period does not completely capture the market risk of positions that cannot be liquidated within one day.

As an example of how to interpret VaR, if an investment bank reports an interest rate trading business VaR of $50 million, this means that, under normal trading conditions, the bank is 95% confident that a change in the value of its interest rate portfolio would not result in a loss of more than $50 million in a single day. A summary of VaR reported by several investment banks is included in Exhibit 5.10.

### Average Daily VaR

Value-at-Risk (VaR) measures the worst expected loss under normal market conditions over a specific time interval at a given confidence level.

In the jargon of VaR, suppose that a portfolio manager has a daily VaR equal to $1 million at 1% (or, 99% confidence level). This means that there is only one chance in 100 that a daily loss bigger than $1 million occurs under normal market conditions.

Note 1: Calculated at 95% confidence level

Note 2: Calculated at 95% confidence level, based on six month period ended December 31, 2008 (JPMorgan moved from a 99% to a 95% confidence level calculation in third quarter of 2008)

Note 3: Calculated at 99% confidence level

Note 4: Calculated at 2008 average exchange rate of CHF/USD at 0.93

Note 5: Calculated at 2008 average exchange rate of EUR/USD at 1.47

Source: Respective 2008 10-K filings

| 2008 Average Daily VaR ($ in millions) | |
| --- | --- |
| Goldman Sachs[1] | $180 |
| Morgan Stanley[1] | $115 |
| JPMorgan Chase[2] | $202 |
| Citigroup[3] | $292 |
| Credit Suisse[3, 4] | $164 |
| UBS[3, 4] | $123 |
| Deutsche Bank[3, 5] | $179 |
| Bank of America[3] | $111 |

**EXHIBIT 5.10**

## Questions

1. When might an investment bank decline participation in an underwriting and why?
2. How do professionals in sales, trading, and research work together?
3. Describe what Prime Brokerage is, including four principal products in this area and the generic name of the financial institutions that are targeted for this business.
4. Explain traders' market-making function.
5. Why would a prospective issuer prefer to hire as underwriter an investment bank that has traders already active in its security?
6. FICC is one of the main Divisions in an Investment Bank. What does FICC stand for? Other than during 2007 and 2008, how does this division typically rank from a profitability point of view, compared to other Divisions? What happened during these two years, and which part of the FICC Division was most responsible for this outcome?
7. Which stock would likely have a lower rebate and why: a stock whose issuer has a large amount of convertible securities outstanding, or a stock whose issuer has no convertible securities and has no significant share-moving news in the near-term?
8. An investor lends 10,000 shares of ABC for two months when the stock is at $50 and requires 102% cash collateral. The market interest on cash collateral is 4.0%. The rebate rate on ABC shares is 2.5%. Calculate the combined profit for the stock lender and investment bank.

9. Suppose Company XYZ has an average daily trading volume of 1 million shares and shows a current short interest ratio of 3.0. It currently has a $100 million convertible outstanding that is convertible into 4 million shares. The hedge ratio on convertible bond is 55%, which means hedge funds investing in the security will sell short 55% of the shares underlying the convertible. Assume all investors in the convertible are hedge funds. Based on this information, estimate the adjusted short interest ratio that is a better representation of the current "bearish sentiment" on the stock.

10. How were senior tranches of a CDO able to obtain investment-grade credit ratings when some of the underlying assets were non-investment-grade?

11. A domestic airline based in the United States has placed a large $10 billion order for new airplanes with French aircraft manufacturer Airbus. Delivery is scheduled in 4 years. Payments are staggered based on a percentage of completion rate. The U.S. airline believes the Euro will appreciate against the Dollar during this time frame. How can the U.S. airline hedge currency risk related to this purchase with an investment bank?

12. What does VaR stand for? What is its definition, and why is it important to investment banks? What are some of the criticisms of VaR?

# Asset Management, Wealth Management, and Research

## Asset Management

Asset Management refers to the professional management of investment funds for individuals, families, and institutions. Investments include stocks, bonds, convertibles, alternative assets (such as hedge funds, private equity funds, and real estate), commodities, indexes of each of these asset classes, and money market investments. Asset managers specialize in different asset classes, and management fees are paid based on the asset class. For alternative assets, additional fees are paid based on investment performance as well. Fees types can be broken down into four major categories, based on asset class:

1. Alternative assets: Management fees can range from 1% to 2% of assets under management (AUM), and additional fees are charged based on the fund manager's performance. Some alternative asset managers receive performance fees of 10% to 20% on the annual increase in value of assets. This means that if a high-net-worth investor entrusted $10 million to an alternative asset manager, and the value of this investment increased to $11.5 million in one year (a 15% increase), the asset manager would be paid as much as 2% × $10 million = $200,000 management fee, plus 20% × ($11.5 million – $10 million) = $300,000 performance fee. So total fees paid would be $500,000, which is, in effect, a 5% fee on the original $10 million investment. Although this may seem high, the investor's net return is still 10% after fees. Therefore, despite the high fee percentage, this may be a suitable fee arrangement for an investor if the net return is better than net returns from other investment choices. Of course, this determination should be made in the context of the riskiness of the investment and the diversification objectives of the investor.

2. Equity and convertible investments: Fees are generally lower for this asset class than for alternative asset investments. Management fees typically range from 0.75% to 1.75% of AUM, depending on the type of equity or convertible investment (U.S. domestic, international, large cap, small cap, etc.). Although it is less common for additional fees to be charged based on the fund manager's performance for this asset class, depending on the type of fund and the manager of the fund, performance fees may be paid.

3. Bond and commodity investments: Fees are generally lower for this asset class than for equity and convertible funds. Investment fees typically range from 0.50% to 1.5% of AUM, depending on the type of fund (U.S. high grade, U.S. low grade, distressed debt, international, etc.). Performance fees are unusual in bond or commodity investments, but possible, depending on the risk and complexity of the investment process.

4. Indexes: Fees for managing indexes are usually even smaller, ranging from 0.10% to 0.50% of AUM.

Asset Management products are offered through separately managed accounts and through commingled vehicles such as mutual funds and private investment funds. A summary of assets under management by some of the largest investment banks is provided in Exhibit 6.1. Invested funds are generally lumped into the following categories when placed in Asset Management accounts at an investment bank: fixed income, equity, alternative investments (comprised principally of hedge fund, private equity, and real estate investments), and money market.

Fund performance is a key metric when evaluating Asset Management capabilities. Investors measure this by relying on different performance measurement firms, such as Morningstar and Lipper, who compile aggregate industry data that demonstrate how individual mutual funds perform against both indexes and peer groups over time. For alternative asset classes such as hedge funds and private equity, there are specialized industry research firms that track fund performance (e.g., Hedge Fund Research and Alpha Magazine track hedge fund performance, while Preqin Global Private Equity Review, among others, track private equity performance). Most funds are ranked into quartiles based on their relative performance each quarter and each year. Inevitably, top quartile funds draw disproportionately more investable funds whenever rankings are announced.

For most asset classes, performance is measured against a benchmark. This benchmark can be either a well-known index for the asset class being managed, or a benchmark created by averaging the returns of a peer group of funds. For mutual funds, where the focus is on relative returns, performance is compared against indexes and peers. For alternative assets such as hedge funds, it is common to measure performance not only on a relative basis but also on an absolute return basis. These funds attempt to achieve a positive (non-negative) return (and not just beat a certain benchmark) through the use of derivatives and by creating short positions in different

**Global Investment Bank Asset Management Divisions**

| Bank | AUM ($bn)[1] |
|------|----------|
| Barclays[2] | 1,495 |
| J.P. Morgan | 1,133 |
| Goldman Sachs | 779 |
| Deutsche Bank | 652 |
| UBS | 544 |
| Morgan Stanley | 399 |
| Credit Suisse | 390 |
| Bank of America[3] | 341 |
| Citigroup[4] | -- |

Note 1: As of year-end 2008.

Note 2: As of August 2009, the shareholders of Barclays approved a plan to sell the bank's asset management division to BlackRock Inc. for $14.2 billion.

Note 3: Bank of America FY2008 AUM excludes Merrill Lynch (the acquisition closed on January 1, 2009). Merrill Lynch has an approximately 50% ownership in BlackRock, which has $1.4 trillion in AUM.

Note 4: Citigroup sold its asset management business to Legg Mason in 2005.

Source: Respective 2008 10-K filings

**EXHIBIT 6.1**

asset classes. As demonstrated by the average industry return of –19% in 2008, hedge funds are not always successful at generating absolute returns.

Performance measurement is often not just focused on returns but on risk-adjusted returns as well. Modern portfolio theory has established the qualitative link that exists between portfolio risk and return. The Capital Asset Pricing Model (CAPM) developed by Sharpe in 1964 highlighted the concept of rewarding risk. This led to the creation of risk-adjusted ratios including the Sharpe ratio, which measures the return of a portfolio in excess of the risk-free rate, compared to the total risk of the portfolio. Subsequent efforts to measure risk-adjusted returns have led to improved performance measurement practices.

## Hedge Fund Investments

Most major investment banks have large hedge funds housed within their Asset Management Division. These funds are managed principally for the benefit of investing clients (although the bank and employees of the bank may also invest in the fund) and are separate from the proprietary investing activities conducted within the Trading Division (which invests solely for the account of the firm, without any outside client investments). For example, Goldman Sachs Asset Management (GSAM), the asset management business within Goldman Sachs, has several hedge funds that invest in a wide range of asset classes and strategies, including commodities, equity, fixed income, and emerging markets. Global Alpha is one of the hedge funds, which had assets of approximately $12 billion at its peak in 2006, but shrunk to approximately $2.5 billion by 2008 (after losses and withdrawals). Investors in this fund include high-net-worth clients, institutional investors, and employees of Goldman Sachs. This quantitative strategies fund has had annual gross returns as high as 51%, but the fund lost a reported 6% during 2006 and about 37% during 2007, before rebounding somewhat during 2008. Global Equities Opportunities Fund, another Goldman Sachs hedge fund, also encountered difficulties during 2007 and required a $3 billion cash infusion (two-thirds from the parent firm). This fund had about $7 billion in assets at its peak, but shrunk to as low as $1 billion in assets during early 2008. Other hedge funds managed by GSAM had substantially better results. Overall, Goldman Sachs manages about 20 hedge funds within GSAM.

J.P. Morgan purchased a majority of hedge fund Highbridge Capital during 2004 (completing the full acquisition during July 2009), creating a flagship hedge fund within the bank's asset management division. Managing several other hedge funds in this division as well, J.P. Morgan's aggregate hedge fund AUM at the end of 2007 stood at $44.7 billion, making the bank the world's largest hedge fund manager. In 2008, however, after suffering from investor redemptions and poor performance at the Highbridge fund, J.P. Morgan saw its AUM drop to $32.9 billion, placing it second, after Bridgewater Associates (a non-investment bank affiliated hedge fund manager).

## Private Equity Investments

Most large investment banks participate in private equity to varying degrees, as indicated by the following summary of selected firms:

1. Goldman Sachs manages private equity fund of funds.
2. J.P. Morgan, Goldman Sachs, and Morgan Stanley invest directly in companies or real estate through management of dedicated funds.
3. Credit Suisse manages private equity co-investment funds.
4. Citigroup and Bank of America invest directly in companies without a fund vehicle.

Investments by these firms may include leveraged buyout, mezzanine, real estate, and infrastructure transactions.

Of the nine largest global investment banks, Goldman Sachs has one of the most comprehensive private equity programs. Since 1992, Goldman Sachs' Merchant Banking Division (part of the Asset Management Division) has raised $119 billion of capital to invest in these transactions, including $28 billion for mezzanine investments (fixed income securities with an associated equity component, which may include an equity warrant) and a $20 billion direct private equity fund which closed in 2007. In addition, Goldman Sachs had $24 billion AUM in private equity fund of funds at the end of 2008.

## Wealth Management

Wealth Management refers to advisors who provide investment advice to selected individual, family, and institutional investing clients. Wealth Management advisors attempt to identify investors who have a significant amount of funds to invest and then work with these investors to make investments in the asset classes just described. In other words, Wealth Management professionals create investment advisory relationships with investors and are not directly involved in the management of asset classes (which is the role of Asset Managers). An investment bank's Wealth Management advisors help investors define their risk tolerance and diversification preferences. They then either assist investors in self-directed investments, or persuade them to entrust the advisor to make investments on their behalf. Wealth Management advisors must exercise good judgment in allocating funds to achieve high investment returns and appropriate diversification relative to client risk objectives.

Wealth Management services include more than providing investment advice. To a certain extent, advisors are also asset allocators, if they have been entrusted to invest funds on behalf of clients. They are also acting in many cases as a financial planning advisor, helping clients obtain retail banking services, estate planning advice, legal resources, and taxation advice. There is also a growing trend for advisors to provide insurance and annuity products to clients. The Wealth Management advisor attempts to help investing clients sustain and grow long-term wealth and meet financial goals, and there are many different non-investment tools that are introduced to facilitate these goals.

Wealth Management advisors typically limit their services to clients that have more than $5 million in investable funds. Some banks require an even higher amount of funds in order to focus attention and limited resources on investing clients. For example, subject to a number of considerations, Goldman Sachs largely limits its Wealth Management efforts to clients that have more than $25 million in investable funds.

Some banks have created a *private client services* business that brings many, but not all, of the bank's services to investors who do not meet the investable fund threshold amount required to be covered by Wealth Management advisors.

Individual investors that have an even lower amount of investable funds are covered by *retail* advisors and brokers who help them invest cash in both the Asset Management products offered by the bank and products offered from external sources. All of the largest investment banks, with the exception of Goldman Sachs, have a retail team. Merrill Lynch, immediately prior to its acquisition by Bank of America in 2008, had the largest retail business, followed by Wachovia (which was acquired by Wells Fargo in 2008). Citigroup's Smith Barney division established a joint venture with Morgan Stanley during early 2009 (majority owned by Morgan Stanley, with the right to acquire 100% ownership over a 5-year period). As of March 2009, the largest retail brokerage teams in the United States were controlled by Morgan Stanley, Wells Fargo, Bank of America, and UBS (see Exhibit 6.2).

### U.S. Brokerage Force Ranking, as of March 2009

| Firm | Number of Brokers | Revenue ($ in millions) | Revenue per Broker | Client Assets ($ in billions) |
|---|---|---|---|---|
| Morgan Stanley Smith Barney[1] | 20,807 | $15,718 | $755,000 | $1,721 |
| Wells Fargo/Wachovia[1,2] | 15,879 | $8,700 | $548,000 | $910 |
| Bank of America/Merrill Lynch[1] | 15,822 | $14,076 | $890,000 | $1,293 |
| UBS (U.S. division) | 8,760 | $5,103 | $583,000 | $619 |

Note 1: As of March 31, 2009 Morgan Stanley controlled the largest brokerage force based on their majority control of Morgan Stanley Smith Barney (a joint venture between Morgan Stanley and Citigroup), Wells Fargo controlled the second largest brokerage team following their acquisition of Wachovia, and Bank of America controlled the third largest brokerage team following their acquisition of Merrill Lynch.

Note 2: Quarterly revenue data on Wells Fargo's brokerage business not available. revenue shown is for full year 2008.

Source: Respective 2008 10-K and Q1-2009 10-Q filings; author's estimates

**EXHIBIT 6.2**

In summary, the largest investment banks have dedicated "sales teams" that focus on one, two, or three different individual investing customer segments, based on the client's investable asset amount and requirement for non-investment services.

Since these sales teams have a duty to help clients achieve the best possible returns in the context of their risk tolerance, in some cases, investing clients may be directed to investment products not provided by the investment bank. Suppose, for example, that an investment bank's Asset Management fund offerings do not include a type of investment that a client wants to invest in, or the performance of an internal fund (from a risk/return perspective) is less than a competing fund at another firm. In this scenario, the advisor may choose to direct part of a client's investment portfolio to an Asset Management product provided by a competitor. However, at many banks, incentive systems are designed to keep all client investments within the bank rather than see funds go to a competing firm, which creates a potential conflict of interest. This became a significant issue at Citigroup and at Merrill Lynch, as discussed in Exhibit 6.3.

Wealth management, private client services, and retail advisors at each bank work closely with colleagues from the Asset Management group to bring appropriate investment offerings to investors. In addition, they also work closely with the bank's capital markets teams to place underwritten new offerings with their investing clients. At some banks, advisors place 10% to 30% of underwritten offerings with their investors (the balance of which goes to institutional investors). Finally, advisors work with some traders in their secondary market making activity, helping to create flow for the traders and meeting the secondary investment interests of their clients.

# Research

Research is provided by all large investment banking firms to selected institutional and individual investing clients on a global basis. This research usually covers equity, fixed income, currency, and commodity markets. Research professionals also focus on economics, portfolio strategy, derivatives, and credit issues, offering insights and ideas based on fundamental research.

**Avoiding Conflict of Interest in Asset Management**

During 2005 and 2006, both Merrill Lynch and Citigroup decided to give up control over their asset management business because, among other reasons, they wanted to avoid a potential conflict of interest between the wealth management advisory function and the asset management function. In 2005, Citigroup entered into an arrangement with Legg Mason, Inc., a leading global asset management firm, whereby the brokerage portion of Legg Mason was bought by Citigroup, while the asset management business of Citigroup was bought by Legg Mason.

In 2006, two months after the Citigroup-Legg Mason deal closed, Merrill Lynch entered into an arrangement with BlackRock, a large investment management firm that had a particularly strong focus in fixed income securities, whereby Merrill Lynch's asset management business merged with BlackRock, creating a new independent company with nearly $1 trillion in assets under management. Merrill Lynch's ownership of the combined asset management company was 49.8%, and it came with a 45% voting interest in a firm that had a majority of independent directors. By giving up control of its asset management business, Merrill Lynch was able to mitigate potential conflict of interest concerns.

**EXHIBIT 6.3**

Equity research focuses on public company specific analysis as well as on industries and geographical regions. This research sometimes coordinates with macro, quantitative, and derivatives research teams to identify investment ideas. Economic research formulates macroeconomic forecasts for economic activity, foreign exchange, and interest rates based on globally coordinated views of regional economists. Fixed income research focuses on corporate debt in the context of the issuer's industry, and is critically dependent on understanding credit risks. Commodities research is a globally focused effort that principally analyzes energy and precious metals. Strategic research groups provide market views, forecasts, and recommendations on asset allocation and strategic investment strategies that could involve other forms of research.

Research is typically, but not always, housed within the Trading Division of an investment bank and is comprised of two different groups. Research that is provided to investing clients of the firm is called *sell-side* research. Research that is provided to proprietary traders who trade for the account of the bank and to the bank's asset managers, who manage money for investing clients, is called *buy-side* research. This is the same type of research that hedge funds produce for their internal traders, or that large mutual funds such as Fidelity produce for their internal fund managers.

Sell-side research has always been an analytically intense area within investment banks. Equity research analysts produce detailed financial models that help them forecast earnings as well as the future value of assets. For example, research is produced by analysts who build models that forecast a company's future revenue and earnings based on several factors, including but not limited to company guidance, economic conditions, historical trends, and new information (e.g., product introductions, customer wins/losses, competitive conditions, and analyst judgment). They then use multiples based on revenue, EBITDA, earnings, book value, and cash flow in order to help assess a company's future share price. In addition, the analyst may also employ other valuation models such as peer comparisons, discounted cash flow analysis, or replacement value. An analyst may then use this information along with other research to formulate an investment opinion, which is then communicated to investors or investment advisors. Many investors rely on analysts' opinions regarding whether or not they should buy or sell a security or other asset. For example, if a company's forecasted value is above the value implied by the current market price, the analyst might use this information to rate a company *overweight* or *buy*. Conversely, if a company's forecasted value is below its implied market value, a rating of *underweight* or *sell* might be given. If the analyst believes the company is trading at or near fair value, then the stock might be given an *equal weight* or *hold* rating.

Equity analysts usually publish research reports quarterly in association with a company's earnings reports. Additional research is published if there are important events announced by a company through a press release, 8-K filing with the SEC (in the United States), or if the analyst has conducted proprietary research. An example may be a recent interview between the analyst and senior management of the company or an investor field trip. Research is provided in both print and electronic form. Some of a firm's most important investing clients are sometimes given direct access to analysts and are able to discuss models and assumptions on an ongoing basis.

The value provided to investing clients by sell-side research on public companies is summarized as follows:

1. In-depth initiation reports that introduce investing clients to new industries or new companies.
2. Quarterly performance reports during earnings season when investors need concise and rapid summaries of results.
3. Previews of expected quarterly performance.
4. Analysis of how an investment thesis changes following material events.
5. Creation of financial models and valuation tables.
6. Proprietary research and interpretation of compelling investment considerations.
7. Summary of investor concerns about an industry or individual companies in the industry.
8. Company or industry updates.
9. Surveys of industries based on field checks and industry conferences.
10. Access to company management by arranging investor meetings, conferences, and non-deal road shows.
11. Due diligence with a company's senior management prior to an IPO where the bank's investment bankers have an underwriting mandate (if the research team decides to pick up coverage).

Research is usually organized into four main segments: equity research, economic research, commodities research, and credit research:

1. Equity research focuses on individual stocks typically in targeted industries, which include communication, media and entertainment, consumer products, financial institutions, industrials, technology, transportation, healthcare, retail, and education.
2. Credit research focuses on corporate debt of issuers in various industry sectors. Teams are divided into Investment-Grade Credit and High-Yield Credit. The focus of this research is on different aspects of a company than what is provided in equity research. In particular, credit research analyzes bond and loan documentation and whether a company's future cash flow is expected to meet all cash payment obligations.
3. Commodities research uses economic models to analyze supply-and-demand fundamentals and creates price forecasts on a range of commodities.
4. Economic research creates macroeconomic forecasts for economic activity, foreign exchange rates, and interest rates.

## Paying for Research

Research has historically received revenue from investing clients through an indirect mechanism: part of the commissions paid by investors to sales professionals when they buy securities is redirected to the research department. This *soft dollar* compensation arrangement has been a key part of sell-side research for decades, since investors are generally reluctant to pay direct fees for the use of research. For example, an investor who values equity research provided by a sell-side analyst at an investment bank might be willing to pay a commission of 3 cents per share for common shares the investor purchases through the bank, and a portion of this commission is redirected to the research department.

Unfortunately for research departments, estimated revenues from sales commission reallocations dropped from an estimated $5 billion in 2005 in the United States to less than $3 billion in 2008. This drop occurred, in part, because large institutional investors expanded their own buy-side research in response to growing concerns about the independence of sell-side research (questions arose about whether research was biased in favor of companies that were clients of the Investment Banking Division of a bank). In addition, Regulation FD, discussed later in this chapter, made some research marginally less valuable to investors.

Most institutional investors do not want to pay direct fees for research through what is called *unbundled research,* because they are concerned that these fees will negatively impact their investment record. For example, when investors buy stock through an investment bank, the stock acquisition cost is net of commissions that are slightly higher than an investor might otherwise pay (to include some compensation for research). Since investors record returns based on the difference between the purchase cost net of commissions and their eventual sales price, if a separate fee is paid for research, with a correspondingly smaller commission, the net purchase price will be higher (since it does not net out the separate fee paid for research), which corresponds to a lower investment return, assuming an eventual sale at a profit.

Notwithstanding investor aversion to paying unbundled fees, during 2006, Fidelity, a major institutional investor, completed agreements with several investment banks to pay a separate fee for research and simultaneously reduce commissions. However, not many other institutional investors have followed suit. As a result, the answers to declining research revenue and the future mechanism for compensating research are unclear. In this environment, investment banking research departments have been pared back and compensation has been reduced. At some investment banks there have been internal discussions regarding whether the research function should be sold since costs of operation exceed allocated and direct revenue. This problem was exacerbated by the 2003 enforcement action against 10 of the top investment banks operating in the United States that, among other things, took away the Investment Banking Division's ability to make payments to the research team as an inducement to help bankers obtain underwriting mandates from corporate clients (see the following section).

## Conflicts of Interest

One of the major problems with sell-side research is its alleged lack of independence. Some banks' Investment Banking Divisions have historically put pressure on research analysts to modify negative views on a company when bankers were soliciting a financing or M&A transaction with a company. Negative equity or fixed income research could upset management, making it problematic for bankers to obtain mandates. As a result, some bankers felt it necessary to press research departments to prioritize their research activities based on the Investment Banking Division's underwriting or M&A effort, rather than on the priorities of the firm's investing clients for objective research. This created a conflict of interest that had far-reaching repercussions.

During April 2003, the SEC, New York's attorney general, the National Association of Securities Dealers (NASD), and the New York Stock Exchange (NYSE) announced enforcement actions against the following 10 investment banks: Bear Stearns, Credit Suisse, Goldman Sachs, Lehman Brothers, J.P. Morgan, Merrill Lynch, Morgan Stanley, Citigroup, UBS, and Piper Jaffray. The banks were required to pay a total of approximately $1.4 billion, comprised of $875 million in penalties and disgorgement, $432.5 million to fund independent research, and $80 million to promote investor education. In addition to the monetary payments, the firms were also required to comply with significant requirements that included eliminating any influence by the Investment Banking Division over the research department, increasing supervision, and making independent research available to investors.

The enforcement actions alleged that all of the firms engaged in acts and practices that created or maintained inappropriate influence by the Investment Banking Division over research analysts, thereby imposing conflicts of interest on research analysts. The allegations, which were neither admitted to nor denied by the firms, also charged that certain firms issued fraudulent research reports, issued research reports that were not based on principles of fair dealing and good faith, and did not provide a sound basis for evaluating facts. In addition, it was alleged that certain research reports contained exaggerated or unwarranted claims about the covered companies and/or opinions for which there were no reasonable bases, and certain firms received payments from companies for research without disclosing such payments. Finally, it was alleged that certain firms engaged in inappropriate "spinning" of "hot" IPO allocations (selling IPO shares that had significant demand to top executives and directors of a company, in exchange for future investment banking business from that company).

By insulating research analysts from Investment Banking Division pressure, the enforcement action was designed to ensure that stock recommendations are not tainted by efforts to obtain investment banking fees. Important reforms required of investment banks included:

1. There must be a physical separation between research and investment banking professionals.
2. The firm's senior management must determine the research department's budget without input from the Investment Banking Division and without regard to specific revenues derived from investment banking activity.
3. Research analysts' compensation may not be based, directly or indirectly, on Investment Banking Division revenues or on input from investment banking personnel.
4. Research management must make all company-specific decisions to terminate coverage, and investment bankers can have no role in company-specific coverage decisions.
5. Research analysts are prohibited from participating in efforts to solicit investment banking business, including pitches and road shows.
6. In addition to providing their own research, investment banks are obligated to furnish independent research to investing clients (this requirement ended during 2009).

## Regulation FD

Regulation FD was implemented by the SEC during 2000. FD stands for fair disclosure. This regulation prohibits a company's executives from selectively disclosing material information that could impact a company's share price. This means that prior to discussing any potential "stock moving" information with research analysts, the company must disclose this information through an SEC filing. The benefit of this regulation is that it levels the playing field, enabling all investors to receive the same information at the same time. Prior to the promulgation of this regulation, some large institutional investors received stock moving information before other investors received it based on private discussions that a company had with a research analyst, which was passed on selectively to favored large investors. Regulation FD was an attempt to bring better transparency and fairness when companies decide to communicate with investors by ensuring that all investors are able to make investment decisions based on the same information at the same time. However, critics claim that because companies must now be more careful in what they say to analysts and investors, and when they say it, less information is distributed in a less timely way. In addition, it is usually filtered through lawyers, causing a dilution in the quality of information. Some investors feel that, as a result of Regulation FD, no one in the investment community, including retail investors, has the same quality or depth of information that they used to receive.

## Questions

1. What is the difference between asset management (AM) and wealth management (WM)?
2. Why would a wealth manager choose to allocate some of a client's asset to another bank?
3. How are the different functions of the sell-side versus the buy-side manifested through their fee structures?
4. What drove the need to separate research and investment banking?
5. How have the U.S. enforcement actions against sell-side research in 2003 heightened the issue of declining research revenues?
6. What are the objectives of Regulation FD? What are the concerns about this U.S.-based regulation?

# Credit Rating Agencies, Exchanges, and Clearing and Settlement

## Credit Rating Agencies

Credit rating agencies play a very important role in the business of investment banking by assigning credit ratings to debt issuers and their debt instruments. Debt instruments include bonds, convertible bonds, and loans. In addition, credit rating agencies assign ratings to structured finance securities that are backed by various types of collateral. Structured finance includes asset-backed securities, residential and commercial mortgage-backed securities, and collateralized debt obligations. Investment banks work closely with credit rating agencies when developing structured finance products in order to secure targeted ratings for these securities. See Exhibit 7.1 for a summary of the role of credit rating agencies.

| Rating Agency Role | |
|---|---|
| *To communicate unbiased opinions on creditworthiness of companies and their debt instruments to the investment community.* | |
| **Corporate and government finance** | **Structured Finance** |
| ▪ Bonds / notes / commercial paper<br>▪ Convertibles<br>▪ Bank notes | ▪ Collateralized debt obligations (CDO)<br>▪ Residential mortgage-backed securities (RMBS)<br>▪ Commercial mortgage-backed securities (CMBS)<br>▪ Asset-backed securities (ABS) |

Source: Standard & Poor's

**EXHIBIT 7.1**

Issuers can be corporations, governments and agencies, special purpose entities, and nonprofit organizations. The ratings process involves an analysis of business risk, including competitive position within the industry, diversity of product lines, and profitability compared to peers; and financial risk, including accounting, cash flow financial flexibility, and capital structure considerations (see Exhibit 7.2). The rating reflects the issuer's credit worthiness (ability to repay the obligation), which affects the interest rate or yield applied to the security being rated. These ratings are used by investors, banks, and governments as an input into their investment, loan, and regulatory decisions. The ratings are independent of influence by others (although this has become the subject of some controversy, as described shortly) and create an easy to understand measurement of relative credit risk. This generally results in increased efficiency in the market, lowering the costs for borrowers, investors and lenders, and expanding the total

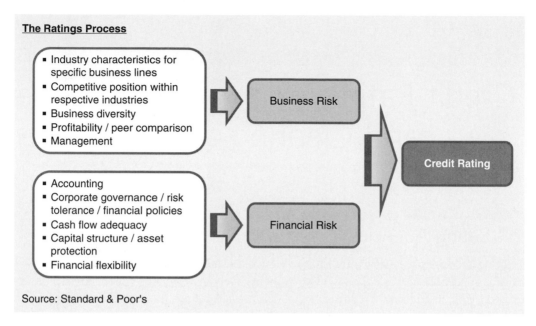

**The Ratings Process**

- Industry characteristics for specific business lines
- Competitive position within respective industries
- Business diversity
- Profitability / peer comparison
- Management

→ **Business Risk**

- Accounting
- Corporate governance / risk tolerance / financial policies
- Cash flow adequacy
- Capital structure / asset protection
- Financial flexibility

→ **Financial Risk**

→ **Credit Rating**

Source: Standard & Poor's

**EXHIBIT 7.2**

supply of capital. In most cases, issuers of public market bonds must receive ratings from at least one agency in order to attract investment interest. In many cases, a bond will be rated by two or three different credit rating agencies based on requests from investors. See Exhibit 7.3 for ratings scales from Standard & Poor's, Moody's, and Fitch, the three largest credit rating agencies, across different levels of credit risk. These rating agencies operate on an issuer-pay model whereby the issuer, not the investor, pays for the rating services. An exception to this is rating agencies' policy toward *unsolicited ratings,* which is intended to protect investors from issuers that withdraw their ratings when performance begins to suffer. If a company has enough debt outstanding to be considered "widely-held" and requests a rating withdrawal, rating agencies reserve the right to assign ratings on an unsolicited basis, so that investors remain informed about credit risk.

During 2006, a law was enacted in the United States that empowered the SEC to accept 10 firms as Nationally Recognized Statistical Rating Organizations (NRSROs). The largest three of these firms are Standard & Poor's, Moody's, and Fitch, who dominate the other seven. Certain regulators require the use of NRSRO-rated securities for certain investments and for regulatory capital determination purposes. For example, the Federal Reserve will only accept investment-grade securities as collateral under its various lending facilities to banks based on ratings from one or more of the big three firms. At the state level, various rules also require ratings from these three rating agencies. There is active debate about whether this "oligopoly" within NRSROs is appropriate. Some go even further by suggesting that the SEC should eliminate regulations altogether that require the use of NRSRO-rated securities so that investors are free to discover their own best methods for judging credit risk, without being required to use the analytical services provided by NRSROs.

## Asset-Backed Securities

Moody's, Standard & Poor's, and Fitch actively rated mortgage-backed securities, providing many such securities with their highest ratings until 2007, when a portion of the mortgages backing these securities defaulted, causing the securities to plummet in value. As a result, the big three

## Credit Rating Scales

### Standard & Poor's and Fitch Credit Rating Scales

| Investment Grade | Non-Investment Grade (High Yield, Junk Bonds) |
|---|---|
| **AAA**: the best quality companies, reliable and stable<br>**AA+, AA, AA-**: quality companies, slightly higher risk than AAA<br>**A+, A, A-**: economic situation can affect financings, but still strong<br>**BBB+, BBB, BBB-**: medium class companies, which are satisfactory at the moment | **BB+, BB, BB-**: more prone to changes in the economy<br>**B+, B, B-**: financial situation varies noticeably<br>**CCC+, CCC, CCC-**: currently vulnerable and dependent on favorable economic condition to meet its commitments<br>**CC**: highly vulnerable, very speculative bonds<br>**C**: highly vulnerable, perhaps in bankruptcy or in arrears but still continuing to pay out on obligations<br>**D**: has defaulted on obligations and expected to generally default on most or all obligations<br>**NR**: not publicly rated |

### Moody's Credit Rating Scales

| Investment Grade | Non-Investment Grade (High Yield, Junk Bonds) |
|---|---|
| **Aaa**: Obligations of the highest quality, with minimal credit risk<br>**Aa1, Aa2, Aa3**: Obligations of high quality and subject to very low credit risk<br>**A1, A2, A3**: Obligations upper-medium grade and subject to low credit risk<br>**Baa1, Baa2, Baa3**: Obligations subject to moderate credit risk: medium-grade and possess certain speculative characteristics | **Ba1, Ba2, Ba3**: Obligations are judged to have speculative elements and are subject to substantial credit risk<br>**B1, B2, B3**: Obligations speculative and subject to high credit risk<br>**Caa1, Caa2, Caa3**: Obligations of poor standing and are subject to very high credit risk<br>**Ca**: Obligations highly speculative and are likely in or very near default, with some prospect of recovery of principal and interest<br>**C**: Obligations are the lowest rated class of bonds and are typically in default, with little prospect for recovery of principal or interest<br>**NR**: Not Rated |

Source: Standard & Poor's, Fitch, and Moody's

**EXHIBIT 7.3**

agencies felt compelled to downgrade across the board many securities in this asset class, which exacerbated their decline in value, causing investors and insurers hundreds of billions of dollars in losses during 2007 and 2008.

Investment banks consult with credit rating agencies to determine the optimal structure for different tranches of mortgage-backed securities and other asset-backed securities. During this process, banks submit contemplated structures and expected ratings to the credit rating agencies for feedback. If there is a divergence between the banker's and the credit rating agency's view on expected ratings, then the process repeats again, with the banker modifying the structure (which could involve increasing the collateral base of the senior tranche or modifying the mix of assets) and resubmitting for feedback. The process repeats until the bankers are confident the targeted rating can be achieved. Frequently, rating agencies will express opinions on the types of assets that must be used to secure the debt offered by an asset-backed security in order to obtain desired credit ratings. There are typically different tranches representing different levels of credit risk in an asset-backed security, based on the cash flow, maturity, and credit support vehicles embedded in each tranche. It is common, for example, to have three separate tranches rated AAA, BBB, and

BB, representing low risk, medium risk, and speculative risk, respectively. Investors require higher interest rates (or yields) for the more risky tranches.

Rating agencies state that their ratings suggest the likelihood a given debt security will fail to pay principal and interest over time, but they are not expressing opinions regarding the volatility of the rated security or the wisdom of investing in that security. Historically, the most highly rated debt exhibited low volatility and high liquidity. This means that the price of the debt did not change much on a day-to-day basis and that there were almost always other buyers willing to purchase the debt. Unlike straight bonds and loans, however, asset-backed securities may sometimes have hundreds or thousands of individual securities embedded in each tranche. These similarly rated securities concentrate risk in such a way that even a small change in the perceived risk of default can mushroom in scale and dramatically affect the security's market price. During the 2007 and 2008 credit crisis, this led to very significant drops in the price of many mortgage-backed securities, especially those backed by subprime mortgages.

## Criticism Against Credit Rating Agencies

Credit rating agencies have been heavily criticized for their role in working with investment banks to create mortgage-backed securities that had higher ratings than they deserved. They are also criticized for not downgrading mortgage-backed securities as early as they should have. Many investors thought that the agencies were both wrong in the first place and slow to make corrections.

Other criticisms of rating agencies relate to their relationship with corporations that issue straight bonds and other non-asset-backed securities. Although investors are the principal users of the credit ratings, they do not pay for this service. Instead, it is the issuer of the debt security that pays for the rating. It has been suggested by some investors, especially those who invest in securities that experience a ratings decline, that the agencies are susceptible to undue influence from corporations since they are the actual paying clients, or they are vulnerable to being mislead. On the other hand, corporate treasury staffs sometimes feel that they have an adversarial relationship with credit rating agencies. When receiving a rating that they believe is unjustifiably low, they sometimes claim that the rating agencies do not understand their business.

## Monoline Insurers' Relationship with Credit Rating Agencies

Investment banks underwrite asset-backed securities and trade them in the secondary market. Before underwriting the securities, they work with rating agencies in structuring each tranche to obtain a designated rating, sometimes injecting credit-enhancing instruments. One such instrument is a guarantee from monoline insurers, which include Ambac, MBIA, and Security Capital Assurance (SCA). These insurers guarantee the repayment of bond principal and interest when an issuer defaults. Since, until recently, these insurers were rated AAA, the result of this insurance was to reduce the required interest rate on a debt obligation. Therefore, if the cost of insurance coverage is less than the effective interest rate savings, it is economical to purchase the insurance. As suggested by its name, monoline insurers only focus on insuring capital markets bonds, whereas multiline insurance companies provide insurance to multiple industries.

As a result of the credit crisis of 2007–2008, the principal monoline insurers experienced a major shakeup based on the guarantees they provided to collateralized debt obligations (CDOs) that were backed by subprime mortgages. As these securities defaulted or declined in value, payments by monolines increased and their future potential payment obligations grew dramatically. This resulted in credit rating agencies downgrading the credit ratings of the monolines, which, in turn, was a factor in the credit rating agencies also downgrading the CDOs guaranteed by the monolines. This vicious circle severely impacted investment banks since, in their underwriting and secondary market-making roles, the banks held a large inventory of these securities that now had to be marked-to-market at much lower values.

During 2008, Ambac and MBIA both lost their AAA ratings, which not only impacted the CDOs they guaranteed, but also the thousands of state and municipal government bonds that were guaranteed by them. The total decline in value during 2007 and 2008 of all of the securities guaranteed by the monolines amounted to hundreds of billions of dollars. SCA disclosed a loss of $1 billion during November 2007, causing the rating agencies to downgrade the insurer to CCC, and forcing them to delist from the NYSE. During July 2008, Merrill Lynch reached a $500 million settlement agreement with SCA, which had guaranteed billions of dollars of mortgage-backed securities owned by Merrill, thereby contributing to Merrill's massive $46 billion in write-downs.

## Credit Rating Advisory Services Provided by Investment Banks

Most companies and governments that issue bonds want credit ratings assigned to their bonds to facilitate investor purchases of the securities at the lowest possible yield. Although most issuers pay for this service, there are a few companies that do not. These companies generally have actively traded debt and unassailable credit strength, which makes demand for their bonds far greater than supply. Purchasers of credit ratings spend considerable time and resources to provide information that helps rating agencies build financial models that reflect well on the company's financial strength. These models are the foundation from which analysts determine credit ratings.

Investment banks provide credit rating advisory services to companies by suggesting the potential credit rating outcome from the issuance of different kinds of financings (bonds, loans, convertibles, preferred shares, or common shares). Bonds and loans weaken an issuer's balance sheet and, subject to the use of proceeds, may reduce cash flow. As a result, rating agencies might consider downgrading a company if the company initiates a large loan or bond transaction. However, if the bond or loan proceeds are used to repay existing debt or to fund an acquisition or new business that is expected to generate significant cash flow, which could be used to pay the coupons on the debt offering, then there may not be a downgrade. Further, if the bond or loan obligation is small relative to the company's capital structure, there may not be a downgrade. If a company issues convertibles or preferred shares, the transaction could positively or negatively impact ratings, depending on maturity and conversion features. If a company issues common shares, this will have a positive impact on ratings if the size of the issue is sufficiently large. Typically, issuers are careful not to raise financing that results in a credit rating agency downgrade of their debt obligations, unless there are very favorable results that otherwise come from the financing.

Investment bankers help prepare clients for an annual or semiannual pilgrimage to New York to meet with the agencies to review the client's business and any material changes that could impact ratings. Sometimes, investment bankers and their issuing clients miscalculate rating agency reaction to a new security issuance or changing business fortunes of a company. When this leads to an unexpected downgrade, there is considerable frustration and anxiety. Normally, investment banks are able to avoid surprises by attempting to replicate the models built by credit rating agencies and advise corporations (or governments) on ratios that they need to meet in relation to interest coverage, total debt, cash flow, and other credit related metrics. Nevertheless, it is not a perfect process and surprises still occur.

To help rating agencies build models that accurately reflect the business and financial risks of companies, senior management from companies (and investment bankers, if retained for this purpose) sometimes provide material non-public information regarding a potential financing to rating agencies prior to initiating the new financing. This enables the agency to incorporate information into their models in advance of the financing, which allows a rating to be issued on the same day as the financing. This is beneficial to investors who want to know the ratings impact of all new securities before they commit to invest in these securities. It is incumbent on rating agencies not to disclose any material non-public information to anyone who can use the information to trade securities of the company prior to the company's announcement of the financing.

Investment bank credit rating advisors are frequently former employees of Moody's or Standard & Poor's and have an in-depth understanding of the models used by their former employers, as well as the personalities and analytical perspectives of their former colleagues. This is helpful in advising companies regarding the probable ratings outcome from different financing alternatives. Investment bankers provide a narrower range of credit rating advisory services to governments.

# Exchanges

Investment banks actively trade stocks, bonds, and derivatives on exchanges around the world. Exchanges enable buyers and sellers to anonymously buy and sell securities at agreed-upon prices through an electronic medium, although some exchanges such as NYSE Euronext still conduct a relatively small volume of trading-floor-based transactions.

Each company that has publicly traded stock must determine the exchange on which to list their securities. Each exchange has its own requirements that a company must meet in order to obtain and maintain a listing. Requirements are imposed for financial reporting and disclosure standards as well as minimum trading volume and stock price standards. If these standards are not met, shares will be delisted (assuming the infractions are not rectified after a certain "grace period"). Listing requirements for NYSE Euronext include at least one million shares of stock worth $100 million and earnings in excess of $10 million over the last 3 years. NASDAQ requirements include 1.25 million shares worth at least $70 million and aggregate 3-year earnings of at least $11 million. The London Stock Exchange requires a minimum market capitalization of £700,000, a minimum public float of one quarter of this amount, and a minimum working capital amount.

The largest stock exchanges in the world by value of shares trading (turnover) are NASDAQ and NYSE Euronext-US in the United States; London Stock Exchange, Frankfurt Stock Exchange (Deutsche Borse), and NYSE Euronext (Europe) in Europe; and Tokyo Stock Exchange and Shanghai Stock Exchange in Asia. As of the end of 2008, turnover for the top seven exchanges (in trillions of U.S. dollars) was NASDAQ ($36.4); NYSE Euronext-US ($33.6); London Stock Exchange ($6.3); Tokyo ($5.6); Frankfurt ($4.7); NYSE Euronext-Europe ($4.4); and Shanghai ($2.6). See Exhibit 7.4 for the ranking of the top 20 exchanges.

## Specialists

Historically, a portion of the business conducted on the NYSE Euronext trading floor was through a specialist system, whereby an individual acts as the official market maker for a given security, providing liquidity to the market, taking the other side of trades when there are buy/sell imbalances, and preventing excessive volatility. However, as electronic communications networks (ECNs) have become more efficient, the specialist system has diminished in importance.

**Top 20 Stock Exchanges**
As of 2008

| Region | Stock Exchange | Total Share Turnover (US $ millions) |
|---|---|---|
| Americas | NASDAQ OMX | 36,446,548.5 |
| Americas | NYSE Euronext (US) | 33,638,937.0 |
| Europe - Africa - Middle East | London SE | 6,271,520.6 |
| Asia-Pacific | Tokyo SE Group | 5,607,321.9 |
| Europe - Africa - Middle East | Deutsche Börse | 4,678,829.0 |
| Europe - Africa - Middle East | NYSE Euronext (Europe) | 4,411,248.7 |
| Asia-Pacific | Shanghai SE | 2,600,208.6 |
| Europe - Africa - Middle East | BME Spanish Exchanges | 2,410,721.2 |
| Americas | TSX Group | 1,710,228.0 |
| Asia-Pacific | Hong Kong Exchanges | 1,629,782.3 |
| Europe - Africa - Middle East | SIX Swiss Exchange | 1,500,366.5 |
| Europe - Africa - Middle East | Borsa Italiana | 1,499,456.5 |
| Asia-Pacific | Korea Exchange | 1,432,479.9 |
| Europe - Africa - Middle East | NASDAQ OMX Nordic Exchange | 1,338,181.1 |
| Asia-Pacific | Shenzhen SE | 1,248,721.8 |
| Asia-Pacific | Australian SE | 1,213,239.6 |
| Asia-Pacific | Taiwan SE Corp. | 829,612.2 |
| Asia-Pacific | National Stock Exchange India | 725,398.7 |
| Americas | BM&FBOVESPA | 724,199.2 |
| Americas | American SE | 561,602.5 |

Source: World Federation of Exchanges

**EXHIBIT 7.4**

In addition, there have been objections to certain aspects of the specialist system. Some of the objections include the possibility of a special interest profit at the expense of investors, higher cost (relative to ECNs), and the possibility of front-running (traders using knowledge of a customer's incoming large order to place their own order ahead of it to benefit from a change in market direction that a large order may induce).

In 2008, in response to these concerns and shifts in the market structure of securities trading, NYSE Euronext moved to eliminate specialists and replaced them with designated market makers (DMMs). A key difference between the new DMMs and specialists is that the issue of front-running is eliminated since DMMs no longer get a first look at electronic orders. In addition, some of the privileges enjoyed by specialists are no longer available, and some restrictions under the specialist format have been removed to allow greater flexibility. In general, the new structure is designed to modernize the market-making function and make it more competitive and effective.

## Derivatives Exchanges

CME Group (CME), headquartered in Chicago, is the world's largest and most diverse derivatives exchange. Derivatives include options, futures, and swaps. *Futures* are contracts to buy or sell an asset on a specific date in the future at a price determined today. This is in contrast to spot contracts, which are for immediate delivery. *Options* are contracts between a buyer and seller that give the buyer the right, but not the obligation, to buy or sell a designated asset at a future date at an agreed upon price. *Swaps* are contracts in which two counterparties agree to exchange one stream of cash flows for another stream of cash flows. Since launching an IPO in 2002, the market capitalization of CME has grown to be the largest of any derivatives exchange in the world, approximately double the value of NYSE Euronext, the most valuable stock exchange. Instead of stocks and bonds, derivatives are traded on this exchange. With customers utilizing a nearly 24-hour electronic trading platform for some products, remarkable trading volume is generated at the CME. The exchange offers futures and options based on benchmark products available across all major asset classes, including interest rates, equity indexes, foreign exchange, energy, agricultural commodities, metals, and alternative products such as weather and real estate. The futures and options contracts for these asset classes enable counterparties a means for hedging, speculation, and asset allocation in relation to risks associated with interest rate sensitive instruments, equity market exposure, changes in the value of foreign currency, and changes in the prices of commodities.

The largest agricultural commodities product is corn, where over 319,000 futures and options contracts trade daily. The largest interest rate product is Eurodollars, where over 2 million futures contracts trade daily, and interest rate futures on 10-year U.S. Treasury Notes, where over 1 million contracts trade daily. The largest equity product is the E-mini S&P 500 futures contract, which trades over 2.5 million contracts daily, and other equity index futures and options, where over 1 million contracts trade daily. In addition, there is daily trading of more than 1.4 million energy futures and options contracts, 600,000 FX futures and options contracts, and 230,000 metals futures and options contracts.

CME is now largely an electronic exchange. All major investment banks trade at the exchange for their own account and on behalf of their investing and hedging clients. All trades require the posting of margin that changes daily based on the value of the futures and options contracts that counterparties enter into. The margin positions must be adjusted daily in order to manage risk properly. Margin obligations are met by cash or performance bonds and vary according to product and associated volatility. The effect of the margin system is to prevent failures to deliver value at contract expiration.

Futures exchanges (a subset of derivatives exchanges) are regulated in the United States principally by the Commodities Futures Trading Commission (CFTC), since futures contracts are not deemed to be securities, which fall under the regulatory scope of the SEC. Other large international futures/derivatives exchanges include Eurex, NYSE Euronext, BM&F Bovespa, and Intercontinental Exchange (ICE).

## Over-the-Counter Market

Securities and derivatives that are listed and traded on an exchange are called listed instruments. Securities and derivatives that trade directly between two parties, without an exchange as intermediary, are called over-the-counter (OTC) instruments. Unlike listed trades, OTC trades are not in the public domain and, unless reported by the parties to the trade, remain confidential. OTC stock trades in the United States are sometimes reported by investment banks to either the OTC Bulletin Board (OTCBB), if the relevant company files required reports with the SEC, and/or to Pink Sheets (so named because stock quotes are printed on pink sheets), if the relevant company does not file required reports with the SEC. With the exception of a few foreign issuers that have issued American Depositary Receipts (ADRs), companies quoted in the Pink Sheets are generally smaller and have thinly traded stock. These companies are usually much riskier than listed companies or OTCBB traded companies.

The OTC market for derivatives is much larger than the market for listed derivatives. Derivatives are financial instruments whose value changes in response to changes in an underlying security or other asset. Derivatives have two uses: reducing risks and allowing speculation. They are tied to many different types of assets, including stocks, bonds, interest rates, exchange rates, commodities, and indexes.

Due to exceptional growth experienced by the global OTC derivatives market, regulators are increasingly concerned about the potential systemic risk posed by this market. The Bank for International Settlements estimates that as of June 2008, the total outstanding notional amount of OTC derivatives was $684 trillion, which is more than eight times higher than the total amount of exchange-traded derivative contracts (see Exhibit 7.5).

Because regulators and politicians believed that financial institutions' involvement in OTC derivatives contributed to the financial crisis in 2008, U.S. regulators announced in May of 2009 a proposal to increase federal regulation of the previously under-regulated OTC market.

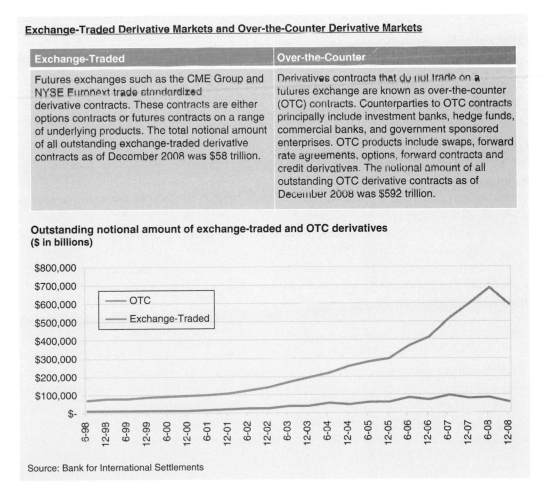

**Exchange-Traded Derivative Markets and Over-the-Counter Derivative Markets**

| Exchange-Traded | Over-the-Counter |
| --- | --- |
| Futures exchanges such as the CME Group and NYSE Euronext trade standardized derivative contracts. These contracts are either options contracts or futures contracts on a range of underlying products. The total notional amount of all outstanding exchange-traded derivative contracts as of December 2008 was $58 trillion. | Derivatives contracts that do not trade on a futures exchange are known as over-the-counter (OTC) contracts. Counterparties to OTC contracts principally include investment banks, hedge funds, commercial banks, and government sponsored enterprises. OTC products include swaps, forward rate agreements, options, forward contracts and credit derivatives. The notional amount of all outstanding OTC derivative contracts as of December 2008 was $592 trillion. |

**Outstanding notional amount of exchange-traded and OTC derivatives ($ in billions)**

Source: Bank for International Settlements

**EXHIBIT 7.5**

These financial regulatory reforms attempt to increase transparency and promote market discipline by requiring many standard OTC derivative contracts to be cleared through regulated central counterparties such as exchanges. These contracts are to be guaranteed by the exchange, mitigating the risk of systemic failure from the collapse of one large counterparty (see additional discussions on transaction clearing in the next section). New reporting requirements for firms with significant positions in complex derivative transactions are also proposed. The legislation is designed to bring a higher level of disclosure across all major players in the derivatives market. Regulators in many of the world's major capital centers are considering adoption of similar regulations in an effort to create greater disclosure and reduce systemic risk.

## Clearing and Settlement

Investment banks are inextricably linked with exchanges in clearing and settling listed securities and derivatives transactions. Clearing and settlement starts with an effort to capture trade data between counterparties and making sure the terms of buyers' and sellers' trade records match perfectly. This is the *front end* of the trade. Clearing also involves *novation,* in which the central counterparty clearinghouse (CCP) substitutes for the original counterparties in relation to future performance of all remaining obligations. For each transaction that is to be cleared, the original contract is replaced with two contracts with the CCP, one where the CCP is the buyer, and one where the CCP is the seller. CCPs use a risk management system that includes the posting of collateral to support a guarantee that is provided by the CCP to transacting parties in a trade. Each exchange has its own clearinghouse, and all members of the exchange are generally required to clear their trades through the clearinghouse.

### Securities Settlement

Securities are accounted for electronically by *book-entry* in an electronic table. Transfer of ownership of a security is based on the simultaneous transfer of funds to pay for the security, which is called *delivery versus payment.* Once title to the security has been passed to the buyer, the clearing and settlement process ends and the custody process begins. Bank CDs and commercial paper settle on the same business day ("for cash"); U.S. Treasury securities settle the next business day ("for regular"); and FX settles 2 business days after the trade ("T + 2"). U.S. equity securities settle 3 business days after the trade ("T + 3").

Settlement default risk arises from two sources. First, the seller either does not have or does not properly deliver securities on the settlement date. This is called a *short fail.* Second, the buyer fails to pay for the security, which is called a *long fail.* Exchanges have automatic procedures that temporarily mitigate both long and short fails, including cash collateral and netting arrangements.

To reduce the number of transactions that must be settled, exchanges have a multilateral netting system. Since most settlements with an exchange are completed between an investment bank and an exchange, and since banks typically have many purchases and sales of the same security, their net delivery obligation is determined by the exchange. All details of settlement obligations must be resolved before the close of business the day after the trade was originally consummated. The funding side of settlement is netted down to a single payment made either by the exchange to an investment bank or by the bank to the exchange.

## Derivatives Settlement

Derivatives are also accounted for electronically through a book-entry system. Other than this initial similarity, clearing and settlement of derivatives is quite different from that of securities. Instead of clearing and settling within 3 days, derivatives often remain outstanding for a much longer time—sometimes months and years. Unlike securities, where the security is delivered and simultaneously paid for in full, derivatives represent an obligation (if a futures or swap contract) or an option (if an options contract) to buy or sell a financial instrument or asset at a future date, which can be weeks, months, or years in the future. As a result, the buyer and seller pose financial risks to an exchange for an extended period of time. Because of this large risk, exchanges require daily mark-to-market posting and adjustment of collateral based on the changing value of the derivatives contract. Derivatives therefore require substantially more complex risk management systems than are required for securities.

As is the case with securities, for exchange-traded derivative transactions, investment banks that initiate trades (on their own behalf or for clients) novate the transactions by substituting the exchange's clearinghouse as the counterparty to the trade. This results in the creation of two new contracts with a guarantee of closing provided by the exchange on both contracts. Novation also allows the liquidation of derivative contracts prior to maturity, which is not possible for a security.

In addition to providing risk management, margining, and collateral management services to investment banks and other users of an exchange, the exchange also provides a performance guarantee and anonymity between counterparties. To protect itself from financial loss that will occur if an investment bank or other counterparty fails to deliver against their trading obligations, exchanges require all counterparties to deposit performance collateral. Generally speaking, this performance collateral is set at levels that should cover at least one day's expected market movement for the instruments that underlie each trade.

## Investment Banking Services

Investment banks collect fees on all transactions that they clear and settle on behalf of investing and hedging clients. In addition, banks act as custodians for securities owned by their clients. This can be a significant source of revenue for banks: for example, in 2008, J.P. Morgan reported Worldwide Securities Services revenue (clearing and custody related revenue) of approximately $4.6 billion (7% of net revenues), with over $13 trillion in assets under custody.

# Questions

1. Compare the different roles provided to the investor community by credit rating analysts and sell-side research analysts.
2. What is the difference between business risk and financial risk?
3. What precipitated the decline in CDO values during the 2007–2008 credit crisis?
4. What are the major criticisms directed at Moody's, Standard & Poor's, and Fitch?
5. In 2001, the NYSE switched from a fractional pricing system (stock priced in increments of 1/8 of a dollar) to a decimal pricing system (stock priced in increments as small as 1 cent). Explain how this might encourage front-running by traders?
6. Why might OTC derivatives be considered more risky than exchange-traded derivatives?
7. How is derivatives settlement different from securities settlement?

# 8

# International Banking

Investment banking is a global business, with most of the largest firms operating in more than 20 countries. This chapter focuses on (a) Euromarkets; (b) financing and advisory activity in Japan, China, and Emerging Markets; (c) the global IPO market; and (d) selected other international banking topics.

## Euromarkets

*Euromarkets* is the generic term used in international capital markets for securities issued and held outside the issuer's country of origin. Bonds that trade in this market are called *Eurobonds*. Euromarkets exist to facilitate cross-border financings by corporations and sovereign entities and were originally created in response to the Cold War during the 1950s. The Soviet Union at that time was concerned that holding U.S. dollar deposits (largely generated from sale of oil) in the United States would enable the U.S. government to freeze these assets. As a result, they deposited their U.S. dollars with European banks in Europe, outside of the control of the U.S. government. Due to restrictions on dollar-lending activities to foreign companies and ceiling limits on interest rates offered for deposits, U.S. banks also moved significant dollar balances to their merchant banking offices in Europe. All of this gave rise to a very large amount of U.S. dollars deposited mostly in London and has led to remarkable growth in the Euromarkets, especially after OPEC countries began depositing U.S. dollars received from oil sales outside of the United States during the 1980s.

Although London is the unofficial center of the Euromarkets, Frankfurt and Paris are large centers as well. One reason European cities dominate this market is due to their geographic convenience to markets in the Americas and Asia. Euromarkets can also be considered to include certain Caribbean countries such as the Cayman Islands, which have significant foreign deposits as well. The Euromarkets are attractive because they are, for the most part, unregulated and sometimes offer higher yields to investors. This market has become a significant source of global liquidity.

Eurobonds are debt instruments that are listed on an exchange in bearer form (i.e., owned by whomever is holding the security instead of in registered form with registered owners). They are issued and traded outside the country whose currency the Eurobond is denominated in, and outside the regulations of a single country. Interest income from these bonds is exempt from withholding tax and the bonds are generally not registered with any regulatory body. For example, while a U.S. corporation's domestic bonds are subject to SEC oversight, its Eurobonds are not (unless offered concurrently to U.S. investors). The market is self-regulated through the International Capital Markets Association (ICMA). Eurobonds are generally issued by multinational corporations or sovereign entities of high credit quality. An international syndicate of banks typically underwrites a Eurobond issuance and distributes bonds to investors in a number of countries (other than the headquarter country of the issuer).

Eurobonds can be issued in many forms, including fixed-rate coupon bonds (interest is usually payable annually and principal is due in bullet form), convertible bonds, zero-coupon bonds, and floating rate notes. Eurobonds issued in U.S. dollars are called *Eurodollar bonds*; Eurobonds issued in Japanese yen are called *Euroyen bonds*. There are many other currencies in which Eurobonds are issued, including pound sterling, euro, and Canadian dollar, among others. In each case, the Eurobond is named after the currency in which it is denominated. Almost all Eurobonds are owned "electronically" rather than in physical form and are settled through either Euroclear or Clearstream, two global electronic depository systems.

## London's Financial Market

One-quarter of the world's largest financial companies have their European headquarters in London. There are more than 550 banks and 170 global securities firms that have London offices, more than any other city in the world. The London foreign exchange market is the largest in the world, with average daily turnover in excess of $500 billion. The London market has captured more than one-third of the OTC derivatives market and manages almost half of European institutional equity capital. The London Inter-Bank Offer Rate (LIBOR), which represents the interest rate that banks charge each other for short-term loans, is recorded every day in London and disseminated worldwide as the most-used base rate in the world for determining loan pricing.

# Japan's Financial Market

During the 1980s, Japan's stock market skyrocketed to remarkable levels. The price to earnings (PE) ratio for the Nikkei-225 stock index reached above 70×, nearly four times higher than the U.S. S&P 500 stock index PE ratio of approximately 18×. This market was buoyed by high real estate prices and an interlocking corporate ownership structure that was common in Japan. Unfortunately, after reaching a high of almost 39,000 in January 1990, the Nikkei-225 index fell more than 50% during that year. Although the market has since seen considerable volatility, it has never returned to the historical high, and as of mid-2009, was below 10,000. An innovative investment banking transaction that relates to Japan's financial market crash is summarized in Chapter 9, in the section on Nikkei Put Warrants.

The principal banking institutions in Japan have changed dramatically through mergers over the past 20 years. There are currently three large banks: Mitsubishi UFJ Financial Group, Mizuho Financial Group, and Sumitomo Mitsui Financial Group. Each of these banks operates principally as a commercial bank, with somewhat limited securities activities. However, during 2008, in the wake of the credit crisis that weakened many of Wall Street's investment banks, Mitsubishi made a significant investment in Morgan Stanley, acquiring approximately 21% of the U.S. firm's stock. The largest pure-play securities firms in Japan are Nomura Securities and Daiwa SMBC. When Lehman Brothers failed during 2008, Nomura Securities acquired most of Lehman's businesses in Asia and Europe, substantially bolstering its global investment banking presence.

## M&A in Japan

Due to a restrictive regulatory environment, the M&A market in Japan had been slow to develop. However, new legislation passed in the past decade helped to accelerate the pace of deal making in Japan. In 2003, a new law permitted non-Japanese companies to use their own stock to acquire Japanese companies that were under Japanese bankruptcy court protection. This was followed by a 2007 law that further extended the ability of foreign companies to use their stock to acquire Japanese companies, as well as other laws that lowered the threshold shareholder approval requirement for an acquisition. As a result, it is likely that M&A activity will increase in Japan in the future.

One of the most successful foreign acquisitions in Japan was initiated by Ripplewood, a U.S.-based private equity firm. Ripplewood led the buyout of Long-Term Credit Bank (LTCB) in 2000, which was suffering a severe financial reversal. As part of the acquisition agreement, the Japanese government agreed to purchase any LTCB assets that fell by 20% or more post-acquisition. As a result, the bank sold its worst assets at above market prices to the government following the acquisition. LTCB was renamed Shinsei Bank, and with new management and Ripplewood's ongoing support, the bank became profitable. Ripplewood subsequently monetized its investment by taking Shinsei Bank public in 2004, achieving a reported profit of over $1 billion for its 4-year holding.

## Equity Financing in Japan

More than 70% of equity underwriting in Japan is conducted by Nomura, Mitsubishi, and Daiwa. Although foreign investment banks can also underwrite Japanese securities, they have limited distribution networks, and therefore most of their underwriting activities are directed to companies whose stocks trade on the Second Section of the Tokyo or Osaka stock exchanges (mid-sized companies trade on the Second Section while large-cap companies trade on the First Section). However, foreign investment banks sometimes are able to act as a co-lead bookrunner in partnership with one of the big three Japanese securities firms when First Section listed companies desire a strong distribution capability outside of Japan.

## Trading Securities in Japan

Japanese government bonds are issued in the form of short-term Treasury bills and longer-term coupon bonds and zero-coupon bonds ranging from maturities of 2 to 30 years. Bond auctions are conducted by the Ministry of Finance (MOF) and can be bid for by Japanese banks and securities firms, as well as by qualified foreign firms.

Japanese corporations have historically relied principally on bank borrowings for their debt financings. As a result, the Japanese corporate bond market is small relative to the country's GDP, when compared to the U.S. or U.K. corporate bond markets. However, over the past 15 years, which has been a difficult time for the Japanese banking sector, the Japanese corporate bond market has grown substantially. Banks are increasingly applying stricter covenants in their loans to corporations and are encouraging many clients to allow them to underwrite bonds, rather than complete bank borrowings. This trend has recently allowed several U.S. and European firms to break into the top bond underwriter rankings in Japan.

Trading in equity securities is largely centered on the Tokyo Stock Exchange (TSE), which accounts for over 80% of all trading volume in the country. In addition to Japanese firms, a limited number of non-Japanese companies list their shares on the TSE. The remainder of the trading volume in Japan is generated from four other equity exchanges: Osaka, Nagoya, Fukuoka, and Sapporo.

# China's Financial Market

China's financial market has seen dramatic growth and increasing sophistication as regulatory barriers have been reduced and the country's economy has grown rapidly. This growth has been facilitated in part by the government's relaxation of its foreign exchange controls in 1996. Under relaxed regulations, current account renminbi (RMB) became convertible (subject to certain restrictions) into other currencies. This was followed in 2002 with the creation of the Qualified Financial Institutional Investor (QFII) program, which allowed qualifying foreign investors to participate in the Chinese equity market via domestic A-shares and in the Chinese debt market. Many non-Chinese financial institutions have since obtained the QFII designation, enabling them to participate in these markets.

## M&A in China

Non-domestic M&A activity in China has historically been limited. However, because of China's accession to the World Trade Organization in 2001, there are now more opportunities for foreign investment. China has restructured many of its state-owned assets and is encouraging some of these enterprises to consolidate into larger companies. As a result, a large number of state-owned enterprises are being made available for restructuring or partnering with foreign companies. There is a high level of government participation in all M&A transactions in China, with the Ministry of Commerce and the State Development and Reform Commission focusing on not only antitrust issues but also on economic and social consequences. In addition, the Ministry of Commerce is the principal foreign investment regulator and has general supervisory and approval authority over M&A transactions. Finally, the State-Owned Assets Supervision and Administration Commission and the China Securities Regulatory Commission are also involved in approving, monitoring, and regulating state-owned or listed company M&A transactions.

Foreign companies are not permitted to operate business directly in China. To conduct business in China, a company must operate through a Foreign Investment Enterprise (FIE). The percentage of foreign ownership allowable in a FIE depends on the industry: 100% ownership is permitted for some industries, but for others, the percentage of foreign ownership is restricted. FIEs can be set up as joint ventures (JVs), wholly owned foreign enterprises (WOFEs), or foreign-invested companies limited by shares (FCLS).

## Equity Financing in China

The Shanghai Stock Exchange and the Hong Kong Stock Exchange are the two largest exchanges in China. The market capitalization of domestic shares trading on both exchanges reached an aggregate high of over $6 trillion in 2007. Although market capitalization fell during 2008 due to the global financial crisis (combined market capitalization at the end of 2008 was $2.8 trillion, less than half the capitalization compared to 2007), these exchanges maintained their rankings as the world's sixth and seventh largest exchanges due to the global impact of the crisis. Stock market valuations rebounded strongly on these two exchanges during 2009. The next largest exchange in China is the Shenzhen Stock Exchange. The market capitalization of shares trading on this exchange was $353 billion at the end of 2008. Plans are under way to designate the Shenzhen Stock Exchange as the Growth Enterprise Market (GEM) for China. This market will be similar to NASDAQ in the United States, specializing in smaller-market capitalization and predominantly high-tech companies. Acceptance of listing applications by the China Securities Regulatory Commission commenced in July 2009.

Chinese companies may issue A-shares or B-shares on the Shanghai or Shenzhen exchanges. A-shares are limited to purchases by only Chinese residents and QFIIs, and are denominated in renminbi. B-shares can be purchased by foreign investors and, as of 2001, by Chinese residents as well. These shares cannot be converted into A-shares and are denominated in renminbi, but traded in either U.S. dollars (in Shanghai) or Hong Kong dollars (in Shenzhen). Dividends and capital gains from B-shares can be sent outside of China, and foreign securities firms can act as dealers for these shares.

Foreign investors can also invest in Chinese shares through purchasing shares listed in Hong Kong (H-shares). These shares are listed to facilitate offshore financing by Chinese companies and can only be traded by foreign investors or Hong Kong residents and not by mainland Chinese residents. H-shares are denominated in Hong Kong dollars. Hong Kong-headquartered companies (which can be incorporated in Hong Kong or certain offshore jurisdictions) that are controlled by mainland Chinese companies, or that derive significant revenue from mainland China customers, issue *Red Chip* stock.

The growth and popularity of the H-share and Red Chip markets in Hong Kong has led to a decline in the B-share markets. Today, there are more than 10 times as many A shares as B-shares trading on the two mainland exchanges, and the aggregate market value of all B-shares is less than 1% of the aggregate market value of A-shares. This decline has led to a gradual withdrawal of foreign institutional funds as liquidity in the B-share markets continues to dwindle. The majority of B-share investors are now domestic retail investors. Due to the diminishing utility of having a separate A- and B-share market, there is speculation that Chinese regulators will merge the B-share market into the A-share market.

UBS, Goldman Sachs, and Morgan Stanley have historically dominated the equity underwriting league tables in Hong Kong for H-shares. In mainland China, Chinese securities firms, including China International Capital Corp. (one-third owned but not managed by Morgan Stanley) and China Galaxy Securities Co. dominate the rankings for A-share underwriting.

## Trading Securities in China

Over 200 bond products trade on the Shanghai Stock Exchange, including Treasury bonds, enterprise bonds (issued by government-owned enterprises), corporate bonds, and convertible bonds. There are also over 1,000 listed companies and more than 25 securities investment funds and 20 warrants listed on the exchange.

The corporate bond market in China is very small, with negligible trading volume. China's banks provide almost all of the debt financing required by borrowers. Only 6% of all Chinese bonds are issued by nonfinancial enterprises, providing just 1.5% of the total financial needs of corporations in China. The Chinese bond market has three major players: the Central Bank is responsible for a 37% market share, the Chinese government has a 31% share, and Chinese policy banks represent a 23% market share.

Chinese government bonds trade both on exchanges and over-the-counter. The Ministry of Finance issues Treasury bonds, construction bonds, fiscal bonds, and other "special" bonds. Policy banks such as Export-Import Bank and China Development Bank issue bonds to support infrastructure projects and strategic industries. These bonds are considered to be only slightly riskier than government bonds. Bonds issued by the government and by policy banks are important tools for the central bank in managing the country's monetary and fiscal policies.

## International Investment Banking Activity in China

Most major investment banks have actively pursued business opportunities in China. However, tight regulatory controls by the Chinese government have limited the entry of these banks to only certain areas of the domestic market. In addition, depending on when the bank entered the

Chinese market, the level of authorization varied according to the legislation in place at that time. In general, these banks can only participate in domestic securities underwriting through JVs set up with Chinese securities firms whereby the foreign bank owns no more than a one-third share in the entity. Goldman Sachs and UBS set up their JVs in 2004 and 2005, respectively, and are the only two foreign banks that have been allowed management control over their JVs. The three other major foreign banks that have domestic securities underwriting approval (Morgan Stanley, Credit Suisse, and Deutsche Bank) only have passive ownership in their JV entities. A summary of major foreign investment bank investments in China is provided in Exhibit 8.1. A summary of foreign investment bank revenue in China is summarized in Exhibit 8.2.

### Foreign Banking Investments in China

- Morgan Stanley entered into a joint venture, China International Capital Corporation (CICC), with China Construction Bank in 1995.

- Citigroup bought 5% of Shanghai Pudong Development Bank for $67 million in 2002.

- Goldman Sachs owns 33% of a joint venture with Gao Hua Securities called Goldman Sachs Gao Hua Securities that was set up at the end of 2004.  This gave Goldman Sachs entrance into the domestic securities underwriting business.

- UBS acquired 20% of Beijing Securities in 2005, which gave the bank its license to underwrite domestic securities.

- Bank of America (then Merrill Lynch) entered into JV agreement with Huaan Securities in 2005, with a 33% stake in the venture. However, in 2007, after failing to get approvals from the Chinese government, the bank cancelled its agreement with Huaan.

- Bank of America (then Merrill Lynch) and Royal Bank of Scotland, with other investors, acquired 10% of Bank of China for $3.1 billion in 2005.

- Credit Suisse entered into a JV with Founder Securities in 2008, and subsequently received regulatory approval in 2009 to underwrite domestic securities.

- Bank of America initially paid $3 billion in 2005 for a 9% in China Construction Bank (CCB); in late 2008, the bank paid an additional $7 billion to increase the holding to 19.1%.  During May, 2009, Bank of America raised $7.3 billion from the sale of a 5.7% stake in CCB.

- Goldman Sachs, Allianz and American Express paid $3.8 billion in 2006 for a 10% ownership in the Industrial and Commercial Bank of China (ICBC). During June, 2009, Goldman Sachs raised more than $1.9 billion from the sale of an almost 1% holding in ICBC, leaving Goldman Sachs with a remaining 4% stake.

- Deutsche Bank entered into a JV with Shanxi Securities in 2009. The new venture is named Zhong De Securities and has regulatory approval to underwrite domestic securities.

- Over 30 other firms have established QFIIs and received permission to invest over $4 billion.

Source: Company press releases

**EXHIBIT 8.1**

## Emerging Financial Markets

Emerging markets countries are countries in a transitional phase between developing and developed status. Examples include India, Mexico, China, most of Southeast Asia, and countries in Eastern Europe and the Middle East (countries included in MSCI Barra's Emerging Market Index are listed in Exhibit 8.3).

### Foreign Investment Banks' Securities Business Revenue in China

Foreign (non-Chinese) investment banks (shaded in light green) have been able to capture a large share of investment banking fees generated in China:

| China M&A, ECM and DCM Revenue Ranking – 2007 | | | | China M&A, ECM and DCM Revenue Ranking – 2008 | | | |
|---|---|---|---|---|---|---|---|
| | Bank | Fees ($m) | % Share | | Bank | Fees ($m) | % Share |
| 1 | UBS | 276.5 | 12.4 | 1 | UBS | 75.6 | 8.0 |
| 2 | Morgan Stanley | 250.4 | 11.2 | 2 | Morgan Stanley | 74.8 | 8.0 |
| 3 | Goldman Sachs | 186.1 | 8.3 | 3 | Credit Suisse | 59.8 | 6.4 |
| 4 | J.P. Morgan | 142.3 | 6.4 | 4 | CITIC Securities | 53.2 | 5.7 |
| 5 | Bank of America Merrill Lynch | 135.4 | 6.1 | 5 | Nomura | 52.8 | 5.6 |
| 6 | Credit Suisse | 107.0 | 4.8 | 6 | China Int'l Capital Corp Ltd | 51.0 | 5.4 |
| 7 | Bank of China Ltd | 101.8 | 4.6 | 7 | Citi | 46.1 | 4.9 |
| 8 | Deutsche Bank | 92.4 | 4.1 | 8 | J.P. Morgan | 44.3 | 4.7 |
| 9 | China Int'l Capital Corp Ltd | 89.9 | 4.0 | 9 | Bank of America Merrill Lynch | 41.8 | 4.4 |
| 10 | Citi | 85.7 | 3.8 | 10 | Goldman Sachs | 37.3 | 4.0 |
| | **Subtotal** | **1,467.4** | **65.8** | | **Subtotal** | **536.4** | **57.0** |
| | **Total** | **2,230.0** | **100.0** | | **Total** | **940.5** | **100.0** |

Source: Dealogic

**EXHIBIT 8.2**

### MSCI Barra's Emerging Market Index

The MSCI Emerging Market Index is designed to measure equity market performance in global emerging markets. This Index is a float-adjusted market capitalization index. As of September, 2009, it consists of indices in 22 emerging economies:

| Brazil | Chile | China | Colombia | Czech Republic |
|---|---|---|---|---|
| Egypt | Hungary | India | Indonesia | Israel |
| Korea | Malaysia | Mexico | Morocco | Peru |
| Philippines | Poland | Russia | South Africa | Taiwan |
| Thailand | Turkey | | | |

Source: MSCI Barra

**EXHIBIT 8.3**

Conducting investment banking activities in emerging markets countries represents both significant revenue opportunities and correspondingly large risks. Some investment banks have prioritized activities in these countries and have been very successful. Included among the most successful banks are Citigroup, Goldman Sachs, UBS, J.P. Morgan, Morgan Stanley, Deutsche Bank, and Credit Suisse. These firms have focused on a broad array of business activities, including securities underwriting, syndicated lending, M&A, and a significant number of trading and investing initiatives.

Incremental risks associated with investment banking business in these countries include currency, political, liquidity, accounting, tax, and volatility risks. Currencies in some of these countries are subject to rapid, sometimes unanticipated changes based on significant dislocations in a country's credit or stock markets. Political risk can significantly impact a securities market if a government expropriates property or if there is a political coup. A country's securities market can also be significantly impacted if liquidity dries up. This can happen based on government limitations on foreign investments or if large blocks of shares are held by founding investors who refuse to share control or profits. Accounting and tax policies can sometimes change in an unanticipated manner in emerging market countries, putting investing and underwriting activities at risk. Finally, high volatility is part and parcel of most emerging market countries, with occasional wild swings in securities prices that are difficult to anticipate and hedge.

In spite of these risks, most large investment banks have prioritized development of their emerging markets business, since these countries are expected to grow significantly and develop more efficient capital markets. Many of these countries are improving their legal system to better support enforcement of contracts. They are also improving disclosure requirements and corporate governance practices. Finally, they are increasing privatization of previously government-owned businesses, allowing individual ownership of shares. All of this suggests that investment banks will be able to profitably expand their activities in these countries if they properly monitor and control risk procedures.

## Bonds

Credit ratings for bonds issued by emerging market countries and for the countries themselves are important considerations in the development of robust securities markets. Ratings are provided by rating agencies such as S&P, Moody's, and Fitch, as well as by specialty publishers such as Institutional Investor (see Exhibit 8.4). In addition to affecting a country's currency, country credit ratings can also have an important impact on the universe of investors able to invest in the country. For example, most institutional investors cannot invest in countries below a certain credit rating. A ratings upgrade, therefore, can potentially increase the pool of investors for a country's securities.

Annual secondary market trading of emerging market bonds and other emerging market debt securities is estimated to exceed $6 trillion. Emerging market debt securities include Brady bonds (discussed shortly), sovereign and corporate Eurobonds, local market debt, and sovereign loans. Approximately 50% of this trading volume is represented by trading in debt instruments denominated and traded in the issuer's home country.

## Syndicated Loans

Syndicated loans have historically been the key source of new capital for emerging markets countries. Unfortunately, during the 1980s most of these loans defaulted. In order to mitigate losses that banks were accruing, Brady bonds were created in 1989: bonds were issued to banks in exchange for their nonperforming loans. In most cases these bonds were tradable and came with guarantees from various governments. In addition, the bonds were usually collateralized by U.S. Treasury 30-year zero-coupon bonds purchased by the debtor country using a combination of IMF, World Bank, and the country's own foreign currency reserves. This allowed banks to remove the bonds from their balance sheets and the borrowers to regain the ability to pay off existing debt and issue new debt. A large share of all Brady bonds has now been repaid.

## Equity

Many emerging market countries have removed most barriers to foreign investor purchases of equity. However, there are still some restrictions that limit the trading activities of international investment banks in most of these countries. Principal equity trading activity in emerging market

## Global Credit Ranking for Emerging Market Countries

| Rank (Mar 2009) | Country | Institutional Investor Credit Rating | One-Year Change |
|---|---|---|---|
| 25 | Taiwan | 78.8 | -1.6 |
| 27 | Chile | 76.7 | -0.7 |
| 32 | Czech Republic | 74.7 | -1.7 |
| 34 | China | 74.1 | -2.4 |
| 36 | South Korea | 72.6 | -7.3 |
| 38 | Poland | 71.5 | -1.5 |
| 39 | Malaysia | 70.3 | -2.6 |
| 43 | Israel | 67.8 | -1.4 |
| 45 | Mexico | 65.7 | -3.6 |
| 47 | Russia | 64.6 | -4.8 |
| 48 | Brazil | 62.5 | 1.9 |
| 50 | South Africa | 61.1 | -4.7 |
| 52 | India | 59.9 | -2.8 |
| 54 | Thailand | 59.6 | -3.5 |
| 55 | Hungary | 59.2 | -7.6 |
| 56 | Peru | 58.8 | 1.1 |
| 60 | Colombia | 55.3 | 0.6 |
| 63 | Morocco | 53.7 | -1.4 |
| 69 | Egypt | 49.9 | -0.8 |
| 72 | Turkey | 49.0 | -3.0 |
| 74 | Indonesia | 47.5 | -0.7 |
| 75 | Philippines | 47.1 | -2.6 |

Source: Institutional Investor

**EXHIBIT 8.4**

countries relates to ADR (American Depositary Receipt) and GDR (Global Depositary Receipt) issues by some of the larger companies in the emerging markets. Another important trading activity of the investment banks is in emerging market exchange-traded funds. These funds, usually benchmarked off of indexes created by MSCI Barra (a spin-off of Morgan Stanley), enable investors to purchase U.S.-dollar-based exposure to different emerging market countries based on country indexes (MSCI Brazil Index Fund, MSCI South Africa Index Fund, or MSCI Taiwan Index Fund, etc.). MSCI Barra also has a broad-based index called MSCI Emerging Index Fund, which captures equity market exposure to the emerging markets countries listed in Exhibit 8.3.

## M&A

Most large investment banks have reasonably active emerging markets M&A businesses. Risks must be carefully balanced against expected returns to be successful in this market. Risks that are especially important to consider include intellectual property, political, legal, currency, operational, and financing risks. All of these risks are much higher in emerging market countries and should be factored into deal considerations. For example, in an M&A DCF valuation, WACC

**Emerging Market M&A League Tables, 2008 and 1H-2009**

| 2008 Latin America Completed M&A Advisor Rankings[1] | | | |
|---|---|---|---|
| Rank | Advisor | Value $bn | No. |
| 1 | Credit Suisse | $30.2 | 38 |
| 2 | J.P. Morgan | $24.4 | 31 |
| 3 | Citi | $22.9 | 30 |
| 4 | UBS | $20.6 | 38 |
| 5 | Goldman Sachs | $19.7 | 16 |
| 6 | Rothschild | $14.1 | 15 |
| 7 | Banco Bradesco SA | $10.2 | 10 |
| 8 | Banco Itau SA | $8.6 | 6 |
| 9 | Morgan Stanley | $6.6 | 15 |
| 10 | Bank of America Merrill Lynch | $5.6 | 18 |

| 2008 Eastern Europe Completed M&A Advisor Rankings[1] | | | |
|---|---|---|---|
| Rank | Advisor | Value $bn | No. |
| 1 | Bank of America Merrill Lynch | $68.8 | 35 |
| 2 | J.P. Morgan | $53.0 | 32 |
| 3 | Credit Suisse | $41.1 | 23 |
| 4 | IFC Metropol | $37.0 | 34 |
| 5 | KIT Finance Holding Co OOO | $31.2 | 22 |
| 6 | Deutsche Bank | $19.8 | 32 |
| 7 | Renaissance Capital | $19.8 | 17 |
| 8 | UBS | $12.1 | 8 |
| 9 | Citi | $12.0 | 15 |
| 10 | Otkritie Financial Corp - OFC | $11.9 | 49 |

| 1H-09 Latin America Completed M&A Advisor Rankings[1] | | | |
|---|---|---|---|
| Rank | Advisor | Value $bn | No. |
| 1 | Morgan Stanley | $17.4 | 7 |
| 2 | Rothschild | $16.6 | 11 |
| 3 | Banco Itau SA | $14.1 | 6 |
| 4 | J.P. Morgan | $9.0 | 16 |
| 5 | Citi | $8.1 | 10 |
| 6 | Credit Suisse | $7.5 | 10 |
| 7 | UBS | $5.3 | 7 |
| 8 | Barclays Capital | $2.8 | 2 |
| 9 | CIBC World Markets | $2.6 | 2 |
| 10 | Atlas Strategic Advisors | $2.5 | 1 |

| 1H-09 Eastern Europe Completed M&A Advisor Rankings[1] | | | |
|---|---|---|---|
| Rank | Advisor | Value $bn | No. |
| 1 | J.P. Morgan | $10.0 | 13 |
| 2 | Bank of America Merrill Lynch | $8.5 | 5 |
| 3 | Credit Suisse | $5.2 | 6 |
| 4 | Deutsche Bank | $5.0 | 6 |
| 5 | Gazprombank | $4.8 | 3 |
| 6 | Citi | $4.3 | 2 |
| 7 | Rothschild | $3.9 | 7 |
| 8 | BNP Paribas | $3.8 | 3 |
| 9 | RBS | $2.8 | 7 |
| 10 | RZB | $2.6 | 9 |

Note 1: Any region involvement – includes acquiror, target or divestor
Source: Dealogic

**EXHIBIT 8.5**

should be adjusted higher, depending on the country. It is also important to consider a wide range of potential growth rates. League tables for M&A activity in emerging markets countries are provided in Exhibit 8.5.

# Global IPO Market

During 2007, global IPO financings raised nearly $300 billion in proceeds, with Brazil, Russia, India, and China, or BRIC countries, accounting for $105 billion (35%) of this volume. Three years earlier, in 2004, this same group of countries comprised just 11% of total global IPO proceeds (see Exhibit 8.6). BRIC's share of the global IPO market temporarily decreased to 22% in 2008, mostly stemming from the ongoing uncertainty and market turmoil caused by the global credit crisis. During 2009, however, BRIC IPOs regained much of their prior momentum and comprised nearly half of global IPOs.

Because of U.S. regulatory restraints, GAAP (Generally Accepted Accounting Principles) reporting requirements, high U.S. costs, and development of other equity capital markets, most of the world's IPOs are now launched outside of the United States (see Exhibit 8.7).

# BRIC IPOs

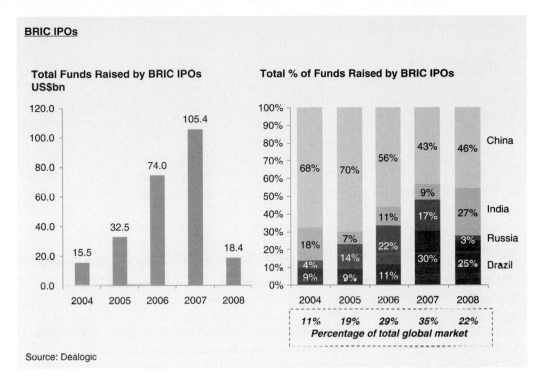

**Total Funds Raised by BRIC IPOs US$bn**

**Total % of Funds Raised by BRIC IPOs**

Source: Dealogic

**EXHIBIT 8.6**

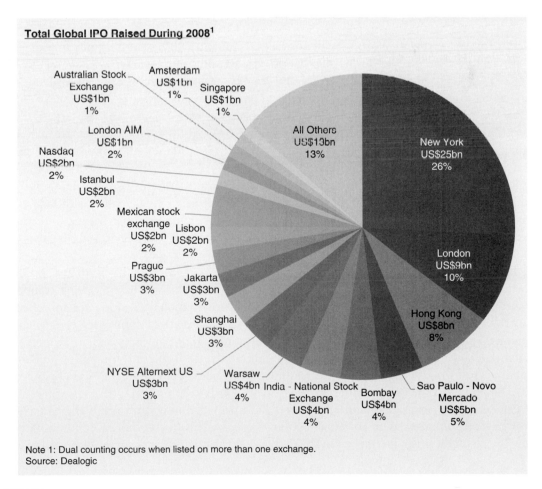

## Total Global IPO Raised During 2008[1]

Note 1: Dual counting occurs when listed on more than one exchange.
Source: Dealogic

**EXHIBIT 8.7**

## Brazil's IPO Market

Brazil became the third largest IPO market in the world in 2007, contributing to more than 10% of global IPOs by funds raised: 64 companies worth $27.3 billion tapped the Brazilian IPO market, a 251% rise from the previous year. Almost all of these companies listed on the Sao Paolo stock exchange (BOVESPA), which went public in 2007, raising $3.2 billion in the country's largest ever IPO. The BOVESPA then went on to merge with the Brazilian Mercantile and Futures Exchange (BM&F) in 2008 to create the new BM&F BOVESPA. U.S.-style corporate governance standards, one-share/one-vote rules, greater transparency, minority shareholder protection, and enhanced quality of disclosed information all combined to draw a record amount of foreign capital into the Brazilian equity market. These foreign investors purchased more than two-thirds of all local Brazilian share offerings during 2007.

The typical business plan for a family-run Brazilian enterprise is to take in private equity or hedge fund money for 25% to 30% of the company to enable growth through acquisitions, and when a sufficient size is achieved, then an IPO is the next source for capital. This, in turn, enables further growth, since the company has a liquid acquisition currency.

In 2008, Standard & Poor's upgraded Brazil's credit rating to BBB- (investment grade status). This was an important step in further expanding the investor base for Brazil's equity and bond markets, since the investment-grade rating enabled international pension funds and other institutions to invest in Brazil for the first time.

## Russia's IPO Market

Russia's capital markets developed rapidly between 2000 and 2007, with the stock market value increasing more than tenfold during this period. Russia's IPO market in 2007 saw fundraising totaling $19 billion, with 20 IPOs at an average deal size of $948 million. The new issuances primarily came from financial services, real estate, and energy and power sectors. The $8 billion offering from Vneshtorgbank, Russia's second-largest state-owned bank, was the largest IPO in the world that year. In all, Russia represented 7% of the global IPO market during 2007. Similar to Brazil, Russia's IPO market slowed down significantly in 2008, as did the rest of the global capital markets, due to the global credit crisis.

Russian companies are legally required to list locally at least 30% of their equity. The Moscow Exchange provides limited liquidity and an opaque pricing system, although many improvements are under way to improve the listing process, market infrastructure, and trading systems. These changes should improve the appeal of this exchange to issuers and investors over time.

The most popular way for large Russian companies to raise equity is to list a Global Depositary Receipt (GDR) issue in London, combined with a Moscow listing, giving companies exposure to both local and international investors. Some international investors are apprehensive about the ambiguity of certain Russian regulations, especially relating to tax, financial statements, and legal restructuring. Until these uncertainties diminish, there may be limited international demand for Russian GDR issues. As an alternative to listing in London, some Russian companies are listing in Hong Kong. In addition, companies in Ukraine and Kazakhstan have listed IPOs in both London and Hong Kong.

Private equity and hedge fund investments have provided important pre-IPO financing for smaller transaction sizes of up to $200 million. As Russian banks withdrew funding with the advent of the credit crisis that began in 2007, these alternative investors filled the funding gap, enabling Russian companies to continue financing acquisitions. The companies that are able to grow via these acquisitions have also positioned themselves to access the IPO market. Once public, many companies have used their shares as an acquisition currency to facilitate further growth.

## India's IPO Market

India's IPO market saw 106 deals during 2007, raising an aggregate $8.8 billion, which represents the largest volume raised in 1 year for the country. Average deal size was $83 million, which is much smaller than in either the Brazilian or the Russian markets. However, during 2008, Reliance Power completed a $3 billion IPO, creating a foundation for future large offerings. The most active Indian IPO issuers come from the industrial, energy and power, financial, and real estate sectors. As India continues to build up its roadways, power plants, and ports, it is expected that the industrial and power sectors will see the most IPO volume going forward, as these industries are direct beneficiaries of infrastructure projects.

Due to strict regulatory limits, a foreign institutional investor can invest in no more than 10% of total issued capital of a listed Indian company. However, in aggregate, foreigners provide approximately three-quarters of the capital coming into the IPO market. Indian companies seeking to complete an IPO are required by law to list on a local exchange such as the Mumbai Stock Exchange or the National Stock Exchange. They are, however, also allowed to dual list on international exchanges. There are two principal routes taken for dual listings. High-tech Indian companies whose customers might be principally U.S. based will dual list in the United States since U.S. investors may have a better understanding of the issuer's value proposition. For metals and mining companies, it is common to dual list in the United Kingdom on the AIM market section of the London Stock Exchange, since it attracts many of the global players in this industry. Most Indian IPOs that raise more than $125 million include a Rule 144A component that enables some funding from qualified institutional buyers in the United States.

In 2007, both the Mumbai Stock Exchange and the National Stock Exchange became 20% owned by foreign investors that included NYSE Euronext, Deutsche Bourse, and the Singapore Exchange. The resulting sharing of management and regulatory practices has facilitated many improvements in these large Indian exchanges. India's growing GDP and high savings rates of approximately 35% have made a huge pool of investable funds available. The strengthening of India's exchanges and higher quality IPOs have led to an increasing allocation of investable funds to equities. In 2005, total Indian savings in equities was less than 2%. By 2007, this had grown to over 5%. Ongoing growth in equity allocation may substantially boost the growth of the equity market in India.

Hedge funds, private equity, and venture capital firms have all invested in pre-IPO companies in India, and these firms have been the key driver for the country's IPO market in recent years. International investor interest in smaller Indian companies should continue to grow following the government's announcement that any fund that is regulated in its home country is welcome to invest in India.

## China's IPO Market

During 2007, Greater China led the world in both IPO funds raised ($66 billion) and number of transactions (259). Proceeds raised that year were almost twice the $34 billion raised in the U.S. IPO market. Under the government's new policy of promoting Shanghai's stock exchange, about two-thirds of funds raised in Shanghai were H-share issues (first-time domestic IPOs by China's biggest companies, which had previously listed in Hong Kong). In addition, many mid-sized IPOs were listed in mainland China, with an average deal size of $255 million. The top four Chinese industries by funds raised during 2007 were financial services, industrials, real estate, and metals and mining. The largest ever Chinese IPO was a $22 billion offering from ICBC during 2006: the IPO raised $16 billion in Hong Kong and another $6 billion in mainland China through a dual-listed transaction. This even eclipsed the largest ever U.S. IPO, which was an offering by VISA that raised proceeds of $19.6 billion during 2008.

Mainland Chinese companies listed on the Shanghai Stock Exchange (A-shares) have historically traded at a premium to mainland Chinese companies listed on the Hong Kong Stock Exchange (H-shares). This is often true for the same company that lists both A-shares and H-shares. In 2007, an index called the Hang Seng China AH Premium Index was launched to track the price disparity between A-shares and H-shares of dual-listed companies. The premium tracked by this index has been as high as 100%. The reason for this anomaly is because of strict capital controls in China that create a supply and demand imbalance. Although the wealth of individuals in China has grown rapidly, capital controls prevent average Chinese investors, who have a very limited range of companies that they can invest in within mainland China, from investing in shares in Hong Kong or in any non-Chinese market overseas. As a result, the limited numbers of investment opportunities available to mainland Chinese investors are bid up through heavy demand. The Chinese government has suggested it will consider allowing mainland Chinese individuals to purchase H-shares (Red Chips) for the first time, which should reduce the price disparity between Hong Kong-listed and Shanghai-listed Chinese companies.

Historically, there have been a number of overseas Chinese listings. However, as part of an effort to develop the Shanghai Stock Exchange into an international financial center, the Chinese government passed provisions in 2006 that made it more difficult for Chinese companies to list anywhere outside of the mainland. Only a limited number of domestic companies may be allowed to dual list in China and on an international exchange, and the process for approval is not very transparent. During 2007, the Chinese e-commerce company Alibaba was the first major Asian technology company not to list on NASDAQ, which historically receives the majority of listings from overseas technology companies. Alibaba achieved a very high PE multiple when it raised $1.7 billion through a listing solely on the Hong Kong exchange. In 2009, China decided to allow qualified foreign companies to float shares and issue GDRs on the Chinese exchange.

Compared with the mainland exchanges, the Hong Kong exchange offers the advantages of better access to global capital, greater brand recognition, higher corporate governance standards, and less volatility. While this exchange caters to foreign investors and settles in HK dollars, the Shanghai and Shenzhen exchanges focus on local retail investors, operate under an exchange control regime, and use the renminbi as the settlement currency. As a result, the Hong Kong and mainland exchanges are not fully comparable, and neither is in a dominant position.

Private Chinese companies that are incorporated offshore can choose where to list their shares (other than in mainland China). Usually, they prefer to list in Hong Kong to access global institutional investors, and include Regulation S or Rule 144A provisions to access European and U.S. institutional markets. Smaller private Chinese companies that are incorporated offshore usually consider listing in Singapore or on London's AIM market. Chinese companies incorporated offshore need to receive approvals from a number of Chinese regulatory agencies before they can list on a foreign exchange.

# American Depository Receipt (ADR)

An ADR represents U.S. investor ownership of non-U.S. company shares. ADRs are issued by U.S. depositary banks and deposited with a custodian (agent of the depositary bank) in the country of issuance. An ADR represents the right for an investor to obtain the non-U.S. shares held by the bank (although in practice investors usually never receive the shares). ADRs are priced in U.S. dollars and pay dividends in U.S. dollars. Although convenient for investors, this results in currency risk embedded in the security. Individual shares of a non-U.S. company represented by an ADR are called American Depositary Shares (ADSs).

ADR investors can obtain ADRs by either purchasing them on a U.S. stock exchange or by purchasing the non-U.S. shares in their original market of issuance and then (a) depositing them with a bank in exchange for a new ADR, or (b) swapping the shares for existing ADRs.

Investment banks are actively involved in helping non-U.S. companies list their shares in the United States in the form of ADRs. Foreign companies utilize the ADR program to raise capital, increase liquidity, and expand U.S. market awareness of the company. Sometimes issuers also use ADRs as an acquisition currency.

An ADR that trades in the U.S. market is priced based on the non-U.S. company's share price in their home market. This price is constantly adjusted for changing FX spot rates, so there is a high degree of volatility in ADR prices. ADR prices are also impacted by home country accounting, legal, and political differences. Although most non-U.S. companies provide GAAP-based financial information, caution is necessary because of the use of estimates, uncertain tax implications, and other adjustments that are unique to the home country. ADRs are registered with the SEC through Form F-6 based on certain exemptions that are available to qualified non-U.S. companies.

A Global Depository Receipt (GDR) is similar to an ADR except that a GDR is offered in two or more markets outside the non-U.S. issuer's home country. A number of other depository instruments exist as well, such as EuroDRs, which trade within the Euro zone and represent ownership of shares in a company headquartered outside of the Euro zone, and SDRs, which trade within Singapore and represent ownership of shares in a company headquartered outside of Singapore.

# Standardized International Financial Reporting

During 2002, the European Union agreed that all listed companies within Europe should report using one financial reporting framework, called International Financial Reporting Standards (IFRS). IFRS, finally adopted in Europe in 2005, has become the key contender to be the global financial reporting language. Canada, India, Brazil, China, Korea, and Japan are expected to adopt IFRS, and when this occurs, approximately 65% of Fortune 500 companies will be reporting their financial results under IFRS. The SEC has announced that foreign private issuers preparing their financial statements in accordance with IFRS will no longer have to include reconciliation to U.S. GAAP. It is now likely that the SEC will also adopt IFRS as a standard financial reporting framework for U.S. companies. In November 2008 the SEC released a roadmap to conversion, which proposed beginning with voluntary conversion in 2009 (for fiscal years ending on or after December 15, 2009) and concluding with mandatory conversion by 2014.

A remaining complication with IFRS relates to the fact that, although IFRS applies to listed (public) companies, it does not apply in some countries to unlisted companies. As a result, unlisted companies must use their national standards and not IFRS when preparing financial statements. For example, in Germany, listed companies prepare their financial statements in accordance with IFRS, but unlisted companies prepare their financial statements in accordance with German GAAP. Therefore, if an unlisted German company initiates an IPO, the company may have to spend considerable resources to convert its financial information from local GAAP to IFRS.

Despite the initial conversion expense, one global financial reporting language means that the cost of doing business across jurisdictions becomes lower, transparency and comparability increase, and global capital-raising initiatives become more compelling. The end result is improved efficiency in global capital markets, lower costs of capital, and enhanced shareholder value. IFRS will enable a harmonization of international regulations and will allow international investors to make more informed decisions, resulting in an expansion of capital available for the world's capital raisers.

## International Investors

Sovereign Wealth Funds (SWFs) have become a major source of funding for international capital raising. According to Deutsche Bank and Boston Consulting Group (BCG), at the end of 2007, SWFs controlled over $3 trillion in investable assets (almost doubling in size since 2003), and they owned 7% of worldwide stock market capitalization. Although many of these funds experienced considerable losses in 2008, the estimated aggregate AUM of SWFs is still over $3 trillion. Some governments have restricted SWF investment in key companies. For example, in 2006 Germany prevented a Russian SWF fund from making a major investment in Deutsche Telekom. In 2008, in an effort to foster closer and more cooperative relationships, the United States signed agreements with Abu Dhabi and Singapore that established a basic code of conduct for SWFs and the countries in which they invest. One of the major principles established in this agreement was the idea of investment decisions driven solely on commercial grounds and not geopolitical motives. Until similar agreements are adopted worldwide to resolve political considerations, the long-term impact of SWFs on the global equity (and M&A) markets is uncertain. The largest SWFs are listed in Exhibit 8.8.

**Largest Sovereign Wealth Funds**

| Country | Fund | Assets (US$bn)[1] | Inception | Origin |
|---|---|---|---|---|
| UAE (Abu Dhabi) | Abu Dhabi Investment Authority | 627 | 1976 | Oil |
| Saudi Arabia | SAMA Foreign Holdings | 431 | n/a | Oil |
| China | State Administration of Foreign Exchange | 347 | n/a | Non-Commodity |
| Norway | Government Pension Fund of Norway | 326 | 1990 | Oil |
| Singapore | Government of Singapore Investment Corp | 247 | 1981 | Non-Commodity |
| Russia | National Welfare Fund | 220 | 2008 | Oil |
| Kuwait | Kuwait Investment Authority | 203 | 1953 | Oil |
| China-Hong Kong | HK Monetary Authority Investment Portfolio | 193 | 1998 | Non-Commodity |
| China | China Investment Corporation | 190 | 2007 | Non-Commodity |
| Singapore | Temasek Holdings | 85 | 1974 | Non-Commodity |
| China | National Social Security Fund | 82 | 2000 | Non-Commodity |
| UAE (Dubai) | Investment Corporation of Dubai | 82 | 2006 | Oil |
| Libya | Libyan Investment Authority | 65 | 2006 | Oil |
| Qatar | Qatar Investment Authority | 62 | 2003 | Oil |
| Algeria | Revenue Regulation Fund | 47 | 2000 | Oil |
| Australia | Australian Future Fund | 42 | 2004 | Non-Commodity |
| Kazakhstan | Kazakhstan National Fund | 38 | 2000 | Oil |
| Brunei | Brunei Investment Agency | 30 | 1983 | Oil |
| France | Strategic Investment Fund | 28 | 2008 | Non-Commodity |
| United States (Alaska) | Alaska Permanent Fund | 27 | 1976 | Oil |
| South Korea | Korea Investment Corporation | 27 | 2005 | Non-Commodity |
| Malaysia | Khazanah Nasional | 23 | 1993 | Non-Commodity |
| Ireland | National Pensions Reserve Fund | 23 | 2001 | Non-Commodity |
| UAE (Abe Dhabi) | Mubadala Development Company | 15 | 2002 | Oil |
| Bahrain | Mumtalakat Holding Company | 14 | 2006 | Oil |

Note 1: Rankings as of April, 2009.
Source: Sovereign Wealth Fund Institute

**EXHIBIT 8.8**

# Questions

1. What are the benefits of issuing and investing in Eurobonds?
2. Why are most corporate Eurobond issuers large, multinational corporations?
3. A put option gives the holder the right, but not the obligation, to sell an underlying asset at an agreed-upon price. Discuss why the Japanese government's guarantee to Ripplewood as part of its buyout of Long Term Credit Bank is similar to granting Ripplewood a put option on the bank's assets.
4. Why did China institute an A-share/B-share system? How has regulatory easing benefited QFIIs?
5. In a comparable transactions analysis, what additional considerations might an investment banker factor in when valuing an emerging market company?
6. Suppose you are a wealth advisor and a client has asked for your recommendation on which of the BRIC countries poses the least risk and most opportunity for investment growth. Briefly compare the perceived risks and benefits of each of the countries and provide support for your selection.

# Convertible Securities and Wall Street Innovation

## Convertible Securities

Most convertibles[1] are underwritten by large investment banks on a best-efforts basis. This means that the issuer bears share price risk during the period of time when the security is being marketed to prospective investors. In the United States, convertibles are typically sold based on a 144A exemption from registration with the SEC. These securities, if held for 180 days (and assuming the issuer is current in their required SEC filings), can be freely sold, as can the underlying common shares, without the need for a registration statement.

### Hedge Funds and Delta Hedging

The principal investors in most convertible securities are hedge funds that engage in convertible arbitrage strategies. These investors typically purchase the convertible and simultaneously sell short a certain number of the common shares that underlie the convertible. The number of shares they sell short as a percentage of the shares underlying the convertible is approximately equal to the risk-neutral probability at that point in time (as determined by a convertible pricing model that uses binomial option pricing as its foundation) that the investor will eventually convert the security into common shares. This probability is then applied to the number of common shares into which the convertible security could convert to determine the number of shares the hedge fund investor should sell short (the *hedge ratio*).

As an example, assume a company's share price is $10 at the time of its convertible issuance. A hedge fund purchases a portion of the convertible, which gives the right to convert into 100 common shares of the issuer. If the hedge ratio is 65%, the hedge fund may sell short 65 shares of the issuer's stock on the same date as the convertible purchase. During the life span of the convertible, the hedge fund investor may sell more shares short or buy shares, based on the changing hedge ratio. To illustrate, if one month after purchasing the convertible (and establishing a 65-share short position) the issuer's share price decreases to $9, the hedge ratio may drop from 65% to 60%. To align the hedge ratio with the shares sold short as a percentage of shares into which the investor has the right to convert the security, the hedge fund investor will need to buy 5 shares in the open market from other shareholders and deliver those shares to the parties who had lent the shares originally. "Covering" five shares of their short position leaves the hedge fund with a new short position of 60 shares. If the issuer's share price 2 months after issuance increases to $11, the hedge ratio may increase to 70%. In this case, the hedge fund investor

---

[1]For a general description of convertible securities, please refer to Chapter 3.

An Introduction to Investment Banks, Hedge Funds, and Private Equity

may want to be short 70 shares. The investor achieves this position by borrowing 10 more shares and selling them short, which increases the short position from 60 shares to 70 shares. This process of buying low and selling high continues until the convertible either converts or matures.

The end result is that the hedge fund investor is generating trading profits throughout the life of the convertible by buying stock to reduce the short position when the issuer's share price drops, and borrowing and selling shares short when the issuer's share price increases. This dynamic trading process is called *delta hedging*, which is a well-known and consistently practiced strategy by hedge funds. Since hedge funds typically purchase between 60% and 80% of most convertible securities in the public markets, a significant amount of trading in the issuer's stock takes place throughout the life of a convertible security. The purpose of all this trading in the convertible issuer's common stock is to hedge share price risk embedded in the convertible and create trading profits that offset the opportunity cost of purchasing a convertible that has a coupon that is substantially lower than the coupon that would be attached to a straight bond from the same issuer with the same maturity.

In order for hedge funds to invest in convertible securities, there needs to be a substantial amount of the issuer's common shares available for hedge funds to borrow, and adequate liquidity in the issuer's stock for hedge funds to buy and sell shares in relation to their delta hedging activity. If there are insufficient shares available to be borrowed or inadequate trading volume in the issuer's stock, a prospective issuer is generally discouraged from issuing a convertible security in the public markets, or is required to issue a smaller convertible, because hedge funds may not be able to participate.

When a new convertible security is priced in the public capital markets, it is generally the case that the terms of the security imply a theoretical value of between 102% and 105% of face value, based on a convertible pricing model. The convertible is usually sold at a price of 100% to investors, and is therefore underpriced compared to its theoretical value. This practice provides an incentive for hedge funds to purchase the security, knowing that by delta hedging their investment, they should be able to extract trading profits at least equal to the difference between the theoretical value and *par* (100%). For a public market convertible with atypical characteristics (e.g., an oversized issuance relative to market capitalization, an issuer with limited stock trading volume, or an issuer with limited stock borrow availability), hedge fund investors normally require an even higher theoretical value (relative to par) as an inducement to invest.

Convertible pricing models incorporate binomial trees to determine the theoretical value of convertible securities. These models consider the following factors that influence the theoretical value: current common stock price; anticipated volatility of the common stock return during the life of the convertible security; risk-free interest rate; the company's stock borrow cost and common stock dividend yield; the company's credit risk; maturity of the convertible security; and the convertible security's coupon or dividend rate and payment frequency, conversion premium, and length of call protection, among other inputs.

## Zero Coupon Convertibles

A Zero Coupon Convertible (ZCC) is similar to a coupon-paying convertible, except instead of paying interest coupons each year, the issuer increases the principal amount of the convertible over time by an amount equal to the unpaid coupon, creating an "accretion" of the bond. Accordingly, as is the case with a zero coupon bond that does not have a conversion feature, the principal amount increases each year until the maturity of the bond. Notwithstanding the zero coupon feature, the conversion premium, which determines the number of underlying shares the security can convert into, is approximately the same for both a coupon-paying convertible and a ZCC of the same issuer (assuming identical maturity and call provisions).[2]

Given the fact that there are approximately the same number of underlying shares for a ZCC and a coupon-paying convertible, and ZCCs' unpaid coupons are "paid" by increasing the principal amount of the convertible, why might a prospective issuer prefer a ZCC to a coupon-paying convertible? The reasons include the following:

1. A U.S. issuer is able to receive tax deductions in relation to the annual accretion of the convertible, creating a positive cash flow bond financing (no cash payments for coupons, but tax deductions equal to the deductions the issuer would receive if a coupon-paying convertible had been issued).

2. There is a lower probability of conversion on the portion of the convertible that is not purchased by hedge funds[3] because an unhedged investor will usually (assuming no credit or illiquidity concerns) only convert into common shares if the value of those shares exceeds the principal cash redemption value of the bond's accreting principal amount, which increases each year.

A ZCC is, therefore, a positive cash flow bond financing with a lower chance of earnings per share (EPS) dilution since conversion is somewhat less likely. Given these benefits, why don't all potential convertible issuers complete ZCC transactions? One reason is that based on tax law symmetry, since issuers receive tax credits based on the accretion, investors must pay income taxes in relation to this annual accretion, or *phantom income*. As a result, typically only nontaxable investors will consider ZCC investments. Another reason is that because coupons are accreted into the bond principal amount instead of paid annually, investors have more credit exposure to a ZCC issuer at maturity. Depending on the issuer, investors may require a small economic benefit as compensation for this risk (such as an up to 1/8% higher yield compared to a conventional coupon-paying convertible, or, as described in footnote 1, a slightly lower conversion premium).

## Mandatory Convertibles

Unlike an optionally converting convertible where the investor has the right, but not the obligation, to convert a bond holding into a predetermined number of the issuer's common shares, a mandatory convertible requires conversion. In an optionally converting convertible, the decision to convert at maturity is based on the company's share price. If the share price does not exceed the conversion price, the investor will require the company to pay off the convertible's principal amount with cash at maturity. As a result, from the perspective of a credit rating agency, on its issuance date, an optionally converting convertible is considered to be similar to debt. In a mandatory convertible, however, because an investor does not hold the right to demand cash repayment in the future (shares will always be delivered instead), credit rating agencies consider this security to be similar to equity. Because of this, a company seeking to issue equity may consider

---

[2]Depending on the credit rating of the issuer, a ZCC might have a slightly lower conversion premium to compensate investors for greater credit risk associated with not receiving annual coupon payments.

[3]Hedge funds generally do not convert their holding into common stock based on the value of shares, since they have delta hedged their position by selling short a percentage of the shares into which they can convert.

a mandatory convertible as an alternative to a common share issuance. Issuing a mandatory convertible has the benefit of receiving almost the same equity content from rating agencies as from a common share issuance, but with fewer shares delivered to investors if the company's share price is higher on the maturity date (which is usually 3 years following issuance).

A mandatory convertible has, in effect, a floating conversion price that changes based on the company's share price at maturity. The formula for determining the shares delivered at maturity is as follows:

1. If, at maturity, the issuing company's share price (Maturity Price) is at or below the share price on the convertible issuance date (Issuance Price), the shares delivered to investors will be identical to the shares that would have been delivered if common shares had been issued instead of the convertible (Shares Issued).
2. If, at maturity, the company's share price has risen but is less than the conversion price (usually set at 20–30% above the share price on the issuance date), the number of shares delivered to investors is equal to: Shares Issued × Issuance Price / Maturity Price.
3. If, at maturity, the company's share price exceeds the conversion price, the number of shares delivered to investors is equal to: Shares Issued × Issuance Price / Conversion Price (see **Case Study 3, "Freeport-McMoRan: Financing an Acquisition,"** to review application of the floating conversion price formula).

Suppose, for example, that company ABC is seeking to raise $100 million. If ABC decides to raise the funds through a $100 million mandatory convertible that has a conversion price of $31.25 (25% conversion premium) when its common stock price is $25, ABC will be obligated to deliver 3.2 million shares at maturity if its share price equals or exceeds the conversion price at maturity ($100 million / $31.25 = 3.2 million shares). This is also the same number of shares that would be delivered if the convertible had been an optionally converting convertible with the same conversion price. If the company had decided to issue common shares when the stock was at $25 per share instead of a mandatory convertible, it would have had to sell 4 million shares to raise $100 million. Assuming ABC's share price at the maturity of the mandatory is equal to or higher than the conversion price, the common share issuance would have resulted in the delivery of 25% more shares compared to a mandatory convertible offering of the same issuance size. If, however, ABC's share price is $25 or lower at maturity of the mandatory convertible, the company will deliver 4 million shares, which is the same number of shares that would have been issued in a common share offering. If the share price is between $25 and $31.25 at maturity, the company will deliver somewhere between 3.2 million shares and 4 million shares, depending on the share price.

Despite the certainty of eventual conversion into common stock, from the perspective of issuers, investors, and rating agencies, a comparison between a mandatory convertible and common shares is somewhat complex. For example, the equity content for one form of mandatory convertible is less than the equity content for a straight common stock offering if the issuer wishes to receive tax benefits from the mandatory convertible issuance (see details in the following paragraph). In addition, the dividend associated with a mandatory convertible is higher than the issuer's common stock dividend. This is because, although mandatory convertible investors bear the same downside risk as common share investors, they do not have the same upside share price benefit (the number of shares received at conversion is lower than the shares that would be received in a common stock offering if the mandatory convertible issuer's share price is higher on the maturity date than on the issuance date).

Mandatory convertibles are issued in two forms. The first one is a Unit Structure, which has two components: (a) a 30-year subordinated debt, and (b) a 3-year stock purchase contract issued by the company to the same investors, which results in a variable share delivery mechanism after 3 years. For U.S.-regulated banks, the Unit Structure has an additional layer, whereby the subordinated debt is issued to a trust vehicle and a simultaneous subordinated trust stake is issued to investors by the trust (including a provision for remarketing the trust stake to other investors after 3 years). See Exhibit 9.1 for an overview of a Unit Structure mandatory convertible issued by Marshall and Ilsley (M&I). The second form of a mandatory convertible is a Non-Unit Structure, which provides for issuance of preferred stock and a variable common share delivery mechanism in 3 years that is linked to the issuer's share price at delivery and with simultaneous retirement of the preferred shares once common shares are delivered (see Exhibit 9.2).

## Unit Structure

A Unit Structure mandatory convertible is described in Exhibit 9.1.

M&I's security is divided into two components: a trust, which purchases M&I subordinated debt, and a stock purchase contract, which requires investors to make a payment in 3 years to receive M&I stock. The subordinated bonds have a 30-year maturity, and they reprice after 3 years when investment bank underwriters of the convertible conduct an auction to sell the trust stake held by investors to new investors. The yield on the trust stake will be reset at the time of the auction so that it will trade at par. The original investors who purchased the trust stake also

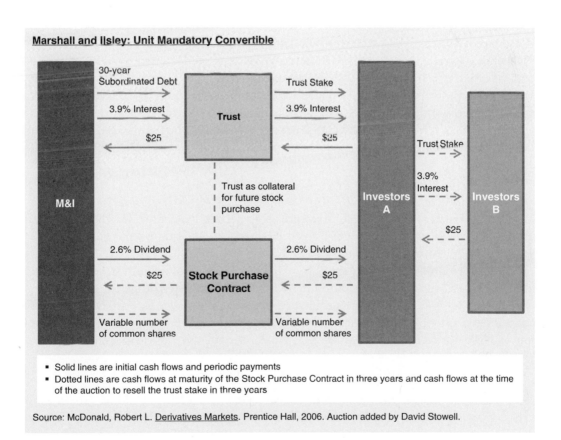

Marshall and Ilsley: Unit Mandatory Convertible

- Solid lines are initial cash flows and periodic payments
- Dotted lines are cash flows at maturity of the Stock Purchase Contract in three years and cash flows at the time of the auction to resell the trust stake in three years

Source: McDonald, Robert L. <u>Derivatives Markets</u>. Prentice Hall, 2006. Auction added by David Stowell.

**EXHIBIT 9.1**

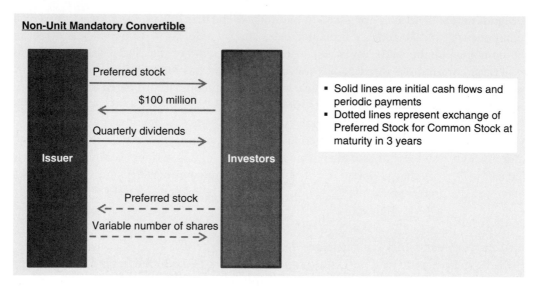

**EXHIBIT 9.2**

enter into the stock purchase contract, which requires them to pay cash for common shares in 3 years. The cash amount payable under the stock purchase contract is exactly equal to the cash that the same investors receive from auctioning the trust stake in 3 years. As a result, investors achieve the same risk/return profile that exists for other mandatory convertible investors, as described earlier and in Exhibit 9.2 (for Non-Unit mandatory convertibles).

Depending on the terms, the Unit Structure provides a company with equity credit of 50% or 75% from rating agencies. The issuer also receives tax deductions on the interest payments associated with the subordinated debt (equivalent to approximately 60% of the annual cash payment obligation of the company, with the remaining 40% relating to dividends paid pursuant to the stock purchase contract). The Unit Structure also receives favorable accounting treatment that results in less EPS dilution on the date of issuance compared to a common stock offering (based on the treasury stock method of accounting).

### Non-Unit Structure

A Non-Unit Mandatory Convertible Structure is preferred by companies that either cannot benefit from tax deductions or want even higher (up to 100%) equity content. A description of this structure may be found in Exhibit 9.2.

In 2007, Freeport-McMoRan (FM) issued a $2.9 billion Non-Unit Structure mandatory convertible underwritten by joint bookrunners J.P. Morgan and Merrill Lynch. FM also simultaneously issued $2.9 billion of common equity, generating total proceeds for the company of $5.8 billion. These transactions, in conjunction with $17.5 billion in debt financing, funded the cash portion of FM's acquisition of Phelps Dodge, which created the world's largest publicly traded copper company.

The mandatory convertible financing achieved a number of objectives for FM:

1. It enabled the company to obtain a larger equity financing than would have been available from sale of common stock only due to limited demand for the company's common shares

beyond $2.9 billion (most of the mandatory convertible investors were funds that would not have purchased the common stock).

2. It provided FM with almost 100% equity credit for the offering, even though common shares would only be issued after 3 years, upon the mandatory conversion of the convertible from its initial preferred share form.

3. For the same amount of proceeds raised, there would be fewer common shares delivered to investors upon conversion in 3 years compared to the simultaneous common stock offering, assuming FM's share price rises during this period, which provides a permanent EPS reporting benefit.

FM chose the Non-Unit Structure mandatory convertible for its ability to maximize equity credit, and was willing to give up tax deductions that are only available in the Unit Structure because the company operated principally outside of the United States and therefore had no U.S. tax obligations. By contrast, M&I chose the Unit Structure in order to take advantage of tax deductions, even though this structure provided less equity credit.

The FM mandatory convertible was issued in the form of 28.75 million preferred shares offered at $100 per share, with a 6.75% dividend and a 3-year maturity. The preferred shares were mandatorily convertible into FM's common shares based on the following schedule.

If FM's share price at maturity is:

- less than or equal to $61.25, the investor receives 1.6327 FM shares;
- between $61.25 and $73.50, the investor receives $100 / current FM share price;
- equal to or greater than $73.50, the investor receives 1.3605 FM shares.

The payoff graph for delivery of FM shares as a function of the company's share price on the maturity date in 3 years is shown in Exhibit 7 of **Case Study 3, "Freeport-McMoRan: Financing an Acquisition."**

This mandatory convertible, at maturity, provided investors with the following:

1. The same number of FM common shares in 3 years as they would have received by buying the company's common stock on the date of the simultaneous offering (with the purchase price in both cases at $61.25), assuming FM's stock price is equal to or less than $61.25 in 3 years.

2. No participation in the upside of any FM share price appreciation in 3 years if FM's stock price falls in the range of $61.25 to $73.50 during this period.

3. Participation in 1/1.2 (83%) of the appreciation in FM share price above $73.50 in 3 years.

Investors in the FM convertible assumed all of the downside risk of owning FM stock over a 3-year period but did not participate in the first 20% appreciation (from $61.25 to $73.40), and participated in only 83% of the appreciation above 20%. As a result, they had to be compensated for the opportunity cost of buying the mandatory convertible compared to purchasing common stock. Compensation was paid, in effect, through 6.75% p.a. dividend payments for 3 years, which was 5.15% p.a. above FM's common stock dividend of 1.6% p.a. at the time of issuance.

## Comparison of Mandatory Convertibles Issued by M&I and FM

There are both differences and similarities between FM's Non-Unit Structure with M&I's Unit Structure. Both securities pay annual cash flows that are greater than the underlying stock's dividend. M&I's security pays an annual cash flow of 6.5% (2.6% dividend under the stock purchase contract and 3.9% coupon for the subordinated bond component, which was tax deductible for M&I), and FM's security pays 6.75% in annual dividends. Both securities have a similar common share payoff structure at maturity. However, M&I's security was divided into two components: a trust that contained M&I subordinated bonds, and a stock purchase contract that required investors to make a payment in 3 years to receive M&I stock. The subordinated bonds have a 30-year maturity and reprice after 3 years so that they trade at par. This enabled investors to sell the subordinated bonds to other investors through an auction conducted by investment banks, receiving the exact amount of cash from this sale necessary for investors to purchase M&I's shares pursuant to the stock purchase contract.

M&I (unlike FM) had U.S. tax obligations, and so chose the Unit Structure over the Non-Unit Structure because of the tax-deductions received on the 3.9% coupons. Under the Unit Structure, tax-deductibility arises in part because 30-year debt is issued rather than preferred shares. The detached nature of the debt and stock repurchase agreement are evidenced by separate documents. Although the investor must pledge the debt against the obligation to purchase M&I stock in 3 years, the investor can substitute treasury securities as collateral. As a result, the two documents and related obligations operate independently.

## Wall Street Innovation

As evidenced by convertible securities, investment banks are creative in achieving the varying objectives of both their issuing and investing clients. New forms of securities must take into account not only client economic priorities but also consider legal, tax, accounting, and political issues. All large investment banks have new product development teams that work with internal and outside advisors, including lawyers, accountants, tax experts, and regulatory experts. This is a very time-consuming and complicated process, and it often includes false starts. Significant resources can be invested in creating a new structure only to conclude at the end that, although it resolves economic, legal, and accounting issues, there is a disadvantageous tax outcome. Or if the tax outcome is acceptable, sometimes regulatory or accounting difficulties may arise. The challenge is making sure all potential issues have been considered and resolved before presenting new products to clients.

When developing new products, a firm must also take its reputation into consideration. Even if all of the key areas are thoroughly analyzed and all issues seem to be resolved, any negative press coverage of the new product (or the client involved in the new product) can be problematic for the bank. In addition, despite strong favorable opinions provided by the bank's legal, accounting, tax, and other advisors, regulators may disagree in the future with one or more of these opinions, creating unforeseen complications for the product. As a result, all banks have a very careful vetting process where committees must approve any new product prior to its launch. Even when all advisors are supportive, clients are interested in the product, and considerable resources have been used to develop it, these committees may veto the product if there are reputational concerns.

Although some of the most innovative products are developed in the convertible securities market, there have been many other successful products developed in other areas, including structured finance, municipal securities, pension funds, M&A, and others. Two examples of investment banking product innovations are discussed in the following sections: Nikkei Put Warrants and Accelerated Share Repurchase Programs.

# Nikkei Put Warrants

The Nikkei Put Warrants program, developed by Goldman Sachs and other firms, exemplifies an investment banking innovation that not only meets the global needs of both issuing and investing clients but also involves principal risk-taking by investment banks.

In 1990, put warrants on the Nikkei 225 stock index (Nikkei Puts) were sold in the United States for the first time. Nikkei Puts enabled U.S. retail investors to receive a cash payment if the Japanese stock market fell. This market had increased dramatically during the preceding 4 years, reaching its historical high of 38,915.90 on the last trading day of 1989, 2 weeks prior to the launch of a Nikkei put offering in the U.S. public market by Goldman Sachs on January 12, 1990. By June of that year, the Japanese stock market had crashed, dropping by more than 50%.

Put Warrants (essentially the same as put options) give their holders the right, but not the obligation, to sell an underlying asset by a certain date for a predetermined price. In the case of Nikkei Puts, a decline in the Japanese stock market would increase the value of Nikkei Puts, and the investor would receive a cash payment equal to the difference between the Nikkei 225 stock index market price and the higher predetermined strike price (a cash-settled option). The first Nikkei Puts were listed on the American Stock Exchange and principally underwritten by Goldman Sachs, with the Kingdom of Denmark as the issuer. At the time a private partnership, Goldman Sachs did not have registration capability with the SEC and therefore could not issue the Nikkei Puts directly. The Kingdom of Denmark had the ability to register with the SEC, which enabled them to sell the Nikkei Puts at the request of Goldman Sachs. Simultaneous to selling the puts to U.S. retail investors, the Kingdom of Denmark also entered into a Nikkei Put purchase contract with Goldman Sachs, thereby fully hedging its exposure (see Exhibit 9.3). The proceeds

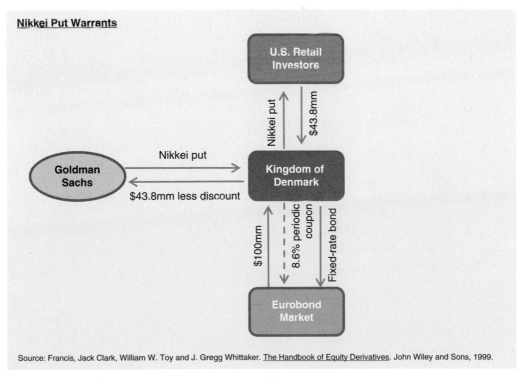

Source: Francis, Jack Clark, William W. Toy and J. Gregg Whittaker. The Handbook of Equity Derivatives. John Wiley and Sons, 1999.

**EXHIBIT 9.3**

from the Nikkei Put sales exceeded the cost of purchasing the hedge, so the remaining proceeds were contributed into a Eurobond transaction, which the Kingdom of Denmark simultaneously sold in London through Goldman Sachs, thereby creating low-cost financing.

U.S. companies with registration statements could have been asked to issue the Nikkei Puts, but the unfavorable accounting consequences of matching Nikkei Put purchase and sales contracts precluded their involvement. The Kingdom of Denmark, on the other hand, had no such accounting concerns. Multiple other Nikkei Put transactions took place in the United States during the first half of 1990, until the Japanese government asked investment banks to discontinue these transactions, following the sharp reversal in Japan's stock market. Prior to this shutdown, U.S. investors actively purchased and traded the Nikkei Puts, making them among the most actively traded instruments on the American Stock Exchange. Investors saw the value of their Nikkei Put investment skyrocket as the Japanese stock market crashed (see the Nikkei 225 stock index history in Exhibit 9.4).

The Nikkei Put sales in the United States marked the tail end of a series of transactions arranged by Goldman Sachs in Japan that also involved the firm's offices and clients in both New York and London. The front end of this story started 2 years earlier in 1988 when Japanese insurance companies purchased hundreds of high-coupon Nikkei-linked bonds from high-quality European issuers. These bonds offered investors above-market coupons in return for accepting the risk of principal loss if the Nikkei 225 Index dropped below a designated level at the maturity of the bonds.

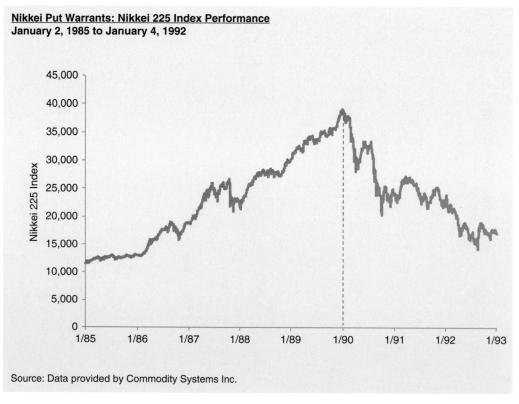

**Nikkei Put Warrants: Nikkei 225 Index Performance**
January 2, 1985 to January 4, 1992

Source: Data provided by Commodity Systems Inc.

**EXHIBIT 9.4**

Economically, these bonds can be analyzed as yen-denominated bonds in which the Japanese investor sold an embedded put warrant on the Nikkei 225 Index to the issuer of the bond (see Exhibit 9.5). The issuer of the bond then sold the embedded put warrant to Goldman Sachs (see Exhibit 9.6 and the discussion that follows). A conventional fixed-rate yen bond from an issuer might have carried a coupon of 5%, but Nikkei-linked bonds often had a coupon of at least 7.5%. The amount by which the Nikkei-linked bond coupon exceeded a conventional coupon represented the warrant (option) premium the Japanese investor received for selling the embedded put warrant to the issuer.

If the Nikkei 225 Index dropped below a designated level at maturity (e.g., 32,000 in Exhibit 9.5), the bond's principal amount paid to the Japanese investor decreased. The amount by which it decreased is equivalent to the settlement value for the embedded put warrant. Therefore, if the Nikkei Index's average dropped below the designated level (strike price), the European issuer repaid the original principal amount through two settlements:

1. The reduced amount of principal is paid to the Japanese investor.
2. An amount equal to the difference between the original principal amount of the bond and the reduced payment to the Japanese investor is paid to Goldman Sachs. This difference is equal to the cash settlement value of the put warrant sold to Goldman Sachs.

Japanese investors were obviously bullish on their domestic stock market when they accepted the downside risk inherent in the Nikkei-linked bonds. However, regulatory factors also motivated these investments. Regulations required that Japanese insurance companies pay dividends to policyholders only from current investment income and not capital gains from stock holdings. Therefore, while dividends received from equity investments and coupons received from bond investments could be paid out, stock market gains could not. This created an incentive to

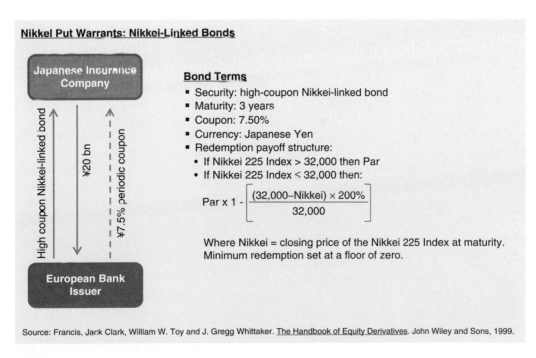

**Nikkei Put Warrants: Nikkei-Linked Bonds**

Japanese Insurance Company

High coupon Nikkei-linked bond

¥20 bn

¥7.5% periodic coupon

European Bank Issuer

**Bond Terms**
- Security: high-coupon Nikkei-linked bond
- Maturity: 3 years
- Coupon: 7.50%
- Currency: Japanese Yen
- Redemption payoff structure:
  - If Nikkei 225 Index > 32,000 then Par
  - If Nikkei 225 Index < 32,000 then:

$$\text{Par} \times \left[ 1 - \frac{(32{,}000 - \text{Nikkei}) \times 200\%}{32{,}000} \right]$$

Where Nikkei = closing price of the Nikkei 225 Index at maturity. Minimum redemption set at a floor of zero.

Source: Francis, Jack Clark, William W. Toy and J. Gregg Whittaker. The Handbook of Equity Derivatives. John Wiley and Sons, 1999.

**EXHIBIT 9.5**

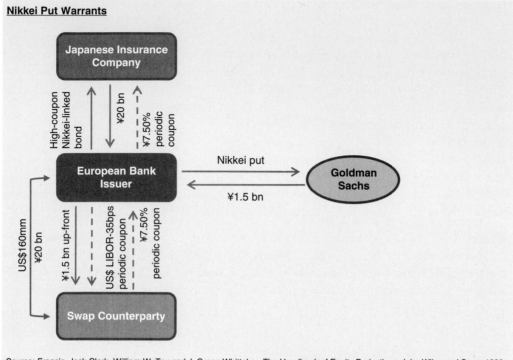

**Nikkei Put Warrants**

Source: Francis, Jack Clark, William W. Toy and J. Gregg Whittaker. <u>The Handbook of Equity Derivatives</u>. John Wiley and Sons, 1999.

**EXHIBIT 9.6**

invest in bonds with high coupons rather than in stock investments with very low dividends (below 1% average).

Because of the Nikkei-linked bonds' higher yield, there was strong demand from Japanese insurance companies for these bonds. As a result, Goldman Sachs (and other investment banks) actively arranged private placements of these bonds for the insurance companies.

The Nikkei-linked bond issuers were mostly AAA-rated European banks and sovereigns that wanted to raise U.S. dollar proceeds at a low interest rate (in the example provided in Exhibit 9.6, a 3-year bond with a net coupon of LIBOR-35 basis points). To achieve this objective, the issuer stripped out the Nikkei put warrant that was embedded in the bond and sold it to Goldman Sachs. The payment from Goldman Sachs for the Nikkei put warrant fully compensated the issuer for the difference between the 7.5% coupon they paid on the Nikkei-linked bonds and the substantially lower LIBOR-35 basis point floating rate payment that was their target (see Exhibit 9.6). In addition, the payment covered the cost of hedging the issuer's currency exposure from yen to U.S. dollars. The issuer was left with a fully hedged U.S.-dollar-denominated financing with a coupon that was below their normal borrowing cost (see Exhibit 9.6).

Goldman Sachs' role in the Nikkei-linked bond transaction was manifold:

1. They located investors (Japanese insurance companies) that were interested in yen-denominated bonds that provided a higher-than-market coupon (7.5% in the example) in exchange for accepting principal repayment risk based on downside exposure to the Nikkei Index.
2. They found highly rated issuers from Europe that were willing to accept a complicated financing structure in order to achieve funding at a below-market interest rate (approximate annual coupon savings of 35 basis points).

3. They arranged a swap counterparty for the issuer to hedge currency exposure from yen to U.S. dollars, with an upfront payment to the counterparty to compensate for risks and costs associated with the swap.
4. They purchased the Nikkei put warrants embedded in the Nikkei-linked bond from the issuer, paying a price equal to the upfront payment required by the swap counterparty to the issuer.

Goldman Sachs paid a price for the Nikkei put warrants that was considerably below the theoretical value of the warrants, creating potential future profit opportunities. With an approximate 2-year gap between when the first Nikkei-linked bonds were originated (resulting in Nikkei put warrant purchases by Goldman Sachs) and when Nikkei put warrants were sold to U.S. retail investors by the Kingdom of Denmark (after purchasing like-warrants from Goldman Sachs), the investment bank had to manage its exposure to the Japanese stock market. Goldman Sachs did this by buying Japanese stocks or futures on these stocks in amounts equal to a portion of the exposure represented by the purchased Nikkei puts, and then *delta hedging* their exposure by buying more shares (or futures) on any future day that the Japanese equity market declined, and selling shares (or futures) when the market increased. As a result of this daily delta hedging, Goldman Sachs was able to transform its exposure from Japanese share price exposure to Japanese stock market volatility exposure, which was easier to manage, until the time that the Nikkei put warrants were sold in the U.S. market (see Exhibit 9.7).

By purchasing Nikkei put warrants at a below theoretical market cost from the Nikkei-linked bond issuer and delta hedging this risk position, Goldman Sachs created the opportunity for significant trading profits (buying when stock prices dropped and selling when they increased) that exceeded the Nikkei put warrant purchase cost. Goldman Sachs was able to succeed in its

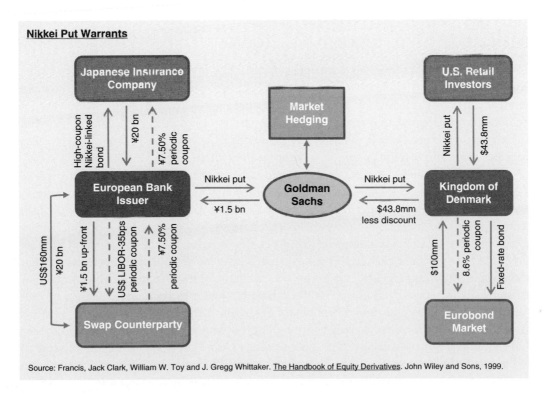

Source: Francis, Jack Clark, William W. Toy and J. Gregg Whittaker. The Handbook of Equity Derivatives. John Wiley and Sons, 1999.

**EXHIBIT 9.7**

strategy because it had accurately estimated that the future volatility of the Nikkei 225 Index would be higher during the delta hedging period than the implied volatility of the Japanese stock market at the time of the purchase of the Nikkei put warrants.

A summary of the activities of Goldman Sachs in relation to the Nikkei put warrant program includes the following:

1. Investment arranger: placed Nikkei-linked bonds with Japanese insurance company investors and Nikkei put warrants with U.S. retail investors.
2. Financing arranger: raised fully hedged low-cost financings for European issuers of Nikkei-linked bonds and Eurobonds for the Kingdom of Denmark and other issuers.
3. Swap arranger: developed the strategy for hedging the Nikkei-linked bond and found swap counterparties.
4. Risk manager: acted as principal in pricing the Nikkei put warrants both in Japan and in the United States, delta hedged the Nikkei put warrant risk position and hedged currency exposure between the yen-denominated Nikkei put warrants purchased and the U.S. dollar-denominated Nikkei put warrants sold.
5. Regulatory catalyst: worked with legal counsel and stock exchange officials to obtain Japanese and U.S. regulatory approvals for the first Nikkei put warrant transaction in the United States.

The Nikkei put warrants transactions created by Goldman Sachs (and several other firms that participated in this effort) offered innovative financing and investing solutions for the firm's issuing and investing clients. By working with its network of offices and clients throughout the world, and undertaking considerable principal risk, the investment bank was able to meet client needs while creating significant risk-adjusted profits.

## Accelerated Share Repurchase Program

Corporations must make decisions each quarter regarding how to allocate available cash. One option is to return cash to shareholders through dividends or share repurchases. Historically, dividend payments represented up to 90% of the total payout to shareholders. However, share repurchases have increased significantly in recent years, and in 2007, cash paid to shareholders from share repurchases eclipsed cash paid in dividends as companies became more focused on earnings per share increases as a vehicle to support their share price.

Normally in the United States, shares are repurchased through an open market share repurchase program whereby the company announces through an SEC filing that they have board approval to purchase either a specified number of shares or a specified dollar amount of shares. The company has no obligation, however, to purchase shares, notwithstanding this announcement, and in some cases never completes the purchases (similar to when a company files an S-3 shelf registration statement that covers future securities issuances but may never issue securities from the registration statement). Assuming the company does initiate a repurchase plan, an investment bank is typically employed as the company's agent to repurchase shares. In order to take advantage of the safe harbor provisions of SEC Rule 10b-18, which mitigates legal risk in repurchases, the agent must limit daily share purchases (with some exceptions) to no more than 25% of the stock's prior 4-week average daily trading volume (ADTV). The result of repurchases is a reduction in the share count in the denominator for EPS reporting. However, with the limitation on daily purchases, it can take more than a year for some companies to purchase the number of shares that the board has authorized, resulting in a slow capture of the EPS benefit from repurchases.

An accelerated share repurchase (ASR) program is designed to capture the EPS benefit of a repurchase program up front, rather than waiting for the benefit to be realized over time. This is accomplished by a contract under which a company purchases a large block of its shares from an investment bank at the closing market price on the date of the purchase, with a cash adjustment to follow at the end of the contract (which might be, for example, one year later). The investment bank borrows the shares it sells to the company from existing shareholders, creating a short position, which it covers through daily open market purchases that are limited to 25% of the company's ADTV. Assuming it takes one year for the investment bank to purchase enough shares to cover its short position, the total cost for the purchases of shares over this period is determined at the end of the year. If the total purchase cost is higher than the payment received by the investment bank from the short sale of shares to the company one year earlier, the company reimburses the investment bank for the difference. If the total purchase cost for the investment bank is less than the payment they received one year earlier, the investment bank reimburses the difference to the company. This adjustment amount after one year is modified based on the returns that the investment bank achieves from investing cash they received from the company upfront (factoring in a reducing cash position each day as cash is used to purchase shares over the one-year period). A further modification to the cash adjustment is made to compensate the bank for their service. See Exhibit 9.8 for a summary of the ASR program.

An ASR program does not create any greater EPS benefit at the end of the repurchase period than if the company purchased its own shares every day over this period. However, the ASR

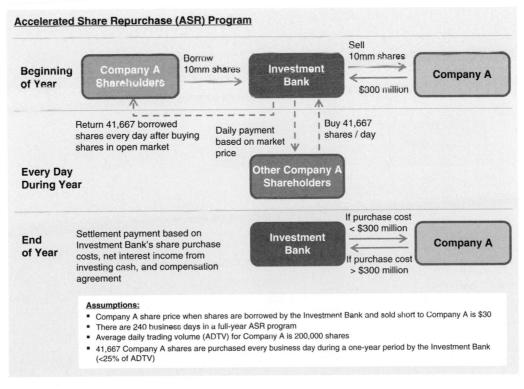

**EXHIBIT 9.8**

program accelerates the EPS benefit to the first day of the period, rather than waiting for the full benefit at the end of the period. This is what motivates some companies to utilize the program. An ASR program also can be linked to equity derivative strategies that create additional potential benefits to the company. For example, call spreads or collars can be included in an ASR program to enable a share repurchasing company to limit the maximum settlement payment they will make at the end of the program.

In addition to creating an earlier EPS benefit, investment banks added an interesting (but short-lived) tax benefit to the ASR in 2007, in conjunction with IBM. In May of 2007, IBM announced that it had completed a $12.5 billion ASR agreement with three investment banks, under which the company repurchased 118.8 million shares (8% of the company's outstanding shares) at $105.18 per share from the investment banks for immediate delivery to the company. The banks were expected to purchase an equivalent number of IBM shares in the open market during the following 9 months, with an adjustment paid (settlement payment) at the end of this period, as just described.

The repurchases were executed through IBM International Group, a wholly owned subsidiary based in the Netherlands, which used $1 billion of its own cash and an $11.5 billion loan from the banks to fund the balance of the purchase. Principal and interest on the loan were to be paid with cash generated by IBM International Group's non-U.S. operating subsidiaries (see Exhibit 9.9).

As a result of this ASR program, IBM was able to purchase $12.5 billion in stock (immediately improving its EPS), and at the same time, lower its tax obligations by using funds from its foreign units to repay the loan instead of repatriating these funds to the United States. Repatriation of funds usually results in a U.S. tax obligation if the money sent back is profit that was taxed overseas at a lower rate. In essence, IBM's use of their overseas unit to purchase stock, with a simultaneous borrowing by the unit, implied that as IBM's overseas businesses produce profits,

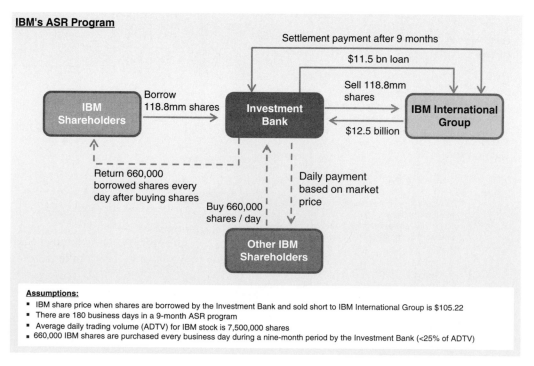

**IBM's ASR Program**

Settlement payment after 9 months

$11.5 bn loan

Sell 118.8mm shares

IBM Shareholders — Borrow 118.8mm shares → Investment Bank → IBM International Group

$12.5 billion

Return 660,000 borrowed shares every day after buying shares

Buy 660,000 shares / day

Daily payment based on market price

Other IBM Shareholders

**Assumptions:**
- IBM share price when shares are borrowed by the Investment Bank and sold short to IBM International Group is $105.22
- There are 180 business days in a 9-month ASR program
- Average daily trading volume (ADTV) for IBM stock is 7,500,000 shares
- 660,000 IBM shares are purchased every business day during a nine-month period by the Investment Bank (<25% of ADTV)

**EXHIBIT 9.9**

these profits would be used to repay the loan raised to finance the repurchase, rather than repatriating the profits to the United States and paying withholding taxes on this repatriation. Assuming a potential repatriation tax rate of 35%, IBM may have reduced their tax bill by approximately $2 billion by applying this rate (minus an estimated 17% credit for foreign taxes paid) to the overseas borrowing of $11.5 billion.

Subsequent to the completion of the IBM ASR transaction and several other similar transactions that reduced repatriation-related taxes, the IRS issued new rules under Section 957(c) that effectively shut down this ASR-related structure. The IRS position was immediately challenged by several corporations.

## Questions

1. After an initial hedge is in place, what do hedge fund investors in convertible bonds do with shares of the underlying stock when the stock price increases or decreases?
2. True or false: Convertible arbitrage hedge funds invest in convertible bonds because the fund managers have a bullish view on the company's stock. Explain your answer.
3. Discuss whether you feel the SEC's temporary ban on short-selling financial stocks in 2008 during the financial crisis unfairly punished convertible arbitrage funds.
4. If companies A and B are identical in every respect except B has higher stock price volatility, which company would likely achieve better convertible pricing? Assuming convertibles issued by A and B have the same terms except for conversion price, would the company you selected have a higher or lower conversion price?
5. WheelCo is raising $200 million via a mandatory convertible bond issuance. Assuming the company's share price on the date of issuance is $20 and the convertible bond carries a 25% conversion premium, what is the number of shares WheelCo has to deliver to investors if its share price at maturity is (a) $19; (b) $22; (c) $26; and (d) $30?
6. Suppose you are a current shareholder in a company that is contemplating capital raising alternatives. Assuming the transaction would have no negative credit repercussions and you want minimal EPS dilution, rank the following types of convertibles from least potential for dilution to most potential for dilution: coupon-paying convertible, mandatory convertible, zero coupon convertible.
7. A U.S.-based BBB-rated company is looking to make a large acquisition. Management believes synergies from the acquisition will create new market opportunities. Unfortunately, these new opportunities will take a few years to realize, and until then, benefits will not be fully reflected in the company's stock price. If the company has rating agency concerns and wants tax deductions from interest payments, what type of security is this company likely to issue in support of its acquisition and why?
8. Why was the Nikkei Put Warrant program so profitable for Goldman Sachs?
9. What is ASR an abbreviation for? Describe this transaction and the principal benefit for a client. What additional benefit did IBM achieve in the ASR program described in this chapter?
10. Assume a company's ADTV is 240,000 shares. How many days would it take to complete a 10.8 million share repurchase program? The company has 120 million shares outstanding, and its estimated EPS for the current fiscal year is $3.40. Assuming the company meets its earnings estimate, what would year-end EPS be under an ASR program for the full 10.8 million shares, assuming it is executed 20 business days before the company's fiscal year end? And under an open market repurchase program?

# Investment Banking Careers, Opportunities, and Issues

Investment banking focuses on (a) giving financial advice to corporate or government-related clients and helping them raise, retire, or risk manage capital; (b) giving strategic advice to corporate clients to enhance shareholder value through acquisitions, divestitures, mergers, or restructurings, (c) taking trading risk positions in financial instruments to provide investment opportunities and liquidity for investing clients; (d) providing financing, risk management, and other securities services to investing clients; (e) providing research for investing clients; (f) investing the firm's own capital on a proprietary basis; (g) providing loans to large corporations that use other investment banking services; (h) managing money for investing clients; and (i) providing support functions for all the aforementioned areas of focus.

Each of these different areas is separately managed and has different responsibilities and compensation systems. Each requires a separate analysis to determine whether there are career fits. All investment banking jobs are time-consuming, intense, and well compensated, but they vary considerably in terms of content and required skills. The nine focus areas just described generally fall into five main business areas: (1) Investment Banking; (2) Trading and Sales; (3) Private Wealth Management, Asset Management, and Research; (4) Principal Investments; and (5) other investment banking functions, such as Operations and Finance.

## Investment Banking

The Investment Banking Division is responsible for (a) giving financial advice to corporate or government-related clients and helping them raise, retire, or risk-manage capital; and (b) giving strategic advice to corporate clients to enhance shareholder value through acquisitions, divestitures, mergers, or restructurings. All bankers in this division have strong analytical and communication skills, but some are better at marketing and others are better at focusing on the technical aspects of transaction execution. Bankers that have marketing skills tend to work in a client relationship management area, and bankers that have greater technical skills often work in a product area such as M&A or capital markets. Of course, there are many exceptions to this general statement, and sometimes bankers move between these areas during their career. In addition, some banks combine M&A and client relationship management into a single area.

This division requires long hours, hard work, and strong analytical skills. Fellow employees and clients are intelligent and demanding, and there is a strong focus on teamwork. The first few years provide an apprenticeship environment where the "trade" is taught and skills are developed. Some of the work during this period is somewhat mundane, and some is highly analytical and creative. Banking operates on a meritocracy system, and those who have or are able to develop the requisite skills and demonstrate the required work ethic can do very well. There is stiff competition to succeed, and not everyone does since there is a culling process to determine the weakest performers every year, who leave the firm either through self-selection or the firm's edict. Depending on the year and the firm, this could be between 5% and 15% of employees. Although compensation generally does not vary much during the first few years, in subsequent years, it can vary dramatically, depending on performance.

There are different entry points into the Investment Banking Division. Analyst positions are available for college graduates and Associate positions are available for a small group of third-year analysts, MBAs, JDs, and, occasionally, professionals from other industries. It is sometimes (but infrequently) possible for professionals from other industries or PhDs to be hired as Vice Presidents or Managing Directors, if they have a unique skill set that is needed at the firm, but these positions are normally filled through internal promotions or hires from other investment banks. At some firms, there are additional levels such as Senior Vice Presidents or Directors (see Exhibit 10.1).

## Analysts

Prospective candidates for analyst positions should develop skills with spreadsheets during their undergraduate years and, ideally, take accounting and economics classes. Finance or investing classes are not essential but could be valuable preparation as well. A summer internship at an investment bank, although difficult to obtain since investment banks limit their summer recruiting to a small number of universities, is very helpful to secure after the sophomore or junior year of college. Analyst positions typically are for a 2- or 3-year period, and most analysts will be asked to leave after this period to pursue an MBA, other academic interests, or to work elsewhere. Depending on the year and the firm, 20% to 40% of analysts will be asked to stay at the firm and are promoted to Associate.

An analyst principally runs analytical models, gathers information, analyzes the information so that it can be incorporated in presentations, and develops presentation materials for Associates, Vice Presidents, and Managing Directors. Analysts usually have multiple projects to work on and are essential members of a client or deal team. Projects generally relate to either M&A or financing transactions. A typical week can involve 80 to 100 hours in the office, sometimes

**Investment Banking Division Positions**

| Position[1] | Source | Period in Position |
|---|---|---|
| Analyst | College graduates | 2 – 3 years |
| Associate | 3rd year analysts, MBAs, JDs, other industries | 3.5 – 5 years |
| Vice President | Experienced associates, other industries | 4 – 10 years |
| Managing Director | Experienced vice presidents, other industries | |

Note 1: Some investment banks also have a Director and/or a Senior Vice President position between Vice President and Managing Director.

EXHIBIT 10.1

including all-nighters, and almost always including work during the weekends. A good attitude, strong analytical skills, attention to detail, and a strong work ethic are essential, as is an ability to work well in a team.

## Associates

MBAs are the principal candidates for the Associate position, although an increasing number of third-year analysts are being promoted into this position. MBA students should focus on developing strong analytical, negotiation, and teamwork skills while in school. A broad array of finance and investing classes are important, as are classes that focus on derivatives, securities analysis, tax planning, restructuring, and M&A. The best MBA candidates have a strong background of extra-curricular and leadership activities and have demonstrated the ability to work well in a group.

Associates manage the day-to-day details of most banking projects and have the principal responsibility to create presentations. They check all analyst work, including financial modeling, and run some of the more complicated models themselves. There is frequent client contact, and, for some smaller deals, an Associate may be responsible for executing the transaction, as well as directly communicating with the client. In addition, they train analysts and recruit future bankers. Work hours are generally not much less than for analysts: 70 to 100 hours per week on average, although there are some differences based on the city and the size of the firms (e.g., outside of New York or smaller firms sometimes require fewer hours).

## Vice Presidents

Associates are generally promoted to Vice President (VP) after 3.5 to 5 years, depending on the firm. VPs are responsible for managing most deals and managing both Associates and Analysts who work on deal teams. They are a principal source of communication with clients and are involved in new business development and client relationship management activities. Negotiating and creating solutions for client problems are a core part of their responsibility. VPs also mobilize resources within the firm to meet client needs, so they need to coordinate with different banking teams and other divisions in the firm.

In addition to deal work, VPs are responsible for recruiting, mentoring, and promoting the firm's overall business activities. They understand internal relationships, resource allocation issues, legal issues (in relation to specific transactions), and ethical standards of the firm. VPs may manage 5 to 10 projects at a time and bear the responsibility for execution of existing transactions and development of new revenue-producing transactions.

## Managing Directors

Managing Directors (MDs) are generally promoted after 4 to 10 years at the Vice President or equivalent level. MDs manage VPs, Associates, and Analysts and have the most senior responsibility for managing client relationships. In addition, they have the greatest burden for developing new business and are asked to achieve a minimum revenue level each year. They must be team-oriented and possess the ability to obtain all the firm's resources necessary to complete deals and meet client needs. They have access to the firm's senior management and frequently call on them to meet with clients. They also have access to resources provided both internally and externally from outside legal, tax, and accounting professionals.

Negotiating with clients and internally for resources is a key part of an MD's job. Proper resource allocation and internal political issues are important areas of focus. Ultimately, Managing Directors are running fairly large businesses with associated revenue that could fall in the range of $10 million to $100 million (or more) a year, depending on the function and the firm. Managing Directors also determine compensation levels and career development paths for members of their team, make capital allocation decisions, and focus on recruiting and training. They usually manage between 5 and 10 revenue-based client projects at a time, while balancing the needs of other clients who are not currently completing transactions but are expected to in the future.

# Trading and Sales

The Trading Division usually has the following focus: (a) taking trading risk positions in financial instruments to provide investment opportunities and liquidity for investing clients; (b) providing financing, risk management, and other securities services to investing clients; (c) providing research for investing clients; and (d) investing the firm's own capital on a proprietary (short-term) basis or through long-term principal investments. Usually, the same titles described for the Investment Banking Division apply to the Trading Division. However, the period of time it takes for promotion could be accelerated for particularly capable employees. Compensation in this Division may initially be comparable or slightly lower than for the Investment Banking Division. However, over time, for especially high-performing employees, the compensation could be higher for Trading Division professionals, since they may have the ability to create greater revenue for the firm.

The entry points into the Trading Division are similar to the Investment Banking Division: Analyst positions are available for college graduates; Associate positions are available for Third-Year Analysts (with many more promoted, compared to the Investment Banking Division), MBAs, and occasionally professionals from other industries. PhDs are also hired as Associates in quant-heavy areas such as fixed income strategy. Sometimes (but infrequently), PhDs and others are hired as Vice Presidents or Managing Directors if they have a unique analytical skill that is needed by the firm.

Descriptions of careers in this division are best provided based on job function rather than job title. The key job functions include Client-Related Trading, Proprietary Trading, and Institutional Sales.

## Client-Related Trading

Client-related traders function as equity, fixed income, currency, or commodity traders. In addition, there is a separate group of derivative traders in each of these areas. Traders have the responsibility to commit the firm's capital in support of purchasing and selling securities with investing clients of the firm. They need to have an inventory of securities at all times in order to actively make bids and offers in reasonable volume for targeted securities. Hedging decisions regarding their inventory and forecasting future valuations are key responsibilities. The ability to make quick, accurate analytical decisions and synthesize a myriad of risks, including political, regulatory, interest rate, credit, and volatility risks, is important. A trader must be able to accept periodic losses and manage a portfolio in an efficient and logical manner. Most of a trader's key decisions are made before noon, when the market is most active, and so a good trader must be able to start early (sometimes 7:00 A.M. or so) and make numerous clear-headed decisions before lunch. Hours are usually shorter than for bankers: often 50 to 60 hours per week. However, time spent on a trading floor can be quite intense.

Client-related traders must be able to work as a team with sales professionals, upon whom they are critically dependent for information and trades. In addition, they must be able to absorb both internal and external research and synthesize this information to build analytical models that facilitate good trading decisions. This is a very fast-paced environment set on a crowded trading floor with, often, hundreds of other traders sharing a large trading area that might have thousands of computer screens and a high noise level. The ability to isolate oneself from the surrounding tumult and rely on carefully built analytical models to guide trading decisions is a key to success in this business.

## Proprietary Trading

Proprietary traders largely need the same skill set as client-related traders. However, they are not integrated with the firm's sales team, as client-related traders are. Proprietary traders may receive investment ideas from internal sales colleagues, but they are also contacted by sales professionals from other firms who consider them to be clients. These traders might have more than a dozen sales professionals calling on them to do trades, and their duty is to execute transactions with whoever can bring the best ideas, best price, and best execution. Assuming the internal and external options are comparable, however, the transaction is likely to be completed in-house, unless there are internal compliance limitations.

There are potential conflicts of interest with the firm's client-related traders, because both sets of traders could be competing for the same trades. As a result, there must be a physical and legal separation between the two groups, as well as restricted communication. In addition, there must be an impermeable *Chinese Wall* between proprietary traders and investment bankers, since the latter are privy to material, non-public information that cannot be shared with anyone outside of a small "need-to-know" group of bankers who are advising clients or executing transactions.

Proprietary traders have the potential to create the largest earnings, as well as the largest losses, within an investment bank. As a result, they can be the best-compensated employees and, if losses are too large, the first to be fired. This is an intense, exciting environment in which confident, highly analytical people with the right personality can thrive. However, it is not for the faint of heart or for those who lose sleep over a loss position. Traders must take a portfolio approach to their trades and make sure that they understand all relevant risks. If 6 or 7 out of 10 trades are profitable and the unprofitable ones have limited losses, a trader can expect a long and successful career.

## Institutional Sales

Institutional sales is divided into equity, fixed income, currency, and commodity areas. There are also separate sales professionals focused on derivative products that relate to these areas. Institutional salespeople work directly with client-related traders in an effort to bring reasonable bids and offers in required sizes to their institutional clients, which include pension funds, endowments, family funds, corporate treasury funds, insurance companies, hedge funds, banks, and mutual funds. Of these clients, hedge funds are the most active traders. It is estimated that hedge fund trading represents approximately 50% of NYSE Euronext and NASDAQ trading, which is by far the largest trading by any of the key institutional investor categories.

### Equity Sales

Equity sales is comprised of four segments. Research sales professionals make stock recommendations to investors based on analysis of internal or external research. Portfolio managers are their client contacts. Sales traders recommend stock trading ideas that are not solely research-based and focus on technical issues that are important to their principal contact, the institutional investor trader. Sales traders have direct contact with their firm's client-related traders to price and execute trades (see Exhibit 5.1 in Chapter 5). Convertibles sales professionals focus exclusively on selling convertible securities to targeted convertible investors. Equity derivative sales professionals cover investing clients who are interested in derivatives transactions.

Sales professionals must always keep abreast of market developments, possess a solid ability to keep track of client's perspectives and priorities, and be creative in finding securities and strategies that help their investing clients achieve good, risk-adjusted trading profits. They stand between internal traders and the investing client, trying to balance the competing interests of both parties.

### Fixed-Income Sales

Fixed-income sales is divided into many different product areas, including (a) investment-grade corporate bonds, (b) high-yield corporate bonds, (c) securitized products, (d) distressed debt, (e) bank loans, (f) U.S. and other sovereign securities, (g) emerging market bonds and loans, (h) municipal securities, (i) preferred stock and commercial paper, (j) money market instruments, (k) foreign exchange, and (l) commodities. Each of these areas is highly specialized, and institutional investors expect focused coverage that provides timely ideas, creative solutions, liquidity, and excellent execution.

This is a very fast-moving market, and volume is the key to achieving profitability, since the margins on many of these products are razor thin. In addition, fixed-income sales includes a separate group of derivatives sales specialists who, in many cases, have overlapping client coverage responsibility. Proper client coverage requires a lot of coordination and good communication.

### Prime Brokerage Sales

Hedge funds are the principal clients of the prime brokerage sales effort. The main products of the prime brokerage area are securities lending and the provision of financing based on sophisticated collateral mechanisms. This group also coordinates securities clearing and provides custody and reporting services. In addition to facilitating trades in stocks, bonds, and convertibles through lending activities, the group also focuses on foreign exchange, precious metals, and derivatives prime brokerage activities. A sales position in Prime Brokerage requires extensive knowledge of the securities market and the ability to work closely with internal sales and trading professionals, as well as with hedge fund clients, who demand excellent service.

## Private Wealth Management

Private Wealth (PW) professionals secure, develop, and manage relationships with high-net-worth individuals, their families, family offices, and foundations. PW helps investing clients build and preserve their financial wealth by creating and implementing long-term asset allocation strategies based on client risk parameters. They also provide clients with access to investment ideas, private banking services, and trust company services. This job requires strong people skills, as well as analytical ability, networking ability, and an understanding of a global array of investment opportunities. Investing clients can make every investment decision and ask the PW sales professional to execute these decisions. Alternatively, investing clients can turn over many decisions to the PW sales team, who will allocate assets according to the client's risk preferences. In this case, the sales effort is a careful balance between introducing clients to investment products offered internally and products offered by external sources. At some investment banks, the PW business is combined with the Asset Management Business in a single division comprised of the two separate business functions. At other firms, the PW business is separate from the Asset Management business. In addition, some firms have a very large "retail" business that works with individual investing clients who have smaller investment portfolios.

## Asset Management

Asset Management (AM) professionals specialize principally in one of the following different areas:

1. Fundamental Equity Investments, which conducts bottom-up research across a broad range of public companies, including both developed and emerging markets globally. This group focuses on both growth equity and value equity investments.
2. Fixed Income Investments, which locates fixed income investing opportunities either locally or throughout the world, focusing in particular on under-researched markets. This group looks at all maturities, including short-term money market instruments and 30-year bonds.
3. Quantitative Investments, which employs advanced quantitative methods to systematically find sources of alpha (risk-adjusted returns in excess of "market returns"). This group utilizes proprietary risk models that actively manage risk and allocations. All securities across all types of investment styles are included in this investment area.
4. Alternative Investments, which includes hedge fund, private equity, fund of fund, and real estate strategies.

AM professionals manage a broad array of funds which target co-investment by many investing clients, whenever suitable. In addition, professionals develop and manage customized investment portfolios and discretionary funds for institutions, corporations, pension funds, governments, foundations, and individuals. They also design and manage families of mutual funds and develop new investment products.

College graduates start at the Junior Analyst or Junior Associate level (title varies depending on firm), which supports the research efforts of buy-side Research Analysts. Some Junior Analysts/Junior Associates leave after two or three years to pursue MBAs, while others are promoted to Associate. Successful Associates are promoted to buy-side Research Analysts, who provide investment recommendations to Portfolio Managers, and some eventually become Portfolio Managers.

The entry points into the AM Division are slightly different from the Investment Banking Division: there are generally fewer positions available for college graduates because entry-level positions are usually offered to MBAs. AM typically has more lateral hires, with candidates coming from consulting, accounting, or investment banking sell-side research. Some AM positions target candidates who have obtained their Chartered Financial Analyst (CFA) certification. PhDs are also hired in areas such as economic research and quantitative research.

# Research

Research is a globally focused business. It covers fundamental research and analysis of selected company debt and equity securities, industries, commodities, and economies. This group provides investment and trading recommendations and strategies for institutional and individual investors, as well as for the Trading Division of the firm. In addition to conducting research and writing reports, research professionals interact with investing and issuing clients, and host conferences and meetings between investors and corporate or government issuers.

Research professionals develop analytical models that capture relevant information (while filtering out noise) and interpret events so that compelling research themes can be developed. In addition to analytical skills, writing skills are essential to facilitate communication. In-depth, nonsuperficial, and timely analysis and reporting is essential to perform well in this function. The entry points for Research are similar to the entry points for AM professionals.

# Principal Investments

Principal Investments is comprised of professionals who focus on (a) acquiring public companies or divisions of companies through leveraged buyout transactions (private equity); (b) infrastructure investments in transport-related projects (toll roads, airports, and ports) and in regulated gas, water, and electrical utilities; (c) mezzanine finance (subordinated debt or preferred shares with equity warrants or conversion rights); (d) private equity fund of funds (investing in multiple external private equity funds as an asset allocator); and (e) real estate investments.

As an example of the meaningful size of the Principal Investments business, Goldman Sachs raised a $6.5 billion infrastructure fund in 2006, a $20 billion private equity fund in 2007, a $20 billion mezzanine fund in 2008, a $5.5 billion private equity secondary fund in 2009, and over $16 billion for real estate investments since 2001. This business also includes a $24 billion private equity fund of funds. Goldman Sachs co-invested in each of these principal investment funds, with an estimated 10–20% of the funds subscribed by the firm, and the balance of the funding coming from institutional and high-net-worth clients.

Professionals who work in the Principal Investments area have a strong investment background and aptitude. Their analytical and negotiation skills are tested in the private equity arena by running LBO models, focusing on debt capital markets to secure leverage, finding high-quality management teams, and determining exit strategies that enable high rates of return.

As the Principal Investments area has grown in recent years, so has the potential for conflicts of interest between this area and the investment bank's large private equity clients such as KKR, TPG, Carlyle, Blackstone, and Bain Capital. The Principal Investments area sometimes competes directly with these firms to secure investment opportunities. This can become problematic, since these same private equity firms usually pay very large fees to investment banks for arranging acquisitions, debt financing, and mezzanine financing. In addition, investment banks are paid fees to arrange exit transactions when private equity clients sell companies they have purchased after a 3- to 7-year holding period. Typical exit strategies include IPOs and M&A sales, both of which are highly profitable businesses for investment banks. Some investment banks have tried to resolve potential conflicts regarding Principal Investments by focusing on joining their private equity clients in *club LBOs,* where an investment bank will co-invest with these clients if the acquisition amount is in excess of the capacity the private equity firms are able to provide. In this case, investment banks claim that they are facilitating private equity client investment objectives, instead of competing against them.

Other potential conflicts of interest arise sometimes when a bank is retained to advise a corporate client that is the target of a potential hostile acquirer. For example, in 2006, Goldman Sachs was acting as an M&A advisor to BAA (the owner and operator of seven British airports) after the company became a target of a hostile takeover attempt. The company was surprised when Goldman Sachs's Principal Investments team indicated their interest to acquire BAA if this prevented the company from falling into the hands of a hostile acquirer. In this case, the company was concerned because, after hiring the firm to protect them from acquirers, Goldman Sachs became a potential acquirer. Goldman, on the other hand, felt that they were acting as a potential "white knight" to preempt a hostile acquisition with a friendly acquisition offer. The result was that BAA fired Goldman Sachs as their M&A advisor, and the original hostile acquirer outbid Goldman Sachs by acquiring $1.9 billion of BAA stock in the open market. Goldman Sachs was criticized by the press in the United Kingdom, which led to their CEO's announcement that the firm needed to be more careful to avoid potential conflict of interest situations in the future.

## Other Investment Banking Functions

The other activities conducted by an investment bank are characterized as service areas designed to facilitate revenue production in the previously described businesses. Included among these service areas are Finance, Operations, Compliance, HR, Legal, Building and Security Management, and Technology. Each of these areas is important for the successful operation of an investment bank. The Operations and Finance areas are summarized in the following sections.

### Operations

The operations activities at an investment bank sometimes represents up to 15% of all employees at a firm. Those in this area assist all of the revenue-generating businesses, serving as internal consultants who develop processes and controls and help specify systems that deliver accurate and timely reporting and execution. This group is involved in risk management and execution activities that protect both the firm's and the client's capital and reputation. It is also a party to the innovation and process improvement activities that create the systems, tools, and workflows that support the firm's transactions, while improving productivity and competitive advantage. This group is also involved in process management activities that create best practices within the firm and solutions to problems faced by clients, the firm, and the industry.

### Finance

Members of an investment bank's finance team are responsible for (a) tracking and analyzing the firm's capital flows; (b) managing relationships with regulators; (c) preparing the firm's statutory financial information and statements for each region; (d) measuring, analyzing, and controlling the risk exposures of the firm; and (e) coordinating with each of the firm's business areas to ensure there is sufficient funding and appropriate allocation of capital. Finance is organized into separate groups that focus on different functions. The controller's group is responsible for safeguarding the firm's assets. The corporate tax team ensures compliance with the tax laws of all countries in which the firm operates. Corporate treasury manages the firm's liquidity and capital structure. The credit department protects the firm's capital against counterparty default. The strategy group develops and executes long-term strategic plans (often working closely in conjunction with the heads of the bank's principal business areas). Market risk management focuses on measuring, analyzing, and controlling the market risk of the firm. Finally, operational risk management analyzes the risk assessment frameworks that identify, measure, monitor, and manage risk exposures.

# Investment Banking Opportunities and Issues

## Mortgage Securitization

Mortgage securitization is the process of combining mortgages into pools and then dividing them into portions (tranches) that can be sold as securities in the capital markets. This process breaks with the tradition of commercial banks holding mortgages on their balance sheets. Instead, banks that originate U.S. mortgages can unwind risk and add liquidity by selling pools of mortgages to government-sponsored enterprises (GSEs)—the Federal National Mortgage Association (FNMA, or Fannie Mae), the Federal Home Loan Mortgage Corporation (FHLMC, or Freddie Mac), or the Government National Mortgage Association (GNMA, or Ginnie Mae)—in addition to private conduit-type customers. By creating a market for previously illiquid mortgages, securitization offers more efficient pricing of mortgages, which lowers interest rates for borrowers and contributes to greater home ownership. The act of pooling mortgages into different tranches, ranging from high coupon to low coupon or short-term to long-term securities, improves the marketability of these investment products by catering to investors with different risk tolerances. Investors can invest in securitized mortgages ranging from senior (lower-risk) securities that pay low interest rates to subordinated (higher-risk) securities that pay high interest rates.

Despite the benefits, the complex nature of securitization can also mask some of the risks involved in owning mortgage-related investments. By immediately selling the mortgages they have originated, commercial banks transfer credit and interest rate risk onto institutional and individual investors, thereby giving lenders little incentive to adhere to strict mortgage underwriting standards. This agent-principal problem contributed to the development of negative amortizing loans, zero principal loans, and no documentation mortgages, as well as the explosion of subprime loans. Subprime mortgages accounted for over 20% of all mortgage originations in 2007, up from 6% in 2002. Securitized mortgages were at the epicenter of the credit crisis of 2007–2008, creating trillions of dollars in investment losses and contributing to significant changes in the investment banking industry landscape.

## Credit Crisis of 2007–2008

After several years of easy credit, excess liquidity, and cheap debt, the financial markets unraveled between the summer of 2007 and the end of 2008. Subprime borrowers began defaulting in mass, pressured by rising interest rates and falling home prices that made refinancing or selling a home a difficult challenge. Investors in mortgage-backed securities (MBS) and collateralized debt obligations (CDO) were the first affected and began reporting large losses as the value of the mortgages underlying these securities dropped. Two Bear Stearns hedge funds that heavily invested in subprime securities declared bankruptcy on July 31, 2007, after failing to meet margin calls. American Home Mortgage, once the tenth largest U.S. mortgage lender, lost the funding it needed to make new loans and filed for bankruptcy on August 6, 2007. Corporate credit spreads responded to these high-profile collapses and began widening dramatically, despite most nonfinancial companies' generous cash holdings. Short-term financing, in the form of commercial paper backed by assets, dried up and threatened the future of a number of financial institutions. The combination of these events led to a full-blown credit crisis that had far-reaching implications for the global economy.

Although governmental response to the subprime mortgage crisis was swift, it failed to improve market conditions. Noting the lack of liquidity in the debt markets, the European Central Bank (ECB) injected €95 billion in overnight credit into the interbank market on August 9, 2007, and the U.S. Federal Reserve quickly followed suit by injecting $38 billion into the U.S. markets on August 10, 2007—the latter's largest cash infusion since the September 11, 2001, terrorist attacks. The Fed then lowered the discount rate by 50 basis points on August 17 and another 50 basis points on September 18. To improve short-term liquidity, the Fed created the Term Auction Facility (which gave banks 28-day loans) in December 2007, and then slashed the Fed funds rate by another 75 basis points in January 2008—its first emergency cut since 1982.

Unfortunately, the Fed's moves only offered short-term relief to the markets and did not stem the losses experienced by mortgage lenders or MBS and CDO investors. Countrywide Financial and Washington Mutual, two of the largest mortgage lenders in the United States, sought cash infusions in order to bolster their capital positions and cover losses. After months of liquidity problems, Countrywide accepted Bank of America's offer in January 2008 to exchange 0.1822 of its shares for each share of Countrywide. Using Bank of America's closing stock price as of April 18, 2008, the deal valued Countrywide at $7.03 per share—a more than 70% discount to where the stock traded one year earlier. IndyMac Bank, a thrift specializing in Alt A loans, saw its loan charge-offs balloon and the value of its assets plummet as the subprime crisis escalated. IndyMac was actively seeking capital after effectively experiencing a bank run, following comments by a senator that raised concerns about the bank's solvency; however, such funding never materialized and the bank was seized by federal regulators on July 11, 2008.

The failure of IndyMac, the tenth largest mortgage lender in the United States, renewed concerns about Freddie Mac and Fannie Mae. Together, these two U.S. government-sponsored enterprises owned or guaranteed about $5.2 trillion of home mortgages (nearly half of mortgage loans outstanding in the United States). Although the majority of loans owned by Freddie Mac and Fannie Mae were prime loans and delinquencies had not risen to worrisome levels, shares of both companies tumbled more than 80% from a year earlier during the summer of 2008, as operating losses mounted and threatened the mortgage companies' capital cushions. The U.S. Treasury and Federal Reserve announced on July 13, 2008, that they would seek approval from Congress to buy equity and give Fannie Mae and Freddie Mac access to the Fed's discount window, signaling to investors that the government was prepared to back these companies in order to stem a housing crisis fallout.

Investment banks were also severely affected by the credit crunch. Large banks such as UBS, Merrill Lynch, and Citigroup announced significant write-downs related to investments in subprime securities, ultimately leading to the resignations of each of these banks' CEOs. Lehman Brothers also took large write-downs and reported a quarterly loss in June 2008 (its first since the investment bank's IPO in 1994), which precipitated the removal of its CFO and COO. With the economy weak and business confidence low, investment banks continued to experience large profit declines in their investment banking, proprietary, and principal investing businesses despite wide-scale staff reductions. Before the end of 2008, Bear Stearns was sold to J.P. Morgan, Merrill Lynch was sold to Bank of America, Wachovia was sold to Wells Fargo, and Lehman Brothers filed for bankruptcy, while Citigroup experienced huge stock declines and required massive public and private capital infusions to stay afloat. See **Case Study 2, "Investment Banking in 2008 (B): A Brave New World,"** for a more complete overview of the crisis during 2007 and 2008 and the new investment banking paradigm that resulted from this crisis.

## Bear Stearns

Bear Stearns, an 85-year-old investment bank with almost $400 billion in assets, was one of the largest casualties of the credit crisis. Following weeks of liquidity and bankruptcy rumors, J.P. Morgan offered to pay $1.2 billion for the firm during March 2008, a fraction of its value just months earlier. Bear Stearns' downfall was striking, considering the firm qualified as "well capitalized" by Fed rules, even when the Fed decided to subsidize the takeover by J.P. Morgan to remove the possibility of a potential collapse. Bear's leverage ratio (as defined by assets / equity) in the fourth quarter of 2007 was approximately 33 times—a high number, but not an outlier among investment banks, as it was in line with peers such as Morgan Stanley.

Bear's ultimate undoing was the perception that it was facing a cash crunch. Despite assurances from CEO Alan Schwartz that the company's balance sheet remained strong, counterparties began placing margin calls in droves on March 13, 2008, leading creditors to pull funding from the bank. The next day, Schwartz announced that Bear had taken an emergency loan out with J.P. Morgan as its "liquidity position in the last 24 hours had significantly deteriorated." The following weekend, Bear negotiated its buyout package with J.P. Morgan, who was the bank's clearing agent for its collateral.

Bear Stearns endured more than its fair share of pitfalls in the 10 months leading up to its demise. The collapse of two of Bear's hedge funds (that were heavily invested in subprime securities) during July 2007 arguably ushered in the start of the credit crisis. Bear's subsequent write-downs on mortgage-related securities and abysmal quarterly results, compounded by its focus on fixed income trading, reinforced the sense that it was struggling relative to the other investment banks. Still, Bear took steps to line up greater long-term funding as the credit crisis unfolded, and had investors not lost confidence in its financial position, Bear may have survived with the Fed's creation of the Primary Dealer Credit Facility (PDCF). The PDCF, which was established the same day the J.P. Morgan–Bear Stearns deal was announced, allows primary dealers to provide investment-grade securities as collateral for short-term loans from the Federal Reserve Bank of New York in order to fund their operations. The demise of Bear Stearns—an institution that had weathered the Great Depression and the Savings and Loan crisis—illustrates how perception can be more influential than reality during times of financial uncertainty. See **Case Study 1, "Investment Banking in 2008 (A): Rise and Fall of the Bear,"** for a more complete summary of the rise and fall of Bear Stearns.

## Short-Term Financing by Investment Banks

Investment banks have historically relied on large amounts of short-term financing to fund their operations. The most popular forms of short-term financing are commercial paper and repurchase (repo) agreements. In a typical repo agreement, a financial institution receives financing by selling securities and repurchasing them at a higher price when the agreement matures (often overnight, or in 1 week or 1 month). In this exchange, the buyer receives securities as collateral to protect against default. Should these assets tumble in value, the seller is forced to come up with additional cash to meet margin calls or risk losing access to credit. Almost 25% of total assets at large investment banks were financed by overnight repos in 2007, an increase from about 12.5% in 2000.

Commercial paper is different from repos in that it is generally unsecured and matures within 1 to 270 days (although most paper matures within 90 days). Investment banks typically refinance or *roll over* maturing paper with new commercial paper issuance.

Short-term financing provides four principal benefits for investment banks:

1. Funding is cheap (below bank loan rates), because historical default risk is low.
2. Availability of funding is typically high.
3. This funding provides considerable flexibility to meet cash needs as they change from day to day.
4. In a normal upward-sloping yield curve environment, the longer-term assets purchased with short-term liabilities carry returns above funding costs, creating earnings based on an asset/liability mismatch.

While short-term financing offers investment banks many benefits, it also exposes them to interest rate and liquidity risk. Specifically, should the banks' assets experience a significant drop in value, the interest rate charged by investors can increase and the availability of short-term financing can evaporate. Investment banks found themselves in this position during October 2008 (following the collapse of Lehman Brothers), when the amount of their commercial paper outstanding shrank to just 25% of its former volume virtually overnight. Instead of issuing more paper to pay back investors, when the market dried up, banks were forced to dump assets at significant discounts. The credit crisis also caused significant value reductions in the collateral backing repo agreements (as well as a general crisis of confidence), resulting in the refusal by many investors to roll over repos. This refusal forced banks to unload more assets at firesale prices, exacerbating the drop in securities values across the globe. After the credit markets ravaged investment banks during 2007 and 2008, these institutions were forced to significantly reduce their reliance on short-term financing and limit their asset/liability mismatch. The end result was higher funding costs, less flexibility, and lower earnings potential.

## Structured Investment Vehicles

First launched by Citigroup in 1988, a structured investment vehicle (SIV) is an operating finance company that engages in market arbitrage. SIVs are designed to earn stable returns above prevailing market interest rates by generating a positive investment spread between their assets and liabilities. Specifically, SIVs make money by selling short-term commercial paper backed by assets and investing the proceeds in longer-term, higher-yielding assets such as mortgage-related securities.

SIVs are structured as special-purpose vehicles (SPVs) so that banks can keep them off their balance sheets. This serves to free up regulatory capital, maintain the bank's credit rating, and protect the operating company against insolvency and other risks. Unlike on-balance sheet entities, SIVs are not required to publicly disclose their investment holdings or leverage.

Most SIVs minimize credit risk by investing in highly rated securities. However, they still face liquidity and interest rate risk due to their investing strategies. SIVs' net interest income suffers during a flattening yield curve, because returns from investments do not increase at a rate commensurate with the rise in funding costs. As a result, profits drop until yields on longer-dated securities improve. This risk may be mitigated somewhat by utilizing hedging instruments. Liquidity risk, however, is far more difficult to manage successfully. SIVs depend on a liquid asset-backed commercial paper market to finance their investments. When refinancing is not possible, an SIV may be forced to sell investments in order to meet its debt obligations.

During the credit crisis, SIVs encountered enormous liquidity risk. A lack of demand for commercial paper combined with plummeting prices for mortgage-related securities threatened the survival of many SIVs. The U.S. Treasury Department responded to the impending crisis during September 2007 by asking the largest commercial banks to consider setting up a super-conduit that would buy the troubled SIVs' assets. This way, SIVs would not be forced to dump their mortgage-backed securities into the market, driving prices even lower and potentially triggering a full-blown meltdown. However, this strategy did not work, as the credit crisis worsened and availability of commercial paper funding for SIVs dried up entirely. As the global credit crisis worsened during 2008, most SIV activities were wound down.

## Leverage at Investment Banks

Banks are heavily leveraged compared to other businesses. The average commercial bank has a leverage ratio (defined as total assets / book equity) in the range of between 10 and 15 to 1, compared to between 1 and 3 to 1 for the average nonfinancial company. Investment banks historically took on more debt than commercial banks, with average leverage ratios of between 20 and 30 to 1. Investment banks use leverage to enhance their return on equity (a closely watched metric for financial services companies). When business plans are realized, leverage boosts returns and profits. However, when losses occur, banks' high leverage can cause outsized losses that reduce equity and deplete capital cushions. During 2007, leverage at investment banks approached (or reached, in several cases) historical highs.

Investment banks frequently adjust their leverage in response to liquidity conditions and the macro economy. As a result, leverage is typically high during business cycle peaks and low during business cycle troughs. During the first half of 2007, investment banks were enjoying a strong period of growth marked by impressive proprietary trading profits. Despite rising value at risk (VaR) estimates, which measure an investment bank's "worst case" losses if conditions quickly deteriorate, investment banks continued to build up leverage to augment their investment returns. Such excessive leverage, however, worked against the banks when the credit markets collapsed during the second half of 2007. At that time, trading losses piled up, and asset prices plunged in response to worries about the value of underlying collateral. Consequently, many investment banks moved from appearing overcapitalized to undercapitalized over the span of 6 months. During 2008 and 2009, investment banks all significantly reduced their leverage following substantial losses and the imposition of regulatory requirements that restricted leverage (see Exhibit 10.2).

## Capital Ratios

Some investors have become increasingly skeptical regarding investment banks' capital ratios. Tier 1 ratios are reported by investment banks based on either Basel I or Basel II guidelines. These ratios compare shareholder's equity to risk-adjusted assets. However, deciding on the proper risk weighting for assets leaves the process open to subjective judgments. Historically, U.S. investment banks compiled assets based on Basel I guidelines and under supervision by the SEC, while commercial banks compiled assets based on Basel II and under the supervision of the Federal Reserve. During late 2008, however, all investment banks shifted to compiling assets under Basel II. Unfortunately, Basel II allows for management judgment and management control over models that determine the risk weighting of assets, which, in effect, gives banks some latitude to set their own capital requirements. As a result, there is a concern that these ratios may not provide reliable information about bank capital. See Exhibit 10.3 for a comparison of Tier 1 ratios as of December 31, 2008.

## Compensation

Historically, investment banks have targeted compensation as a percent of total net income to be at or below 50%. At J.P. Morgan's investment bank, this percentage was 41% in 2006, 44% in

**Leverage at Investment Banks**

| Firm | Leverage (Assets / Equity) | | | |
|---|---|---|---|---|
| | YE-06 | YE-07 | YE-08 | Mid-09 |
| Bank of America | 10.8 | 11.7 | 10.3 | 10.0 |
| Barclays[1] | 39.2 | 41.4 | 49.8 | 41.0 |
| Bear Stearns[2] | 28.9 | 33.5 | -- | -- |
| Citigroup | 15.7 | 19.3 | 13.7 | 12.1 |
| Credit Suisse | 28.8 | 31.5 | 36.2 | 30.1 |
| Deutsche Bank[1] | 34.3 | 50.8 | 71.7 | 50.5 |
| Goldman Sachs | 23.4 | 26.2 | 13.7 | 14.2 |
| JPMorgan Chase | 11.7 | 12.7 | 13.0 | 13.1 |
| Lehman Brothers[2] | 26.2 | 30.7 | -- | -- |
| Merrill Lynch[2] | 21.6 | 31.9 | -- | -- |
| Morgan Stanley | 31.7 | 33.4 | 13.0 | 14.5 |
| UBS[1] | 48.2 | 61.7 | 61.9 | 47.7 |

Note 1: Barclays, Deutsche Bank and UBS financials are presented under IFRS standards. All other banks are presented according to U.S. GAAP. A major difference between IFRS and U.S. GAAP is the accounting for derivatives, non-derivative trading assets, and reverse repos/borrowed securities. The former shows gross exposures while the latter shows values on a net basis. For example, after taking into consideration the netting impact of U.S. GAAP accounting, Deutsche Bank's total assets at year-end 2008 drops from EUR 2,202 billion to EUR 1,030 billion. According to Deutsche Bank's targeted leverage ratio definition, which has adjustments for U.S. GAAP netting rules (and some additional minor adjustments), its adjusted assets / adjusted equity ratio was 28 at December 31, 2008.

Note 2: Bear Stearns and Merrill Lynch were acquired by JPMorgan Chase and Bank of America, respectively, in 2008. Lehman Brothers filed for Chapter 11 bankruptcy protection in 2008 and subsequently sold its U.S. investment banking operations to Barclays.

Source: Respective 10-K and 10-Q filings; Deutsche Bank roadshow presentation from February 19 – 20, 2009

EXHIBIT 10.2

**Capital Cushions: Bank Tier-1 Ratios**
As of Year-End 2008[1]

| Global Investment Banks | |
|---|---|
| Bank of America | 9.2% |
| Barclays | 8.6% |
| Citigroup | 11.9% |
| Credit Suisse | 13.3% |
| Deutsche Bank | 10.1% |
| Goldman Sachs | 15.6% |
| J.P. Morgan | 10.9% |
| Morgan Stanley | 17.9% |
| UBS | 11.0% |

Note 1: Bank of America, Barclays, Citigroup, Credit Suisse, Deutsche Bank, J.P. Morgan, and UBS as of fiscal year ended December 31, 2008; Goldman Sachs and Morgan Stanley as of fiscal year ended November 30, 2008.

Source: Respective 2008 10-K filings

EXHIBIT 10.3

2007, and 63% in 2008. Bonuses usually make up more than half of a firm's compensation expense. During profitable years, a year-end bonus might be more than three times the size of the salary for a successful Vice President or Managing Director. Following the financial crisis of 2007–2008, governments around the world attempted to influence investment bank compensation decisions in an effort to reduce excessive risk taking that led to losses during these years. France, Germany, and the Netherlands limited the size of bonuses paid to senior bankers. In the United States, firms that received TARP funding from the government were forced to reduce senior management and trader bonuses. However, efforts to remake broad-based financial rules regarding compensation became bogged down amid infighting between federal regulators and opposition from lawmakers who believed that further expanding the government's reach would only create new problems. An industry consensus emerged nonetheless that multiyear employment contracts should be avoided, and up to 50% of bonus compensation should be paid in the form of stock, which vests over multiple years and becomes unrestricted only if legacy risk positions remain profitable over time.

## New Power Brokers in the Capital Markets

An ongoing study by the McKinsey Global Institute examines four groups of investors that are having a major impact on the global capital markets: Asian governments, oil exporters, hedge funds, and private equity firms. Their influence significantly impacts investment banking activities, since they have amassed an increasingly large pool of capital. These new investor groups have expanded their investment strategies and increased the use of private financing as an alternative to the public markets.

The combined financial assets of these four investor groups is in excess of $12 trillion (see Exhibit 10.4). As Asian countries' trade surpluses and oil-exporting countries' petro-profits continue to grow, it is possible their assets may eventually reach the size of assets under management by insurance companies. Although the credit crisis that started during mid-2007 reduced somewhat the growth rate of private equity and hedge funds, investor appetite for alternative investment returns should continue for diversification reasons, even as returns have dropped.

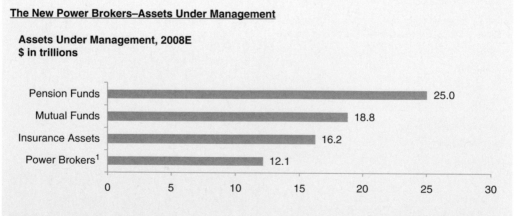

**The New Power Brokers–Assets Under Management**

Assets Under Management, 2008E
$ in trillions

| | |
|---|---|
| Pension Funds | 25.0 |
| Mutual Funds | 18.8 |
| Insurance Assets | 16.2 |
| Power Brokers[1] | 12.1 |

Note 1: Power brokers include Asian governments, oil export countries, hedge funds, and private equity funds.
Source:  McKinsey Global Institute; International Financial Services, London; Hedge Fund Research, Inc.; Investment Company Insititute; Preqin

**EXHIBIT 10.4**

Since private equity funds and hedge funds can leverage their investments, the buying power of their combined $2.3 trillion in assets under management may be approximately $5 to $6 trillion, based on this leverage.

As the power brokers' wealth has increased, so has their influence. Citigroup, UBS, Barclays, and Morgan Stanley have all received substantial investments from Asian governments and oil exporters in recent years (see Exhibit 10.5). Petrodollar investors include the six states of the Gulf Cooperation Council (Bahrain, Kuwait, Oman, Qatar, Saudi Arabia, and the United Arab Emirates) and other oil exporters in the Middle East and North Africa, as well as Norway, Russia, Venezuela, Nigeria, and Indonesia. These investors include central banks, sovereign wealth funds, companies, and wealthy individuals from these regions. Overall, government entities control about 60% of petrodollar foreign assets, and wealthy individuals and companies control the remaining 40%. High oil prices have elevated petroleum exporters into the ranks of major foreign investors, including Russia, which in 2008 made $330 billion in new foreign investments (see Exhibit 10.6).

Asian sovereign investors include central banks, which hold about 85% of foreign assets, and sovereign wealth funds, which hold 15% of assets. Apart from Singapore, Asian governments manage most of their foreign assets through central banks, who have traditionally invested in low-risk, fixed-income securities (in particular, U.S. Treasuries). The two largest central bank investors are China, with $1.9 trillion in foreign reserve assets, and Japan, with $1 trillion. When compared with asset managers on a global basis, the Chinese central bank's AUM is greater than that of the largest private asset manager in the world, Barclays Global Investors (see Exhibit 10.7).

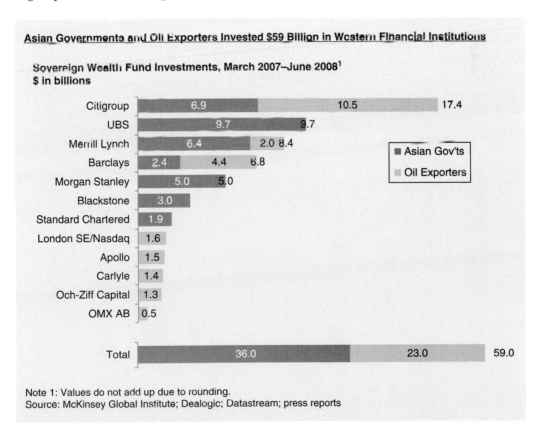

**Asian Governments and Oil Exporters Invested $59 Billion in Western Financial Institutions**

Sovereign Wealth Fund Investments, March 2007–June 2008[1]
$ in billions

| | Asian Gov'ts | Oil Exporters | Total |
|---|---|---|---|
| Citigroup | 6.9 | 10.5 | 17.4 |
| UBS | 9.7 | 9.7 | |
| Merrill Lynch | 6.4 | 2.0 | 8.4 |
| Barclays | 2.4 | 4.4 | 6.8 |
| Morgan Stanley | 5.0 | 5.0 | |
| Blackstone | 3.0 | | |
| Standard Chartered | 1.9 | | |
| London SE/Nasdaq | 1.6 | | |
| Apollo | 1.5 | | |
| Carlyle | 1.4 | | |
| Och-Ziff Capital | 1.3 | | |
| OMX AB | 0.5 | | |
| Total | 36.0 | 23.0 | 59.0 |

Note 1: Values do not add up due to rounding.
Source: McKinsey Global Institute; Dealogic; Datastream; press reports

**EXHIBIT 10.5**

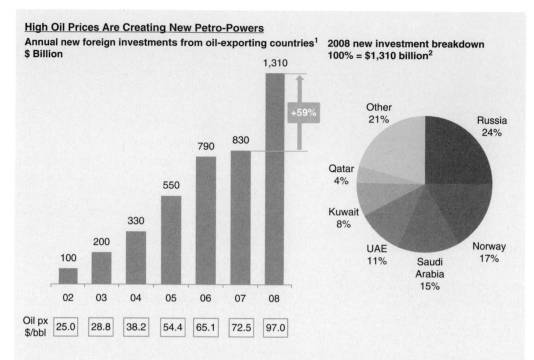

**High Oil Prices Are Creating New Petro-Powers**

Annual new foreign investments from oil-exporting countries[1]
$ Billion

2008 new investment breakdown
100% = $1,310 billion[2]

Note 1: Oil-exporting countries include the Gulf Cooperation Council states (Bahrain, Kuwait, Oman, Qatar, Saudi Arabia, and the UAE), Algeria, Indonesia, Iran, Libya, Nigeria, Norway, Russia, Syria, Venezuela, and Yemen.
Note 2: Values do not add up due to rounding.
Source: McKinsey Global Institute; Institute for International Finance; International Monetary Fund; U.S. Department of Energy; McKinsey Global Institute Cross-Border Investment Database

**EXHIBIT 10.6**

**China's Central Bank Would Rank as the Largest Asset Manager in the World**

Largest 10 asset managers by AUM, 2008; $ Trillion

Source: McKinsey Global Institute; company reports; International Financial Services, London; Investment Alliance; Investment Company Institute; Nelson Marketplace Web; People's Bank of China; Bank of Japan

**EXHIBIT 10.7**

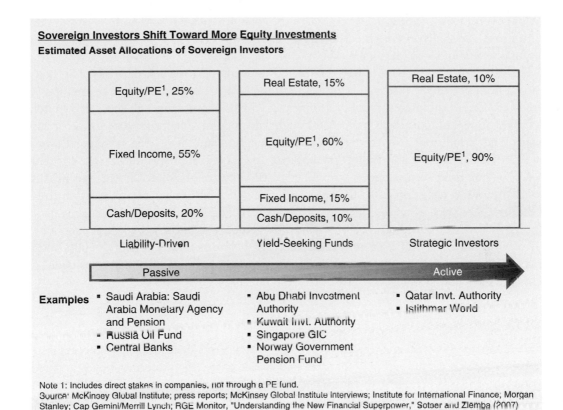

Sovereign Investors Shift Toward More Equity Investments
Estimated Asset Allocations of Sovereign Investors

EXHIBIT 10.8

Among sovereign investors, there is an increasing appetite for a broader array of investments, many of which carry much higher risk (see Exhibit 10.8).

The credit crisis significantly impacted private equity funds. The spread between high-yield bond rates over swap rates, which is a measure of private equity's cost of credit, increased from 190 basis points in June 2007 to 539 basis points in March 2008. This dramatic financing cost increase, combined with limited availability of credit for leveraged buyouts, reduced the ability of private equity firms to raise capital and substantially reduced the volume of buyouts. However, private equity firms are finding alternative ways to deploy capital and have expanded their activity in Private Investment in Public Equity (PIPEs), emerging market investments, investments in smaller companies that require less leverage, investments in banks that are recapitalizing, and investments in distressed debt.

The credit crisis also significantly impacted hedge funds. This crisis led to lower hedge fund returns and several fund blow-ups. Total hedge fund industry average returns were negative during the first quarter of 2008 for the first time since 2004 and ended 2008 down over 19% for the year, before rebounding to positive territory during the first half of 2009. Bear Stearns' hedge funds, Peloton Partners, Sailfish Capital Partners, Focus Capital, and UBS's Dillon Read were all large hedge funds that shut down during 2007 and 2008. Hedge fund leverage dropped by about 40% between early 2007 and late 2008, reducing the industry's ability to achieve historical returns. However, with consolidations favoring the largest funds and permanent capital already raised by several hedge funds in IPO transactions, capital managed by the industry should continue to grow, especially among the 100 largest hedge funds, which already control 74% of all hedge fund assets under management.

The rapid rise of the new power brokers poses a number of potential risks. For example, additional liquidity might foster asset price inflation: Asian and petrodollar investors may have lowered U.S. long-term interest rates by as much as 75 basis points through their large purchases of U.S. Treasuries and corporate bonds. Although this may have helped create low-cost capital, the easy money conditions also led to rising real estate prices and then to the subsequent mortgage crisis. Another risk is the concern that state investors might use their spending power for political purposes, as has been seen in the antics of Venezuela's President Hugo Chavez and in Russia's stoppage of natural gas supplies to Ukraine. Systemic risk is also a concern in relation to hedge fund failures. This was a major concern at the time of Long-Term Capital Management's near-collapse and also a concern during the 2007–2008 credit crisis. Finally, bad investments by private equity during 2006 and 2007 may result in a significant increase in credit defaults and poor returns for these vintage year investments. Hedge fund and private equity challenges could result in ongoing credit and earnings concerns for investment banks.

## Credit Default Swaps

Credit default swaps (CDSs) are derivative contracts designed to spread risk and reduce exposure to credit events such as default or bankruptcy. In a CDS, one party (the protection buyer) makes periodic payments to a second party (the protection seller) in exchange for a payoff in the event a third party (the reference entity) defaults on its debt obligations. For protection buyers, a CDS resembles an insurance policy, as it can be used to hedge against a default or bankruptcy by the reference entity. For protection sellers, a CDS creates annual income in exchange for the risk they undertake.

Unlike most other financial products, CDS contracts have historically been unregulated. Although contracts specify the identity of protection sellers and the scheduled termination date of default protection, some contracts have not required the seller to hold assets as collateral for the transaction. Without a self-regulatory organization (SRO) to mandate standard terms and practices, there is no universal way of valuing the securities involved in these contracts. Furthermore, CDS contracts are heavily traded, with contracts often changing hands many times over the course of their life. As a result, the protection buyer often does not know whether the protection seller has sufficient capital to cover a security's loss and provide payment to the protection buyer.

According to the International Swaps and Derivatives Association (ISDA), the CDS market exploded over the past decade to more than $54 trillion notional amount in mid-2008, which is more than twice the market capitalization of the U.S. stock market. CDS emerged as a popular portfolio management tool due to its flexibility in customizing exposure to corporate credit. Investors could effectively establish a short position without making an initial cash outlay. These instruments also allowed investors to exit credit positions during periods of low liquidity.

The strong economy of the mid-1990s drove the growth of the CDS market. Protection sellers believed the odds of corporate default were low and viewed the premiums received as an easy way of enhancing investing returns. For many years, this was the case, and investment banks, commercial banks, some insurance companies (notably AIG), and hedge funds profited from the CDS market.

However, returns quickly evaporated with the onset of the subprime crisis. Credit spreads widened significantly, negatively impacting the performance of CDS contracts that were increasingly used to hedge against default for poor quality companies. According to Fitch Ratings, 40% of CDS protection sold worldwide in July 2007 was on companies or securities that were rated below investment grade, up from 8% in 2002. With bond defaults rising, investors began to worry about counterparty risk and questioned whether sellers had adequate reserves to cover losses. This concern precipitated the Fed's bailout of Bear Stearns and AIG (both active sellers of CDSs). Counterparties to Bear and AIG began withdrawing cash from these firms, and regulators feared the repercussions of large-scale bankruptcies.

In response to these events and concerns that the CDS market could unravel, new regulations were issued that required protection sellers to disclose the nature and terms of the credit derivative, the reason it was entered into, the current status of its payment and performance risk, the amount of future payments it might be required to make, the fair value of the derivative, and whether there are provisions that would allow the seller to recover money or assets from third parties.

## Bridge Loans

Investment banks have made large bridge loan commitments to M&A clients to fund cash acquisitions, with the expectation that the loans will only be funded if a long-term securities offering such as a high-yield bond transaction or a secured syndicated loan is not completed. The bridge loan often has a commitment fee, a takedown fee when the loan is drawn down, and a significant credit spread over a floating interest rate. In addition, the provider of the bridge loan generally secures the right to arrange the take-out financing, which includes underwriting and placement fees.

Although participating in bridge loans helps investment banks secure additional lucrative business from private equity firms (such as debt underwriting and M&A advisory), there can also be considerable risk. For example, during 2006 and 2007, private equity firms pushed investment banks to provide large bridge loans to fund many large acquisitions from which the investment banks were receiving M&A advisory fees. When the credit crunch hit, a large number of buyout-related bridge loans were fully drawn down at a time when the capital markets were unable to provide take-out financing in the form of high yield bonds or long-term syndicated loans. As a result, investment banks unexpectedly had to fund what turned out to be long-term loans that tied up considerable bank capital and caused significant losses for the banks as credit conditions deteriorated. As of the end of August 2007, it was estimated that the nine largest investment banks held more than $250 billion of unwanted *hung* bridge loans provided to private equity clients to fund their leveraged buyouts (see Exhibit 10.9).

## Investment Banking Future

Investment banking industry revenue tumbled during 2007 and 2008 due to weak financing and M&A markets, reductions in leverage available to support proprietary trading, and massive write-offs from mortgage-related businesses, bridge loans, and SIV arrangements. During 2009, a partial recovery in the M&A and financing markets bolstered revenue and provided a foundation for stabilizing the industry. Goldman Sachs, J.P. Morgan, and Morgan Stanley sit at the top of global investment banking revenue rankings, and they have the momentum to maintain this lead. The other six largest global firms should be able to maintain their competitive position overall, while boutique investment banks may be able to make inroads in the M&A advisory market.

### LBO Bridge Loans

- A large volume of mega private equity deals in 2007 combined with an escalating credit crisis starting in the second half of 2007 created a significant amount of hung bridge loans stuck on banks' balance sheets. By Q3 of 2007, there were an estimated $300 billion in outstanding bridge loans.

- Although not a lucrative business for banks, the intense competition for M&A and financing fees from private equity clients persuaded most large banks to participate in this lending practice.

- Ironically, although pressure from the private equity firms caused this predicament for the banks, private equity firms were also among those that took advantage of lenders' woes, by raising dedicated funds to purchase these loans at discounted prices from the banks.

| Hung Bridge Loans (Q3 07) | | Dedicated Hung Bridge Funds | |
|---|---|---|---|
| Company | Estimated Outstanding "Hung Bridges" | Fund | Fund Size |
| Citigroup | $51 billion | Goldman Sachs Fund | $1 billion |
| J.P. Morgan | $41 billion | Lehman Brothers Special Situations | $2 billion |
| Goldman Sachs | $32 billion | Oaktree Fund | $4 billion |
| Deutsche Bank | $27 billion | TPG Credit Fund | $1 billion |
| Credit Suisse | $27 billion | Apollo | $1 billion |
| Lehman Brothers | $22 billion | Blackstone | $1 billion |
| Morgan Stanley | $20 billion | | |
| Bank of America | $18 billion | | |
| Merrill Lynch | $16 billion | | |

Source: Reuters Loan Pricing Corp.; Deponte, Kelly: "Hung Bridge" Funds, Probitas Partners, Sep. 2007; company filings; author's estimates

**EXHIBIT 10.9**

Equity, equity derivatives, FX, and prime brokerage businesses, which have been somewhat less affected by the credit crunch, should be able to perform well going forward. Some businesses that have been more directly affected, such as securitization and credit derivatives, will require portfolio adjustments and a strengthened talent base in order to produce required returns in the future. The fixed income business will need to become less reliant on leverage in general and short-term financing in particular. Banks will need to avoid repeating the mistake of replacing shrinking client margins with proprietary trading that is not always linked to specific capabilities. The key to future trading activity may be to concentrate more risk-taking on facilitating client transactions and less on leveraged investments unrelated to clients.

Going forward, there will be reduced appetite for risk and leverage in the investment banking industry. This may lead to lower returns on equity, unless firms can make technological progress in driving costs down, more fully capture share-of-wallet opportunities with clients, and create new sources of revenue from products and services that have yet to be developed. Historically, the industry has been remarkably resourceful in reinventing itself and driving earnings through new products and services. In spite of tighter regulations, including greater control over balance sheets and compensation practices, as the global economy improves, the industry should be able to continue creating value for clients and good returns on invested capital.

# Questions

1. What are the core differences between Investment Banking (IB) and Sales and Trading career paths?
2. Describe what a *Chinese Wall* is and which U.S. regulator would be concerned with issues involving the wall.
3. What advancement in the mortgage market set the foundation for the subprime crisis and why?
4. Describe a Credit Default Swap (CDS). What are regulators trying to do to mitigate risk in the CDS market?
5. Under what scenarios will the SIV market arbitrage model fail to work?
6. Why were U.S. investment banks allowed to operate at higher leverage ratios compared to commercial banks?
7. How does the phrase "perception is reality" apply to Bear Stearns?
8. How do Asian and petrodollar investors fit into the genesis of the financial crisis during 2007–2008? Structure your answer around the themes of easy credit, excess liquidity and cheap debt.
9. Discuss how CDS can be used for hedging and speculative purposes.

# Hedge Funds and Private Equity

# 11

# Overview of Hedge Funds

In the United States, the Securities and Exchange Commission (SEC) has stated that the term hedge funds "has no precise legal or universally accepted definition."[1] But most market participants agree that hedge funds have the following characteristics: (1) almost complete flexibility in relation to investments, including both long and short positions; (2) ability to borrow money (and further increase leverage through derivatives) in an effort to enhance returns; (3) minimal regulation; (4) some illiquidity since an investor's ability to get an investment back is restricted through lock-up agreements (that may prevent any liquidity during the first 1 or 2 years of a hedge fund's life) and quarterly disbursement limitations thereafter (subject to *gates*, which may further limit disbursements); (5) investors include only wealthy individuals and institutions such as university endowments, pension funds, and other qualified institutional buyers (except through fund of fund investments, which are available to a broader array of investors); and (6) fees that reward fund managers for performance.

A typical fee structure for hedge funds includes both a management fee and a performance fee, whereas a typical mutual fund does not require a performance fee and has a smaller management fee. Hedge fund management fees are usually around 2% of net asset value (NAV), and performance fees are approximately 20% of the increase in the fund's NAV. This *2 and 20* fee structure is significantly higher than for most other money managers, with the exception of private equity fund managers, who enjoy similarly high fees.

Hedge funds target *absolute returns*, which are investment returns that theoretically do not depend on the performance of broad markets and the economy, unlike the returns associated with mutual funds. One of the historical claims made by hedge funds (which is a subject of dispute following large losses by many hedge funds during 2008) is that their returns are "uncorrelated" with market returns for traditional investments such as stocks and bonds. A lack of correlation is an attractive characteristic for investors who are attempting either to lower risk in their investment portfolio while keeping returns unchanged or to increase returns in their portfolio without increasing risk.

This category of investment management started during 1949 when Alfred W. Jones created a fund that utilized short selling of assets to hedge other assets that were purchased to create an investment portfolio. His fund neutralized the effect of changes in the general market by buying assets that were expected to increase in value and selling short assets that were expected to fall in value. This created a hedge that was designed to remove overall market risk. Others followed Jones in using hedging strategies within an investment fund, creating the investment fund category called *hedge funds*. However, many funds that do not use hedging in their investment strategy are still called hedge funds if they exhibit the characteristics described in the first paragraph of this chapter. Most hedge funds, in fact, are not hedged, as established by several academic studies

---

[1]"Implications of the Growth of Hedge Funds." Staff Report to the United States Securities and Exchange Commission, 2003.

An Introduction to Investment Banks, Hedge Funds, and Private Equity

on the subject. For example, a 2001 study showed that broad hedge fund exposure to the S&P 500 (measured in one-month intervals) had a beta of 0.84 when adjusting for stale pricing (when pricing does not accurately reflect current values) of assets held.[2] A study in 2009 using more recent market data (and further adjusting for illiquidity) led to similar conclusions. The aggregate hedge fund industry's market exposure to the S&P 500 was a beta of 0.44.[3]

Hedge funds have been exempt from some securities regulations in the United States and in many other countries based on the fact that they invite investment from only sophisticated institutional investors and high-net-worth investors. In addition, there are limitations in some cases on the total number of investors in a fund. As a result, hedge funds have been exempt from regulations that govern leverage, the use of derivatives, short selling, fees, reporting, and investor liquidity. Mutual funds by contrast, are not exempt from these regulations. This freedom from some (but not all) regulation enables hedge funds to participate in a broad variety of investment strategies and allows them to change courses and strategies opportunistically and rapidly, taking advantage of changing market circumstances. In the United States, as of December 2009, legislative proposals provided that advisors to hedge funds should register with the SEC under the Investment Company Act. Although many hedge funds have resisted registration, over 1,900 hedge fund advisors have already voluntarily registered with the SEC.

## Leverage

Hedge funds frequently borrow (creating *leverage*) in order to increase the size of their investment portfolio and increase returns (if asset values increase). For example, if a hedge fund received $100 million from investors, the fund might purchase securities worth $400 million by borrowing $300 million from banks, using the $400 million of purchased securities as collateral against the $300 million loan. This is called a *margin loan*. Another form of leverage used by hedge funds is created through repurchase agreements, where a hedge fund agrees to sell a security to another party for a predetermined price and then buy the security back at a higher price on a specified date in the future. In addition, leverage is provided by selling securities short and using the proceeds to purchase other securities and through derivatives contracts that enable hedge funds to create exposure to an asset without using as much capital as would be required by buying the asset directly (see Exhibit 11.1).

When hedge funds borrow money, their losses, as well as their gains, are magnified. For example, if a hedge fund receives $100 million from investors and then borrows $300 million to make investments totaling $400 million, a 25% fall in the value of its $400 million investment portfolio would result in a total loss of the investor's capital if the hedge fund closed down. If, alternatively, the investment portfolio increased by 25%, investors would receive a 100% return on their investment, before subtracting management fees and operating costs.

Hedge funds had over $1.9 trillion in investor capital at the end of 2007. When including leverage obtained through debt and derivative positions, total hedge fund investable assets were estimated to be $6.5 trillion, which is a 3.4 times implied leverage ratio. This amount was slightly less than one-third of the total investments controlled by insurance companies and slightly more than one-fourth of the investments held by pension funds. In the aftermath of the 2007–2008 credit crisis, however, hedge fund leverage decreased significantly to an estimated 2.0 times investor capital by the first quarter of 2009. Total investable assets decreased by 64% to $2.4 trillion (see Exhibit 11.2).

---

[2]Asness, C., R. Krail, and J. Liew. "Do Hedge Funds Hedge?" *Journal of Portfolio Management*. 28 (2001): 6–19.

[3]Connor, Gregory, Lisa Goldberg, and Robert Korajczyk. *Portfolio Risk Analysis*. Princeton University Press (forthcoming).

### How Hedge Fund Leverage Works

Hedge fund investor capital can be leveraged in several ways to enhance overall returns.

**Direct forms of leverage:**

#### Bank borrowings

Hedge funds can take out margin loans (buying securities on margin) from banks. For example, assuming a 20% margin on security ABC, a hedge fund could buy $10 worth of securities by paying only $2 upfront and having the bank supply the remaining $8 in the form of a loan. To protect its loan balance, the bank requires the hedge fund to deposit an agreed amount of securities as collateral. If the market value of the ABC securities drops, the bank can require additional collateral from the hedge fund (margin call) to further protect itself.

#### Repossession agreements ("repos")

Usually used by hedge funds to finance debt security purchases, a repo transaction involves one party agreeing to sell a security to another party for a given price and then buying it back later at a higher price.

**Implicit forms of leverage:**

#### Short selling

Short selling is the practice of selling securities borrowed from banks or other counterparties. Funds raised from the sale of these borrowed securities are used to buy other securities – a practice known as long/short trading.

#### Off-balance-sheet leverage through derivatives and structured products

Derivatives include options, swaps, and futures. Investors can gain much larger risk exposures to an asset class through the use of derivatives than from buying the assets directly. Investments in the high-risk portions of structured products such as collateralized debt obligations (CDOs) also provide implicit leverage.

Through the first half of 2008, total hedge fund industry leverage was estimated to be three to four times investor capital.

Source: Farrell, Diana, et al. "The New Power Brokers: How Oil, Asia, Hedge Funds and Private Equity Are Shaping the Global Capital Markets." McKinsey Global Institute Oct. 2007.

**EXHIBIT 11.1**

## Growth

Hedge funds grew at a remarkable rate between 1990 and 2007, from 530 funds with under $39 billion in assets to more than 7,600 funds with assets of almost $1.9 trillion (see Exhibits 11.3 and 11.4). This growth resulted from the following developments:

1. **Diversification.** Investors were looking for portfolio diversification beyond *long-only* investment funds. Hedge funds provided this portfolio diversification to investors through exposure to a broader range of assets and risks.
2. **Absolute returns.** Investors found the absolute return focus of hedge funds appealing. Most traditional investment fund managers try to beat market averages such as the S&P 500 Index, claiming excellent management skills if their fund outperforms the relevant index. However, if the index return is negative, the outcome would be inferior to a hedge fund that achieves an absolute return (meaning a return greater than 0%). Of course, notwithstanding the absolute return focus, some hedge funds have in fact achieved negative returns.
3. **Increased institutional investing.** After seeing several university endowments such as Yale's endowment achieve spectacular returns from investing up to 50% of their entire portfolio in alternative assets such as hedge funds, private equity, real estate, and commodities

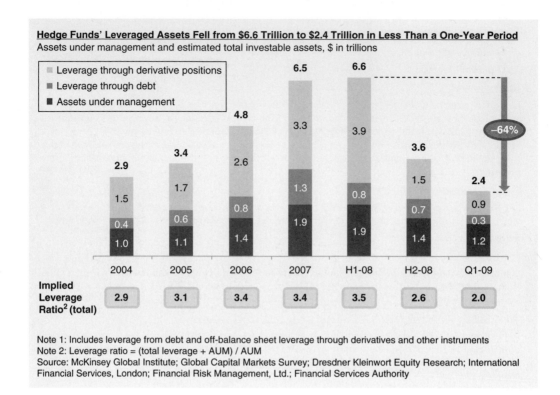

**EXHIBIT 11.2**

(achieving an average annual return of over 23% between 2001 and 2007), many large institutional investors such as pension funds and petrodollar funds (as well as other university endowment funds) substantially increased their exposure to hedge funds.

4. **Favorable market environment.** This period was characterized by a very benign market environment. Since hedge funds rely on leverage to augment returns, low interest rates, the availability of credit, flexibility in credit terms, strong equity market performance, and accommodating tax and regulatory conditions fueled the hedge fund boom.

5. **Human capital growth.** Some of the best financial and investing talent in the world moved into the hedge fund arena. Hedge funds were able to draw talent from investment banks and asset managers because of very high compensation and the opportunity to be more independent. During 2006, 26 hedge fund managers earned more than $130 million, including James Simons, founder of Renaissance Technologies, who earned an estimated $1.5 billion. This amount was topped during 2007 and 2008, when John Paulson, President of Paulson & Co., was estimated to have earned over $3.7 billion, after directing his firm to take bearish positions in mortgage-backed securities.

6. **Financial innovation.** Hedge funds' ability to execute increasingly complex and high-volume trading strategies has been made possible by product and technology innovations in the financial market and by reductions in transaction costs. Electronic trading platforms for futures and swaps and *direct market access* tools allowed hedge funds to profitably trade a broad range of financial assets, while at the same time more effectively manage their risks.

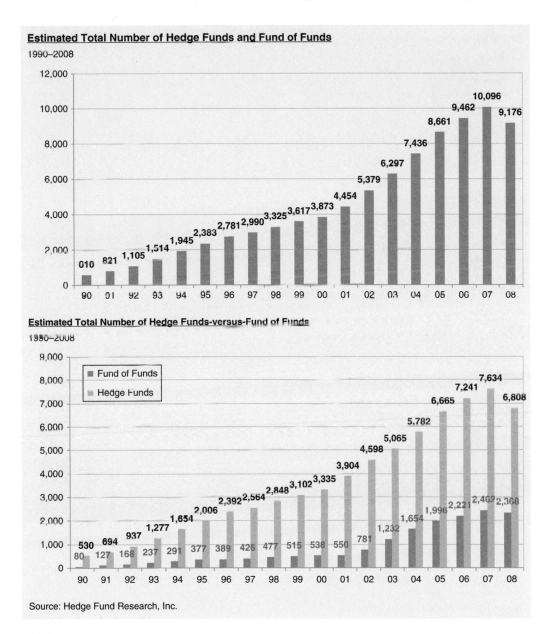

**EXHIBIT 11.3**

# Composition of Investors

High-net-worth individuals used to make up the largest share of hedge fund investors, holding more than half of all hedge fund assets through 2000. While this investor class has doubled in number and assets over the past decade, its share of all hedge fund assets declined to 30% during 2008. Most other investor classes have grown at a faster pace during this period: institutional investors such as pension funds, insurance companies, endowments, and foundations now account for 38% of hedge fund assets (up from just 25% in 1997). High-net-worth individuals, family offices, and institutional investors also invest in hedge funds through funds-of-funds, which accounted for 32% of hedge fund assets during 2008 (more than double its 1997 share of 14%). See Exhibit 11.5.

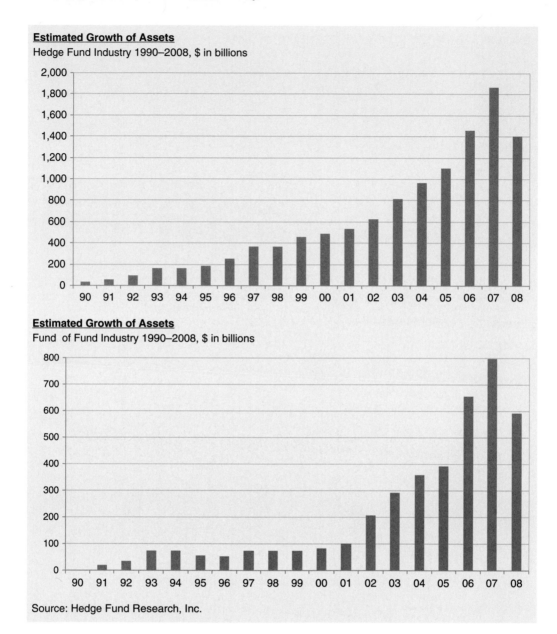

**EXHIBIT 11.4**

# Industry Concentration

The hedge fund industry is dominated by the largest participants. The ten largest hedge funds at the end of 2008 are listed in Exhibit 11.6. During 2008, the 100 largest hedge funds controlled 74% of all hedge fund assets (this means that approximately 1.5% of funds controlled 74% of assets). Over 75% of all hedge fund assets are held by U.S.-based funds, and over 15% of assets are held by European-based funds. Hedge fund revenue is highly concentrated in the top 205 funds. At the end of 2006, it was estimated that within a global hedge fund revenue pool of $33 billion, the top 205 hedge funds received $24.4 billion, or 74% of total revenue (see Exhibit 11.7).

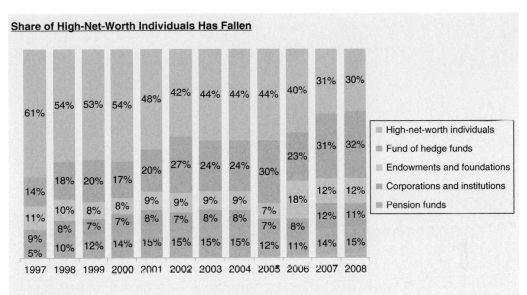

**Share of High-Net-Worth Individuals Has Fallen**

Source: McKinsey Global Institute; Hennessee Group LLC; International Financial Services, London estimates

EXHIBIT 11.5

**Top 10 Hedge Funds by Assets Under Management at the End of 2008**

| Firm | Region | AUM ($bln) |
|---|---|---|
| Bridgewater Associates | U.S. | 38.6 |
| J.P. Morgan | U.S. | 32.9 |
| Paulson & Co. | U.S. | 29.0 |
| D.E. Shaw Group | U.S. | 28.6 |
| Brevan Howard[1] | Europe | 26.8 |
| Och-Ziff Capital Management | U.S. | 22.1 |
| Man AHL[1] | Europe | 22.0 |
| Soros Fund Management | U.S. | 21.0 |
| Goldman Sachs Asset Management[1] | U.S. | 20.6 |
| Farallon Capital Management[2] | U.S. | 20.0 |
| Renaissance Technologies[2] | U.S. | 20.0 |

Note 1: As of December 31, 2008. All other figures as of January 1, 2009.
Note 2: Tied for 10th place.
Source: Absolute Return Billion Dollar Club, March 2009 rankings

EXHIBIT 11.6

# Performance

The average annual returns (after fees are deducted) by hedge funds between 1996 and 2006 was only slightly higher than broad equity market returns during this period. For example, Hedge Fund Research's HFRI Fund Weighted Composite Index (HFR index) showed average annual

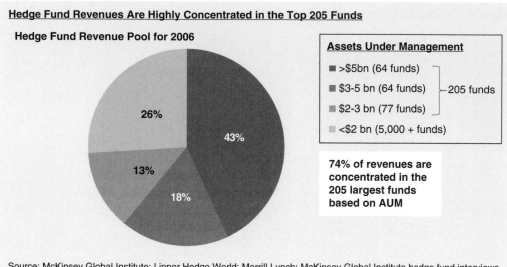

**EXHIBIT 11.7**

returns during this period of 10.6%, compared to an average annual return for the MSCI–World Equity Index (MSCI index) of 8.1% over the same period. However, the standard deviation of returns in the HFR index was lower: 2.1% for the HFR index compared to 4.2% for the MSCI index.[4] During 2007 and 2008 (a period of significant market dislocation), the average annual return for the HFR index was –5%, compared to –20% for the MSCI index. From 2002 to 2008, median returns of top-performing hedge funds were significantly higher than industrywide returns: the top decile of hedge funds outperformed the HFR Fund Weighted Composite Index by an average of 45.8%. As a result, the average hedge fund slightly outperforms the broad equity market in a normal market environment (and with lower risk), but it substantially outperforms during unstable markets. For those investors who have money invested in the top-performing hedge funds, overall returns are substantially better than average hedge fund returns.

Unfortunately, because hedge funds are not required to follow any prescribed reporting protocol by regulators, hedge fund databases have a number of biases than can skew returns. For example, there is a survivorship bias (some funds are dropped from the database when they are liquidated or fail) and a backfill bias (when new funds are added to the database they may only report positive past returns). If these biases are excluded, hedge fund returns may be lower. For example, it has been determined that when excluding biases during a survey period of January 1995 through April 2006, the compound annual returns of hedge funds was 9% (net of fees), compared to the S&P 500 return of 11.6% during the same period.[5] However, during this period it was also found that hedge funds created *alpha* returns (returns that are uncorrelated with the broad market) of 3% p.a. This means that hedge funds provided beneficial diversification, excluding biases, even though they underperformed the S&P 500 during the survey period. During the financial crisis that started in mid-2007, the correlations between hedge fund returns

---

[4]Ferguson, Roger, and David Laster. "Hedge Funds and Systemic Risk." Banque de France Financial Stability Review, 2006.

[5]Ibbotson, Roger, and Peng Chen. "The ABCs of Hedge Funds: Alphas, Betas, and Costs." Yale ICF Working Paper No. 06-10. 2006.

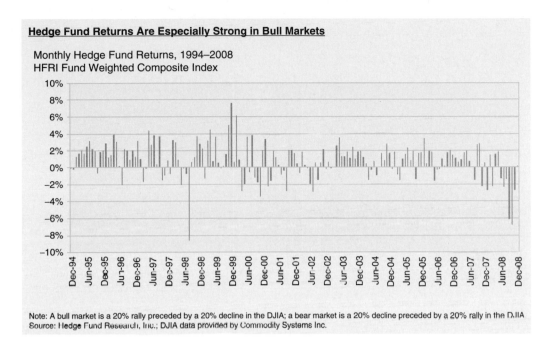

**Hedge Fund Returns Are Especially Strong in Bull Markets**

Monthly Hedge Fund Returns, 1994–2008
HFRI Fund Weighted Composite Index

Note: A bull market is a 20% rally preceded by a 20% decline in the DJIA; a bear market is a 20% decline preceded by a 20% rally in the DJIA
Source: Hedge Fund Research, Inc.; DJIA data provided by Commodity Systems Inc.

**EXHIBIT 11.8**

and the returns of broad-based equity indexes increased, reducing the diversification benefit seen in previous years that were not characterized by extreme market events.

Average hedge fund returns have been positive during every year except 1998 and 2008 over the period 1995–2008. Their overall performance has been especially strong during bull markets (see Exhibit 11.8). When comparing risk-adjusted returns over the period of 1990 to 2008, hedge fund strategies have garnered higher average annual returns than both all-equities and all-bonds portfolios (see Exhibit 11.9). In addition, data from the 2001 to 2007 period show that returns from top quartile hedge funds are significantly higher than returns generated from U.S. equities and bonds (see Exhibit 11.10). As the hedge fund industry continues to mature, increasing amounts of data will become available to assess the industry's performance. A number of academic papers in recent years have begun to analyze hedge fund returns and whether they really deliver alpha. See Exhibit 11.11 for a summary of these findings.

## 2008 Slowdown

During 2008, an unprecedented decline in global equity and credit markets caused many financial assets, including convertible bonds and bank debt, to fall out of favor and become dislocated in either price or liquidity (or both). A growing uncertainty about the stability of the global financial sector caused counterparties (including prime brokers) to reevaluate the amount and terms of credit they extended to hedge funds, resulting in a broad-scale reduction in leverage and subsequent liquidations of many hedge fund portfolios during September and October. An unprecedented number of requests from investors for withdrawals during the third and fourth quarters of 2008 resulted from their own sudden liquidity needs, which forced many hedge funds to liquidate out-of-favor positions and portfolios into already dislocated markets, exacerbating security mispricings and subsequently causing further erosion to already poor fund performance results.

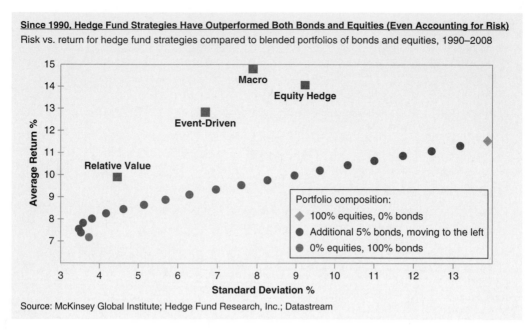

**EXHIBIT 11.9**

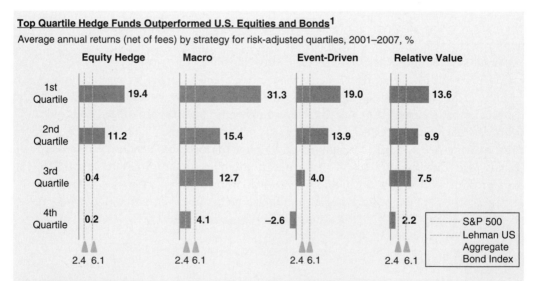

**EXHIBIT 11.10**

The Credit Suisse/Tremont Hedge Fund Index was down 19.1% in 2008, making it the worst year ever for hedge funds. However, this decline compared favorably with the 38.5% decline in the S&P 500 Index over the same period. Therefore, although 2008 was a bad year for hedge funds, as a group, they outperformed the S&P 500 Index by over 19%. Refer to Exhibit 11.12 for a performance comparison. Because of significant losses in 2008, over 900 hedge funds

## Academic Research on Hedge Fund Performance

Due to limitations in the availability of hedge fund performance data, a clear assessment of industry performance is difficult to obtain.  However, based on what is available through the small but growing number of academic papers on hedge funds, a number of observations can be made:

- Hedge funds in aggregate have slightly outperformed the public equities market.

  o Top-quartile hedge funds significantly out-perform equities.

- Hedge funds in aggregate are slightly less volatile than the public equities market.

- Absolute returns ("alpha", or returns uncorrelated with the broader market) have been more elusive:

  o For many hedge fund strategies, over 70% of returns reflect returns of common market indices.[1]

  o Fund of funds delivered no alpha.[2]

  o 3% of annual hedge fund returns can be attributed to alpha.[3]

  o Top quartile hedge funds are able to achieve outsized alphas (as high as 15% annually), based on data from a period of a few years.[4]

These findings suggest that investing in market indices can be a reasonable and less expensive alternative to expensive hedge funds (with the exception of top performing hedge funds).

It is important to note that there are limitations to these observations as imperfect data can create a number of biases:

- Selection bias: participation in hedge fund databases is voluntary.

- Survivorship bias: unsuccessful funds that have folded are not included in most hedge fund databases.

- Backfill bias: once a hedge fund registers with a database, returns from years prior to registration are provided and incorporated into the database as well.  Funds are typically included in databases after they have accumulated a good performance track record.

- Liquidation bias: returns are no longer reported before a fund enters into final liquidation.

Although difficult to aggregate the effect of all of these biases, by some estimates, just survivorship and backfill bias together can inflate industry returns by as much as 4%.[5]

Note 1: Hasanhodzic, Jasmina and Andrew W. Lo, "Can hedge-fund returns be replicated?: The linear case." *Journal of Investment Management*, Q2 2007, Vol. 5, No. 2.
Note 2: Fung, William, et al. "Hedge funds: Performance, risk, and capital formation." AFA 2007 Chicago Meetings paper, 19 Jul. 2006.
Note 3: Ibbotson, Roger G. and Peng Chen. "The A,B,Cs of hedge funds: Alphas, betas and costs." Yale ICF working paper, Sep. 2006.
Note 4: Kosowski, Robert, et al. "Do hedge funds deliver alpha? A Bayesian and bootstrap analysis." *Journal of Financial Economics*, Vol. 84, No. 1, Apr. 2007, pp. 229-64.
Note 5: Fung, William and David Hsieh. "Hedge funds: An industry in its adolescence." *Federal Reserve Bank of Atlanta. Economic Review*, Q4 2006, Vol. 91, No. 4.
Source: Farrell, Diana, et al. "The New Power Brokers: How Oil, Asia, Hedge Funds and Private Equity Are Shaping the Global Capital Markets." McKinsey Global Institute Oct. 2007.

**EXHIBIT 11.11**

closed, reducing the total number of hedge funds by year-end 2008 to 9,176 (including fund of funds) and assets under management to $1.4 trillion (down by over $500 billion from a peak of over $1.9 trillion, recorded during mid-2008). During the fourth quarter of 2008, hedge funds saw $152 billion in redemptions. Both poor- and good-performing funds experienced net asset outflows as investors looked to raise cash from all possible sources. Investors in funds that were experiencing liquidity problems were unable to withdraw money from those funds, so they turned to other funds with "friendly" gate policies as a source for cash. This meant even strong performers, such as Caxton Associates, which saw its largest fund gain 13% but overall assets drop by 27% in 2008, were not completely immune to the outflow. See Exhibit 11.13 for a discussion of the travails of the hedge fund market during 2008.

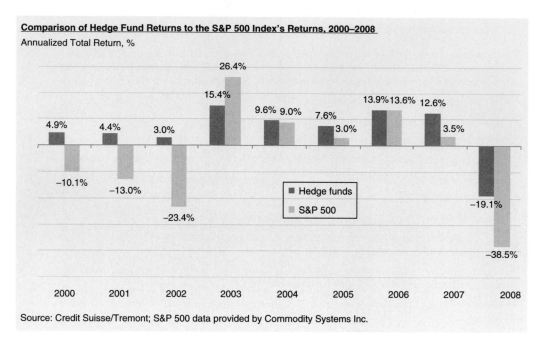

**Comparison of Hedge Fund Returns to the S&P 500 Index's Returns, 2000–2008**

Annualized Total Return, %

Source: Credit Suisse/Tremont; S&P 500 data provided by Commodity Systems Inc.

**EXHIBIT 11.12**

During 2009, hedge funds began to recover some of the losses they experienced in 2008, and industry average returns were 9.5% at the end of June (compared to flat performance during this period by the S&P 500 index). Almost all major fund strategies were up for the 6-month period, with some of the worst-performing strategies in 2008 exhibiting strong recoveries. For example, emerging markets, down by 37% in 2008, was up 20% at the end of June 2009. Similarly, convertible arbitrage, down over 33% in 2008, was up 29% during the first half of 2009. See Chapter 15 for additional discussion of hedge fund performance.

During the second quarter of 2009, hedge fund assets increased for the first time since the industry's peak in mid-2008. The increase was driven entirely by investment gains, as investors redeemed $43 billion during the quarter. Industry assets increased modestly from $1.41 trillion at December 31, 2008, to $1.43 trillion at June 30, 2008. Fund closings and consolidations continued in 2009, however. The estimated total number of hedge funds (including fund of funds) decreased during both first and second quarter 2009 to reach 8,923 funds by the end of June.

## Market Liquidity and Efficiency

Hedge funds have a significant impact on global capital markets. Because they actively trade securities, hedge funds account for more than one-third of trading in many of the largest equity and debt markets (see Exhibit 11.14). For example, hedge funds represent up to one-half of all stock trades on NYSE Euronext and on the LSE. For debt securities, it is estimated that they represent 47% of distressed debt trading, 30% of U.S. government bond trading, and 25% of high-yield bond trading. In plain vanilla credit derivatives, hedge funds may represent 60% of all trading volume.

Hedge fund trading has significantly increased liquidity in markets around the world and increased financial options for institutional investors, corporations, governments, and individuals.

**Travails of the Hedge Fund Market in 2008**

Hedge funds are supposed to thrive in rough markets.

Not in 2008. A historic decline in stocks, and troubles in almost every part of the bond market, dealt hedge funds their worst year on record. By the end of the year, investors were scrambling to get out, bringing an end to years of industry growth and creating uncertainty about the future of major components of the business.

Through December 2008, hedge funds globally lost 19% on average, according to Hedge Fund Research, a Chicago firm that tracks the industry. Although that's better than the 38% loss on the Standard & Poor's 500-stock index (including dividends) over the same period, it's far from the gains most funds posted for more than a decade. The biggest fund category within hedge funds, long-short funds (where the strategy is to buy some shares while betting against others), was down 23% on average. Funds that invest in emerging markets dropped 31%.

Assets controlled by hedge funds tumbled to $1.4 trillion from nearly $2 trillion at the start of the year, according to Hedge Fund Research, and continued falling in 2009.

Fund managers and their investors are trying to figure out what went wrong. One conclusion: Too many funds bought the same assets. As markets fell in September and October, and hedge funds came under pressure, many moved to sell investments, sending prices even lower and causing losses for other funds that hadn't yet sold.

Stocks favored by hedge funds performed even worse than the overall market, according to data from Goldman Sachs. An index of 50 stocks "that matter most" to hedge funds lost nearly 45%, including dividends, compared with a loss of 38.5% on the S&P 500.

One problem for many hedge funds was the amount they hold of hard-to-trade assets, such as loans, real-estate holdings, and stakes in small, private companies. These illiquid investments at one time accounted for 20% of some fund portfolios, estimated to total about $400 billion. As financial markets come under pressure, it becomes harder to get out of these investments, or even to value them accurately.

Another problem for the industry was the fallout from December 2008's arrest of Bernard Madoff for a $50 billion Ponzi scheme. While Madoff wasn't a hedge-fund manager, his business of overseeing private accounts for wealthy individuals in tight-knit social circles from Palm Beach, to Long Island, as well as for charities and private-banking clients all across Europe, rattled investor trust in private-investment managers in general.

The scandal also tainted fund of funds, the professional investment firms that raise money from clients to invest in a portfolio of other investment funds. Several such firms channeled billions of dollars to Madoff through feeder funds, raising questions about how much due diligence those firms performed and whether clients' investments are as diversified and safe as they should be.

Source: Zuckerman, Gregory and Jenny Strasburg. "For Many Hedge Funds, No Escape." Wall Street Journal 2 Jan. 2009.

EXHIBIT 11.13

This has led to many new hedging vehicles that are designed to reduce investment risk. Active trading by hedge funds has also created greater price discovery in financial markets, which has led to a reduction in pricing inefficiencies.

Hedge funds have significantly augmented the growth of credit derivatives, which had swelled to over $60 trillion in notional amount during 2007, but then contracted down to $39 trillion at the end of 2008 as a result of the credit crisis. According to the McKinsey Global Institute, hedge funds were responsible for over one-third of contracts sold through 2006, having delivered approximately $6.4 trillion in notional credit protection ($800 billion on a net basis). In addition, hedge funds have been large buyers of asset-backed securities (ABS) and collateralized debt obligations (CDO) created from ABS. As a result of this activity, banks were able to originate more loans and take credit risks off their own balance sheet. This, in turn, enabled both

**Hedge Funds Account for a Significant Share of Trading Volume**
Hedge Fund's Estimated Share of Trading, %

| | |
|---|---|
| Cash Equity on NYSE and LSE | 50 |
| U.S. Government Bonds | 30 |
| High-Yield Bonds | 25 |
| Credit Derivatives - Plain Vanilla | 60 |
| Credit Derivatives - Structured | 30 |
| Emerging Market Bonds | 45 |
| Distressed Debt | 47 |
| Leveraged Loans | 32 |

Source: McKinsey Global Institute; NYSE; LSE; U.S. Bond Market Association; IMF; Greenwich Associates; Financial News; Gartmore; Stern School of Business; British Bankers' Association; ISDA; McKinsey CIB practice

**EXHIBIT 11.14**

consumers and companies to access new sources of capital. Although hedge fund activity has created many benefits, the expanded access to capital is, unfortunately, also one of the causes of the financial crisis that started during mid-2007, because too many mortgages were originated for individuals who should not have qualified to receive credit.

Hedge funds have provided many loans to private equity funds in support of their leveraged buyout activity. S&P estimates that hedge funds committed over $70 billion in leveraged loans to private equity firm portfolio companies and below-investment-grade companies during 2006, which represented approximately 13% of all such loans during that year.

## Financial Innovation

Hedge funds have been significant users of new products developed by investment banks and others that allow exposure to different asset classes more efficiently, at a lower cost, and with less transparency. This has given rise to an increase in quantitative trading activities (using computers to analyze anomalous financial prices and then engaging in automated trading to exploit the anomalies) and more robust arbitrage trading activity (investing in two related financial instruments in an effort to exploit price inefficiencies). The newly created financial products are available on exchanges and in the over-the-counter (OTC) market. These products have given hedge funds the opportunity to acquire consumer loans, mortgages, and credit card debt that were previously only held by banks.

New products also include total return swaps, credit default swaps, and other synthetic products that create exposures to asset classes that were previously not accessible to hedge funds, as well as hedging vehicles that promote expansion of risk taking. In addition, hedge funds have been the beneficiaries of significant improvement in reporting and risk management systems, which has enabled them to engage in ever more complex and robust trading activities. However, the complexities of many of these products has also led to some unanticipated risks, resulting in increased concerns among regulators and practitioners of the possibility for large losses (many of which have already occurred). There is substantial disagreement about whether the benefits of this innovation have been outweighed by the systemic and individual risks they have created (see Chapter 14).

## Illiquid Investments

Hedge funds have historically limited their participation in illiquid investments, preferring to match their investment horizon to the typically 1-year lock-up periods that their investors agree to. However, many hedge funds have increasingly invested in illiquid assets in an effort to augment returns. For example, they have invested in private investments in public equity (PIPEs), acquiring large minority holdings in public companies. Their purchases of CDOs and CLOs (collateralized loan obligations) are also somewhat illiquid, since these fixed-income securities are difficult to price and there is a limited secondary market during times of crisis. In addition, hedge funds have participated in loans (Och-Ziff provided a large loan to finance the takeover of Manchester United, one of the world's most popular football/soccer teams), and invested in physical assets (e.g., purchasing Indonesian oil rigs). Sometimes, investments that were intended to be held for less than 1 year have become long-term, illiquid assets when the assets depreciated and hedge funds decided to continue holding the assets until values recovered, rather than selling at a loss (see the discussion of side pockets in the following section). It is estimated that more than 20% of total assets under management by hedge funds are illiquid, hard-to-price assets. This makes hedge fund asset valuation difficult and has created a mismatch between hedge fund assets and liabilities, giving rise to significant problems when investors attempt to withdraw their cash at the end of lock-up periods.

## Lock-ups, Gates, and Side Pockets

Hedge funds generally focus their investment strategies on financial assets that are liquid and able to be readily priced based on reported prices in the market for those assets or by reference to comparable assets that have a discernable price. Since most of these assets can be valued and sold over a short period of time to generate cash, hedge funds permit investors to invest in or withdraw money from the fund at regular intervals, and managers receive performance fees based on quarterly mark-to-market valuations. However, in order to match up maturities of assets and liabilities for each investment strategy, most hedge funds have the ability to prevent invested capital from being withdrawn during certain periods of time. They achieve this through *lock-up* and *gate* provisions that are included in investment agreements with their investors.

A *lock-up* provision provides that during an initial investment period of, typically, 1 to 2 years, an investor is not allowed to withdraw any money from the fund. Generally, the lock-up period is a function of the investment strategy that is being pursued. Sometimes, lock-up periods are modified for specific investors through a side letter agreement. However, this can become problematic because of the resulting different effective lock-up periods that apply to different investors who invest at the same time in the same fund. Also, this can trigger "most favored nations" provisions in other investor agreements.

A *gate* is a restriction that limits the amount of withdrawals during a quarterly or semiannual redemption period after the lock-up period expires. Typically gates are percentages of a fund's capital that can be withdrawn on a scheduled redemption date. A gate of 10% to 20% is common. A gate provision allows the hedge fund to increase exposure to illiquid assets without facing a liquidity crisis. In addition, it offers some protection to investors who do not attempt to withdraw funds, because if withdrawals are too high, assets might have to be sold by the hedge fund at disadvantageous prices, causing a potential reduction in investment returns for remaining investors. During 2008 and 2009, as many hedge fund investors attempted to withdraw money

**Gating**

The illiquidity of hedge funds often means that, even if investors realize the manager of their fund has run into trouble, it could be months before they can get their money back. Even then, arrangements called "gates" may restrict the proportion of an investor's holdings that can be redeemed. Hedge fund managers use gates to control redemptions during difficult markets. For example, in the throes of the subprime mortgage meltdown of 2007, an article in the *New York Times* blog "DealBook" described how the Bear Stearns Asset-Based Securities Fund "had moved to suspend investor redemptions." According to a Bear spokesman, "[...] we believe by suspending redemptions we can ensure the best long term results for our investors [...] we don't believe it is prudent or in the interest of our investors to sell assets in the current market environment." The ability of the Bear Stearns hedge fund managers to suspend investor redemptions illustrates the power of gating. Because the fund had incurred serious losses, investors in the fund likely would have pulled their money out were they not bound by gates. Thus, gating allows hedge fund managers to have greater control over their investors' funds by preventing investors from obtaining redemptions at inopportune times.

Source: DealBook, "Third Bear Stearns Fund Skids on Mortgages." <u>New York Times</u> 1 Aug. 2007.

**EXHIBIT 11.15**

based on poor returns and concerns about the financial crisis, there was considerable frustration and some litigation directed at hedge fund gate provisions (see Exhibit 11.15).

Hedge funds sometimes use a *side pocket* account to house comparatively illiquid or hard-to-value assets. Once an asset is designated for inclusion in a side pocket, new investors don't participate in the returns from this asset. When existing investors withdraw money from the hedge fund, they remain as investors in the side pocket asset until it is either sold or becomes liquid through a monetization event such as an IPO. Management fees are typically charged on side pocket assets based on their cost, rather than a mark-to-market value of the asset. Incentive fees are charged based on realized proceeds when the asset is sold. Usually, there is no requirement to force the sale of side pocket investments by a specific date. Sometimes, investors accuse hedge funds of putting distressed assets that were intended to be sold during a 1-year horizon into a side pocket account to avoid dragging down the returns of the overall fund. Investors are concerned about unexpected illiquidity arising from a side pocket and the potential for even greater losses if a distressed asset that has been placed there continues to decline in value.

Fund managers sometimes use even more drastic options to limit withdrawals, such as suspending all redemption rights (but only in the most dire circumstances).

## Comparison with Private Equity Funds and Mutual Funds

Hedge funds are similar to private equity funds in a number of ways. They are both private pools of capital that pay high management fees and high performance fees based on the fund's profits (2 and 20), and they are both lightly regulated. However, hedge funds generally invest in relatively liquid assets, and purchase minority positions in company stocks and bonds and in many other assets (taking both long and short positions for many investments). Private equity funds, by contrast, typically purchase entire companies, creating a less liquid investment that is often held for 3 to 7 years. Although there is an intention to create liquidity after this period, since exit events often include an IPO (where only a portion of the investment is sold) or an M&A sale (where the consideration could be in shares of another company rather than cash), liquidity is not assured even then.

Hedge funds are pools of investment capital, as are mutual funds. However, the similarity stops there. Mutual funds must price assets daily and offer daily liquidity, compared to the typical quarterly disclosure of asset values to hedge fund investors and liquidity that is subject to certain limitations, as described earlier. In the United States, hedge funds are limited to soliciting investments only from accredited investors, but mutual funds have no such limitation. Mutual funds are heavily regulated in the United States by the SEC, while hedge fund regulation, although subject to change (see Chapter 14), is limited. The hedge fund fee structure is also significantly different: mutual funds usually receive management fees that are substantially lower than fees paid to hedge funds, and mutual funds generally do not receive the performance fees that hedge funds receive. While mutual funds typically do not use leverage to support their investments, leverage is a hallmark of hedge funds. Finally, hedge funds engage in a much broader array of trading strategies, creating both long and short investment positions, utilizing derivatives and many other sophisticated financial products to create the exposures that they want. Mutual funds generally have less investment flexibility.

Recently, a small number of mutual funds have introduced performance-based fees, and some mutual funds are pursuing more aggressive, flexible trading strategies in an effort to keep investors from defecting to hedge funds.

## High-Water Marks and Hurdle Rates

A high-water mark relates to payment of performance fees. Hedge fund managers typically receive performance fees only when the value of the fund exceeds the highest net asset value it has previously achieved. For example, if a fund is launched with a net asset value (NAV) of $100 per share and NAV was $120 at the end of the first year, assuming a 20% performance fee, the hedge fund would receive a performance fee of $4 per share. If, however, at the end of the second year NAV dropped to $115, no performance fee would be payable. If, at the end of the third year, NAV was $130, the performance fee would be $2 instead of $3, because of the high-water mark: ($130 − $120) × 0.2. Sometimes, if a high-water mark is perceived to be unattainable, a hedge fund may be motivated to close down. See Chapter 15 for more discussion of high-water marks. In addition, some hedge funds agree to a hurdle rate whereby the fund receives a performance fee only if the fund's annual return exceeds a benchmark rate, such as a predetermined fixed percentage, or a rate determined by the market, such as LIBOR or a T-bill yield.

## Public Offerings

In Europe, Man Group PLC launched the first ever hedge fund IPO in 1994. On February 9, 2007, Fortress Investment Group (FIG), which is an alternative asset manager that includes hedge fund, private equity, and real estate investment businesses, launched an IPO in the United States at a price of $18.50, and their shares closed on the first trading day at $31, which reflected a price that was 40 times the previous year's earnings per share. This contrasted with Goldman Sachs's price/earnings ratio of 11 times and Legg Mason, a mutual fund, which had a price/earnings ratio of 24 times. FIG's very high price/earnings ratio prompted other U.S. hedge funds and private equity funds to consider an IPO. In June 2007, GLG Partners, a large European hedge fund, launched an IPO in the United States, raising $3.4 billion. Och-Ziff, one of the largest U.S. hedge funds, launched an IPO on November 12, 2007, at a price of $32. All of the hedge fund IPOs offered a stake in a management company, and the offerings were organized through a master

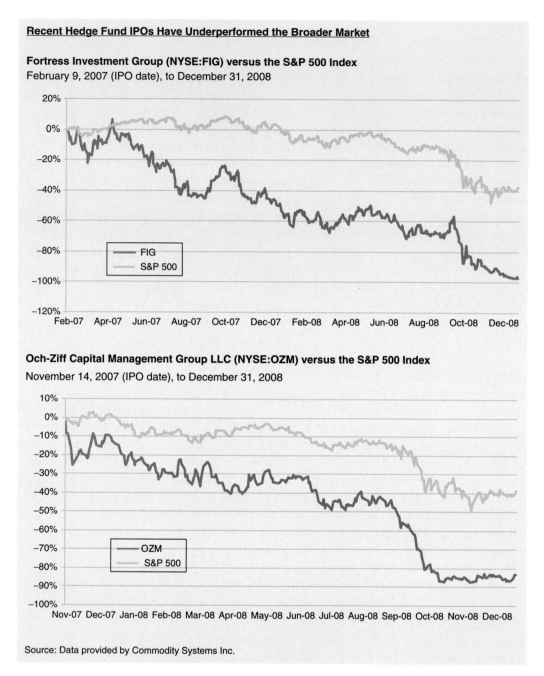

**Recent Hedge Fund IPOs Have Underperformed the Broader Market**

**Fortress Investment Group (NYSE:FIG) versus the S&P 500 Index**
February 9, 2007 (IPO date), to December 31, 2008

**Och-Ziff Capital Management Group LLC (NYSE:OZM) versus the S&P 500 Index**
November 14, 2007 (IPO date), to December 31, 2008

Source: Data provided by Commodity Systems Inc.

**EXHIBIT 11.16**

limited partnership that gave public investors limited say in the firm's governance. Citadel was the first U.S. hedge fund to file a registration statement with the SEC to enable a public bond offering. In December 2007, they sold a $500 million bond to institutional investors. Several other hedge funds considered, but aborted, U.S. IPO initiatives during 2007 and 2008 after seeing the share price of Fortress and Och-Ziff fall precipitously as the market turned negative during those years (see Exhibit 11.16).

# Fund of Funds

A *fund of funds* is an investment fund that invests in a portfolio of other investment funds, rather than investing directly. A fund of hedge funds attempts to provide a broad exposure to the hedge fund industry and risk diversification. They typically charge a management fee of 1% to 1.5% of AUM and also receive performance fees that range from 10% to 20%. As a result, if a fund of funds invests in a dozen hedge funds that charge "2 and 20" fees on average, total management and performance fees paid by fund of fund investors could be about 3.25% and 35%, respectively. For some investors, these fees outweigh the benefits of investing in hedge funds. However, many investors who may not qualify to invest in hedge funds because they have insufficient capital to invest, or are not recognized as qualified investors in the United States by the SEC, will invest in a fund of funds as the only vehicle through which they can invest in hedge funds. In addition, since many fund of funds have investments in 10 or more different hedge funds, they provide more diversification than some investors might achieve directly due to limited amounts of investable capital. See Exhibit 11.17.

Some high-net-worth and institutional investors will channel money through a fund of funds because they value the *due diligence* process by which fund of funds weed out poor hedge fund managers. However, there are many recent examples of inadequate due diligence, where fund of funds have performed at or worse than hedge fund indexes, based on poor investment decisions that reflect inadequate investigation of hedge fund practices and investment strategies. For example, many investors were distraught when they were told that their fund of funds at Goldman Sachs and Man Group had invested in Amaranth Advisors, a hedge fund that declared bankruptcy in 2006. Another example is the Madoff Ponzi scheme: during December 2008, a number of fund of funds acknowledged that they invested in Bernard Madoff's funds, which may result in overall investor losses of multiple billions of dollars. Even though Madoff's funds were not considered hedge funds, hedge funds were nonetheless tainted by this disaster. Allegations of poor due diligence by fund of funds has created more intense scrutiny of the investigation practices of these funds. See Exhibit 11.17.

Some hedge funds welcome fund of fund investments because it gives them a new source of cash and the investment amount is typically large. Other hedge funds limit fund of fund investment because they worry that fund of funds take a short-term view and are quick to withdraw money if performance declines.

The fund of funds industry is dominated by European firms such as the fund of fund arms of Man Group, UBS, HSBC, Société Générale, Credit Suisse, and Julius Baer. In the United States, Permal (controlled by Legg Mason) and Chicago-based Grosvenor are among the largest. At the end of 2008, fund of funds represented approximately 32% of all investments in hedge funds (see Exhibit 11.5). See Chapter 15 for additional discussion of fund of funds.

**Why Use a Fund of Funds Firm?**

- Diversification and access
    - o    Immediate diversification with relatively modest capital investment
    - o    Access to certain managers who might otherwise be closed for investment

- Value-added investment process
    - o    Fundamental knowledge of many different investment strategies
    - o    Network of industry relationships assists in filtering manager universe
    - o    Staffing resources and expertise necessary for manager due diligence and monitoring
    - o    Understanding of quantitative and qualitative portfolio construction issues
    - o    Dynamic process that requires constant attention

- Operational efficiencies
    - o    Legal due diligence and document negotiation
    - o    Consolidated accounting, performance and financial reporting
    - o    Cash flow management

Source: Grosvenor Capital Management

**EXHIBIT 11.17**

## Questions

1. Unlike most mutual funds, why are hedge funds able to charge performance fees on top of management fees?
2. Describe side pockets.
3. Where does the name *hedge funds* come from?
4. Describe a margin loan.
5. Why is it especially important to adjust hedge fund returns data for survivorship bias in the aftermath of the 2007–2008 financial crisis?
6. Looking at the comparison of hedge fund returns versus the S&P 500 index's returns in Exhibit 11.12, even if hedge funds are not always successful at generating absolute returns, what benefit do they seem to offer investors?
7. What are some positive consequences resulting from the proliferation of hedge funds?
8. What are some unforeseen consequences resulting from the proliferation of hedge funds?
9. Discuss the dangers of asset/liability mismatch. What are some strategies that hedge funds employ to mitigate this issue?
10. Why do you think there is a fund of fund market for hedge funds, but not for mutual funds?
11. Although hedge funds are less regulated than mutual funds, what type of indirect regulation affects the hedge fund industry?
12. What are the three key benefits touted by fund of funds? Do you think that fund of funds achieved these benefits during 2008? Why or why not?

# Hedge Fund Investment Strategies

The material in this chapter should be cross-referenced with **Case Study 6, "Kmart, Sears, and ESL: How a Hedge Fund Became One of the World's Largest Retailers."**

Hedge funds employ dynamic investment strategies designed to find unique opportunities in the market and then actively trade their portfolio investments (both long and short) in an effort to maintain high and diversified absolute returns (often using leverage to enhance returns). By contrast, most mutual funds only take long positions in securities and are less active in trading their portfolio investments (usually without leverage) as they attempt to create returns that track (and ideally outperform) the market. Some hedge funds attempt to exploit price anomalies in the market by, for example, taking advantage of a pricing mismatch between two related bonds. Other funds use computer models to identify anomalous relationships between different equity securities. There are also hedge funds that simply make un-hedged directional bets on market movements, after analyzing macroeconomic fundamentals. In addition, some hedge funds use extensive bottoms-up research and analysis to pick stocks or bonds that show appreciation potential. Regardless of their strategy, most hedge funds are much more active traders, compared to mutual funds. As a result, hedge funds account for a significant share of all financial asset trading activity worldwide.

There are four broad groups of hedge fund strategies: arbitrage, event-driven, equity-related, and macro. The first two groups in many cases attempt to achieve returns that are uncorrelated with general market movements. Managers of these strategies try to find price discrepancies between related securities, using derivatives and active trading based on computer-driven models and extensive research. The second two groups are impacted by movements in the market, and they require intelligent anticipation of price movements in stocks, bonds, foreign exchange, and physical commodities based on extensive research and model building. A summary of the four broad groups of hedge fund strategies is found in Exhibit 12.1.

Hedge fund strategies have become more diversified in order to reduce investment risk. For example, in 1990, macro investments by hedge funds comprised 39% of all hedge fund assets. By 2008, this strategy comprised only 20% of hedge fund assets. During the same period of time, arbitrage and event-driven strategies combined grew from 24% to 48% of all hedge fund assets (see Exhibit 12.2).

## Equity-Based Strategies

### Equity Long/Short

A hedge fund manager that focuses on equity long/short investing starts with a fundamental analysis of individual companies, combined with research on risks and opportunities particular to a company's industry, country of incorporation, competitors, and the overall macroeconomic environment in which the company operates. Managers consider ways to reduce volatility by either

## Hedge Fund Strategies Can be Grouped into Four Major Categories

| | Subcategory | Description |
|---|---|---|
| **Arbitrage** | Fixed-income based arbitrage | Exploits pricing inefficiencies in fixed-income markets, combining long/short positions of various fixed income securities |
| | Convertible arbitrage | Purchases convertible bonds and hedges equity risk by selling short the underlying common stock |
| | Relative value arbitrage | Exploits pricing inefficiencies across asset classes-e.g., pairs trading, dividend arbitrage, yield curve trades |
| **Event Driven** | Distressed securities | Invests in companies in a distressed situation (e.g. bankruptcies, restructuring), and/or shorts companies expected to experience distress |
| | Merger arbitrage | Generates returns by going long on the target and shorting the stock of the acquiring company |
| | Activism | Seeks to obtain representation in companies' board of directors in order to shape company policy and strategic direction |
| **Equity Based** | Equity long/short | Consists of a core holding of particular equity securities, hedged with short sales of stocks to minimize overall market exposure |
| | Equity non-hedge | Commonly known as "stock picking"; invests long in particular equity securities |
| **Macro** | Global Macro | Leveraged bets on anticipated price movements of stock markets, interest rates, foreign exchange, and physical commodities |
| | Emerging markets | Invests a major share of portfolio in securities of companies or the sovereign debt of developing or "emerging" countries; investments are primarily long |

Source: McKinsey Global Institute; Hedge Fund Research, Inc.; David Stowell

**EXHIBIT 12.1**

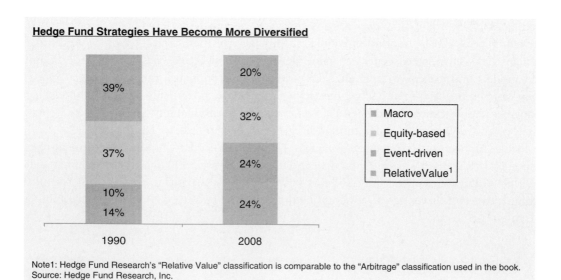

### Hedge Fund Strategies Have Become More Diversified

Note1: Hedge Fund Research's "Relative Value" classification is comparable to the "Arbitrage" classification used in the book.
Source: Hedge Fund Research, Inc.

**EXHIBIT 12.2**

diversifying or hedging positions across industries and regions and hedging undiversifiable market risk. However, the overall risk in this strategy is determined by whether a manager is attempting to prioritize returns (by having more concentration and leverage) or low risk (by creating lower volatility through diversification, lower leverage, and hedging). The core rationale of a long/short strategy is to shift principal risk from market risk to manager risk, which requires skilled stock selection to generate alpha. To do this, a manager concurrently buys and sells similar securities in an attempt to exploit relative mispricings, while decreasing market risk. An overview of a long/short strategy is found in Exhibit 12.3.

## Non-Hedged Equity

This strategy is common to hedge funds, mutual funds, and other investors. There is usually no hedge involved, and investments are long only (not short). This stock-picking strategy relies on fundamental research on individual companies and industries. Usually, this area is divided into a regional or global focus and includes market capitalization diversification.

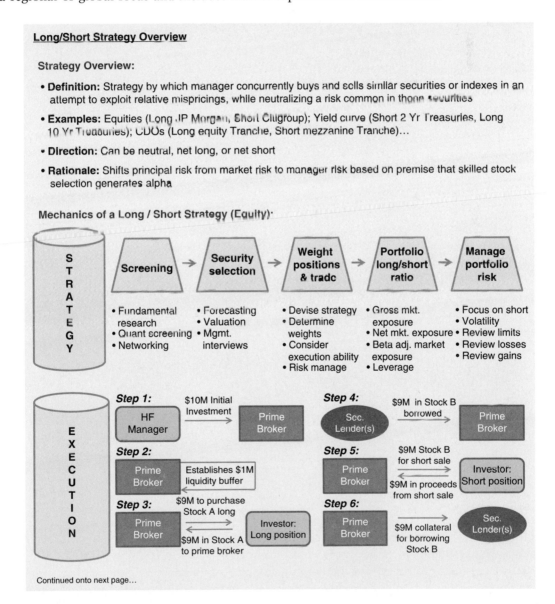

**Long/Short Strategy Overview**

**Strategy Overview:**

- **Definition:** Strategy by which manager concurrently buys and sells similar securities or indexes in an attempt to exploit relative mispricings, while neutralizing a risk common in those securities

- **Examples:** Equities (Long JP Morgan, Short Citigroup); Yield curve (Short 2 Yr Treasuries, Long 10 Yr Treasuries); CDOs (Long equity Tranche, Short mezzanine Tranche)...

- **Direction:** Can be neutral, net long, or net short

- **Rationale:** Shifts principal risk from market risk to manager risk based on premise that skilled stock selection generates alpha

**Mechanics of a Long / Short Strategy (Equity):**

STRATEGY

Screening → Security selection → Weight positions & trade → Portfolio long/short ratio → Manage portfolio risk

- Fundamental research
- Quant screening
- Networking

- Forecasting
- Valuation
- Mgmt. interviews

- Devise strategy
- Determine weights
- Consider execution ability
- Risk manage

- Gross mkt. exposure
- Net mkt. exposure
- Beta adj. market exposure
- Leverage

- Focus on short
- Volatility
- Review limits
- Review losses
- Review gains

EXECUTION

**Step 1:** HF Manager → $10M Initial Investment → Prime Broker

**Step 2:** Prime Broker Establishes $1M liquidity buffer

**Step 3:** Prime Broker ← $9M to purchase Stock A long / $9M in Stock A to prime broker → Investor: Long position

**Step 4:** Sec. Lender(s) → $9M in Stock B borrowed → Prime Broker

**Step 5:** Prime Broker ← $9M Stock B for short sale / $9M in proceeds from short sale → Investor: Short position

**Step 6:** Prime Broker → $9M collateral for borrowing Stock B → Sec. Lender(s)

Continued onto next page...

**EXHIBIT 12.3A**

**Long/Short Strategy Return Sources and Costs:**

**Return Sources:**
- Performance
  - Alpha on long position plus alpha on short position
- Interest rebate
  - Short sale proceeds invested by prime broker in short term securities
  - Rebate = Interest on short sale proceeds – prime broker lender fee and expenses
  - Rebate is usually = 75-90% of interest on short sale proceeds
- Liquidity buffer interest
  - Liquidity buffer posted to pay for daily mark to market adjustments and to pay dividends to stock lenders (arranged by prime brokers)
  - Liquidity buffer earns short term interest

**Costs:**
- Share borrow costs
- Margin costs on short position
- Transaction costs

**Return Attribution:**

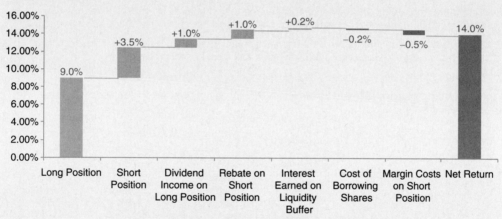

EXHIBIT 12.3B

# Macro Strategies

## Global Macro

A macro-focused hedge fund makes leveraged bets on anticipated price movements in stock and bond markets, interest rates, foreign exchange, and physical commodities. A macro strategy also takes positions in financial derivatives such as forwards, options, and swaps on assets such as stocks, bonds, commodities, loans, and real estate, and on indexes that are focused on interest rates, stock and bond markets, exchange rates, and instruments that relate to inflation. A macro-focused fund considers economic forecasts, analysis about global flow of funds, interest rate trends, political changes, relations between governments, individual countries, political and economic policies, and other broad systemic considerations. A well-known practitioner of a global macro investment is George Soros, who sold short more than $10 billion of pound sterling in 1992, successfully profiting from the Bank of England's reluctance to either raise its interest rates to levels comparable to rates in other European countries or to float its currency. Although the Bank of England resisted both initiatives, market forces ultimately forced it to withdraw its currency from the European Exchange Rate Mechanism and to devalue the pound sterling. Soros earned an estimated $1.1 billion from his bearish macro position on the pound sterling.

## Emerging Markets

An emerging-market-focused hedge fund invests most of its funds in either the securities of companies in developing (emerging) countries or the sovereign debt of these countries. Emerging markets is a term used to describe a country's social or business activity that is characterized by rapid growth and industrialization. Typically investors demand greater returns because of incremental risks.

# Arbitrage Strategies

Arbitrage is possible when one of three conditions are met: (1) the same asset does not trade at the same price in all markets; (2) two assets with identical cash flows do not trade at the same price; or (3) an asset with a known price in the future does not trade today at its future price, discounted by the risk-free interest rate.

## Fixed-Income-Based Arbitrage

Fixed-income arbitrage funds attempt to exploit pricing inefficiencies in fixed income markets by combining long/short positions of various fixed income securities. For example, historically, because of the limited liquidity of the Italian bond futures market, the currency-hedged returns from this market in the short term were lower than the short-term returns in the very liquid U.S. Treasury bond market. However, over a longer period of time, the hedged returns became nearly identical. Fixed-income arbitrageurs benefited from the eventual convergence of hedged yields between currency-hedged Italian bond futures and U.S. Treasury bonds by shorting relatively expensive U.S. Treasury bonds and purchasing relatively cheap Italian bond futures.

Another example involves 30-year on-the-run and off-the-run U.S. Treasury bonds. Liquidity discrepancies between the most recently issued 30-year Treasury bonds (called on-the-run bonds) and 29.75-year Treasury bonds that were originally issued one quarter earlier (called off-the-run bonds) sometimes causes a slight difference in pricing between the two bonds. This can be exploited by buying cheaper off-the-run bonds and shorting the more expensive on-the-run bonds. Since the price of the two bonds should converge within 3 months (both bonds becoming off-the-run bonds), this trading position should create a profit for the arbitrageur.

## Convertible Arbitrage

A convertible bond can be thought of as a fixed-income security that has an embedded equity call option. The convertible investor has the right, but not the obligation, to convert (exchange) the bond into a predetermined number of common shares. The investor will presumably convert sometime at or before the maturity of the bond if the value of the common shares exceeds the cash redemption value of the bond. The convertible therefore has both debt and equity characteristics and, as a result, provides an asymmetrical risk and return profile. Until the investor converts the bond into common shares of the issuer, the issuer is obligated to pay a fixed coupon to the investor and repay the bond at maturity if conversion never occurs. A convertible's price is sensitive to, among other things, changes in market interest rates, credit risk of the issuer, and the issuer's common share price and share price volatility.

An analysis of convertible bond prices factors in three different sources of value: investment value, conversion value, and option value. The investment value is the theoretical value at which the bond would trade if it were not convertible. This represents the security's floor value, or the minimum price at which it should trade as a nonconvertible bond. The conversion value represents the value of the common stock into which the bond can be converted. If, for example, these shares are trading at $30 and the bond can convert into 100 shares, the conversion value is $3,000. The investment value and conversion value can be considered, at maturity, the low and high price boundaries for the convertible bond. The option value represents the theoretical value of having the right, but not the obligation, to convert the bond into common shares. Until maturity, a convertible trades at a price between the investment value and the option value.

A Black-Scholes option pricing model, in combination with a bond valuation model, can be used to price a convertible security. However, a binomial option model, with some adjustments, is the best method for determining the value of a convertible security. See Chapters 3 and 9 for a more complete description of convertible securities, which includes a discussion of convertible preferred shares and mandatory convertibles.

Convertible Arbitrage is a market neutral investment strategy that involves the simultaneous purchase of convertible securities and the short sale of common shares (selling borrowed stock) that underlie the convertible. An investor attempts to exploit inefficiencies in the pricing of the convertible in relation to the security's embedded call option on the convertible issuer's common stock. In addition, there are cash flows associated with the arbitrage position that combine with the security's inefficient pricing to create favorable returns to an investor who is able to properly manage a hedge position through a dynamic hedging process. The hedge involves selling short a percentage of the shares that the convertible can convert into based on the change in the convertible's price with respect to the change in the underlying common stock price (delta), and the change in delta with respect to the change in the underlying common stock (gamma). The short position must be adjusted frequently in an attempt to neutralize the impact of changing common share prices during the life of the convertible security. This process of managing the short position in the issuer's stock is called *delta hedging*.

If hedging is done properly, whenever the convertible issuer's common share price decreases, the gain from the short stock position should exceed the loss from the convertible holding. Equally, whenever the issuer's common share price increases, the gain from the convertible holding should exceed the loss from the short stock position.

In addition to the returns produced by delta hedging, the investor will receive returns from the convertible's coupon payment and interest income associated with the short stock sale. However, this cash flow is reduced by paying a cash amount to stock lenders equal to the dividend that the lenders would have received if the stock were not loaned to the convertible investor, and further reduced by stock borrow costs paid to a prime broker. In addition, if the investor leveraged the investment by borrowing cash from a prime broker, there will be interest expense on the loan. Finally, if an investor chooses to hedge credit risk of the issuer, or interest rate risk, there will be additional costs associated with credit default swaps and a short Treasury position. See Exhibit 12.4 for a more thorough review of the convertible arbitrage strategy.

This strategy attempts to create returns that exceed the returns that would be available from purchasing a nonconverting bond with the same maturity issued by the same issuer, without being exposed to common share price risk. Most convertible arbitrageurs attempt to achieve double-digit annual returns from convertible arbitrage.

## Mechanics of Convertible Arbitrage

A convertible arbitrageur attempts to purchase undervalued convertibles and simultaneously short a number of common shares that the convertible can convert into (the "conversion ratio"). The number of shares sold short depends on the conversion ratio and the delta. The delta measures the change in the convertible's price with respect to the change in the underlying common stock price, which represents the convertible's equity sensitivity for very small stock price changes. The arbitrageur's objective is to create an attractive rate of return regardless of the changing price of the underlying shares. This is achieved by capturing the cash flows available on different transactions that relate to the convertible as well as directly from the convertible and by profiting from buying a theoretically cheap convertible. Many convertibles are originally issued at a price below their theoretical value because the stock price volatility assumed in the convertible pricing is below the actual volatility that is expected during the life of the convertible. A summary of potential convertible returns is as follows:

1.  **Income Generation**

    The arbitrageur tries to generate income while hedging the risks of various components of a convertible bond. Income from a convertible hedge comes from the following: Coupon + interest on Short Proceeds – Stock Dividend – Stock Borrow Cost. This income is increased if the arbitrageur leverages the investment (two or three times leverage is common). However, costs associated with hedging interest rate and credit risks reduce the income. An example of income generation, which is linked to Figure 2, follows:

    > Assuming that an issuer's common stock price is $41.54 and dividend yield is 1% when a $1,000 convertible is issued and the convertible has a 2.5% coupon, a conversion ratio of 21.2037, 53% average short stock position (with 2% interest income available from this position) and a stock borrow cost of 0.25% on the short proceeds, over a one year horizon, the total income from a delta hedged convertible would be $28.50, which is equal to 2.9% of the $1,000 convertible:

    | | | |
    |---|---|---|
    | Coupon | 2.5% on $1,000 convertible | = $25.00 |
    | + Short Interest | 2% on $466.83* short proceeds | = $9.34 |
    | – Stock Dividend | 1% on $466.03* short proceeds | = ($4.67) |
    | – Stock Borrow Cost | 0.25% on $466.83* short proceeds | = ($1.17) |
    | Total | | = $28.50 |

    > * The $1,000 convertible can convert into 21.2037 shares (the conversion ratio).
    > $41.54 (current share price) x 21.2037 = $880.80. Since there is a 53% short position, the value of the shares sold short is $880.80 x 0.53 = $466.83

2.  **Monetizing Volatility**

    Because of the nonlinear relationship between prices for the convertible and for the underlying stock, there is an additional gain potential in creating a delta neutral position between the convertible and the stock. This is explained in Figure 1. At point 1, the green line represents the long convertible position, whereas the dotted line represents the delta neutral exposure. Therefore, if the stock price were to fall from position 1, the gain on the short stock position is greater than the loss from the long convertible position (position A). However, if the stock were to gain, the loss on the short would be less than the gain on the convertible (position B). To demonstrate this, consider Figure 2 on the following page.

Continued onto next page...

**EXHIBIT 12.4A**

## Relative Value Arbitrage

Relative value arbitrage exploits pricing inefficiencies across asset classes. An example of this is *pairs trading*. Pairs trading involves two companies that are competitors or peers in the same industry that have stocks with a strong historical correlation in daily stock price movements. When this correlation breaks down (one stock increases in price while the other stock decreases in price) a pairs trader will sell short the outperforming stock and buy the underperforming stock,

This convertible trades at a price of 101.375% of par, has a delta of 53% and is convertible into 21.2037 shares per $1,000 convertible security. This Figure describes the process for "monetizing the volatility," or generating trading profits by rehedging the position as the stock moves. It would cost $1,013.75 to purchase the convertible, and there would be $466.83 in short stock proceeds, resulting in a net cash outlay of $546.93. If the stock price subsequently increases by 5%, because of the nonlinearity of the convertible, the convertible appreciated more than the loss on the short position, creating profit of $.98. At this point, the convertible delta exposure is neutralized at the new hedge delta level by shorting more stock, since the delta has increased. Conversely, if the stock decreases by 5%, the convertible depreciates less than the gain on the short position, creating a profit of $1.37. The convertible delta exposure is neutralized at the new delta level by purchasing stock to reduce the short position because the delta is lower at this point. And so, the investor makes a profit, regardless of whether the stock goes up or down. Assuming that there is, on average, a $1.17 annual profit from monetizing volatility [($1.37 + .98)/2] for every 5% change in share price, and assuming there are monthly 5% changes, this represents a hypothetical profit of 12 x $1.17, which is equal to 1.4% of the $1,000 convertible. Transaction costs are not included in this analysis, which will reduce the profits in both directions.

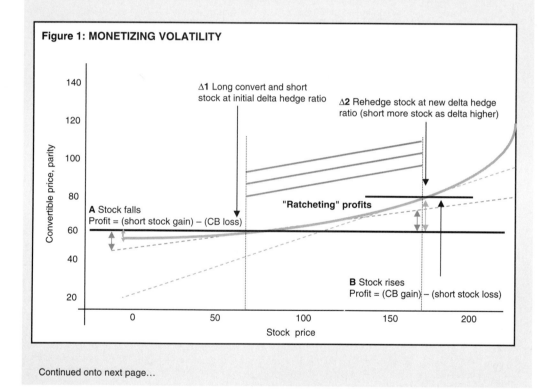

Figure 1: MONETIZING VOLATILITY

Continued onto next page...

EXHIBIT 12.4B

betting that the *spread* between the two stocks will eventually converge. When and if convergence occurs, there can be significant trading profits. Of course, if divergence occurs, this trade can lose money.

Another example of a relative value arbitrage involves the New York Stock Exchange (NYSE) and the Chicago Mercantile Exchange (MERC). A stock trading on the NYSE should have a strong correlation with the futures price for that stock trading on the MERC. If the prices for the stock and its futures contract unexpectedly diverge, fast computers operated by highly quantitative traders recognize the divergence and immediately initiate trades. When the stock

Figure 2: **CONVERTIBLE ARBITRAGE TRADE**

| | | Convertible arbitrage fund |
|---|---|---|
| Stock Px = $41.54 | **initial case** | Long convertible 101.375 par = $1,013.75 |
| Convertible delta = 53% | | Amount of short shares 21.2037*53% = 11.24 |
| Conv. Ratio = 21.2037 shares | | Short value = 11.24 (shares)*41.54 (price) = $466.82 |
| Convertible Px = 101.375% par | | Net cash outlay = $546.93 |
| | **+5% scenario** | Current share price = $43.617 |
| | | Loss from short = $466.82 − (11.24*43.617) = $23.34 |
| | | Gain from convertible = (1,038.07[1] − 1,013.75) = $24.32 |
| | | Net gain = 24.32-23.34 = $.98 |
| | | New hedge delta = 58.11% |
| | **-5% scenario** | Current share price = $39.463 |
| | | Gain from short = $466.82 − (11.24*39.463) = $23.34 |
| | | Loss from convertible = (1,013.75 − 991.78[2]) = $21.97 |
| | | Net gain = 23.34-21.97 = $1.37 |
| | | New hedge delta = 46.73% |

Note: calculations are not rounded.

See Figure 3 below to compare a convertible arbitrage trade with an unhedged (long-only) convertible purchase. For a convertible arbitrage trade, if the underlying stock increases by 5%, the profit is $.98, compared with an unhedged convertible purchase profit of $24.32. If the underlying stock decreases by 5%, a convertible arbitrage trade produces a profit of $1.37, compared to a loss of $21.97 for an unhedged convertible.

Figure 3: **LONG-ONLY TRADE (ONE YEAR)**

| | | Long-only fund |
|---|---|---|
| Stock Px = $41.54 | **initial case** | Long convertible 101.3755 par = $1,013.75 |
| Convertible delta = 53% | | Net cash outlay = $1,013.75 |
| Conv. Ratio = 21.2037 shares | **+5% scenario** | Current share price = $43.617 |
| Convertible Px = 101.375% par | | Gain from convertible = (1,038.07[1] − 1,013.75) = $24.32 |
| | | Coupon for 1 year = 2.5 |
| | | Net gain = $26.82 |
| | **-5% scenario** | Current share price = $39.463 |
| | | Loss from convertible = (1,013.75 − 991.78[2]) = $21.97 |
| | | Coupon for 1 year = 2.5 |
| | | Net loss = $19.47 |

Note: calculations are not rounded.

Continued onto next page...

**EXHIBIT 12.4C**

outperforms the futures contract, the trade is to short the stock and buy the futures contract. When the futures contract outperforms the stock, the trade is to short the futures contract and purchase the stock. In the case of a stock and its futures contract, the two prices will almost always converge, creating a trading profit. This profit will likely be very small (and fleeting), since many traders/computers will see the same divergence and quickly set up this arbitrage. As a result, for the arbitrage position to be profitable, traders/computers need to look for small pricing discrepancies and then quickly complete a large volume of long and short trades in the stock and futures contract in order to make an adequate trading profit.

3. **Purchasing Undervalued Convertible**

An important source of additional potential profit comes from purchasing a convertible at a price that is below its theoretical value, from an implied volatility perspective. When this happens and the convertible exposures are properly neutralized through delta hedging, incremental profits will be created over time based on the below-market purchase. These profits will be even higher if there is an increase in volatility during the holding period. However, if volatility decreases, this potential profit opportunity can turn into a potential loss. If a convertible is purchased at a 2% discount to theoretical value, this could result in a profit of $20 (2% of the $1,000 convertible).

4. **Summary of Returns**

The total one-year convertible return in this hypothetical, hedged convertible is comprised of Income Generation (2.9%), Monetizing Volatility (1.4%), and Purchasing an Undervalued Convertible (2%, calculated for a one-year holding period). This results in a hypothetical return of 6.3%.

If one-half of this convertible is purchased with $500 borrowed from a Prime Broker at 2%, the total one-year return from this investment would be approximately 10.6% ($1,000 x 6.3% = $63. $63 - $10 interest cost = $53. $53/$500 = 10.6%)

Notes 1 and 2:  Value of the convertible based on changes in the underlying share price as determined by a convertible pricing model.
Source: Basile, Davide. "Convertible bonds: Convertible arbitrage versus long-only strategies." Morgan Stanley Investment Management Journal, Issue 1, Volume 2, 2006.

**EXHIBIT 12.4D**

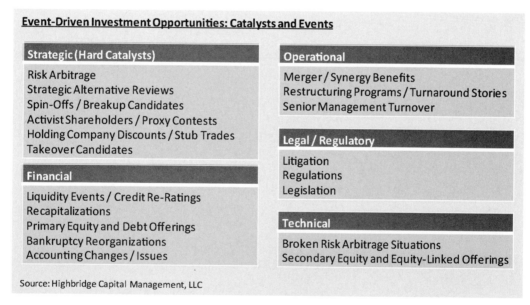

**Event-Driven Investment Opportunities: Catalysts and Events**

**Strategic (Hard Catalysts)**

Risk Arbitrage
Strategic Alternative Reviews
Spin-Offs / Breakup Candidates
Activist Shareholders / Proxy Contests
Holding Company Discounts / Stub Trades
Takeover Candidates

**Financial**

Liquidity Events / Credit Re-Ratings
Recapitalizations
Primary Equity and Debt Offerings
Bankruptcy Reorganizations
Accounting Changes / Issues

**Operational**

Merger / Synergy Benefits
Restructuring Programs / Turnaround Stories
Senior Management Turnover

**Legal / Regulatory**

Litigation
Regulations
Legislation

**Technical**

Broken Risk Arbitrage Situations
Secondary Equity and Equity-Linked Offerings

Source: Highbridge Capital Management, LLC

**EXHIBIT 12.5**

# Event-Driven Strategies

Event-driven strategies focus on significant transactional events such as M&A transactions, bankruptcy reorganizations, recapitalizations, and other specific corporate events that create pricing inefficiencies. Refer to Exhibit 12.5 for a summary of the types of events and catalysts fund managers look for when generating investment ideas.

**Merger Arbitrage Summary**

- The concept of risk arbitrage involves "betting" that an announced merger or acquisition will ultimately close
- When a company (Acquirer) announces the potential merger or acquisition of another public company (Target), there is a time lag between the announcement and the actual closing of the deal
  - The price of the Target's stock moves up close to the value of the takeover bid, but almost always to a price slightly lower than the announcement price
- The spread between the Target's stock price after announcement and the price offered is the "arbitrage spread" and represents the risk that the deal will not be completed
- An arbitrageur will
  - Buy shares of the Target
  - Short the shares of the Acquirer (if it is a stock deal)
- If the deal is closed at the offered price, the arbitrageur will then receive the spread plus any dividends received as profit

**EXHIBIT 12.6**

## Activist

Activist shareholders take minority equity or equity derivative positions in a company and then try to influence the company's senior management and board to consider initiatives that the activist considers important in order to enhance shareholder value. Activist investors often attempt to influence other major investors to support their recommendation to the company, which sometimes leads to proxy solicitations designed to change the management composition of the company. Activist investors commonly push for lower costs, lower cash balances, greater share repurchases, higher dividends, and increased debt, among other things. Chapter 13 provides a more complete explanation of activist shareholder activities and their impact on corporations.

## Merger Arbitrage

Merger arbitrage, which is also called *risk arbitrage*, is an investment strategy that attempts to achieve gains based on the spread between an acquirer's purchase price offer and a target's stock price after announcement of the intended acquisition or merger. See Exhibit 12.6 for a summary of the basic strategy for a share-for-share merger arbitrage transaction.

In a merger where the acquirer has agreed to deliver its own stock as consideration (a share-for-share merger), an arbitrageur will sell short the acquirer's stock and simultaneously buy the stock of the target. If the merger is completed, the target's stock will be converted into the stock of the acquirer based on an exchange ratio that is usually determined at the time of the merger announcement (unless there is a collar established, as described below). Upon receiving the acquiring company's stock in exchange for the target company stock, an arbitrageur will deliver the acquiring company stock to the party that lent shares to create the short position (covering the short).

Sometimes, a share-for-share merger includes a collar arrangement whereby the number of acquirer shares delivered at closing is subject to change depending on whether the acquirer's share price has increased or decreased between the announcement date and closing date, and if so, by how much. Collar provisions make the merger arbitrage process more complicated, depending on the structure of the collar. Sometimes, mergers also include preferred stock, warrants, or other securities, which makes the arbitrage activity even more challenging.

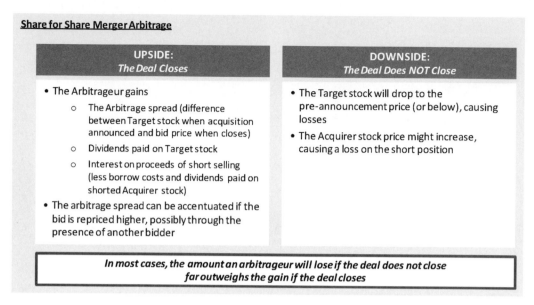

**EXHIBIT 12.7**

In a merger where the consideration is cash, an acquirer offers to purchase the shares of the target company for a fixed cash price. During the period of time until the merger closes (which could be one month to one year or longer), the target company's stock typically trades below the bid price, since there is some probability that the merger does not close. An arbitrageur who thinks that the merger will be consummated will simply buy the target company stock after the merger announcement and achieve profits equal to the difference between the arbitrageur's purchase price and the higher price paid by the acquiring company if the transaction closes.

The Upside and Downside of a share-for-share merger arbitrage transaction is summarized in Exhibit 12.7. See Exhibit 12.8 for a comparison of cash and share-for-share merger arbitrage transactions. See Exhibit 12.9 for a summary of merger arbitrage spreads for both successful and unsuccessful merger arbitrage efforts. The expected return of a cash merger arbitrage is summarized in Exhibit 12.10.

## Distressed Securities

Distressed securities investment strategies are directed at companies in distressed situations, such as bankruptcies and restructurings, or companies that are expected to experience distress in the future. Distressed securities are stocks, bonds, and trade or financial claims of companies in, or about to enter or exit, bankruptcy or financial distress. The prices of these securities fall in anticipation of financial distress and many holders choose to sell rather than remain invested in a financially troubled company. If a company that is already distressed appears ready to emerge from this condition, the prices of the company's securities may increase. Due to the market's inability to always properly value these securities, and the inability of many institutional investors to own distressed securities, these securities can sometimes be purchased at significant discounts to their risk-adjusted value. See Exhibit 12.11.

As shown in Exhibits 12.12 and 12.13, an investor can purchase and hold the securities of a company that is about to enter into a restructuring process until the company emerges from this

**Comparison of Cash and Share for Share Transactions**

Cash Transactions
• Arbitrageur only buys the Target company's stock
    o   Stock sells at a discount to the acquisition price
    o   Arbitrageur holds the Target until merger consummation and receives cash

Share for Share Transactions
• Arbitrageur will buy the shares of the Target as in a cash transaction, but will also sell short the stock of the Acquirer
    o   The amount to be shorted is based on the exchange ratio in the bid:
        –   If the proposed exchange ratio is 1:2 (1 share of the Acquirer will be issued for every 2 shares of the Target), then
        –   If the Arbitrageur buys 1,000 shares of the Target, there would be a simultaneous shorting of 500 shares of the Acquirer
    o   Arbitrageur holds the Target shares until the acquisition is consummated and then receives Acquirer stock, which is used to cover the short position

**EXHIBIT 12.8**

**Median Arbitrage Spread**

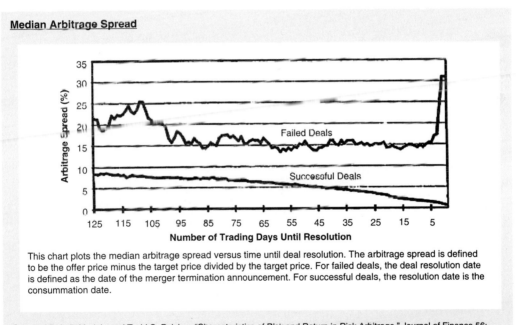

This chart plots the median arbitrage spread versus time until deal resolution. The arbitrage spread is defined to be the offer price minus the target price divided by the target price. For failed deals, the deal resolution date is defined as the date of the merger termination announcement. For successful deals, the resolution date is the consummation date.

Source: Mitchell, Mark L. and Todd C. Pulvino. "Characteristics of Risk and Return in Risk Arbitrage." Journal of Finance 56: 2135-2176.

**EXHIBIT 12.9**

process and the value of the security increases. As shown in Exhibit 12.14, an investor can also purchase the securities held by creditors in a bankruptcy. Alternatively, an investor can capitalize on mispricing between different securities of the same issuer that have senior or junior positions in the company's capital structure. When a distressed situation occurs, senior securities should appreciate in value relative to junior securities. This suggests that an investor should purchase

**Expected Return for Cash Merger**

> **Expected Return = [C*G-L(100%-C)]/Y*P**

Where:
- C is the expected chance of success (%)
- G is the expected gain in the event of a success (usually takeover price – current price)
- L is the expected loss in the event of a failure (current price – original price)
- Y is the expected holding time in years (usually the time until the acquisition takes place)
- P is the current price of the security

**Example:**
Company A makes a tender offer at $25 a share for Company B, currently trading at $15. The deal is expected to close in 3 months. The stock of Company B immediately increases to $24

- C = 96%
- G = $1.00
- L = $9.00 ($24-$15)
- Y = 25% (3/12 months)
- P = $24

> Exp. Return = [0.96*$1 - $9*(1 – 0.96)]/(0.25*$24) = 10%

EXHIBIT 12.10

**Distressed Securities Return**

Capitalize on the knowledge, flexibility, and patience that creditors of a company do not have

| | |
|---|---|
| Bonds | Many institutional investors, like pension funds, are barred by their charters or regulators from directly buying or holding below investment-grade bonds (Ba1/ BB+ or lower) |
| Bank Debt | Banks often prefer to sell their bad loans to remove them from their books and use the freed-up cash to make other investments |
| Trade Claims | Holders of trade claims are in the business of producing goods or providing services and have limited expertise in assessing the likelihood of being paid once a distressed company files for bankruptcy |

EXHIBIT 12.11

the senior securities and sell short the junior securities if they can do this before prices diverge. The success of distressed securities strategies usually depends on negotiations with other investors and lenders who have claims on the company and decisions made by bankruptcy court judges and trustees.

A successful distressed securities investment strategy uses an investment process that focuses on fundamental analysis, historical performance, causes of distress, capital structure, debt covenants, legal issues, trade execution, and the nature of claims and liabilities in the target's capital structure (see Exhibit 12.15).

Distressed securities investment strategies can be active or passive. Active investors will try to influence the restructuring and the refinancing process through participation in a creditor committee, and take a "hands-on" approach to ensure that the workout process is handled on a fair basis and that the investor's interests are protected or augmented. Active investors will get involved with many legal aspects of the workout and will attempt to reorganize the company

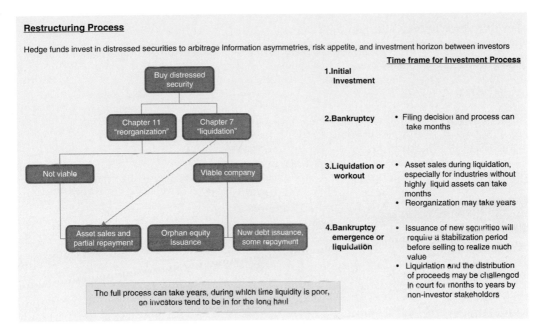

**Restructuring Process**

Hedge funds invest in distressed securities to arbitrage information asymmetries, risk appetite, and investment horizon between investors

EXHIBIT 12.12

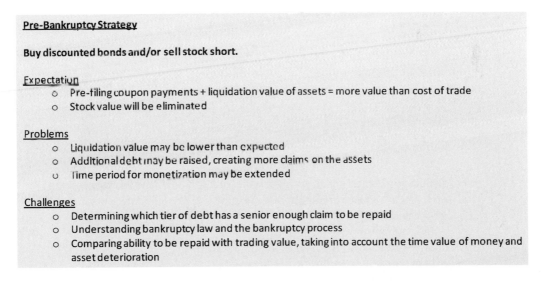

EXHIBIT 12.13

in a way that is most beneficial to their interests. In contrast, passive investors are less proactive and look for less complicated and less time-intensive investments in distressed situations (see Exhibit 12.16).

An example of a distressed securities investment in Barney's, a large clothing retailer, is found in Exhibit 12.17. Another example of a distressed securities investment is found in **Case Study 6, "Kmart, Sears, and ESL: How a Hedge Fund Became One of the World's Largest Retailers."** A summary of downside risks and opportunities is provided in Exhibit 12.18.

## In Bankruptcy Strategy

**Purchase shares issued to creditors in bankruptcy, or buy junior debt securities in anticipation of shares being issued during reorganization.**

Expectation
- o  Lack of analyst coverage and sales by impatient creditors creates undervalued shares
- o  Value will climb as firm emerges from bankruptcy

Problems
- o  Firm liquidates and shares become worthless
- o  Firm goes back into Chapter 11 a second time ("Chapter 22") and shares become worthless

Challenges
- o  Difficult to determine that the core business is viable and valuable

**EXHIBIT 12.14**

## Investment Process

Analyze:
- Fundamental/Quantitative analysis
- Historical performance and cause of distress
- Capital structure
- Debt structure covenants
- Legal issues
  - o  Bankruptcy proceedings
  - o  Tax issues
  - o  Public documents
  - o  Rights of subordinated creditors
  - o  Enforceability of derivatives
- Trade execution
  - o  Understand market trading dynamics
  - o  Arbitrage risk models that analyze individual relationships among securities
  - o  Liquidity analysis to understand how long it takes to liquidate a position
  - o  Potential politics involved in bankruptcy proceedings
  - o  Multi-scenario valuation models
- Nature of claims and liabilities in target's capital structure
  - o  Size of claims
  - o  Relative seniority
  - o  Composition of claims
  - o  Security liens
  - o  Guarantees
  - o  Relationship agreements among equity holders
  - o  Contingent liabilities
  - o  Intrinsic value

**EXHIBIT 12.15**

**Active Versus Passive Distressed Investing**

| Active | | Passive |
|---|---|---|
| **Control** | **Non-Control** | **Passive** |
| • Requires 1/3 block and 1/2 to control: may require partners <br> • Heavy lifting, private equity style investing, restricted <br> • Exit: 2-3 years <br> • Mid/small cap focus <br> • Opportunities: all credit environments | • Senior secured/senior unsecured <br> • Influence process, sometimes restricted <br> • Exit: 1-2 years <br> • Mid/small cap focus <br> • Opportunities: all credit environments | • Invest in undervalued securities trading at distressed levels <br> • Trading oriented; long, short, and capital arbitrage <br> • Exit: 6-12 months <br> • Large cap focus <br> • Opportunities: cyclical |

**EXHIBIT 12.16**

**Example Transaction**

- When Barney's filed Chapter 11 bankruptcy protection in early 1996 after it was unable to make the rent payments on its stores, many clothing designers chose to sell their trade claims and recoup a portion of their money
- Two hedge funds, Bay Harbour Management and Whippoorwill Associates Inc., acquired the company's distressed unpaid bills in secondary markets for $240 million – Bay Harbour paid about 30 cents on the dollar and Whippoorwill paid about 50 cents on the dollar – and subsequently rejected bids from retailers interested in buying Barney's:
    - Saks Fifth Avenue offered $290 million in 1997
    - Dickson Poon, a Hong Kong entrepreneur whose Dickson Concepts also owns Britain's Harvey Nichols department store, bid $280 million in 1997
    - DFS Group, airport duty-free store operator, bid approximately $280 million in 1998
- In January 1999, a bankruptcy court handed control over to the creditors: Bay Harbour and Whippoorwill became the two largest shareholders of common stock, collectively holding 85% of the shares
    - The bankruptcy process was lengthy (three years) and complicated due to a JV partnership with Isetan Company Limited, a Japanese department store operator that had funded Barney's expansion strategy with over $600 million
    - Isetan came away with a stake of about 7% as well as various concessions
    - Other equity holders included the company's President and CEO (6%) and the Pressman (founding) family (2%)
- Barney's was sold to Jones Apparel Group, Inc. for $401 million in December 2004

**EXHIBIT 12.17**

# Summary

Hedge fund investment strategies attempt to increase returns, reduce volatility of returns, and achieve positive returns even in difficult markets. Sometimes they are successful in achieving these objectives, and sometimes they are unsuccessful. This chapter has summarized some of the most actively utilized investment strategies, but there are dozens of other strategies that are employed by hedge funds. Many of these strategies involve short-selling, use arbitrage techniques, employ derivatives, involve significant corporate events, and incorporate sophisticated trading and financial vehicles, which are principally supplied by the prime brokerage, trading, and credit providing desks of investment banks.

To facilitate greater understanding of specific investment strategies, Exhibits 12.19 to 12.22 provide simplified numerical examples for transactions involving Merger Arbitrage, Pairs Trading, Distressed Investing, and Global Macro strategies.

## Risks and Opportunities

### Downside Risks

- High exposure to company/sector risks
- Miscalculation of firm liquidation value
- Timing of market and short-term losses
- Company fraud or misrepresentation
- Debt can turn into worthless equity
- Other creditors are uncompromising
- Reorganization lasts longer than expected
- Securities are not liquid
- At mercy of bankruptcy court
- Increased competition
- Regulatory changes
- Management motivation for a low exit value (when they receive low-strike options)

### Opportunities

- Ability to influence the distribution process, new equity issuance and future of new company
- Forced selling leads to discounted prices
- Many distressed firms not "covered" by Wall Street
- Can adapt style to particulars of deal and are not constrained by ratings
- Replace management / implement cost controls

**EXHIBIT 12.18**

## Merger Arbitrage

### Rationale

- Widget Makers Inc (WMI) has offered to purchase Sofa Makers Inc (SMI) for 2 shares of WMI stock per share of SMI. Just prior to announcement of the offer, WMI was trading at $52 per share and SMI was trading at $74 per share (the offer was at an approximately 40% premium to SMI's share price)
- WMI and SMI both do not pay dividends
- We expect that the offer will be accepted by SMI shareholders and will be completed in the next 2 to 3 months
- Post announcement, WMI is trading at $50 per share and SMI is trading at $95 per share

### Trade

- Buy 100 shares of SMI at $95
- Sell short 200 shares of WMI at $50

### Expected Result

- The merger will complete and we can close the short position in WMI through the exchange of SMI shares, making a profit of $5 per SMI share purchased over a 3 month period
- *Example*: If WMI rises to $60 per share and SMI rises to $120 upon completion, we do not have any additional cash flow in the future and make $5 per share from the initial investment
- *Example*: If WMI falls to $45 per share and SMI falls to $90 upon completion, we again do not have any additional cash flow in the future and make $5 per SMI share from the initial investment

### Additional Upside

- If a competitive bidding situation arises for SMI, we may see the price of SMI increase (and potentially WMI further decrease as it works to sweeten its bid)
- *Example*: If WidgeFactory (WF), comes in and bids $120 per share in cash for SMI, we could see SMI increase up to $118 per share (or even higher as WMI may be expected to counter bid) and WMI stay at $50 per share. If we close the position, we would enjoy a profit of $23 per share on SMI or $2300 from our trade

### Downside Risk

- If the transaction fails to complete, we may see SMI's price fall and WMI's price rebound, causing a potentially significant loss
- *Example*: If the transaction is blocked by regulators, we could see SMI's price revert to $74 and WMI return to $52 per share. In this case, we would lose $21 per share on SMI and $2 per share on WMI for a loss of $2500

### Mitigating Risk Position Partway Through

- If we grow concerned regarding the prospects of the merger, we may consider closing our position or purchasing options to limit our downside risk
- *Example*: If WMI stays at $50 per share and SMI rises to $98, we may consider closing our position, rather than waiting for completion
- *Example*: If WMI stays at $50 per share and SMI rises to $98, we may consider purchasing out of the money puts for SMI at for example $95 to lower the loss in case the merger does not complete. If these options cost $1, in case of completion we would make $4 per SMI share or a profit of $400. If the merger does not complete and SMI's price reverts to $74 and WMI returns to $52 per share, we would lose $2 per share on WMI, and nothing on SMI, and would have paid for the put, for a loss of $500 (much better than the $2500 expressed above)

**EXHIBIT 12.19**

## Pairs Trading

### Rationale

- Widget Makers Inc (WMI) has developed a new product which we believe will make Widget Makers' product much more desirable than that of its main competitor WidgetFactory (WF)
- We expect WMI will take more market share from WF
- WMI and WF both do not pay dividends

### Trade

- Buy 100 shares of WMI at $52
- Sell short 100 shares of WF at $45

### Expected Result

- We expect that over time the spread between WMI and WF will widen
- *Example*: If we think that in 1 year WMI will rise to $65 per share and WF will rise to $50 per share → make $13 per WMI share and lose $5 per WF share → make $800 profit from our trade (returns $1500 on $700 investment)
- *Example*: If WMI falls to $40 and WF falls to $30, we lose $12 per share on WMI and we make $15 per share on WF → make $300 from our trade (returns $1000 on $700 investment)

### Additional Upside

- The upside in this trade comes from the spread widening – it may be more than we expect

### Downside Risk

- We may be incorrect in our belief that the new product will be liked by the market (think "New Coke") and we may see the spread tighten or even WM overtake WMI
- For example, if WMI increases to $55 and WF increases to $54, we would gain $3 per share from WMI and lose $9 per share from WF for a loss of $600 on a $700 investment

### Mitigating Risk Position Partway Through

- If we grow concerned regarding the prospects for the new product, we may consider closing our position or purchasing options to limit our exposure
- *Example*: We may consider buying puts and selling calls on WMI and selling puts and buying calls on WF. While this will limit our upside potential, it will also limit our downside risk based upon the spreads we bake into these option positions and their net cost

**EXHIBIT 12.20**

## Distressed Investing

### Rationale

- Investment Power Producer (IPP) operates in the unregulated segment of the highly regulated energy market
- With its input costs increasing at a faster rate than its output revenue over the last several years, IPP has had negative cash flow and negative earnings for the last few years and may be forced into bankruptcy in the near term
- IPP is financed primarily with $10 billion of 5% debt which matures in 10 years, and is trading at a deep discount of $30 per $100 face – IPP's debt has a below investment grade rating
- IPP's stock is trading at $3 per share with 100 million shares outstanding
- IPP has sufficient cash for approximately 2 years of operation and debt service at current cash burn rates ($1.5 billion per year of which $0.5 billion is debt service)
- IPP's debt covenants impose that significant asset sales can trigger a put on the bonds (at the bondholder's discretion)
- We expect IPP will be forced into bankruptcy after 2 years
- In liquidation, we expect the assets could be sold for $3.5 billion (which would take roughly 1 year from the time bankruptcy is entered)

### Trade

- Buy 1 bond ($1000 face) of IPP at $30 per $100 face
- Sell short 100 shares of IPP at $3

### Downside Risk

- Given the regulated nature of the industry, we may see a shift in regulation which could lead to a generally worse scenario with much greater volatility for IPP (for example, regulated utilities must now purchase a set percentage of their power from unregulated power producers such as IPP and newly purchased assets will be subject to additional environmental requirements, thus lowering the value of assets in a sale)
- *Example*: This change in regulation could mean that the assets are worthless. But if a regulated power producer buys its energy from IPP and the company's enterprise value is $20 billion (which happens with a probability of 10%), then the share price would increase to $10 per $100 face (get paid back in full with 10% probability and worthless otherwise) → this would make our trade lose $200 per bond and $7 per share for a loss of $900

### Expected Result

- As our initial portfolio is zero cost by construction, let us examine the cash flows from the trade: we will get coupon payments of $50 per year for the first two years, and then the company will be liquidated resulting in payment of $350 ($35 per $100 face to bondholders)
- The shares will be worthless, creating an economic gain of $300 and no future cash flow

### Additional Upside

- If the company looks to negotiate with bondholders sooner than expected, we may see better returns as there will be more assets left to distribute to claimants – for example – if the company liquidates in one year, the value of assets would be $3.5B plus the additional $1.5B in cash remaining, leaving the bondholders $50 per $100 face

### Mitigating Risk Position Part Way Through

- Given the risks associated with this position, it may be difficult to attach additional instruments to limit risk exposure. Given that the equity is already behaving like an option, it is unlikely that there will be a liquid market in equity options in which to transact which would offer any advantages versus transacting in equity
- We may consider going long the credit default swap index for non-regulated power producers to hedge since CDS spreads typically increase with rising stock volatilities
- We may consider closing our stock position

**EXHIBIT 12.21**

**Global Macro**

**Rationale**

- Elbonia is a developed, industrialized country with a stable government
- Although commodity and Elbonian stock markets have been rallying for the past few quarters, the Elbonian market remains focused on the risks of deflation and continued deterioration of the Elbonian economy
- The Elbonian central bankers have stated that they will "do whatever needs to be done" in order to inflate the economy
- We believe that the market has not accurately priced market implied inflation rates in Elbonia given the relatively low Elbonian CPI readings of 2%
- Current prices are in line given inflation expectations of 1% going forward
- We expect inflation will stay at 2% going forward

**Trade**

- Buy 1 Elbonian National Bond Inflation-Protected Security (ENBIPS) maturing in 5 years at 2% at 1000
- Sell short 1 Elbonian National Bond (ENB) at 3% at 1000
- ENB is a Nominal Note so its yield is Nominal Yield = "Real" Yield + Expected inflation
- ENBIPS provides a "Real" Yield
- → ENB Yield minus ENBIPS Yield = Market-Implied Inflation

**Expected Result**

- *Example*: our long position is expected to generate a payoff of $1,217 [(1+.02 Real Yield +.02 Inflation)^5] for gains of $217 over 5 years while our short position is expected to grow $1,159 [(1+.03 Nominal Yield)^5] over the 5 years for a net gain of $57

**Additional Upside**

- Given the macroeconomic environment and the central bank's stated policy, it is possible that inflation will increase more than expected
- *Example*: If inflation increases to 4% over the lifetime, the value of our long position will grow to $1,338 [(1+.02 Real Yield + .04 Inflation)^5] while our short position remains at $1,159 [(1 + .03 Nominal Yield)^5] creating a gain of $179

**Downside Risk**

- If deflation does occur, we could experience losses
- *Example*: If we experience deflation of 1% per year, the value of our ENBIPS would increase only to $1,051 [(1+.02 Real Yield -.01 Inflation)^5] over time while our ENB would still grow to $1,159 [(1+.03 Nominal Yield)^5], causing a net loss of $108

**Mitigating Risk Position Part Way Through**

- *Example*: We may consider purchasing an option which would allow us to enter into a forward contract on the ENBIPS to reduce our loss in case deflation is worse that initially expected

**EXHIBIT 12.22**

# Questions

1. During the height of the financial crisis in late 2008, the yield curve flattened and the yield on the 30-year Treasury bond reached an all-time low of 2.52%. As a hedge fund manager, suppose you think the market has overreacted and will eventually correct itself, leading to a steepening in the yield curve. What trades might you execute in a long/short strategy to take advantage of the situation?

2. Precious metals such as gold and silver experienced significant gains during the financial crisis as investors purchased tangible assets that have more perceived value stability. In October 2008, you notice that a gold/silver precious metals closed-end fund is trading at a historically high premium relative to its net asset value. What trade might you employ to take advantage of the situation (assuming you believe the worst is over)?

3. ABC and DEF operate in the same industry, and you have just attended a trade show where they have unveiled their new product lines that are coming out this month. ABC's offering looks like a winner, whereas you have serious doubts about DEF's new products. ABC and DEF both trade at $50 per share. ABC 1-year $50 calls trade at $3, and DEF 1-year $50 calls trade at $4. ABC 1-year $50 puts trade at $3.50, and DEF 1-year $50 puts trade at $3.50. Interest rates are 2%. Neither ABC nor DEF pay dividends nor are expected to pay dividends in the coming years. As a long/short hedge fund investor, what options trade should you execute in this scenario?

4. Why did convertible arbitrage strategies perform so poorly in 2008?

5. Assume you buy $1,000 of a convertible bond at par, which was offered at a 2.5% discount to its theoretical value. The stock price on the day of purchase is $35 and carries a 1% dividend yield. The convertible bond has a 4% coupon, a conversion premium of 20%, and a delta of 56%. Interest income from the short position is 1.5%, and stock borrow cost is 0.25%. During a 1-year holding period, the stock moves three times.

The percentage change in stock price, corresponding convertible bond value, and new delta ratio, in sequential order, are as follows: +7% / $1,037.12 / 61%; –5% / $1,012.11 / 58%; +4% / $1,032.71 / 60%. Calculate the returns generated from this investment after one year, broken out by Income Generation, Monetizing Volatility, and Purchasing an Undervalued Convertible. Ignore transaction costs for the purposes of this exercise.

6. When is merger arbitrage an attractive investment strategy? What are the downside risks of this strategy?

7. MNO makes a tender offer for PRS at 1.5 MNO shares per PRS share. MNO was trading at $40 per share prior to announcement and fell to $38 on announcement. PRS was trading at $40 per share prior to announcement and is now trading at $50. If you are pursuing a merger arbitrage strategy, what is the position you would set up to create potential investment value? What derivative transaction could you use to mitigate your risk?

8. Calculate the expected return for the following cash merger arbitrage transaction: offer per Target share is $30.25. Target's share price just prior to the announcement is $20.00, and $28.50 immediately following the announcement. The deal is expected to close with a 95% certainty. The deal is expected to close in 4 months.

9. Why do you think distressed/restructuring hedge fund strategies did so poorly in 2008 (down 25% for the year)?

10. Generally speaking, in which two hedge fund strategies would you expect to see more volatile returns?

11. Merger arbitrage is considered a market-neutral strategy. Under what conditions would this no longer be the case?

12. What are some ways to neutralize market risk in an equity long/short transaction?

# 13
# Shareholder Activism and Impact on Corporations

The material in this chapter should be cross-referenced with **Case Study 7, "McDonald's, Wendy's, and Hedge Funds: Hamburger Hedging? Hedge Fund Activism and Impact on Corporate Governance,"** and **Case Study 8, "Porsche, Volkswagen, and CSX: Cars, Trains, and Derivatives."**

Certain hedge funds focus on shareholder activism as a core investment strategy. An activist shareholder acquires a minority equity position in a public corporation and then applies pressure on management in order to increase shareholder value through changes in corporate policy. Some of the common changes advocated by activist shareholders include reducing corporate costs, repurchasing common shares, increasing corporate leverage, increasing dividends, reducing CEO compensation, reducing cash balances, and divesting certain businesses. In addition, activist shareholders will sometimes campaign against proposed acquisitions or allocation of cash for purposes that are not perceived to create shareholder value. Activists sometimes also pursue a sale of a target company or a break-up of the company through a piecemeal sale or spin-off of significant operations. See Exhibit 13.1.

Activist shareholders usually acquire between 1% and 10% of a target company's shares, or create an equity exposure by entering into equity derivative transactions, such as purchasing call options on the company's stock, simultaneously purchasing call options and selling put options on the company's stock, entering into forward transactions to purchase the company's stock, or

---

**Shareholder Activism**

- Some corporations are vulnerable to hostile initiatives by activist shareholders
- Hedge funds can be vocal investors who demand change in the corporate governance landscape in a number of ways:
    - Publicly criticizing/challenging Boards and managements
    - Nominating Board candidates and pursuing their agenda through proxy contests
    - Supporting other activists
- Hedge funds' activist strategy has been successful by taking advantage of:
    - Like-minded hedge funds' herd mentality
    - Ability to overcome reputation for short-term focus
    - Ability to skillfully use a deep arsenal of securities and financial instruments
    - Familiarity with M&A and legal regulations and rights
    - Readiness to go to battle and devote significant resources to full-blown public relations battles

Source: Morgan Stanley

**EXHIBIT 13.1**

entering into equity swaps in relation to the company's stock. These derivative alternatives will be discussed later in this chapter and are described in Case Studies 7 and 8. A relatively small shareholding or equity derivative position established by an activist shareholder may enable the investor to launch a campaign to make significant changes in the company, without the added cost and time required by a complete acquisition. To be effective, however, the activist shareholder generally must obtain the support of other large shareholders. This can sometimes be obtained through large-scale publicity campaigns, shareholder resolutions, or, in the extreme, proxy battles for control over the board of directors.

Shareholder activism became an active force during 1985, when the Supreme Court of Delaware decided four cases relating to corporate governance: Unocal, Household, Van Gorkom, and Revlon. Pension funds, mutual funds, and activist hedge funds joined the movement at that time and activity increased every year until 2002, when shareholder activism gained considerable momentum because of the Enron and WorldCom corporate blowups and the subsequent passage of the Sarbanes-Oxley Act of 2002.

## Shareholder-Centric vs. Director-Centric Corporate Governance

A key issue in corporate governance is whether the corporate board of directors will survive as the governing organization of the public corporation, or if shareholder activism will ultimately invalidate the role of the board. In other words, will corporations become more shareholder-centric and less director-centric in their governance?

Some critics of shareholder-centric governance indicate that this movement is causing a shift in the board's role from guiding strategy and advising management to ensuring compliance and performing due diligence. This shift can create a wall between the board and the CEO, removing the "trusted advisor" role of board members, as CEOs become increasingly wary of sharing concerns with investigative and defensive boards. Based on concern about litigation, directors sometimes become so focused on their individual committee responsibility that they are less able to focus on the broad objectives of maximizing shareholder value. They become "Balkanized" into powerful committees of independent directors, unable to broadly coordinate the focus of the entire board. Even when the board is able to focus on the business of the corporation in cooperation with the CEO, activist investors create pressure on boards to manage for short-term share price performance rather than long-term value creation. This may result in short-changing the company's relationships with its employees, customers, suppliers, and communities, as well as reducing investment in R&D and capital projects that are critical to a company's long-term success.

Another criticism of shareholder-centric governance is that shareholder activists could ultimately wrest substantial control from boards, causing companies to bring almost every important decision to a shareholder vote. This would largely shut down the normal operating procedures of the company, slowing down decisions and creating competitive disadvantages, as previously confidential decisions that were made by the board are put in the public domain. There is also concern that activist shareholders can create inappropriate pressure on boards through nondocumented alignments between different activists to achieve their objectives. Activists take advantage of the ambiguity of concepts like group, acting in concert, and investment intent, testing the limits of securities, reporting, and antitrust rules. This activity is explored in more detail in **Case Study 8, "Porsche, Volkswagen, and CSX: Cars, Trains, and Derivatives."**

RiskMetrics Group (RMG), through its Institutional Shareholder Services (ISS) division, focuses on corporate governance and proxy voting among institutional investors. This organization, which influences the thinking of institutional investors, has increasingly supported shareholder-centric initiatives. During 2009, RMG recommended that its institutional investor clients "withhold votes" whenever they disapprove of company policies. For example, RMG has recommended a withhold vote whenever a board "lacks accountability and oversight," coupled with "sustained poor performance" relative to the company's peers.[1] RMG has for many years attacked shareholder rights plans (poison pills), pushing for a 20% or higher triggering threshold and a shareholder redemption feature, which substantially reduces the effectiveness of a rights plan. RMG's policy is to recommend withholding votes against an entire board of directors, if the board adopts or renews a rights plan without shareholder approval, does not commit to putting the rights plan to a shareholder vote within one year of adoption, or reneges on a commitment to put the rights plan to a vote. This policy could be challenging for corporations that are the subject of potential hostile or unsolicited takeover attempts.

In spite of RMG's fight against shareholder rights plans, during 2008, 76 U.S. public companies adopted their first-ever poison pill, compared to 42 original pill adoptions in 2007. Many shareholders who used to follow activist leaders in pressuring companies to eliminate their poison pills or declassify their boards now encourage companies to protect their interests through prudent takeover defenses. However, the debate continues.

Corporate boards and CEOs are increasingly focused on the threat of activist shareholders and the frequently adversarial positions of organizations like RMG. They turn to investment bankers and outside law firms for direction in shoring up their defenses against hostile takeovers and unfriendly activist shareholder initiatives. See Exhibit 13.2 for a corporate checklist of matters to be considered by a company regarding how to prevent or respond to hedge fund activism.

## Activist Hedge Fund Performance

Activist hedge fund activity was negatively impacted during a 2-year period that started in mid-2007, when the financial crisis took its toll on activists' capital and credibility. Prior to the crisis, for a 5 year period, hedge fund activists had been very successful in persuading companies to repurchase stock, which contributed to rising share prices (stock repurchases in the United States exceeded $1.7 trillion between mid-2002 and mid-2007, more than doubling repurchase amounts compared to the previous 5-year period). The gains related to share repurchase, combined with large gains achieved when activists were successful in initiatives to push companies into a sale to private equity or other buyers, resulted in strong returns for activist shareholders. The financial crisis took away available credit (from both activists and companies), which resulted in reduced share repurchases and fewer M&A transactions, creating correspondingly lower investment returns for activist investors. As a consequence, the track records of several hedge fund investors were tarnished: Kirk Kerkorian took positions in both Ford and General Motors stock and agitated for change, but ultimately he sold these positions at a significant loss. Carl Icahn pushed Time Warner into buying back $20 billion in stock when it traded at $18 during 2006, but the company's shares dropped to a low of around $7 at the end of 2008. Activists also pressured Home Depot and Motorola, among others, to purchase shares prior to a steep share price decline. Exhibit 13.3 shows activist hedge fund returns during 2005–2008.

---

[1] "U.S. Proxy Voting Manual." Risk Metrics Group, 15 Jan. 2009.

## Dealing with Activist Hedge Funds

- Create Team to Deal with Hedge Fund Activism
  - A small group (2-5) of key officers plus lawyer, investment banker, proxy soliciting firm, and public relations firm
  - Ensure ability to convene special meeting of board within 24 to 48 hours
  - Continuing contact and periodic meetings of the team are important
  - A periodic fire drill with the team is the best way to maintain the state of preparedness
  - Periodic updates of board
  - Warlist of contacts updated regularly

- Shareholder Relations
  - Review dividend policy, analyst presentations and other financial public relations
  - Prepare fiduciary holders with respect to takeover tactics designed to panic them
  - Review trustees for various company plans and determine if change is required
  - Monitor changes in institutional holdings on a regular basis
  - Plan for contacts with institutional investors (including maintenance of an up-to-date list of holdings and contacts) and analysts and with media, regulatory agencies and political bodies
  - Remain informed about activist institutional investors and about corporate governance and proxy issues
  - Role of arbitrageurs and hedge funds

- Prepare the Board of Directors to Deal with the Activist Situation
  - Maintaining a unified board consensus on key strategic issues is essential to Success
  - Schedule periodic presentations by lawyers and investment bankers to familiarize directors with the takeover scene and the law and with their advisors
  - Company may have policy of continuing as an independent entity
  - Company may have policy of not engaging in takeover discussions
  - Directors must guard against subversion by raider and should refer all approaches to the CEO
  - Avoid being put in play; psychological and perception factors may be more important than legal and financial factors in avoiding being singled out as a takeover target
  - Review corporate governance guidelines and reconstitution of key committees

- Monitor Trading
  - Stock watch service, Schedule 13F filings
  - Watch for Schedule 13D and Hart-Scott-Rodino Act filings
  - Monitor parallel trading and group activity (the activist "wolf pack")

- Responding to an Activist Approach
  - Responses to Non-Public Communications
    - No duty to discuss or negotiate
    - No duty to disclose unless leak comes from within
    - Response to any particular approach must be specially structured; team should confer to decide proper response
    - Keep board advised
    - Be prepared for public disclosure by activist
  - Response to Public Communication
    - No response other than "will call you back" (no outright rejection; no substantive discussion—try to learn as much as possible by listening)
    - Assemble team; inform directors
    - Call special board meeting to meet with team and consider the communication
    - Determine board's response and whether to meet with attacker
    - Avoid mixed messages
    - Be prepared and willing to defend vigorously and attack the attackers

Source: Wachtell, Lipton, Rosen & Katz: memo from Martin Lipton, "Takeover Response Checklist and Dealing with Activist Hedge Funds," Apr. 2009.

**EXHIBIT 13.2**

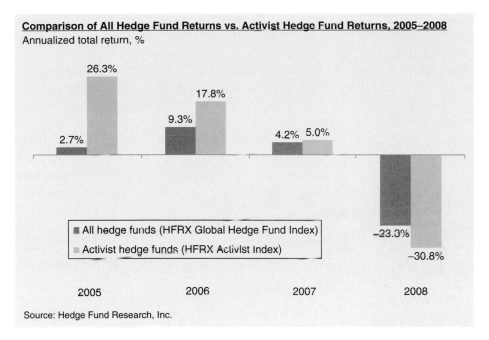

Comparison of All Hedge Fund Returns vs. Activist Hedge Fund Returns, 2005–2008

Source: Hedge Fund Research, Inc.

**EXHIBIT 13.3**

According to academic studies, the number of public companies targeted for poor performance by hedge funds grew more than tenfold between 1994 and 2006.[2] Despite the prevalence of hedge fund activism, however, the studies identified an apparent contradiction in the notion that a hedge fund portfolio manager with a short-term financial goal would have the time, energy, or expertise to improve the long-term performance of a public company. When examining the effectiveness of hedge fund activism in producing value for shareholders, the studies found that unless a target company was ultimately sold following activist investment, there was little change (during the 18 months following the first activist filing) in the company's stock price or financial results. This was true even when the company took other steps urged by the activists, such as replacing the CEO, changing the composition of the board or buying back stock. The studies also confirmed that investments by activist funds increase the likelihood that target companies will get sold.

In an environment where private equity funds have a more difficult time securing debt financing to support acquisitions, activist hedge fund investors are less threatening to corporations. The historically symbiotic relationship between activist hedge funds and buyout firms increases when credit markets free up and leveraged buyout activity grows.

## Activist Hedge Fund Accumulation Strategies

For an activist investor, timing is everything. Their objective is to accumulate enough ownership in a targeted company to influence change, but they want to accumulate shares without drawing attention from the target and without attracting tag-along investors, whose purchases can drive

---

[2]Greenwood, Robin, and Michael Schor. "Investor Activism and Takeovers." *Journal of Financial Economics* 92 (2009): 362–375.

up the stock price, making it too expensive to accumulate additional stock (see Exhibit 13.4). Some activist investors have utilized derivatives to help them create a large exposure to a company, without alerting either the target or other potential investors.

The SEC requires investors that own 5% or more of a company's equity to disclose their ownership through a 13D filing within 10 days of acquisition. To avoid tipping their hand, however, some activist investors have used cash-settled equity swaps to create an equity exposure to the target. These derivative contracts do not require 13D disclosure. (See the next section, "CSX vs. TCI," and **Case Study 8, "Porsche, Volkswagen, and CSX: Cars, Trains, and Derivatives."**)

An equity swap is typically entered into with an investment bank counterparty, which causes the bank to buy shares as a hedge against their obligation to pay the returns of the stock ownership (appreciation or depreciation, plus dividends) to the activist hedge fund in exchange for payments that are based on a floating rate of interest (typically LIBOR) plus an appropriate

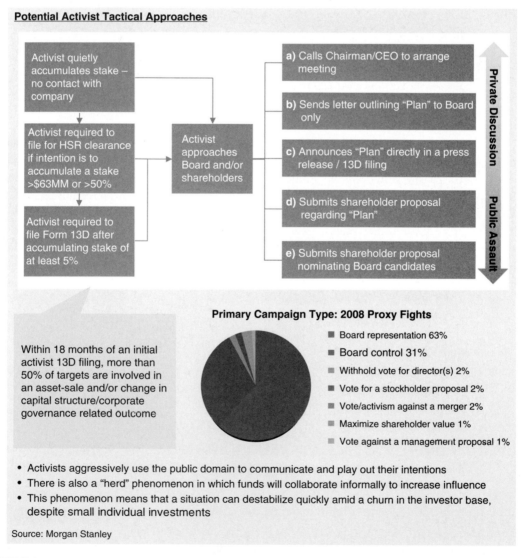

**Potential Activist Tactical Approaches**

Activist quietly accumulates stake – no contact with company

Activist required to file for HSR clearance if intention is to accumulate a stake >$63MM or >50%

Activist required to file Form 13D after accumulating stake of at least 5%

Activist approaches Board and/or shareholders

a) Calls Chairman/CEO to arrange meeting

b) Sends letter outlining "Plan" to Board only

c) Announces "Plan" directly in a press release / 13D filing

d) Submits shareholder proposal regarding "Plan"

e) Submits shareholder proposal nominating Board candidates

Private Discussion → Public Assault

Within 18 months of an initial activist 13D filing, more than 50% of targets are involved in an asset-sale and/or change in capital structure/corporate governance related outcome

**Primary Campaign Type: 2008 Proxy Fights**

- Board representation 63%
- Board control 31%
- Withhold vote for director(s) 2%
- Vote for a stockholder proposal 2%
- Vote/activism against a merger 2%
- Maximize shareholder value 1%
- Vote against a management proposal 1%

- Activists aggressively use the public domain to communicate and play out their intentions
- There is also a "herd" phenomenon in which funds will collaborate informally to increase influence
- This phenomenon means that a situation can destabilize quickly amid a churn in the investor base, despite small individual investments

Source: Morgan Stanley

**EXHIBIT 13.4**

credit spread. In some equity swaps, the hedge fund has the right to purchase the underlying shares from the counterparty under certain circumstances, at which point the hedge fund would disclose ownership of the shares (but not before the shares are delivered). The key question under this arrangement is who controls votes attached to the shares that are the subject of the equity swap? Since the activist does not own the shares, they technically do not own the voting rights and therefore may not be required by the SEC to disclose ownership under 13D rules. However, since the hedge fund might be able to receive these shares before a future vote on the election of directors, the activist can theoretically own the shares when it matters most. It is important to note, however, that many banks expressly refuse to deliver shares or to vote in proxy contests.

Sometimes activist hedge funds have acted in concert with other hedge funds to both buy shares and enter into equity swaps. For example, two funds could each purchase 4.9% of a company's shares without entering into any written agreement to act together, and each could also enter into an equity swap on 4.9% of the company's shares. Even though this may mean that, at the time of a critical corporate event such as election of directors, the two hedge funds might effectively control a combined 19.6% of a company's stock and vote their shares in the same way at that time, neither fund must disclose their position until immediately before the election. In this case, the two hedge funds will enjoy the benefit of surprise and could wield significant influence on the outcome of an election. It is important to note that if, in fact, hedge funds act in concert, there may be legal complications, as discussed in the next section.

## CSX vs. TCI

Equity swaps have enabled hedge funds to participate in activist shareholder initiatives for many years, creating the following benefits: (1) maximizing the activist's profit potential by avoiding the market bidding up shares in anticipation of a control contest; (2) allowing the activist to strategically time the disclosure of intent to influence corporate policy (potentially permitting the activist to ambush a company with an undisclosed holding greater than 5%); and (3) enabling an activist to swiftly acquire shares by unwinding the swaps through physical settlement (if the counterparty consents to do so), allowing the activist to potentially acquire the common shares held by swap counterparties as a hedge.

During 2007, The Children's Investment Fund (TCI), a major European-based hedge fund, acquired a 4.2% ownership in CSX, the fourth-largest U.S. rail operator. TCI then announced its intent to propose a slate of directors for CSX's board at the company's annual meeting during June 2008. Subsequent to this announcement, the two parties battled in court and in the court of public opinion, with CSX launching a lobbying campaign among U.S. legislators. In March 2008, CSX accused TCI and another hedge fund (3G Capital Partners) of violating disclosure laws by building up a coordinated stake through equity swap contracts. The two hedge funds at that time held a combined 8.7% shareholding in the company and an economic exposure to the stock, based on the equity swaps, equal to an additional 11.5% of outstanding shares. In April, TCI filed a countersuit against CSX, alleging the company withheld material facts and violated insider-trading policies.

Although investors that hold 5% or more of a U.S. company's stock are required to report stock holdings with the SEC, investors that create exposure to the stock through derivatives do not face the same requirements in some situations. Equity swaps are derivatives that do not grant direct voting rights to the swap counterparty. This is why the hedge funds believed that they had no disclosure obligation. The International Swaps and Derivative Association Inc. and the

Securities Industry and Financial Markets Association filed a legal brief supporting the hedge funds and their position regarding nondisclosure. Moreover, during June 2008, the SEC also sided with the hedge funds, stating that there is no 13D disclosure requirement for holders of cash-settled equity swaps.

Ultimately, TCI and 3G Capital Partners entered into swaps with eight bank counterparties, which in aggregate gave them economic exposure to more than 14% of CSX's shares, with a notional value in excess of $2.5 billion. It was alleged by CSX that most, if not all, of the swap counterparties hedged their exposure by accumulating an equal position in CSX shares. The SEC ruled that "standard cash-settled equity swap agreements" do not confer either voting or investment power to the swap party over shares acquired by its counterparty to hedge the relevant swaps, a conclusion that is not changed by the presence of economic or business incentives that the counterparty may have to vote the shares as the other party wishes or to dispose of the shares to the other party.[3] The SEC therefore rejected CSX's position that TCI and 3G Capital Partners had acquired beneficial ownership over the CSX shares purchased by counterparties to hedge their exposure to the swaps. As a result, the SEC ruled that the hedge funds were therefore not subject to reporting requirements under Rule 13D (see Exhibit 13.5).

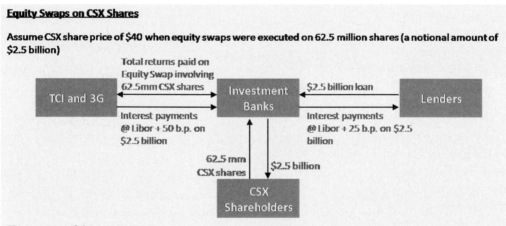

**Equity Swaps on CSX Shares**

Assume CSX share price of $40 when equity swaps were executed on 62.5 million shares (a notional amount of $2.5 billion)

The outcome of this transaction is:

- TCI and 3G receive economic exposure to 62.5 million CSX shares since they receive/pay total returns from/to investment bank counterparties (quarterly appreciation/depreciation of CSX share price + dividends)

- Since TCI and 3G don't own shares (investment banks purchased 62.5 million CSX shares to hedge their equity swap position) the hedge funds may not need to report beneficial ownership of these shares to the SEC

- The investment banks receive a spread of 25 basis points between their cost of borrowing $2.5 billion and the payments received from TCI and 3G under the equity swap

- The hedge fund may have the right to unwind the equity swap in the future before a proxy vote by paying $2.5 billion to the investment banks in exchange for 62.5 million CSX shares

**EXHIBIT 13.5**

Shortly after the SEC ruling, however, a federal judge found that the two hedge funds had consciously avoided securities laws in their proxy battle with CSX, a decision that stands to reshape how activist investors move on their corporate targets. The judge rebuked the funds by saying they sought to justify their actions "on the basis of formalistic arguments," even when they

---

[3]Amicus curiae letter of the SEC Division of Corporate Finance filed in CSX Corp. v The Children's Investment Fund Management et al. (June 4, 2008).

had "defeated the purpose of the law."[4] The court's decision gave ammunition to CSX as it continued its proxy fight based on the judicial view that the hedge funds had together plotted a bid for control of the company, but consciously, and illegally, failed to disclose their intentions. The court also found that the hedge funds delayed publicly disclosing that they were coordinating their CSX-related actions. Finally, the court noted that, although TCI had no legal right to vote or dispose of the hedged shares, as an important client of the investment bank counterparties, they could possibly influence the voting decision of the banks that held CSX shares as a hedge to their equity swap position.

This federal ruling was not a complete victory for CSX, however, since the judge said that it was too late to reverse their actions, and that he was legally prevented from "sterilizing" or neutralizing their votes when shareholders chose new members of their board of directors on June 25, 2008, including representatives from the hedge funds.[4]

The Federal Court position appears to be at odds with the SEC's position. However, the Federal ruling represents a strong challenge to hedge funds who attempt to conceal their true economic position through the use of derivatives. See **Case Study 8, "Porsche, Volkswagen, and CSX: Cars, Trains, and Derivatives,"** for further discussion of this topic.

## Changing Rules That Favor Activists

Activist investors have become adept at initiating proxy contests to obtain shareholder votes in support of the activist's platform. There are many factors that influence shareholder votes, including the makeup of a company's institutional shareholder base, the extent to which these investors are susceptible to influence by third-party advisory services such as RiskMetrics/ISS or Glass Lewis, and the involvement of the retail investor base and associated broker discretionary votes. In 2009, the SEC decided to eliminate broker discretionary voting for the election of directors, which shifts additional power to activists in director elections. Historically, brokers have been allowed to vote on behalf of their retail clients who hold shares in public companies if the shareholder fails to vote. Brokers typically vote these shares in-line with management's recommendations, including for incumbent directors. With the SEC elimination of the NYSE rule that allowed for the broker discretionary voting in director elections, there will likely be fewer votes in favor of management.

The elimination of broker discretionary voting is particularly important since almost 45% of S&P 500 companies have adopted a majority vote election standard, replacing plurality voting. In plurality voting, the nominees for available directorships who receive the highest number of votes cast are elected, irrespective of the number of votes cast, including withheld votes. Under this system, a nominee could theoretically be elected as a director based on receiving, for example, two affirmative votes in an election where there was one vote cast against the director and millions of withheld votes. For companies that have adopted the majority vote requirement for directors, nominees are typically required to receive the affirmative vote of at least 50% of the votes of all shareholders in order to remain in office for another term. Previously, the broker discretionary voting rule change would have had limited impact since nearly all companies had a plurality voting system. But, with a majority voting standard, disgruntled investors, including activist hedge funds, may be more successful in "just vote no" campaigns to remove incumbent directors.

---

[4]Slater, Dan. "Judge Kaplan Reprimands Hedge Funds in Takeover Battle with CSX." The Wall Street Journal, 12 June 2008.

## Daniel Loeb and 13D Letters

Daniel Loeb is a hedge fund manager and founder of Third Point LLC. He is well known for writing public letters in which he expresses disapproval of the performance and decision making of senior management of selected companies. His letter writing is a form of shareholder activism. These letters are often sent directly to a company's CEO or board, and are sometimes attached to 13D filings with the SEC when Loeb's holdings in a company exceed 5%. Loeb's goal is to shame companies into replacing their CEOs, shaking up their boards, or doing other things that will boost the value of his investment. After Loeb bought shares in Potlatch Corporation and the share price dropped, he branded CEO Pendleton Siegel a "CVD"—chief value destroyer. He wrote to Star Gas Partners L.P. CEO Irik Sevin: "Do what you do best. Retreat to your waterfront mansion in the Hamptons where you can play tennis and hobnob with your fellow socialites." Sevin subsequently resigned from the company. See Loeb's letter to the CEO of InterCept, Inc. in Exhibit 13.6.[5]

## Lehman Brothers' Erin Callan vs. David Einhorn of Greenlight Capital

Erin Callan was promoted to the position of CFO of Lehman Brothers in December 2007, but was removed from this position in June 2008 after a 6-month verbal battle with activist shareholder David Einhorn of Greenlight Capital. Greenlight set up a short position in Lehman Brothers' stock starting in July 2007 because Einhorn felt that Lehman was undercapitalized and had massive exposure to CDOs that were not recorded properly. He also claimed that Lehman Brothers was using dubious accounting practices in their financial filings. Starting in April 2008, Einhorn talked publicly about his Lehman short position. During May, Callan had a private call with Einhorn and his analysts in an attempt to explain discrepancies that had been uncovered between Lehman's latest financial filing and what had been discussed during its conference call about that filing. Einhorn indicated that Callan fumbled some of her responses to questions on Lehman's asset valuations, and he took his concerns public. She then publicly disputed Einhorn's positions several times, but each time Lehman's stock fell further. Lehman ultimately filed for bankruptcy protection during September 2008, and Greenlight Capital achieved significant gains from its short position in Lehman stock.

## Carl Icahn vs. Yahoo

During February 2008, Microsoft offered to buy Yahoo at $31 per share, but Yahoo's CEO and founder rejected the offer. Following this rejection, Carl Icahn started accumulating a position in Yahoo stock, attempting to benefit from an eventual sale to Microsoft. During May 2008, Icahn initiated a proxy fight against Yahoo after acquiring an equity equivalent position of 59 million Yahoo shares. This position was comprised of 9.9 million common shares and equity collars on 49 million Yahoo shares. The equity collars were created through the purchase of call options on Yahoo (American-style calls with an unknown strike price and maturity) and the simultaneous sale of put options on Yahoo (European-style puts with a strike price of $19.50, maturing in

---

[5]Gopinath, Deepak. "Hedge Fund Rabble-Rouser," Bloomberg Markets, Oct. 2005.

## Daniel Loeb Letter to Intercept, Inc.

June 24, 2004

Mr. John W. Collins
Chairman of the Board and Chief Executive Officer
Intercept, Inc.
3150 Holcomb Bridge Road
Suite 200
Norcross, GA 30071

Dear Mr. Collins:

I am writing to inform you that we agree with the market's determination that InterCept, Inc (the *"Company"*) should be worth substantially more with your imminent involuntary extraction from the position of Chief Executive Officer, which we would expect to result from the likely sale of the Company. Accordingly, we have increased our stake in the Company to 1,750,000 shares, 8.6% of the outstanding common valued at approximately $29 million

As you know from our letter to you dated May 27, 2004, we have grave doubts about your managerial skill, fitness to run a public company and business judgment. All of these criticisms were substantiated by the investigation that we conducted and the numerous examples that were provided. For these reasons and the others identified here and in our prior correspondence, we will be pleased to withhold authority for a vote in favor of your re-election whenever the postponed annual meeting is held.

Unfortunately, your depiction of Third Point Management as a *"sleazy hedge fund"* in the June 12, 2004 Atlanta Journal-Constitution is totally baseless and possibly libelous. For someone who acquired iBill, a purported *"merchant processing business"* whose real activity is primarily to provide billing services to hard core pornographic websites, your credibility as moral arbiter is not strong. Perhaps from your vantage point in the porno industry, you find it unsavory that I support a children's cancer hospital (Tomorrow's Children's Fund), education for the disadvantaged youth (Prep for Prep), women's rights in third world countries (Equality Now) and numerous other charities. Maybe it is the fact that, since inception, my business has generated over $600 million in profits and provided numerous jobs, which you find offensive.

In any event, calling your second largest shareholder *"sleazy"* is further evidence of your poor judgment and exemplifies the type of behavior that should provide you with ample opportunity to join your son-in-law on the golf course in the not too distant future.

Sincerely,

Daniel S. Loeb

Source: Company filings

**EXHIBIT 13.6**

November 2010). See Exhibit 13.7 for an example of how this transaction may have been structured.

The equity collars provided the following potential benefits for Icahn: (1) The estimated cost for the equity collars could be zero, compared to the over $1.23 billion cost that Icahn would have paid to purchase 49 million Yahoo shares at the $25.15 opening share price on the date the collars were entered into; and (2) entering into a collar transaction was less visible than purchasing 49 million shares, enabling Icahn to secure his position without competing directly in the market for shares. The options can be settled physically, by delivery of shares, or if Icahn does not want to buy Yahoo shares if options are exercised, he can *cash settle* the options. Cash settlement means that, if an option is exercised, the economic equivalent of a physical settlement will be paid

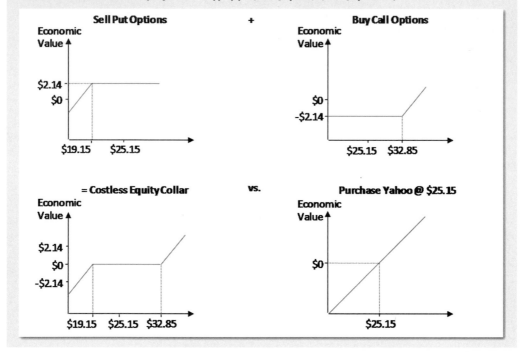

**Equity Collars on Yahoo Stock**

- Assume Yahoo share price of $25.15 when the equity collar is executed
- Put options on 49 million Yahoo shares at a strike price of $19.15 and an 18 month maturity can be sold for proceeds of:

    (i)   $2.14/option

- Call options on 49 million Yahoo shares at a strike price of $32.85 and an 18 month maturity can be purchased for a cost of:

    (ii)   $2.14/option

- Total cost for a "Cashless Equity Collar" = (i) - (ii) = $2.14/option - $2.14/option = $0

EXHIBIT 13.7

in cash: payment to Icahn if Yahoo's share price exceeds $32.85, or from Icahn if the share price falls below $19.15.

Icahn, along with two other directors who supported him, ultimately joined Yahoo's board in July 2008 in an arrangement that ended the proxy fight that he initiated. Although Icahn stated at that time that he "continue[d] to believe that the sale of the whole company or the sale of its Search business in the right transaction and must be given full consideration," he agreed not to interfere with the full board's decisions regarding whether or not to sell the company.[6] By the end of 2008, Microsoft had not renewed its offer for Yahoo, and the company's share price dropped below $13, suggesting a bad economic outcome for Icahn. During July 2009, the two companies announced a partnership in Internet search and advertising in an effort to better compete with Google, without a full acquisition by Microsoft. One week after this announcement, Yahoo's share price was $14.50.

---

[6]Yahoo! Inc. 21 July 2008. Yahoo! Announces Settlement with Carl Icahn [Press Release].

# Bill Ackman vs. McDonald's, Wendy's, Ceridian, Target, and MBIA

Bill Ackman launched Pershing Square Capital Management, which was considered to be an activist hedge fund, in 2004. This fund has purchased common shares (or call options to purchase common shares in the future) in many companies, including Wendy's, McDonald's, Ceridian, Barnes & Noble, Borders, Sears, Sears Canada, Dr. Pepper Snapple, General Growth Properties, Longs Drug, and Target. The fund has also purchased a number of financial company stocks, including Greenlight Capital, Visa, MasterCard, AIG, and Wachovia.

Pershing Square's experience with McDonald's and Wendy's is described in **Case Study 7, "McDonald's, Wendy's, and Hedge Funds: Hamburger Hedging?"** In the Ceridian investment, Ackman acquired 15% of the company's shares and tried to fill the company's board with his own independent nominees, while pushing for a spin-off of its strongest division. The company ultimately sold itself to a private equity firm and a private insurer for $36 a share, a price that was about double Pershing Square's purchase price.

Ackman set up Pershing Square IV during 2007 to invest solely in Target Corporation, the second largest U.S. discount retailer. The investment totaled $2 billion, creating economic exposure to more than 10% of the company through purchase of common shares and through swap and option positions. Target's stock price dropped by approximately 21% during the fund's 2007 holding period, and this resulted in an over 43% loss in the fund's value because of leverage. During 2008, because of further drops in Target's share price, combined with the fund's leveraged position, the value of Pershing Square IV dropped an additional 68%.

Ackman, based on his fund's large position, pushed Target to buy back shares, sell its credit card unit, and extract more value through its real estate holdings (Ackman wanted Target to spin-off the land on which the company's stores were built into a REIT (real estate investment trust), with the REIT to lease attached buildings to Target for 75 years). The company resisted any real estate initiatives, but ultimately agreed to purchase $10 billion in shares and sell almost 50% of its credit card portfolio for $3.6 billion.

During October 2008, Target responded to Ackman's REIT proposal by stating that his "analysis raises serious concerns on a number of important issues, including:

1. The validity of assumptions supporting Pershing Square's market valuation of Target and the separate REIT entity;
2. The reduction in Target's financial flexibility due to the conveyance of valuable assets to the REIT and the large expense obligation created by the proposed lease payments, which are subject to annual increase;
3. The adverse impact the company believes the proposed structure would have on Target's debt ratings, borrowing costs, and liquidity, exacerbated by current market conditions;
4. The frictional costs and operational risks, including tax implications, of executing Pershing Square's ideas;
5. The risk of diverting management's focus away from core business operations over an extended time period to execute such a complex transaction in the current environment."[7]

---

[7]Target Corporation. 29 Oct. 2008. Target Corporation Addresses Real Estate Structure Ideas from Pershing Square, LLP [Press Release].

In addition to investing in the stock of underperforming companies, Pershing Square created large short positions in a number of companies, including Fannie Mae, Freddie Mac, and MBIA. MBIA is the largest provider of financial guarantees to states and municipalities. In addition, MBIA has provided a significant amount of guarantees in support of subprime mortgages and related obligations. Ackman established a large short position in MBIA's stock after flagging the company's over $18.7 billion in subprime exposure through guarantees of mortgage-backed securities and CDOs (collateralized debt obligations), which represented more than 280% of the company's statutory capital. Embedded within this exposure were guarantees of $9 billion in support of CDO-squared obligations (a riskier form of CDOs). This short position was one of the principal drivers for Pershing Square's strong performance in several funds during 2007–2008, as MBIA's share price dropped from over $70 to under $4. During this period, Moody's reduced the company's credit rating from Aaa to Baa1. Ackman's short positions in the stocks of both Fannie Mae and Freddie Mac during 2008 also produced significant profits for Pershing Square funds, after these two stocks both dropped in value by over 90%. See Exhibit 13.8 for a summary of Bill Ackman's advice to activist and traditional investors.

### Bill Ackman's Advice for Activist and Traditional Investors

**Do your homework:** Ackman gets most of his ideas not from sophisticated tips but just by "brute force," from reading annual reports and looking for ways in which companies are undervalued by the stock market. Then he can pull just a few simple levers to boost the companies' stock valuations to where he believes it should be.

**Find a theme and export it:** Ackman invested in Sears and Sears Canada because the retailing companies financed their credit-card receivables on their own balance sheets, which wasn't well-understood by the markets. He used the same kind of thinking to tackle Target, which he believed was a strong company with a solid debt profile and also one of the only retailers to still finance its credit cards in-house. In the case of Sears, Ackman evaluated it based on its component parts, including Sears Hardware, Home Services, Sears Canada, Land's End and Sears Mexico (all of that is before considering the company's extensive real estate value).

**Don't get emotional:** Ackman describes himself as a totally rational being "at least when it comes to investing." He said it was the same with his continuing battle with MBIA and other bond insurers. Though to outside observers the MBIA clash seemed especially personal, he says it was a matter of seeing that MBIA had a triple-A rating and was levered 140 to 1, which didn't make sense.

**Dive into the deep end:** "We don't do anything unless we do it in a big way. We're not the kind of firm that buys 1%, puts our toe in the water and buys another few percent more," he said. Because he targets liquid, large-cap companies, there are risks: "The hard thing is to figure out how the market is going to react...I don't disagree with the fundamental view that this is a difficult business at a difficult time. I just disagree with what the underlying outcome is going to be.

**Be persistent:** Ackman once described himself as "a persistent cuss," and that perhaps is the trait of many short-sellers and activists. On MBIA, Ackman said, "it took five years for the rest of the world to come around to my point of view. There was some pain....You have to be convinced you're right and everyone else is wrong, which is not easy. But if you're not confident, you'll never pull the trigger." He is in a business where too much self-confidence can lead a person to ignore the facts. "There are a lot of good analysts who can run models and spreadsheets. But temperament is a big part of success," he noted.

**Get out of the office:** Ackman gets his best epiphanies when he's away from his desk. "This is not a business where you want to spend 24 hours a day in the office....The key is not working 80 hours a week."

Source: Moore, Heidi N. "Bill Ackman Part II: Eight Easy Steps to Becoming a Short-Seller." Wall Street Journal, 12 Jun. 2008.

**EXHIBIT 13.8**

**Notable Activist Investors**

| Fund | AUM ($bn) | Key Individual(s) | Selected Investments | Comments |
|---|---|---|---|---|
| Icahn Associates | 12.1 | Carl Icahn | • Time Warner  • Yahoo<br>• Motorola  • Biogen<br>• Kerr-McGee  • BEA Systems | • Most prolific activist<br>• Frequently seeks Board seats<br>• Not deterred by market capitalization of target<br>• Access to significantly more capital through Icahn's personal wealth |
| Harbinger Capital Partners | 19.0 | Philip Falcone | • New York Times<br>• Cleveland Cliffs | • Successfully added two directors to the New York Times Board<br>• Opposed Cleveland Cliffs' proposed acquisition of Alpha Natural Resources |
| Children's Investment Fund (TCI) | 8.7 | Chris Hohn | • CSX<br>• Euronext / Deutsche Borse<br>• ABN AMRO | • Corporate governance focus<br>• Historically European-focused, but recently active in U.S.<br>• Violations of securities laws in CSX situation did not prevent success story in proxy fight<br>• Opposed Deutsche Borse's bid for the London Stock Exchange |
| JANA Partners | 4.5 | Barry Rosenstein | • Time Warner  • CNET<br>• Kerr-McGee | • Regularly partners with Icahn<br>• Managed by former protégé of Asher Edelman |
| Pershing Square Capital Management | 5.6 | William Ackman | • Borders  • Ceridian<br>• McDonald's  • Target<br>• Wendy's | • Recent focus on retail/real estate plays |
| Atticus Capital Management | 8.4 | Timothy Barakett | • Phelps Dodge<br>• Euronext/ Deutsche Borse | • Unlikely to lead proxy contest, but very vocal and well-regarded given recent high-profile successes<br>• Frequently makes entire sector bets and seeks to catalyze strategic activity |
| Trian Fund Management | 2.8 | Nelson Peltz<br>Peter May | • Heinz  • Chemtura<br>• Wendy's  • Cadbury's | • High profile given Peltz's background<br>• Experience of principals suggests likely focus on consumer/retail sector |
| Relational Investors | 5.6 | David Batchelder<br>Ralph Whitworth | • Sprint  • SPX<br>• Home Depot  • Sovereign Bancorp | • Corporate governance focus, very targeted<br>• Exceptionally high incidence of CEO change at targets |
| Steel Partners | 4.8 | Warren Lichtenstein | • United Industrials  • Brinks<br>• KT&G Corp | • Has partnered with Icahn<br>• Recent focus has been more international, particularly Asia |

Source: Morgan Stanley

**EXHIBIT 13.9**

## Summary

There is disagreement on whether hedge fund shareholder activism makes companies stronger or merely generates short-term gains that principally benefit the activist at the expense of long-term shareholders. During 2008, there were more than 75 U.S. hedge funds dedicated to event-driven, activist-style investing, and these funds managed more than $50 billion in assets. See Exhibit 13.9 for a list of notable activist hedge funds. Some significant institutional investors have lined up with these hedge funds to push boards to be more responsive to shareholders. In a number of cases, it appears that improvements have been made in companies that, in the absence of shareholder activism, may not have occurred. In other cases, large share repurchases pushed by activists and executed by companies created large opportunity costs when the repurchases occurred before subsequent steep share price drops. In addition, a number of acquisitions pushed by activist shareholders have seen significant share price drops since closing.

## Questions

1. Before the elimination of the broker vote, which type of company would have made an easier target for an activist investor and why: a company with mostly large institutional shareholders, or one with many small retail shareholders?
2. In the environment immediately following the credit crisis of 2007–2008, what are factors that encouraged and hampered the activities of activists?
3. What's the benefit of staggering the election of board of directors?

4. Cumulative voting is the practice of allowing shareholders to cast all of their votes for a single nominee for the board of directors when the company has multiple openings on its board. Does this practice help or hinder activists?

5. Describe what is meant by a "13D letter."

6. If Company A owns Company B's stock (which is currently trading at $30), and A purchases a 2-year put on B's stock with a strike price of $25 and sells a 2-year call on B stock with a strike price of $34, what is this equity derivative structure called? What are its benefits and disadvantages?

7. What timing mismatch issue exists for activist hedge fund investment strategy?

8. Activist funds need to devote more time and resources to investments compared to most other fund strategies. What added risk does this produce for activist funds?

9. Describe a total return swap (sometimes called an *equity swap*) and the benefits of this strategy for a hedge fund.

10. In the legal battle between CSX, TCI, and 3G, the SEC and the Federal Court judge that presided over the lawsuit held differing views of the case. Which had a more rules-based approach, and which had a more principles-based approach?

# 14
# Risk, Regulation, and Organizational Structure

The material in this chapter should be cross-referenced with **Case Study 5, "A Tale of Two Hedge Funds: Magnetar and Peloton."**

## Investor Risks

Hedge fund investors are exposed to portfolio level risks at each hedge fund they invest in, as summarized in Exhibit 14.1. In addition, they are exposed to hedge fund investment level risks, which include business risks, people risks, investment strategy risks, and systemic risks.

Another way of looking at hedge fund investor risk is to focus on five incremental risks that are more pronounced in hedge funds than in many other investment funds. These incremental risks relate to leverage, regulation, short selling, transparency, and risk tolerance.

---

**Risks in Hedge Fund Investing**

| Portfolio Level Issues | | |
|---|---|---|
| Liquidity<br>Transparency<br>Benchmarking | Survivorship Bias<br>Complexity<br>Leverage | UBTI[1]<br>Headline Risk<br>Terms and Conditions |

| Investment Level Issues | | | |
|---|---|---|---|
| **Business** | **People** | **Investment Process/Strategy** | **Systemic** |
| Operational Controls | Key-Person | Strategy Failure | Regulatory Change |
| Client Composition | Integrity/Behavior | Style Drift | Failure of Prime Broker |
| Changes in Capital Base | Focus, Drive, Motivation | Leverage | Correlation Spike in Stressed Markets |
| Counterparty Risk | Depth & Breadth of Team | Liquidity | Failure of Major Financial Institution |
| Conflicts of Interest | | Concentration | |
| Compensation Structure | | Unstable Correlations | |

Note 1: UBTI, Unrelated Business Taxable Income, is income regularly generated by tax-exempt entities by means of taxable activities. In the case of hedge funds, it includes debt-financed income, on which tax-exempt investors would then need to pay taxes. This issue can be circumvented through the use of offshore hedge funds.
Source: Grosvenor Capital Management

**EXHIBIT 14.1**

---

## Leverage

Most, but not all, hedge funds use leverage to increase their returns. In addition, many hedge funds utilize a significant amount of off-balance sheet leverage through derivatives. Exhibit 14.2 shows leverage on balance sheets of hedge funds. Leverage works well when returns are positive, but it backfires when returns are negative. The average leverage applied depends on the investment strategy and the hedge fund. Assuming that a hedge fund borrows $70 after receiving $30 from investors and a $100 investment is made with the total proceeds, if the investment declines by 10%, investors suffer a loss of 33%. By the same token, if the investment increases by 10%, investors gain 33%. Some investors are uncomfortable with the variability in potential returns represented by a leveraged hedge fund investment strategy. Leverage is also cited as a significant factor in increasing the risk of a systemic disturbance, since hedge fund leverage creates more vulnerability to liquidity shocks (see discussion of systemic risk below). Over a 5-year period from 2004 to 2008, the average leverage employed by hedge funds ranged from 40% for many equity long/short strategies to over 400% for some fixed income arbitrage strategies.

It should be noted that a large proportion of hedge fund leverage is collateralized by assets, so although notional leverage amounts can be very large, marginal leverage (uncollateralized by assets) is much smaller.

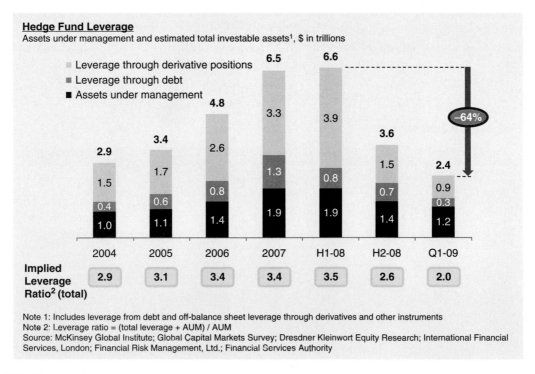

**Hedge Fund Leverage**
Assets under management and estimated total investable assets[1], $ in trillions

- Leverage through derivative positions
- Leverage through debt
- Assets under management

| | 2004 | 2005 | 2006 | 2007 | H1-08 | H2-08 | Q1-09 |
|---|---|---|---|---|---|---|---|
| Implied Leverage Ratio[2] (total) | 2.9 | 3.1 | 3.4 | 3.4 | 3.5 | 2.6 | 2.0 |

Note 1: Includes leverage from debt and off-balance sheet leverage through derivatives and other instruments
Note 2: Leverage ratio = (total leverage + AUM) / AUM
Source: McKinsey Global Institute; Global Capital Markets Survey; Dresdner Kleinwort Equity Research; International Financial Services, London; Financial Risk Management, Ltd.; Financial Services Authority

**EXHIBIT 14.2**

## Regulation

U.S. hedge funds are able to rely on the *private adviser exemption* to reporting under the Investment Advisers Act of 1940 (1940 Act), as long as a hedge fund adviser has fewer than 15 clients and neither holds himself out generally to the public as an investment adviser nor acts as an investment adviser to a registered investment company. Since nearly all hedge fund advisers manage fewer than 15 separate hedge funds, they are not currently compelled to register under the 1940 Act. As a result, U.S. hedge funds are not subject to as much direct oversight from financial regulators compared to mutual funds and most other investment managers who are not exempt from the 1940 Act. Similarly, non-U.S.-based hedge funds generally have less regulation compared to most other investment funds in their respective countries. However, banks (the principal counterparties to hedge funds in trading and lending transactions) are highly regulated, therefore "indirect" regulation (including the U.S. Fed's Reg T limitations on margin) applies to hedge funds.

## Short Selling

Many hedge funds sell securities short as a way to express a bearish view. This short-selling action creates a theoretically limitless exposure if the shorted security increases in value. A long position in a security has a loss potential that is limited by the value of the security, but there is no such limit in a short position. However, short-sale positions that are hedges against a long holding are considered risk mitigators rather than risk augmenters.

## Transparency

Hedge funds frequently engage in investment and hedging activities that attempt to arbitrage pricing inefficiencies in the market. To the extent that many funds identify the same opportunities, the profitability of an arbitrage strategy can be impaired. As a result, some hedge funds are very secretive about their investment strategies in order to protect the alpha sources they have identified and, as a result, provide limited information to investors. Investors therefore have limited ability to monitor hedge fund activities that could potentially impair investment values. In addition, even if investors had more transparency, gates and other liquidity limitations minimize investor alternatives.

## Risk Tolerance

Many hedge funds managers are inherently more comfortable taking risks compared to non-hedge-fund managers. They are willing to consider a much broader array of investment alternatives and new, innovative securities. In addition, hedge funds frequently use derivatives, which sometimes carry risks that are problematic to analyze and value. However, derivatives can also mitigate risk, if used properly.

# Systemic Risk

Systemic risk is typically defined as a financial shock that brings with it the reality—or the clear and present danger—of inflicting significant damage on the entire financial system and the economy. In other words, systemic risk relates to the possibility that many financial institutions fail simultaneously in response to a single major event. Hedge funds can create systemic risk in two ways: (1) the failure of several large hedge funds at the same time could create contagion across many classes of financial and real assets as the failing funds are required to unwind all of their investment positions at firesale prices, and (2) hedge funds can potentially create large losses for the banks that lend to them if collateral is inadequate or valuation methodologies are inaccurate. Large losses incurred by banks from their exposure to hedge funds could have a cascading effect on other financial institutions.

The activities of hedge funds were heavily scrutinized following the failure of Long-Term Capital Management (LTCM), which was bailed out during 1998 by 14 major investment banks, operating under the coordination of the U.S. Federal Reserve. These banks and the Fed took the view that excessive leverage employed by LTCM, in combination with a misguided liquidity expectation, caused the fund's collapse and that many other financial institutions would have been dragged into bankruptcy if the bailout had not occurred.

The main themes that emerged from analyzing the LTCM debacle and subsequent hedge fund failures are the importance of liquidity and leverage, and the correlations among instruments and portfolios that are under extreme stress (which in a normal market environment are considered uncorrelated).

The failure of Amaranth Advisors in 2006, combined with increasing bank exposure to hedge funds, refocused attention on whether hedge funds posed substantial risks to the general market. Some regulators and central banks, including the Bank of England, concluded that, although hedge funds can create systemic risk, there are even bigger systemic risks posed by other financial market participants. The Bank's Deputy Governor for Financial Stability stated in 2006 that traditionally central banks and regulators believed that the greatest risk to financial stability was posed by the key intermediaries at the center of the financial system. In his view, hedge funds were not even among the top 12 main sources of vulnerability in the system. He also stated that, in fact, hedge funds allowed for the transfer of risk from parties who do not want it to parties who do, potentially reducing systemic risk as a result.[1]

There are many who disagree with this position. For example, in a study that was referred to in the Federal Reserve Bank of Atlanta's Economic Review, the study's authors concluded, among other things, that massive fund inflows have had a material impact on hedge fund returns and a corresponding increase in risks, and that risks facing hedge funds are nonlinear and more complex than those facing traditional asset classes. The study determined that because of the dynamic nature of hedge fund investment strategies and the impact of fund flows on leverage and performance, hedge fund risk models require more sophisticated analytics and are susceptible to greater error.[2] This study and similar studies conclude that hedge funds create systemic risk that alters the risk/reward landscape of financial investments. These studies support the view that, although hedge funds have historically outperformed many other forms of investment management, they have also created corresponding risks that differ in important ways from more traditional investments. Such differences may have implications in the consideration of systemic risk.

Actions initiated by bank counterparties to hedge funds can also create systemic risk. As a result of substantial losses suffered during the 2007–2008 credit crisis, banks were forced to shore up their capital base and drastically reduce the amount of credit provided to their borrowing clients, including hedge funds. Many hedge funds were put at risk when banks went bankrupt or reduced funding available to the funds through margin calls (in an effort to strengthen their own balance sheets).

In a scenario where several large and highly leveraged hedge funds experience a significant dislocation in the market and are forced by their lenders to quickly unwind positions, there could be a significant drop in prices for the securities being sold. This could, in turn, cause contagion across other, normally uncorrelated asset classes, which ultimately might create significant losses

---

[1]Sir John Gieve, Deputy Governor, Bank of England: 17 October 2006 speech on Hedge Funds and Financial Stability given at the HEDGE 2006 Conference.

[2]Chan, Nicholas; Getmansky, Mila; Haas, Shane M.; and Lo, Andrew W. "Do Hedge Funds Increase Systemic Risk?" Federal Reserve of Atlanta Economic Review, 4th Quarter (2006).

for other investors and spark a flight to safety, as investors panic and sell many securities at a loss to mitigate investment risk. This scenario was played out to a certain extent during the 2-year period starting mid-2007. For example, during August 2007, several large quantitative arbitrage hedge funds experienced significant losses when the credit market became troubled, and stress from this market bled into the equity market. The leverage employed by a number of these funds, combined with the rapid, massive, computer-driven selling of similar securities by the quantitative hedge funds, caused billions of dollars of losses for these funds. This, in turn, prompted fund of hedge funds to redeem their investments in hedge funds, which caused more liquidations of hedge fund positions to raise cash to meet these redemptions, which further exacerbated equity and fixed income market declines. Throughout 2007 and 2008, hedge funds sold assets based on margin calls from counterparties and increased investor redemptions. The result was to put further downside pressure on securities that were already suffering pricing erosion from the effects of the subprime mortgage asset debacle. See Exhibit 14.3 for an example of how leverage can accelerate forced selling. In this example, if a stock price drops by 5%, a hedge fund will need to sell $20 worth of stock in order to maintain a required leverage ratio. However, a lender might also ask for a lower leverage ratio, causing sale of an additional $15 worth of stock. This selling activity is likely to put additional downside pressure on the stock. See **Case Study 5, "A Tale of Two Hedge Funds: Magnetar and Peloton."**

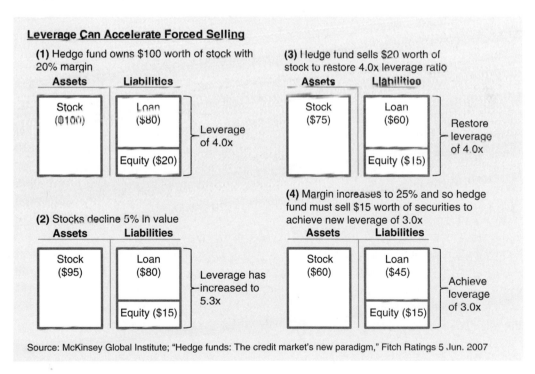

Source: McKinsey Global Institute; "Hedge funds: The credit market's new paradigm," Fitch Ratings 5 Jun. 2007

**EXHIBIT 14.3**

## Bank Exposure to Hedge Funds

A number of large banks carry significant exposure to hedge funds. This exposure includes revenue exposure, since hedge funds are the single most important commission-based clients of the trading division of these banks. It is estimated that total revenue associated with the provision by banks of trading and prime brokerage services to hedge funds was over $33 billion during 2008.

These services include trading securities, clearing and custody, securities lending, financing (including margin loans, repos, and sometimes, permanent capital), and customized technology and reporting tools. The large fees gained from providing these services leaves certain large banks vulnerable to significant reductions in revenue if a number of their largest hedge fund clients fail.

In addition, some banks have a very large exposure to credit risk in relation to their cash loans to hedge funds. Although these loans are collateralized, margin adjustments sometimes do not keep up with the changing value of the underlying collateral. During the massive financial market dislocation that spanned a 2-year period starting in the summer of 2007, banks were forced to significantly tighten their margin protocols and reduce overall credit exposure to hedge funds. As a result of bank credit limitations, hedge funds were required to reduce the leverage employed in their investment strategies. In spite of their large credit exposure to hedge funds, historically, banks have suffered minimal losses because of the assets that backed their loans to the funds.

Finally, a number of large banks are the principal counterparties to hedge funds in derivative contracts. For example, hedge funds have entered into a massive amount of credit default swaps (CDS) with banks. A CDS is a privately negotiated agreement that explicitly shifts credit risk from one party to the other. According to the International Swaps and Derivatives Association (ISDA), the outstanding notional value of credit derivative contracts rose from an estimated $700 billion at year-end 2001 to an estimated $54.6 trillion at mid-year 2008. Banks are also counterparties to hedge funds in equity swaps and other derivative contracts.

## Mitigating Systemic Risk

The key to mitigating systemic risk associated with hedge funds is for (1) banks to employ more conservative lending strategies; (2) hedge funds to become less leveraged and more diversified in their investment activity; and (3) regulators to apply good judgment in efforts to increase regulation of hedge funds. Severe regulatory action directed at hedge funds to mitigate systemic risk is not necessarily the best answer. In fact, if regulation of hedge funds becomes too burdensome, some of the liquidity that hedge funds provide may evaporate. This, in turn, could eliminate important sources of capital when credit markets freeze up. For example, when investors are forced to sell distressed securities to meet liquidity requirements, the buyers of these securities are frequently hedge funds. Without a bid from hedge funds for distressed assets there might not be any buyers, which could further push down the price of the distressed assets. In effect, hedge funds have become "lenders (or investors) of last resort," helping to put a floor on declining asset values. Efforts should be made to appropriately mitigate systemic risk through reasonable regulation of hedge funds, but regulators must be careful to avoid a sharp curtailment in the liquidity that hedge funds provide, since this could exacerbate systemic risk.

# Regulation

In the United States, a public investment company such as a mutual fund is required to register with the SEC under the Investment Company Act of 1940 (1940 Act). After registration, they are required to report information on a regular basis and are subject to many limitations, including limitations on leverage, short selling, and performance fees. Hedge funds, by contrast, are not deemed to be public investment companies, since they operate pursuant to exemptions from registration requirements, and so do not have the same limitations imposed on them.

The exemptions utilized by hedge funds are included in Sections 3(c)1 and 3(c)7 of the 1940 Act, which are available for funds that have 100 or fewer investors and funds where the investors are *qualified purchasers*, respectively. A qualified purchaser is an individual who has investment assets that exceed $5 million. A 3(c)1 fund cannot have more than 100 investors, but a 3(c)7 fund can have unlimited number of investors, although more than 499 investors would subject the fund to registration under the Securities Exchange Act of 1934.

In addition, managers of hedge funds maintain exemption from registration as investment advisers under the Investment Advisers Act of 1940 (Advisers Act) by advising fewer than 15 funds. For this purpose, an individual hedge fund counts as a single fund, regardless of the number of underlying investors in the fund. Finally, in order to avoid *plan assets* issues under ERISA (Employee Retirement Income Security Act), most funds limit benefit plan participation to less than 25% of total fund assets.

In order to obtain exemptions from registration, hedge funds are sold through private placement offerings, which means that funds cannot be offered or advertised to the general public and are normally offered under Regulation D. This process basically limits hedge fund offerings to accredited investors. An accredited investor is an individual with a minimum net worth of $1.5 million or, alternatively, a minimum income of $200,000 in each of the previous 2 years and a reasonable expectation of reaching the same income level in the current year.

There have been a number of attempts to change the regulatory landscape for hedge funds. In December 2004, the SEC issued a rule change that required most hedge fund advisers to register with the SEC under the Advisers Act by February 1, 2006. This requirement applied to firms that managed in excess of $25 million and that had over 15 investors. However, the rule was challenged in the U.S. Court of Appeals for the District of Columbia, and in June 2006 the court overturned the SEC rule. The SEC has subsequently examined how to address this ruling but has not mounted a successful challenge. During February 2007, the President's Working Group on Financial Markets rejected further regulation of hedge funds and recommended that the industry should instead adopt voluntary guidelines. However, after significant hedge fund and fund of fund losses that occurred during 2007 and 2008 (including the billions of dollars in losses associated with former NASDAQ Chairman Bernard Madoff's investments business), active regulatory and congressional discussion about imposing new regulations on the hedge fund industry was renewed in 2009. See Exhibit 14.4 for a summary of U.S. laws and regulations that impact hedge funds.

Although regulation has historically been minimal in the United States and the United Kingdom, politicians in continental Europe have actively advocated greater regulation. For example, in May 2007, Germany tried to push other countries at a G8 meeting to agree to a code of conduct for the industry. Although all eight countries could not agree on standards, the Germans continued to advocate a standardized global framework for regulating hedge funds. Some hedge fund managers have agreed with the need for more regulation, suggesting a concern that low- or non-standardized regulation may discourage additional investment into hedge funds.

## Alternative Regulatory Approaches

Regulators worry about three main issues:

1. The possibility of hedge funds defrauding investors: To combat this potential problem regulators have tried to limit the kind of investors allowed to invest in hedge funds to sophisticated investors who can perform their own assessment (or pay someone else to do this for them).

**Summary of Hedge Fund Laws and Regulations**

- Securities Act of 1933
  - o Interest in a fund are "securities"
  - o Regulation D "safe harbor"
    - Rule 506
      - No limit on amount of sales
      - Generally only sold to "accredited investors" ($1 million net worth or $200K in income in last two years)
      - Can have up to 35 non-"accredited investors"
    - No general advertising
    - File Form D with SEC within 15 days of sale
- Securities Exchange Act of 1934
  - o Funds with 500 investors and $10 million in equity must register
- Investment Company Act of 1940
  - o Hedge funds exempted under Section 3(c)(1) and 3(c)(7)
    - Section 3(c)(1) funds:
      - No more than 100 investors
      - Accredited investor
      - Qualified client (natural person with net worth of >$1.5 million)
    - Section 3(c)(7) funds:
      - <500 investors (if >500, would have to be registered)
      - Qualified purchaser (natural person with liquid net worth of $5 million)
- Investment Advisors Act of 1940
  - o Requires investment advisors to register with the SEC
    - <$25 million AUM: state registration only
    - $25 – $30 million AUM: SEC or state registration
    - >$30 million: SEC registration
  - o Exemption under Section 203(b)(3) for advisors who have less than 15 clients over a 12 month period
- Potential new legislation proposed in 2009:
  - o Hedge Fund Transparency Act of 2009 (applies to funds with AUM of $50 million or more)
    - Would broaden definition of "Investment Company" and strike the Section 3(c)(1) and 3(c)(7) exemptions
    - Required anti–money laundering program
    - Currently unregistered investment advisors may need to register as well, even if they have less than 15 clients, if Section 3(c)(1) and 3(c)(7) exemptions no longer apply to their funds
  - o Hedge Fund Advisor Registration Act of 2009—this would amend the '40 Act and remove the <15 clients exemption rule

Source: Mallon P.C.; Morrison & Foerster LLP

**EXHIBIT 14.4**

2. Trading by hedge funds using insider information: To address this problem regulators generally apply the same rules that they apply to other investment firms in relation to market abuse.
3. Hedge fund destabilization of the financial system and, by extension, the economy: To address this problem regulators have principally focused on timely and accurate collateral valuations and on the overall level of borrowing by hedge funds (and limiting such borrowing by applying more stringent lending standards on banks, which they directly regulate).

However, in spite of common concerns, each country takes a somewhat different regulatory approach. For example, in Portugal, the use of derivatives is carefully controlled, whereas in France there is less focus on derivatives, but more focus on leverage. French regulators have also been very concerned about potential collusion by hedge funds in attempts to push companies to agree to takeover bids. In Russia, regulators are substantially more restrictive than in other G8 countries.

U.K. regulators have been fairly consistent with the regulators in the United States, but they have taken a particularly strict view on side letters in an effort to avoid favoring some investors over others.

For many, the best answer is self-regulation. An organization called Alternative Investment Management Association (AIMA) has published a Guide to Sound Practices for Hedge Fund Valuation, which suggests, among other things, the appointment of an independent valuation service provider, the use of multiple pricing sources, and the disclosure of any material involvement by a hedge fund manager in the determination of a fund's net asset value (NAV).

As an increasing number of hedge funds become public companies, allowing any investor to invest in their stock (e.g., Och-Ziff Capital Management in the U.S. and Man Group in the U.K.), a laissez-faire attitude of regulators to hedge funds may come under pressure. As less sophisticated investors gain exposure to hedge funds by investing in public hedge fund stock, some regulators may feel compelled to step up the pressure for more stringent regulation. The counter to this concern is that, by filing the required registration statement with regulators before launching IPOs, hedge funds are already subjecting themselves to additional regulation as a publicly reporting company.

# Organizational Structure

A hedge fund's organizational structure is generally developed with a principal focus on how to minimize taxes and regulatory constraints. See Exhibit 14.5 for an overview of a typical hedge fund investment partnership.

## Domicile

Many hedge funds are registered offshore. The principal offshore locations include the Cayman Islands (55%), British Virgin Islands (15%), and Bermuda (10%). Onshore hedge fund registrations are principally in the Unites States (65%, mostly in Delaware) and in Europe (31%). The domicile chosen depends on the tax and regulatory environment of the fund's investors. By creating an offshore domicile, the fund can avoid paying taxes on the increase in the value of its portfolio. However, investors in the fund will still pay individual taxes on any profit realized in their investment with the fund. In addition, the hedge fund manager will pay taxes on management fees.

## Legal Entity

Hedge funds usually organize as a limited partnership for U.S.-based taxable investors. The general partner of the limited partnership is usually the hedge fund investment manager, and investors are limited partners. Offshore investors that are non-U.S. entities and U.S. entities that do not pay taxes (such as pension funds) invest through a separate offshore vehicle. Both onshore and offshore funds usually invest in a master feeder fund, which then co-invests in a master fund. The assets of the master fund are managed by the hedge fund investment manager. This structure creates optimal tax and regulatory advantages for both onshore and offshore investors, while enabling the investment manager to manage all invested funds together. The hedge fund investment manager does not retain an interest in the master fund. If organized properly, this structure enables taxable investors to avoid paying taxes twice, and also enables tax-exempt investors to participate in the same investment management pool as taxable investors.

To create an optimal legal structure, a hedge fund will employ the services of accountants, lawyers, auditors, an administrator (who completes reports and arranges issuance and

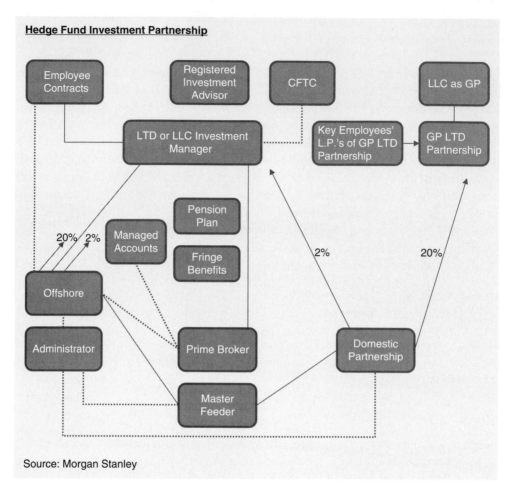

**Hedge Fund Investment Partnership**

Source: Morgan Stanley

**EXHIBIT 14.5**

redemption of interests), an independent valuation party (who determines the net asset value, or NAV, of the fund), and a prime broker (who lends money and shares, acts as derivatives counter-party, and provides trade execution, clearing, and settlement services).

## Open-Ended Partnership

Hedge funds typically operate as open-ended partnerships. An open-ended fund is able to periodically issue additional partnership interests or shares directly to new investors at a price that is equal to NAV/share or interest. Investors are able to redeem their interests or shares at the prevailing NAV/share or interest on the date of redemption. Shares or interests in open-ended funds are typically not traded. Profits associated with these shares or interests are usually not distributed to investors before redemption. By contrast, a closed-end fund distributes profits to shareholders and allows shares to be traded.

## Taxes

This section focuses only on U.S. tax matters, and is subject to change as the laws change. Other countries have different tax laws that may provide different tax outcomes. Hedge funds based in the United States are organized as investment partnerships. For these funds, the general partners are both investors in and managers of the fund. By contrast, offshore funds, which can be formed in various locations, including the Cayman Islands and Bermuda, are organized as limited duration companies, or in the form of non-pass-through vehicles. The offshore funds are advised by an investment advisor under contract (who has ownership in the funds).

U.S. domestic partnerships pay annual management fees to the management company, which is usually formed as a limited partnership or an LLC, and performance fees, which are allocated to the general partner. For offshore funds, the fund pays management and incentive fees to the management company (which is taxed as ordinary income). For U.S.-based managers, the management fee is taxed as ordinary income. The tax characterization for performance allocation is more complex. If the fund's profits are from the sale of capital assets held for more than one year (it is estimated that less than one-third of investments are held for more than one year), the profits will "flow through" to the limited partner investors and the general partner as long term capital gains. This enables U.S.-based limited partners to pay the lower capital gains tax rate of 15%, as opposed to the maximum tax rate on ordinary income of 35% (or whatever the applicable tax rate is). The performance allocation paid to the general partner is either deemed an unrealized gain or taxed in the same tax category as a partnership, including dividend interest and long-term gains. Since the partnership is not a business, it does not pay payroll taxes (or the 2.9% in Medicare taxes on performance fees that qualify as long term capital gains). As a result, under certain circumstances, U.S.-based hedge fund managers may, in effect, pay total taxes on their performance income that equals 15% for assets held for more than one year, compared to taxes of up to 37.9% that, with a less permissive tax regime, would be payable. According to a study put together by the committee on taxation at the U.S. House of Representatives, these performance fee–related tax savings projected across a 10-year period could exceed $30 billion (this amount includes private equity funds, whose performance fees are subject to the same benefit).[3]

The Alternative Minimum Tax Relief Act of 2008 contained a provision that would have taxed performance fees at ordinary income rates. That Act passed the House of Representatives in June 2008 but failed to pass in the Senate. As a result, hedge fund managers continue to save up to 22.9% in taxes for all assets they manage that can be characterized as capital assets held for over one year. Some or all of this tax advantage is expected to be eliminated at some point by Congress. However, it is useful to point out that any changes in U.S. tax policy may affect only a small portion of profits, since most hedge funds generate the majority of their income from short-term investments.

In addition to potentially benefiting from the low tax rate on performance fees, U.S.-based hedge fund managers have historically enjoyed tax benefits in relation to management fees. In 2008, however, the U.S. government eliminated a tax benefit that allowed for the deferral of income taxes on deferred compensation, which impacted all taxpayers, including hedge fund managers. Prior to the enactment of this code (Internal Revenue Code Section 457), hedge fund managers had been able to defer management fees for income tax purposes, whereby no current income was recognized on deferred fees or interest and investment return attributable to deferred fees. Managers recognized income only when, at the manager's election, cash was received based on the deferred amount plus investment return on this amount. Through this arrangement, managers had been able to limit income received each year to only the amount needed to spend or invest outside the hedge fund. The remainder was saved on a tax-deferred basis. As a result of the new tax code, 2008 was the last year that fund managers benefited from the deferral.

---

[3]Committee on Taxation. "Estimated Revenue Effects of H.R. 6275, The 'Alternative Minimum Tax Relief Act Of 2008,' Scheduled for Markup by the Committee on Ways and Means on June 18, 2008" (JCX-51-08) (2008).

268 HEDGE FUNDS AND PRIVATE EQUITY

## Questions

1. Which two core hedge fund activities can either create incremental risk or act as a risk mitigator?
2. Explain the importance of hedge funds to investment banks, including revenue, types of business, and which division is most relevant. In addition, with which investment banking areas do hedge funds principally compete?
3. Suppose a hedge fund manager buys $15 million of ABC shares on 20% margin. The maximum allowable leverage ratio is 4.0×. The next day, unexpected negative news about ABC is released and its stock closes down 7%. One day later, the hedge fund's prime broker notifies the manager that leverage ratios now need to come down to 3.0×. What percentage of the original balance of ABC shares is left in the investment fund at the end of the day after selling shares to comply with the new leverage requirement? Assume the fund's sales of ABC stock does not further depress its share price.
4. What are two of the key checks and balances in place to help manage the incremental risks associated with the hedge fund industry?
5. What are some of the major market events in the last three decades that have raised the issue of systemic risk?
6. Based on the current regulatory environment, even if a U.S. hedge fund is exempt from registration under the 1940 Act, what type of regulations does it need to adhere to?
7. Under current U.S. laws, when does a fund (and its advisors) need to register with the SEC?

# 15
# Hedge Fund Issues and Performance

## Hedge Fund Performance

2008 was a watershed year in the hedge fund industry. Assets under management (AUM) by hedge funds dropped by unprecedented levels, and the concept of managing for absolute returns (positive returns) was, in part, invalidated by significant losses (see Exhibit 15.1). As a result of these losses, investor withdrawals increased substantially. This withdrawal activity, combined with reductions in asset values, resulted in a drop in AUM by approximately 25%, from almost $1.9 trillion at the end of 2007 to just over $1.4 trillion by the end of 2008. Part of the problem during 2008 was that too many funds bought the same assets. As markets fell, many hedge funds sold these assets to gain liquidity, pushing prices even lower. Compounding this problem was the need for some investors to raise cash when the equity market decline caused minimum equity allocation benchmarks to be breached, triggering a need to take money out of hedge funds and reinvest directly in equity instruments.

Hedge funds that invested in Russia and China, which provided big gains during previous years, were among the worst performers in 2008, with losses of 70% to 90% during the year. Contrasting with these losses were a few hedge funds such as Paulson Advantage Plus, which was up more than 35% during 2008, based on bearish positions in toxic mortgage-related securities.

The Fund Weighted Composite Index tracked by Hedge Fund Research (HFR) fell by 19.0% during the year compared to the drop in Standard & Poor's 500 stock index of 38.5%, including

| A Difficult Year for the Industry | |
| --- | --- |
| **HFRI Index** | **2008 Returns** |
| **HFRI Fund Weighted Composite Index** | **-19.0%** |
| HFRI Convertible Arbitrage Index | -33.7% |
| HFRI Distressed/Restructuring Index | -25.2% |
| HFRI Equity Hedge Index | -26.6% |
| HFRI Equity Market Neutral Index | -6.0% |
| HFRI Event Driven Index | -22.1% |
| HFRI Macro Index | 4.8% |
| HFRI Merger Arbitrage Index | -5.0% |
| HFRI Relative Value Arbitrage Index | -18.0% |

Source: Hedge Fund Research, Inc.

**EXHIBIT 15.1**

dividends. Therefore, even though hedge fund losses were significant, they were substantially less than the broader equity market. 2008 marked only the second calendar year of negative returns for hedge funds since 1990. As seen in Exhibit 15.2, approximately two-thirds of the decline in assets during 2008 was a result of poor hedge fund performance. The remaining one-third came from clients withdrawing their assets. Fund of hedge funds, operating under the premise of greater asset diversification, underperformed hedge funds, losing 21.3% for the year. Emerging market funds and many other funds also performed poorly. With very few exceptions, hedge funds returned negative results for the year, regardless of investment strategy (see Exhibit 15.3). Despite the overall poor performance, however, it is important to reemphasize that hedge funds, both in aggregate and across the major investment strategies, still outperformed the broader market.

In 2009, hedge funds regained some of their historical momentum and ended in positive return territory for the first half of the year. The Fund Weighted Composite Index was up 9.5% at the end of June. This compares to a 1.8% gain over the same period for the S&P 500. Several of the worst performing strategies in 2008 experienced the strongest growth during the first half of 2009. Emerging markets, down by 37% in 2008, were up 20% at the end of June 2009. Similarly, convertible arbitrage, down over 33% in 2008, was up 29% during the first half of 2009. See Exhibits 15.3 and 15.4 for a comparison of fund returns during the two periods. Despite the strong gains, however, it is important to point out that the industry as a whole is still below its high-water mark set in October 2007. According to Hedge Fund Research as of June 30, 2009, its Fund Weighted Composite Index needed to gain another 14.7% before regaining the prior peak.

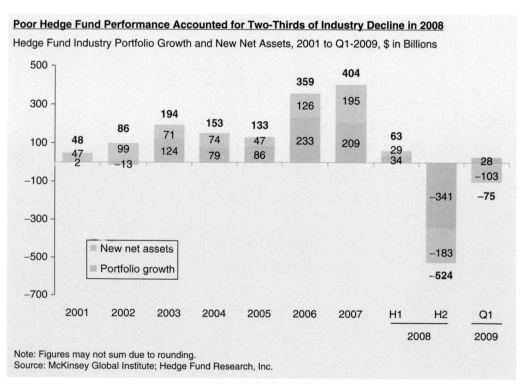

**Poor Hedge Fund Performance Accounted for Two-Thirds of Industry Decline in 2008**

Hedge Fund Industry Portfolio Growth and New Net Assets, 2001 to Q1-2009, $ in Billions

Note: Figures may not sum due to rounding.
Source: McKinsey Global Institute; Hedge Fund Research, Inc.

EXHIBIT 15.2

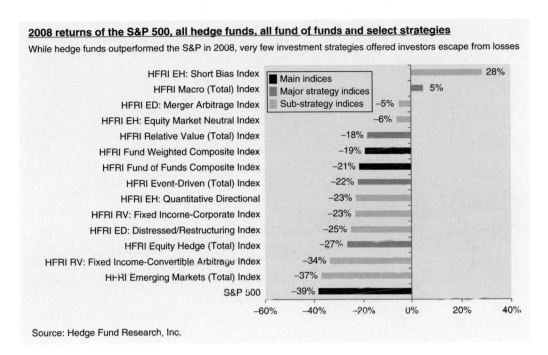

**2008 returns of the S&P 500, all hedge funds, all fund of funds and select strategies**

While hedge funds outperformed the S&P in 2008, very few investment strategies offered investors escape from losses

Source: Hedge Fund Research, Inc.

**EXHIBIT 15.3**

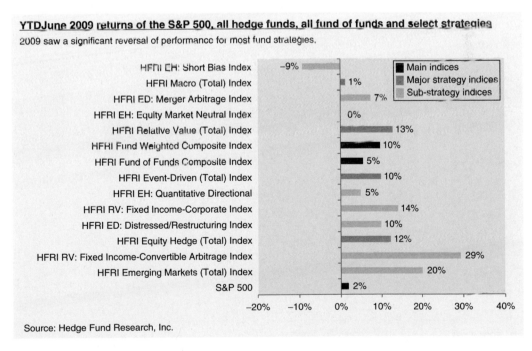

**YTDJune 2009 returns of the S&P 500, all hedge funds, all fund of funds and select strategies**

2009 saw a significant reversal of performance for most fund strategies.

Source: Hedge Fund Research, Inc.

**EXHIBIT 15.4**

Despite the strong performance in 2008 by short bias funds, which focus on shorting companies perceived to be overvalued, these funds produced the worst returns during the first half of 2009. Indeed, when the investment horizon is lengthened, these funds have offered investors surprisingly little value appreciation (see Exhibit 15.5). The compounded annual return of HFR's

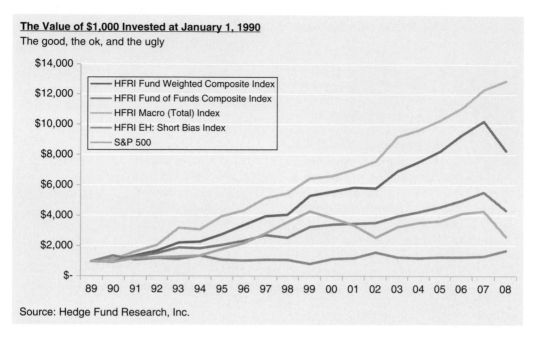

**The Value of $1,000 Invested at January 1, 1990**
The good, the ok, and the ugly

Source: Hedge Fund Research, Inc.

**EXHIBIT 15.5**

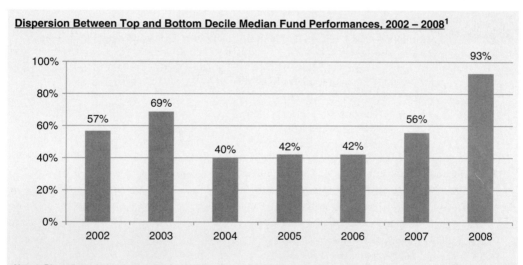

**Dispersion Between Top and Bottom Decile Median Fund Performances, 2002 – 2008[1]**

Note 1: Dispersion calculated as median fund performance of the top decile less the median fund performance of the bottom decile.
Source: Hedge Fund Research, Inc.

**EXHIBIT 15.6**

Short Bias Index from 1990 to 2008 was just 2.8%. In comparison, the compounded annual returns during this period for the S&P 500 and the broader composite hedge fund index were 5.2% and 11.8%, respectively. Macro-focused strategies performed especially well over this period, providing investors compounded annual returns of 14.4%.

When looking at hedge fund performance at the top and bottom deciles, the extreme market volatility of 2008 translated to the most significant dispersions in returns since HFR started tracking this data. At year-end 2008, the dispersion between the median returns of top and bottom deciles was 93%, compared to an average dispersion of 51% for the prior 6 years (see Exhibit 15.6).

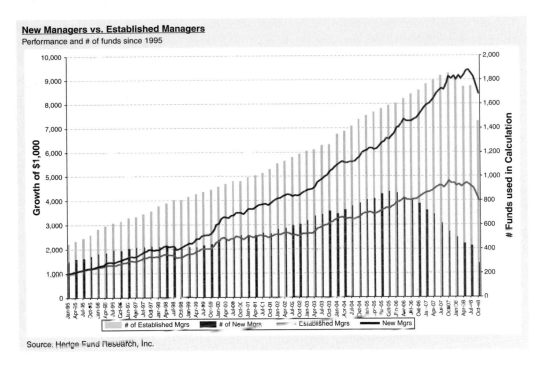

**New Managers vs. Established Managers**
Performance and # of funds since 1995

Source: Hedge Fund Research, Inc.

**EXHIBIT 15.7**

Finally, an analysis of whether the length of a manager's experience is any indication of expected returns brings interesting results. Comparing the performance of new managers (as defined by those in operation for less than 24 months) against established managers, new managers consistently outperform, even when adjusted for backfill. See Exhibit 15.7.

# Fund of Funds

The year 2008 ended on a bad note with the disclosure of billions of dollars in losses experienced by those who invested in Bernard Madoff's investment funds. While Madoff was not a hedge fund manager, a number of fund of funds that allocate investor money to hedge funds also allocated money to Madoff through feeder funds. This created concern about the quality of fund of funds' due diligence processes. The ensuing crisis of confidence in fund of funds resulted in many investors withdrawing money from these funds, which in turn, caused money to be taken out of hedge funds.

Fund of funds have sold themselves to investors on the basis that they offer three key benefits: diversification, access to sought-after managers, and due diligence. The financial crisis weakened the first two benefits from the perspective of many investors; the Madoff scandal significantly undermined the third benefit. As a result, assets under management by fund of funds dropped during 2008 from a high of $826 billion at the end of June 2008 to $593 billion by the end the year, according to Hedge Fund Research.

Compounding the difficulties of fund of funds was the leverage employed by these funds. Many fund of funds borrowed money to supplement investor money when they made investments in various hedge funds. Since most of the hedge funds they invested in were already leveraged, this doubling up of leverage created enhanced losses beyond the losses of the underlying funds. In part because of this leverage, average losses from fund of hedge funds during 2008 were 21%, compared to average losses for hedge funds during the year of 19%.

With lenders retracting credit, fund of funds were forced to dump assets, putting further pressure on hedge funds and the markets in general. As a result, a number of high-profile hedge funds liquidated or froze redemptions during 2008, traumatizing the investor base and triggering additional requests for redemption by some investors who sought liquidity wherever they could find it (even from hedge funds that were generating positive returns).

## Absolute Return

Historically, many investors have viewed hedge funds as an investment class that created absolute returns through the use of sophisticated hedging vehicles and by investing (both long and short) in a very diverse array of global assets. However the financial crisis of 2007 and 2008 forced investors to reconsider this view. Although the flexibility and skill of hedge funds kept the industry from suffering losses as large as the overall market, it is clear that the concept of achieving consistent positive returns is not always sustainable. In the face of extreme market duress, hedge funds are carried downstream along with relative return investment managers, although at a slower pace.

The negative returns realized by hedge funds occurred during 2008 just as the funds had expanded their investor base to a broader group of institutional investors that were attracted to the concept of absolute returns. Seeing hedge fund investment values drop, this new investor base became increasingly skeptical about what hedge funds are able to deliver, and decreased their allocations to this asset class at the same time that many other investors withdrew funds based on liquidity concerns. The resulting asset outflow caused some hedge funds to virtually implode. Withdrawals occurred at the same time that some hedge funds had begun investing in less liquid investments. In effect, these hedge funds started to compete with private equity funds for longer-term assets. Unfortunately, since hedge funds typically have lock-up periods of 2 years or less (as compared to lock-ups of 10 years or longer for private equity funds), unexpected withdrawals forced funds to sell liquid assets at firesale prices, exacerbating their losses and causing, in some cases, the need to close down the fund.

It is increasingly problematic for hedge funds to market themselves as absolute return funds. Instead, they now have to focus more on the key of delivering diversification. In other words, they are now perceived increasingly as relative value funds, but because of the broad array of investment and hedging tools at their disposal, they are still able to apply a partial breaking mechanism in bad markets. In a down market, many hedge funds may not produce positive returns, but as was proven during 2008, most will outperform other investment managers because they produce *diversified beta*, defined by Partners Group, a Swiss-based alternative asset manager, as "diversif[ication] across a large spectrum of return drivers that balances the investment risk of each individual underlying risk."[1]

## Benefits Revisited

Historically, hedge fund managers have articulated the following benefits for investors who place money in their funds:

1. Attractive risk-adjusted returns, focusing on positive returns, low volatility, and capital preservation.
2. Low correlation with major equity and bond markets.

---

[1]Jaeger, Lars. "Jaeger predicts year of alternative beta, the death of 'black boxes'. Advocates 'scenario based' portfolio construction." AllAboutAlapha.com, 19 Jan. 2009.

3. Investment flexibility to invest long or short, using a variety of instruments, investing in segments of the market that suffer from structural inefficiencies and in smaller asset pools.
4. Focus on marketable securities.
5. Structural advantages, including performance-based compensation (focus on performance instead of asset gathering), managers' personal investment (which aligned interests), and the ability to attract the "best and brightest."

An analysis of these benefits in light of the major dislocations of the market during 2007 and 2008 suggests the following about hedge funds:

1. Achievement of positive (absolute) returns has become a problematic objective during periods of major market dislocation.
2. Achievement of low correlation with major equity and bond markets is difficult to obtain during periods of major market dislocation.
3. Investment flexibility continues to be a major benefit of hedge funds.
4. Some hedge funds have invested a portion of their assets in nonmarketable securities, creating a mismatch between asset maturities and investor withdrawal requirements.
5. Structural advantages continue, including performance-based compensation and aligned interests.

## Transparency

Hedge fund investors historically have not required a significant amount of investment transparency from hedge fund managers. However, many investors are now pushing for greater position-level transparency. There will be ongoing pressure for more transparency, but there will also be corresponding pushback from some managers based on their concern that disclosure of strategies will benefit competitors and cause arbitrage opportunities to disappear.

Managers are generally willing to provide organizational and process transparency regarding assets under management, profit and loss attribution, key investment themes, new product initiatives, and personnel. In addition, risk transparency is usually provided through disclosure of credit exposure, volatility exposure, long versus short positions, leverage, geographic focus, portfolio concentration, industry focus, and market capitalization focus. However, hedge fund managers will attempt to keep specific investment strategies and ideas confidential. Investors must therefore decide whether the level of overall transparency provided is adequate in the context of the risks and benefits associated with investing in hedge funds.

## Fees

Following the poor industry performance during 2008, some hedge funds decided to reduce fees. For example, Renaissance Technologies, one of the largest and most successful hedge funds, waived all management fees for 2009 for its Renaissance Institutional Futures fund. In addition, the fund agreed not to receive any performance fees until 2008 losses of 12% were recovered. Other funds, including Highbridge Capital Management, launched new share classes with lower fees in exchange for longer lock-up periods.

At the end of 2008, Citadel Investment Group gave back about $300 million in fees it had previously collected, after completing a money-losing year. Other firms also gave back fees and remained committed to not receiving performance fees until they reached their high-water marks. At most funds, fee cuts came principally from performance fees rather than management fees.

As a result, 1% to 2% management fees continue to be the norm. Hedge funds maintain that when poor performance eliminates performance fees, management fees are essential to keeping the funds operational.

## High-Water Mark

A hedge fund high-water mark is a mechanism that is implemented to make sure that managers do not take a performance fee in the current period when the fund has had negative performance over previous performance fee periods. The high-water mark is the colloquial term for a *cumulative loss account*. A cumulative loss account starts with a zero balance at the beginning of any performance period (monthly, quarterly, or yearly, as determined by the firm), and it records net losses during that period. See Exhibit 15.8 for an example of high-water-mark calculation.

It was estimated that only 1 in 10 hedge funds received performance fees during 2008 because of losses and application of high-water marks. This created significant compensation pressures for many funds since their management fees were insufficient to keep the business going, which resulted in significant downsizing of headcount and office space.

---

**High Water Mark Example**

An example of the mechanical application of the cumulative loss account and high water mark calculation is below:

Hedge fund NAV 01/01/06: $1,000,000

Hedge fund NAV 12/31/06:      $1,200,000 (total after expenses, including the management fee expense)
Gain: $200,000
Less Performance fee: $40,000 [20% of $200,000]
Cumulative loss account: $0

Hedge fund NAV 01/01/07: $1,160,000

Hedge fund NAV 12/31/07:      $1,000,000 (total after expenses, including the management fee expense)
Gain: ($160,000)
Less Performance fee: $0
Cumulative loss account: $160,000

Hedge fund NAV 01/01/08: $1,000,000

Hedge fund NAV 12/31/08      $1,100,000 (total after expenses, including the management fee expense)
Gain: $100,000
Less Performance fee: $0
Cumulative loss account: $60,000

Hedge fund NAV 01/01/09: $1,100,000

Hedge fund NAV 12/31/09      $1,300,000 (total after expenses, including the management fee expense)
Gain: $200,000
Less Performance fee: $28,000 [20% of $140,000]
Cumulative loss account: $0

The concept of the high water mark is theoretically similar to the "claw-back" provision found in many private equity funds in that its purpose is to make sure the manager is not overcompensated for underperformance. However, the high water mark is distinctly different in that it is prospective in nature (whereas the claw-back is retrospective in nature). The high water mark is applied to a hedge fund manager on a going forward basis and so the manager will need to get the fund's account back up to the high water mark before a performance fee can be taken.

**EXHIBIT 15.8**

The high-water mark is designed to benefit investors by preventing a manager from taking a performance fee on the same gains more than once. However, the high-water mark also creates a perverse incentive for the hedge fund manager to either take extra risk to generate returns high enough to deplete the cumulative loss account so that a performance fee will be paid or to close down the fund and start again. Both of these actions could be damaging to investors, forcing them either to make a redemption at an inopportune time, or continue with their investment, with a potentially higher risk profile. If a hedge fund manager shuts down a fund, the investor might suffer disproportionate losses as assets are sold in a firesale environment. However, to keep money invested in the fund under a higher risk profile may also not be in the investor's best interest. Moreover, taking money out to invest with another manager might subject the investor to the same high-water-mark issue.

As a result of this conundrum, in some cases it might make sense for investors to consider modification of the high-water mark. An alternative to the standard hedge fund high-water mark is a modified high-water mark: resetting the high-water mark to the current fund level under circumstances where to do so better aligns everyone's interest, amortizing losses over a several-year period to enable some modest level of performance fees during the current period, or rolling the high-water mark over a more extended period.

A modified high-water mark may create value for investors by keeping a manager in the game and reducing the incentive of the manager to take excessive risk. As a quid pro quo, some hedge fund managers may be willing to accept lower performance fees.

## Searching for Returns

Hedge funds have traditionally been associated with *alpha-based* returns, which are independent of market conditions, but increasingly, hedge funds participate in the same investment activity as traditional fund managers. To differentiate themselves, hedge fund managers have had to search for new sources of returns in new markets. This search has pushed them into less liquid investments, including private equity investments and other private transactions. This activity extends their investment horizon, requires longer lock-ups, and results in the need to hire new managers who have long-term investment expertise. Hedge funds have become active participants in leveraged bank loans, mezzanine financings, insurance-linked securities, and LBO transactions. In other words, hedge funds have moved a significant amount of their investment base from short-term liquid transactions to longer-term less liquid transactions, in their search for alpha-based returns.

## Future Developments

Hedge funds suffered significant pain during 2007–2009: redemptions created loss of income and forced sales of assets that compounded losses; fees were reduced as performance waned; regulators reached toward greater regulation and more taxes; and many investors became concerned with the hedge fund model. As a result, a number of significant developments should continue in the future:

1. Hedge funds have more limited access to leveraged financing, which in particular impacts convertible arbitrage, fixed income arbitrage, and statistical arbitrage investment strategies.

2. The ability to maintain confidentiality over investment strategies has been reduced as investors demand more transparency and liquidity. Losses, gates, and fraud have forced hedge funds to become more open in their activities and more willing to share details of their business and associated risks with investors.

3. Fees have been reduced from the typical 2/20 schedule to a lesser fee system that allows greater returns to investors and acknowledges the lower return environment.

4. The decline in alpha is well documented, and many hedge funds are now viewed as creating diversified beta instead of finding significant returns from market inefficiencies. This still represents value added, but differentiation from many well-managed traditional investment funds is more difficult.

5. Hedge funds are subject to additional regulatory constraints, which limit somewhat their flexibility, especially in long/short equity, event-driven, and other equity-based strategies.

6. A less favorable tax environment will result in reduction in after-tax compensation received by hedge fund managers.

7. As hedge funds adjust to the new realities of the market, they are developing longer lock-up arrangements that better match the lengthening maturity profile of their investments. This enables them, in turn, to expand long-term investment activity to take advantage of higher yields available for patient capital.

8. The balance of power has shifted from general partners to limited partners. The result is that limited partners have been successful in obtaining better transparency, improved liquidity (or better match with assets), and the other benefits described above.

## Merging of Functions

Hedge funds, private equity funds, and investment banks compete against each other and are, at the same time, major sources of revenue for each other. Each of the largest participants in these three industries conducts business activities in all three areas. For example, Goldman Sachs has an industry-leading investment banking business, providing M&A and underwriting services to corporate and municipal clients, and to private equity firms. Goldman Sachs also has an industry-leading sales and trading business, providing trading and lending services to institutional and individual investors, including hedge funds. In fact, private equity funds and hedge funds are the two most important clients of Goldman Sachs' investment banking division and trading division, respectively. In addition, Goldman Sachs conducts one of the world's largest hedge fund businesses, between their proprietary trading desk and their Asset Management Division. Finally, Goldman Sachs conducts one of the world's largest private equity businesses, between their principal investment area and their Asset Management Division (see Exhibit 15.9). As a result, Goldman Sachs is both a critically important provider of services to hedge funds and private equity funds, as well as one of their principal competitors.

Fortress Investment Group is a global alternative investment and asset management firm that completed an IPO in the United States during 2007. They invest in the areas of hedge funds, private equity funds, and real estate. Fortress also actively uses investment banking services to find private equity investment opportunities, finance investments, and buy, sell, and borrow securities for its hedge fund investment platform (see Exhibit 15.10).

Cerberus Capital Management established a significant investor following based on its hedge-fund-related investments in distressed debt. This experience provided a foundation to

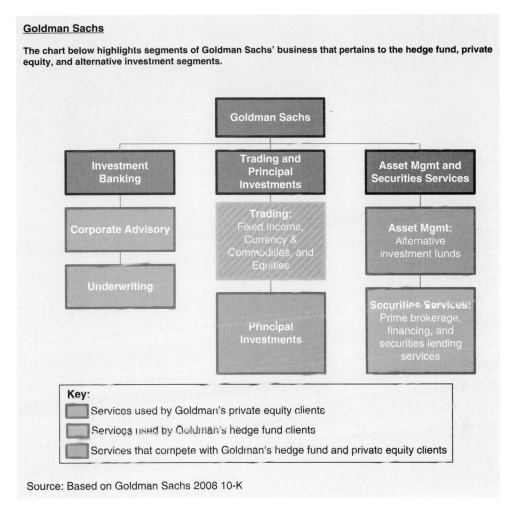

**Goldman Sachs**

The chart below highlights segments of Goldman Sachs' business that pertains to the hedge fund, private equity, and alternative investment segments.

Source: Based on Goldman Sachs 2008 10-K

EXHIBIT 15.9

understand long-term investments, as many of its early distressed debt investments were transformed through bankruptcy courts into equity exposure. As a result, in addition to its hedge-fund-based investments, Cerberus has become one of the largest private equity funds in the world (see Exhibit 15.11 and **Case Study 10, "Cerberus and the U.S. Auto Industry"**).

The Blackstone Group was created by Peter Peterson and Stephen Schwarzman, two former investment bankers. This firm is an alternative asset manager that focuses on private equity, hedge fund investing, and real estate. In addition, Blackstone has become involved in providing M&A advice in direct competition to investment banks (see Exhibit 15.12).

Citadel Investment Group is an alternative asset manager that principally focuses on hedge fund investments, but their investment portfolio has broadened beyond traditional hedge fund investments. Citadel has also developed a large hedge fund administration business that competes with the prime brokerage operations of major investment banks by providing securities loans, and reporting and administrative services to other hedge funds. In addition, Citadel expanded beyond its traditional trading-based businesses when it launched an investment banking advisory division in May 2009.

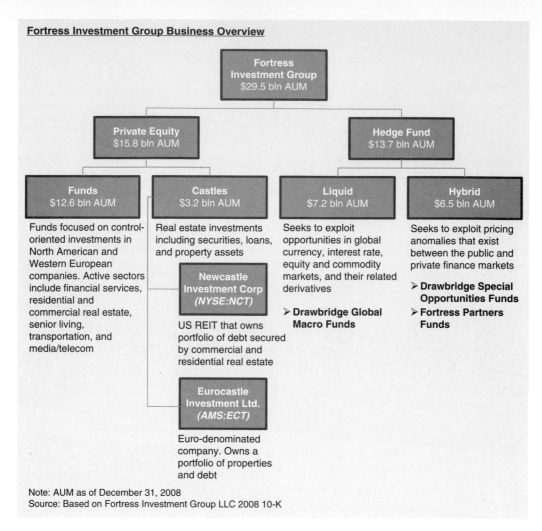

**EXHIBIT 15.10**

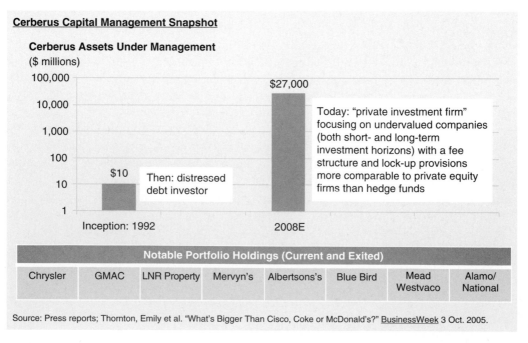

**EXHIBIT 15.11**

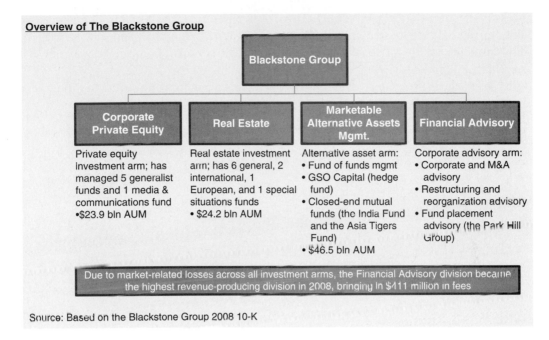

**Overview of The Blackstone Group**

Source: Based on the Blackstone Group 2008 10-K

EXHIBIT 15.12

Some of the largest hedge funds also provide investment banking services and invest in private equity assets. Investment banks manage funds that are already included among the world's largest hedge funds and private equity funds. Private equity funds are developing hedge fund investing businesses and providing investment banking services. As a result, the merging of hedge funds, private equity, and investment banks is well underway and this process should accelerate in the future.

## Questions

1. Describe the key characteristics and benefits of hedge funds.
2. The performance disparity between established managers and new managers was especially sizable in 2008. Describe what may have attributed to this.
3. Based on the returns of the various strategies in Exhibits 15.3 and 15.4, which strategy seems to be most successful at achieving absolute returns?
4. Assume that an investor invests in a fund of hedge funds (FHF). FHF employs 2.0× leverage. Now suppose FHF invests all its money in 10 hedge funds (HF) that each employ 25% margin/4.0× leverage. What happens to the investor's money (% decrease) if investments in each of the HF's portfolios drop 5% in value?
5. Assuming the same size and profitability, which fund would you expect to have more in tax liabilities: Active Trading or Activist Investing?
6. Hedge fund AlphaBeta has a NAV of $1 million and a zero balance in its cumulative loss account on January 1, 2006. Now suppose AlphaBeta's annual performance (net of management fees) matches that of the Credit Suisse/Tremont hedge fund index as shown in Exhibit 11.12. AlphaBeta charges a 20% performance fee. Based on the high-water mark reached in 2007, what minimum percentage gain does the fund need to achieve in 2009 before performance fees can be taken again?

7.  Classifying some of the largest hedge funds as Tier 1 financial holding companies would subject these funds to requirements regarding capital, liquidity, and risk management. The rationale for this is that a large hedge fund, on its own, could pose systemic risk to the financial system. Discuss the merits of this argument.

8.  What is the benefit of a hedge fund like Citadel expanding into a hedge fund services business such as market making and fund administration?

# 16

# Overview of Private Equity

Private equity can be broadly defined to include the following different forms of investment:

1) **Leveraged Buyout:** Leveraged buyout (LBO) refers to the purchase of all or most of a company or a business unit by using equity from a small group of investors in combination with a significant amount of debt. The targets of LBOs are typically mature companies that generate strong operating cash flow.

2) **Growth Capital:** Growth capital typically refers to minority equity investments in mature companies that need capital to expand or restructure operations, finance an acquisition, or enter a new market, without a change of control of the company.

3) **Mezzanine Capital:** Mezzanine capital refers to an investment in subordinated debt or preferred stock of a company, without taking voting control of the company. Often these securities have attached warrants or conversion rights into common stock.

4) **Venture Capital:** Venture capital refers to equity investments in less mature non-public companies to fund the launch, early development, or expansion of a business.

Although private equity can be considered to include all four of these investment activities, it is common for private equity to be the principal descriptor for LBO activity. Venture capital, growth capital, and mezzanine capital are each considered a separate investment strategy, although some large private equity firms participate in all four investment areas. This chapter principally focuses on LBO activities of private equity firms. See Exhibit 16.1 for a summary of the growth of leveraged buyout assets under management.

Investment firms that engage in LBO activity are called private *equity firms*. These firms are also called *buyout firms* or *financial sponsors*. The term financial sponsor comes from the role a private equity firm has as the "sponsor," or provider, of the equity component in an LBO, as well as the orchestrator of all aspects of the LBO transaction, including negotiating the purchase price and, with investment banker assistance, securing debt financing to complete the purchase.

Private equity firms are considered *financial buyers*, because they do not bring synergies to an acquisition, as opposed to *strategic buyers*, who are generally competitors of a target company and will benefit from synergies when they acquire or merge with the target. As a result, in auctions conducted by targets, strategic buyers are usually able to pay a higher price than the price offered by financial buyers. However, there are many instances in which financial buyers win auction bids because of antitrust issues or because financial buyers use aggressive assumptions regarding future cash flow (based on a more leveraged capital structure and more effective management direction), favorable debt financing terms, and aggressive exit strategies.

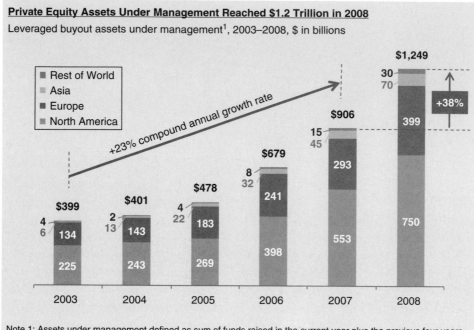

**Private Equity Assets Under Management Reached $1.2 Trillion in 2008**

Leveraged buyout assets under management[1], 2003–2008, $ in billions

Note 1: Assets under management defined as sum of funds raised in the current year plus the previous four years.
Source: McKinsey Global Institute; Preqin

EXHIBIT 16.1

## Characteristics of a Private Equity Transaction

Key characteristics of a private equity transaction include:

1. In a private equity transaction a company or a business unit is acquired by a private equity investment fund that has secured debt and equity funding from institutional investors such as pension funds, insurance companies, endowments, and fund of funds, or from high-net-worth individuals, sovereign wealth funds, hedge funds, or banks. The equity investment portion of an acquisition has historically represented 30% to 40% of the purchase price, with the balance of the acquisition cost coming from debt financing.
2. Relatively high debt levels utilized to fund the transaction increase the return on equity for the private equity buyer (although this increase should be risk adjusted). There are different levels of debt used: senior debt, which is provided by banks and is usually secured by the assets of the target company, and subordinated debt, which is usually unsecured and raised in the high-yield capital markets.
3. If the target company is a public company (as opposed to a private company or a division of a public company), the buyout results in the target company *going private*, with the view that this newly private company will be resold in the future (typically 3 to 7 years) through an IPO or private sale to another company (or to another private equity firm).
4. The private equity firm's targeted internal rate of return (IRR) during the holding period for their investment has historically been above 20%, but actual IRR depends on the amount of leverage, the ability of the target's cash flow to pay down some of the debt, dividend pay-outs, and the eventual exit strategy (and the IRR should be risk-adjusted to reflect higher leverage).

5. The *general partners* of the private equity fund commit capital to the transaction alongside *limited partners*, who are the equity investors just described. In addition, management of the target company usually also have a meaningful capital exposure to the transaction.

## Target Companies for Private Equity Transactions

For an LBO transaction to be successful, the target company must generate a significant amount of cash flow to pay high debt interest and principal payments and, sometimes, dividends to the private equity shareholders. Without this ability, investors will not achieve acceptable returns and the eventual exit strategy may be impaired. To achieve strong cash flow, management of the target company must be able to reduce costs while growing the company. The best potential target companies generally have the following characteristics:

1. Motivated and competent management: It is crucial that management be willing and able to operate a highly leveraged company that has little margin for error. If existing management is not capable of doing this, new management must be brought in. Some private equity firms have a cadre of operating executives that they bring in either to take over or supplement management activities in order to create value and grow the company.

2. Robust and stable cash flow: Private equity funds look for robust and stable cash flow to pay interest that is due on large amounts of debt and, ideally, to also pay down debt over time. The fund initially forecasts cash flow that incorporates cost savings and operational initiatives designed to increase cash-flow post-acquisition. This forecast includes the risk-adjusted maximum amount of debt that can be brought into the capital structure, which leads to determination of the amount of equity that must be invested, and the corresponding potential return based on the equity investment. The greater the projected cash flow, the greater the amount of debt that can be utilized, creating a smaller equity investment. The lower the equity investment, the greater the potential return.

3. Leveragable balance sheet: If a company already has significant leverage, and if their debt is not structured efficiently (e.g., not callable, carries high interest payment obligations, and other unfavorable characteristics), the company may not be a good target. An ideal target company has low leverage, an efficient debt structure, and assets that can be used as collateral for loans.

4. Low capital expenditures: Since capital expenditures use up cash flow available for debt service and dividends, ideal target companies have found a balance between making capital expenditures that provide good long-term returns on investment and preserving cash to pay interest and principal payments on debt, and potential dividends. As a result, many private equity firms steer away from high-tech and biotech companies that require high capital expenditures (with a few notable exceptions that have resulted in questionable return opportunities, as described in Chapter 18).

5. Quality assets: A good target company has strong brands and quality assets that have been poorly managed, or has unrealized growth potential. Generally speaking, service-based companies are less ideal targets compared to companies that have significant tangible assets of high quality, because a service company's value is significantly linked to employees and intangible assets such as intellectual property and goodwill. These types of assets don't provide collateral value for loans, compared to assets such as inventories, machinery, and buildings.

6. Asset sales and cost-cutting: A target company may have assets that are not used in the production of cash flow. For example, the company might have too many corporate jets or

unproductive real estate used for entertainment or other less productive uses. A private equity firm focuses on any assets that do not facilitate growth in cash flow, and sales of these assets are initiated to create cash to pay down acquisition debt. Another reason to sell assets is to facilitate diversification objectives. The ability to cut costs is also important to create incremental value. Sometimes this leads to a reduction in personnel, or in entertainment and travel budgets. However, for certain target companies, the principal focus is on facilitating growth rather than cutting costs.

## Private Equity Transaction Participants

The key participants in a private equity transaction include the following:

1. Private equity firm (as noted, this firm is also called a financial sponsor, buyout firm, or LBO firm): The private equity firm (a) selects the LBO target (often with the assistance of an investment bank); (b) negotiates the acquisition price, secures senior and subordinated debt financing (again, often with the assistance of an investment bank); (c) completes the acquisition through a closing event; (d) as owner and controlling member of the board of directors, operates the acquired company through either existing management or new management; (e) oversees the activities and decision-making of senior management; (f) makes all major strategic and financial decisions; and (g) decides when and how to sell the company (by initiating an exit strategy, usually with the assistance of an investment bank).

2. Investment banks: Investment banks (a) introduce potential acquisition targets to private equity firms; (b) help negotiate the acquisition price; (c) often either provide loans (as a participant in a syndicated bank loan facility) and/or underwrite high-yield bond offerings; (d) occasionally assist in recapitalizations by underwriting debt or providing loans that fund the distribution of a large dividend to the private equity owner; and (e) assist in the eventual sale of the company through either an M&A-related sale or an IPO transaction. As a result, private equity funds represent a significant source of revenue for investment banks. Several large private equity firms paid over $500 million in fees to investment bankers during 2006 at the height of the private equity boom.

3. Investors: Institutional and high-net-worth investors become limited partners in a fund organized by a private equity firm, as opposed to investing directly in the firm. Fund of funds are also limited partners based on their significant investing capacity. Investors sign investment contracts that lock up their money for as long as 10 to 12 years. Typically, however, distributions are made to investors as soon as investments are turned into cash through completion of an exit strategy such as an IPO or sale of the company. Limited partners commit to provide capital over time, rather than in a single amount upfront. The general partner's draw on this capital depends on when investment opportunities are identified (both to acquire companies and to expand company operations through acquisitions or product extensions). As a result, it may be a number of years after the original commitment of capital before all of the limited partner funds are drawn down.

4. Management: Management of companies co-invest with the private equity fund in the new equity of the acquired company, which aligns management's interests with the interests of the fund. In addition, management usually receive stock options. This effectively eliminates agency issues and provides the incentive to work hard and create significant value. The end result is wealth creation for management if they are successful in managing the company until a successful exit is completed (usually 3 to 7 years after acquisition). If problems

develop during the holding period, or if exits are significantly delayed, management will not only forego significant exit-related compensation but may also lose their job.

5. Lawyers, accountants, tax experts, and other professionals: There is a significant amount of work by professionals who advise private equity funds and investment banks in the full array of private equity activities described. As a result, there are many professional service firms that have dedicated staff that focus principally, or only, on private equity transactions.

## Structure of a Private Equity Fund

Private equity firms are usually organized as management partnerships or limited liability partnerships that act as holding companies for several private equity funds (and sometimes, other alternative asset funds) run by general partners. At the largest private equity firms there may be 20 to 40 general partners. These general partners invest in the fund and also raise money from institutional investors and high-net-worth individuals, who become limited partners in the fund.

Private equity firms receive cash from several sources. They receive an annual management fee from limited partners that generally equals between 1% and 3% of the fund's assets under management (see Exhibit 16.2). They also receive a portion of the profits generated by the fund, which is called *carry* or *carried interest*. The carry is typically approximately 20% of profits, which provides a strong incentive for the private equity firms to create value for the fund. The balance of profits is paid out to limited partners. Finally, the companies that the fund invests in (called *portfolio companies*) sometimes pay transaction fees to the fund in relation to various services rendered, such as investment banking and consulting services, which are typically calculated as a percentage of the value of the transaction, and sometimes, *monitoring fees*. Some (but not all) funds credit these fees against management fees payable by limited partners.

Partnership agreements between the general partners and limited partners are signed at the inception of each fund, and these agreements define the expected payments to general partners. The management fee resembles fees paid to mutual funds and hedge funds (higher than mutual funds and about the same level as hedge funds). The carry has no analogue among most mutual funds and is similar to the performance fee received by hedge funds (although hedge fund managers receive performance fees annually based on the value of assets under management, whereas private equity fund general partners only receive carry when their investment is monetized, which often is after a 3- to 7-year holding period). Successful private equity firms stay in business by raising a new fund every 3 to 5 years. Each fund is expected to be fully invested within 5 years and is designed to realize an exit within 3 to 7 years of the original investment.

## Capitalization of a Private Equity Transaction

A private equity portfolio company has a capital structure that, historically, included up to 70% debt. This debt includes collateralized bank borrowing through revolving credit facilities and term loans, mezzanine debt, high-yield bonds sold in the public capital markets, and subordinated notes placed principally with banks and institutional investors (see Exhibit 16.3). The amount of debt that is included in capital structures increased through mid-2007 and then decreased as the market's tolerance for leverage diminished during the credit crisis that started at that time.

**General Partner Fee Structure, Excerpt from "The Economics of Private Equity Funds"**

"GPs earn the bulk of fixed revenue – which is not based on the performance of the fund – through management fees. To see how management fees are calculated, we need to define several terms. Over the lifetime of the fund, some of the committed capital is used for these fees, with the remainder used to make investments. We refer to these components of committed capital as lifetime fees and investment capital, respectively. At any point in time, we define the invested capital of the fund as the portion of investment capital that has already been invested into portfolio companies. Net invested capital is defined as invested capital, minus the cost basis of any exited investments. Similarly, contributed capital is defined as invested capital plus the portion of lifetime fees that has already been paid to the fund, and net contributed capital is equal to contributed capital minus the cost basis of any exited investments. The typical fund has a lifetime of ten years, with general partners allowed to make investments in new companies only during the first five years (the investment period), with the final five years reserved for follow-on investments and the exiting of existing portfolio companies.

Most funds use one of four methods for the assessment of management fees. Historically, the most common method was to assess fees as a constant percentage of committed capital. For example, if a fund charges 2 percent annual management fees on committed capital for ten years, then the lifetime fees of the ten-year fund would be 20 percent of committed capital, with investment capital comprising the other 80 percent. In recent years, many funds have adopted a decreasing fee schedule, with the percentage falling after the investment period. For example, a fund might have a 2 percent fee during five-year investment period, with this annual fee falling by 25 basis points per year for the next five years.

The third type of fee schedule uses a constant rate, but changes the basis for this rate from committed capital (first five years) to net invested capital (last five years). Finally, the fourth type of fee schedule uses both a decreasing percentage and a change from committed capital to net invested capital after the investment period. For any fee schedule that uses net invested capital, the estimation of lifetime fees requires additional assumptions about the investment and exit rates...

...The most common initial fee level is 2 percent, though the majority of funds give some concessions to LPs after the investment period is over; e.g., switching to invested capital basis ([84.0 percent]), lowering the fee level ([45.1 percent]), or both ([38.9 percent]). Based on these facts, we should expect lifetime fees to be less than 20 percent of committed capital for most funds."

Source: Metrick, Andrew and Ayako Yasuda. "The Economics of Private Equity Funds (June 9, 2009)". Review of Financial Studies, Forthcoming.

**EXHIBIT 16.2**

See Exhibit 16.4 for a summary of average LBO equity contribution through 2008. See Exhibit 16.5 for a summary of LBO Debt/EBITDA.

## Assets Under Management

Assets under management (AUM) have increased by more than 10 times between 1995 and 2008 (see Exhibit 16.6). The principal investors in these assets are private equity fund of funds, public pension funds, and corporate pension funds (see Exhibit 16.7). Assuming that the average private equity fund has employed two parts debt to one part equity, it is estimated that the total capitalization controlled by private equity funds was approximately $3.7 trillion as of 2008. This amount may have dropped to under $2 trillion by mid-2009, after considering the estimated drop in the market value of existing investments (estimated to be more than $300 billion by McKinsey Global Institute) and lower available leverage of approximately one part debt to one part equity.

**Portfolio Company Capitalization**

- Debt (~60-70% of overall cap structure)
  - o  Senior bank debt, two types:
    - ▪  Revolving credit facility (Revolver) which can be paid down and re-borrowed as needed
    - ▪  Term debt (senior and subordinated) with floating rates
  - o  Junior debt, two types:
    - ▪  High yield (typically public markets)
    - ▪  Mezzanine debt (subordinated notes, typically sold to banks, institutions and hedge funds)
    - ▪  Other key features:
      - −  Warrants
      - −  Payment-in-kind (PIK) toggle allows no interest payment and increase in principal
- Equity (~30-40% of overall cap structure)
  - o  Preferred stock
  - o  Common stock

**EXHIBIT 16.3**

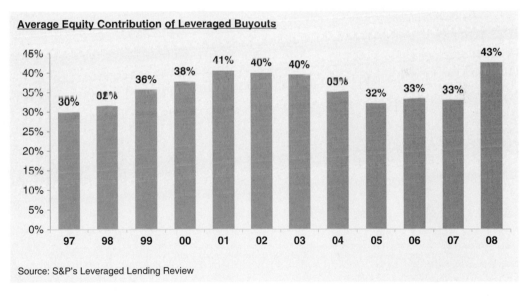

Source: S&P's Leveraged Lending Review

**EXHIBIT 16.4**

# History

The first LBO transaction was completed in 1955, using a publicly traded holding company as an investment vehicle to borrow money and then acquire a portfolio of investments in corporate assets. This activity gained momentum during the 1960s when Warren Buffet (through Berkshire Hathaway) and Nelson Peltz (through Triarc) made leveraged investments. During the 1970s a group of bankers at Bear Stearns, including Jerome Kohlberg and Henry Kravis, completed a number of leveraged investments, but in 1976 these bankers left Bear Stearns to organize their own firm, which was called Kohlberg Kravis & Roberts (KKR). In 1982, William Simon (a former U.S. Treasury Secretary) completed an LBO of Gibson Greetings, a producer of greeting

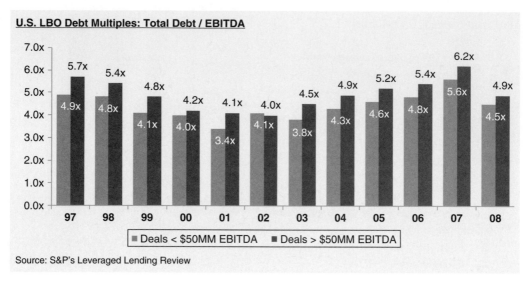

**EXHIBIT 16.5**

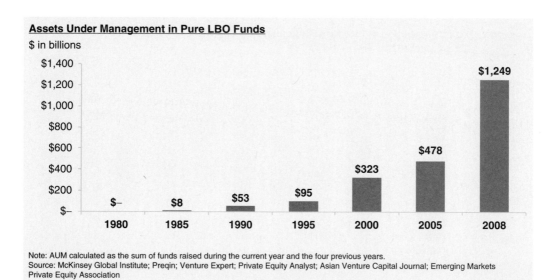

**EXHIBIT 16.6**

cards, for $80 million using a minimal amount of equity, and then sold a portion of the company less than 18 months later for $290 million through an IPO. The significant media attention received by this transaction brought many other investors into this fledgling market.

During the 1980s, many LBO transactions were labeled by the press as *corporate raids*, especially those transactions that featured a hostile takeover, asset stripping, and major layoffs. Carl Icahn, Nelson Peltz, Kirk Kerkorian, and T. Boone Pickens were some of the notable "raiders" during this period. The largest and last major LBO during the 1980s was the $31.1 billion takeover of RJR Nabisco by KKR, which attracted significant attention because of the enormous size of the transaction (which was not matched in size until 2006). By the end of the 1980s a number of large buyouts ended in bankruptcy, including Federated Department Stores and Revco.

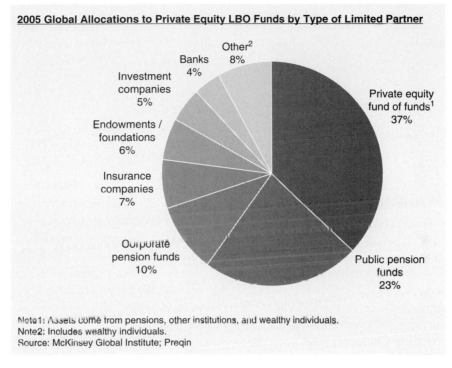

**2005 Global Allocations to Private Equity LBO Funds by Type of Limited Partner**

Note1: Assets come from pensions, other institutions, and wealthy individuals.
Note2: Includes wealthy individuals.
Source: McKinsey Global Institute; Preqin

**EXHIBIT 16.7**

A few years later, KKR was forced to contribute an additional $1.7 billion in equity to RJR Nabisco in a recapitalization designed to salvage this investment. One of the principal reasons for the growth in LBOs during this period was the development of the high-yield bond (junk bonds) market that was propelled by Drexel Burnham Lambert (Drexel). Drexel's junk bond effort was led by Michael Milken, who was indicted in 1989 on charges of racketeering and securities fraud as the result of an insider trading investigation. Drexel filed for bankruptcy protection in 1990, and Milken served 2 years in prison. These events virtually closed down the junk bond market and substantially reduced LBO activity during the first half of the 1990s.

In 2002, the stage was set for remarkable growth in the LBO market. A period of benign interest rates, a resurgent junk bond market, a robust bank loan market, and remarkably lenient lending standards opened the door to an explosive market. The passage of the Sarbanes-Oxley Act in the United States during July 2002 added to growth of the LBO market as a large number of companies recognized the benefits of avoiding increasingly burdensome regulations that were imposed on public companies based on this Act. By "going private," companies were not required to file all of the information required by the Act (and by other securities regulations) and were relieved of millions of dollars of legal and accounting costs that were necessary to remain in compliance. In addition, many companies recognized the benefit of being able to manage their business on a long-term basis as a private company, instead of managing to meet public company quarterly analyst expectations.

Between 2002 and mid-2007, a remarkable number of transactions were completed, many of which were in excess of $30 billion. During 2006, private equity firms bought 654 U.S. companies, spending $375 billion. Globally, private equity firms raised $281 billion during the year, and another $301 billion in the following year. In July 2007, the credit crisis that started earlier in the mortgage markets spilled over into the junk bond and leveraged loan markets, substantially reducing the appetite of the debt markets for private equity transactions. Credit spreads widened considerably during the second half of 2007 and the entire leveraged finance market came to a near standstill. By the end of 2007, there was virtually no debt available to support large private equity transactions (see "Impact of Financial Services Meltdown on Private Equity" at the end of this chapter).

# Financing Bridges

## Bridge Loans

A bridge loan is an interim financing for a private equity fund to facilitate an acquisition until permanent debt financing can be obtained. Bridge loans are typically more expensive than permanent financing to compensate for the additional risk of the loan. The bridge loan commitment will not be drawn down unless permanent debt funding is not available, creating the need for a bridge in a troubled capital market. Investment banks generally provide bridge loans to private equity firms when they are confident that the bridge funding will not be necessary, because they expect to be able either to syndicate a term bank credit facility or successfully place a high-yield bond offering in the capital markets. During 2007 and 2008, because of the global financial crisis, many bridge loans were unexpectedly funded when investment banks were unsuccessful in securing permanent debt financing. See Chapter 10 for more information on bridge loans provided by investment banks to facilitate private equity acquisition activity.

## Equity Bridges

Target companies require private equity funds to provide an equity commitment letter prior to signing a purchase agreement. If the fund is unable to cover the entire equity commitment at that time, or is waiting for a limited partner to make a co-investment but the timing for this co-investment does not coincide with the purchase agreement signing date, the private equity firm might ask banks that are receiving fees from underwriting debt, providing loans, or advising on the acquisition, to provide an equity bridge to the private equity firm to cover the gap. To put an equity bridge in place, the private equity firm enters into a separate commitment with the bank that provides for fees, including utilization fees if the bridge equity is funded, and additional fees if the lenders' equity has not been purchased within a specified period of time. The expectation is that the bridge is a short-term commitment and will be rapidly sold down to permanent equity sources. The equity bridge provider usually has the right to collect a pro rata portion of any break-up fee that might be paid by the target if the deal is terminated, but may resist payment of any reverse break-up fee if the private equity firm walks away from the deal. In some cases, banks are asked, essentially, to take equity exposure to target companies that approaches or exceeds the equity committed to by private equity funds. The worst-case outcome for banks occurs if they cannot sell down the equity exposure they have assumed and are left holding equity stakes in companies that they otherwise have no intention of investing in, with no near-term source for repayment. Because private equity firms have historically paid investment banks billions of dollars in fees each year, fierce competition for future fees persuaded many banks to participate in this highly risky practice.

During 2007, banks that had provided equity bridges to support large LBO transactions found themselves unable to sell their equity exposure to others. This, combined with bridge loans unexpectedly provided to private equity portfolio companies when capital and loan markets froze up, resulted in hundreds of billions in "hung" loans and deteriorating equity stakes held by banks. Some of these positions were eventually sold at discounts of more than 50%.

## Covenant-Lite Loans and PIK Toggles

During the permissive loan environment of 2006 through mid-2007, a large number of private equity transactions were completed using *covenant-lite* loans. These loans lacked the financial triggers that historically allowed banks to shut off credit and force loans to become due and payable. This type of loan reduces the likelihood of a loan default, but at the same time delays the ability of banks to intervene, because they are prevented from acting on early warning signs of a problem.

Covenant-lite loans come in many forms, including elimination of covenants that require a borrower to maintain certain financial ratios, leaving lenders to rely only on covenants that restrict a company from *incurring*, or actively engaging in certain actions. For example, a covenant that requires a company to maintain a ratio of debt to EBITDA can be breached if the financial condition of the company deteriorates when the covenant is measured quarterly. In a typical covenant-lite package, this maintenance is eliminated and replaced with a covenant that only restricts a company from incurring new debt, which cannot be violated simply based on a deteriorating financial condition. Rather, the company has to take affirmative action by raising new debt to breach it. Another alternative in a covenant-lite package is a carve-out in a traditional maintenance covenant that forgives in advance predetermined deviations from the covenant. A related benefit often attached to covenant lite loans are *equity cure* provisions that enable a private equity firm to cure a covenant deficiency by adding more equity into a deal and calling the equity EBITDA, thereby curing the breach.

A *PIK toggle* feature in high-yield bonds and leveraged loans provides a borrower with a choice regarding how to pay accrued interest for each interest period: (1) pay interest completely in cash; (2) pay interest completely "in kind" by adding it to the principal amount (or by issuing new debt having a principal amount equal to the interest amount due); or (3) pay half of the interest in cash and half in kind.

Covenant-lite loans and PIK toggle features allowed private equity firms to secure more favorable debt transactions in support of their acquisition activity during the height of the private equity boom. Default rates were at historically low levels (less than 1% during 2006) and the supply of debt exceeded demand: banks were emboldened by the low default rate and the opportunity to secure high fees from completing underwriting and M&A transactions with private equity firms, while hedge funds brought a new source of debt financing to private equity firms, creating competition for the banks. As a result, private equity funds were able to secure low-cost financing with very favorable covenant and interest payment packages. This came to an abrupt halt during the second half of 2007 as the credit crisis gained momentum and default rates jumped substantially.

## Club Transactions and Stub Equity

When the size of a potential acquisition by a private equity firm exceeds around 10–15% of the capital in a fund sponsored by the firm, the possibility of a *club transaction* is considered. In a club deal, 2 to 5 different private equity firms coordinate to co-invest in a target company. The benefits that club transactions create include spreading economic risk, sharing expertise, pooling of relationships with financing sources, reduction of costs per firm, and reduction in competition. The challenges include increasing exposure to a single large transaction for limited partners who have capital invested in more than one of the club members; politics regarding which advisors to hire (investment banks and law firms); determining which firm will coordinate the bidding process; determining the price that all club members accept; agreeing on co-investors sponsored by each club member (usually from their limited partner pool); regulator antitrust concerns; and the ultimate exit strategy. During 2005–2007, when many transactions exceeded $5 billion, formation of clubs was common. Since mid-2007, when most transactions have been for smaller amounts, very few clubs have been formed.

*Stub equity* refers to the practice of letting public shareholders of a target continue to own equity in a company that is purchased by private equity funds. Stub equity is usually only offered when major shareholders of a target company are unwilling to sell their shares because they believe the offered price is too low. Stub equity allows these shareholders to participate in valuation growth alongside the private equity funds. Usually, stub equity is limited to no more than 30% of post-acquisition equity and, if a U.S. transaction, it is SEC registered but will not be listed on an exchange, substantially reducing the liquidity of the shares. Importantly, unlike the general partners in the fund, owners of stub equity do not participate in carry.

The advantages of stub equity include reduced litigation risk for the private equity sponsor; smaller equity investment required; limitation on governance rights for the stub holders; and sometimes improved accounting results from a recapitalization, since the company may qualify for recapitalization accounting, which avoids the write-up of the target's fixed assets or identified intangibles and subsequent depreciation and amortization of these assets (which reduces earnings). The disadvantages of stub equity include SEC disclosure requirements; ongoing SEC reporting requirements; potential fiduciary duty to minority shareholders; lower leverage applied to the private equity firm's investment; and the potential for future mark-to-market valuations in the event that shares (which are not traded on an exchange) become listed on *pink sheets* and are traded over-the-counter, potentially giving rise to mark-to-market valuations that do not reflect true value for the private equity funds, based on the illiquidity of a pink sheet market.

## Teaming Up with Management

Private equity firms typically make arrangements with management of a target company regarding terms of employment with the surviving company, post-closing option grants and rollover equity (the amount of stock that management must purchase to create economic exposure to the transaction) prior to executing definitive agreements with the target. When the target is a U.S. public company, these arrangements with management are problematic because of securities law regulations that govern such arrangements. For example, the first question is whether a special committee of the board of the target company is needed to oversee agreements with management. The firm must be careful that the transaction does not lose the benefit of the presumption of fair dealing. In a transaction where a private equity fund teams up with a *controlling* shareholder to take a public company private, the actions of the target's board become subject to the *entire fairness* test, a standard of review that is more exacting than the traditional business judgment rule. There is no bright-line test regarding whether a shareholder is controlling. For example, a Delaware court found that a 40% holder who was the target's CEO fell into the category of controlling. Other courts, however, have applied smaller percentages in determining controlling interest. If a transaction's fairness is challenged, the burden of proof is held by the target. However, if a special committee of independent directors has been formed to review the transaction, then the burden of proof may shift to the plaintiff challenging the fairness of the deal. Even when there is no controlling shareholder involved, a target board will frequently decide to create a special committee to forestall challenges to the transaction, especially when senior management has a significant equity stake in the target (see Exhibit 16.8).

### Kinder Morgan LBO

**Background:**
- Kinder Morgan management approached Goldman Sachs in February 2006 for a strategic alternatives review to enhance shareholder value.
- Among the options considered were share repurchase programs, a going-private transaction, and a leverage buyout.
- During April, Goldman requested to become the principal investor in a buyout transaction. Top management at Kinder, including President C. Park Sharper and founder, Chairman and CEO Richard Kinder (who owned an 18% share of the company) were to be members of the buyout group.
- From April through mid-May, management and Goldman (both the advisory and investment arms) worked together to explore the viability of the buyout option and counseled with outside legal and ratings advisors.
- On May 13 the board was notified for the first time of the current strategic review and on May 28, a $100/share offer was presented. Subsequent to receipt of the offer, the board of directors formed a special committee and enlisted the help of Morgan Stanley and Blackstone to evaluate the proposal and seek higher offers.

**Issues:**
- There is an inherent potential conflict of interest when management joins with the acquiring party.
  - While the board is most concerned with maximizing shareholder value through increasing the number of bidders, the management team may prefer having its own bid succeed.
  - As a member of the buyout group, management can participate in the future upside potential of the company through an equity rollover in the transaction, but other shareholders cannot participate when they sell their shares.
- Goldman's role in the transaction also presents potential concerns.
  - The firm stands to earn large fees through its role as the advisor and also as the lead loan arranger on the transaction. It would also potentially achieve significant gains in its investment in Kinder.
- Because the offer was already announced and there were no other buyers that had already performed the amount of diligence that Goldman and the management team had completed, initiating an auction for competing bids was risky. If Kinder started an auction but no interested parties come forward, the special committee's ability to negotiate with the buyout group could be hindered.

**Outcome:**
- Morgan Stanley and Blackstone contacted 35 parties, but none were interested in putting in a competing bid. The board was very unhappy with how Goldman and management developed the transaction, but they were able to leverage that displeasure in a negotiation for a higher offer price of $107.50/share, which shareholders ultimately approved. The deal closed on May 30, 2007.

Source: Press reports

**EXHIBIT 16.8**

Teaming up with management can potentially trigger a target's takeover defenses, including poison pills, if management owns more than 15% of the target's stock. Another problem that can arise relates to disclosure. Pre-signing arrangements with management might require mandatory early disclosure of the transaction, based on Section 13(d) of the Securities Exchange Act. Counsel for the target must determine whether pre-announced disclosure is required if the private equity fund neither enters into a pre-signing voting agreement with management nor holds equity in the target.

Public company acquisitions are normally either structured as a one-step merger or as a tender offer followed by a back-end merger. However, tender offers have become rare for transactions that include management participation, because according to U.S. securities laws, the bidder in a tender offer is required to pay all of the holders of the target's stock the highest price paid to any single holder. Since private equity transactions that include management participation usually involve negotiation at an early stage regarding employment agreements, rollover equity, and post-closing option grants, the issue arises whether these arrangements run afoul of securities laws that require a common price paid to all holders of equity.

When the management of a company approaches a private equity fund to team up on a buyout, and management assumes the leading role in orchestrating a going private transaction, this is called a management buyout (MBO). The same issues just described apply to an MBO. However, there are even more issues that complicate the transaction, because management's horizon for the investment is usually longer than for a private equity firm and return objectives may be different as well.

## Leveraged Recapitalizations

A leveraged recapitalization of a private equity fund portfolio company involves the issuance of debt by the company some time after the acquisition is completed, with the proceeds of the debt transaction used to fund a large cash dividend to the private equity owner. This action increases risks for the portfolio company by adding debt, but enhances the returns for the private equity fund. Although the providers of debt in a leveraged recapitalization are undertaking considerable risk, they are generally paid for this incremental risk through high interest payments and fees. However, the new debt can cause the value of outstanding debt to decline as the company's risk profile increases. The other stakeholders that can be harmed by leveraged recapitalizations are employees and communities. If the increased leverage results in destabilization of the company because of inability to meet interest and principal payment obligations, employees can lose their jobs (and, potentially, their pensions) and communities can lose their tax base if the company is dissolved through a bankruptcy process.

A notable example of a leveraged recapitalization occurred during late 2005 when Hertz, the car rental company, was purchased from Ford Motor Co. in a $15 billion buyout by Clayton, Dubilier & Rice, Merrill Lynch Global Private Equity, and The Carlyle Group. The private equity firms invested $2.3 billion, with the balance funded by debt. Six months after the deal was completed, Hertz borrowed $1 billion and used this cash to pay a dividend to the private equity investors, reducing their exposure by almost half. These firms then completed an IPO of Hertz at the end of 2006, resulting in a significant gain for a holding period that amounted to approximately one year (see Exhibit 16.9).

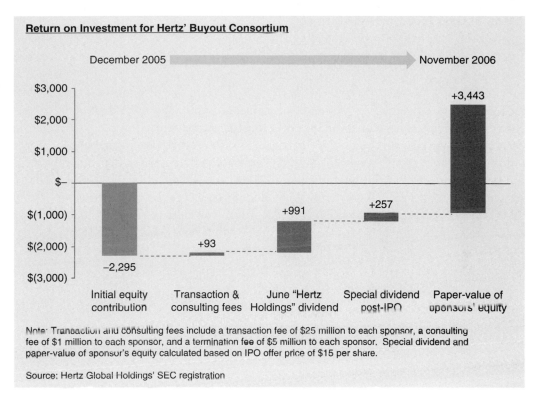

**Return on Investment for Hertz' Buyout Consortium**

December 2005 ⟶ November 2006

Note: Transaction and consulting fees include a transaction fee of $25 million to each sponsor, a consulting fee of $1 million to each sponsor, and a termination fee of $5 million to each sponsor. Special dividend and paper-value of sponsor's equity calculated based on IPO offer price of $15 per share.

Source: Hertz Global Holdings' SEC registration

EXHIBIT 16.9

# Secondary Markets for Private Equity

A secondary market has developed for private equity as banks and other financial institutions attempt to sell their private equity investments to reduce the volatility of earnings and rebalance portfolios. In addition, individuals and institutional investors are also sellers of limited partnership interests in private equity funds. Secondary market sales fall into one of two categories: the seller transfers a limited partnership interest in an existing private equity fund that continues its existence undisturbed by the transfer, or the seller transfers a portfolio of private equity investments in operating companies. Sellers of private equity investments sell both their investments in a fund and also their remaining unfunded commitments to the fund. In most cases, the consent of the general partner is required in order to transfer a partnership interest. The principal tax issue in a secondary transfer is determining whether the transfer will cause the fund to become a *publicly traded partnership* that is taxable as a corporation. This can generally be avoided if an exchange is not used and if there are a limited number of partners that remain invested.

Sellers come principally from three different groups: distressed parties such as large banks and insurance companies that need to sell assets to raise cash; quasi-distressed investors such as funds of funds, hedge funds, and other direct investors that are no longer self-funding when private equity distributions stop; and other non-distressed sellers including endowments, whose long-term view of the private equity market changes. The principal buyers include specialist funds that raise pools of capital to take advantage of favorable pricing, including funds set up by Goldman Sachs, Credit Suisse, Coller Capital, and Pomona Capital. Other leading secondary investment firms include Lexington Partners, AXA Private Equity, HarbourVest Partners, Partners Group, J.P. Morgan, and Morgan Stanley.

## Fund of Funds

A private equity fund of funds consolidates investments from many individual and institutional investors to make investments in a number of different private equity funds. This enables investors to access certain private equity fund managers that they otherwise may not be able to invest with, diversifies their private equity investment portfolio, and augments their due diligence process in an effort to invest in high-quality funds that have a high probability of achieving their investment objectives. Private equity fund of funds represent the largest portion of committed capital in the private equity market. The largest private equity fund of funds include AlpInvest Partners, AXA Private Equity, Goldman Sachs, and Credit Suisse (see Exhibit 16.10).

**Top Private Equity Fund of Funds**

| Top 10 Private Equity Fund of Funds (Ranking as of August 2009) | | |
| --- | --- | --- |
| Company | Committed Capital | Headquarters |
| AlpInvest Partners | $57.0 billion | Netherlands |
| AIG Investments | $29.0 billion | U.S. |
| AXA Private Equity | $25.0 billion | France |
| Goldman Sachs Private Equity | $24.0 billion | U.S. |
| Credit Suisse Customized Fund Investment Group | $24.0 billion | U.S. |
| Pantheon Ventures | $23.1 billion | U.K. |
| Pathway Capital Management | $20.6 billion | U.S. |
| Adams Street Partners | $20.0 billion | U.S. |
| Capital Dynamics | $20.0 billion | Switzerland |
| NB Alternatives | $19.0 billion | U.S. |

Source: Preqin

**EXHIBIT 16.10**

## Private Equity Goes Public

Both The Blackstone Group and Fortress Management Group completed IPOs during 2007, listing shares for their management companies on the New York Stock Exchange. Blackstone raised $7.3 billion and Fortress raised $2.2 billion. Since these offerings, both firms' share price dropped significantly (see Exhibit 16.11). Apollo Management completed a listing of a closed-end debt fund on NASDAQ during 2004, raising $2.2 billion, and then completed a listing for a feeder to its U.S.-based fund on Euronext during 2006, raising $1.6 billion. Also during 2006, KKR completed a listing for a feeder to its U.S.-based fund on Euronext, raising $3.9 billion. Although several

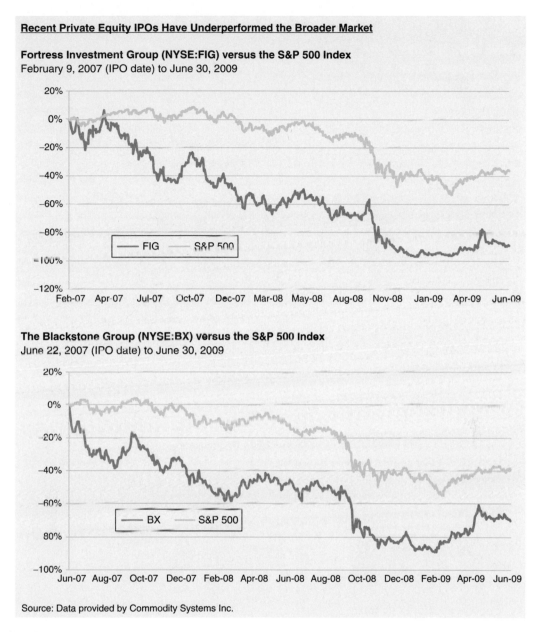

**Recent Private Equity IPOs Have Underperformed the Broader Market**

**Fortress Investment Group (NYSE:FIG) versus the S&P 500 Index**
February 9, 2007 (IPO date) to June 30, 2009

**The Blackstone Group (NYSE:BX) versus the S&P 500 Index**
June 22, 2007 (IPO date) to June 30, 2009

Source: Data provided by Commodity Systems Inc.

**EXHIBIT 16.11**

other firms, including KKR, attempted to issue IPOs in the United States for their management companies during 2007 and 2008, market conditions forced these firms to abort their efforts.

In July 2009, as the markets stabilized and KKR returned to profitability, the firm resumed its attempt to go public via a reverse merger with KKR Private Equity Investors (K.P.E.), its Euronext-listed affiliate. Under terms of the transaction, KKR will own 70% of the combined business while K.P.E. investors will own the remaining 30%, and the fund has the right to switch its listing to the NYSE.

# Impact of Financial Services Meltdown on Private Equity

From 2002 through 2005, LBO activity boomed, but leverage levels and acquisition multiples remained reasonable. Most deals completed during this period have provided or will provide strong returns for their investors (see Exhibit 16.12). From 2006 through mid-2007, a bubble developed in the private equity market, with debt and acquisition multiples rising above historical norms. Some of the deals completed during this period will experience difficulties and produce lower returns (see Exhibit 16.13). Following mid-2007, after the credit crisis hit, many deals experienced significant problems. Investment banks could not syndicate LBO debt, creating a backlog of around $390 billion. Many transactions were pulled and others were renegotiated (see Exhibit 16.14). In addition, a significant number of transactions became the subject of large lawsuits (see Exhibit 16.15). As a result, the nature and structure of private equity transactions changed: smaller in size, more equity contribution, less favorable debt terms, lower number of transactions, less debt-dependant transactions, more co-investments with corporate partners, and longer holding periods (see Exhibits 16.16 to 16.22). The result of these changes going forward may be lower investment returns and lower risk transactions, with lower amounts of capital committed to this asset class (see Exhibit 16.23). However, in spite of these significant changes, the private equity market may flourish in the future if quality investments are made at historically low prices, since the vintage year of investment has always been the principal driver of returns in the private equity industry.

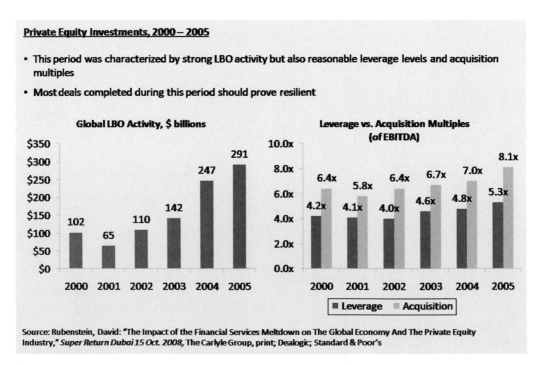

EXHIBIT 16.12

**Private Equity Investments, 2006 – 1H 2007**

- A bubble developed in the private equity market during this period, with leverage and acquisition multiples rising considerably above historical norms

- As a result, some companies acquired during this period may experience financial difficulties

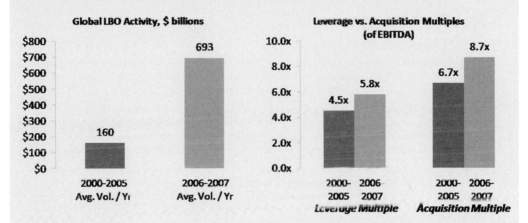

Source: Rubenstein, David: "The Impact of the Financial Services Meltdown on The Global Economy And The Private Equity Industry," *Super Return Dubai 15 Oct. 2008,* The Carlyle Group, print; Dealogic; Standard & Poor's; Morgan Stanley Financial Sponsors Group

EXHIBIT 16.13

**Private Equity Investments Post-Mid 2007: Busted and Restructured Deals**

- Many deals experienced difficulty in closing after the onset of the credit crisis

- Investment banks were unable to syndicate LBO debt, which led to a significant $389 billion debt backlog

- As a result, many deals were pulled ("busted") while others were renegotiated on more favorable terms to the buyers and lenders

| Busted Deals | | Restructured Deals | |
|---|---|---|---|
| Company | Value | Company | Value |
| Sallie Mae | $25.5 billion | Clear Channel Communications | $27.3 billion |
| Huntsman Corp | $10.6 billion | First Data | $26.3 billion |
| Harman International | $8.2 billion | Harrah's Entertainment | $26.2 billion |
| Affiliated Computer Services | $8.0 billion | Biomet | $11.4 billion |
| Alliance Data | $7.8 billion | HD Supply | $8.5 billion |
| Penn National Gaming | $6.1 billion | Thompson Learning | $7.8 billion |

Source: Rubenstein, David: "The Impact of the Financial Services Meltdown on The Global Economy And The Private Equity Industry," *Super Return Dubai 15 Oct. 2008,* The Carlyle Group, print; Morgan Stanley Financial Sponsors Group

EXHIBIT 16.14

**Huntsman vs. Apollo – the Aftermath of a Collapsed Private Equity Transaction**

- May 2007 – Huntsman puts itself up for sale, contacting, among others, Apollo-owned Hexion Specialty Chemicals and Basell, a subsidiary of Access Industries.

- June 2007 – Huntsman signs a merger agreement with the Dutch chemical company Basell for $25.25/share, with a $200 million termination fee.

- July 2007 – After increasingly higher offers from Hexion, Huntsman finally agrees at $28/share to go with Apollo/Hexion, with a $325 million deal termination fee. The higher offer is made in spite of greater closing risks due to a longer anticipated regulatory approval process, especially given the deteriorating credit environment.

- May 2008 – Huntsman reports Q1 2008 profits were down by 31%.

- June 2008 – Hexion is informed by its financial advisors that based on the new financials, the merged entity would not be solvent. Hexion subsequently sues Huntsman, claiming it has met the requisite conditions for terminating the deal without incurring the $325 million termination fee.

- June 2008 – Huntsman countersues Hexion's parent, Apollo Management, as well two of the private equity firm's founders, Leon Black and Josh Harris, for pursuing "a strategy designed to cause [Huntsman] to terminate with Basell and accept promises [Apollo] never intended to keep." In the suit with Apollo, Huntsman seeks $3 billion in damages and $100 million to cover its half of the Basell breakup fee.

- September 2008 – A Delaware judge issues an opinion that refuses to allow Apollo/Hexion from walking away from the deal and orders them to use best efforts to close the deal at the original $28/share offer price (or pay the $325 million breakup fee to walk away). The judge believed that deteriorating financial performance did not qualify as a material adverse effect.

- December 2008 – Huntsman agrees to settle with Apollo for $1 billion in payments:

  - $325 million breakup fee (Hexion has commitments from the original lenders of the deal, Deutsche Bank and Credit Suisse, to fund the fee).

  - $425 million in cash payments from Apollo's affiliates.

  - $250 million payment from Apollo affiliates in exchange for 10-year convertible notes of Huntsman.

  - Huntsman sues Deutsche Bank and Credit Suisse for withdrawing their commitment to finance the deal and conspiring with Apollo to interfere with Huntsman's prior pact with Basell.

- June 2009 – Huntsman reaches agreement with Deutsche Bank and Credit Suisse for the banks to pay $632 million in cash and provide $1.1 billion in loans to resolve their dispute. Following announcement, Huntsman's share price dropped to $5, less than one fifth the original $28 offer price from Apollo/Hexion.

Source: Press reports

**EXHIBIT 16.15**

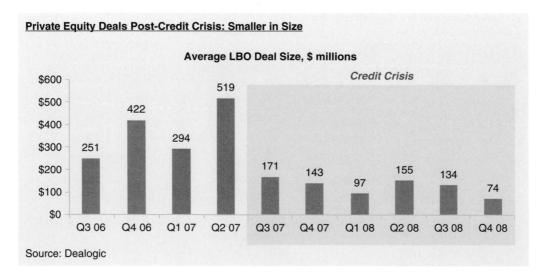

**Private Equity Deals Post-Credit Crisis: Smaller in Size**

Average LBO Deal Size, $ millions

Source: Dealogic

**EXHIBIT 16.16**

**Private Equity Deals Post-Credit Crisis: More Equity and Less Debt**

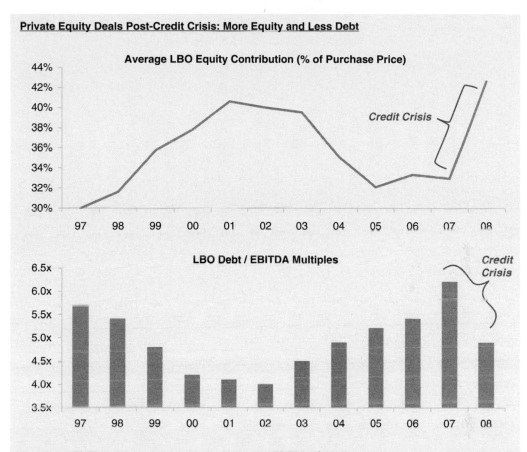

**Average LBO Equity Contribution (% of Purchase Price)**

*Credit Crisis*

**LBO Debt / EBITDA Multiples**

*Credit Crisis*

Note: Debt / EBITDA multiples shown for deals with adjusted EBITDA > $50 million
Source: Rubenstein, David: "The Impact of the Financial Services Meltdown on The Global Economy And The Private Equity Industry," *Super Return Dubai 15 Oct 2008*, The Carlyle Group, print; Dealogic

**EXHIBIT 16.17**

**Private Equity Deals Post-Credit Crisis: More Expensive Debt**

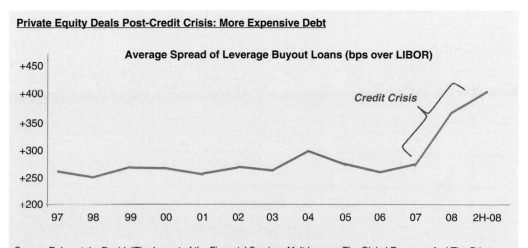

**Average Spread of Leverage Buyout Loans (bps over LIBOR)**

*Credit Crisis*

Source: Rubenstein, David: "The Impact of the Financial Services Meltdown on The Global Economy And The Private Equity Industry," *Super Return Dubai 15 Oct 2008*, The Carlyle Group, print; Dealogic

**EXHIBIT 16.18**

**Private Equity Deals Post-Credit Crisis: Fewer Deals**

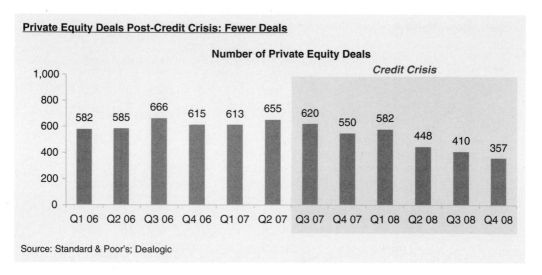

Source: Standard & Poor's; Dealogic

**EXHIBIT 16.19**

**Private Equity Deals Post-Credit Crisis: Less Debt-Dependent**

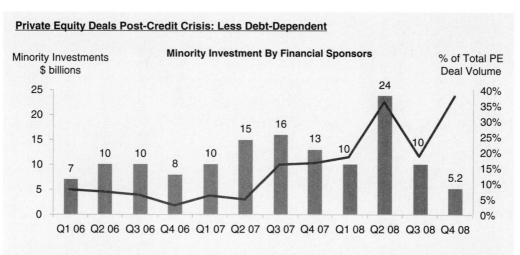

Source: Rubenstein, David: "The Impact of the Financial Services Meltdown on The Global Economy And The Private Equity Industry," *Super Return Dubai 15 Oct 2008,* The Carlyle Group, print; Dealogic

**EXHIBIT 16.20**

**Private Equity Deals Post-Credit Crisis: Additional Trends**

- Private equity firms are increasingly investing alongside corporate partners or sovereign wealth funds.
  - Ex: Blackstone, Bain Capital and NBC Universal teamed up in 2008 for the $3.5 billion joint acquisition of the Weather Channel.
- Investment holding periods are becoming longer as private equity firms spend more time building value by improving the operational performance of their portfolio companies.
  - Many exits will by delayed in order to create targeted exit values.

Source: Rubenstein, David: "The Impact of the Financial Services Meltdown on The Global Economy And The Private Equity Industry," Super Return Dubai 15 Oct. 2008, The Carlyle Group, print

**EXHIBIT 16.21**

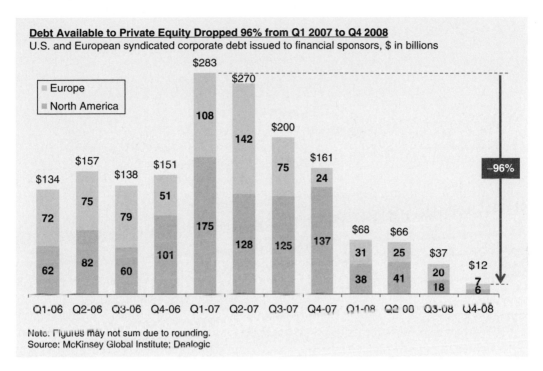

**Debt Available to Private Equity Dropped 96% from Q1 2007 to Q4 2008**
U.S. and European syndicated corporate debt issued to financial sponsors, $ in billions

Note: Figures may not sum due to rounding.
Source: McKinsey Global Institute; Dealogic

**EXHIBIT 16.22**

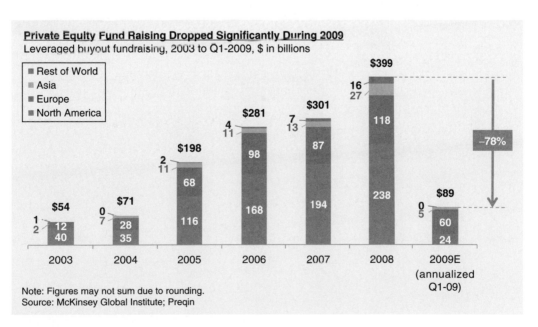

**Private Equity Fund Raising Dropped Significantly During 2009**
Leveraged buyout fundraising, 2003 to Q1-2009, $ in billions

Note: Figures may not sum due to rounding.
Source: McKinsey Global Institute; Preqin

**EXHIBIT 16.23**

## Questions

1. Are private equity firms financial buyers or strategic buyers and why? Which type of buyer should generally be able to pay more in an M&A auction and why? Why might that not always be the case?

2. Provide two examples: one of a publicly traded company that would be a good LBO target, and one that would not be an ideal candidate. Explain your choices.

3. What type of management is generally needed to run a portfolio company owned by a private equity firm? Describe the characteristics of these managers.

4. What are the five principal financing sources for an LBO transaction?

5. How is the commitment and redemption of capital different in private equity compared to hedge funds?

6. Why would a proposal to eliminate the tax benefits of carried interest (performance fees) have a greater impact on the private equity industry?

7. Why are general partners typically only allowed to make investments in new companies during the first 5 years of a fund's life?

8. Suppose a private equity fund has $100 million in committed capital and its base rate for management fees is 2%. The fund invested in 10 companies during the first 5 years and begins to exit its investments in year 6 at a pace of two exits per year until the end of year 10, when all investments have been exited. Assume the original cost basis for each investment is $10 million. Also assume fees calculated on net invested capital is based on year-end balances. How much in lifetime management fees does the firm earn, based on each of the four methods described in Exhibit 16.2?

9. What type of concessions were private equity firms able to get from investment banks during 2006 and the first half of 2007 that normally would not be possible?

10. When a private equity fund teams up with management for a potential buyout, why would they want to avoid having early disclosure of the transaction?

11. Why do you think more companies do not recapitalize their balance sheets by adding more debt in order to replicate the returns achieved by private equity fund portfolio companies? Do investment banks ever recommend a leveraged recapitalization of public companies? Why or why not?

12. Since private equity firms seek to minimize their equity contribution in a deal in order to maximize returns, the amount of debt used to finance transactions should (wishing away financial risk) be the maximum amount of leverage for the company that debt providers will accept. Why, then, are these companies allowed to take on even more debt for leveraged recapitalizations?

# ::: 17
# LBO Financial Model

The material in this chapter should be cross-referenced with **Case Study 9, "The Toys 'R' Us LBO."**

As previously discussed, targets for LBO transactions are typically companies in mature industries that have stable and growing cash flow that can be used to service large debt obligations and, potentially, pay dividends to the financial buyers. In addition, targets usually have low capital expenditures, low leverage, and assets that can be sold. Financial buyers generally target an exit event within 3 to 7 years, which is usually accomplished through either an IPO or M&A sale to a strategic buyer or, sometimes, to another financial buyer. Financial buyers have historically targeted an IRR on their investments of above 20%. The possibility of achieving a high return is augmented by purchasing a company at the lowest possible price using the maximum amount of sustainable leverage that is available and, correspondingly, minimizing the equity contribution.

Management of the target company will be asked to grow the company's market share and improve margins, creating growth in free cash flow. Sometimes, as a result of operating improvements, the company can achieve an enterprise value/EBITDA multiple expansion (see Chapter 4), but this is unusual. To realize a target IRR return for a private equity investor, the company must grow cash flow in order to pay down debt over the holding period (resulting in an increase in equity), and then a sale must be accomplished in the future at a multiple of the increased cash flow level (see Exhibit 17.1). Exhibit 17.2 shows three potential ways to achieve IRR returns by deleveraging, improving margins, or through multiple expansion.

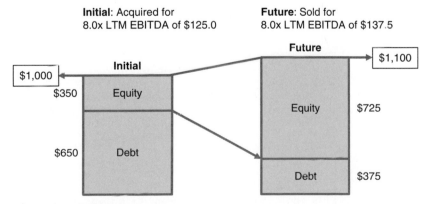

**LBO Objective: Pay Down Debt During Holding Period**

**Initial**: Acquired for 8.0x LTM EBITDA of $125.0

**Future**: Sold for 8.0x LTM EBITDA of $137.5

Source: Training the Street, Inc.

**EXHIBIT 17.1**

An Introduction to Investment Banks, Hedge Funds, and Private Equity

**LBO: Three Ways to Create Returns**

Assume the Target company was acquired for 8.0x LTM EBITDA of $125.0

| | 1. Deleveraging | 2. Deleverage & Improve Margins | 3. Deleverage, Improve Margins & Multiple Expansion |
|---|---|---|---|
| **Sources of Funds** | | | |
| Total Debt | $650.0 | $650.0 | $650.0 |
| Total Equity | 350.0 | 350.0 | 350.0 |
| Total | $1,000.0 | $1,000.0 | $1,000.0 |
| | | | |
| **Year 5 Assumptions** | | | |
| Cumulative Excess Cash to Repay Debt | $167.6 | $212.3 | $212.3 |
| Projected EBITDA | 125.0 | 164.5 | 164.5 |
| Assumed Exit Multiple | 8.0x | 8.0x | 9.0x |
| Transaction Value | 1,000.0 | 1,316.0 | 1,480.5 |
| +/- Net Debt[1] | (482.4) | (437.7) | (437.7) |
| Equity Value | $517.6 | $878.2 | $1,042.8 |
| | | | |
| **IRR Returns (5-Yr Exit)** | 8.1% | 20.2% | 24.4% |

Note 1: Total Debt – Cumulative Excess Cash to Repay Debt = Net Debt
Source: Training the Street, Inc.

**EXHIBIT 17.2**

An LBO analysis includes cash flow projections, terminal value projections (the price at which a financial buyer thinks the company can be sold in 3 to 7 years), present value determination (the price that a financial buyer will pay for a company today), and the analysis solves for the IRR of the investment (the discount rate applied). LBO models require an assumption of a minimum IRR required by financial buyers, based on risks associated with the investment and market conditions. The model solves for the purchase price that creates this targeted IRR. Basically, the LBO analysis answers the question: What is the highest purchase price that can be paid for a company in order to earn a compound annual rate of return that meets the investor's risk-adjusted return requirement?

The LBO analysis considers whether there is enough projected cash flow to operate the company and also pay debt principal and interest payments. In addition, the analysis determines if there is sufficient cash flow to pay dividends at some point to the private equity investor. An ability to retire debt and pay dividends results in a higher IRR.

## Determining Cash Flow Available for Debt Service and Debt Sources

The starting point in an LBO analysis is to determine the cash flow available to service a target company's future debt obligations. This can be done by increasing net income by adding depreciation and amortization and then either increasing it further (or decreasing it) by changes in deferred taxes, other non-cash charges, and changes in net working capital. The result is cash flow from operations, which should be reduced by capital expenditures to create cash flow available for debt service (see Exhibit 17.3). When cash flow available for debt service has been calculated, the total debt available to purchase the target can be determined through discussion with investment bankers who will advise regarding the market's tolerance for debt, given the cash flow and risk characteristics of the target company and the target company's industry (see Exhibit 17.4). Bankers and their financial sponsor clients sometimes scale back the amount of debt they attempt to secure if associated risks seem too high. When the maximum appropriate amount of debt to finance an acquisition is determined, investment bankers and the financial sponsor can then determine the sources of debt, which include senior credit facilities, second lien loans, high-yield debt, and mezzanine financing (see Exhibits 17.5 and 17.6).

## Determining Financial Sponsor IRR

The next step in an LBO analysis is to calculate the IRR. This is done by determining the equity portion of the purchase price, dividend payments to be made, if any, during the investment horizon, and the expected market value of the equity on the exit date. Usually, a range of purchase

**Determining Cash Flow Available for Debt Service**

|   | Net Income |
|---|---|
| + | Depreciation and amortization |
| +/- | Changes in deferred taxes |
| +/- | Other non-cash changes |
| +/- | Changes in net working capital |
| = | Cash flow from operations |
| - | Capital expenditures |
| = | Cash flow available for debt service |

**EXHIBIT 17.3**

**What Determines Debt Capacity?**

| Industry Risk | Company Risk | Structural Risk |
|---|---|---|
| • Growth rate and size<br>• Cyclicality<br>• Barriers to entry<br>• Capital intensity<br>• Relative strength of suppliers and customers<br>• Rate of technological change/ threat of substitution<br>• Environmental issues<br>• Regulatory risk | • Competitive position<br>• Historical performance<br>• Achievability of projections<br>• Depth and quality of management<br>• Qualitative:<br> o Information quality<br> o Ownership support | • Quantitative<br> o Size<br> o Leverage<br> o Coverage<br>• Security (second way out)<br>• Sources of repayment<br> o Are assumptions credible?<br>• Valuation/equity cushion<br>• Comparable transactions<br>• Other successful LBOs in that industry<br>• Growth capability given leverage constraints |

Source: Training the Street, Inc.

**EXHIBIT 17.4**

**Typical Capital Structure**

- Senior credit facility
  - Revolver
  - Term loans
- Second lien loans
- High yield debt
  - Senior notes
  - Senior subordinated notes
- Mezzanine / PIK / warrants / preferred stock
- Common equity

Source: Training the Street, Inc.

**EXHIBIT 17.5**

**Common Financing Parameters**

| | |
|---|---|
| • Key Credit Statistics: | • Typical Range:[1] |
| o  Total Debt/EBITDA | o  3.5 – 5.5x |
| o  Senior Bank Debt/EBITDA | o  2.5 – 3.5x |
| o  EBITDA /Interest Coverage | o  >2.0x |
| o  EBITDA - CapEx/Interest Coverage | o  >1.6x |
| o  Bank Debt Payoff | o  6 – 8 years |
| o  Equity Contribution | o  At least 20 – 35% |

- Factors affecting credit statistics:
  - EBITDA determination
  - Maintenance versus growth in CapEx
  - Average versus peak working capital requirements
  - Off-balance sheet financing

Note 1: These ranges applied prior to the credit crisis, which started during the second half of 2007. Subsequently, market conditions worsened, resulting in lower debt ratios, higher interest coverage ratios and higher equity contribution requirements. For a few transactions during 2006 to mid-2007, Total Debt/EBITDA multiples reached 8x.

Source: Training the Street, Inc.

**EXHIBIT 17.6**

prices is considered along with a corresponding equity investment amount (which is determined after calculating the maximum debt amount available for the purchase, as described). The equity amount must, in combination with the projected cash flow and the final projected equity value on the exit date (factoring in the risks associated with cash flow and equity exit value projections) create an IRR that is acceptable to the financial sponsor. If the resulting IRR is below an acceptable level, the financial sponsor must either lower the purchase price or lower the equity contribution, while increasing the debt component of the purchase price, subject to the additional debt being accessible. In other words, this is an iterative process, which sometimes requires the financial sponsor to either reduce the minimum IRR level or give up the investment opportunity, depending on the price expectations of the target company and pricing from competing buyers. Further, the IRR accepted by the financial sponsor depends on the risk of the investment: lower-risk investments allow lower IRR requirements, and higher-risk investments require higher IRR requirements.

Ultimately, financial sponsors are focused on the profitability of an investment, its risk, and the time it takes to exit the investment. They consider the multiple of the expected equity at the time of exit relative to the initial equity invested, striking a balance between maximizing IRR and maximizing the total cash amount taken out of the investment when the exit is achieved. For example, even if an IRR of 30% is achievable after 2 years, a sponsor may choose a 25% IRR alternative based on an exit in 4 years if the "profit" of the transaction (equity value at exit − equity invested at inception = profit) is substantially higher in the 4-year exit alternative (see Exhibit 17.7). By holding the investment for 4 years, the sponsor gives up IRR but increases the multiple of investment from 1.69× to 2.44×. The IRR give-up relates principally to investor desire to remain invested based on their aversion to new risks and costs associated with redeployment of funds and financial buyer interest in achieving high multiples of investment (which creates an effective marketing metric for future fundraising).

**Comparison of IRR vs. Multiple of Investment**

| Initial Equity Invested | Investment Holding Period | IRR | Value of Equity at Exit | Profit | Multiple of Investment |
|---|---|---|---|---|---|
| $1,000 | 2 years | 30% | $1,690 | $690 | 1.69x |
| $1,000 | 4 years | 25% | $2,441 | $1,441 | 2.44x |
| $1,000 | 6 years | 20% | $2,986 | $1,986 | 2.99x |

**EXHIBIT 17.7**

# Determining Purchase Price and Sale Price

Financial sponsors generally determine a purchase price for a target based on a multiple of enterprise value to EBITDA. In consultation with investment bankers, they determine purchase price multiples that strategic buyers might apply to an acquisition, and then decide if they are able to offer a higher multiple based on their targeted IRR. (Normally, financial buyers cannot pay as high a multiple as strategic buyers because they lack synergies, but leverage can level the playing field.) The IRR, in turn, is determined based on the amount of debt financing available and the cash flow available for debt service. The decision regarding a purchase price is therefore based on an iterative process. Financial sponsors usually project a future sale price based on the same multiple used in the initial purchase price determination. Sometimes, however, a comparable company multiple is used if the ultimate sale is expected to be initiated through an IPO, or a comparable transactions multiple may be appropriate if an M&A sale is expected. In addition, the sale multiple could be increased if positive changes in the industry or in management are expected, or decreased if negative changes are expected. See Chapter 4 for a more complete discussion of valuation multiples.

# LBO Analysis Example

A simplified example of an LBO analysis is provided in the next sections, based on the acquisition of Toys "R" Us (Toys) by a consortium of buyers consisting of KKR, Bain Capital, and Vornado Realty Trust during 2005. This consortium will be referred to as "KKR."

## Forecast Revenue, Margins, D&A, CapEx, Working Capital, Interest Rate, and Tax Rate

The LBO analysis starts with a review of the target company's financial statements. See Toys financial statements in Exhibits 17.8, 17.9, and 17.10. KKR would have completed a summary similar to Exhibit 17.11 to determine historical sales growth and margins. They would have then performed due diligence to determine the likelihood that Toys would be able to continue producing similar (or better) margins and sales growth. KKR would also have completed a forecast of Toys' balance sheet, income statement, and cash flow statement for their expected investment horizon in an effort to determine cash flow projections that would be utilized to establish the future value of the company. This future value would be calculated by multiplying projected EBITDA on the date of a future sale by the expected enterprise value/EBITDA multiple that would be relevant at that time.

As part of the creation of future expected balance sheets, income statements, and cash flow statements, KKR would have made assumptions regarding growth in revenues. When these projections are made, other parts of the income statement (including cost of goods sold; selling, general, and administrative expenses; and depreciation and amortization) are expected to remain constant (or to decline slightly) as a percentage of revenues (see Exhibit 17.12).

For CapEx, it is commonly assumed that annual CapEx is equal to annual depreciation in order to keep the asset base constant.[1] However, KKR may have decided to improve Toys' asset base by increasing CapEx above depreciation, or they might have decided to decelerate CapEx, allowing Toys' asset base to reduce.

Although working capital can be set at a percentage of revenues, KKR probably calculated working capital based on individual balance sheet items, with changes in Toys' working capital resulting from the projected balance sheet (see Exhibit 17.13). Toys' FYE 2005 federal tax rate of 35% (state and local taxes might increase the tax rate to as much as 38%) was used as a base from which KKR could project future tax rates, which could be constant, increasing, or decreasing, depending on known and future expected tax developments. The interest rate assumption used for Toys was higher than the company's historical rate in order to reflect higher leverage and correspondingly higher risk to lenders (see Exhibit 17.14).

## Calculate Acquisition Multiples

On March 17, 2005, Toys announced that it had reached a definitive agreement to sell the entire company to KKR for $26.75 per share in a $7.7 billion transaction, including all transaction fees. The purchase price represented a total transaction value (enterprise value + transaction fees) that was 9.9× Toys' FYE 2005 EBITDA and an enterprise value that was 9.4× Toys' FYE 2005 EBITDA. The equity amount contributed by KKR was $1.3 billion (see Exhibits 17.15 and 17.16). KKR's purchase price was a 63% premium to Toys' share price on the day before the

---

[1]To account for inflation, however, CapEx is often projected to increase at a higher rate than depreciation so that the real value of physical capital like plant and equipment does not decline.

**Consolidated Financial Results ($ in millions, except per share data)**

|  | For the Year Ended | | |
| --- | --- | --- | --- |
|  | 2/1/2003 | 1/31/2004 | 1/29/2005 |
| Net sales | $11,305 | $11,320 | $11,100 |
| Growth |  | 0.1% | −1.9% |
| Cost of sales | (7,799) | (7,646) | (7,506) |
| Gross margin | $3,506 | $3,674 | $3,594 |
| Growth |  | 4.8% | −2.2% |
| Margin | 31.0% | 32.5% | 32.4% |
|  |  |  |  |
| SG&A | ($2,724) | ($3,026) | ($2,932) |
| Growth |  | 11.1% | −3.1% |
| Margin | −24.1% | −26.7% | −26.4% |
| Reported EBITDA (pre-restructuring charges) | $782 | $648 | $662 |
| Growth |  | −17.1% | 2.2% |
| Margin | 6.9% | 5.7% | 0.0% |
|  |  |  |  |
| D&A | ($330) | ($368) | ($354) |
| Restructuring and other charges | 0 | (03) | (4) |
| EBIT | $443 | $217 | $304 |
| Growth |  | −51.0% | 40.1% |
| Margin | 3.9% | 1.9% | 2.7% |
|  |  |  |  |
| Interest expense | ($119) | ($142) | ($130) |
| Interest and other income | 9 | 10 | 19 |
| Pretax income | 000 | $93 | $193 |
| Growth |  | −72.1% | 107.5% |
| Margin | 2.9% | 0.8% | 1.7% |
|  |  |  |  |
| Income tax (expense)/benefit | (120) | (30) | 59 |
| Net income | $213 | $63 | $252 |
| Growth |  | −70.4% | 300.0% |
| Margin | 1.9% | 0.6% | 2.3% |
|  |  |  |  |
| Diluted EPS | $1.02 | $0.29 | $1.16 |
| Growth |  | −71.6% | 300.0% |
|  |  |  |  |
| Adjusted consolidated EBITDA |  |  |  |
| Reported EBITDA (pre-restructuring charges) | $782 | $648 | $662 |
| Add-back of one-time items in Toys "R" Us—U.S.[a] | 0 | 0 | 118 |
| Adjusted consolidated EBITDA | $782 | $648 | $780 |
| Growth |  | −17.1% | 20.4% |
| Margin | 6.9% | 5.7% | 7.0% |

**EXHIBIT 17.8**

company announced it was exploring a sale of the global toy business. KKR may have decided to offer a high premium based on an analysis of comparable transactions that included acquisition premiums and because of Toys' significant real estate holdings (which KKR may have felt was not fully valued by the market). Regardless, KKR would have completed financial projections that showed growth in cash flow over their investment horizon. Multiples applied against cash

**Consolidated Balance Sheet ($ in millions)**

|  | For the Year Ended | |
| --- | --- | --- |
|  | 1/31/2004 | 1/29/2005 |
| ASSETS | | |
| Cash and cash equivalents | $1,432 | $1,250 |
| Short-term investments | 571 | 953 |
| Accounts and other receivables | 146 | 153 |
| Merchandise inventories | 2,094 | 1,884 |
| Net property assets held for sale | 163 | 7 |
| Current portion of derivative assets | 162 | 1 |
| Prepaid expenses and other current assets | 161 | 159 |
| Total current assets | $4,729 | $4,407 |
|  | | |
| Property, plant, and equipment | | |
| Real estate, net | $2,165 | $2,393 |
| Other, net | 2,274 | 1,946 |
| Total PP&E | $4,439 | $4,339 |
|  | | |
| Goodwill, net | 348 | 353 |
| Derivative assets | 77 | 43 |
| Deferred tax asset | 399 | 426 |
| Other assets | 273 | 200 |
|  | | |
| Total assets | $10,265 | $9,768 |
|  | | |
| LIABILITIES AND STOCKHOLDERS' EQUITY | | |
| Short-term borrowings | $0 | $0 |
| Accounts payable | 1,022 | 1,023 |
| Accrued expenses and other current liabilities | 866 | 881 |
| Income taxes payable | 319 | 245 |
| Current portion of long-term debt | 657 | 452 |
| Total current liabilities | $2,864 | $2,601 |
|  | | |
| Long-term debt | 2,349 | 1,860 |
| Deferred income taxes | 538 | 485 |
| Derivative liabilities | 26 | 16 |
| Deferred rent liability | 280 | 269 |
| Other liabilities | 225 | 212 |
| Minority interest in Toysrus.com | 9 | 0 |
| Total liabilities | $6,291 | $5,443 |
|  | | |
| Stockholders' equity | | |
| Common stock | $30 | $30 |
| Additional paid-in capital | 407 | 405 |
| Retained earnings | 5,308 | 5,560 |
| Accumulated other comprehensive loss | (64) | (7) |
| Restricted stock | 0 | (5) |
| Treasury shares, at cost | (1,707) | (1,658) |
| Total stockholders' equity | $3,974 | $4,325 |
|  | | |
| Total liabilities and stockholders' equity | $10,265 | $9,768 |

EXHIBIT 17.9

**Consolidated Statement of Cash Flow ($ in millions)**

| | For the Year Ended | | |
|---|---|---|---|
| | 2/1/2003 | 1/31/2004 | 1/29/2005 |
| CASH FLOWS FROM OPERATING ACTIVITIES | | | |
| Net earnings | $213 | $63 | $252 |
| | | | |
| Adjustments to reconcile net earnings to net cash from operating activities: | | | |
| Depreciation and amortization | $339 | $368 | $354 |
| Amortization of restricted stock | 0 | 0 | 7 |
| Deferred income taxes | 99 | 27 | (40) |
| Minority interest in Toysrus.com | (14) | (8) | (6) |
| Other non-cash items | (9) | 1 | 2 |
| Non-cash portion of restructuring and other charges | 0 | 63 | 4 |
| | | | |
| Changes in operating assets and liabilities: | | | |
| Accounts and other receivables | 8 | 62 | (5) |
| Merchandise inventories | (100) | 133 | 221 |
| Prepaid expenses and other operating assets | (118) | 28 | 76 |
| Accounts payable, accrued expenses, and other liabilities | 109 | 117 | (45) |
| Income taxes payable | 48 | (53) | (74) |
| Net cash provided by operating activities | $575 | $801 | $746 |
| | | | |
| CASH FLOWS FROM INVESTING ACTIVITIES | | | |
| Capital expenditures, net | ($395) | ($262) | ($269) |
| Proceeds from sale of fixed assets | 0 | 0 | 216 |
| Purchase of SB Toys, Inc. | 0 | 0 | (42) |
| Purchase of short-term investments and other | 0 | (572) | (382) |
| Net cash used in investing activities | ($395) | ($834) | ($477) |
| | | | |
| CASH FLOWS FROM FINANCING ACTIVITIES | | | |
| Short-term borrowings, net | $0 | $0 | $0 |
| Long-term borrowings | 548 | 792 | 0 |
| Long-term debt repayment | (141) | (370) | (503) |
| Decrease/(increase) in restricted cash | (60) | 60 | 0 |
| Proceeds from issuance of stock and contracts to purchase stock | 266 | 0 | 0 |
| Proceeds from exercise of stock options | 0 | 0 | 27 |
| Net cash (used in)/provided by financing activities | $613 | $482 | ($476) |
| | | | |
| Effect of exchange rate changes on cash and cash equivalents | ($53) | ($40) | $25 |
| | | | |
| CASH AND CASH EQUIVALENTS | | | |
| (Decrease)/increase during year | $740 | $409 | ($182) |
| Beginning of year | 283 | 1,023 | 1,432 |
| End of year | $1,023 | $1,432 | $1,250 |

**EXHIBIT 17.10**

flow on the projected future sale date would create a final equity amount, which when compared with the initial KKR equity contribution, would result in an IRR that was acceptable to KKR.

## Determine Target's Capitalization after Acquisition

Post-acquisition, Toys had a capitalization of (a) $2.3 billion of assumed existing debt plus $4.4 billion of new debt for a total of $6.7 billion in debt (see Exhibit 17.17); and (b) $1.3 billion of

**Financial Performance by Segment ($ in millions)**

| | 2/1/2003 | % of Total | 1/31/2004 | % of Total | 1/29/2005 | % of Total | 2/1/2003 | 1/31/2004 | 1/29/2005 |
|---|---|---|---|---|---|---|---|---|---|
| | For the Year Ended | | | | | | For the Year Ended | | |
| NET SALES BY SEGMENT | | | | | | | GROWTH BY SEGMENT (%) | | |
| Toys "R" Us—U.S. | $6,755 | 59.8 | $6,326 | 55.9 | $6,104 | 55.0 | | −6.4 | −3.5 |
| Toys "R" Us—International | 2,161 | 19.1 | 2,470 | 21.8 | 2,739 | 24.7 | | 14.3 | 10.9 |
| Babies "R" Us | 1,595 | 14.1 | 1,738 | 15.4 | 1,863 | 16.8 | | 9.0 | 7.2 |
| Toysrus.com | 340 | 3.0 | 371 | 3.3 | 366 | 3.3 | | 9.1 | −1.3 |
| Kids "R" Us | 454 | 4.0 | 415 | 3.7 | 28 | 0.3 | | −8.6 | −93.3 |
| Consolidated net sales | $11,305 | 100.0 | $11,320 | 100.0 | $11,100 | 100.0 | | 0.1 | −1.9 |
| | | | | | | | | | |
| OPERATING EARNINGS BY SEGMENT | | | | | | | MARGIN BY SEGMENT (%) | | |
| Toys "R" Us—U.S. | $256 | 49.4 | $70 | 20.4 | $4 | 0.9 | 3.8 | 1.1 | 0.1 |
| Toys "R" Us—International | 158 | 30.5 | 166 | 48.4 | 220 | 51.9 | 7.3 | 6.7 | 8.0 |
| Babies "R" Us | 169 | 32.6 | 192 | 56.0 | 224 | 52.8 | 10.6 | 11.0 | 12.0 |
| Toysrus.com | (37) | −7.1 | (18) | −5.2 | 1 | 0.2 | −10.9 | −4.9 | 0.3 |
| Kids "R" Us[1] | (28) | −5.4 | (67) | −19.5 | (25) | −5.9 | −6.2 | −16.1 | −89.3 |
| Segment operating earnings | $518 | 100.0 | $343 | 100.0 | $424 | 100.0 | 4.6 | 3.0 | 3.8 |
| Corporate/other expenses[2] | (75) | | (63) | | (116) | | | | |
| Restructuring charges | 0 | | (63) | | (4) | | | | |
| Reported operating earnings | $443 | | $217 | | $304 | | 3.9 | 1.9 | 2.7 |
| | | | | | | | | | |
| ADJUSTED EBITDA BY SEGMENT | | | | | | | MARGIN BY SEGMENT (%) | | |
| Toys "R" Us—U.S.[3] | $447 | 55.1 | $264 | 39.3 | $322 | 37.4 | 6.6 | 4.2 | 5.3 |
| Toys "R" Us—International | 210 | 25.9 | 227 | 33.8 | 295 | 34.3 | 9.7 | 9.2 | 10.8 |
| Babies "R" Us | 197 | 24.3 | 223 | 33.2 | 262 | 30.5 | 12.4 | 12.8 | 14.1 |
| Toysrus.com | (33) | −4.1 | (16) | −2.4 | 1 | 0.1 | −9.7 | −4.3 | 0.3 |
| Kids "R" Us[1] | (10) | −1.2 | (27) | −4.0 | (20) | −2.3 | −2.2 | −6.5 | −71.4 |
| Adjusted segment EBITDA | $811 | 100.0 | $671 | 100.0 | $860 | 100.0 | 7.2 | 5.9 | 7.7 |
| Corporate/other expenses[2] | (75) | | (63) | | (116) | | | | |
| Add-back: other D&A | 46 | | 40 | | 36 | | | | |
| Consolidated adjusted EBITDA | $782 | | $648 | | $780 | | 6.9 | 5.7 | 7.0 |

Note 1: Includes markdowns of $49 million and accelerated depreciation of $24 million in 2003 related to the closing of all stores.

Note 2: Includes corporate expenses, the operating results of Toy Box, and the equity in net earnings of Toys "R" Us—Japan. Increase in amount is due to our strategic review expenses and Sarbanes-Oxley Section 404 compliance totaling $29 million. In addition, we incurred charges of $8 million relating to our 2004 restructuring of the Company's corporate headquarters operations, and a $19 million increase in incentive compensation costs.

Note 3: EBITDA for FY 2005 adjusted by adding back $132 million in inventory markdowns and excluding $14 million related to a lawsuit settlement—$118 million net add-back in FY 2005.

Source: Toys "R" Us FYE 2005 10-K Filing

**EXHIBIT 17.11**

### Income Statement

($ in millions)

**Base Case**

| For the FYE January 31 | Actual | | | Projected | | | | | | | | | |
|---|---|---|---|---|---|---|---|---|---|---|---|---|---|
| | 2003 | 2004 | 2005 | 2006 | 2007 | 2008 | 2009 | 2010 | 2011 | 2012 | 2013 | 2014 | 2015 |
| Consolidated Net Sales | $11,305.0 | $11,320.0 | $11,100.0 | $10,875.2 | $10,456.3 | $10,405.8 | $10,741.8 | $11,140.9 | $11,554.9 | $11,984.2 | $12,429.4 | $12,891.2 | $13,370.2 |
| Growth | | 0.1% | −1.9% | −2.0% | −3.9% | −0.5% | 3.2% | 3.7% | 3.7% | 3.7% | 3.7% | 3.7% | 3.7% |
| COGS & SG&A by Segment | $10,494.0 | $10,649.0 | $10,240.0 | $9,986.4 | $9,569.5 | $9,501.9 | $9,799.4 | $10,155.5 | $10,532.8 | $10,924.1 | $11,330.0 | $11,750.9 | $12,187.5 |
| Margin | 92.8% | 94.1% | 92.3% | 91.8% | 91.5% | 91.3% | 91.2% | 91.2% | 91.2% | 91.2% | 91.2% | 91.2% | 91.2% |
| EBITDA by Segment | $811.0 | $671.0 | $860.0 | $888.7 | $886.9 | $903.9 | $942.5 | $985.5 | $1,022.1 | $1,060.1 | $1,099.4 | $1,140.3 | $1,182.7 |
| Margin | 7.2% | 5.9% | 7.7% | 8.2% | 8.5% | 8.7% | 8.8% | 8.8% | 8.8% | 8.8% | 8.8% | 8.8% | 8.8% |
| Corporate / Other Expenses | 29.0 | 23.0 | 80.0 | 27.9 | 26.8 | 26.7 | 27.6 | 28.6 | 29.6 | 30.7 | 31.9 | 33.1 | 34.3 |
| Margin | 0.3% | 0.2% | 0.7% | 0.3% | 0.3% | 0.3% | 0.3% | 0.3% | 0.3% | 0.3% | 0.3% | 0.3% | 0.3% |
| Consolidated EBITDA | $782.0 | $648.0 | $780.0 | $860.8 | $860.0 | $877.2 | $914.9 | $956.9 | $992.4 | $1,029.3 | $1,067.6 | $1,107.2 | $1,148.4 |
| Growth | | −17.1% | 20.4% | 10.4% | −0.1% | 2.0% | 4.3% | 4.6% | 3.7% | 3.7% | 3.7% | 3.7% | 3.7% |
| Margin | 6.9% | 5.7% | 7.0% | 7.9% | 8.2% | 8.4% | 8.5% | 8.6% | 8.6% | 8.6% | 8.6% | 8.6% | 8.6% |
| D&A by Segment | 293.0 | 328.0 | 318.0 | 304.4 | 288.5 | 284.6 | 293.2 | 303.8 | 315.1 | 326.8 | 339.0 | 351.5 | 364.6 |
| Margin | 2.6% | 2.9% | 2.9% | 2.8% | 2.8% | 2.7% | 2.7% | 2.7% | 2.7% | 2.7% | 2.7% | 2.7% | 2.7% |
| Other D&A | 46.0 | 40.0 | 36.0 | 35.3 | 33.9 | 33.7 | 34.8 | 36.1 | 37.5 | 38.9 | 40.3 | 41.8 | 43.4 |
| Margin | 0.4% | 0.4% | 0.3% | 0.3% | 0.3% | 0.3% | 0.3% | 0.3% | 0.3% | 0.3% | 0.3% | 0.3% | 0.3% |
| Restructuring Charges | 0.0 | 63.0 | 4.0 | 0.0 | 0.0 | 0.0 | 0.0 | 0.0 | 0.0 | 0.0 | 0.0 | 0.0 | 0.0 |
| Consolidated EBIT | $443.0 | $217.0 | $422.0 | $521.1 | $537.6 | $558.9 | $586.8 | $616.9 | $639.9 | $663.6 | $688.3 | $713.9 | $740.4 |
| Growth | | −51.0% | 94.5% | 23.5% | 3.2% | 4.0% | 5.0% | 5.1% | 3.7% | 3.7% | 3.7% | 3.7% | 3.7% |
| Margin | 3.9% | 1.9% | 3.8% | 4.8% | 5.1% | 5.4% | 5.5% | 5.5% | 5.5% | 5.5% | 5.5% | 5.5% | 5.5% |
| Interest Expense | | | | | | | | | | | | | |
| Assumed Debt | | | | $139.0 | $116.8 | $100.3 | $88.2 | $74.1 | $57.8 | $39.4 | $18.7 | $3.9 | $0.0 |
| Senior Secured Credit Facility | | | | 47.3 | 50.8 | 54.3 | 57.8 | 61.3 | 64.8 | 66.5 | 66.5 | 54.5 | 22.5 |
| Unsecured Bridge Loan | | | | 209.0 | 209.0 | 209.0 | 209.0 | 209.0 | 209.0 | 209.0 | 209.0 | 209.0 | 209.0 |
| Secured European Bridge Loan | | | | 90.0 | 90.0 | 90.0 | 90.0 | 90.0 | 90.0 | 90.0 | 90.0 | 90.0 | 90.0 |
| Mortgage Loan Agreements | | | | 64.0 | 64.0 | 64.0 | 64.0 | 64.0 | 64.0 | 64.0 | 64.0 | 64.0 | 64.0 |
| Total Interest Expense | | | | $549.2 | $530.5 | $517.5 | $509.0 | $498.3 | $485.6 | $468.9 | $448.2 | $421.4 | $385.5 |
| Interest Income on Cash Balance | | | | 40.5 | 46.8 | 53.0 | 59.2 | 65.5 | 71.7 | 77.9 | 77.9 | 77.9 | 77.9 |
| Pre-Tax Income | | | | $12.4 | $53.9 | $94.3 | $137.1 | $184.1 | $226.0 | $272.7 | $318.0 | $370.4 | $432.8 |
| Use of NOLs | | | | 0.0 | 0.0 | 0.0 | 0.0 | 0.0 | 0.0 | 0.0 | 0.0 | 0.0 | 0.0 |
| Taxes          35.0% | | | | 4.3 | 18.9 | 33.0 | 48.0 | 64.4 | 79.1 | 95.4 | 111.3 | 129.7 | 151.5 |
| Net Income | | | | $8.1 | $35.0 | $61.3 | $89.1 | $119.6 | $146.9 | $177.3 | $206.7 | $240.8 | $281.3 |
| Growth | | | | | 334.2% | 75.1% | 45.3% | 34.3% | 22.8% | 20.7% | 16.6% | 16.5% | 16.8% |
| Margin | | | | 0.1% | 0.3% | 0.6% | 0.8% | 1.1% | 1.3% | 1.5% | 1.7% | 1.9% | 2.1% |
| Proceeds from Store Sales (After-Tax) | | | | 217.7 | 185.8 | 0.0 | 0.0 | 0.0 | 0.0 | 0.0 | 0.0 | 0.0 | 0.0 |
| Dividends | | | | 0.0 | 0.0 | 0.0 | 0.0 | 0.0 | 0.0 | 0.0 | 0.0 | 0.0 | 0.0 |
| Retained Earnings | | | | $225.8 | $220.8 | $61.3 | $89.1 | $119.6 | $146.9 | $177.3 | $206.7 | $240.8 | $281.3 |

**EXHIBIT 17.12**

## Balance Sheet

($ in millions)

**Base Case**

| For the FYE January 31 | Actual | | | Projected | | | | | | | | | |
|---|---|---|---|---|---|---|---|---|---|---|---|---|---|
| | 2003 | 2004 | 2005 | 2006 | 2007 | 2008 | 2009 | 2010 | 2011 | 2012 | 2013 | 2014 | 2015 |
| **ASSETS** | | | | | | | | | | | | | |
| Cash and Cash Equivalents | | | $1,247.0 | $1,247.0 | $1,247.0 | $1,247.0 | $1,247.0 | $1,247.0 | $1,247.0 | $1,247.0 | $1,247.0 | $1,247.0 | $1,247.0 |
| Accounts and Other Receivables | | | 153.0 | 149.9 | 144.1 | 143.4 | 148.1 | 153.6 | 159.3 | 165.2 | 171.3 | 177.7 | 184.3 |
| Merchandise Inventories | | | 1,884.0 | 1,837.3 | 1,760.6 | 1,748.2 | 1,802.9 | 1,868.4 | 1,937.9 | 2,009.9 | 2,084.5 | 2,162.0 | 2,242.3 |
| Other Current Assets | | | 167.0 | 163.6 | 157.3 | 156.6 | 161.6 | 167.6 | 173.8 | 180.3 | 187.0 | 193.9 | 201.2 |
| Total Current Assets | | | $3,451.0 | $3,397.9 | $3,309.1 | $3,295.2 | $3,359.6 | $3,436.6 | $3,518.0 | $3,602.4 | $3,689.9 | $3,780.6 | $3,874.8 |
| Net, PP&E | | | 4,339.0 | $4,216.8 | $4,103.5 | $3,993.3 | $3,880.0 | $3,762.9 | $3,641.4 | $3,515.4 | $3,384.8 | $3,249.2 | $3,108.6 |
| Goodwill, net | | | 0.0 | 0.0 | 0.0 | 0.0 | 0.0 | 0.0 | 0.0 | 0.0 | 0.0 | 0.0 | 0.0 |
| New Goodwill | | | 2,684.0 | 2,684.0 | 2,684.0 | 2,684.0 | 2,684.0 | 2,684.0 | 2,684.0 | 2,684.0 | 2,684.0 | 2,684.0 | 2,684.0 |
| Other Assets | | | 669.0 | 669.0 | 669.0 | 669.0 | 669.0 | 669.0 | 669.0 | 669.0 | 669.0 | 669.0 | 669.0 |
| **Total Assets** | | | $11,143.0 | $10,967.7 | $10,765.6 | $10,641.5 | $10,592.7 | $10,552.5 | $10,512.4 | $10,470.8 | $10,427.6 | $10,382.8 | $10,336.4 |
| **LIABILITIES & STOCKHOLDERS' EQUITY** | | | | | | | | | | | | | |
| Accounts Payable | | | $1,023.0 | $997.7 | $956.0 | $949.3 | $979.0 | $1,014.6 | $1,052.2 | $1,091.3 | $1,131.9 | $1,173.9 | $1,217.6 |
| Accrued Expenses & Other Current Liabilities | | | 1,126.0 | 1,098.1 | 1,052.3 | 1,044.8 | 1,077.5 | 1,116.7 | 1,158.2 | 1,201.2 | 1,245.9 | 1,292.1 | 1,340.2 |
| Total Current Liabilities | | | $2,149.0 | $2,095.8 | $2,008.3 | $1,994.1 | $2,056.5 | $2,131.3 | $2,210.4 | $2,292.6 | $2,377.7 | $2,466.1 | $2,557.7 |
| Assumed Debt | | | $2,312.0 | $1,964.1 | $1,628.7 | $1,457.4 | $1,257.1 | $1,022.6 | $756.4 | $455.4 | $120.3 | $0.0 | $0.0 |
| Senior Secured Credit Facility | | | 700.0 | 700.0 | 700.0 | 700.0 | 700.0 | 700.0 | 700.0 | 700.0 | 700.0 | 446.4 | 27.0 |
| Unsecured Bridge Loan | | | 1,900.0 | 1,900.0 | 1,900.0 | 1,900.0 | 1,900.0 | 1,900.0 | 1,900.0 | 1,900.0 | 1,900.0 | 1,900.0 | 1,900.0 |
| Secured European Bridge Loan | | | 1,000.0 | 1,000.0 | 1,000.0 | 1,000.0 | 1,000.0 | 1,000.0 | 1,000.0 | 1,000.0 | 1,000.0 | 1,000.0 | 1,000.0 |
| Mortgage Loan Agreements | | | 800.0 | 800.0 | 800.0 | 800.0 | 800.0 | 800.0 | 800.0 | 800.0 | 800.0 | 800.0 | 800.0 |
| Total Debt | | | $6,712.0 | $6,364.1 | $6,028.7 | $5,857.4 | $5,657.1 | $5,422.6 | $5,156.4 | $4,855.4 | $4,520.3 | $4,146.4 | $3,727.0 |
| Deferred Income Taxes | | | 485.0 | 485.0 | 485.0 | 485.0 | 485.0 | 485.0 | 485.0 | 485.0 | 485.0 | 485.0 | 485.0 |
| Other Liabilities | | | 497.0 | 497.0 | 497.0 | 497.0 | 497.0 | 497.0 | 497.0 | 497.0 | 497.0 | 497.0 | 497.0 |
| **Total Liabilities** | | | $9,843.0 | $9,441.9 | $9,019.0 | $8,833.5 | $8,695.6 | $8,535.8 | $8,348.8 | $8,129.0 | $7,880.1 | $7,594.5 | $7,266.7 |
| **Stockholders' Equity** | | | | | | | | | | | | | |
| New Preferred Stock | | | $0.0 | $0.0 | $0.0 | $0.0 | $0.0 | $0.0 | $0.8 | $0.0 | $0.0 | $0.0 | $0.0 |
| Sponsor Equity | | | 1,300.0 | 1,300.0 | 1,300.0 | 1,300.0 | 1,300.0 | 1,300.0 | 1,300.0 | 1,300.0 | 1,300.0 | 1,300.0 | 1,300.0 |
| Retained Earnings | | | 0.0 | 225.9 | 446.6 | 508.0 | 597.1 | 716.7 | 863.6 | 1,040.9 | 1,247.6 | 1,488.4 | 1,769.7 |
| Total Stockholders' Equity | | | $1,300.0 | $1,525.8 | $1,746.6 | $1,800.0 | $1,897.1 | $2,016.7 | $2,163.6 | $2,340.9 | $2,547.6 | $2,788.4 | $3,069.7 |
| **Total Liabilities & Stockholders' Equity** | | | $11,143.0 | $10,967.7 | $10,765.6 | $10,641.5 | $10,592.7 | $10,552.5 | $10,512.4 | $10,470.8 | $10,427.6 | $10,382.8 | $10,336.4 |
| Check | | | $0.000 | $0.000 | $0.000 | $0.000 | $0.000 | $0.000 | $0.000 | $0.000 | $0.000 | $0.000 | $0.000 |

**EXHIBIT 17.13**

## Interest Rate and Working Capital Assumptions

($ in millions)

**Base Case**

| For the FYE January 31 | Actual | | | Projected | | | | | | | | | |
|---|---|---|---|---|---|---|---|---|---|---|---|---|---|
| | 2003 | 2004 | 2005 | 2006 | 2007 | 2008 | 2009 | 2010 | 2011 | 2012 | 2013 | 2014 | 2015 |
| **Interest Rate Assumptions** | | | | | | | | | | | | | |
| LIBOR | | | 2.75% | 3.25% | 3.75% | 4.25% | 4.75% | 5.25% | 5.75% | 6.00% | 6.00% | 6.00% | 6.00% |
| Interest Earned on Cash | | | 2.75% | 3.25% | 3.75% | 4.25% | 4.75% | 5.25% | 5.75% | 6.25% | 6.25% | 6.25% | 6.25% |
| **Cash Interest Rate on Debt** | | LIBOR Spread | Fixed Rate | | | | | | | | | | |
| Assumed Debt | | | 6.50% | 6.50% | 6.50% | 6.50% | 6.50% | 6.50% | 6.50% | 6.50% | 6.50% | 6.50% | 6.50% |
| Senior Secured Credit Facility | | 3.50% | | 6.75% | 7.25% | 7.75% | 8.25% | 8.75% | 9.25% | 9.50% | 9.50% | 9.50% | 9.50% |
| Unsecured Bridge Loan | | | 11.00% | 11.00% | 11.00% | 11.00% | 11.00% | 11.00% | 11.00% | 11.00% | 11.00% | 11.00% | 11.00% |
| Secured European Bridge Loan | | | 9.00% | 9.00% | 9.00% | 9.00% | 9.00% | 9.00% | 9.00% | 9.00% | 9.00% | 9.00% | 9.00% |
| Mortgage Loan Agreements | | | 8.00% | 8.00% | 8.00% | 8.00% | 8.00% | 8.00% | 8.00% | 8.00% | 8.00% | 8.00% | 8.00% |
| **Working Capital Assumptions** | | | | | | | | | | | | | |
| Accounts and Other Receivables | | $146.0 | $153.0 | $149.9 | $144.1 | $143.4 | $148.1 | $153.6 | $159.3 | $165.2 | $171.3 | $177.7 | $184.3 |
| Days Outstanding | | 4.7 | 5.0 | 5.0 | 5.0 | 5.0 | 5.0 | 5.0 | 5.0 | 5.0 | 5.0 | 5.0 | 5.0 |
| Merchandise Inventories | | $2,094.0 | $1,884.0 | $1,837.3 | $1,760.6 | $1,748.2 | $1,802.9 | $1,868.4 | $1,937.9 | $2,009.9 | $2,084.5 | $2,162.0 | $2,242.3 |
| Turns | | 5.1 | 5.4 | 5.4 | 5.4 | 5.4 | 5.4 | 5.4 | 5.4 | 5.4 | 5.4 | 5.4 | 5.4 |
| Other Current Assets | | $486.0 | $167.0 | $163.6 | $157.3 | $156.6 | $161.6 | $167.6 | $173.8 | $180.3 | $187.0 | $193.9 | $201.2 |
| Days Outstanding | | 15.7 | 5.5 | 5.5 | 5.5 | 5.5 | 5.5 | 5.5 | 5.5 | 5.5 | 5.5 | 5.5 | 5.5 |
| Accounts Payable | | $1,022.0 | $1,023.0 | $997.7 | $956.0 | $949.3 | $979.0 | $1,014.6 | $1,052.2 | $1,091.3 | $1,131.9 | $1,173.9 | $1,217.6 |
| Days Outstanding | | 35.0 | 36.5 | 36.5 | 36.5 | 36.5 | 36.5 | 36.5 | 36.5 | 36.5 | 36.5 | 36.5 | 36.5 |
| Accrued Expenses & Other Current Liabilities | | $1,185.0 | $1,126.0 | $1,098.1 | $1,052.3 | $1,044.8 | $1,077.5 | $1,116.7 | $1,158.2 | $1,201.2 | $1,245.9 | $1,292.1 | $1,340.2 |
| Days Outstanding | | 40.6 | 40.1 | 40.1 | 40.1 | 40.1 | 40.1 | 40.1 | 40.1 | 40.1 | 40.1 | 40.1 | 40.1 |
| Total Current Assets | | $2,726.0 | $2,204.0 | $2,150.9 | $2,062.1 | $2,048.2 | $2,112.6 | $2,189.6 | $2,271.0 | $2,355.4 | $2,442.9 | $2,533.6 | $2,627.8 |
| Total Current Liabilities | | 2,207.0 | 2,149.0 | 2,095.8 | 2,008.3 | 1,994.1 | 2,056.5 | 2,131.3 | 2,210.4 | 2,292.6 | 2,377.7 | 2,466.1 | 2,557.7 |
| Working Capital | | $519.0 | $55.0 | $55.1 | $53.8 | $54.1 | $56.1 | $58.4 | $60.5 | $62.8 | $65.1 | $67.5 | $70.0 |
| (Increase) / Decrease in Accounts and Other Receivables | | | ($7.0) | $3.1 | $5.8 | $0.7 | ($4.6) | ($5.5) | ($5.7) | ($5.9) | ($6.1) | ($6.4) | ($6.6) |
| (Increase) / Decrease in Merchandise Inventories | | | 210.0 | 46.7 | 76.7 | 12.4 | (54.7) | (65.5) | (69.4) | (72.0) | (74.7) | (77.4) | (80.3) |
| (Increase) / Decrease in Other Current Assets | | | 319.0 | 3.4 | 6.3 | 0.8 | (5.1) | (6.0) | (6.2) | (6.5) | (6.7) | (6.9) | (7.2) |
| Increase / (Decrease) in Accounts Payable | | | 1.0 | (25.3) | (41.7) | (6.7) | 29.7 | 35.6 | 37.7 | 39.1 | 40.5 | 42.1 | 43.6 |
| Increase / (Decrease) in Accrued Expenses & Other Current Liabilities | | | (59.0) | (27.9) | (45.9) | (7.4) | 32.7 | 39.2 | 41.5 | 43.0 | 44.6 | 46.3 | 48.0 |
| **(Increase in) Reduction of Working Capital** | | | $464.0 | ($0.1) | $1.3 | ($0.3) | ($2.0) | ($2.3) | ($2.2) | ($2.2) | ($2.3) | ($2.4) | ($2.5) |
| (Increase) / Decrease in Long-Term Assets | | | 0.0 | 0.0 | 0.0 | 0.0 | 0.0 | 0.0 | 0.0 | 0.0 | 0.0 | 0.0 | 0.0 |
| Increase / (Decrease) in Long-Term Liabilities | | | 0.0 | 0.0 | 0.0 | 0.0 | 0.0 | 0.0 | 0.0 | 0.0 | 0.0 | 0.0 | 0.0 |

**EXHIBIT 17.14**

equity. As a result, equity represented only 16.3% of post-acquisition Toys capitalization, and debt represented 83.7% of capitalization. This compares to a pre-acquisition equity and debt of approximately 65% and 35%, respectively. As a result, Toys' capitalization became significantly more leveraged based on the LBO transaction (see Exhibit 17.18).

**Transaction Summary**

| ($ in millions) | Value |
|---|---|
| Equity Price per Share | $26.75 |
| Implied Shares Purchased (millions of shares) | 220.6 |
| Equity Value | $5,900 |
| Other Transaction Value (Ex Fees) | 394 |
| Assumed Debt | 2,312 |
| Remaining Cash on Balance Sheet | (1,247) |
| Enterprise Value | $7,359 |
| Transaction Fees | 362 |
| Enterprise Value w/Fees | $7,721 |
| FYE 2005 EBITDA | $780 |
| EV (Excluding Fees) / FYE 2005 EBITDA | 9.4x |
| EV (with Fees) / FYE 2005 EBITDA | 9.9x |

Note: The model assumes transaction closed on FYE January 29, 2005. Actual deal closed on July 21, 2005.

**EXHIBIT 17.15**

**Sources and Uses ($ in millions)**

| Sources | | Uses | |
|---|---|---|---|
| Cash on balance sheet | $956 | Purchase of common stock | $5,900 |
| Senior secured credit facility | 700 | Purchase of stock options and restricted stock | 227 |
| Unsecured bridge loan | 1,900 | Settlement of equity security interests | 114 |
| Secured European bridge loan | 1,000 | Purchase of all warrants | 17 |
| Mortgage loan agreements | 800 | Transaction fees | 362 |
| Sponsor equity | 1,300 | Severance and bonus payments | 36 |
| *Total* | $6,656 | *Total* | $6,656 |

| Summary of Fees | |
|---|---|
| Advisory fees and expenses | $78 |
| Financing fees | 135 |
| Sponsor fees | 81 |
| Other | 68 |
| *Total* | $362 |

Note: Senior secured credit facility has $2.0 billion of availability.

This exhibit reflects actual sources and uses for the Toys transaction that closed on July 21, 2005: the $956 million cash used is included in the model, which assumes (for simplicity) a closing on January 29, 2005 (see Exhibit 17.18).

Source: Toys "R" Us, Form 10-Q, July 30, 2005

**EXHIBIT 17.16**

**Leverage Summary ($ in millions)**

| LEVERAGE ANALYSIS | | Cumul. Multiple |
|---|---|---|
| Approximate existing debt | $2,312 | 3.0x |
| $2 billion senior secured credit facility | 700 | 3.9x |
| Unsecured bridge loan | 1,900 | 6.3x |
| Secured European bridge loan | 1,000 | 7.6x |
| Mortgage loan agreements | 800 | 8.6x |
| Total | $6,712 | 8.6x |
| Remaining cash and short-term investments on balance sheet assumed by the consortium | (1,247) | |
| Net leverage | $5,465 | 7.0x |

Note: The model assumes transaction closed on FYF January 29, 2005. Actual deal closed on July 21, 2005.

**EXHIBIT 17.17**

## Determine Cash Flow Available for Debt Service

KKR determined the cash flow available for debt service by subtracting CapEx from projected EBITDA and then making adjustments based on changes in working capital and other long-term assets and liabilities and payment of cash taxes. In addition, because KKR expected to receive cash from the sale of stores, the projected after-tax proceeds of these sales increased cash. The result was a forecast of cash available for debt service through 2015 (see Exhibit 17.19). This amount was then reduced to reflect interest expense netted against interest income to create cash available for debt repayment. Normally, this cash is used to pay down debt, and, in the case of Toys, Exhibit 17.19 suggests that the $2.3 billion of debt assumed on the date of acquisition is paid off first, and then the senior secured credit facility receives partial repayment. The end result of using available cash flow to retire debt is the reduction in total debt over time and improvement in debt/EBITDA ratios (see Exhibits 17.19 and 17.20). The reduction in debt combined with the increase in EBITDA creates growth in equity for a financial sponsor. This in turn creates the opportunity for the sponsor to achieve its targeted IRR (see Exhibit 17.1).

The Toys projected cash flow statement (Exhibit 17.19) shows that there should be $347.9 million in cash available during 2006 to repay a portion of the debt assumed at the time of the acquisition.[2] Payment of this debt reduces total debt from $6.712 billion in 2005 to $6.364 billion in 2006 (see Exhibit 17.20). This total debt amount continues to decrease from debt repayment through 2010, when it reaches $5.423 billion (net debt of $4.176 billion). LBO models typically assume that all excess cash is used to pay down debt. This is because the financial sponsor usually thinks that this is the best use for excess cash. However, if there is a compelling investment opportunity, or if the sponsor wants the company to pay a large dividend, this cash can be diverted, unless lenders include loan covenants that prevent or minimize dividends and other large cash payments (which they usually do).

[2]Sometimes, a range of cash flows is projected, since it is increasingly difficult to be precise the farther out in time the projection continues. A variable cash flow projection will reveal alternative IRR outcomes and the riskiness of the debt brought onto the balance sheet.

**Consolidated Balance Sheet @ Transaction Close**

| ($ in millions) | Actual For the Fiscal Year Ended | | Acquisition | Adjusted |
| | 1/31/2004 | 1/29/2005 | Adjustments | Balance Sheet @ Close |
|---|---|---|---|---|
| **ASSETS** | | | | |
| Cash and Cash Equivalents | $2,003 | $2,203 | ($956) | $1,247 |
| Accounts and Other Receivables | 146 | 153 | | 153 |
| Merchandise Inventories | 2,094 | 1,884 | | 1,884 |
| Other Current Assets | 486 | 167 | | 167 |
| Total Current Assets | $4,729 | $4,407 | ($956) | $3,451 |
| Net, PP&E | $4,439 | $4,339 | | $4,339 |
| Goodwill, net | 348 | 353 | (353) | 0 |
| New Goodwill | 0 | 0 | 2,684 | 2,684 |
| Other Assets | 749 | 669 | | 669 |
| **Total Assets** | $10,265 | $9,768 | $1,375 | $11,143 |
| **LIABILITIES & STOCKHOLDERS' EQUITY** | | | | |
| Accounts Payable | 1,022 | 1,023 | | 1,023 |
| Accrued Expenses & Other Current Liabilities | 1,185 | 1,126 | | 1,126 |
| Total Current Liabilities | $2,207 | $2,149 | $0 | $2,149 |
| Assumed Debt | 3,006 | 2,312 | | 2,312 |
| Senior Secured Credit Facility | 0 | 0 | 700 | 700 |
| Unsecured Bridge Loan | 0 | 0 | 1,900 | 1,900 |
| Secured European Bridge Loan | 0 | 0 | 1,000 | 1,000 |
| Mortgage Loan Agreements | 0 | 0 | 800 | 800 |
| Total Debt | 3,006 | 2,312 | 4,400 | 6,712 |
| Deferred Income Taxes | 538 | 485 | | 485 |
| Other Liabilities | 540 | 497 | | 497 |
| **Total Liabilities** | $6,291 | $5,443 | $4,400 | $9,843 |
| *Stockholders' Equity* | | | | |
| New Preferred Stock | $0 | $0 | | $0 |
| Sponsor Equity | 0 | 0 | 1,300 | 1,300 |
| Retained Earnings | 3,974 | 4,325 | (4,325) | 0 |
| Total Stockholders' Equity | $3,974 | $4,325 | ($3,025) | $1,300 |
| **Total Liabilities & Stockholders' Equity** | $10,265 | $9,768 | $1,375 | $11,143 |

Note: Cash includes short-term investments. The model assumes transaction closed on January 29, 2005. Actual deal closed on July 21, 2005.

**Note: Goodwill Calculation**

| | |
|---|---|
| Equity Purchase Price (Incl. Fees) | $6,656 |
| Less Tangible Net Worth | 3,972 |
| New Goodwill | $2,684 |

Note: Tangible Net Worth calculated as Retained Earnings - Goodwill

**EXHIBIT 17.18**

## Calculate Credit Ratios

Lenders in an LBO transaction take considerable risks based on their exposure to highly leveraged companies like Toys. As a result, they require controls on the company's total amount of debt and on the cash flow available to pay interest when due. As a condition for lending, therefore, two different kinds of credit ratios are imposed by lenders: leverage ratios and coverage ratios.

Leverage ratios limit the amount of total debt and net debt that the target company is allowed to undertake relative to EBITDA. In the Toys transaction, post-acquisition total debt/EBITDA during 2005 was 8.61×. Net debt/EBITDA during 2005 was 7.01× (see Exhibit 17.20).

## Cash Flow Statement
($ in millions)

**Base Case**

| For the FYE January 31 | Actual | | | Projected | | | | | | | | | |
| --- | --- | --- | --- | --- | --- | --- | --- | --- | --- | --- | --- | --- | --- |
| | 2003 | 2004 | 2005 | 2006 | 2007 | 2008 | 2009 | 2010 | 2011 | 2012 | 2013 | 2014 | 2015 |
| Consolidated EBITDA | | | | $860.8 | $860.0 | $877.2 | $914.9 | $956.9 | $992.4 | $1,029.3 | $1,067.6 | $1,107.2 | $1,148.4 |
| Net Capex | | | | 217.5 | 209.1 | 208.1 | 214.8 | 222.8 | 231.1 | 239.7 | 248.6 | 257.8 | 267.4 |
| EBITDA - Capex | | | | $643.3 | $650.9 | $669.1 | $700.1 | $734.1 | $761.3 | $789.6 | $819.0 | $849.4 | $881.0 |
| (Increase) / Decrease in Working Capital | | | | ($0.1) | $1.3 | ($0.3) | ($2.0) | ($2.3) | ($2.2) | ($2.2) | ($2.3) | ($2.4) | ($2.5) |
| (Increase) / Decrease in Other LT Assets | | | | 0.0 | 0.0 | 0.0 | 0.0 | 0.0 | 0.0 | 0.0 | 0.0 | 0.0 | 0.0 |
| Increase / (Decrease) in Other LT Liabilities | | | | 0.0 | 0.0 | 0.0 | 0.0 | 0.0 | 0.0 | 0.0 | 0.0 | 0.0 | 0.0 |
| Cash Taxes | | | | (4.3) | (18.9) | (33.0) | (48.0) | (64.4) | (79.1) | (95.4) | (111.3) | (129.7) | (151.5) |
| Cash on Balance Sheet in Excess of Minimum Balance | | | | 0.0 | 0.0 | 0.0 | 0.0 | 0.0 | 0.0 | 0.0 | 0.0 | 0.0 | 0.0 |
| Other Sources / (Uses) of Cash | | | | ($4.4) | ($17.6) | ($33.3) | ($50.0) | ($66.7) | ($81.3) | ($97.7) | ($113.6) | ($132.1) | ($154.0) |
| Proceeds from Store Sales (After-Tax) | | | | 217.7 | 185.8 | 0.0 | 0.0 | 0.0 | 0.0 | 0.0 | 0.0 | 0.0 | 0.0 |
| Cash Available for Debt Service | | | | $856.6 | $819.1 | $635.8 | $650.1 | $667.4 | $680.1 | $691.9 | $705.3 | $717.3 | $727.0 |
| Total Interest Expense | | | | $549.2 | $530.5 | $517.5 | $509.0 | $498.3 | $485.6 | $468.9 | $448.2 | $421.4 | $385.5 |
| Interest Income on Cash Balance | | | | 40.5 | 46.8 | 53.0 | 59.2 | 65.5 | 71.7 | 77.9 | 77.9 | 77.9 | 77.9 |
| Cash Available for Debt Amortization / Repayment | | | | $347.9 | $335.4 | $171.3 | $200.4 | $234.5 | $266.2 | $301.0 | $335.1 | $373.9 | $419.4 |
| Assumed Debt Repayment | | | | ($347.9) | ($335.4) | ($171.3) | ($200.4) | ($234.5) | ($266.2) | ($301.0) | ($335.1) | ($120.3) | $0.0 |
| Senior Secured Credit Facility Repayment | | | | $0.0 | $0.0 | $0.0 | $0.0 | $0.0 | $0.0 | $0.0 | $0.0 | ($253.6) | ($419.4) |
| Excess Cash After Debt and Credit Facility Repayment | | | | $0.0 | $0.0 | $0.0 | $0.0 | $0.0 | $0.0 | $0.0 | $0.0 | $0.0 | $0.0 |
| Minimum Cash Balance | | | | 1,247.0 | 1,247.0 | 1,247.0 | 1,247.0 | 1,247.0 | 1,247.0 | 1,247.0 | 1,247.0 | 1,247.0 | 1,247.0 |
| Ending Cash Balance | | | | $1,247.0 | $1,247.0 | $1,247.0 | $1,247.0 | $1,247.0 | $1,247.0 | $1,247.0 | $1,247.0 | $1,247.0 | $1,247.0 |
| **Credit Statistics** | | | | | | | | | | | | | |
| Total Debt / EBITDA | | | 8.61x | 7.39x | 7.01x | 6.68x | 6.18x | 5.67x | 5.20x | 4.72x | 4.23x | 3.74x | 3.25x |
| Net Debt / EBITDA | | | 7.01x | 5.94x | 5.56x | 5.26x | 4.82x | 4.36x | 3.94x | 3.51x | 3.07x | 2.62x | 2.16x |
| EBITDA / Interest Expense | | | | 1.57x | 1.62x | 1.69x | 1.80x | 1.92x | 2.04x | 2.20x | 2.38x | 2.63x | 2.98x |
| (EBITDA-Capex) / Interest Expense | | | | 1.17x | 1.23x | 1.29x | 1.38x | 1.47x | 1.57x | 1.68x | 1.83x | 2.02x | 2.29x |
| **Tax Loss Carryforward** | | | | | | | | | | | | | |
| Beginning Balance | | | | $0.0 | $0.0 | $0.0 | $0.0 | $0.0 | $0.0 | $0.0 | $0.0 | $0.0 | $0.0 |
| Additions | | | | 0.0 | 0.0 | 0.0 | 0.0 | 0.0 | 0.0 | 0.0 | 0.0 | 0.0 | 0.0 |
| Use of NOLs | | | | 0.0 | 0.0 | 0.0 | 0.0 | 0.0 | 0.0 | 0.0 | 0.0 | 0.0 | 0.0 |
| Ending Balance | | | | $0.0 | $0.0 | $0.0 | $0.0 | $0.0 | $0.0 | $0.0 | $0.0 | $0.0 | $0.0 |

**EXHIBIT 17.19**

## Returns Summary
($ in millions)

**Base Case**

| | Actual | Projected | | | | | CAGR |
| --- | --- | --- | --- | --- | --- | --- | --- |
| | 2005 | 2006 | 2007 | 2008 | 2009 | 2010 | '05-'10 |
| Consolidated EBITDA | $780.0 | $860.8 | $860.0 | $877.2 | $914.9 | $956.9 | 4.2% |
| Growth | 20.4% | 10.4% | -0.1% | 2.0% | 4.3% | 4.6% | |
| Margin | 7.0% | 7.9% | 8.2% | 8.4% | 8.5% | 8.6% | |
| Capex | | $217.5 | $209.1 | $208.1 | $214.8 | $222.8 | |
| Total Interest Expense | | $549.2 | $530.5 | $517.5 | $509.0 | $498.3 | |
| Total Debt | $6,712 | $6,364 | $6,029 | $5,857 | $5,657 | $5,423 | |
| Cash and Cash Equivalents | 1,247 | 1,247 | 1,247 | 1,247 | 1,247 | 1,247 | |
| Net Debt | $5,465 | $5,117 | $4,782 | $4,610 | $4,410 | $4,176 | |
| Total Debt / EBITDA | 8.61x | 7.39x | 7.01x | 6.68x | 6.18x | 5.67x | |
| Net Debt / EBITDA | 7.01x | 5.94x | 5.56x | 5.26x | 4.82x | 4.36x | |
| EBITDA / Interest Expense | | 1.57x | 1.62x | 1.69x | 1.80x | 1.92x | |
| (EBITDA-Capex) / Interest Expense | | 1.17x | 1.23x | 1.29x | 1.38x | 1.47x | |

**Returns (Including Sponsor Fee)**

| EBITDA Multiple | ROI | Gain | ROI w/Fee | Gain |
| --- | --- | --- | --- | --- |
| 7.00x | 13.0% | $1,100.4 | 14.5% | $1,181.4 |
| 7.50x | 16.8% | 1,531.0 | 18.4% | 1,612.0 |
| 8.00x | 20.2% | 1,961.6 | 21.8% | 2,042.6 |
| 8.50x | 23.2% | 2,392.2 | 24.8% | 2,473.2 |
| 9.00x | 26.0% | 2,822.8 | 27.6% | 2,903.8 |
| 9.50x | 28.5% | 3,253.4 | 30.2% | 3,334.4 |
| 10.00x | 30.8% | 3,684.0 | 32.5% | 3,765.0 |

**EXHIBIT 17.20**

Note that these ratios reduce each year based on the repayment of debt until 2010, when total debt/ EBITDA is 5.67× and net debt/EBITDA is 4.36×.

Coverage ratios require the company to produce cash flow, at a minimum, in excess of annual interest payments. For example, EBITDA must exceed interest payments due in any year by a certain ratio. In the Toys transaction, EBITDA/interest expense during 2006 was 1.57×. (EBITDA-CapEx)/interest expense was 1.17× during 2006. Through the repayment of debt, these ratios improve each year until 2010, when EBITDA/interest expense increases to 1.92× and (EBITDA-CapEx)/interest expense increases to 1.47×.

## Calculate the Equity Value, IRR, and Multiple of Investment on Projected Exit Date

To calculate equity value, IRR, and multiple of investment on the projected exit date, start with EBITDA on the projected exit date year (2010 in the Toys case; see Exhibit 17.21) and multiply that EBITDA by a range of enterprise value/EBITDA multiples that might apply as of the exit date. This creates an expected enterprise value. After the enterprise value alternatives are determined, equity value as of the exit date can be calculated by subtracting debt and adding cash. A further step sometimes involves determining the equity value of options held by non-sponsor holders (such as management) and reducing the equity value for the sponsor by this amount.

The most relevant multiple to use in forecasting the exit equity value for the sponsor depends on who the expected buyer is on the exit date (IPO sale, or M&A sale to a strategic buyer or to another financial sponsor) and the multiple used to value the investment on the original acquisition date. Generally, sponsors use the same multiple for entering and exiting an investment, but this depends on the facts and circumstances of the investment.

After a range of equity values is determined, the IRR of the investment can be calculated based on the number of years the investment is expected to be held, and the entry and exit equity values derived from the analysis. The IRR is the discount rate that causes the present value of the future cash flow (including the equity value on the exit date) to equal the equity investment at

**Returns Summary**

($ in millions)

Base Case

| | | Exit Multiple | Enterprise Value | Less: Debt | Plus: Cash | Net Debt | Equity Value | Value of Mgmt Options | Net Sponsor Equity Value |
|---|---|---|---|---|---|---|---|---|---|
| Assumed Exit Year | 2010 | 7.00x | $6,698.3 | ($5,422.6) | $1,247.0 | ($4,175.6) | $2,522.7 | $122.3 | $2,400.4 |
| EBITDA | $956.9 | 7.50x | 7,176.7 | ($5,422.6) | $1,247.0 | ($4,175.6) | $3,001.1 | 170.1 | 2,831.0 |
| | | 8.00x | 7,655.1 | ($5,422.6) | $1,247.0 | ($4,175.6) | $3,479.6 | 218.0 | 3,261.6 |
| | | 8.50x | 8,133.6 | ($5,422.6) | $1,247.0 | ($4,175.6) | $3,958.0 | 265.8 | 3,692.2 |
| | | 9.00x | 8,612.0 | ($5,422.6) | $1,247.0 | ($4,175.6) | $4,436.5 | 313.6 | 4,122.8 |
| | | 9.50x | 9,090.5 | ($5,422.6) | $1,247.0 | ($4,175.6) | $4,914.9 | 361.5 | 4,553.4 |
| | | 10.00x | 9,568.9 | ($5,422.6) | $1,247.0 | ($4,175.6) | $5,393.4 | 409.3 | 4,984.0 |

**Sponsor Return**

| | 2005 | 2006 | 2007 | 2008 | 2009 | 2010 | ROI | Gains |
|---|---|---|---|---|---|---|---|---|
| 7.00x | ($1,300.0) | $0.0 | $0.0 | $0.0 | $0.0 | $2,400.4 | 13.0% | $1,100.4 |
| 7.50x | (1,300.0) | 0.0 | 0.0 | 0.0 | 0.0 | 2,831.0 | 16.8% | 1,531.0 |
| 8.00x | (1,300.0) | 0.0 | 0.0 | 0.0 | 0.0 | 3,261.6 | 20.2% | 1,961.6 |
| 8.50x | (1,300.0) | 0.0 | 0.0 | 0.0 | 0.0 | 3,692.2 | 23.2% | 2,392.2 |
| 9.00x | (1,300.0) | 0.0 | 0.0 | 0.0 | 0.0 | 4,122.8 | 26.0% | 2,822.8 |
| 9.50x | (1,300.0) | 0.0 | 0.0 | 0.0 | 0.0 | 4,553.4 | 28.5% | 3,253.4 |
| 10.00x | (1,300.0) | 0.0 | 0.0 | 0.0 | 0.0 | 4,984.0 | 30.8% | 3,684.0 |

**Sponsor Return Including Initial Fees**

| | 2005 | 2006 | 2007 | 2008 | 2009 | 2010 | ROI with Fee | Gains with Fee |
|---|---|---|---|---|---|---|---|---|
| 7.00x | ($1,219.0) | $0.0 | $0.0 | $0.0 | $0.0 | $2,400.4 | 14.5% | $1,181.4 |
| 7.50x | (1,219.0) | 0.0 | 0.0 | 0.0 | 0.0 | 2,831.0 | 18.4% | 1,612.0 |
| 8.00x | (1,219.0) | 0.0 | 0.0 | 0.0 | 0.0 | 3,261.6 | 21.8% | 2,042.6 |
| 8.50x | (1,219.0) | 0.0 | 0.0 | 0.0 | 0.0 | 3,692.2 | 24.8% | 2,473.2 |
| 9.00x | (1,219.0) | 0.0 | 0.0 | 0.0 | 0.0 | 4,122.8 | 27.6% | 2,903.8 |
| 9.50x | (1,219.0) | 0.0 | 0.0 | 0.0 | 0.0 | 4,553.4 | 30.2% | 3,334.4 |
| 10.00x | (1,219.0) | 0.0 | 0.0 | 0.0 | 0.0 | 4,984.0 | 32.5% | 3,765.0 |

**EXHIBIT 17.21**

time zero. This IRR can be calculated on most financial calculators by including the time horizon (n), which was 5 years in the Toys case, the original investment (PV), which was –$1.3 billion (without fees) for Toys, and the exit equity value (FV), which, assuming a 9.0× multiple, was $4.12 billion for Toys. Assuming no interim dividend payments (PMT), solving for the IRR (i) based on the 9× multiple results in an IRR of 26%.

In Exhibit 17.21, the original equity investment by KKR in Toys during 2005 was $1.3 billion. Assuming a 5-year holding period (an exit during 2010), the sponsor's equity value at exit ranges from $2.4 billion to just under $5.0 billion, depending on the enterprise value/EBITDA multiple used. Since the 2005 multiple (excluding fees) was 9.4×, it is reasonable to assume an exit multiple of between 9.0× and 9.5×, which suggests that the IRR for KKR in the Toys transaction may have been expected to be between 26.0% and 28.5%. Including fees, the expected return may have been 26.7% to 30.2%.

If an exit multiple of 9.0× had been used, the expected exit equity value would have been $4.12 billion, producing a gain of $2.82 billion (not including initial fees), since the original equity investment was $1.3 billion. As a result, the expected multiple of investment would have been $4.12 billion/$1.3 billion = 3.17 times (equity exit value/entry equity value).

## LBO Analysis Post-Credit Crisis

Although when KKR initiated the Toys LBO the expected IRRs may have been 26%, or higher, and expected multiple of investment at 3.17×, or higher, there was considerable risk associated with this transaction. It is likely, therefore, that KKR completed several *stress test* scenarios that projected worsening credit, real estate, and retailing markets. Based on this risk adjusted analysis, they may have expected lower returns. Indeed, in the post-credit-crisis environment, returns for most financial sponsors were significantly diminished. This happened, in part, because creditors were unwilling to provide as much leverage in support of LBO transactions (and the cost of leverage increased). With less leverage available, financial sponsors were required to commit more upfront equity, which reduced returns. In addition, because of a massive inflow of new private equity funding that came from investors during 2006–2008, there was significantly more competition for acquisition targets, which also resulted in a reduction in returns. During 2009, many sponsors accepted IRRs of 10% to 15%, while other sponsors decided to seek returns from nontraditional sources.

## Questions

Please also refer to questions in **Case Study 9, "The Toys 'R' Us LBO."**

1. What does an LBO analysis include, what does it solve for, and what question is answered by the analysis?
2. What are the three ways to create returns through an LBO transaction?
3. What is the formula for determining cash flow available for debt service?
4. What are the key credit statistics in an LBO financing?

# ▦ 18
# Private Equity Impact on Corporations

The material in this chapter should be cross-referenced with **Case Study 10, "Cerberus and the U.S. Auto Industry."**

## Private Equity-Owned Companies: Management Practices and Productivity

The credit crisis that started in mid-2007 caused private equity acquisition activity to drop substantially when access to debt financing became limited. As a result, the private equity ownership model came under increasing scrutiny, and questions arose regarding whether this asset class could create sustainable value without "financial engineering."

In response to this question, the authors of the World Economic Forum's publication "The Economic Impact of Private Equity Report 2009" concluded that private equity-owned companies are, on average, better managed than other forms of companies, including government-, family-, and privately owned firms, even after controlling for characteristics such as country, industry, size, and employee skills. This is because there are very few badly managed firms that are controlled by private equity firms, whereas other companies include a "tail" of very badly managed companies.

Although the results for private equity-controlled companies versus dispersed shareholding companies are not statistically significant, private equity portfolio companies have slightly higher management practices scores. Private equity-owned company management quickly adopts merit-based hiring, firing, pay, and promotion practices. These companies have tough evaluation metrics, which are focused on both short-term and long-run objectives, and the metrics are well understood by employees and are linked to the company's performance. Private equity-owned companies are also very good at operational management practices such as adoption of lean management, focusing on continuous improvement, and implementing comprehensive performance documentation processes.

The World Economic Forum's publication concluded that private equity-owned companies are more productive than companies with other ownership structures. A key finding is that the net impact of private equity ownership on employment was quite modest: although these companies shed jobs at a considerably higher pace immediately after the acquisition is completed, in the subsequent 3 years they added back many of these jobs. In addition, when factoring in productivity and worker earnings, private equity-owned companies compared favorably with other forms of company ownership. See Exhibit 18.1 to review the publication's key findings.

In summary, the World Economic Forum's conclusions are that private equity firms do more than apply financial engineering to their target companies. Research has demonstrated that private equity-owned companies have high scores on a wide range of management practices and,

**An Excerpt on Private Equity and Target Company Productivity from:**
**The Global Economic Impact of Private Equity Report 2009**

...[T]arget manufacturing firms experience an intensification of creative destruction. Job creation and job destruction activity, establishment entry and exit, and establishment acquisition and divestiture (all relative to controls) are intensified in the wake of private equity transactions. The same patterns hold for private equity targets in the private sector as a whole.

Firms acquired by private equity groups experience productivity growth in the two-year period after the transaction that is on average two percentage points more than at controls. About 72% of this out-performance differential reflects more effective management of existing facilities, including gains from accelerated reallocation of activity among the continuing establishments of target firms. About 36% of the differential reflects the productivity contribution of more entry and exit at target firms. It was also found that firms acquired by private equity had higher productivity than their peers at the time of the original acquisition by the private equity group.

The probability of establishment shut-down is less likely for more productive facilities for both private equity targets and comparable firms, but the relationship is much stronger for private equity-backed firms. In other words, private equity investors are much more likely to close underperforming establishments at the firms they back, as measured by labour productivity.

Both targets and controls tend to share productivity gains with workers in the form of higher wages, but the relationship between productivity gains and wage increases is slightly stronger at targets. Establishments with higher than average productivity growth have higher than average earning per worker growth.

The positive productivity growth differential at target firms (relative to controls) is larger in periods with an unusually high interest rate spread between AAA-rated and BB-rated corporate bonds. The higher productivity growth at target firms during periods of financial stress reflects greater reallocation of activity to more productive establishments and a higher rate of closure at less productive ones.

Source: "The Globalization of Alternative Investments Working Papers Volume 2: The Global Economic Impact of Private Equity Report 2009." World Economic Forum Jan 2009.

**EXHIBIT 18.1**

during the first 2 years after acquisition, productivity grows faster than at control companies. In addition, the research demonstrates that productivity gains at private equity-owned companies are shared more with employees in the form of higher wages as compared to non-private equity-controlled companies.

# Private Equity-Owned Company Failures

In spite of the favorable research that supports the private equity-ownership model, there have been a number of notable failures.

## Hawaiian Telecom Communications (HTC)

HTC (at the time, Hawaii's largest telephone carrier) filed for bankruptcy protection in December 2008. The Carlyle Group purchased HTC from Verizon Communications in 2005 for $1.6 billion, using $425 million in equity and debt financing for the balance. Unfortunately, Carlyle faced problems from the start, as state utility regulators delayed the closing of the acquisition, and billing and customer-service issues plagued the company while it was creating a new back-office system. As a result, many customers dropped both cable and wireless services and the company's revenues fell, creating large losses. By February 2008, three consecutive quarterly losses compelled Carlyle to bring in a turnaround expert as an interim CEO, replacing CEO Michael Ruley. In May, yet another new CEO was brought in. Seven months later, the company filed for Chapter 11 bankruptcy protection.

## Washington Mutual, Inc. (WaMu)

An investment group led by Texas Pacific Group (TPG) purchased Washington Mutual, Inc. (WaMu) for $7 billion during April 2008. In September 2008, WaMu, the largest savings and loan association in the United States, was placed in receivership by the Federal Deposit Insurance Corporation (FDIC). The FDIC then sold the banking subsidiaries of the company to J.P. Morgan for $1.9 billion, after invalidating all debt and equity claims. The holding company (without the banking subsidiaries) subsequently filed for Chapter 11 bankruptcy protection. TPG had invested $1.35 billion in WaMu, and the firm's losses were spread between three of TPG's investment funds: $475 million loss in $15 billion TPG V; $475 million loss in $20 billion TPG VI; and $400 million loss in $6 billion TPG Financial Partners.

## Scorecard During 2008

Of the 287 companies (with assets over $1 million or revenues over $10 million) that filed for bankruptcy protection in the United States during 2008, 71 (almost 25%) were either currently owned or previously owned by private equity firms.[1] From 2005 to 2008, according to Standard & Poor's, private equity-owned firms added $475 billion of debt to company balance sheets. In stable economic periods, this debt may have been manageable, but during the very problematic economy of 2008, it appears that many private-equity-related companies could not tolerate their additional debt burden.

# Private Equity Purchase Commitment Failures

## BCE, Inc.

Eighteen months after Ontario Teachers' Pension Plan, Providence Equity, Madison Dearborn Partners, and Merrill Lynch Global Private Equity signed a merger agreement to acquire BCE, Canada's largest telephone company, the deal collapsed. This would have been the largest private equity-led acquisition in history (at the time of announcement), based on its original valuation of $41 billion. There was an express condition of closing that a solvency opinion be provided. The BCE transaction collapsed when a valuation expert at KPMG issued an opinion that the acquisition would result in an insolvent entity, thereby releasing the four equity providers from their obligation to close the transaction. These firms stated that because of the failure to receive a solvency opinion, they were also released from an obligation to pay a $1.2 billion break-up fee. Because the equity providers walked away from the deal, four banks that had committed to provide $34 billion in debt financing also walked away. These banks were Citigroup, Deutsche Bank, Royal Bank of Scotland Group, and Toronto Dominion Bank. It was estimated that, given the poor condition of the credit markets, if these banks had been forced to provide financing based

---

[1]Capital IQ.

on the terms of their original commitment, they might have absorbed up to $12 billion in theoretical losses.

The biggest losers from this failed transaction were BCE shareholders, who expected to be bought out at around $34 per share. When the transaction collapsed during December 2008, BCE's share price was $18.29, resulting in a total loss of value to shareholders of approximately $12.6 billion.

## Huntsman Corporation

On December 15, 2008, 18 months after an initial agreement was reached, Huntsman Corporation, a manufacturer and marketer of differentiated chemicals, announced that it terminated its $6.5 billion merger agreement with Hexion Specialty Chemicals, a company owned by Apollo Management. Huntsman sued Hexion and Apollo in an effort to force them to proceed with the leveraged buyout of the company, but Huntsman withdrew the lawsuit based on a settlement agreement totaling $1 billion in payments to Huntsman. This payment obligation was shared between Apollo, who paid $425 million (and an additional $250 million in exchange for 10-year convertible notes issued by Huntsman), and Credit Suisse and Deutsche Bank (originally committed to provide debt financing for the transactions), who paid a $325 million break-up fee.

In spite of the payment by Credit Suisse and Deutsche Bank, Huntsman pursued claims against the banks based on, among other things, an allegation that the banks conspired with Apollo and tortuously interfered with Huntsman's prior merger agreement with Basell. This dispute was settled out of court during June 2009.

Huntsman had reached an agreement to sell their company at $25.25 per share to Basell, a large European-based chemical company, but changed its course when Apollo made a $28 per share offer and advised that it had financing commitments in place with the banks.

The company's share price fell to $10 when the LBO transaction with Apollo and Hexion fell through, creating a loss of $3.6 billion for Huntsman shareholders. See Exhibit 16.15 in Chapter 16 for a more complete summary.

# Private Equity Portfolio Companies Purchased During 2006–2007

The largest private equity acquisitions during 2006 and 2007 are listed in Exhibit 18.2. During 2008 and 2009, the valuations for all of these companies were marked down considerably below the original acquisition valuations. Evidence of the decline in valuations is provided by Blackstone Group, which is a publicly reporting company. Blackstone posted a fourth-quarter 2008 loss of $415.2 million and a full-year loss of $1.16 billion. During the fourth quarter of 2008, it marked down the equity value of its holdings by 20%, on average, following a 7% reduction during the previous quarter. Valuation declines in portfolio companies drove down Blackstone's own stock price by 88% from its June 2007 IPO price to its price on March 31, 2009. A summary of six of the private equity transactions listed in Exhibit 18.2 follows.

## TXU Energy (TXU)

TXU provides electricity and related services to 2.3 million customers in Texas though 41 generating plants. A $44 billion acquisition was announced on February 26, 2007, and closed on October 10, 2007. The principal purchasers were KKR, TPG, and Goldman Sachs, with Lehman

**Large Private Equity Transactions During 2006 and 2007**

| Target Name | Sponsor(s) Involved | Transaction Value ($mm) |
|---|---|---|
| TXU | Citigroup, GSCP, KKR, LEH PE, MS PE, TPG | $ 44.2 |
| Equity Office Properties | Blackstone | $ 39.0 |
| HCA Inc. | Bain, KKR, ML Private Equity | $ 33.5 |
| First Data Corp. | KKR | $ 30.8 |
| Alltel Corp. | GS, TPG | $ 27.8 |
| Clear Channel Communications Inc. | Bain, TH Lee | $ 26.8 |
| Hilton Hotels Corp. | Blackstone | $ 26.5 |
| Harrah's Entertainment Inc. | Apollo, TPG | $ 25.6 |
| Kinder Morgan Inc. | GSCP, Carlyle, Riverstone, Management | $ 21.6 |
| Albertsons Inc. | SuperValu, CVS, Cerberus | $ 17.1 |
| Freescale Semiconductor Inc. | Blackstone, Carlyle, Permira, TPG | $ 16.0 |
| Intelsat Ltd. | BC Partners | $ 15.9 |
| Univision Communications Inc. | MDP, Providence, TPG, TH Lee | $ 13.9 |
| VNU NV | Blackstone, Carlyle, KKR, TH Lee, H&F, AlpInvest | $ 11.5 |
| Philips Semiconductors | KKR, Silver Lake, AlpInvest | $ 11.2 |
| Biomet | Blackstone, GSCP, KKR, TPG | $ 10.9 |
| Home Depot Supply | Bain Capital, CD&R, Carlyle | $ 10.3 |
| **Total Transaction Value** | | **$ 383.2** |

Source: Thomson Financial

EXHIBIT 18.2

Brothers, Citigroup, and Morgan Stanley as co-investors. The transaction was announced at the peak time for securing financial leverage, but was funded after the credit markets started freezing up. The investment banks considered paying a $1 billion break-up fee to get out of their debt funding commitment, but agreed to fund, taking an estimated $900 million in theoretical or actual debt underwriting losses. See Exhibits 18.3, 18.4, and 18.5 for a summary of the transaction. TXU, which was renamed Energy Future Holdings Corporation (EFH) after the acquisition was completed, had a fourth quarter 2008 loss of $8.86 billion, causing KKR to write down the value of their holding by 30%. EFH shut down 15 generating plants in Texas during 2008 (22% of capacity), because they could not operate these plants profitably. In spite of these difficulties, and a $38 billion debt load, KKR and TPG said that their investment was well positioned to survive an extended downturn. However, debt holders were not as sanguine during March 2009, given the 60 cents on the dollar trading level for senior secured bonds and 48 cents on the dollar trading level for the company's high-yield bonds at that time. Loans to EFH represent the largest single position in KKR's fixed income investment vehicle, compounding the firm's overall exposure to the company.

## TXU: Investment Summary

**Full Valuation**

- 8.9x closing enterprise value / EBITDA multiple was a 10-25% premium to other independent power producers
- Implied valuation due to a promised consumer price reduction was 9.0 – 10.0x

**Pre-Close Commitment**

- A price reduction of 10% and commitment not to raise prices through Sept 2009 created a potential $500 million EBITDA reduction
- There was also a $400 million commitment to invest in demand-side energy reduction initiatives

**Solid Industry Fundamentals**

- ✓ Low-beta industry
- ✓ Historical solid returns
- ✓ Stated 5-year investment horizon: (i) fully leveraged strong projected industry growth; and (ii) allowed financing markets to rebound

**Cash Cow**

- ✓ Enormous cash-generator
- ✓ ~$800 million in annual dividends to investors
- ✓ Selling 20% ownership interest in a subsidiary was expected to generate $1 billion
- ✓ Eliminate near-term CapEx in coal plants and ramp-up in nuclear

Source: Deal data based on press reports

**EXHIBIT 18.3**

## TXU: Sources and Uses / Closing Capital

| | | | Capital Structure | | | | | |
|---|---|---|---|---|---|---|---|---|
| $ in MMs | | % of | EBITDA | | | | | |
| Sources | $ | Capital | Multiple [1] | Interest Rate | Tenor | Uses | | $ |
| Revolver ($2,700MM) | $0 | 0.0% | 0.00x | L+ 3.50% | 6 yrs | Purchase of TXU Equity | | $32,105 |
| Letter of Credit Facility ($1,125MM) | $0 | 0.0% | 0.00x | 3.50% | 6 yrs | Existing Debt Assumed | | 8,000 |
| Term Loan | 16,450 | 36.1% | 3.20x | L+ 3.50% | 6 yrs | Refinancing of Existing Debt | | 4,000 |
| Delay-Draw Term Loan ($4,100MM) | 2,150 | 4.7% | 0.42x | L+ 3.50% | 7 yrs | Transaction Fees and Expenses | | 1,500 |
| **Senior Secured Debt** | **18,600** | **40.8%** | **3.62x** | | | | | |
| New Senior Unsecured Bridge / HY Notes | 11,250 | 24.7% | 2.19x | 10.25-11.25% | 8-10 yrs | | | |
| Existing Senior Unsecured Notes | 2,978 | 6.5% | 0.58x | Various | Various | | | |
| Pollution / Other Control Bonds | 5,022 | 11.0% | 0.98x | Various | Various | | | |
| **Total Senior Unsecured Debt** | **19,250** | **42.2%** | **3.74x** | | | | | |
| KKR Equity | 2,500 | 5.5% | 0.49x | | | | | |
| TPG Equity | 2,500 | 5.5% | 0.49x | | | | | |
| GS / Lehman / CITI / MS Equity | 2,755 | 6.0% | 0.54x | | | | | |
| **Total New Cash Equity** | **7,755** | **17.0%** | **1.51x** | | | | | |
| **Total Transaction Sources** | **45,605** | **100.0%** | **8.86x** | | | **Total Transaction Uses** | | **$45,605** |

[1] Estimated FYE 2007 EBITDA $5,145MM.

- $12 billion of pre-acquisition debt, but nearly $38 billion post-acquisition
- Substantial senior secured and total leverage of 3.6x and 7.4x, respectively

Source: Company filings

**EXHIBIT 18.4**

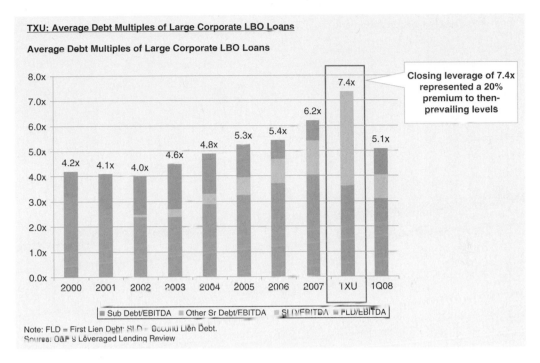

TXU: Average Debt Multiples of Large Corporate LBO Loans

**EXHIBIT 18.5**

## Equity Office Properties (EOP)

When the $39 billion EOP transaction was agreed to in February 2007, the buyers were able to take advantage of the "best ever" debt financing environment for LBO transactions (see Exhibit 18.6). EOP (controlled by Sam Zell) was the largest U.S. publicly traded owner and manager of office buildings, with 580 properties boasting over 100 million square feet. The buyer was the real estate arm of The Blackstone Group, which competed with Vornado Realty Trust for over one month, before finally winning (see Exhibits 18.7 and 18.8). Within 3 weeks of completing the transaction, Blackstone had sold $20.6 billion of EOP's real estate, leaving them with $19 billion of net assets. See Exhibits 18.9 and 18.10 for a summary of the transaction's financing and valuation.

## Hospital Corporation of America (HCA)

HCA is the largest private operator of healthcare facilities in the world. As of the transaction date, they owned 169 hospitals and 108 surgery centers in 21 states, the United Kingdom, and Switzerland. The LBO was announced in July 2006 and closed in November 2006, for a total enterprise value of $33 billion. The private equity consortium included Bain Capital, KKR, Merrill Lynch Private Equity, and HCA founder Thomas F. Frist Jr. and members of his family, who contributed $800 million in equity. Exhibit 18.11 summarizes the transaction's valuation and the sources and uses of funds. HCA operated in a difficult industry environment, and shareholders had grown frustrated with poor stock market performance. To secure an acceptable IRR, the buyers relied on a challenging assumption that margins would not decline in the future (see Exhibit 18.12). An overview of the financing commitments is summarized in Exhibit 18.13.

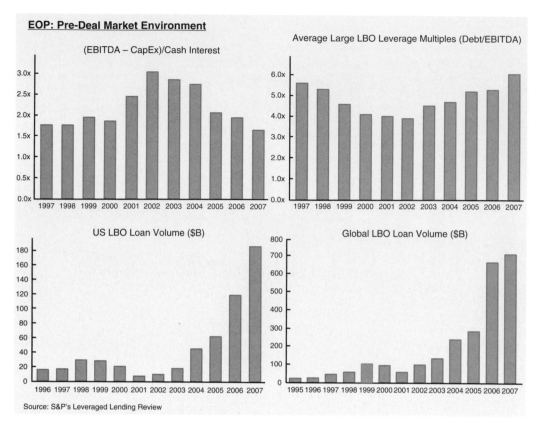

**EOP: Pre-Deal Market Environment**

Source: S&P's Leveraged Lending Review

**EXHIBIT 18.6**

**EOP: How Did the Bidding War for EOP Unfold?**

- Throughout 2006, EOP engages several parties regarding a potential sale
- November 2006: EOP accepts an all-cash offer by Blackstone to be acquired for $48.50/share, with a $200 million break-up fee, but before closing, the following events occurred:

**Timeline of Events: January 17, 2007 – February 5, 2007**

| January 17 | January 25 | January 31 |
|---|---|---|
| Consortium of Vornado, Starwood Capital, and Walton Street submits a bid for $52/share using 40% stock and 60% cash | Blackstone raises its all-cash offer to $54/share and break-up fee increased to $500 mm. EOP board re-affirms support | Vornado submits an offer for $56 using 45% stock and 55% cash |

| February 4 | February 5 | |
|---|---|---|
| Vornado revises bid to include up-front cash for 55% of the shares | Blackstone raises its offer to $55.50/share and break-up fee increased to $720 mm. EOP board re-affirms support | |

Source: Press reports and company press releases

**EXHIBIT 18.7**

## EOP: Why was Blackstone's Offer Superior?

On February 7, Vornado withdrew its proposal and EOP shareholders unanimously approved Blackstone's offer of $55.50/share, a 37.8% premium over the three month trading price

| Comparison of Proposals | | | |
|---|---|---|---|
| | Blackstone Transaction | Vornado Proposal | Considerations / Issues |
| Price / Share | $55.50 | $56.00 | EOP board preferred all cash offer to mix of cash/stock |
| Form of Consideration | 100% cash | 55% in cash; 45% Vornado stock | Use of stock adds complexity and valuation risk |
| Closing | Immediate | Uncertain | Vornado's closing was subject to shareholder approval of stock issuance |

EOP's board preferred the greater speed and certainty of closing offered by Blackstone

Source: Press reports and company press releases

**EXHIBIT 18.8**

## EOP: Valuation Analysis

| Valuation Metrics | | | | | |
|---|---|---|---|---|---|

**NAV & DCF Valuations**

**Net Asset Value**

| | Implied Share Price | |
|---|---|---|
| Gross Value Net of Liabilities | $45.6 | $49.1 |
| Gross Value Net of Liabilities & Transaction Costs | $43.8 | $47.2 |
| 2007 Nominal Cap Rates | 5.4% | 5.7% |
| Values Per Square Ft | $349.0 | $367.0 |

**Discounted Cash Flow**

| | Implied Share Price | |
|---|---|---|
| DCF Valuation | $41.3 | $46.1 |
| Terminal Value Multiples (2011 EBITDA) | 17.5x | 18.5x |
| Discount Rates | 7.25% | 7.75% |

**Comparable Companies Valuation**

**Comparable Companies Analysis**

| | Multiple | | Implied Share Price | |
|---|---|---|---|---|
| Funds From Operations (FFO) | 18.0x | 20.0x | $41.0 | $45.6 |
| 2007 EBITDA | 17.5x | 18.5x | $44.6 | $48.4 |

**Comparable Transaction Analysis**

| | Multiple | | Implied Share Price | |
|---|---|---|---|---|
| 2007 EBITDA | 18.0x | 19.0x | $46.0 | $49.8 |
| | Cap Rate | | | |
| 2007 Net Operating Income | 5.25% | 5.75% | $44.4 | $50.8 |

**Transaction Pricing Metrics**

| | |
|---|---|
| Offer Price | $55.5 |
| Equity Value | $24,631 |
| Net Debt | 12,743 |
| Preferred | 213 |
| Minority Interest | 1,396 |
| Total Transaction Value ($38.983 billion) | $38,983 |
| 2007 FFO Multiple (Funds from Operations) [1] | 23.8x |
| 2007 EBITDA Multiple [2] | 20.2x |

(1) Based on FirstCall consensus estimate of $2.33 as of February 5, 2007
(2) Based on Wall Street Research

**Transaction Premiums**

| | | |
|---|---|---|
| Closing Date | | 2/9/07 |
| Offer Price | | $55.50 |
| Premium to 11/1/06 unaffected price | $42.95 | 29.2% |
| Premium to 11/17/06 price | $44.72 | 24.1% |
| Premium to 3-month average | $40.26 | 37.9% |
| Premium to 6-month average | $38.24 | 45.1% |

Source: Company filings; analyst reports

**EXHIBIT 18.9**

## Harrah's Entertainment (Harrah's)

Harrah's is the world's largest provider of branded casino entertainment, and its business is operated through 50 casinos in six countries. The company's brand names in the United States are Harrah's, Caesars, and Horseshoe. The $26 billion acquisition of Harrah's by Apollo Global

## EOP: How was the Transaction Financed?

| EOP Post-LBO Capitalization ($ in billions) | | | | |
|---|---|---|---|---|
| **Initial** | | | **Post-Asset Sale** | |
| Equity – Blackstone | $4.3 | $20.6 billion of asset sales in 3 weeks, leaving $19.0 billion of net assets | Equity – Blackstone | $4.3 (est.) |
| Bridge – GS, Bear, B of A | $3.3 | | Bridge – GS, Bear, B of A | --- |
| Assumed Debt | $2.3 | | Assumed Debt | $1.2 |
| New Debt | $29.7 | | CMBS & Mezzanine[1] | $13.5 (est.) |
| Total | $39.6 | | Total | $19.0 |

Note 1: Completed at tight levels with range of LIBOR plus 100 to 300 b.p.
Source: Press reports

**EXHIBIT 18.10**

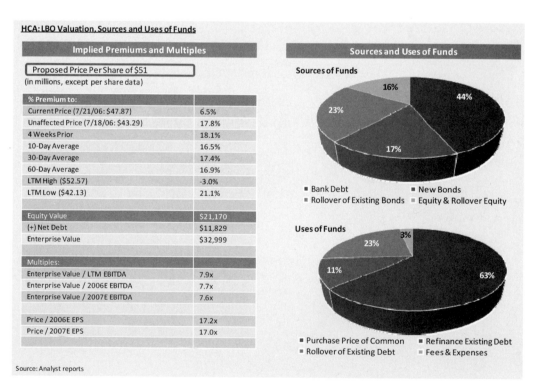

### HCA: LBO Valuation, Sources and Uses of Funds

**Implied Premiums and Multiples**

Proposed Price Per Share of $51
(in millions, except per share data)

| % Premium to: | |
|---|---|
| Current Price (7/21/06: $47.87) | 6.5% |
| Unaffected Price (7/18/06: $43.29) | 17.8% |
| 4 Weeks Prior | 18.1% |
| 10-Day Average | 16.5% |
| 30-Day Average | 17.4% |
| 60-Day Average | 16.9% |
| LTM High ($52.57) | -3.0% |
| LTM Low ($42.13) | 21.1% |
| | |
| Equity Value | $21,170 |
| (+) Net Debt | $11,829 |
| Enterprise Value | $32,999 |
| | |
| Multiples: | |
| Enterprise Value / LTM EBITDA | 7.9x |
| Enterprise Value / 2006E EBITDA | 7.7x |
| Enterprise Value / 2007E EBITDA | 7.6x |
| | |
| Price / 2006E EPS | 17.2x |
| Price / 2007E EPS | 17.0x |

**Sources and Uses of Funds**

Sources of Funds

16% / 44% / 23% / 17%

- Bank Debt
- New Bonds
- Rollover of Existing Bonds
- Equity & Rollover Equity

Uses of Funds

3% / 23% / 11% / 63%

- Purchase Price of Common
- Refinance Existing Debt
- Rollover of Existing Debt
- Fees & Expenses

Source: Analyst reports

**EXHIBIT 18.11**

Management and TPG Capital was announced during October 2006 and, after besting a competing offer from Penn National, closed during January 2008, following the Nevada Gaming Commission's granting of final approval. This transaction carried very high debt levels, with total debt at almost 10× EBITDA. In addition, some of the debt utilized PIK toggles (an important

## HCA: Transaction Rationale

| | |
|---|---|
| *Buyers' Perspective* | • Difficult industry environment and depressed valuations made industry attractive to sponsors<br>  ○ Good LBO candidate:<br>    – Low entry multiple: 7.9x LTM EBITDA of $4.1 billion vs. comp range of 8.0x – 9.5x<br>    – Margin improvement through divestiture of underperforming assets<br>    – Possible multiple expansion through IPO: HCA already had a successful LBO, with an IPO exit in 1993, creating ~39% IRR for sponsors<br>• Low probability of competition for deal |
| *Management Perspective* | • Greater operating flexibility in tough industry environment<br>• Create shareholder value – best alternative based on review of strategic alternatives<br>• Participate in future upside potential of Company through equity rollover in transaction |
| *Shareholders' Perspective* | • Poor stock price performance since 2002 despite share repurchases<br>• Offer price likely best offer due to size of company and management involvement |
| *Risks* | • Financing – capital markets' appetite for $27 billion of new debt<br>• Target IRR difficult to achieve if margins contract 1 – 2% due to increasing bad debt and competition<br>• Difficulty in gaining shareholder approval due to relatively low 18% premium |

**EXHIBIT 18.12**

## HCA: Summary of Debt Financing Commitments

• The Buyer Group submitted debt commitment letters from Merrill Lynch, Citigroup, Bank of America and J.P. Morgan
  ○ $16.8 billion of senior secured credit facilities, $5.7 billion of senior secured second lien bridge loans
• Financing commitments were not subject to the successful syndication of new credit facilities
• Bridge loan facility committed to by banks, with funding drawn down if bonds not placed prior to closing
  ○ Funding of bridge conditioned upon delivery of offering memorandum no less than 20 business days prior to funding
  ○ Company must use commercially reasonable efforts to ensure underwriters have 20 consecutive business days to market the bonds after receipt of offering memorandum
• Commitment letters have the same conditionality as in the Merger Agreement
  ○ Material Adverse Effect definition conformed, Representations matched Merger Agreement
  ○ Termination date consistent with Merger Agreement End Date
• Equity requirement equal to 15% of pro forma capitalization
  ○ Equity commitment letters delivered by the Buyer Group, with limited conditionality

**EXHIBIT 18.13**

feature to keep the company afloat if future cash flow is squeezed). Returns for this transaction are highly dependent on operating improvements and a reduction in CapEx. A key reason why the market accepted such high leverage was because of the creative separation of loans collateralized by Harrah's land from loans provided directly to the casino operations of the company (see Exhibit 18.14). Sources and uses for the LBO transaction are summarized in Exhibit 18.15.

**Harrah's: Real Estate Holdings**

- Harrah's owns approximately 350 acres, both developed and undeveloped, in Las Vegas and in other locations around the world

- Harrah's real estate holdings were used to raise $7.5 billion through commercial mortgage-backed securities

- TPG/Apollo leveraged the company's land holdings separately from the casino operations, enabling greater overall leverage

- Sale of unencumbered real estate may become an important source of cash to retire debt in the future

Source: Company filings

**EXHIBIT 18.14**

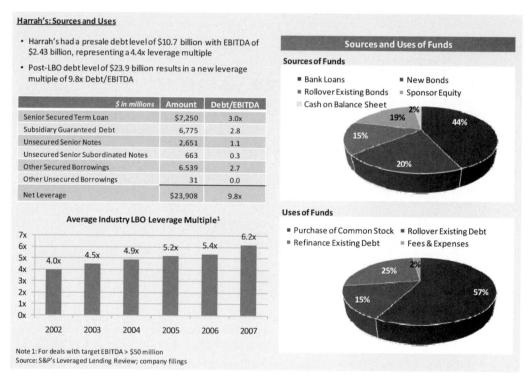

**Harrah's: Sources and Uses**

- Harrah's had a presale debt level of $10.7 billion with EBITDA of $2.43 billion, representing a 4.4x leverage multiple

- Post-LBO debt level of $23.9 billion results in a new leverage multiple of 9.8x Debt/EBITDA

| $ in millions | Amount | Debt/EBITDA |
|---|---|---|
| Senior Secured Term Loan | $7,250 | 3.0x |
| Subsidiary Guaranteed Debt | 6,775 | 2.8 |
| Unsecured Senior Notes | 2,651 | 1.1 |
| Unsecured Senior Subordinated Notes | 663 | 0.3 |
| Other Secured Borrowings | 6.539 | 2.7 |
| Other Unsecured Borrowings | 31 | 0.0 |
| Net Leverage | $23,908 | 9.8x |

**Average Industry LBO Leverage Multiple[1]**

Note 1: For deals with target EBITDA > $50 million
Source: S&P's Leveraged Lending Review; company filings

**EXHIBIT 18.15**

During February 2009, Harrah's massive debt package was restructured in order to keep the company out of bankruptcy court. Harrah's entered into a debt-exchange offer, exchanging their debt for new notes priced at a discount and with longer maturities. The company was required to offer a more senior position in their capital structure to the exchange parties to induce them to complete this transaction. New tax laws associated with the U.S. economic stimulus program allowed Harrah's to delay paying tax up front when the exchange occurred. Prior to the new law, a company that reduced the principal amount of debt through an exchange was required to pay taxes on the amount reduced, since it was considered taxable income. Now, taxes on cancellation of debt can be deferred for 5 years and then paid over a subsequent 5-year period. At the time of the exchange, Harrah's loans traded at 58 cents on the dollar, and their high-yield bonds traded at 6 cents on the dollar.

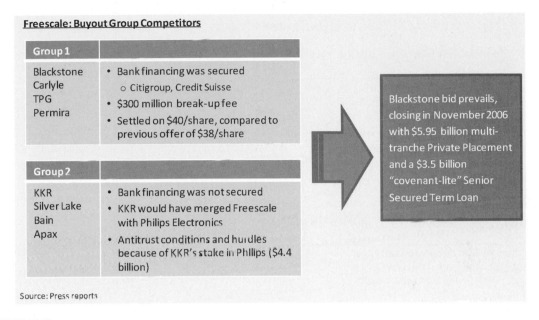

Source: Press reports

**EXHIBIT 18.16**

## Freescale Semiconductor (Freescale)

Freescale was formed in 2004 when Motorola spun off its Semiconductor Products Division. The company manufactures chips for wireless, networking, and automotive sectors. During September 2006, Blackstone led a consortium bid at $38 per share for Freescale, a 24% premium to the company's pre-announcement share price. Another consortium led by KKR quickly topped this by offering $42. Nevertheless, Blackstone's group (including Carlyle, TPG, and Permira) eventually won the bidding in November 2006 with a $40 price and a total consideration of $17.6 billion (see Exhibit 18.16). A *go-shop* provision allowed the company to solicit other proposals for 50 days, subject to a $300 million break-up fee, but no one else stepped up with a higher price. Leverage, at 5.7× EBITDA, was very high for a technology company acquisition, given the unpredictable cash flow represented by this company (and industry) and $3.5 billion of this leverage included *covenant-lite* and *PIK toggle* features. See Exhibit 18.17 for a summary of leverage, sources, and uses. This investment became problematic for the buyers: orders from Motorola, the principal customer, dropped significantly; the company's credit ratings were cut; and the pricing of both outstanding loans and bonds fell sharply in the secondary market. The buyers were forced to renegotiate with debt providers, entering into a debt exchange offer that reduced outstanding debt and extended maturities in exchange for higher interest rates and a more senior position in the capital structure.

## Univision

Univision is a Spanish language television, radio, music, and Internet company. The company was acquired by a consortium comprised of Madison Dearborn Partners, Provident Equity, Saban Capital Group, Texas Pacific Group, and Thomas H. Lee Partners for a total consideration of $13.6 billion. Leading up to the acquisition, Univision's EBITDA margin had grown from 34% to 38.5%, leverage had dropped to a debt-to-assets ratio of 16%, their television network was the most watched Spanish-language network, and their radio stations were in the top 5 in the

**Freescale: Sources and Uses and Leverage Analysis**

**Sources and Uses ($ in millions)**

| Sources | | Uses | |
|---|---|---|---|
| Cash on B/S | 2,365 | Purchase of Common Stock | 16,534 |
| Senior Term Loan | 3,500 | Total Rights/Warrants/Options | 675 |
| Private Placement | 5,950 | Assumed Net Liabilities | 1,523 |
| Sponsor Equity | 7,150 | Other | 233 |
| Total | 18,965 | Total | 18,965 |

| | |
|---|---|
| EBITDA LTM July 2006: | $ 1,559 |
| Implied EV | $ 15,122 |
| Implied EV/EBITDA | 9.7x |
| Implied EV/Revenues | 2.4x |

**Leverage Analysis ($ in millions)**

| | Amount | Debt/EBITDA (cumulative) |
|---|---|---|
| $3.5b Senior Secured Term Loan | $ 3,500 | 2.2x |
| $2.35b Senior Unsecured Notes | 2,350 | 3.8x |
| $1.6b Senior Subordinated Notes | 1,600 | 4.8x |
| $1.5 PIK Notes | 1,500 | 5.7x |
| $0.5m Floating Rate Notes | 500 | 6.1x |
| Total | 9,450 | 6.1x |
| | | |
| Remaining cash on B/S | 635 | |
| | | |
| Net Leverage | $ 8,815 | 5.7x |

Source: Press reports; Capital IQ

**EXHIBIT 18.17**

16 markets they competed in. The bidding process to acquire Univision started during February 2006, when the board announced their interest in considering alternatives to enhance shareholder value. A broad auction ensued that pitted a range of both financial buyers and strategic buyers. Ultimately, five parties qualified to submit bids, including three private equity consortiums, leading to closure during March 2007 (see Exhibit 18.18). A valuation analysis for the transaction is found in Exhibit 18.19, and a sources and uses analysis is found in Exhibit 18.20. This transaction included covenant-lite debt and a PIK toggle feature. A key criticism of the transaction is that projected EBITDA of $863 million was barely enough to cover combined annual interest costs plus capital expenditures.

## Private Equity Value Proposition for Corporations

There are three main areas where private equity investments may bring value to corporations: financial engineering, operational engineering, and governance engineering.

Financial engineering refers to efforts to add value by improving a company's capital structure. Improvement means making the capital structure more efficient by reducing the cost of capital. This is achieved by adding leverage from new outside sources.

Operational engineering refers to efforts by private equity firms to improve their portfolio companies through formal and informal consulting services. This consulting may help improve production processes, marketing, and product mix decisions, and ultimately increase working capital.

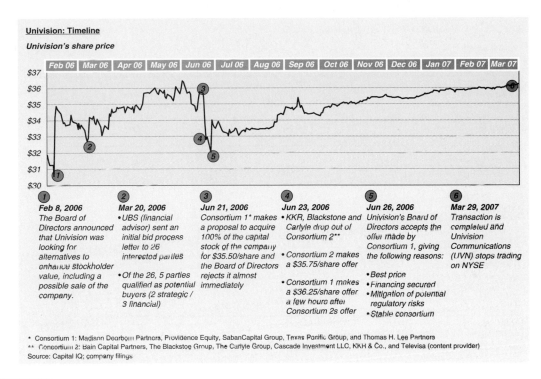

**Univision: Timeline**

*Univision's share price*

| | | | | | | | | | | | | | |
|---|---|---|---|---|---|---|---|---|---|---|---|---|---|
| | Feb 06 | Mar 06 | Apr 06 | May 06 | Jun 06 | Jul 06 | Aug 06 | Sep 06 | Oct 06 | Nov 06 | Dec 06 | Jan 07 | Feb 07 | Mar 07 |

| ① | ② | ③ | ④ | ⑤ | ⑥ |
|---|---|---|---|---|---|
| **Feb 8, 2006** | **Mar 20, 2006** | **Jun 21, 2006** | **Jun 23, 2006** | **Jun 26, 2006** | **Mar 29, 2007** |
| The Board of Directors announced that Univision was looking for alternatives to enhance stockholder value, including a possible sale of the company. | • UBS (financial advisor) sent an initial bid process letter to 26 interested parties<br><br>• Of the 26, 5 parties qualified as potential buyers (2 strategic / 3 financial) | Consortium 1* makes a proposal to acquire 100% of the capital stock of the company for $35.50/share and the Board of Directors rejects it almost immediately | • KKR, Blackstone and Carlyle drop out of Consortium 2**<br><br>• Consortium 2 makes a $35.75/share offer<br><br>• Consortium 1 makes a $36.25/share offer a few hours after Consortium 2s offer | Univision's Board of Directors accepts the offer made by Consortium 1, giving the following reasons:<br><br>• Best price<br>• Financing secured<br>• Mitigation of potential regulatory risks<br>• Stable consortium | Transaction is completed and Univision Communications (UVN) stops trading on NYSE |

\* Consortium 1: Madison Dearborn Partners, Providence Equity, SabanCapital Group, Texas Pacific Group, and Thomas H. Lee Partners
\*\* Consortium 2: Bain Capital Partners, The Blackstone Group, The Carlyle Group, Cascade Investment LLC, KKR & Co., and Televisa (content provider)
Source: Capital IQ; company filings

**EXHIBIT 18.18**

**Univision: Transaction Values Overview**
*($ in millions)*

*Enterprise Value and Leverage Summary*

| | Amount | Multiple of LTM EBITDA |
|---|---|---|
| Transaction Proceeds (excl. fees) | $12,397 | |
| Approximate Existing Debt | 970 | |
| Remaining Cash on Balance Sheet | 104 | |
| Enterprise Value | $13,470 | 19.4x |
| Transaction Fees | 144 | |
| Total Transaction Value | $13,614 | 19.6x |
| LTM EBITDA | $694 | |

| Trading Multiples | | | |
|---|---|---|---|
| | Total Enterprise Value / | | |
| **Comparables** | LTM EBITDA (x) | 2006E EBITDA(x) | 2007E EBITDA (x) |
| High | 14.0x | 13.1x | 12.2x |
| Low | 8.2x | 7.7x | 7.5x |
| Median | 10.8x | 10.0x | 11.0x |
| **Univision** | | | |
| Pre-Announcement Price | 18.0x | 14.8x | 13.1x |
| Univision at $36.25 Offer | 19.4x | 16.7x | 15.1x |

Source: Company filings

| Premium Analysis (@ $36.25 ) | | |
|---|---|---|
| | Price | Premium |
| **Strategic Announcement (February 8, 2006)** | | |
| One-day prior | $30.54 | 18.7% |
| 30-day average | $31.36 | 15.6% |
| | | |
| **Transaction Announcement (June 26, 2006)** | | |
| One-day prior | $32.95 | 10.0% |
| One-week prior | $35.70 | 1.5% |
| One month prior | $36.09 | 0.4% |
| 30-day average | $35.23 | 2.9% |

**EXHIBIT 18.19**

Governance engineering refers to initiatives by private equity firms to create value in portfolio companies by improving incentives and creating monitoring processes that focus on improvements in cash flow through cost reductions and increases in revenues. Many other areas

**Univision: Transaction Sources and Uses and Leverage Analysis**

*Sources & Uses*
($ in millions)

| Sources | | Uses | |
|---|---|---|---|
| Cash on Balance Sheet | $103.5 | Purchase of Common Stock | $11,247 |
| Senior Secured Term Loan Facility | 7,000 | Purchase of Stock Options | 130 |
| Senior Notes | 1,500 | Purchase of all Warrants | 994 |
| Second Lien-Asset Sale Bridge | 500 | Restricted Stock | 26 |
| Sponsor Equity (Approx) | 3,437 | Merger Related Expenses | 144 |
| **Total** | **$12,541** | | **$12,541** |

*Merger Related Expenses*

| | |
|---|---|
| Share-based compensation expense | $46 |
| Change in control payments to employees | $42 |
| Advisory success fee | $33 |
| Legal fees | $16 |
| Other non-compensation expenses | $4 |
| Other compensation expenses | $3 |
| **Total** | **$144** |

*Leverage Analysis*

| | | | Cumul. Multiple | |
|---|---|---|---|---|
| Bank revolving credit facility | $0 | (up to $750) | 0.0x | |
| Bank senior secured term loan facility | 7,000.0 | | 10.1x | |
| Bank second-lien asset sale bridge loan | 500.0 | | 10.8x | |
| Senior notes – 9.75%/10.50% due 2015 | 1,500.0 | (with PIK interest) | 13.0x | |
| Senior notes – 7.85% due 2011 | 525.3 | | 13.7x | Portion of |
| Senior notes – 3.875% due 2008 | 246.1 | | 14.1x | "old" debt |
| Senior notes – 3.5% due 2007 | 198.4 | | 14.4x | |
| Total | $9,970 | | 14.4x | |
| Remaining Cash on Balance Sheet | (104) | | -0.1x | |
| Net Leverage | $9,866 | | 14.2x | |

Source: Company filings

**EXHIBIT 18.20**

are monitored as well to determine results against expectations. Managers are directly compensated based on performance in achieving targeted results.

Some portfolio companies respond well to these three forms of engineering, creating significantly more value for a private equity firm than they had previously produced as a public company with a distributed shareholder ownership model. Other portfolio companies have done poorly, unable to operate well with higher leverage, and not able to respond well to the operational and governance models imposed on them by private equity owners.

## Corporate Rationale for Completing Private Equity Transactions

Companies that have strong cash flow, leveragable balance sheets, low capital expenditures, high-quality assets, and the ability to raise cash through asset sales, are good targets for private equity firms. Sometimes, these companies sell to private equity firms simply because their senior management and board can obtain a very high sale premium, and they conclude that this is the best way to maximize shareholder value. Examples of other companies that might consider a sale to a private equity firm follow.

## Alternative to an IPO

Private companies that need new capital to facilitate growth opportunities may consider an IPO. Family-owned companies that have no succession plan when a founder is ready for retirement may also consider an IPO. An alternative to an IPO is a sale to a private equity fund if the owners want a significant reduction in their exposure to the company. An IPO typically results in the sale of less than 50% of a company (and sometimes as low as 15%), but a sale to a PE firm would result in the transfer of a majority position.

## Corporate Orphans

Some companies operate multiple business units under a holding company ownership structure. Normally, all of these business units have activities that are somewhat related and benefit from common ownership. However, sometimes, business activities change or markets change, and one business unit might not be as related or synergistic with other business units. In this case, a holding company might consider the sale of the *orphan* business. Private equity firms are sometimes the best buyers of an orphan business because they (1) avoid potential antitrust concerns that may arise in a sale to a strategic buyer and (2) minimize disclosure concerns.

## Ignored Public Companies

Equity research is a somewhat scarce resource since it is expensive to provide, and a series of regulatory changes in the United States during 2003 resulted in more limited coverage of public companies. Because of the lack of equity analyst coverage, some public companies' shares are not actively purchased by large institutional investors. As a result, their stock price may be negatively impacted. This can happen to an entire industry as well if the industry has suffered a major upheaval. For companies suffering from a sustained weakness in share price, a private equity buyer might be able to pay a significant premium to the company's current share price if the company has strong cash flow, a leveragable balance sheet, and the other characteristics of a good target, as described.

## Operating or Financial Weakness

If a company has operating weakness in sourcing, distribution, or other operating processes, a private equity firm may be able to bring in new resources to fix these problems. Private equity firms can also significantly bolster a company's access to new sources of financing.

## Mandated Divestitures

Sometimes a regulator requires the sale of a business unit as part of an M&A transaction in order to resolve a restraint of trade concern. The required sale is designed to mitigate concerns that regulators such as the Federal Trade Commission have in relation to their antitrust oversight responsibilities. A private equity firm is frequently the preferred buyer, compared to another company in the same industry, because a strategic buyer might create the same restraint of trade concern that gave rise to the original regulator-mandated sale order.

# Private Equity as an Alternative Model of Corporate Governance

The two principal historical models of corporate ownership are (1) dispersed public ownership across many shareholders; and (2) family-owned or closely held. Private equity ownership is a hybrid between these two models.

The main advantages of public ownership include giving a company the widest possible access to capital, and for start-up companies, more credibility with suppliers and customers. The key disadvantages are that a public listing of stock brings constant scrutiny by regulators and the media, incurs significant costs (listing, legal, and in the U.S., Sarbanes-Oxley and other regulatory compliance costs), and a significant focus on short-term financial results from a dispersed base of shareholders, many of whom are not well informed. Most investors in public companies have limited ability to influence a company's decision making because ownership is so dispersed. As a result, if a company performs poorly, these investors are inclined to sell shares instead of attempting to engage with management through the infrequent opportunities to vote on important corporate decisions. This unengaged oversight opens the possibility of managers potentially acting in ways that are contrary to the interests of shareholders.

Family-owned or closely held companies avoid regulatory and public scrutiny. The owners also have a direct say in the governance of the company, minimizing potential conflicts of interest between owners and managers. However, the funding options for these private companies are mainly limited to bank loans and other private debt financing. Raising equity capital through the private placement market is a cumbersome process that often results in a poor outcome.

Private equity firms offer a hybrid model that is sometimes more advantageous for companies that are uncomfortable with both the family-owned/closely held and public ownership models (see Exhibit 18.21). Companies owned by private equity firms avoid public scrutiny and

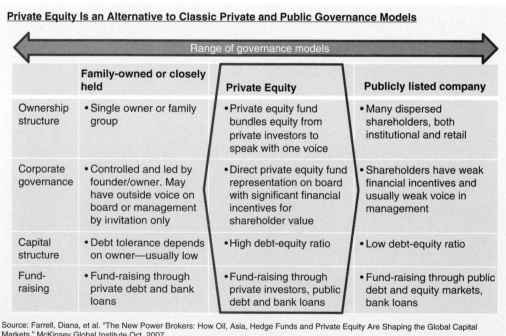

**Private Equity Is an Alternative to Classic Private and Public Governance Models**

Range of governance models

|  | Family-owned or closely held | Private Equity | Publicly listed company |
|---|---|---|---|
| Ownership structure | • Single owner or family group | • Private equity fund bundles equity from private investors to speak with one voice | • Many dispersed shareholders, both institutional and retail |
| Corporate governance | • Controlled and led by founder/owner. May have outside voice on board or management by invitation only | • Direct private equity fund representation on board with significant financial incentives for shareholder value | • Shareholders have weak financial incentives and usually weak voice in management |
| Capital structure | • Debt tolerance depends on owner—usually low | • High debt-equity ratio | • Low debt-equity ratio |
| Fund-raising | • Fund-raising through private debt and bank loans | • Fund-raising through private investors, public debt and bank loans | • Fund-raising through public debt and equity markets, bank loans |

Source: Farrell, Diana, et al. "The New Power Brokers: How Oil, Asia, Hedge Funds and Private Equity Are Shaping the Global Capital Markets." McKinsey Global Institute Oct. 2007.

**EXHIBIT 18.21**

quarterly earnings pressures. Because private equity funds typically have an investment horizon that is longer than the typical mutual fund or other public investor, portfolio companies can focus on longer-term restructuring and investments. Private equity owners are fully enfranchised in all key management decisions, because they appoint their partners as non-executive directors to the company's board and sometimes bring in their own managers to run the company. As a result, they have strong financial incentives to maximize shareholder value. Since the managers of the company are also required to invest in the company's equity alongside the private equity firm, they have similarly strong incentives to create long-term shareholder value. However, the significant leverage that is brought into a private equity portfolio company's capital structure puts pressure on management to operate virtually error free. As a result, if major, unanticipated dislocations occur in the market, there is a higher probability of bankruptcy compared to either the family-owned/closely held or public company model, which includes less leverage.

## Private Equity Influence on Companies

In addition to impacting the companies that they purchase, private equity firms also influence other companies' managers and boards, as well as the broader capital markets (see Exhibit 18.22).

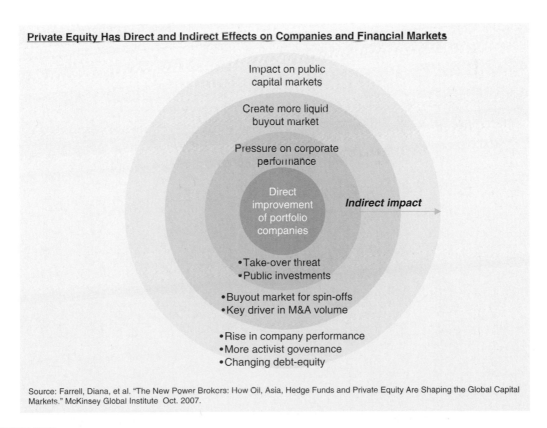

**Private Equity Has Direct and Indirect Effects on Companies and Financial Markets**

Source: Farrell, Diana, et al. "The New Power Brokers: How Oil, Asia, Hedge Funds and Private Equity Are Shaping the Global Capital Markets." McKinsey Global Institute Oct. 2007.

**EXHIBIT 18.22**

## Pressure on Corporate Performance

Private equity funds create competitive pressures on companies that want to avoid being acquired. CEOs and boards of public companies have been forced to review their performance and take steps to improve. In addition, they have focused more on anti-takeover strategies. Many companies have initiated large share-repurchase programs as a vehicle for increasing earnings per share (sometimes using new debt to finance repurchases). This effort is designed, in part, to make a potential takeover more expensive and therefore less likely.

## Changing Capital Structure

Companies consider adding debt to their balance sheet in order to reduce the overall cost of capital and achieve higher returns on equity. This strategy is sometimes pursued as a direct response to the potential for a private equity takeover. However, increasing leverage runs the risk of lower credit ratings on debt, which increases the cost of debt capital and reduces the margin for error. Although some managers are able to manage a more leveraged balance sheet, others are ill equipped, which can result in a reduction in shareholder value through mismanagement.

## Reduction in Public Market Capitalization

During 2006 and 2007, more companies were delisted from NYSE Euronext (the New York Stock Exchange) and taken private than companies that listed IPOs on this exchange. The same thing occurred on the London Stock Exchange during these years. Overall, the reduction in market capitalization resulting from private equity acquisitions exceeded the new market capitalization created from IPOs on both exchanges during this period.

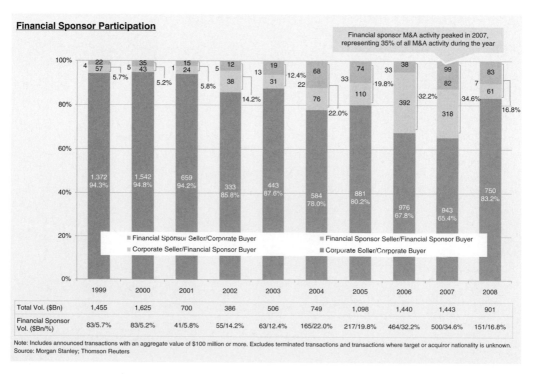

**EXHIBIT 18.23**

## Mergers and Acquisitions

Companies have historically been purchased principally by other companies in their same industry since these companies can find synergies through the acquisition, thereby justifying a large premium to the pre-announcement share price of the target company. However, with the availability of low-cost debt financing to private equity firms through mid-2007, a large number of M&A auctions were won by private equity firms, in spite of the fact that they usually could not match the synergy-based rationale for a high purchase price. Instead, private equity firms were competitive, in part, because they included a highly leveraged capital structure assumption in their valuation analysis to justify a high purchase price offer. As shown in Exhibit 18.23, almost 35% of all M&A transactions completed during 2007 involved a private equity firm.

# Questions

1. What are some measurable benefits from private equity ownership of corporations?
2. What were the World Economic Forum's principal conclusions regarding private equity firms?
3. What were the principal perceived benefits for the PE consortium's acquisition of TXU?
4. In hindsight, what were some of the errors committed by the buyout group for TXU?
5. What were the principal risks faced by the PE consortium when they made their bid to acquire HCA?
6. What aspect of Harrah's business makes it *not* a good buyout target?
7. What is the impact of highly leveraged deals on the portfolio companies' ability to compete in their industries?
8. Describe the three main areas where private equity investments may bring value to corporations.
9. Which of the three private equity value propositions for corporations has become most problematic in recent years?
10. What is a benefit of having a financial buyer versus a strategic buyer in an M&A transaction?
11. Why did financial sponsor participation in the global M&A market drop from 2007 to 2008? What percentage of the market did financial sponsor activity represent during these 2 years?
12. Based on the description of the ideal buyout target in the beginning of the section titled "Corporate Rationale for Private Equity Transaction," which of the companies described in the section "Private Equity Portfolio Companies Purchased During 2006–2007" were the most suitable buyout targets?

# 19

# Organization, Compensation, Regulation, and Limited Partners

## Organizational Structure

A private equity fund is usually structured as a limited partnership that is owned jointly by a private equity firm (General Partner) and other investors, such as pension funds, insurance companies, high-net-worth individuals, family offices, endowments, foundations, fund of funds, and sovereign wealth funds (all of which are Limited Partners). The General Partner manages and controls the private equity fund (see Exhibit 19.1).

Private equity investments are often channeled through a new company (NewCo) that receives equity investments from a private equity fund and (usually) management of the target company. NewCo also obtains debt financing from lenders. The proceeds of the debt and equity capital received by NewCo are then used to acquire the target company (see Exhibit 19.2).

The organizational structure of the private equity fund is developed with a view to maximizing incentive compensation for the General Partner. In this regard, tax considerations are paramount. The General Partner earns compensation based on the management of the fund, receiving management fees that usually equal about 2% of the assets under management and

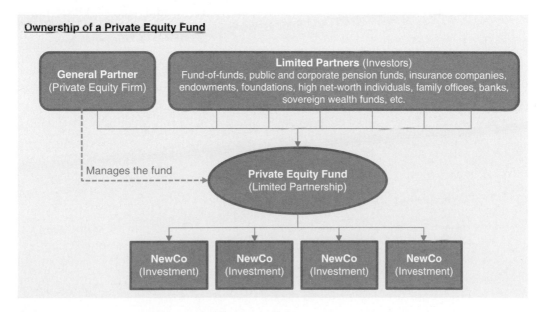

**Ownership of a Private Equity Fund**

**General Partner**
(Private Equity Firm)

**Limited Partners** (Investors)
Fund-of-funds, public and corporate pension funds, insurance companies, endowments, foundations, high net-worth individuals, family offices, banks, sovereign wealth funds, etc.

Manages the fund

**Private Equity Fund**
(Limited Partnership)

**NewCo**
(Investment)

**NewCo**
(Investment)

**NewCo**
(Investment)

**NewCo**
(Investment)

**EXHIBIT 19.1**

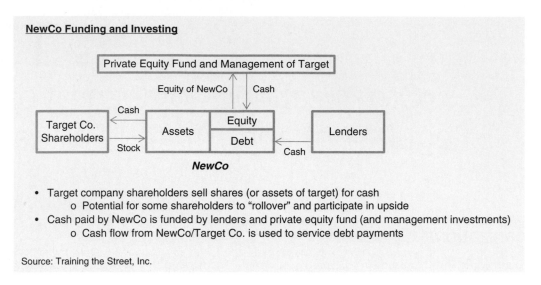

**EXHIBIT 19.2**

an interest in the profits of the investment activity, referred to as *carried interest*. Carried interest is normally considered for tax purposes as an allocation of a portion of the partnership's profits, which allows capital gains treatment. In the United States, a new tax bill may change this tax treatment, which, if passed, would tax carried interest received by fund managers as ordinary income instead of capital gains.

As discussed in previous chapters, the average carried interest is about 20% of profits. However, General Partners and Limited Partners must negotiate how the carried interest will be applied. For example, in the United States, a private equity fund is normally required to maintain capital accounts in accordance with the accounting method used by the tax partnership for Federal income tax purposes, where each partner has its own capital account. Conceptually, the capital accounts of all partners combined correspond to the consolidated stockholders' equity account in a corporate balance sheet.

The capital account of each partner is credited with the amount of any capital contributions by that partner and increased by the amount of net income of the partnership allocated to that partner. Equally, each partner's capital account is decreased whenever distributions are made to partners. In the event of a net loss from any investment, each partner receives an appropriate loss allocation. All net income and net loss must be allocated, since the partnership is not itself a taxpayer. The net worth of a partnership is, in effect, the sum of the interests of all partners.

## Closed-End Funds

Most private equity funds are *closed-end* funds, meaning that Limited Partners commit to provide cash for investments in companies and pay for certain fees and expenses, but they cannot withdraw their funds until the fund is terminated. This compares with mutual funds, where investors can withdraw their money any time. The General Partner in a private equity fund usually commits at least 1% of the total capital, and the balance is committed by Limited Partners. These funds are normally invested over a 4- to 5-year period, then there is a 5- to 8-year period during which the fund will exit investments and return capital and profits to all partners.

During the period of time that capital is invested, Limited Partners have very limited influence on how the capital is spent as long as the fund adheres to the basic covenants of the fund agreement. Some of these covenants relate to restrictions on how much capital can be invested in any one company and the types of securities in which the fund can invest. In addition to management fees and carried interest, the General Partner sometimes receives deal and monitoring fees from portfolio companies in which the fund has invested. Some Limited Partners have objected to this arrangement and insist on applying deal and monitoring fees to reduce the management fees or splitting such fees 50/50 or 80/20 with the General Partner.

Private equity funds purchase public companies at premiums to their current share price that typically range from 10% to more than 50%, depending on the dynamics of the market and the industry of the target company. The purchase price has historically been financed with more than 50% (and sometimes as high as 80%) debt, which comes principally from senior secured loans and junior unsecured high-yield bonds. In the aftermath of the credit crisis of 2007 and 2008, the amount of debt available for transactions dropped significantly. The balance of the purchase price comes from the fund's *equity* capital. The providers of loans include banks, hedge funds, and historically, collateralized loan obligation managers (who bundled many different loans into a portfolio and then segmented the portfolio into different tranches based on seniority, before selling debt tranches to institutional investors).

## Exits

Private equity firms attempt to purchase companies at the lowest possible cost. They generally secure as much debt as possible (after considering associated risks), on the best possible terms (including low interest rates and flexible covenants) to fund the purchase price. At the same time, they consider how to retire debt and, potentially, pay dividends with the cash flow that the acquired company is expected to create. Finally, private equity firms consider alternative exit strategies at the end of the investment holding period, including an IPO, sale to a strategic buyer, sale to an LBO-backed company, sale to another private equity fund, recapitalization, or sale to management. In addition to these exit strategies, an eventual disposition of the company may be a bankruptcy or other unanticipated outcome.

Exhibit 19.3 shows the exit characteristics of leveraged buyouts over time. Based on this sample, the most common exit is a sale to a strategic buyer (38%), followed by sale to another private equity fund through a secondary buyout (24%), and then an IPO (14%). Bankruptcy is the exit outcome for 6% of the companies in the sample. By spreading this bankruptcy rate over an average holding period of 5.5 years, the rate per year is actually lower than the 1.6% average annual default rate for all U.S. corporate bond issuers during 1980–2002 (based on information from Moody's). This is counterintuitive, given that private equity portfolio companies have significantly higher leverage than the average company in Moody's universe. However, the 11% "unknown exits" category found in Exhibit 19.3 might bias this conclusion, since there may be unidentified foreclosures or other bankruptcies/receiverships in this category. For the 2005–2007 vintage year investments by private equity funds, the default rate is likely to be higher than the rate provided in this Exhibit because of relatively higher leverage and purchase prices, combined with the global financial crisis that started in mid-2007.

**Exit Characteristics of Leveraged Buyouts Across Time**

| Year of original LBO | 1970-1984 | 1985-1989 | 1990-1994 | 1995-1999 | 2000-2002 | 2003-2005 | 2006-2007 | Whole period |
|---|---|---|---|---|---|---|---|---|
| **Type of exit:** | | | | | | | | |
| Bankruptcy | 7% | 6% | 5% | 8% | 6% | 3% | 3% | 6% |
| IPO | 28% | 25% | 23% | 11% | 9% | 11% | 1% | 14% |
| Sold to strategic buyer | 31% | 35% | 38% | 40% | 37% | 40% | 35% | 38% |
| Secondary buyout | 5% | 13% | 17% | 23% | 31% | 31% | 17% | 24% |
| Sold to LBO-backed firm | 2% | 3% | 3% | 5% | 6% | 7% | 19% | 5% |
| Sold to management | 1% | 1% | 1% | 2% | 2% | 1% | 1% | 1% |
| Other/unknown | 26% | 18% | 12% | 11% | 10% | 7% | 24% | 11% |
| **No exit by Nov. 2007** | 3% | 5% | 9% | 27% | 43% | 74% | 98% | 54% |
| **% of deals exited within** | | | | | | | | |
| 24 months (2 years) | 14% | 12% | 14% | 13% | 9% | 13% | | 12% |
| 60 months (5 years) | 47% | 40% | 53% | 41% | 40% | | | 42% |
| 72 months (6 years) | 53% | 48% | 63% | 49% | 49% | | | 51% |
| 84 months (7 years) | 61% | 58% | 70% | 56% | 55% | | | 58% |
| 120 months (10 years) | 70% | 75% | 82% | 73% | | | | 76% |

Note: The table reports exit information for 17,171 worldwide leveraged buyout transactions that include every transaction with a financial sponsor in the Capital IQ database announced between 1/1/1970 and 6/30/2007. The numbers are expressed as a percentage of transactions, on an equally-weighted basis. Exit status is determined using various databases, including Capital IQ, SDC, Worldscope, Amadeus, Cao, and Lerner (2007), as well as company and LBO firm web sites.

Source: Kaplan, Steven N. and Per Strömberg. "Leveraged Buyouts and Private Equity." Journal of Economic Perspectives, Vol. 23, No. 1, Winter 2009, p129.

**EXHIBIT 19.3**

## Compensation

There are four sets of fees and expenses in a typical private equity agreement between General Partners and Limited Partners:

1. Management Fee: Usually 2% of total capital commitments until the end of a 4- to 5-year investment horizon, and then 2% of unreturned funded capital thereafter (declining as investments are sold or realized). This fee is payable semi-annually in advance. In addition, Limited Partners bear all organizational expenses incurred in the formation of the fund (often subject to a cap).

2. Carried Interest: This is an incentive payment that will be paid only after a certain rate of return is obtained by Limited Partners (see next section, "Preferred Returns"). The purpose of this payment is to create an approximate 80/20 split in profits above the return of capital plus preferred returns between Limited Partners and General Partners (subject to a Claw-back, as described below). For General Partners to receive carried interest, private equity funds must sell their portfolio companies, realizing gains at the time of sale. Alternatively, carried interest may be paid following interim dividends, distributions, partial sales, or reca-pitalizations before an ultimate sale. Profits or losses are generally recognized at the time of any of these corporate events.

3. Portfolio Company Fees and Expenses: These fees and expenses are paid directly by portfolio companies to the private equity firm. Potential fees and expenses include (1) transaction

fees when purchasing and (sometimes) when selling companies; (2) expenses related to proposed but unconsummated investments; (3) tax and accounting, litigation, general legal, and annual meeting expenses; (4) advisory and monitoring fees; and (5) director fees.

4. Additional Costs: In some cases, a number of additional costs can be imposed. For example cash proceeds can be retained by the General Partner for up to 3 months before being distributed to Limited Partners. In addition, distributions of marketable securities can be in kind (including selling restrictions), which can create extra costs for Limited Partners. Finally, Limited Partners may have to pay penalties for selling their stakes, or for defaults on a capital call.

Unrealized loss in portfolio companies has become an increasingly important issue for the industry, as valuation assumptions for many private equity fund portfolio companies declined significantly during 2008 and 2009. Another issue relates to whether management fees should be included as an expense for purposes of calculating profits that are subject to carried interest. Limited Partners have pressed to include these fees as an expense, since they are evaluated by their investors based on a cash out/cash in basis. There is now strong precedent for including management fees as an expense, although this is the subject of ongoing negotiations for some private equity firms.

## Preferred Returns

Most compensation arrangements include preferred returns, which must be paid to Limited Partners (after return of capital) before carried interest is paid to General Partners. Since Limited Partners invest in private equity funds based on an expectation of higher returns and somewhat higher risk, a preferred return helps to align interests between all partners by linking carried interest to superior returns.

There are two different ways to apply preferred returns: pure preferred returns and hurdle rates. A pure preferred returns approach provides that the carried interest percentage is applied only to profits in excess of a specified return. The effect of this is to reduce carried interest as a percentage of total profits. A hurdle rates approach includes a "catch-up" provision that eliminates this negative outcome for the General Partner if total investment returns are high enough (see Exhibit 19.4). This approach usually provides that a carried interest percentage is applied after returns exceed a predetermined hurdle rate, such as the yield on 1-year U.S. treasuries, LIBOR, or a market index such as the S&P 500.

## Timing Issues

The determination of carried interest and preferred returns is impacted by timing considerations. A private equity fund will normally make a number of different portfolio company investments over a 3- to 5-year investment horizon. Holding periods for each of these investments can vary dramatically, but generally they are for periods of 3 to 7 years. Compensation determination for both carried interest and preferred returns depends on how and when a fund calculates profits. For example, this determination can be made based on the sales date for portfolio companies, or alternatively, based on an averaging or netting process that allows earlier compensation allocations.

Most private equity funds apply an *aggregation* process by netting gains and losses from different portfolio investments as a mechanism to maintain General Partner focus on all

**Preferred Returns Catch-Up Provision**

- A General Partner catch-up provision can eliminate the negative consequences of a pure preferred return carve out for Limited Partners if investment returns are high enough. An example follows:
  - o For ease of reference, assume the following carried interest formula:
    1) 100% of profits (after investor capital is returned) are allocated to Limited Partners until they have received a pure preferred return of 8%, after which
    2) 100% of profits are allocated to the General Partner until the General Partner has received 20% of cumulative profits.
    3) All remaining profits are allocated 80% to the Limited Partners and 20% to the General Partner (the General Partner also shares in the 80% profit allocations to the extent of its investment in the fund).
- In this example, if total profits equal or exceed a 10% return, the General Partner receives 20% of total profits and the interim allocations of the preferred return are ultimately without economic substance. At lower return levels, the outcome is different.
- Therefore, an important factor in evaluating a carried interest formula which has a preferred return is whether there is a General Partner catch-up. This is an area where there remains substantial variation.
- While the General Partner catch-up allocation is often 100%, it is not uncommon to see interim allocations of 80% to the General Partner and 20% to the Limited Partners.

Source: Schell, James M. _Private Equity Funds: Business Structure and Operations_. Law Journal Press, 1999, pp2-16.

**EXHIBIT 19.4**

investments in their portfolio (see "Clawbacks" in the next section). A transaction-by-transaction approach to calculating carried interest is flawed from the perspective of alignment of interests. It can create a bias in favor of higher risk and potentially higher return investments. Although General Partners will lose their share of capital for a bad investment, since they are compensated at 20% of profits above the preferred return, they might reach for higher return investments (which carry correspondingly higher risk). By aggregating all gains and losses, there is less of an incentive for General Partners to make individual portfolio investments that bear disproportionate risk.

A fund must establish in advance whether the preferred return distribution waterfall (in which investor capital is returned first, then any recognized losses, followed by preferred returns and then carried interest) is based on the entire capital commitment from Limited Partners, or only on the percentage of capital that was initially allocated to the portfolio company being sold. Normally, the preferred return is based on the portion of capital initially allocated to fund each investment. This enables a larger carried interest payment to the General Partner and mitigates the possibility that the General Partner will alter the optimal timing for sale of a portfolio company.

Limited Partners do not know that their investment will be profitable until their original capital commitment has been recovered. In addition, the exact amount of profit from their investment is not known until the fund is liquidated and wound up. Although the uncertainty associated with interim determinations of a fund's profitability could be reduced by restricting carried interest distributions until after Limited Partner capital commitments are fully recovered, almost all private equity funds provide for carried interest payments to General Partners coincident with successful portfolio company exits. Limited Partners, therefore, implicitly assume that all remaining unrealized investments will generate proceeds at least equal to their carrying value.

## Clawbacks

Most funds have contractual provisions governing allocations and distributions of carried interest before 100% of Limited Partner capital commitments have been recovered. Based on this, initial investment gains that result in payment of carried interest to General Partners, when followed by investment losses, result in Limited Partners having the ability to recapture some of the carried interest paid. It is not uncommon for a fund to record significant profits during early years, as successful investments are exited, leaving less successful investments to be exited in the later years of a fund. In other words, successful portfolio companies are often sold fairly quickly, while troubled companies usually need time to be fixed before they can be sold. Moreover, when they are sold, the fix often does not restore full value, resulting in capital losses.

A *clawback* is a contractual provision that adjusts distortions in compensation to General Partners based on the timing of gains and losses. Normally, clawback provisions are effective at the time of liquidation and winding up of a fund. Depending on the carried interest formula and the cumulative performance of the fund, the General Partner may be obligated to return a portion of prior distributions of carried interest. Amounts returned are then distributed to Limited Partners.

Aggregation principles are achieved through a clawback, enabling early carried interest distributions, but recapturing some of these distributions if losses occur at later stages. This mitigates Limited Partner risk in terms of sharing early profits, and the risk that a General Partner might sub-optimally sell portfolio companies early in an effort to accelerate earnings.

Usually, General Partners limit the clawback to after-tax portions of prior distributions of carried interest, because they do not want to return a cash portion that they never received. In practice, the clawback provision usually refers to a hypothetical tax rate rather than the actual tax paid by the principals who operate the General Partner, because of different tax determinations that may apply to each principal. Even more important than tax considerations is the triggering event for the clawback. In many cases, the triggering event relates to a circumstance in which the General Partner receives more than 20% of profits, or if Limited Partners do not receive return of capital plus the full preferred return over the life of the fund.

Since carried interest and other distributions to the General Partner are normally immediately redistributed to principals of the General Partner, if a clawback obligation is triggered at the end of the underlying fund, the General Partner probably will not have sufficient cash to pay the clawback. As a result, Limited Partners often require principals of the General Partner to guarantee (often on a joint and several basis) the clawback obligations of the General Partner. Alternatively, sometimes Limited Partners require a portion of carried interest payments to be held as escrow by the General Partner in order to satisfy the clawback.

## Taxes

During February 2009, the U.S. administration pushed for tax changes that would affect private equity funds. Historically, carried interest was taxed based on the long-term capital gains rate of 15%, rather than ordinary income treatment, which could be as high as 37%, or the corporate capital gains tax rate of 35%. It appears unfair to many that a private equity fund that operates as a partnership is allowed to pay less than half the tax rate that public corporations pay for capital gains. Equally unfair to some is the fact that principals of private equity funds receive compensation through carried interest that is taxed at less than half the rate that applies to the compensation packages of employees of traditional asset management funds who receive salary and bonus-based compensation rather than carried interest. Although there are efficiency arguments against increasing taxes on managers of private equity funds (which would decrease the number of participants, causing less competition, and would change manager behavior, resulting in inefficient allocation of resources), the arguments favoring a more egalitarian tax structure may result in higher taxes for General Partner principals.

# Regulations

Historically, in the United States, the SEC has generally not imposed registration requirements on managers of private equity funds, because most managers of private equity funds manage 14 or less funds, and therefore qualify for exemption from registration under the Investment Advisers Act of 1940. However, a new bill (Private Fund Investment Advisers Registration Act of 2009) would eliminate this exemption, and if passed, all managers of private equity funds with assets under management of greater than $30 million will need to register as investment advisers with the SEC. Although the bill does not subject private equity funds to the same expansive regulation as mutual funds and other types of registered investment companies, private equity funds are subject under the bill to reporting, books and records, and anti–money laundering requirements. In addition, they must cooperate with SEC examination requests.

Private equity funds and their managers historically have relied on several key exemptions from the Investment Company Act and the Investment Advisers Act:

1. Investment Company Act: Funds do not need to register with the SEC based on exemptions contained in either Section 3(c)(1), for funds held exclusively by no more than 100 beneficial owners and that are not offered publicly, or 3(c)(7), for funds held exclusively by "qualified purchasers" and that are not offered publicly.
2. Investment Advisers Act: Fund managers do not need to register with the SEC as an investment advisor based on exemptions contained in Section 203(b)(3). Under these exemptions, private advisors do not need to register with the SEC if they have less than 15 clients (in the case of private equity, less than 15 funds), do not advise registered investment companies, and do not hold themselves out to the public as investment advisors.

New legislation would replace these exemptions, making it clear that a private equity fund is an *investment company* for purposes of the Investment Company Act, and that a private equity manager is an *investment advisor* for the purposes of the Investment Advisers Act. However, in the case of the Investment Company Act, this does not mean that funds that register under the new provisions are subject to the regulatory provisions that apply to public mutual funds. They will be exempt from certain provisions of the Investment Company Act if they register with the SEC, file an information form, maintain such books and records as the SEC requires, and cooperate with any request for information or examination by the SEC.

## Using Intermediaries

During May 2009, the State of New York entered into an agreement with The Carlyle Group, one of the largest private equity firms, regarding the use of intermediaries to obtain public pension fund investments. Carlyle paid the State of New York $20 million and agreed to comply with the following code of conduct: a ban on placement agents; a ban on campaign contributions to avoid *pay to play*; increased transparency through disclosure; a higher fiduciary standard of conduct; and strengthened conflicts of interest policies.

This agreement, in effect, limits the use of intermediaries by private equity funds in securing new Limited Partner investments, while creating more transparency and avoiding potential conflicts of interest.

## Perception and Reality

Although there are fewer regulations imposed in the United States on private equity funds compared to mutual funds, private equity funds and fund managers must comply with a number of regulations under federal law, including the following:

1. **Annual Privacy Notices.** Private equity funds are required to have and comply with a privacy policy, and to send a privacy notice to all Limited Partners who are individuals at the start of the partner's relationship with the fund and annually thereafter. The privacy notice must describe the fund's policy regarding disclosure of current and former Limited Partners' non-public information.
2. **Supplemental Filings Pursuant to the Investment Advisers Act of 1940.** All registered investment advisors must file with the SEC certain amendments on an annual basis and offer to provide a brochure with designated information to Limited Partners on an annual basis.
3. **Filings Pursuant to the Securities Exchange Act of 1934.** Filings of Form 13D, Schedule 13G and Form 4 following certain purchases and sales of securities must be made. In addition, filings may need to be made periodically with the SEC depending on circumstances, including Form 5 (directors, officers, and 10% stockholders regarding beneficial ownership); Form 13F, for holdings of over $100 million of Section 13(f) securities; and Schedule 13G (beneficial owners of public company issuers who are exempt from filing requirements of 13D).
4. **ERISA-Related Filing.** For funds in which more than 25% of the investors are pension plans, annual certification must be given to avoid *plan assets* regulations under the Employee Retirement Income Security Act of 1974. In addition, annual audited, and sometimes quarterly unaudited, financial reports must be delivered to Limited Partners.
5. **Private Placement Limitations.** U.S. private equity funds are typically sold via private placement and must adhere to limitations on private placements imposed by the Securities Act of 1933. Funds can only offer investment opportunities to investors with whom the fund or its sponsor has a preexisting relationship and who are accredited investors (individuals with a minimum net worth of $1 million or, alternatively, a minimum income of $200,000, $300,000 with spouse, in each of the previous 2 years and a reasonable expectation of reaching the same income level in the current year).
6. **Antifraud Rule.** The SEC's antifraud rule applies to registered and unregistered investment advisors. Pooled investment vehicles such as hedge funds and private equity funds are, among other restricted communications or practices, prohibited from making materially false or misleading statements regarding investment strategies that will be pursued by the pooled investment vehicle, the experience and credentials of the advisor and associated persons, the risks associated with investing in the pool, the performance of the pool and other funds advised by the advisor), the valuation of the pool and corresponding investor accounts, and practices the advisor follows in the operation of its advisory business such as how investment opportunities are allocated.
7. **Investment Advisors Act of 1940.** As mentioned earlier, under the Investment Advisors Act of 1940, advisors who have 15 or more clients (in the case of private equity funds, 15 or more funds) and $30 million or more in assets under management must register with the SEC. In addition, assuming legislation proposed by the Private Fund Investment Advisors

Registration Act of 2009 passes, the less-than-15 registration exemption would no longer apply, and any investment advisor with $30 million or more in assets under management will need to register with the SEC. Once registered, the advisors will be subject to regulatory reporting requirements, disclosure requirements to investors, creditors, and other counterparties, strong conflict of interest and antifraud prohibitions, robust SEC examination and enforcement authority, and recordkeeping requirements, and requirements for establishing a comprehensive compliance program.

8. **Investment Company Act of 1940.** As mentioned earlier, funds that do not meet the exemptions from the definition of an investment company must register as an investment company. In addition, assuming legislation proposed in 2009 to remove these exemptions passes, most private equity funds will need to register with the SEC as an investment company.

# Limited Partners

## Defaults

When a Limited Partner fails to make a scheduled payment, private equity funds must consider how to cover the missed contribution, how to treat the Limited Partner, and how and whether to replace the unfunded commitment. Most partnership agreements permit the defaulted amount to be called from other Limited Partners, but there are sometimes caps on the replacement amounts that can be called. Some agreements allow the partnership to borrow to cover the defaulted amount or to offset amounts distributable to cover the defaulted amount.

In the event of a default, the General Partner generally has sole discretion regarding what measures to take. In theory, the General Partner may be able to convince a court to require a Limited Partner to honor its capital contribution obligations. However, General Partners have historically been reluctant to sue their investors based on the concern that this action would have a negative impact on future fundraising. However, it is possible that under certain circumstances a General Partner may conclude that its duty to the other Limited Partners requires it to take action to enforce the terms of the partnership agreement.

The General Partner has a fiduciary duty to all partners (unless waived in the partnership agreement), requiring it to consider what action is in the fund's best interest, including the precedent that their decision will have in future potential defaults, the impact on existing credit facilities (which may trigger acceleration of outstanding loans), the potential effect on D&O (directors and officers) insurance policies (including pricing), audited financial and other reporting obligations, and voting and representation on advisory committees.

## Disclosure

When private equity fund industry average returns turned negative during 2008 and 2009, many Limited Partners asked for increased and more frequent disclosure. Instead of quarterly mark-to-market disclosure, some investors pushed for monthly disclosure so they could compare valuations with secondary market pricing and make more frequent risk management decisions.

## Fees

Many Limited Partners also pushed for and obtained fee reductions during this period, as the balance of power shifted to investors. Some private equity firms reduced management fees from 2% to 1.5% and performance fees from 20% to 15%, and some agreed to more favorable clawback arrangements. Competition from secondary market buying opportunities, where purchases could be made at up to 50% discounts, forced many private equity firms to become more accommodating in relation to fees.

## Secondary Market

A private equity secondary market enables Limited Partners and new investors to buy and sell private equity investments or remaining unfunded commitments to funds. Private equity investments are intended to be long-term investments. However, sometimes Limited Partners need to free up cash, or they become disillusioned with hypothetical losses and want to exit their investment. There is no listed public market for most private equity investments, but the secondary market that is facilitated by investment banks and others has grown substantially. This market creates a certain amount of liquidity to enable Limited Partners to sell their interest in a private equity fund to another party. These sales also remove from the selling Limited Partner any remaining unfunded obligations to the fund. Normally, the General Partner must give consent to any sale. See Exhibit 19.5.

The secondary market has grown considerably over the past 7 years (see Exhibit 19.6) and expectations are for continued growth. This is due, in part, to the fact that many Limited Partners became over-allocated to private equity following the significant decline in both public equity and debt markets during the financial crisis of 2008. There were an estimated $50 billion in private equity secondary trades during 2009, double the volume seen in 2008. Secondary bid spreads have declined every year since 2005, providing evidence for a more liquid market (see Exhibit 19.7).

During January 2009, Harvard University's endowment fund attempted to sell up to $1.5 billion of its private equity holdings through secondary market transactions, but the indicated pricing from prospective secondary buyers was not acceptable to the fund. Endowment funds from Duke University, Columbia University, and several other universities have sold portions of

Note 1: The most basic secondary transaction involves an investor selling its limited partnership interest in a fund. In some instances, however, a portfolio of direct company interests may be sold instead.

**EXHIBIT 19.5**

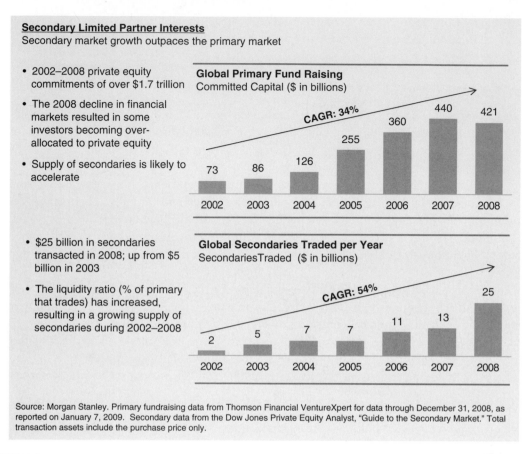

**EXHIBIT 19.6**

their private equity holdings in secondary transactions. The lack of cash coming out of private equity investments (because of a problematic exit environment), large drops in expected private equity valuations, and the need to fund university expenses all contributed to the focus by many large universities on selling part of their private equity portfolios in secondary markets during 2008 and 2009.

During May 2009, Goldman Sachs closed a new $5.5 billion fund designed to purchase private equity Limited Partner interests in the secondary market. Other prominent secondary-fund firms include Lexington Partners, Coller Capital, and Pomona Capital. During 2009, these funds focused on purchasing assets at prices of between 50% and 70%.

## FASB 157

Following November 15, 2008, the Financial Accounting Standards Board's (FASB) Statement No. 157 became effective. This statement defines fair value, establishes a framework for measuring fair value in GAAP (Generally Accepted Accounting Principles), and expands disclosures about fair value measurements. FASB 157 was not specifically promulgated with private equity funds in mind, and private equity funds have historically reported investment values to Limited Partners. However, FASB 157 changes the method for deriving fair value and the amount of disclosure regarding how fair value is determined. FASB 157 provides a hierarchy of inputs that must be used as the basis for determining value, including comparable company transactions and performance multiples.

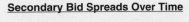

**Secondary Bid Spreads Over Time**

- Strong returns through 2007 attracted more capital and competition
- Thus, pricing for larger intermediated deals rose steadily
- During 2008, an environment of increased supply and uncertain asset values altered the bid spreads materially

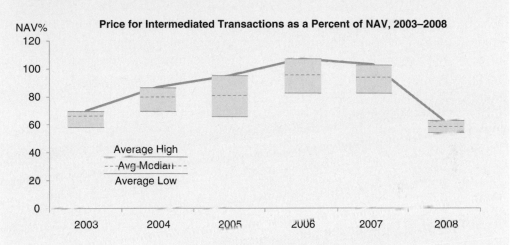

Source: Morgan Stanley. Reported data from funds marketed and sold by Cogent Partners. 2008 reported data consists of 56% Buyout funds, 38% Venture Funds, and 6% other funds. Data reflects the period from January 1, 2003 through December 31, 2008.

**EXHIBIT 19.7**

Historically, private equity funds valued assets at cost or used the latest round of financing as the basis for determining fair value. This approach is no longer consistent with the fair value determination requirements of FASB 157. As a result, during 2008 and 2009, Limited Partners received valuation disclosures for some portfolio companies that showed dramatically lower values than were previously disclosed. This is because, among other things, earnings for most companies dropped significantly during this period and, at the same time, enterprise value/EBITDA multiples contracted because of concerns about a long recession. For example, for a hypothetical buyout in 2007, a company's EBITDA may have been $100 million and a private equity fund may have purchased the company at an enterprise value/EBITDA multiple of 10×, funding the purchase with 60% debt ($600 million) and 40% equity ($400 million). If, during 2008, the company's EBITDA dropped to $66.7 million and comparable companies multiples dropped to 9×, the portfolio company's equity would be wiped out, assuming an unchanged debt amount of $600 million (9 × $66.7 = $600 million, which equals the debt obligation, leaving no equity value).

## Questions

1. What is a difference between the organizational structure of private equity funds and hedge funds?
2. What are similarities and differences in the compensation structure for private equity funds and hedge funds?
3. Based on the fee structure in Exhibit 19.4, calculate the amount of profits allocated to the General Partner and Limited Partners in year 5 and year 6 based on the following: Fund

ABC has $100 million in committed capital. In year 5, the fund monetizes its first holding, generating $10.5 million in the sale. The fund invested $10 million originally in the company. In year 6, the fund sells its second holding, generating $18 million in proceeds for the fund. The original equity investment was $12 million. For simplicity's sake, assume the holding period for each company was one year. Also, there have been no other divestitures, dividends, recapitalizations, etc.

4. Now assume that the fund in Question 3 sells another portfolio company, but this time, records a loss. The original equity investment was $8 million, but the fund was only able to generate $5 million in proceeds after the sale. Assume the holding period was also one year (so just under the threshold for long-term capital gains treatment). The applicable tax rate is 37%. How much will the GP need to return as an after-tax clawback?

5. In the United States, which provisions have private equity funds historically relied on to avoid registration with the SEC?

6. Why is there a secondary market for private equity funds but not hedge funds?

7. Based on HCA buyout Exhibits 18.11–18.13, calculate the value of the financial sponsors' equity stake in HCA, based on FASB 157's fair value determination requirements. Assume HCA's EBITDA dropped by 20% from its LTM EBITDA at the time of the transaction, no debt has been paid down, and valuation multiples have decreased to 6.5×.

# 20

# Private Equity Issues and Opportunities

From 2002 through 2007, a benign interest rate environment, combined with low default rates and ample credit, enabled private equity funds to grow dramatically. Assets under management increased by more than 10 times, and individual transaction values increased to more than $40 billion. This remarkable period came to an abrupt halt during the second half of 2007, as the world entered the worst credit crisis in over 75 years. Many of the private equity deals that closed during 2005–2007 became big disappointments, with equity values dropping on some of these investments to 50 cents on the dollar and lower. During 2008 and 2009, bankruptcy courts became busy focusing on private equity portfolio company failures, and investors became more cautious in channeling money into private equity funds. In spite of the difficulties faced by the industry, as of mid-2009, private equity funds had over $1 trillion in cash to invest. Many of these funds viewed the low corporate valuations caused by a global recession, combined with their huge war chest of funds, as an excellent opportunity to create strong future investment returns.

## PIPEs

During 2008 and 2009 many private equity funds took the view that the distressed equity values seen in many quality companies represented an excellent opportunity to put cash to work, even though the credit markets were moribund. As a result, investment activity continued (although at a slower pace and in smaller transaction sizes), based in many cases on non-control acquisitions of common shares in public companies. The term for this type of investment is private investments in public equity, or PIPEs. For example, Warburg Pincus took a minority investment in MBIA, Carlyle bought a minority interest in Boston Private Financial, Blackstone acquired a 4.5% stake in Deutsche Telecom, General Atlantic invested $1 billion in Bolsa de Mecadorias and Futuros, a Brazilian financial exchange, and J.C. Flowers made a minority investment in MF Global. PIPE transactions can involve a variety of securities, including straight common stock, preferred stock (convertible or nonconvertible), convertible debt, or a combination of all of these securities.

One of the most heavily negotiated issues in large PIPE transactions is the extent to which the investor will be protected if the target company issues new capital on more favorable terms following closing of the investment. Usually this protection is provided for up to a 2-year period of time. In most cases, an equity stake of around 10% is required to gain the right to designate board members. As PIPEs investors have sought greater equity stakes in an issuer, standstill provisions restricting additional share accumulations and "hostile" actions by the investor have become routine. The standstill period typically terminates when the investor owns less than a specified percentage (usually 5%) of the outstanding common stock or voting power of the issuer.

An Introduction to Investment Banks, Hedge Funds, and Private Equity

Private equity firms often trade liquidity for increased governance rights and better terms. In the United States, most if not all PIPE transactions are structured based on the issuance to private equity firms of unregistered securities with trailing registration rights. A registration rights agreement typically requires the issuer to meet a specified timetable for an effective shelf registration and grants the private equity investor additional, but limited, demand and piggyback registration rights. There are typically transfer restrictions that include a lock-up period of up to 3 years, during which no issued shares can be transferred other than to specified permitted transferees, including Limited Partners and existing shareholders.

## Equity Buyouts

Unlike PIPE transactions, which are non-control investments, equity buyouts enable private equity firms to achieve control over companies by purchasing most, but not all, of a target company. In an equity buyout, the entire purchase is completed without borrowing any portion of the purchase price. However, the private equity investor expects that when credit markets permit, they will borrow to fund a future large dividend that reduces their equity exposure. If companies can be acquired at a low enough cost, private equity funds may be able to achieve high returns on their equity investment even without initial leverage. Equity buyouts carry greater risk, because firms are investing more of their own capital up-front, compared to leveraged buyout transactions. They also lose the tax-shelter benefits of interest payments on debt, which increases the overall cost of capital. However, these issues are mitigated if the original purchase price is low enough.

An advantage of an equity buyout is that this transaction may enable a private equity fund to invest in companies without triggering a change-of-control clause that requires the target company to repay debt. For most leveraged buyouts, a private equity fund needs to raise incremental amounts of debt to repay outstanding recalled loans. An equity buyout that does not trigger debt repayment is a significant benefit, because it avoids refunding fees and enables completion of a transaction even in a problematic credit environment.

An example of how a private equity fund may be able to achieve the same IRR return through either a leveraged buyout purchase of a target company at 11 times EBITDA, or an equity buyout purchase of the same target company (in a depressed valuation environment) at 7 times EBITDA is found in Exhibit 20.1. To make the comparison more straightforward in this example, it is assumed that the equity buyout is 100% of the target company, as is the case for a leveraged buyout.

## Distressed Assets

Some private equity firms make loans to troubled companies that are trying to avoid bankruptcy court and need new cash resources. Other firms prowl through bankruptcy courts to find assets that can be purchased at significant discounts. Yet other firms focus on capitalizing on government stimulus programs and, in particular, on infrastructure spending projects and distressed banks. When markets and businesses blow up, private equity funds are, with lots of available capital, in a good position to make a wide variety of investments in distressed assets and loans at potentially advantageous prices. Broadening their investment toolbox to include nontraditional investment securities and assets has enabled private equity funds to put more money to work, while creating IRR outcomes that could potentially reach double digits. At The Carlyle Group, approximately 16% of total assets under management were in leveraged finance and distressed loans as of mid-2009.

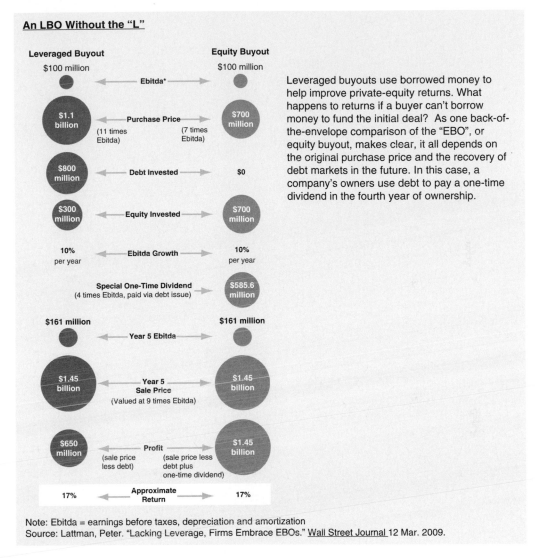

**An LBO Without the "L"**

**Leveraged Buyout**
$100 million

**Equity Buyout**
$100 million

Ebitda*

$1.1 billion

Purchase Price
(11 times Ebitda)    (7 times Ebitda)

$700 million

$800 million

Debt Invested

$0

$300 million

Equity Invested

$700 million

10% per year

Ebitda Growth

10% per year

Special One-Time Dividend
(4 times Ebitda, paid via debt issue)

$585.6 million

$161 million

$161 million

Year 5 Ebitda

$1.45 billion

Year 5 Sale Price
(Valued at 9 times Ebitda)

$1.45 billion

$650 million

Profit
(sale price less debt)    (sale price less debt plus one-time dividend)

$1.45 billion

17%

Approximate Return

17%

Leveraged buyouts use borrowed money to help improve private-equity returns. What happens to returns if a buyer can't borrow money to fund the initial deal?  As one back-of-the-envelope comparison of the "EBO", or equity buyout, makes clear, it all depends on the original purchase price and the recovery of debt markets in the future. In this case, a company's owners use debt to pay a one-time dividend in the fourth year of ownership.

Note: Ebitda = earnings before taxes, depreciation and amortization
Source: Lattman, Peter. "Lacking Leverage, Firms Embrace EBOs." Wall Street Journal 12 Mar. 2009.

**EXHIBIT 20.1**

# M&A Advisory

Some of the larger private equity firms have attempted to diversify their investment activities by adding M&A advisory services to their business mix. The Blackstone Group, in particular, has aggressively focused on providing advice on mergers, acquisitions, and restructurings, pulling in over $410 million in fees from this business during 2008. Blackstone and other large private equity firms are trying to fill the void left by the bankruptcy of Lehman Brothers and the merging of Merrill Lynch into Bank of America and Bear Stearns into J.P. Morgan. Blackstone's advisory clients ranged from troubled insurer AIG to the Ukrainian government. Ford Motor hired Blackstone, along with Goldman Sachs, to rework the debt of the company and persuade bondholders to exchange $1.8 billion in debt for $1.3 billion in equity. The Carlyle Group has also developed an M&A advisory business that focuses, in particular, on bank mergers. For example, Carlyle advised ABN Amro in the sale of LaSalle Bank to Bank of America for $21 billion.

## Capital Markets Activity

During June 2009, KKR reached agreement with Fidelity Investments to exclusively sell portfolio company IPOs through Fidelity, the world's biggest mutual fund company (with over 12 million brokerage clients). This initiative enabled KKR to bypass investment banking firms, who historically underwrote all of KKR's IPOs.

The arrangement with Fidelity provided a distribution channel to KKR's fledgling capital markets business, which underwrites both stock and bond offerings for the companies it owns. After having paid out billions of dollars in underwriting fees to investment banks over 33 years, KKR decided to build an internal capital markets business to capture a large portion of underwriting fees for itself. This initiative is one of several efforts to diversify KKR's private equity business, which suffered a reported $1.2 billion loss during 2008, based on significant drops in valuations for its portfolio companies.

In the first quarter of 2007, during the height of the LBO boom, private equity firms paid a total of $4.3 billion to investment banks. KKR's promotion of an internal capital markets business enabled the firm to save a considerable amount of underwriting fees, but put it in direct competition with investment banks that are instrumental in bringing many acquisition opportunities to the firm. Not all of the other major firms followed KKR's initiative in capital markets, but most have embarked on diversification strategies that make them less reliant on their historical private equity business.

## Hedge Fund and Real Estate Investments

Most of the largest private equity firms conduct hedge fund and real estate investing businesses. At Carlyle, a real estate investment business operated through 10 funds and, as of mid-2009, had invested in 414 properties worldwide, with a total capitalization of $36.2 billion. Over 12% of Carlyle's assets under management were in real estate as of this date. Significant real estate write-downs occurred during 2008 and 2009 in the real estate investment businesses controlled by Carlyle and other private equity funds.

Hedge fund investment activity at private equity firms suffered a big jolt during the 2007–2009 credit crisis. For example, Carlyle Capital Corporation, the hedge fund arm of the Carlyle Group, accrued large losses from its investments in mortgage-backed securities and ended up defaulting on more than $16 billion in related loans during 2008. KKR Financial, the hedge fund arm of KKR, also encountered difficulties during the credit crisis based on bad mortgage-related investments. These investments caused credit rating agencies to lower ratings on KKR Financial, and the company's share price dropped precipitously (KKR Financial had completed an IPO on the NYSE during 2004, reducing KKR's ownership of the firm). During March of 2009, KKR Financial disclosed losses of $1.2 billion for the fourth quarter of 2008 based principally on write-downs and realized losses from investing in leveraged loans to KKR's portfolio companies.

## 2008 Losses and Future Expectations

Based on a combination of write-downs on portfolio companies and realized losses, private equity funds recorded industry average losses estimated at 20% in 2008, which was comparable to the industry average losses suffered by hedge funds during that year. However, the private equity losses were considerably less than U.S. stock market losses during 2008 of approximately 38.5% (S&P 500 Index). During 2009, U.S. corporate pension funds assumed that private equity funds would return on average at least 10% per annum over the 5-year period ending in 2013, exceeding their annual return expectation of just below 8% for hedge funds over the same period of time, according to Greenwich Associates. The reasonably robust return expectations for private equity, however, relate to surviving private equity firms that are able to refinance their portfolio companies in an effort to stave off bankruptcies. Firms that are unable to secure new debt financing for portfolio companies will lose significant amounts of capital and may be forced to close. As of mid-2009, Boston Consulting Group estimated that between 20% and 40% of all private equity firms will disappear over a 3-year period based on their inability to refinance portfolio companies.

## Boom and Bust Cycles

Over the past 30 years, it is clear that credit market conditions are the principal determinants of successful private equity portfolio investments. This is probably because private equity investors attempt to exploit systematic mispricings in the capital markets. When the cost of debt is low compared to the cost of equity (as was the case during 2002–2007), private equity firms attempt to borrow more money and secure more favorable borrowing terms and conditions. For example, private equity funds were able to borrow at an interest rate spread of around 250 basis points over the benchmark LIBOR during the highly permissive credit markets found in 2006. During 2008, as the credit markets froze up, this interest rate spread increased to 500 basis points. As a result, it can be argued that there was an up to 250 basis point mispricing in the credit markets during 2006, which encouraged private equity funds to do more deals, and larger deals than ever before. This, in turn, led to the bust years of 2008 and 2009, where private equity activity dropped precipitously.

The evidence is strong that boom and bust cycles will continue in private equity. Whenever there is a sustained period of high equity returns and a benign interest rate environment, private equity transactions will increase. This boom cycle is characterized by ample credit and loose debt covenants. However, this will be followed by lower activity when credit is tight and corporate earnings are weak. The resultant bust cycle is characterized by debt defaults and bankruptcies.

## Annex Funds

The 2008–2009 recession forced private equity funds into longer than anticipated holding periods for portfolio companies and created capital shortages for many of these companies. This was especially true for struggling companies that required add-ons or operational improvements prior to a sale of the company by the private equity fund. In an effort to resolve the shortage of capital, private equity firms created annex funds. Annex funds usually take the form of a new parallel investment vehicle to an existing fund, and Limited Partners are given the opportunity to participate in the fund.

Annex funds usually have a narrow investment mandate, with funds earmarked for well-defined purposes, such as follow-on investments in current portfolio companies, which are often specifically designated. For example, KKR raised a $500 million annex fund during mid-2009 specifically to prop up companies in its second European buyout fund.

Dilution is a significant concern for the original Limited Partners when they are approached with an annex fund initiative. This is because the annex fund may bring in new investors who may be able to invest in portfolio companies at a lower price than the original Limited Partners.

In addition, fees and other terms related to the annex fund are often more favorable. Of course, if original Limited Partners invest in the annex fund, these concerns are mitigated. However, some may not want to increase their exposure to a portfolio company by investing in the annex fund. Without an annex fund, a portfolio company may not be able to exit in a timely way, delaying returns to the original Limited Partners. Because of this, in spite of their concerns, Limited Partners are usually supportive of annex funds.

## Limited Partner Pull-Backs

When the general equity market dropped precipitously during 2008, many Limited Partners (LPs) found their investment portfolio over-allocated to private equity, because General Partners (GPs) were not able to return capital when exit alternatives evaporated. As a result, many LPs slowed down or discontinued investments in private equity. However as GP write-downs were disclosed during the first half of 2009, allocation percentages normalized, relieving some pressure on LPs to reallocate. In addition, many LPs determined that they did not want to miss out on a potentially favorable vintage year in 2009 for private equity investments, given the significant drop in equity values that occurred during 2008. Further, they didn't want to slow down development of talented staff that was focused on private equity investments, nor jeopardize relationships with strong GPs who expected continued investments through good times and bad.

## Risk Factors

Private equity firms undertake many risks, which were publicly outlined for the first time in Blackstone's 2007 SEC registration statement. These risks include operating in potentially difficult market conditions, uncertainty regarding the timing and receipt of carried interest, highly variable cash flow, uncertainty regarding exit strategies, and uncertainty regarding the future availability of credit, among other risks. A list of some of the principal risks included in Blackstone's IPO prospectus is included in Exhibit 20.2.

## Asian Private Equity Activities

Most Asian private equity investments have been in China and Japan, where over 82% of all Asian investments by U.S. private equity firms have been centered. In China, majority-stake transactions are possible in some industries, but most investments involve minority investments in growth companies. With GDP growth of more than 6% expected for the foreseeable future, and 40 million more people expected to enter China's middle-class each year, significant growth in domestic consumption is forecasted. This has prompted a number of large private equity funds to expand in China, including Bain Capital, Blackstone, Carlyle, KKR, Warburg Pincus, and TPG, which operates through Newbridge Capital. During 2009, TPG sold part of its $1.5 billion controlling stake in Shenzhen Development Bank after a 5-year holding period. Since TPG paid $150 million for this equity position in 2004, the firm achieved a return on its original investment of approximately 10 times. During June 2009, Bain Capital agreed to pay over $400 million to acquire a significant stake in Gome Electrical Appliance, one of the biggest retailers in China.

In Japan, a stagnant market and strong ties between banks and corporations has stymied significant private equity investments over many years. However, some investment activity has

**Principal Risks Included in Blackstone's IPO Prospectus**

- Portfolio Companies: ... During periods of difficult market conditions or slowdowns in a particular sector, companies in which we invest may experience decreased revenues, financial losses, difficulty in obtaining access to financing and increased funding costs...

- Prior Club Deals: ...Consortium transactions generally entail a reduced level of control by Blackstone over the investment because governance rights must be shared with the other private equity investors. Accordingly, we may not be able to control decisions relating to the investment, including decisions relating to the management and operation of the company and the timing and nature of any exit...

- New Investments: ...In addition, during periods of adverse economic conditions, we may have difficulty accessing financial markets, which could make it more difficult or impossible for us to obtain funding for additional investments and harm our assets under management and operating results...

- Valuation Uncertainty: ...Because there is significant uncertainty in the valuation of, or in the stability of the value of illiquid investments, the fair values of such investments as reflected in an investment fund's net asset value do not necessarily reflect the prices that would actually be obtained by us on behalf of the investment fund when such investments are realized...

- In a Rearview Mirror, Future Returns Are Not As Big As They Appear: ...Our investment funds' returns have benefited from investment opportunities and general market conditions that may not repeat themselves, including favorable borrowing conditions in the debt markets...

- Dark Side of Leverage: ... The incurrence of a significant amount of indebtedness by an entity could...give rise to an obligation to make mandatory prepayments of debt using excess cash flow, which might limit the entity's ability to respond to changing industry conditions...[Significant leverage could also] limit the entity's ability to obtain additional financing or increase the cost of obtaining such financing, including for capital expenditures, working capital or general corporate purposes...

- Exiting: ...The ability of many of our investment funds, to dispose of investments is heavily dependent on the public equity markets. large holdings of securities can often be disposed of only over a substantial length of time, exposing the investment returns to risks of downward movement in market prices during the intended disposition period...

Source: Company filing

**EXHIBIT 20.2**

resulted in good returns, and a meaningful increase in investments is anticipated for the future. Many retirement-aged business owners in Japan will consider selling their companies to private equity firms when equity valuations rise. In addition, large conglomerates that have nonstrategic assets to sell will consider bids from private equity firms when valuations increase. Dallas-based Lone Star Funds is one of the most active U.S. private equity firms focusing on Japan, having closed almost 40 investments in this country. Other active firms include Bain Capital, Carlyle, and The Riverside Company. During June 2009, SG Investments, a private equity investment arm of Goldman Sachs, and Hong Kong private equity firm MBK Partners, teamed up to acquire Universal Studios Japan for $1.2 billion.

## Strategic Alliances

Historically, corporations (strategic investors) and private equity (financial investors) have competed with each other to acquire companies, but during the financial crisis that started in mid-2007, an increasing number of co-investments between the two parties occurred. For example, during September 2008, Blackstone and Bain Capital joined NBC Universal (a unit of General Electric Co.) in a $3.5 billion acquisition of The Weather Channel. Private equity firms now look at strategic investors for deal sourcing, sector expertise, and capital. This alliance is particularly effective for investments in regulated industries, where having a strategic investor may provide comfort to regulators that the target company will be operated prudently and in accordance with industry standards. Strategic investors view private equity firms as an important source of capital, and they benefit from private equity firms' strong deal execution expertise.

Challenges in operating a partnership arise when considering corporate governance. Usually but not always, control over the board of the target company and appointment of the CEO falls to the party that provides the most capital. Exit considerations can also be problematic, since private equity firms generally focus on a medium-term investment horizon, while corporate partners may be focused on building a long-term asset with connectivity to its core business. Usually, a private equity firm will view the strategic investor as a potential acquirer of the business when they are ready to exit. In any event, the future sale of shares is usually subject to a right of first offer to the other party.

## Private Equity IPOs

Four U.S.-headquartered firms that conduct private equity business completed IPOs during 2006 and 2007: Blackstone, Apollo, Fortress, and KKR. All four of these IPOs have fared poorly, with share price declines of between 64% and 85% over the 2-year period from mid-2007 to mid-2009. See Exhibits 20.3 through 20.6.

## Focus on Portfolio Management

The financial crisis that started in mid-2007 forced private equity firms to increasingly focus on improving the operating value of portfolio companies as the most important value creation lever, compared to multiple expansion (increasing exit multiples above entry multiples), multiple arbitrage (increasing portfolio company multiples to match industry multiples), and financial leverage (see Exhibit 20.7). This means that more private equity firms have increased their involvement in portfolio company management and, in turn, extended their holding timeline (see Exhibit 20.8). Although viewed as critical, operations garners only about 19% of due diligence attention during the acquisition evaluation period (see Exhibit 20.9), and post-acquisition focus on operational initiatives takes only 22% of private equity fund time allocated to assisting portfolio companies (see Exhibit 20.10). These percentages will need to increase to enable better portfolio management.

Key themes of portfolio management include: (1) much more time is required to focus on portfolio companies following the credit crisis of 2007–2009; (2) private equity firms must concentrate more on maintaining adequate cash to meet the covenant requirements of banks through weekly review of accounts receivable, accounts payable, and inventory; (3) banks require much more information and are reluctant to provide waivers, making cash flow errors very costly; (4) managers who are not skilled at operating efficiently during a downturn sometimes must be removed, even if they are excellent managers during a normal economy; and (5) companies that are operationally strong, but suffer from unpredictable demand, are good targets for add-on acquisitions to normalize demand and achieve scale.

## Private Equity IPOs

### Fortress Investment Group

**The Offering: Feb 2007, NYSE (FIG)**
- 34.3 million Class A shares issued at $18.50 by Fortress Investment Group LLC, raising $634M
- Oversubscribed
- Principals kept all Class B shares: equal to 77.7% of FIG
- Class A shares equaled 23.3% of FIG. Public holding of these shares was 8.6% after the IPO
- Voting rights: One share, one vote, but Principals have control plus "approval rights" on structural business issue

**Use of Proceeds:**
- Pay down $250M outstanding under term loan and $85M under revolving credit facilities
- Fund $169M of commitments to existing PF funds and $29M for general purposes
- Pay quarterly dividend at GP discretion only to Class A shareholders

### The Blackstone Group

**The Offering: June 2007, NYSE (BX)**
- 133 million common units issued at $31 by Blackstone Group L.P., raising $4.1B
- 10x oversubscribed
- Limited voting rights: No right to elect GPs
- GPs retain a right to carried interest; thus, carried interest is not necessarily distributed to all unit holders
- Approximately 80% partner and employee owned with lock ups through 2016

**Use of Proceeds:**
- Pay down $340M revolving credit facility
- Fund a portion of GP commitments to Blackstone's various carry funds (including its corporate private equity funds, real estate funds and certain credit-oriented funds)
- Strategic acquisitions and general business purposes
- Pay quarterly dividend to common unit holders at GP discretion

Source: Company filings

**EXHIBIT 20.3**

## Private Equity IPOs

### KKR

**The Offering: May 2006**
**Eurolist by Euronext (KPE.AS)**
- KKR raised $5B for KPE.AS
- A total of 200M common units were sold at $24.80
- Increased shares from 60m to 200m due to oversubscription
- Fund invests through KKR Private Equity Investors LP, its sole LP
- During May 2007, KKR also listed KFN, a specialty finance company and wholly owned subsidiary
- During July 2007, KKR filed a registration statement for a $1.25B NYSE IPO, but aborted the IPO effort because of poor market conditions

**Use of Proceeds:**
- KPE co-invests in KKR deals through its LP
- Invests 75% in KKR investments and 25% opportunistically

### Apollo Management

**The Offering: June 2006**
**Eurolist by Euronext (AAA)**
- Apollo raised ~$2B for affiliate Apollo Alternative Assets, a publicly traded private equity closed-ended LP
  - 75m common units were initially sold in June at $20
  - Another 18.7m common units were sold between June and August, 2006, bringing total funds raised to just under $2B
- Earlier in the year, Apollo also listed affiliate Apollo Investment Corporation (AINV) on the Nasdaq: AINV is a middle-market focused, business development fund that invests in mezzanine debt, senior secured loans and direct equity

**Use of Proceeds:**
- AAA was formed to invest alongside Apollo's main PE and hedge funds
- Co-Invests with Apollo Funds VI and VIII
- Invests in Apollo Strategic Value Fund (50% of funds raised), Europe Limited investment fund, Asia Opportunity Fund and Euro Principal Finance Fund

Source: Company filings

**EXHIBIT 20.4**

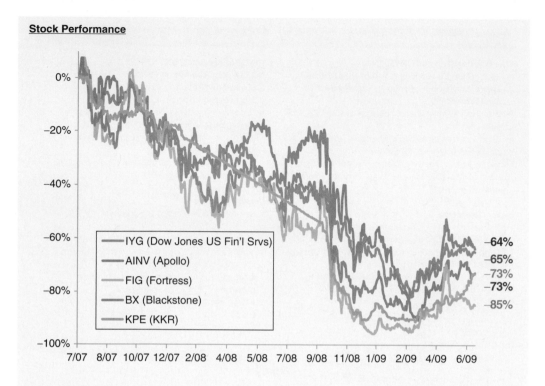

Note: IYG tracks Dow Jones U.S. financial services stocks; AINV is a fund of Apollo Investment Management that invests in middle market equity and mezzanine securities.
Source: Data provided by Commodity Systems Inc. and Morningstar, Inc.

**EXHIBIT 20.5**

## Factors Contributing to Declines in Private Equity Public Share Prices

- Macro-economic conditions
    - ○ High acquisition multiples and the end of cheap financing had a significant impact on these firms
- Opaque business model
    - ○ Difficult to determine "fair value" of shares due to complex financial accounts and subjective accounting
    - ○ Investors don't have access to enough data to make an intelligent decision
- Industry lacks track record in the public market; IPOs priced too high
    - ○ In early 2007, many experts recommended that most investors avoid this "hot part" of the market
    - ○ Blackstone and Fortress went public at peak of PE "fad"
    - ○ Firms are professional investors, making it questionable when they want to sell you a piece of their own firm
- Firms maintained culture of privacy
    - ○ Blackstone declared that management would still retain full control, including decisions on how to allocate large salaries
    - ○ Firms don't disclose enough detail about how funds will be used and don't have to answer to public markets about decisions regarding portfolio companies
- Shareholders lack traditional rights
    - ○ Shareholders don't have traditional voting rights and can't participate in annual shareholder meetings

**EXHIBIT 20.6**

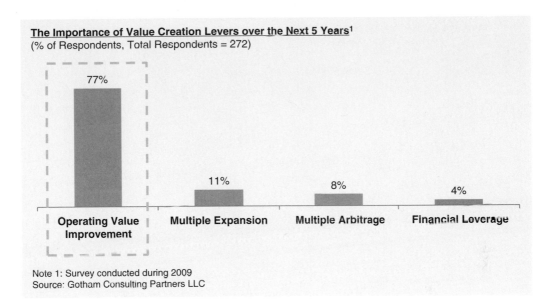

The Importance of Value Creation Levers over the Next 5 Years[1]
(% of Respondents, Total Respondents = 272)

Note 1: Survey conducted during 2009
Source: Gotham Consulting Partners LLC

**EXHIBIT 20.7**

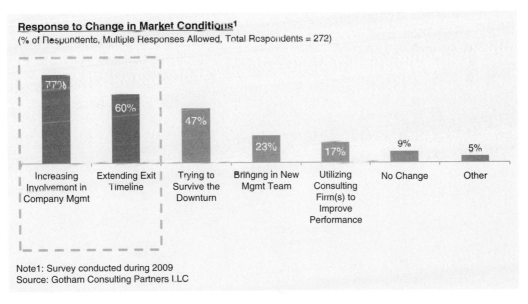

Response to Change in Market Conditions[1]
(% of Respondents, Multiple Responses Allowed, Total Respondents = 272)

Note1: Survey conducted during 2009
Source: Gotham Consulting Partners LLC

**EXHIBIT 20.8**

## Comparison of Private Equity Firms

A ranking of firms that raised private equity investment capital between January 2004 and April 2009 is provided in Exhibit 20.11. The amount of capital raised during this period ranged from #1 TPG (New York-based), which raised $52.35 billion, to #100 Montagu Private Equity (London-based), which raised $2.97 billion. The 50 largest firms raised $813 billion, or 55% more equity capital than the next 250 firms (see Exhibit 20.12). As Exhibit 20.13 shows, 65%

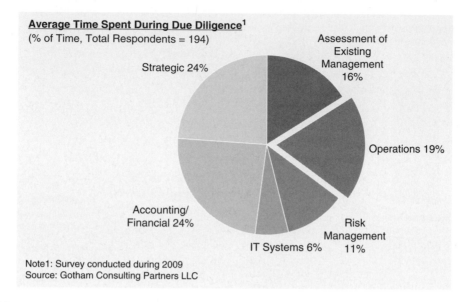

**Average Time Spent During Due Diligence[1]**
(% of Time, Total Respondents = 194)

Assessment of Existing Management 16%

Strategic 24%

Operations 19%

Accounting/ Financial 24%

Risk Management 11%

IT Systems 6%

Note1: Survey conducted during 2009
Source: Gotham Consulting Partners LLC

**EXHIBIT 20.9**

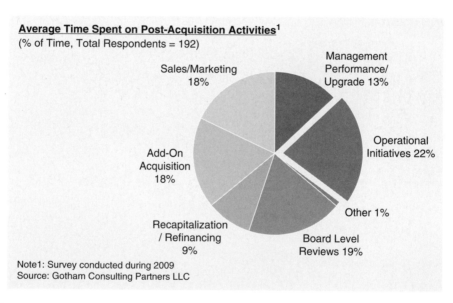

**Average Time Spent on Post-Acquisition Activities[1]**
(% of Time, Total Respondents = 192)

Management Performance/ Upgrade 13%

Sales/Marketing 18%

Operational Initiatives 22%

Add-On Acquisition 18%

Other 1%

Recapitalization / Refinancing 9%

Board Level Reviews 19%

Note1: Survey conducted during 2009
Source: Gotham Consulting Partners LLC

**EXHIBIT 20.10**

of the 300 largest firms are headquartered in the U.S. Exhibit 20.14 shows how the 300 largest firms spent $1.81 trillion in funds raised (more than 31% in telecommunications and healthcare). Finally, Exhibit 20.15 compares the 13.45% IRR of the 50 largest private equity funds with the 13.38% IRR of the top 300 private equity funds. This exhibit also demonstrates that non-U.S.-based firms have historically outperformed U.S.-based firms.

## Profile of The Carlyle Group

The Carlyle Group, which was founded in 1987, had more than 1,300 investors from 68 countries as of 2009, including pension funds, endowments, financial institutions, and high-net-worth individuals. The firm had 480 investment professionals in offices in 20 countries and a total of 900 employees. Carlyle had $85 billion in assets under management (invested through 64 funds),

### Ranking of Private Equity Firms Based on Private Equity Capital Raised from January 2004–April 2009

| Rank | Name of Firm | Headquarters | Capital Raised Over Reference Period ($M) |
|---|---|---|---|
| 1 | TPG | Fort Worth (Texas) | $52,350 |
| 2 | Goldman Sachs Principal Investment Area | New York | $48,990 |
| 3 | The Carlyle Group | Washington DC | $47,730 |
| 4 | Kohlberg Kravis Roberts | New York | $40,460 |
| 5 | Apollo Global Management | New York | $35,180 |
| 6 | Bain Capital | Boston | $34,950 |
| 7 | CVC Capital Partners | London | $33,730 |
| 8 | The Blackstone Group | New York | $30,800 |
| 9 | Warburg Pincus | New York | $23,000 |
| 10 | Apax Partners | London | $21,330 |
| 11 | First Reserve Corporation | Greenwich (Connecticut) | $20,890 |
| 12 | 3i Group | London | $18,390 |
| 13 | American Capital | Bethesda (Maryland) | $17,990 |
| 14 | Hellman & Friedman | San Francisco | $17,900 |
| 15 | Providence Equity Partners | Providence (Rhode Island) | $16,360 |
| 16 | Advent International | Boston | $16,130 |
| 17 | Terra Firma Capital Partners | London | $14,210 |
| 18 | General Atlantic | Greenwich (Connecticut) | $14,100 |
| 19 | Fortress Investment Group | New York | $14,080 |
| 20 | Silver Lake | Menlo Park | $14,000 |
| 21 | Cerberus Capital Management | New York | $13,900 |
| 22 | Permira | London | $12,670 |
| 23 | Clayton Dubilier & Rice | New York | $11,720 |
| 24 | Lehman Brothers Private Equity | New York | $11,710 |
| 25 | PAI Partners | Paris | $11,500 |
| 26 | Bridgepoint | London | $10,870 |
| 27 | EQT Partners | Stockholm | $10,820 |
| 28 | Madison Dearborn Partners | Chicago | $10,600 |
| 29 | Charterhouse Capital Partners | London | $10,560 |
| 30 | Teachers' Private Capital | Toronto | $10,240 |
| 31 | Thomas H. Lee Partners | Boston | $10,210 |
| 32 | Cinven | London | $10,170 |
| 33 | Onex | Toronto | $9,590 |
| 34 | Riverstone Holdings | New York | $9,400 |
| 35 | AXA Private Equity | Paris | $9,370 |
| 36 | JC Flowers & Co. | New York | $8,900 |
| 37 | Oaktree Capital Management | Los Angeles | $8,850 |
| 38 | BC Partners | London | $8,750 |
| 39 | Candover | London | $8,450 |
| 40 | Welsh Carson Anderson & Stowe | New York | $8,420 |
| 41 | Nordic Capital | Stockholm | $8,180 |
| 42 | WL Ross & Co. | New York | $7,770 |
| 43 | Lindsay Goldberg | New York | $7,690 |
| 44 | Sun Capital Partners | Boca Raton (Florida) | $7,500 |
| 45 | NGP Energy Capital Management | Dallas | $7,470 |

Continued onto next page...

**Ranking of Private Equity Firms Based on Private Equity Capital Raised from January 2004–April 2009**

| Rank | Name of Firm | Headquarters | Capital Raised Over Reference Period ($M) |
|---|---|---|---|
| 46 | AlpInvest Partners | Amsterdam | $7,260 |
| 47 | Kelso & Co. | New York | $7,200 |
| 48 | Citi Alternative Investments | New York | $7,080 |
| 49 | Marfin Investment Group | Athens | $6,860 |
| 50 | MatlinPatterson | New York | $6,830 |
| 51 | TA Associates | Boston | $6,827 |
| 52 | New Mountain Capital | New York | $6,687 |
| 53 | EnCap Investments | Houston | $6,575 |
| 54 | Abraaj Capital | Dubai | $6,493 |
| 55 | Doughty Hanson | London | $6,396 |
| 56 | Oak Hill Capital Partners | Stamford (Connecticut) | $6,300 |
| 57 | Stone Point Capital | Greenwich (Connecticut) | $6,226 |
| 58 | Summit Partners | Boston | $6,101 |
| 59 | Investcorp | Manama (Bahrain) | $5,958 |
| 60 | ArcLight Capital Partners | Boston | $5,800 |
| 61 | Barclays Private Equity | London | $5,405 |
| 62 | HIG Capital Management | Miami | $5,342 |
| 63 | Leonard Green & Partners | Los Angeles | $5,300 |
| 64 | Technology Crossover Ventures | Palo Alto | $5,300 |
| 65 | Eurazeo | Paris | $4,847 |
| 66 | Arcapita | Manama (Bahrain) | $4,839 |
| 67 | Actis | London | $4,442 |
| 68 | CCMP Capital | New York | $4,318 |
| 69 | LS Power Group | New York | $4,285 |
| 70 | Altor Equity Partners | Stockholm | $4,158 |
| 71 | Crestview Partners | New York | $4,150 |
| 72 | TowerBrook Capital Partners | New York | $4,130 |
| 73 | Oak Investment Partners | Westport (Connecticut) | $4,110 |
| 74 | Citadel Capital | Cairo | $4,100 |
| 75 | MBK Partners | Seoul | $4,060 |
| 76 | One Equity Partners | New York | $4,000 |
| 77 | Pacific Equity Partners | Sydney | $3,835 |
| 78 | Lion Capital | London | $3,756 |
| 79 | Platinum Equity Partners | Los Angeles | $3,700 |
| 80 | Quantum Energy Partners | Houston | $3,665 |
| 81 | Vestar Capital Partners | Boston | $3,650 |
| 82 | Babson Capital | Boston | $3,636 |
| 83 | The Jordan Company | New York | $3,600 |
| 84 | New Enterprise Associates | Chevy Chase (Maryland) | $3,600 |
| 85 | Mid Europa Partners | London | $3,500 |
| 86 | Affinity Equity Partners | Hong Kong | $3,500 |
| 87 | Advantage Partners | Tokyo | $3,433 |
| 88 | American Securities Capital Partners | New York | $3,300 |

Continued onto next page...

including $3.3 billion of capital committed by the firm's senior managers. These assets are housed within four fund families: leveraged buyouts; real estate; leveraged finance; and growth capital. Carlyle is a private partnership, owned by a group of senior Carlyle professionals and two institutional investors: CalPERS, the California Public Employees Retirement System, owns 5.1%, and Mubdala Development, a strategic development company headquartered in Abu Dhabi, owns 7.5%. See Exhibits 20.16 and 20.17.

### Ranking of Private Equity Firms Based on Private Equity Capital Raised from January 2004 – April 2009

| Rank | Name of Firm | Headquarters | Capital Raised Over Reference Period ($M) |
|------|--------------|--------------|-------------------------------------------|
| 89   | IK Investment Partners | Stockholm | $3,300 |
| 90   | Softbank Group | Tokyo | $3,263 |
| 91   | GI Partners | Menlo Park | $3,250 |
| 92   | Tenaska Capital Management | Omaha (Nebraska) | $3,238 |
| 93   | Hopu Investment Management | Beijing | $3,232 |
| 94   | Yucaipa Companies | Los Angeles | $3,225 |
| 95   | Centerbridge Capital Partners | New York | $3,200 |
| 96   | KRG Capital | Denver | $3,184 |
| 97   | Court Square Capital Partners | New York | $3,100 |
| 98   | Berkshire Partners | Boston | $3,100 |
| 99   | HSBC Principal Investments | London | $3,000 |
| 100  | Montagu Private Equity | London | $2,970 |

Note: "Private equity": The definition of private equity for the purposes of the PEI 300 means capital raised for a dedicated program of investing directly into businesses. This includes equity capital for diversified private equity, buyouts, growth equity, venture capital, turnaround or control-oriented distressed investment capital, and mezzanine debt. Rankings do not take into account funds of funds capital, capital raised for primarily real estate strategies, hedge fund capital, infrastructure and debt capital. Mezzanine debt raised by firms that are primarily engaged in private equity investing is counted (only equity raised for these funds, not the leveraged "buying power"). Mezzanine debt frequently involves warrants for equity stakes, and has historically been counted alongside buyout capital by industry media and data services groups.

Source: "PEI 50 2009," Private Equity International

**EXHIBIT 20.11**

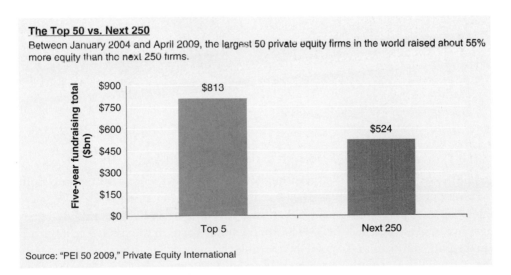

### The Top 50 vs. Next 250

Between January 2004 and April 2009, the largest 50 private equity firms in the world raised about 55% more equity than the next 250 firms.

Source: "PEI 50 2009," Private Equity International

**EXHIBIT 20.12**

Difficulties experienced by Carlyle during 2008 included three portfolio company bankruptcies, consisting of Edscha, a German auto parts manufacturer, SemGroup, a midstream oil and gas logistics and marketing company, and Hawaiian Telecom, a full-service telecommunications provider in Hawaii. In addition, Carlyle Capital Corporation, which invested primarily in AAA

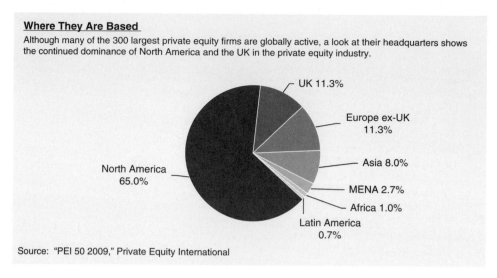

**Where They Are Based**

Although many of the 300 largest private equity firms are globally active, a look at their headquarters shows the continued dominance of North America and the UK in the private equity industry.

UK 11.3%
Europe ex-UK 11.3%
Asia 8.0%
MENA 2.7%
Africa 1.0%
Latin America 0.7%
North America 65.0%

Source: "PEI 50 2009," Private Equity International

**EXHIBIT 20.13**

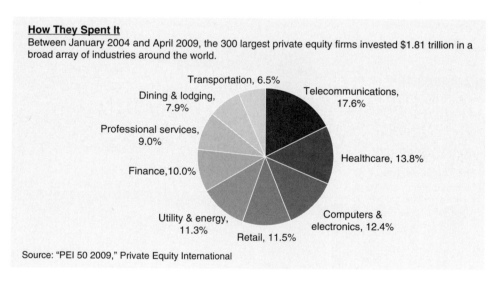

**How They Spent It**

Between January 2004 and April 2009, the 300 largest private equity firms invested $1.81 trillion in a broad array of industries around the world.

Transportation, 6.5%
Dining & lodging, 7.9%
Professional services, 9.0%
Finance, 10.0%
Utility & energy, 11.3%
Retail, 11.5%
Computers & electronics, 12.4%
Healthcare, 13.8%
Telecommunications, 17.6%

Source: "PEI 50 2009," Private Equity International

**EXHIBIT 20.14**

mortgage-related securities issued by government-backed agencies, was placed into liquidation. Also, the firm liquidated Carlyle Blue Wave, a multistrategy hedge fund.

In spite of these difficulties, as of 2009, the firm had an optimistic attitude regarding its future, given its global presence, knowledge, and capital base, and expected to take advantage of depressed equity values to make good long-term investments. The firm expected operating conditions for portfolio companies to remain challenging, fewer (and smaller) transactions requiring more equity (and less debt), longer hold periods, and lower returns.

## Future Issues and Opportunities

Some of the major issues impacting private equity include: (1) whether the historical private equity business model will be effective; (2) future credit availability, given the credit crisis of

### Private Equity Performance

The 50 largest private equity firms slightly outperformed the next 250 largest firms and the industry as a whole (tracked by the SSPE Index). Non-U.S. firms lead U.S. firms by a clear margin.

|  | PEI 50 IRR | PEI 300 IRR | SSPE Index IRR |
|---|---|---|---|
| Pooled Average | 13.45% | 13.38% | 12.92% |
| *By Location* | | | |
| U.S. | 13.36% | 13.31% | 12.47% |
| Non-U.S. | 15.67% | 15.48% | 15.61% |

Note: Based on data compiled from 1437 private equity funds, including fully liquidated partnerships, formed between 1990 and 2008 Q3. IRR: Pooled Average IRR is net of fees, expenses and carried interest. Pooled average IRR treats sample funds as a single "fund" by adding together all cash flows and net asset values. Rather than averaging returns for each sample fund, returns are calculated on the underlying "pooled" portfolio.

Source: "PEI 50 2009," Private Equity International

EXHIBIT 20.15

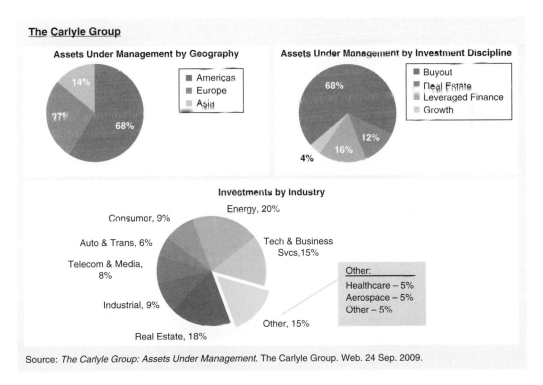

Source: *The Carlyle Group: Assets Under Management.* The Carlyle Group. Web. 24 Sep. 2009.

EXHIBIT 20.16

2007–2009; (3) the sustainability of investor interest in this model; (4) how much distributions and returns will fall for existing limited partners, given the large number of underwater investments that were entered into during 2005–2007; (5) the level of interest from high-net-worth individuals following the Madoff scandal, together with large losses in global equity and fixed income markets; (6) the sustainability of the *2 plus 20* fee model; (7) regulatory and tax changes (see

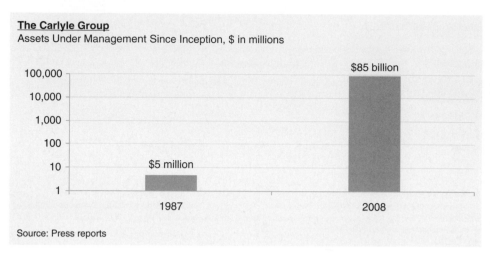

**EXHIBIT 20.17**

Chapter 19); (8) FASB 157 (see Chapter 19); (9) the massive amount of debt that portfolio companies will need to repay when it falls due during 2011–2013, and whether replacement funding for this debt is available; and (10) if replacement debt is not available, whether many portfolio companies will fall into bankruptcy.

All of these issues represent threats to the industry, but there are opportunities as well, including: (1) opportunity to use over $500 billion of available capital to acquire companies at historically low valuation levels; (2) ability to "rescue" financial institutions during their period of greatest need, resulting in potentially advantageous terms; (3) opportunity to partner with corporations and governments in co-investment initiatives; (4) opportunity to use well-honed investment and execution skills to turn around troubled companies; and (5) improvement in management, board, and government attitudes toward private equity as the industry moves to help economies in crisis.

## The New Landscape

Over time, the most successful private equity firms may fall into one of two categories: global private equity firms that have scale, and have diversified their investment and advisory activities; and smaller "niche" private equity firms that have a well-defined, differentiated strategy based on their operating/investing model or industry expertise. The middle tier firms that do not have an area of specialization or differentiation may find it more difficult to raise funding and meet investment objectives.

For as long as credit limitations exist, private equity firms will need to rely increasingly on effective management of portfolio companies in order to deliver expected returns. Successful firms will create greater industry specialization and develop expertise in the areas of working capital, sales force management, pricing, procurement, and other operational areas. Firms will either need to build this capability or acquire it to be successful. Without these operational skills and industry specialization, sole reliance on leverage and financial engineering may result in failure.

Some firms will become successful in identifying different parts of the capital structure to pursue in an effort to achieve the best risk-adjusted returns. Other firms will learn how to better control relationships with the executives who run their portfolio companies. These firms will find ways to better align the interests of owners and managers based on increasing communication and a greater effort to collaborate, rather than police.

Private equity firms will need to determine what percent of their current portfolio is comprised of companies that have significant debt renegotiation requirements, and determine whether they have the skill set needed to be successful in upcoming discussions. This can become a major time commitment and will saddle these firms with significant risks, given the massive amount of debt that is coming due. Other firms need to determine if they have enough capital to fund what may be unique value investment opportunities. If current capital is not sufficient, a considerable amount of time will be needed for fundraising in a problematic climate, with an uncertain outcome.

Leveraged transactions will be smaller and less frequent. The limited supply of large deals will cause some private equity firms to revise their strategy and focus increasingly on distressed transactions, other types of debt transactions, and PIPE investments. Relationships with Limited Partners will change, as they require greater alignment in economics, including reductions in management fees and tighter fund documentation, including limitations on *style drift*, in exchange for improvements in carry. The new landscape will likely have fewer private equity firms, lower returns, a broader array of investments across the capital structure, and greater operational capability.

## Questions

1. why do you think U.S. corporate pension funds projected annual returns for private equity to be higher than that of hedge funds for the 2009–2013 period?
2. Why were LBO funds so successful from 2002 through July 2007? Describe what has happened since then.
3. What is a possible negative consequence of investing during private equity boom cycles?
4. From the perspective of existing Limited Partners (LPs) in a private equity fund, what are the benefits and considerations of annex funds?
5. How are private equity firms adapting to an environment where debt is limited and expensive?
6. Why have larger private equity firms been successful in diversifying into the advisory business traditionally dominated by the major investment banks?
7. Annex funds attempt to address which of the principal risks outlined in Blackstone's IPO prospectus (Exhibit 20.2)?
8. Discuss *multiple expansion* in the context of value creation for private equity investments made following a financial crisis.
9. What might contribute to non-U.S.-based PE firms outperforming U.S.-based PE firms on average?

# SECTION III

# Case Studies

# Investment Banking in 2008 (A): Rise and Fall of the Bear

*Posit: People think a bank might be financially shaky. Consequence: People start to withdraw their money. Result: Pretty soon it IS financially shaky. Conclusion: You can make banks fail.*

—*Sneakers (1992)*

Gary Parr, deputy chairman of Lazard Frères & Co. and Kellogg class of 1980, could not believe his ears.

"You can't mean that," he said, reacting to the lowered bid given by Doug Braunstein, JP Morgan head of investment banking, for Parr's client, legendary investment bank Bear Stearns. Less than eighteen months after trading at an all-time high of $172.61 a share, Bear now had little choice but to accept Morgan's humiliating $2-per share, Federal Reserve sanctioned bailout offer. "I'll have to get back to you."[1]

Hanging up the phone, Parr leaned back and gave an exhausted sigh. Rumors had swirled around Bear ever since two of its hedge funds imploded as a result of the subprime housing crisis, but time and again, the scrappy Bear appeared to have weathered the storm. Parr's efforts to find a capital infusion for the bank had resulted in lengthy discussions and marathon due diligence sessions, but one after another, potential investors had backed away, scared off in part by Bear's sizable mortgage holdings at a time when every bank on Wall Street was reducing its positions and taking massive write-downs in the asset class. In the past week, those rumors had reached a fever pitch, with financial analysts openly questioning Bear's ability to continue operations and its clients running for the exits. Now Sunday afternoon, it had already been a long weekend, and it would almost certainly be a long night, as the Fed-backed bailout of Bear would require onerous negotiations before Monday's market open. By morning, the eighty-five-year-old investment bank, which had survived the Great Depression, the savings and loan crisis, and the dot-com implosion, would cease to exist as an independent firm. Pausing briefly before calling CEO Alan Schwartz and the rest of Bear's board, Parr allowed himself a moment of reflection.

How had it all happened?

## Bear Stearns

Founded with just $500,000 of capital in 1923 by Joseph Bear, Robert Stearns, and Harold Mayer, Bear Stearns needed to show its soon-to-be trademark tenacity and agility in the market

---

[1] Kate Kelly, "Bear Stearns Neared Collapse Twice in Frenzied Last Days," *Wall Street Journal*, May 29, 2008, http://online.wsj.com/article/SB121202057232127889.html (accessed July 17, 2008).

merely to survive its first decade. Originally conceived as an equity trading house to take advantage of a roaring 1920s bull market, Bear instead relied upon its trading in government securities to last through the Great Depression, managing not only to avoid layoffs but also to continue paying employee bonuses. Despite the sagging national and global economy, Bear grew from its seven original employees to seventy-five by 1933, and began to expand with the acquisition of Chicago-based Stein, Brennan.[2]

The firm quickly developed a reputation as a maverick in the white-shoe culture of New York investment banking. Unlike more polished firms, who catered to the world's most prestigious companies and earned most of their revenues from equity underwriting and advisory services, Bear had a cutthroat, renegade culture that stemmed from its dominant position in bond trading, where the slightest turn in the market can make the difference between a profitable trade and a losing one. CEO Salim "Cy" Lewis reinforced this trader's culture after joining the company in 1938 as head of the firm's institutional bond trading department, running the firm almost as a holding company of independent profit centers that frantically sought his approval. Imposing at six foot four, Lewis's audacity, brash demeanor, and relentless work ethic set the tone at Bear until his death in 1978, when he suffered a stroke at his own retirement party at the Harmonie Club in New York City.[3]

In stark contrast to the WASP-y, cliquish atmosphere of its competitors, Bear set the standard for diversity among its employees, valuing initiative and tenacity over pedigree in its hiring. As Lewis's successor, Alan "Ace" Greenberg, put it, "If somebody with an MBA degree applies for a job, we will certainly not hold it against them, but we are really looking for people with PSD degrees," meaning poor, smart, and with a deep desire to become very rich.[4]

"It was unique," said Muriel Siebert, founder of brokerage house Muriel Siebert & Co. "It didn't matter what your last name was. They had a mixture of all kinds of people and they were there to make money." Long before its clubbier competitors embraced hiring diversity, the scrappy, trading-focused Bear had cultivated a roster of Jewish, Irish, and Italian employees who lacked the Ivy League pedigrees required for positions at white-shoe firms such as Morgan Stanley or Lehman Brothers.

When it went public in 1985, the firm diversified its operations, becoming a full-service investment bank with divisions in investment banking, institutional equities, fixed-income securities, individual investor services, and mortgage-related products.[5] Bear's investment banking unit got off to a rough start, battered by the collapse of the mergers and acquisitions boom in the second half of the decade. The firm remained resilient, however, drawing inspiration from its leader on one of the worst trading days in history: October 19, 1987, or Black Monday. As the Dow Jones fell more than 500 points, Greenberg—who did not play golf—pantomimed a golf swing and announced to the assembled throng of traders that he would be taking the following day off.[6]

---

[2]Bear Stearns Companies, Inc., "Company History," http://www.answers.com/topic/the-bear-stearns-companies-inc?cat=biz-fin (accessed July 11, 2008).

[3]Kris Frieswick, "Journey Without Maps," *CFO Magazine*, March 2005, http://www.cfo.com/article.cfm/3709778/1/c_3710920 (accessed July 11, 2008).

[4]Max Nichols, "One of Our Most Remarkable Leaders," *Oklahoma City Journal Record*, April 12, 2001, http://findarticles.com/p/articles/mi_qn4182/is_20010412/ai_n10145162 (accessed July 11, 2008).

[5]Bear Stearns, "Company History."

[6]Kate Kelly, "Fear, Rumors Touched Off Fatal Run on Bear Stearns," *Wall Street Journal*, May 28, 2008, http://online.wsj.com/article/SB121193290927324603.html (accessed July 16, 2008).

By the time James Cayne succeeded Greenberg as CEO in 1993, the firm found itself at the top of the equity underwriting league tables in Latin America and its research department had flourished. Its *Early Look at the Market: Bear Stearns Morning View* became one of the most widely read pieces of market intelligence.

## Long Term Capital Management

Long Term Capital Management, or LTCM, was a hedge fund founded in 1994 by John Meriwether, the former head of Salomon Brothers's domestic fixed-income arbitrage group. Meriwether had grown the arbitrage group to become Salomon's most profitable group by 1991, when it was revealed that one of the traders under his purview had astonishingly submitted a false bid in a U.S. Treasury bond auction. Despite reporting the trade immediately to CEO John Gutfreund, the outcry from the scandal forced Meriwether to resign.[7]

Meriwether revived his career several years later with the founding of LTCM. Amidst the beginning of one of the greatest bull markets the global markets had ever seen, Meriwether assembled a team of some of the world's most respected economic theorists to join other refugees from the arbitrage group at Salomon. The board of directors included Myron Scholes, a coauthor of the famous Black-Scholes formula used to price option contracts, and MIT Sloan professor Robert Merton, both of whom would later share the 1997 Nobel Prize for Economics. The firm's impressive brain trust, collectively considered geniuses by most of the financial world, set out to raise a $1 billion fund by explaining to investors that their profoundly complex computer models allowed them to price securities according to risk more accurately than the rest of the market, in effect "vacuuming up nickels that others couldn't see."[8]

One typical LTCM trade concerned the divergence in price between long-term U.S. Treasury bonds. Despite offering fundamentally the same (minimal) default risk, those issued more recently—known as "on-the-run" securities—traded more heavily than those "off-the-run" securities issued just months previously. Heavier trading meant greater liquidity, which in turn resulted in ever-so-slightly higher prices. As "on-the-run" securities become "off-the-run" upon the issuance of a new tranche of Treasury bonds, the price discrepancy generally disappears with time. LTCM sought to exploit that price convergence by shorting the more expensive "on-the-run" bond while purchasing the "off-the-run" security.

By early 1998 the intellectual firepower of its board members and the aggressive trading practices that had made the arbitrage group at Salomon so successful had allowed LTCM to flourish, growing its initial $1 billion of investor equity to $4.72 billion (Exhibit 1). However, the miniscule spreads earned on arbitrage trades could not provide the type of returns sought by hedge fund investors. In order to make transactions such as these worth their while, LTCM had to employ massive leverage in order to magnify its returns. Ultimately, the fund's equity component sat atop more than $124.5 billion in borrowings for total assets of more than $129 billion. These borrowings were merely the tip of the iceberg; LTCM also held off-balance-sheet derivative positions with a notional value of more than $1.25 *trillion*.

---

[7]Roger Lowenstein, *When Genius Failed: The Rise and Fall of Long-Term Capital Management* (New York: Random House, 2000).

[8]Ibid.

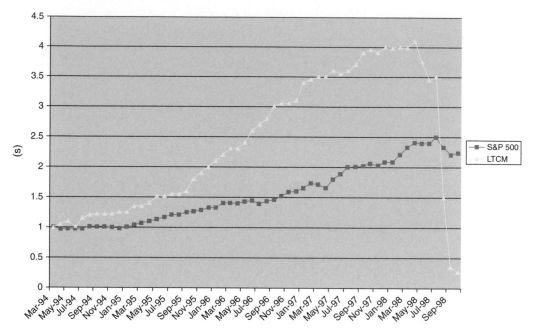

**EXHIBIT 1** Value of $1 Invested in LTCM vs. S&P 500. *Source*: Roger Lowenstein, When Genius Failed: The Rise and Fall of Long-Term Capital Management (New York: Random House, 2000)

The fund's success began to pose its own problems. The market lacked sufficient capacity to absorb LTCM's bloated size, as trades that had been profitable initially became impossible to conduct on a massive scale. Moreover, a flood of arbitrage imitators tightened the spreads on LTCM's "bread-and-butter" trades even further. The pressure to continue delivering returns forced LTCM to find new arbitrage opportunities, and the fund diversified into areas where it could not pair its theoretical insights with trading experience. Soon LTCM had made large bets in Russia and in other emerging markets, on S&P futures, and in yield curve, junk bond, merger, and dual-listed securities arbitrage.

Combined with its style drift, the fund's more than 26× leverage put LTCM in an increasingly precarious bubble, which was eventually burst by a combination of factors that forced the fund into a liquidity crisis. In contrast to Scholes's comments about plucking invisible, riskless nickels from the sky, financial theorist Nassim Taleb later compared the fund's aggressive risk-taking to "picking up pennies in front of a steamroller," a steamroller that finally came in the form of 1998's market panic. The departure of frequent LTCM counterparty Salomon Brothers from the arbitrage market that summer put downward pressure on many of the fund's positions, and Russia's default on its government-issued bonds threw international credit markets into a downward spiral. Panicked investors around the globe demonstrated a "flight to quality," selling the risky securities in which LTCM traded and purchasing U.S. Treasury securities, further driving up their price and preventing a price convergence upon which the fund had bet so heavily.

None of LTCM's sophisticated theoretical models had contemplated such an internationally correlated credit market collapse, and the fund began hemorrhaging money, losing nearly 20 percent of its equity in May and June alone. Day after day, every market in which LTCM traded turned against it. Its powerless brain trust watched in horror as its equity shrank to $600 million in early September without any reduction in borrowing, resulting in an unfathomable 200× leverage ratio. Sensing the fund's liquidity crunch, Bear Stearns refused to continue acting as a clearinghouse for the fund's trades, throwing LTCM into a panic. Without the short-term credit that enabled its entire trading operations, the fund could not continue and its longer-term securities grew more illiquid by the day.[9]

Obstinate in their refusal to unwind what they still considered profitable trades hammered by short-term market irrationality, LTCM's partners refused a buyout offer of $2.50 million by Goldman Sachs, ING Barings, and Warren Buffet's Berkshire Hathaway.[10] However, LTCM's role as a counterparty in thousands of derivatives trades that touched investment firms around the world threatened to provoke a wider collapse in international securities markets if the fund went under, so the U.S. Federal Reserve stepped in to maintain order. Wishing to avoid the precedent of a government bailout of a hedge fund and the moral hazard it could subsequently encourage, the Fed invited every major investment bank on Wall Street to an emergency meeting in New York and dictated the terms of the $3.625 billion bailout that would preserve market liquidity. The Fed convinced Bankers Trust, Barclays, Chase, Credit Suisse First Boston, Deutsche Bank, Goldman Sachs, Merrill Lynch, JP Morgan, Morgan Stanley, Salomon Smith Barney, and UBS—many of whom were investors in the fund—to contribute $300 million apiece, with $125 million coming from Société Générale and $100 million from Lehman Brothers and Paribas. Eventually the market crisis passed, and each bank managed to liquidate its position at a slight profit. Only one bank contacted by the Fed refused to join the syndicate and share the burden in the name of preserving market integrity.

That bank was Bear Stearns.

Bear's dominant trading position in bonds and derivatives had won it the profitable business of acting as a settlement house for nearly all of LTCM's trading in those markets. On September 22, 1998, just days before the Fed-organized bailout, Bear put the final nail in the LTCM coffin by calling in a short-term debt in the amount of $500 million in an attempt to limit its own exposure to the failing hedge fund, rendering it insolvent in the process. Ever the maverick in investment banking circles, Bear stubbornly refused to contribute to the eventual buyout, even in the face of a potentially apocalyptic market crash and despite the millions in profits it had earned as LTCM's prime broker. In typical Bear fashion, Cayne ignored the howls from other banks that failure to preserve confidence in the markets through a bailout would bring them all down in flames, famously growling through a chewed cigar as the Fed solicited contributions for the emergency financing, "Don't go alphabetically if you want this to work."[11]

Market analysts were nearly unanimous in describing the lessons learned from LTCM's implosion; in effect, the fund's profound leverage had placed it in such a precarious position that it could not wait for its positions to turn profitable. While its trades were sound in principal, LTCM's predicted price convergence was not realized until long after its equity had been wiped out completely. A less leveraged firm, they explained, might have realized lower profits than the 40 percent annual return LTCM had offered investors up until the 1998 crisis, but could have weathered the storm once the market turned against it. In the words of economist John Maynard Keynes, the market had remained irrational longer than LTCM could remain solvent. The crisis further illustrated the importance not merely of liquidity but of perception in the less regulated

---

[9]Ibid.

[10]Andrew Garfield et al., "Bear Stearns' $500m Call Triggered LTCM Crisis," *London Independent*, September 26, 1998, http://findarticles.com/p/articles/mi_qn4158/is_19980926/ai_n14183149 (accessed July 12, 2008).

[11]Ibid.

derivatives markets. Once LTCM's ability to meet its obligations was called into question, its demise became inevitable, as it could no longer find counterparties with whom to trade and from whom it could borrow to continue operating.

The thornier question of the Fed's role in bailing out an overly aggressive investment fund in the name of market stability remained unresolved, despite the Fed's insistence on private funding for the actual buyout. Though impossible to foresee at the time, the issue would be revisited anew less than ten years later, and it would haunt Bear Stearns.

With negative publicity from Bear's $38.5 million settlement with the SEC regarding charges that it had ignored fraudulent behavior by a client for whom it cleared trades and LTCM's collapse behind it, Bear Stearns continued to grow under Cayne's leadership, with its stock price appreciating some 600 percent from his assumption of control in 1993 until 2008. However, a rapid-fire sequence of negative events began to unfurl in the summer of 2007 that would push Bear into a liquidity crunch eerily similar to the one that felled LTCM.

## The Credit Crisis

Beginning in the late 1990s, consistent appreciation in U.S. real estate values fueled a decade-long boom in the housing market. During this period, the mortgage business was revolutionized from its traditionally local focus with banks lending directly to homebuyers to a global industry with banks issuing mortgages and then selling them to a diverse pool of investors. Eager to add new products that provided underwriting fees, investment banks began "securitizing" the mortgages, slicing them into various securities differentiated on the basis of the geography of the underlying mortgages, the estimated default risk, and whether the purchaser of the security would receive the interest accruing on the mortgages or the payback of the principal. Investment banks then sold these securities to various investor groups depending on their preferences regarding risk, interest rate exposure, and myriad other factors. Issuance of these collateralized debt obligations, or CDOs, grew to a peak of $421.6 billion in 2006 and $266.9 billion in 1H 2007 in the United States alone (Exhibit 2).[12] In the process, the structure of the mortgage industry changed (Exhibit 3).[13]

Previously, small, mostly regional banks had conducted mortgage lending using the funds deposited by their retail customers, which limited the total dollar amount any one bank could lend. More importantly, banks had to rely upon their own due diligence to make sure that mortgage terms remained reasonable—that the homebuyer had sufficient income and credit history to repay the loan, or that the appraisal on the property justified the amount lent. The surge of investor appetite for CDOs in the early 2000s allowed lenders to issue mortgages and then immediately securitize them through investment banks, who sold the various tranches of those securities in the mortgage bond market. One can easily recognize the sea change in incentives for lenders; without the loan resting on the bank's balance sheet, the best way to boost profits was to originate more—rather than safer—mortgages before flipping them to investment banks, which reissued them through CDOs. Issuance ballooned.

However, the suddenly lucrative CDO market suffered from inherent limitations on the base of potential homebuyers. Moreover, with interest rates remaining historically low and stable for

[12]Securities Industry and Financial Markets Association, "Global CDO Market Issuance Data," http://www.sifma.org/research/pdf/SIFMA_CDOIssuanceData2008.pdf (accessed July 11, 2008).

[13]IMF Global Financial Stability Report, "Financial Market Turbulence: Causes, Consequences, and Policies," 2007.

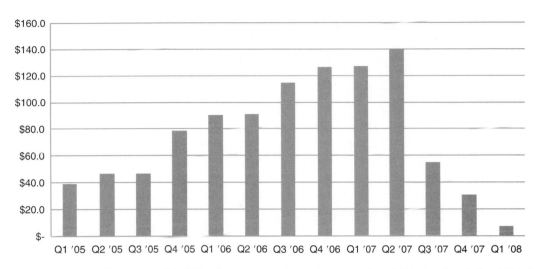

**EXHIBIT 2** U.S. Quarterly CDO Issuance ($ in billions). *Source*: Securities Industry and Financial Markets Association, "Global CDO Market Issuance Data," http://www.sifma.org/research/pdf/SIFMA_CDOIssuanceData2008.pdf (accessed July 11, 2008)

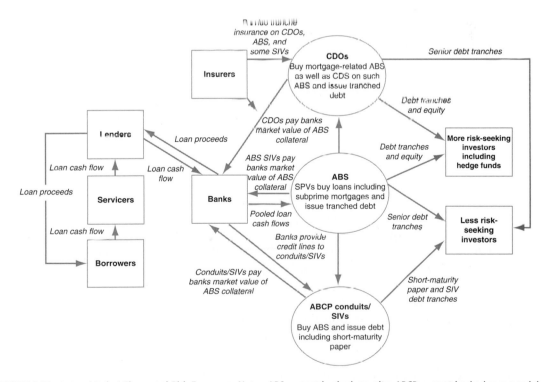

**EXHIBIT 3** Mortgage Market Flows and Risk Exposures *Notes*: ABS = asset-backed security; ABCP = asset-backed commercial paper; CDO = collateralized debt obligation; CDS = credit default swap; SIV = structured investment vehicle; SPV = special purpose vehicle *Source*: IMF Global Financial Stability Report, "Financial Market Turbulence: Causes, Consequences, and Policies," 2007

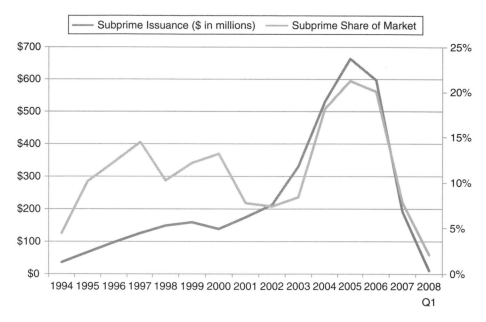

**EXHIBIT 4** Subprime Issuance and Share of Market. *Source*: Ellen Schloemer et al., "Losing Ground: Foreclosures in the Subprime Market and Their Cost to Homeowners," Center for Responsible Learning, December 2006, http://www.responsiblelending.org/pdfs/foreclosure-paper-report-2-17.pdf (accessed July 19, 2008)

the better part of a decade, investors—particularly hedge fund investors, who entered the CDO market in earnest in 2004 and 2005[14]—began seeking higher returns by taking on additional risk. The twin pressures of investors seeking higher returns and lenders trying to grow their market led to the boom in higher-risk mortgages to less creditworthy homebuyers, or "subprime" mortgages (Exhibit 4).

Officially referring to loans that did not meet the more stringent guidelines of Fannie Mae or Freddie Mac, subprime mortgages were geared toward riskier homebuyers with lower incomes and spottier credit histories. As a result, such mortgages frequently carried higher interest rates, increasing investor return but also the likelihood of homeowner default. One common subprime structure was the "2/28" adjustable rate mortgage (ARM), a floating rate loan that featured a low interest rate for the first two years before resetting to a significantly higher rate for the final twenty-eight years of the loan, often 500 or more basis points over LIBOR. The long historical trend in rising real estate values and the ready availability of credit in the market convinced many that they could refinance their mortgages before the ARM adjusted to the higher interest rate, allowing them in effect to gain significant equity in the home without significant cash outlay.

The sudden pullback in U.S. housing prices in the summer of 2006 changed all of that (Exhibit 5). With the collapse of housing markets in Arizona, California, Florida, and the northeast corridor of the United States, many owners found themselves holding negative equity, meaning the appraised value of the property was less than the mortgage debt outstanding on their loan (Exhibit 6). Foreclosures spiked, and suddenly wary lenders stopped issuing new loans almost entirely.

---

[14]Peter Cockhill and James Bagnall, "Hedge Fund Managers Expand Into CDOs and Private Equity," *Hedgeweek*, October 1, 2005, http://www.hedgeweek.com/articles/detail.jsp?content_id=12879 (accessed July 12, 2008).

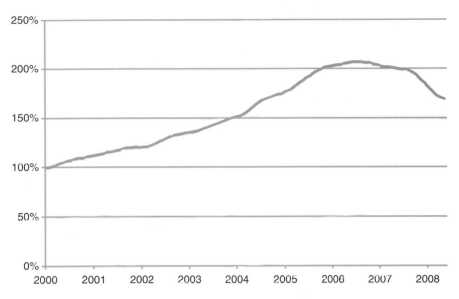

**EXHIBIT 5** S&P/Case-Shiller Home Price Index (SPSC20R) Appreciation Since 2000. *Source*: Schloemer et al., "Losing Ground: Foreclosures in the Subprime Market and Their Cost to Homeowners."

## Bear Stearns Asset Management

Like many of its competitors, Bear Stearns saw the rise of the hedge fund industry during the 1990s and began managing its own funds with outside investor capital under the name Bear Stearns Asset Management (BSAM). Unlike its competitors, Bear hired all of its fund managers internally, with each manager specializing in a particular security or asset class. Objections by some Bear executives, such as co-president Alan Schwartz, that such concentration of risk could raise volatility were ignored, and the impressive returns posted by internal funds such as Ralph Cioffi's High-Grade Structured Credit Strategies Fund quieted any concerns.

Cioffi's fund invested in sophisticated credit derivatives backed by mortgage securities. When the housing bubble burst in 2006, Cioffi's trades turned unprofitable, but like many successful Bear traders before him he redoubled his bets, raising a new Enhanced Leverage High-Grade Structured Credit Strategies Fund that would use 100× leverage (as compared to the 35× leverage employed by the original fund).[15] The market continued to turn disastrously against the fund, which was soon stuck with billions of dollars worth of illiquid, unprofitable mortgages. In an attempt to salvage the situation and cut his losses, Cioffi launched a vehicle named Everquest Financial and sold its shares to the public. But when journalists at the *Wall Street Journal* revealed that Everquest's primary assets were the "toxic waste" of money-losing mortgage securities, Bear had no choice but to cancel the public offering. With spectacular losses mounting daily, investors attempted to withdraw their remaining holdings. In order to free up cash for such redemptions, the fund had to liquidate assets at a loss, selling that only put additional downward pressure on its already underwater positions. Lenders to the fund began making margin calls and threatening to seize its $1.2 billion in collateral, leading to a hastily arranged

---

[15]Bryan Burrough, "Bringing Down Bear Stearns," *Vanity Fair*, August 2008, http://www.vanityfair.com/politics/features/2008/08/bear_stearns200808 (accessed July 13, 2008).

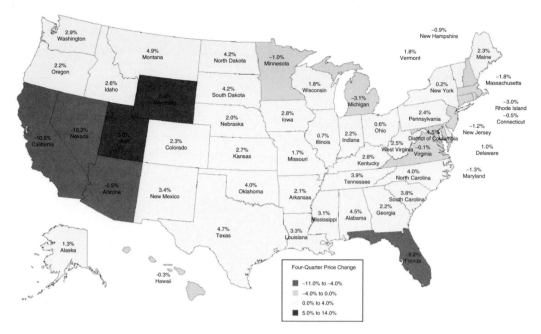

**EXHIBIT 6** Four-Quarter Housing Price Changes by State (2Q 2007–1Q 2008). *Source*: Office of Federal Housing Enterprise Oversight, "Decline in House Prices Accelerates in First Quarter," May 22, 2008, http://www.ofheo.gov/media/hpi/1q08hpi.pdf (accessed July 19, 2008)

conference with creditors in which Bear trader and co-president Warren Spector claimed that lenders from Merrill Lynch and JP Morgan Chase did not understand the fund's operations and that Cioffi would turn it around.

In a less turbulent market it might have worked, but the subprime crisis had spent weeks on the front page of financial newspapers around the globe, and every bank on Wall Street was desperate to reduce its own exposure. Insulted and furious that Bear had refused to inject any of its own capital to save the funds, Steve Black, JP Morgan Chase head of investment banking, called Schwartz and said, "We're defaulting you."[16]

The default and subsequent seizure of $400 million in collateral by Merrill Lynch proved highly damaging to Bear Stearns's reputation across Wall Street. In a desperate attempt to save face under the scrutiny of the SEC, Cayne made the unprecedented move of using $1.6 billion of Bear's own capital to prop up the hedge funds. The bailout later revealed deeper problems at the bank when a front-page *Wall Street Journal* article claimed that Cayne had been absent at the height of the scandal, off on a ten-day golf and bridge-playing vacation in Nashville without a cell phone or e-mail device. The article further alleged ongoing marijuana usage by Cayne, who denied the specific 2004 incident identified in the article but refused to make a blanket statement denying any such usage in the past.

By late July 2007 even Bear's continued support could no longer prop up Cioffi's two beleaguered funds, which paid back just $300 million of the credit its parent had extended. With their holdings virtually worthless, the funds had no choice but to file for bankruptcy protection. The following day, Cayne returned from Nashville and set about trying to calm shareholder fears

---

[16]Ibid.

that Bear was not standing on solid financial ground. Spector would not survive the weekend, with Cayne forcing him out in a sort of public bloodletting to show that things were once again under control. Ironically, his departure may have done more harm than good. After opening an August 3 conference call with a statement of assurance that the company had $11.4 billion in cash and was "taking the situation seriously," Cayne turned the call over to chief financial officer Samuel Molinaro, Jr., and stepped out to speak with an attorney regarding Spector's resignation. When the conversation turned to Q&A, an equity research analyst's question posed to Cayne met with deafening silence. Cayne later returned to the room, but callers were not told this, contributing to the impression of Cayne as a disinterested, absentee CEO.[17]

## The Calm Before the Storm

On November 14, just two weeks after the *Journal* story questioning Cayne's commitment and leadership, Bear Stearns reported that it would write down $1.2 billion in mortgage-related losses. (The figure would later grow to $1.9 billion.) CFO Molinaro suggested that the worst had passed, and to outsiders, at least, the firm appeared to have narrowly escaped disaster.

Behind the scenes, however, Bear management had already begun searching for a white knight, hiring Gary Parr at Lazard to examine its options for a cash injection. Privately, Schwartz and Parr spoke with Kohlberg Kravis Roberts & Co. founder Henry Kravis, who had first learned the leveraged buyout market while a partner at Bear Stearns in the 1960s. Kravis sought entry into the profitable brokerage business at depressed prices, while Bear sought an injection of more than $2 billion in equity capital (for a reported 20 percent of the company) and the calming effect that a strong, respected personality like Kravis would have upon shareholders. Ultimately the deal fell apart, largely due to management's fear that KKR's significant equity stake and the presence of Kravis on the board would alienate the firm's other private equity clientele, who often competed with KKR for deals. Throughout the fall Bear continued to search for potential acquirers, with private equity firm J. C. Flowers & Co., JP Morgan Chase, and Berkshire Hathaway CEO Warren Buffett all kicking the tires before ultimately passing. With the market watching intently to see if Bear shored up its financing, Cayne managed to close only a $1 billion cross-investment with CITIC, the state-owned investment company of the People's Republic of China.

Meanwhile, a battle raged within the firm, with factions pitted against each other on how to proceed with Bear's mortgage holdings, which were still valued at $56 billion despite steady price declines. With traders insisting that any remaining mortgage positions be cut, head mortgage trader Tom Marano instituted a "chaos trade," essentially a massive short on the ABX, a family of subprime indexes. They also shorted commercial mortgage indexes and the stocks of other financials with mortgage exposure, such as Wells Fargo and Countrywide Financial.

Bear's executive and risk committees met in late September 2007 to review the trades, just after negotiations to sell a 10 percent stake in Bear to Allianz SE's Pacific Investment Management Co. had failed. With Cayne recovering from an infection, all eyes turned to Greenberg, who had become increasingly active throughout the crisis. Uncomfortable with the size of Bear's remaining mortgage holdings and the potential volatility of the chaos trade, the

[17]Kate Kelly, "Bear CEO's Handling of Crisis Raises Issues," *Wall Street Journal*, November 1, 2007, http://online.wsj.com/public/article_print/SB119387369474078336.html (accessed July 14, 2008).

veteran trader insisted that the firm reduce its exposure. "We've got to cut!" he shouted, invoking the firm's historical aggressiveness in trimming unprofitable positions.

Despite the fact that the hedges had returned close to half a billion dollars, Schwartz followed Greenberg's advice, requesting trades to offset specific assets in Bear's portfolio instead of the broader, more market-based chaos trade.

Morale sunk to demoralizing lows as fall turned to winter, with bankers squabbling over a greatly diminished bonus pool and top Bear executives clamoring for Cayne's dismissal as CEO. Top performers at Bear demanded that Schwartz oust Cayne or else face a mass exodus. Matters worsened on December 20, when Bear posted the first quarterly loss since its founding some eighty-five years earlier. The next day it received an e-mail from colossal bond manager PIMCO indicating its discomfort with exposure to the financial sector and its desire to unwind billions of dollars worth of trades with Bear. An emergency conference call to Bear alumnus and PIMCO managing director William Powers convinced the fund to hold off on any such drastic moves at least until a meeting with Bear executives, but Powers's admonition came through loud and clear: "You need to raise equity."[18]

In an attempt to stem the tide of quality employees fleeing what appeared to be a sinking ship, Schwartz conversed with the board and received approval to ask for Cayne's resignation, which he tendered on January 8. Cayne remained chairman of the board, with Schwartz stepping in as the new CEO. Schwartz immediately turned his sights to the Q1 numbers, desperate to ensure that Bear would post a quarterly profit and hopefully calm the growing uneasiness among its shareholders, employees, creditors, and counterparties in the market.

## Run on the Bank

Bear's $0.89 profit per share in the first quarter of 2008 did little to quiet the growing whispers of its financial instability (Exhibit 7). It seemed that every day another major investment bank reported mortgage-related losses, and for whatever reason, Bear's name kept cropping up in discussions of the by-then infamous subprime crisis. Exacerbating Bear's public relations problem, the SEC had launched an investigation into the collapse of the two BSAM hedge funds, and rumors of massive losses at three major hedge funds further rattled an already uneasy market. Nonetheless, Bear executives felt that the storm had passed, reasoning that its almost $21 billion in cash reserves had convinced the market of its long-term viability (Exhibit 8).

Instead, on Monday, March 10, 2008, Moody's downgraded 163 tranches of mortgage-backed bonds issued by Bear across fifteen transactions.[19] The credit rating agency had drawn sharp criticism in its role in the subprime meltdown from analysts who felt the company had over-estimated the creditworthiness of mortgage-backed securities and failed to alert the market of the danger as the housing market turned. As a result, Moody's was in the process of downgrading nearly all of its ratings, but as the afternoon wore on, Bear's stock price seemed to be reacting far more negatively than competitor firms.

---

[18]Kate Kelly, "Lost Opportunities Haunt Final Days of Bear Stearns," *Wall Street Journal*, May 27, 2008, http://online.wsj.com/article/SB121184521826521301.html (accessed July 16, 2008).

[19]Sue Chang, "Moody's Downgrades Bear Stearns Alt-A Deals," *MarketWatch*, March 10, 2008, http://www.marketwatch.com/news/story/moodys-downgrades-bear-stearns-alt-deals/story.aspx?guid=%7B9989153A-B0F4-43B6-AE11-7B2DBE7E0B9C%7D (accessed July 19, 2008).

**EXHIBIT 7   Condensed Consolidated Statements of Income, Three Months Ended (US$ in millions, except share and per share data)**

| | February 29, 2008 | February 28, 2007 |
|---|---|---|
| REVENUES | | |
| Commissions | 330 | 281 |
| Principal transactions | 515 | 1,342 |
| Investment banking | 230 | 350 |
| Interest and dividends | 2,198 | 2,657 |
| Asset management and other income | 154 | 168 |
| Total revenues | 3,427 | 4,798 |
| Interest expense | 1,948 | 2,316 |
| Revenues, net of interest expense | 1,479 | 2,482 |
| | | |
| NON-INTEREST EXPENSES | | |
| Employee compensation and benefits | 754 | 1,204 |
| Floor brokerage, exchange, and clearance fees | 79 | 56 |
| Communications and technology | 154 | 128 |
| Occupancy | 73 | 57 |
| Advertising and market development | 40 | 37 |
| Professional fees | 100 | 72 |
| Other expenses | 126 | 93 |
| Total non-interest expenses | 1,326 | 1,647 |
| Income before provision for income taxes | 153 | 835 |
| Provision for income taxes | 38 | 281 |
| Net income | 115 | 554 |
| Preferred stock dividends | 5 | 6 |
| Net income applicable to common shares | 110 | 548 |
| Basic earnings per share | $0.89 | $4.23 |
| Diluted earnings per share | $0.86 | $3.82 |
| Weighted average common shares outstanding | | |
| Basic | 129,128,281 | 133,094,747 |
| Diluted | 138,539,248 | 149,722,654 |
| Cash dividends declared per common share | $0.32 | $0.32 |

Wall Street's drive toward ever more sophisticated communications devices had created an interconnected network of traders and bankers across the world. On most days, Internet chat and mobile e-mail devices relayed gossip about compensation, major employee departures, and even sports betting lines. On the morning of March 10, however, it was carrying one message to the exclusion of all others: Bear was having liquidity problems.

At noon, CNBC took the story public on *Power Lunch*. As Bear's stock price fell more than 10 percent to $63, Ace Greenberg frantically placed calls to various executives, demanding that someone publicly deny any such problems. When contacted himself, Greenberg told a CNBC correspondent that the rumors were "totally ridiculous," angering CFO Molinaro, who felt that denying the rumor would only legitimize it and trigger further panic selling, making prophesies of Bear's illiquidity self-fulfilling.[20] Just two hours later, however, Bear appeared to have dodged a bullet. News of New York governor Eliot Spitzer's involvement in a high-class prostitution ring

---

[20]Burrough, "Bringing Down Bear Stearns."

## EXHIBIT 8 Condensed Consolidated Balance Sheets, Three Months Ended (US$ in millions, except share and per share data)

| | February 29, 2008 | February 28, 2007 |
|---|---|---|
| ASSETS | | |
| Cash and cash equivalents | 20,786 | 21,406 |
| Cash and securities deposited with clearing organizations or segregated in compliance with federal regulations | 14,910 | 12,890 |
| Securities received as collateral | 15,371 | 15,599 |
| Collateralized agreements | | |
| Securities purchased under agreements to resell | 26,888 | 27,878 |
| Securities borrowed | 87,143 | 82,245 |
| Receivables | | |
| Customers | 41,990 | 41,115 |
| Brokers, dealers, and others | 10,854 | 11,622 |
| Interest and dividends | 488 | 785 |
| Financial instruments owned, at fair value | 118,201 | 122,518 |
| Financial instruments owned and pledged as collateral, at fair value | 22,903 | 15,724 |
| Total financial instruments owned, at fair value | 141,104 | 138,242 |
| Assets of variable interest entities and mortgage loan special purpose entities | 29,991 | 33,553 |
| Net PP&E | 608 | 605 |
| Other assets | 8,862 | 9,422 |
| Total assets | 398,995 | 395,362 |
| LIABILITIES AND STOCKHOLDERS' EQUITY | | |
| Unsecured short-term borrowings | 8,538 | 11,643 |
| Obligation to return securities received as collateral | 15,371 | 15,599 |
| Collateralized financings | | |
| Securities sold under agreements to repurchase | 98,272 | 102,373 |
| Securities loaned | 4,874 | 3,935 |
| Other secured borrowings | 7,778 | 12,361 |
| Payables | | |
| Customers | 91,632 | 83,204 |
| Brokers, dealers, and others | 5,642 | 4,101 |
| Interest and dividends | 853 | 1,301 |
| Financial instruments sold, but not yet purchased, at fair value | 51,544 | 43,807 |
| Liabilities of variable interest entities and mortgage loan special purpose entities | 26,739 | 30,605 |
| Accrued employee compensation and benefits | 360 | 1,651 |
| Other liabilities and accrued expenses | 3,743 | 4,451 |
| Long-term borrowings (includes $9,018 and $8,500 at fair value as of February 29, 2008 and November 30, 2007, respectively) | 71,753 | 68,538 |
| Total liabilities | 387,099 | 383,569 |
| STOCKHOLDERS' EQUITY | | |
| Preferred stock | 352 | 352 |
| Common stock | 185 | 185 |
| Paid-in capital | 5,619 | 4,986 |
| Retained earnings | 9,419 | 9,441 |
| Employee stock compensation plans | 2,164 | 2,478 |
| Accumulated other comprehensive income (loss) | 25 | −8 |
| Shares held in RSU trust | −2,955 | — |
| Treasury stock, at cost | −2,913 | −5,641 |
| Total stockholders' equity | 11,896 | 11,793 |
| Total liabilities and stockholders' equity | 398,995 | 395,362 |

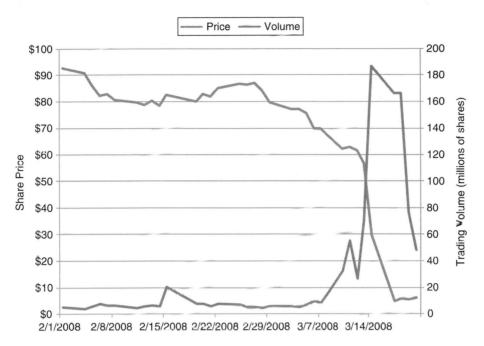

**EXHIBIT 9** Share Price and Trading Volume.

wiped any financial rumors off the front page, leading Bear executives to believe the worst was once again behind them.

Instead, the rumors exploded anew the next day, as many interpreted the Federal Reserve's announcement of a new $200 billion lending program to help financial institutions through the credit crisis[21] as aimed specifically toward Bear Stearns. The stock dipped as low as $55.42 before closing at $62.97 (Exhibit 9). Meanwhile, Bear executives faced a new crisis in the form of an explosion of novation requests, in which a party to a risky contract tries to eliminate its risky position by selling it to a third party. Credit Suisse, Deutsche Bank, and Goldman Sachs all reported a deluge of novation requests from firms trying to reduce their exposure to Bear's credit risk. The speed and force of this explosion of novation requests meant that before Bear could act, both Goldman Sachs and Credit Suisse issued e-mails to their traders holding up any requests relating to Bear Stearns pending approval by their credit departments. Once again, the electronically linked gossip network of trading desks around the world dealt a blow to investor confidence in Bear's stability, as a false rumor circulated that Credit Suisse's memo had forbidden its traders from engaging in any trades with Bear.[22] The decrease in confidence in Bear's liquidity could be quantified by the rise in the cost of credit default swaps on Bear's debt. The price of such an instrument—which effectively acts as five years of insurance against a default on $10 million of Bear's debt—spiked to more than $626,000 from less than $100,000 in October, indicating heavy betting by some firms that Bear would be unable to pay its liabilities.[23]

Internally, Bear debated whether to address the rumors publicly, ultimately deciding to arrange a Wednesday morning interview of Schwartz by CNBC correspondent David Faber.

---

[21]Chris Reese, "Bonds Extend Losses After Fed Announcement," Reuters News, March 11, 2008, http://www.reuters.com/article/bondsNews/idUSNYD00017820080311 (accessed July 16, 2008).

[22]Kelly, "Fear, Rumors Touched Off Fatal Run on Bear Stearns."

[23]Ibid.

**EXHIBIT 10** Differences in Regulation—Commercial Banks vs. Investment Banks

|  | Commercial Banks | Investment Banks |
| --- | --- | --- |
| General business model | Accept deposits and lend them out in a variety of products, provide financial services for individuals and businesses | Underwrite equity and debt offerings, trade stocks and bonds, provide advisory (e.g., M&A) services |
| Federally insured? | Yes | No (pre-2008) |
| Primary source of assets at risk | Depositors | Shareholders |
| Restrictions on leverage | Significant—10% capital ratio considered "well-capitalized" | None |
| Primary oversight | Federal Reserve | Securities and Exchange Commission |
| Restriction of activities | Prohibited from investing in real estate and commodities; new activities require Fed approval | None |

Not wanting to encourage rumors with a hasty departure, Schwartz did the interview live from Bear's annual media conference in Palm Beach. Chosen because of his perceived friendliness to Bear, Faber nonetheless opened the interview with a devastating question that claimed direct knowledge of a trader whose credit department had temporarily held up a trade with Bear. Later during the interview Faber admitted that the trade had finally gone through, but he had called into question Bear's fundamental capacity to operate as a trading firm. One veteran trader later commented, "You knew right at that moment that Bear Stearns was dead, right at the moment he asked that question. Once you raise that idea, that the firm can't follow through on a trade, it's over. Faber killed him. He just killed him."

Despite sentiment at Bear that Schwartz had finally put the company's best foot forward and refuted rumors of its illiquidity, hedge funds began pulling their accounts in earnest, bringing Bear's reserves down to $15 billion. Additionally, repo lenders—whose overnight loans to investment banks must be renewed daily—began informing Bear that they would not renew the next morning, forcing the firm to find new sources of credit. Schwartz phoned Parr at Lazard, Molinaro reviewed Bear's plans for an emergency sale in the event of a crisis, and one of the firm's attorneys called the president of the Federal Reserve to explain Bear's situation and implore him to accelerate the newly announced program that would allow investment banks to use mortgage securities as collateral for emergency loans from the Fed's discount window, normally reserved for commercial banks (Exhibit 10).[24]

Bear executives struggled to placate an increasingly mutinous employee base. Bruce Lisman, head of equities, stood on his desk and implored traders to remain focused and weather the storm, pointing out Bear's historical resilience. Greenberg once again pretended to swing a golf club on the trading floor, as if to suggest that Bear had survived far greater crises.

Regardless of their effect on employees, such assurances had no effect on the market. The trickle of withdrawals that had begun earlier in the week turned into an unstoppable torrent of cash flowing out the door on Thursday. Meanwhile, Bear's stock continued its sustained nosedive, falling nearly 15 percent to an intraday low of $50.48 before rallying to close down 1.5 percent. At lunch, Schwartz assured a crowded meeting of Bear executives

---

[24]Burrough, "Bringing Down Bear Stearns."

that the whirlwind rumors were simply market noise, only to find himself interrupted by Michael Minikes, senior managing director.

"Do you have any idea what is going on?" Minikes shouted. "Our cash is flying out the door! Our clients are leaving us!"[25]

Hedge fund clients jumped ship in droves. Renaissance Technologies withdrew approximately $5 billion in trading accounts, and D. E. Shaw followed suit with an equal amount. That evening, Bear executives assembled in a sixth-floor conference room to survey the carnage. In less than a week, the firm had burned through all but $5.9 billion of its $18.3 billion in reserves, and was still on the hook for $2.4 billion in short-term debt to Citigroup. With a panicked market making more withdrawals the next day almost certain, Schwartz accepted the inevitable need for additional financing and had Parr revisit merger discussions with JP Morgan CEO James Dimon that had stalled in the fall. Flabbergasted at the idea that an agreement could be reached that night, Dimon nonetheless agreed to send a team of bankers over to analyze Bear's books.

Parr's call interrupted Dimon's fifty-second birthday celebration at a Greek restaurant just a few blocks away from Bear headquarters, where a phalanx of attorneys had begun preparing emergency bankruptcy filings and documents necessary for a variety of cash injecting transactions. Facing almost certain insolvency in the next twenty-four hours, Schwartz hastily called an emergency board meeting late that night, with most board members dialing in remotely. Cayne missed most of the conversation while playing in a bridge tournament in Detroit.

Bear's nearly four hundred subsidiaries would make a bankruptcy filing impossibly complicated, so Schwartz continued to cling to the hope for an emergency cash infusion to get Bear through Friday. As JP Morgan's bankers pored over Bear's positions, they balked at the firm's precarious position and the continued size of its mortgage holdings, insisting that the Fed get involved in a bailout they considered far too risky to take on alone. Fed officials had been gathered down the hall for hours, and discussions continued into early Friday morning between the Fed and JP Morgan as Schwartz and Molinaro ate cold pizza, the decision now out of their hands.

Its role as a counterparty in trillions of dollars' worth of derivatives contracts bore an eerie similarity to LTCM, and the Fed once again saw the potential for financial Armageddon if Bear were allowed to collapse of its own accord. An emergency liquidation of the firm's assets would have put strong downward pressure on global securities prices, exacerbating an already chaotic market environment. Facing a hard deadline of credit markets' open on Friday morning, the Fed and JP Morgan wrangled back and forth on how to save Bear. Working around the clock, they finally reached an agreement wherein JP Morgan would access the Fed's discount window and in turn offer Bear a $30 billion credit line that, as dictated by a last-minute insertion by Morgan general counsel Steven Cutler, would be good for twenty-eight days. As the press release went public, Bear executives cheered; Bear would have almost a month to seek alternative financing.

## Bear's Last Weekend

Where Bear had seen a lifeline, however, the market saw instead a last desperate gasp for help. Incredulous Bear executives could only watch in horror as the firm's capital continued to fly out of its coffers. On Friday morning Bear burned through the last of its reserves in a matter of hours. A midday conference call in which Schwartz confidently assured investors that the credit

[25]Kelly, "Fear, Rumors Touched Off Fatal Run on Bear Stearns."

line would allow Bear to continue "business as usual" did little to stop the bleeding, and its stock lost almost half of its already depressed value, closing at $30 per share.[26]

All day Friday, Parr set about desperately trying to save his client, searching every corner of the financial world for potential investors or buyers of all or part of Bear. Given the severity of the situation, he could rule out nothing, from a sale of the lucrative prime brokerage operations to a merger or sale of the entire company. Ideally, he hoped to find what he termed a "validating investor," a respected Wall Street name to join the board, adding immediate credibility and perhaps quiet the now deafening rumors of Bear's imminent demise. Sadly, only a few such personalities with the reputation and war chest necessary to play the role of savior existed, and most of them had already passed on Bear.

Nonetheless, Schwartz left Bear headquarters on Friday evening relieved that the firm had lived to see the weekend and secured twenty-eight days of breathing room. During the ride home to Greenwich, an unexpected phone call from New York Federal Reserve President Timothy Geithner and Treasury Secretary Henry Paulson shattered that illusion. Paulson told a stunned Schwartz that the Fed's line of credit would expire Sunday night, giving Bear forty-eight hours to find a buyer or file for bankruptcy. The demise of the twenty-eight-day clause remains a mystery; the speed necessary early Friday morning and the inclusion of the clause by Morgan's general counsel suggest that Bear executives had misinterpreted it, although others believe that Paulson and Geithner had soured both on Bear's prospects and on market perception of an emergency loan from the Fed as Friday wore on. Either way, the Fed had made up its mind, and a Saturday morning appeal from Schwartz failed to sway Geithner.

All day Saturday prospective buyers streamed through Bear's headquarters to pick through the rubble as Parr attempted to orchestrate Bear's last-minute salvation. Chaos reigned, with representatives from every major bank on Wall Street, J. C. Flowers, KKR, and countless others poring over Bear's positions in an effort to determine the value of Bear's massive illiquid holdings and how the Fed would help in financing. Some prospective buyers wanted just a piece of the dying bank, others the whole firm, with still others proposing more complicated multiple-step transactions that would slice Bear to ribbons. One by one, they dropped out, until J. C. Flowers made an offer for 90 percent of Bear for a total of up to $2.6 billion, but the offer was contingent on the private equity firm raising $20 billion from a bank consortium, and $20 billion in risky credit was unlikely to appear overnight.[27]

That left JP Morgan. Apparently the only bank willing to come to the rescue, Morgan had sent no fewer than three hundred bankers representing sixteen different product groups to Bear headquarters to value the firm. The sticking point, as with all the bidders, was Bear's mortgage holdings. Even after a massive write-down, it was impossible to assign a value to such illiquid (and publicly maligned) securities with any degree of accuracy. Having forced the default of the BSAM hedge funds that started this mess less than a year earlier, Steve Black cautioned Schwartz and Parr not to focus on Friday's $32 per share close and indicated that any Morgan bid could be between $8 and $12.[28]

On its final 10Q in March, Bear listed $399 billion in assets and $387 billion in liabilities, leaving just $12 billion in equity for a 32× leverage multiple. Bear initially estimated that this included $120 billion of "risk-weighted" assets, those that might be subject to subsequent write-downs. As Morgan's bankers worked around the clock trying to get to the bottom of Bear's

[26]Kelly, "Bear Stearns Neared Collapse Twice in Frenzied Last Days."

[27]Burrough, "Bringing Down Bear Stearns."

[28]Ibid.

balance sheet, they came to estimate the figure at nearly $220 billion. That pessimistic outlook, combined with Sunday morning's *New York Times* article reiterating Bear's recent troubles, dulled Morgan's appetite for jumping onto what appeared to be a sinking ship. Later, one Morgan banker shuddered, recalling the article. "That article certainly had an impact on my thinking. Just the reputational aspects of it, getting into bed with these people."[29]

On Saturday morning Morgan backed out and Dimon told a shell-shocked Schwartz to pursue any other option available to him. The problem was, no such alternative existed. Knowing this, and the possibility that the liquidation of Bear could throw the world's financial markets into chaos, Fed representatives immediately phoned Dimon. As it had in the LTCM case a decade ago, the Fed relied heavily on suasion, or "jawboning," the longtime practice of attempting to influence market participants by appeals to reason rather than a declaration by fiat. For hours, Morgan's and the Fed's highest-ranking officials played a game of high-stakes poker, with each side bluffing and Bear's future hanging in the balance. The Fed wanted to avoid unprecedented government participation in the bailout of a private investment firm, while Morgan wanted to avoid taking on any of the "toxic waste" in Bear's mortgage holdings. "They kept saying, 'We're not going to do it,' and we kept saying, 'We really think you should do it,'" recalled one Fed official. "This went on for hours … They kept saying, 'We can't do this on our own.'"[30] With the hours ticking away until Monday's Australian markets would open at 6:00 p.m. New York time, both sides had to compromise.

On Sunday afternoon, Schwartz stepped out of a 1:00 emergency meeting of Bear's board of directors to take the call from Dimon. The offer would come somewhere in the range of $4–5 per share.

Hearing the news from Schwartz, the Bear board erupted with rage. Dialing in from the same bridge tournament in Detroit, Cayne exploded, ranting furiously that the firm should file for bankruptcy protection under Chapter 11 rather than accept such a humiliating offer, which would reduce his 5.66 million shares—once worth nearly $1 billion—to less than $30 million in value. In reality, however, bankruptcy was impossible. As Parr explained, changes to the federal bankruptcy code in 2005 meant that a Chapter 11 filing would be tantamount to Bear falling on its sword, because regulators would have to seize Bear's accounts, immediately ceasing the firm's operations and forcing its liquidation. There would be no reorganization.

Even as Cayne raged against the $4 offer, the Fed's concern over the appearance of a $30 billion loan to a failing investment bank while American homeowners faced foreclosures compelled Treasury Secretary Paulson to pour salt in Bear's wounds. Officially, the Fed had remained hands-off in the LTCM bailout, relying on its powers of suasion to convince other banks to step up in the name of market stability. Just ten years later, they could find no takers. The speed of Bear's collapse, the impossibility of conducting true due diligence in such a compressed time frame, and the incalculable risk of taking on Bear's toxic mortgage holdings scared off every buyer and forced the Fed from an advisory role into a principal role in the bailout. Worried that a price deemed at all generous to Bear might subsequently encourage moral hazard—increased risky behavior by investment banks secure in the knowledge that in a worst-case scenario, disaster would be averted by a federal bailout—Paulson determined that the transaction, while rescuing the firm, also had to be punitive to Bear shareholders. He called Dimon, who reiterated the contemplated offer range.

---

[29]Ibid.
[30]Ibid.

"That sounds high to me," Paulson told the JP Morgan chief. "I think this should be done at a very low price." It was moments later that Braunstein called Parr. "The number's $2."

Under Delaware law, executives must act on behalf of both shareholders and creditors when a company enters the "zone of insolvency," and Schwartz knew that Bear had rocketed through that zone over the past few days. Faced with bankruptcy or Morgan, Bear had no choice but to accept the embarrassingly low offer that represented a 97 percent discount off its $32 close on Friday evening. Schwartz convinced the weary Bear board that $2 would be "better than nothing," and by 6:30 p.m., the deal was unanimously approved.

After eighty-five years in the market, Bear Stearns ceased to exist.

# Investment Banking in 2008 (B): A Brave New World

## The Aftermath of Bear Stearns

Furious Bear Stearns shareholders found a loophole in the hastily arranged merger documents. In the rush to consummate the deal, JP Morgan had accidentally agreed to honor Bear's trades for up to a year irrespective of shareholder approval of the merger. This oversight created the terrifying specter of Morgan failing to acquire Bear but nonetheless remaining on the hook for billions in potential losses from Bear trades gone awry. Holding negotiating leverage for the first time since the crisis began, newly minted Bear CEO Alan Schwartz pushed JP Morgan CEO James Dimon to up the final offer price from $2. In the ensuing week-long fracas, Bear once again appeared headed for bankruptcy, this time via a Chapter 7 liquidation that would have put downward pressure on securities prices around the world. With the Fed's reluctant approval, Morgan finally increased its bid to $10 per share for a total transaction value of $1.2 billion. The Fed lent JP Morgan $30 billion, taking Bear's mortgage holdings as collateral. Morgan assumed responsibility for the first $1 billion of any potential losses, leaving U.S. taxpayers with $29 billion in exposure to Bear portfolios. The transaction was so difficult to value that Gary Parr's Lazard approved fairness opinions on both the $2- and $10-per-share offers within the span of one week.

As Dimon began the herculean undertaking of integrating two financial colossi with sprawling, overlapping operations and profoundly different cultures, market observers attempted to make sense of the shocking speed with which Bear went from a viable investment bank to a party with whom no one in the market wanted to trade. Some observers pointed to its extreme leverage and its excessive exposure to risky subprime securities, but many Bear executives, largely off the record, claimed that Bear had fallen victim to a pernicious group of rumor-mongering hedge funds that had taken out massive short positions on Bear's stock in an effort to depress its stock price. So convinced were Bear executives that so called "shorts" were out to get them that mortgage head Tom Marano rebuffed an offer of help from Citadel Investment Group CEO Kenneth Griffin, claiming, "There's such concern that you're short that I wouldn't even go there."[1] While others pointed out the irony of the notoriously vicious Bear accusing others of sharp practices and foul play, these rumors gained steam on July 15, when the SEC subpoenaed more than fifty hedge funds (including Citadel, a major Bear client) as part of an investigation into the bank's demise. Additionally, the SEC took the unprecedented step of temporarily banning short sales of financial institution stocks. Unfortunately, this ban on short selling effectively shut down a large portion of the convertible securities market, as 659 convertible securities issued during the first eight months

---

[1]Kate Kelly, "Bear Stearns Neared Collapse Twice in Frenzied Last Days," *Wall Street Journal*, May 29, 2008, http://online.wsj.com/article/SB121202057232127889.html (accessed July 19, 2008).

of 2008 came from financial companies, including Bank of America and Citigroup. The shutdown stemmed from the fact that hedge funds acted as the principal investors in convertible securities, simultaneously selling convertible issuer stock as a hedge to their purchase of the convertible note or preferred stock to create a theoretically market-neutral position. The ban caused massive losses in hedge fund portfolios and dissuaded them from making additional investments, denying would-be issuers access to needed capital.

The SEC's emergency order also placed a ban on so-called "naked" shorting, or selling shares in a company without a formal agreement to borrow the shares for the sale. In effect, this reduced the total amount of short interest that could accumulate in a stock. The irony that many of these newly protected financial institutions' trading operations had significant short positions themselves was not lost on financial journalists, one of whom dubbed the emergency order "Operation Stocks Go Up Always."[2] The SEC defended the order on the grounds that unusual market conditions required an extreme response, and that the unique vulnerability of financial institutions to rumors of creditworthiness differentiated such institutions from more traditional operating companies.

At the heart of the rumors that consumed Bear Stearns were novation orders, requests sent by Bear clients to other investment banks asking them to assume contracts agreeing to buy or sell securities to Bear in exchange for a fee. Bear managers alleged that the concentration of such requests at three major banks (Goldman Sachs, Credit Suisse, and Deutsche Bank) represented an attempt to flood those banks' credit departments, resulting in delays in clearing that further fueled the gossip that Bear's credit was no good. If so, it worked; both Goldman and Credit Suisse did delay such requests, and the rumor got back to the market with devastating speed. Allegations that a group of hedge fund managers had toasted Bear's collapse at a breakfast the Sunday morning of the deal and planned a subsequent attack on Lehman Brothers further fueled such speculation.[3] Lehman survived the summer, however, largely because the Fed's acceleration of its emergency lending program allowed it and other banks to access the discount window that had been closed to Bear. Many opined that Bear came up just a week short, for the ability to pledge mortgage securities as collateral against such emergency loans might have allowed it to survive as an independent bank.

Perhaps the greatest amount of speculation surrounded the topic of the Fed's role in the bailout and whether New York Fed President Timothy Geithner acted appropriately; he had prevented a major financial market meltdown, but had he gotten the best possible deal for American taxpayers, now on the hook for $29 billion in potential losses from Bear's mortgage holdings? Geithner's palpably tense interrogation by the Senate Banking Committee on April 3 revealed widespread legislator sentiment that the bailout had benefited Wall Street at the expense of Main Street.[4] Defenders pointed out that Henry Paulson forced a painfully low share price (albeit one that climbed after the offer) so as to discourage banks from taking on similar risk, but critics questioned the Fed's involvement in the first place.

Whatever the implications, bankers and regulators sighed with relief at Bear's rescue, assuming that the Fed's bailout of the beleaguered bank had averted crisis while its insistence that JP

[2]David Gaffen, "Four at Four: Operation Stocks Go Up Always," *Marketbeat*, July 15, 2008, http://blogs.wsj.com/marketbeat/2008/07/15/four-at-four-operation-stocks-go-up-always (accessed July 19, 2008).

[3]Bryan Burrough, "Bringing Down Bear Stearns," *Vanity Fair*, August 2008, http://www.vanityfair.com/politics/features/2008/08/bear_stearns200808 (accessed July 19, 2008).

[4]Gary Weiss, "The Man Who Saved (or Got Suckered by) Wall Street," *Portfolio.com*, June 2008, http://www.portfolio.com/executives/features/2008/05/12/New-York-Fed-Chief-Tim-Geithner (accessed July 19, 2008).

Morgan assume responsibility for the first billion dollars in losses from the loan had dissuaded further irresponsible risk-seeking. In truth, the worst was yet to come, for the tangled roots of 2008's global financial meltdown lay in the previous decade of financial and banking deregulation.

## Gramm-Leach-Bliley and the Fall of Glass-Steagall

On April 6, 1998, Citicorp announced its plans for the largest corporate merger in history by joining with the Travelers Group. The $70 billion deal would merge America's second-largest commercial bank with a sprawling financial conglomerate offering banking, insurance, and brokerage services. Just a year earlier, Travelers had become the country's third-largest brokerage house with its 1997 acquisition of Salomon Brothers, the investment banking firm that first inspired the industry's shift away from traditional advisory services to proprietary trading. Touting the pressures of technological change, diversification, globalization of the banking industry, and both individual and corporate customers' desire for a "one-stop shop" as justification, both companies lobbied hard for the merger's regulatory approval.[5]

The proposed transaction violated portions of 1933's Glass-Steagall Act, part of sweeping securities and banking regulations enacted in the wake of the Great Depression. The Act prohibited the combination of a depository institution, such as a bank holding company, with other financial companies, such as investment banks and brokerage houses. Citigroup successfully obtained a temporary waiver for its violation of the Act, completed the merger, and then intensified the decades-old effort to repeal Glass-Steagall. Inspired by a desire to make U.S. investment banks competitive with foreign deposit-taking investment banks such as UBS, Deutsche Bank, and Credit Suisse First Boston, a Republican Congress and President Clinton passed the Gramm-Leach-Bliley Financial Services Modernization Act in 1999, permitting insurance companies, investment banks, and commercial banks to compete on equal footing across products and markets. The subsequent Commodity Futures Modernization Act of 2000 further deregulated the industry by weakening regulatory control over futures contracts and credit default swaps.

Both liberated and revolutionized, the banking industry embarked upon a decade of acquisitions that concentrated the world's financial power in fewer and fewer hands. Acquisitions of investment banks by commercial banks became commonplace, with FleetBoston buying Robertson Stephens, Bank of America buying Montgomery Securities, Chase Manhattan buying JP Morgan (and the combined entity JPMorgan Chase acquiring Bank One and, later, Bear Stearns), PNC Bank purchasing Harris Williams, Orix buying a controlling interest in Houlihan Lokey, and Wells Fargo buying Barrington (Exhibit 1). As international banking barriers fell and the global markets grew less segmented, the drive for consolidation accelerated, spurred on by the apparent success of the "universal bank" model.

Advocates of the universal bank model argued that customers preferred to do all of their business—whether life insurance, retail brokerage, retirement planning, checking accounts in the case of an individual consumer or payroll services, mergers and acquisitions (M&A) advisory, underwriting, and commercial lending in the case of a corporate customer—with one financial institution. There was some evidence that such mergers between commercial and investment

[5]"Financial Powerhouse," NewsHour with Jim Lehrer transcript, April 7, 1998, http://www.pbs.org/newshour/bb/business/jan-june98/merger_4-7.html (accessed July 19, 2008).

## EXHIBIT 1   Major Bank Mergers Since 1997

| Year | Acquirer | Target | Name of Merged Entity | Transaction Value |
|------|----------|--------|------------------------|-------------------|
| 1997 | U.S. Bancorp | First Bank System, Inc. | U.S. Bancorp | |
| | NationsBank Corp. | Boatmen's Bancshares | NationsBank Corp. | $9.6 billion |
| | Washington Mutual | Great Western Financial Corp. | Washington Mutual | |
| | First Union Corp. | Signet Banking Corp. | First Union Corp. | |
| | National City Corp. | First of America Bank | National City Corp. | |
| 1998 | NationsBank Corp. | Barnett Banks, Inc. | NationsBank Corp. | |
| | First Union Corp. | CoreStates Financial Corp. | First Union Corp. | |
| | NationsBank Corp. | BankAmerica Corp. | Bank of America Corp. | |
| | Golden State Bancorp | First Nationwide Holdings, Inc. | Golden State Bancorp | |
| | Norwest Corp. | Wells Fargo Corp. | Wells Fargo Corp. | |
| | Star Banc Corp. | Firstar Holdings Corp. | Firstar Corp. | |
| | Banc One Corp. | First Chicago NBD Corp. | Bank One Corp. | |
| | Travelers Group | Citicorp | Citigroup | $140 billion |
| | SunTrust Bank | Crestar Financial Corp. | SunTrust Banks, Inc. | |
| | Washington Mutual | H.F. Ahmanson & Co. | Washington Mutual | |
| 1999 | Fleet Financial Corp. | BankBoston Corp. | FleetBoston Financial Corp. | |
| | Deutsche Bank AG | Bankers Trust Corp. | Deutsche Bank AG | |
| | HSBC Holdings plc | Republic New York Corp. | HSBC Bank USA | |
| | Firstar Corp. | Mercantile Bancorp., Inc. | Firstar Corp. | |
| | AmSouth Bancorp. | First American National Bank | AmSouth Bancorp. | $6.3 billion |
| 2000 | Chase Manhattan Corp. | JP Morgan & Co. | JP Morgan Chase & Co. | |
| | Washington Mutual | Bank United Corp. | Washington Mutual | $1.5 billion |
| | Wells Fargo & Co. | First Security Corp. | Wells Fargo & Co. | |
| 2001 | Firstar Corp. | U.S. Bancorp | U.S. Bancorp | |
| | First Union Corp. | Wachovia Corp. | Wachovia Corp. | |
| | Fifth Third Bancorp | Old Kent Financial Corp. | Fifth Third Bancorp | |
| | Standard Federal Bank | Michigan National Bank | Standard Federal Bank N.A. | |
| | FleetBoston Financial Corp. | Summit Bancorp | FleetBoston Financial Corp. | |
| 2002 | Citigroup Inc. | Golden State Bancorp | Citigroup Inc. | |
| | Washington Mutual | Dime Bancorp, Inc. | Washington Mutual | |
| 2003 | BB&T Corp. | First Virginia Banks, Inc. | BB&T Corp. | |
| | M&T Bank | Allfirst Bank | M&T Bank | |
| 2004 | New Haven Savings Bank | Savings Bank of Manchester, Tolland Bank | NewAlliance Bank | |
| | Bank of America Corp. | FleetBoston Financial Corp. | Bank of America Corp. | $47 billion |
| | JP Morgan Chase & Co. | Bank One | JPMorgan Chase & Co. | |
| | Banco Popular | Quaker City Bank | Banco Popular | |

*(Continued)*

## EXHIBIT 1—Cont'd

| Year | Acquirer | Target | Name of Merged Entity | Transaction Value |
|------|----------|--------|-----------------------|-------------------|
| | Regions Financial Corp. | Union Planters Corp. | Regions Financial Corp. | $5.9 billion |
| | SunTrust | National Commerce Financial | SunTrust | $6.98 billion |
| | Wachovia | SouthTrust | Wachovia | $14.3 billion |
| 2005 | PNC Bank | Riggs Bank | PNC Bank | $0.78 billion |
| | Capital One Financial Corp. | Hibernia National Bank | Capital One Financial Corp. | $4.9 billion |
| | Bank of America | MBNA Corp. | Bank of America Card Services | $35 billion |
| 2006 | Wachovia | Westcorp Inc. | Wachovia | $3.91 billion |
| | NewAlliance Bank | Cornerstone Bank | NewAlliance Bank | |
| | Capital One Financial Corp. | North Fork Bank | Capital One Financial Corp. | $13.2 billion |
| | Wachovia | Golden West Financial | Wachovia | $25 billion |
| | Regions Financial Corp. | AmSouth Bancorp. | Regions Financial Corp. | $10 billion |
| 2007 | Citizens Banking Corp | Republic Bancorp | Citizens Republic Bancorp | $1.048 billion |
| | Banco Bilbao Vizcaya Argentaria | Compass Bancshares | Banco Bilbao Vizcaya Argentaria | $9.8 billion |
| | Bank of America | LaSalle Bank | Bank of America | $21 billion |
| | State Street Corp. | Investors Financial Services Corp. | State Street Corp. | $4.2 billion |
| | Bank of New York | Mellon Financial Corp. | Bank of New York Mellon | $18.3 billion |
| | Wachovia | World Savings Bank | Wachovia | $25 billion |
| | Bank of America | U.S. Trust | Bank of America Private Wealth Management | |
| 2008 | JPMorgan Chase | Bear Stearns | JPMorgan Chase | $1.1 billion |
| | Bank of America | Merrill Lynch | Bank of America | $50 billion |
| | JPMorgan Chase | Washington Mutual | JPMorgan Chase | $1.9 billion |
| | Wells Fargo | Wachovia | Wells Fargo | $15.1 billion |
| | 5/3 Bank | First Charter Bank | 5/3 Bank | |
| | PNC Financial Services | National City Corp. | PNC Financial Services | $5.08 billion |

banks had on average destroyed value[6] and anti-tying legislation prevented universal banks from making, for example, a loan's approval contingent on a company's agreement to retain the investment banking arm of the bank for more lucrative M&A activity. However, the perception that traditional "pure-play" investment banks would struggle to compete with combined banking entities that could provide a full range of banking products led to rapid consolidation in the industry.

This consolidation created an uphill battle for the remaining pure-play bulge bracket investment banks: Lehman Brothers, Merrill Lynch, Goldman Sachs, Morgan Stanley, and Bear Stearns. As public companies, pure-play banks faced pressure to deliver return on equity comparable to that of universal banks, even as those banks put competitive pressure on traditional advisory businesses such as M&A, underwriting, and sales and trading. In response, pure-play banks resorted to the two advantages they had over non-depository institutions: unlimited, unregulated leverage capacity, and increasing reliance on proprietary trading to deliver earnings. Their successful efforts in 2004 to convince the SEC to abolish the "net capital" rule—which restricted the amount of debt their brokerage units could take on—demonstrated this growing appetite for leverage.[7] These two synergistic effects slowly but decisively transformed pure-play investment banks from advisory institutions to disguised hedge funds, a process PIMCO manager Paul McCulley has referred to as the rise of the "shadow banking" industry.[8] By the winter of 2008, increased leverage and proprietary trading would ravage the investment banking industry, leading to the collapse, merger, or restructuring of all five major pure-play banks on Wall Street.

## Lehman Brothers

By late 2007, the 150-year-old Lehman Brothers had become one of the five largest investment banks in the United States, and appeared poised to continue its stellar growth with record earnings of $1.1 billion and $1.3 billion in Q1 and Q2 2007, respectively. Since the turn of the century, Lehman had grown increasingly reliant on its fixed income trading and underwriting division, which served as the primary engine for its strong profit growth throughout the first half of the decade (Exhibit 2). Meanwhile, the bank significantly increased its leverage over the same timeframe, going from a debt-to-equity ratio of 23.7× in 2003 to 35.2× in 2007 (Exhibit 3). As leverage increased, the ongoing erosion of the mortgage-backed industry in the summer of 2007 began to impact Lehman significantly. The firm's stock price began to fall from its June 2007 peak of $81.30 to an August low of $51.57. The bank closed BNC Mortgage, its subprime mortgage arm, and began a layoff of more than 2,000 employees worldwide. However, Lehman executives remained optimistic, with CFO Chris O'Meara stating, "I think the worst of this credit correction is behind us." [9]

---

[6]J. F. Houston and M. Ryngaert, "The Overall Gains from Large Bank Mergers," *Journal of Banking and Finance* 18 (1994): 1155–1176; D. A. Becher, "The Valuation Effects of Bank Mergers," *Journal of Corporate Finance* 6 (2000): 199–214; and J. F. Houston, C. James, and M. Ryngaert, "Where Do Merger Gains Come From? Bank Mergers from the Perspective of Insiders and Outsiders," *Journal of Financial Economics* 60 (2001): 285–332.

[7]Stephen Labaton, "Agency's '04 Rule Let Banks Pile Up New Debt," *New York Times*, October 2, 2008, http://www.nytimes.com/2008/10/03/business/03sec.html (accessed November 3, 2008).

[8]Paul McCulley, "Global Central Bank Focus," *PIMCO.com*, August/September 2007, http://www.pimco.com/LeftNav/Featured+Market+Commentary/FF/2007/GCBF+August-+September+2007.htm (accessed November 3, 2008).

[9]Dan Wilchins, "Lehman Earnings Fall Amid $830 Million Writedown," Reuters News, December 13, 2007, http://www.reuters.com/article/businessNews/idUSWEN294620071214 (accessed November 4, 2008).

**EXHIBIT 2**  Lehman Brothers' Financial Performance Since 1999

|  | Sales ($ in millions) | Total Net Income ($ in millions) | Net Margin (%) | EPS ($) |
|---|---|---|---|---|
| 1999 | 18,925 | 1,174 | 6.2 | 2.04 |
| 2000 | 26,313 | 1,831 | 7.0 | 3.19 |
| 2001 | 22,340 | 1,311 | 5.9 | 2.19 |
| 2002 | 16,696 | 1,031 | 6.2 | 1.73 |
| 2003 | 17,146 | 1,771 | 10.3 | 3.17 |
| 2004 | 20,456 | 2,393 | 11.7 | 3.95 |
| 2005 | 31,476 | 3,260 | 10.4 | 5.43 |
| 2006 | 45,296 | 3,960 | 8.7 | 6.73 |
| 2007 | 57,264 | 4,192 | 7.3 | 7.26 |

|  | Total Assets ($ in millions) | Current Liabilities ($ in millions) | Long-Term Debt ($ in millions) | Total Liabilities ($ in millions) | Shareholders' Equity ($ in millions) |
|---|---|---|---|---|---|
| 1999 | 222,225 | 185,251 | 30,691 | 215,942 | 6,283 |
| 2000 | 259,093 | 216,079 | 35,233 | 251,312 | 7,781 |
| 2001 | 285,407 | 238,647 | 38,301 | 276,948 | 8,459 |
| 2002 | 298,304 | 250,684 | 38,678 | 289,362 | 8,942 |
| 2003 | 354,280 | 297,577 | 43,529 | 341,106 | 13,174 |
| 2004 | 413,654 | 342,248 | 56,486 | 398,734 | 14,920 |
| 2005 | 463,962 | 393,269 | 53,899 | 447,168 | 16,794 |
| 2006 | 583,628 | 484,354 | 81,178 | 565,532 | 18,096 |
| 2007 | 814,213 | 668,573 | 123,150 | 791,723 | 22,490 |

Lehman's 2007 annual report in December noted a distinct change in the bank's outlook. More than 6,000 layoffs had continued throughout the fall, and the bank wrote down $830 million in subprime-related mortgages as part of a $3.5 billion package of write-downs in the fourth quarter.[10] Lehman still beat analysts' earnings estimates of $1.42 per share, but newly appointed CFO Erin Callan[11] alluded to potential further write-downs, stating, "We're trying not to be too optimistic … that this is the bottom."[12]

The new year brought little salve to the company's growing wounds. In January 2008 Lehman exited its domestic wholesale mortgage lending unit, cutting an additional 1,300 jobs, a measure that did little to stanch the hemorrhaging of cash from the firm's ongoing subprime exposure. As Bear collapsed in mid-March, Lehman stock fell 48 percent on news that Standard & Poor's had revised its outlook on the firm from "stable" to "negative," noting that revenues would likely decline by more than 20 percent after write-downs.[13] A week later, Lehman reported net income of $489 million in its first quarter 10Q, down 57 percent year-over-year, with $30 billion in cash and $64 billion in highly liquid assets. As rumors flew that the same aggressive

---

[10]Jessica Dickler, "Lehman Layoffs, the Tip of the Iceberg," *CNNMoney.com*, September 21, 2008, http://money.cnn.com/2008/09/15/news/companies/lehman_jobs (accessed November 4, 2008).

[11]Effective December 1, 2007, O'Meara transitioned into a new role as global head of risk management.

[12]Wilchins, "Lehman Earnings Fall."

[13]John Spence, "S&P Puts Negative Outlook on Goldman, Lehman," *MarketWatch*, March 21, 2008, http://www.marketwatch.com/news/story/sp-puts-negative-outlook-goldman/story.aspx?guid=%7BE3B0D7FE-7498-48D7-BE29-FB95B33D0A41%7D (accessed November 4, 2008).

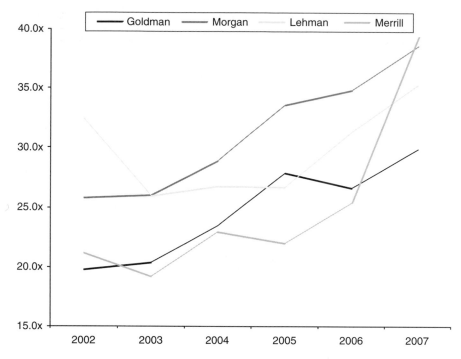

**EXHIBIT 3** Increase in Leverage Among Bulge Bracket Investment Banks

shorts that had allegedly brought down Bear planned to make a run at Lehman, the firm announced the sale of $4 billion in convertible preferred stock. Lehman stock rose 11 percent on the news, as investors assumed that the injection of capital would allow the firm to avoid Bear's fate. Warning signs remained, however, as Oppenheimer & Co. analyst Meredith Whitney prognosticated, "While this capital raise is expensive on a near-term historical basis, it will only get progressively more expensive to raise capital as the year evolves."[14]

Despite the cash infusion, Lehman continued to slip down the path first trod by Bear. In a move eerily reminiscent of Bear's ill-fated efforts to prop up its faltering BSAM hedge funds a year earlier, Lehman bailed out five of its own short-term debt funds by taking $1.8 billion worth of their assets onto its books.[15] Meanwhile, it announced another 1,500 layoffs and its plans to raise an additional $6 billion in new capital via a combined common and convertible preferred stock sale in June 2008, even as it estimated a $3 billion loss in Q3 based on mortgage-related write-downs. The following week, Lehman's board of directors replaced Joseph Gregory as COO with Herbert H. McDade, and terminated Erin Callan's brief tenure as CFO, replacing her with Ian Lowitt.

With the company's stock price in freefall throughout the summer of 2008, CEO Richard Fuld contemplated a go-private transaction, abandoning the idea when it became clear that the company could not arrange the necessary financing to consummate the deal. In a desperate move, Fuld then attempted to locate buyers for $30 billion worth of Lehman's illiquid commercial

---

[14]Yalman Onaran, "Lehman Sells $4 Billion Shares to Help Calm Investors," *Bloomberg.com*, April 1, 2008, http://www.bloomberg.com/apps/news?pid=20601087&sid=aUd7LP996GL0 (accessed November 4, 2008).

[15]"Lehman Says It Bailed Out Money Market, Cash Funds," MP Global Financial News, April 10, 2008, http://www.mpgf.com/mp-gf/pop/news.aspx?newsID=6081 (accessed November 4, 2008).

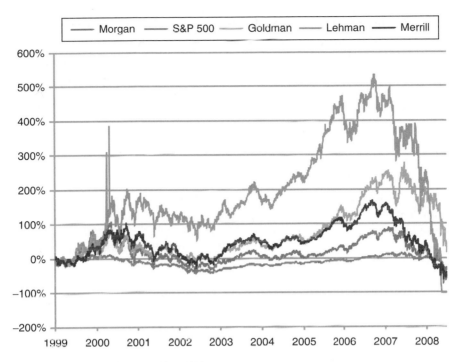

**EXHIBIT 4** Investment Bank Stock Performance Since 1999

mortgage holdings, and launched merger discussions with government-owned Korea Development Bank (KDB) and China's Citic Securities, whose cross-investment with Bear a year earlier
failed to turn market sentiment in the firm. KDB contemplated a two-stage process wherein it
would buy a 25 percent stake from Lehman directly before purchasing an additional 25 percent
in the open market. Ultimately, talks stalled when Lehman refused to budge on price, demanding
a 50 percent premium to its nebulous book value.[16] Discussions with Citic similarly stalled, as
had a potential acquisition by Royal Bank of Canada, who passed in July when it could not get
comfortable with the firm's tenuous liquidity position.[17] Rapidly running out of potential white
knights, Lehman limped toward a September earning report in which analysts predicted an additional $4 billion in write-downs, bringing the total to $12 billion.

Six months after the tumultuous weekend that consumed Bear, Lehman stock fell 30 percent
on September 9, 2008, reducing its market capitalization to $6.8 billion, down from $54.7 billion
at the beginning of 2007 (Exhibit 4). The share price collapse continued the following day as Lehman announced a $3.9 billion loss in Q3 and its intentions to restructure by spinning off $30 billion of its commercial real estate portfolio into a separate, publicly traded entity, selling 55% of
investment advisory subsidiary Neuberger Berman, and selling $4 billion of its European real
estate holdings to Black Rock. These moves would eliminate the goodwill from Lehman's 2003
acquisition of Neuberger, improve the firm's Tier 1 ratio,[18] and increase its tangible book value

---

[16]Henny Sender and Francesco Guerrera, "Lehman's Secret Talks To Sell 50% Stake Stall," *Financial Times*, August 20,
2008, http://www.ft.com/cms/s/0/586ed412-6ee6-11dd-a80a-0000779fd18c.html (accessed November 4, 2008).

[17]"Royal Bank of Canada Considered Buying Lehman," Reuters UK News, September 7, 2008, http://uk.reuters.com/
article/asiaPrivateEquityNews/idUKL722941620080907 (accessed November 4, 2008).

[18]The Tier 1 capital ratio is the ratio of a bank's core equity capital to its total risk-weighted assets, a metric regulators
frequently use to evaluate a bank's financial strength.

by more than $3 billion.[19] However, with the stock price closing at just over $3 per share, these efforts merely bolstered suspicions that the embattled bank would have to seek a buyer. More perniciously, rumors circulated that other market players had begun refusing to honor Lehman's trades, effectively crippling its ability to remain in business, with such speculation further fueled by the Fed's acknowledgement that it had met with various Wall Street firms and the SEC in an effort to resolve Lehman's liquidity crisis.

Unfortunately, the political dominos from Bear's bailout had fallen against Lehman. The public outcry over taxpayer assumption of $29 billion in potential Bear losses made repeating such a move politically untenable just weeks before one of the most contentious presidential elections in history. The surreal scene of potential buyers traipsing into an investment bank's headquarters over the weekend to consider various merger or spin-out scenarios repeated itself once again, with the hard deadline of the next day's market open forcing Lehman to consider any and all offers. This time, the Fed refused to back the failing bank's liabilities, attempting instead to play last-minute suitors Bank of America, HSBC, Nomura Securities, and Barclay's off each other, jawboning them by arguing that failing to step up to save Lehman would cause devastating counterparty runs on their own capital positions. Meanwhile, Lehman hired Weil, Gotshal, and Manges to prepare an emergency bankruptcy filing in case negotiations faltered.

The Fed's desperate attempts to arrange its second rescue of a major U.S. investment bank in six months failed when it refused to backstop losses from Lehman's toxic mortgage holdings. Complicating matters was Lehman's reliance on short-term repo loans to finance its balance sheet; like Bear, Lehman financed more than 25 percent of its assets with repos.[20] Unfortunately, such loans required constant renewal by counterparties, who had grown increasingly nervous that Lehman would lose the ability to make good on its trades. With such sentiment swirling around Wall Street, the last bidder at the table, Barclay's, dropped out when it determined that it could not obtain timely shareholder approval for the acquisition. After Barclay's threw in the towel, Lehman announced the largest Chapter 11 filing in U.S. history, listing assets of $639 billion and liabilities of $768 billion.[21]

The second domino had fallen. It would not be the last.

## Merrill Lynch

Long considered the Irish Catholic bastion on Wall Street, Merrill Lynch grew to prominence on the strength of its massive retail brokerage operations, which allowed its investment banking arm to place underwritten securities directly with brokerage clients. Its 1978 acquisition of White Weld & Co. bolstered its investment banking operations, which flourished in the last decades of the twentieth century alongside its private client services and sales and trading arms. Like Lehman, however, it had grown increasingly reliant on its proprietary trading arm following the deregulation of the banking industry, which fueled its more than 13 percent annual stock price

---

[19]"Lehman Plans Sale, Spin-Off of Assets," Reuters News, September 10, 2008, http://www.reuters.com/article/topNews/idUSN1040161420080910 (accessed November 4, 2008).

[20]Prince of Wall Street, "Goldman's Contrarian Move," April 7, 2008, https://www.istockanalyst.com/article/viewarticle+articleid_1692967.html (accessed November 10, 2008).

[21]Drew G. L. Chapman, "Lehman Brothers Holdings, Inc.'s Bankruptcy Filing Raises Pressing Issues for Hedge Funds," DLA Piper Alternative Asset Management Alert, September 17, 2008, http://www.dlapiper.com/files/upload/Alternative_Asset_Management_Alert_Sep08.html (accessed November 4, 2008). Given the strict federal regulations for insolvent brokerage houses, Lehman's retail brokerage operations did not file, but continued business as usual while the firm sought an outside buyer.

**EXHIBIT 5**   Merrill Lynch's Financial Performance Since 1999

|  | Sales ($ in millions) | Total Net Income ($ In millions) | Net Margin (%) | EPS ($) |
|---|---|---|---|---|
| 1999 | 34,586 | 2,887 | 8.3 | 3.11 |
| 2000 | 43,885 | 3,979 | 9.1 | 4.11 |
| 2001 | 38,232 | −335 | −0.9 | −0.45 |
| 2002 | 27,368 | 1,708 | 6.2 | 1.77 |
| 2003 | 26,432 | 3,836 | 14.5 | 3.87 |
| 2004 | 31,165 | 4,436 | 14.2 | 4.38 |
| 2005 | 45,000 | 4,815 | 10.7 | 4.86 |
| 2006 | 64,500 | 7,097 | 11.0 | 7.18 |
| 2007 | 64,865 | −8,637 | −13.3 | −10.73 |

|  | Total Assets ($ in millions) | Current Liabilities ($ in millions) | Long-Term Debt ($ in millions) | Total Liabilities ($ in millions) | Shareholders' Equity ($ in millions) |
|---|---|---|---|---|---|
| 1999 | 360,900 | 294,121 | 54,043 | 348,164 | 12,802 |
| 2000 | 474,709 | 386,182 | 70,223 | 456,405 | 18,304 |
| 2001 | 510,340 | 412,989 | 76,572 | 489,561 | 20,787 |
| 2002 | 533,021 | 427,227 | 81,713 | 508,940 | 24,081 |
| 2003 | 582,645 | 467,239 | 86,502 | 553,761 | 28,884 |
| 2004 | 750,703 | 596,728 | 122,605 | 719,333 | 31,370 |
| 2005 | 816,516 | 645,415 | 135,501 | 780,916 | 35,600 |
| 2006 | 1,026,512 | 802,261 | 185,713 | 987,474 | 39,038 |
| 2007 | 1,286,177 | 988,118 | 266,127 | 1,254,245 | 31,932 |

return from 2000 to 2006 (Exhibit 4). Merrill similarly exhibited a significant increase in leverage over the same time frame, going from a 19.2× leverage ratio in 2003 to a 39.3× ratio in 2007 (Exhibit 3 and Exhibit 5).

At the height of the credit boom in late 2006, Merrill announced its $1.3 billion acquisition of First Franklin, one of the largest originators of subprime residential mortgage loans. The deal closed in January 2007, and brought Merrill's mortgage portfolio to more than $70 billion.[22] Analysts met the deal with mixed reviews; some noted that it had plugged gaps in Merrill's business lines and expanded its client base, while others expressed concern that Merrill had missed the lending boom, buying at a high price and overlooking the significant integration and absorption issues First Franklin would pose.[23]

The first cracks began to appear with the default of the Bear Stearns hedge funds during the summer of 2007. As one of the funds' key lenders, Merrill seized $800 million of the funds' assets and began an auction process, managing to sell off some of the higher-grade products but struggling to generate bids on the toxic lower-rated tranches. Bear's subsequent decision

[22]Merrill Lynch press release, "Merrill Lynch Announces Agreement to Acquire First Franklin from National City Corporation," September 5, 2006, http://www.ml.com/index.asp?id=7695_7696_8149_63464_70786_70780 (accessed November 4, 2008) and Gabriel Madway, "National City Completes First Franklin Sale to Merrill," *MarketWatch*, January 2, 2007, http://www.marketwatch.com/news/story/national-city-completes-first-franklin/story.aspx?guid=%7BB1E0DE9C-7FA0-48C3-98FF-6F43EA09D169%7D (accessed November 4, 2008).

[23]Shaheen Pasha, "Merrill Strategy Threatened by Bad Loan Market," *CNNMoney.com*, February 21, 2007, http://money.cnn.com/2007/02/21/news/companies/merrill_acquisitions/index.htm (accessed November 4, 2008).

to bail out the funds ended the auction process, but the fiasco highlighted Merrill's significant exposure to the subprime crisis.[24]

Soon thereafter, Merrill announced a $4.5 billion loss from CDOs and U.S. subprime mortgage-backed securities, which it later revised to $7.9 billion. As losses in the firm's credit portfolios mounted, chairman and CEO Stan O'Neal made the mistake of approaching Wachovia Corporation about a potential merger without notifying his board of directors. Infuriated, the board dismissed O'Neal, naming NYSE Euronext CEO John Thain as his replacement in December. The appointment came on the heels of Merrill's announcement that it would write down an additional $11.5 billion in mortgage-backed securities and take a $2.6 billion loss on hedges related to CDOs. The company's stock price slid 46 percent to $48.57 in February 2008, down from its $89.37 high in May 2007.

Desperate to stop the bleeding, Merrill announced layoffs of 2,900 employees, having already eliminated 1,100 positions worldwide since the previous summer. Its first-quarter 2008 results—which included an additional $3.09 billion in mortgage-related write-downs—did little to comfort a market with memories of Bear's implosion fresh in its mind. Moody's Investors Service placed the bank's long-term debt on review for a possible downgrade based on its forecast of an additional $6 billion in write-downs in coming quarters.[25]

Troubles continued in the second quarter, when Merrill suffered $3.5 billion in losses from U.S. super-senior CDOs and negative credit valuation adjustments of $2.9 billion related to hedges. The bank also lost $1.7 billion in its investment portfolios and $1.3 billion from residential mortgage exposures. Amidst the staggering losses, Thain attempted to avoid Bear's fate by raising capital while it was still available. In July 2008 Merrill sold its 20 percent stake in Bloomberg L.P. back to Bloomberg Inc. for $4.425 billion and began negotiations to sell a controlling interest in Financial Data Services, its in-house provider of administrative functions for mutual funds, retail banking products, and other wealth management services.

Even the injection of capital from the Bloomberg transaction could not guarantee Merrill's ongoing independence after more than $52 billion in cumulative write-downs. Complicating matters, Merrill held billions in credit default swaps with troubled insurance giant AIG as the counterparty, exposure that further weakened Merrill's tenuous financial position. The bank's situation turned critical in early September when it became clear that Lehman Brothers would not survive the month. In a last-ditch effort to salvage some shareholder value, Thain reached out to Bank of America CEO Ken Lewis.

Bank of America's investment banking efforts had achieved only middling success following its 1997 acquisition of San Francisco-based boutique Montgomery Securities and the later integration of the remnants of Robertson Stephens, which came in its 2004 acquisition of FleetBoston Financial. While certain groups had excelled—the healthcare and real estate industry groups, and the debt underwriting and private equity placement product groups, for example—the bank had struggled to attract the top-tier talent necessary to compete with other bulge bracket banks. By 2008 the bank had begun to shrink its investment banking operations, laying off more than 1,100 employees in the wake of mortgage-related write-downs. Lewis's comment in 2007 that he had "had all the fun I can stand in investment banking" contributed to perceptions of the

---

[24]Ivy Schmerken, "Credit Crisis in Sub-Prime Mortgages Affects Hedge Funds Trading in Other Asset Classes," September 30, 2007, http://www.advancedtrading.com/ems-oms/showArticle.jhtml?articleID=201805585 (accessed November 4, 2008).

[25]Louise Story, "At Merrill, Write-Downs and More Layoffs," *New York Times*, April 18, 2008, http://www.nytimes.com/2008/04/18/business/18merrill.html (accessed November 4, 2008).

bank's faltering commitment to building the investment banking unit's brand, and prompted defections by junior bankers pessimistic on the group's future.[26]

However, Merrill presented what Lewis later described as "the strategic opportunity of a lifetime." During the very same cataclysmic weekend that claimed Lehman, talks accelerated, with Bank of America finally agreeing to pay $50 billion to acquire Merrill Lynch, a price less than half of Merrill's market capitalization at its 2007 peak. The transaction more than doubled the size of Bank of America's investment banking unit and created the largest retail brokerage unit on Wall Street, while significantly increasing Bank of America's exposure to mortgage-backed securities. Standard & Poor's immediately reduced its long-term counterparty credit rating on Bank of America from AA to AA-, and put the bank's credit ratings on CreditWatch with "negative implications."

And then there were two.

## Goldman Sachs and Morgan Stanley

Unlike its peers, Goldman largely avoided excessive exposure to the mortgage industry, and wrote down just $2 billion in residential mortgages and leveraged loans. Observers expressed skepticism at Goldman's seeming imperviousness to the most catastrophic market environment in history. "I'm not sure what to think; it's almost too good to be true," said Robert Lagravinese of Trinity Funds. "I'm not sure how they avoid every problem that every other investment bank has. No one is that good, smart, or lucky."[27]

During the summer of 2008 Goldman reduced its leveraged loan exposure to $14 billion from $52 billion six months earlier, and reduced its residential and commercial real estate holdings by $6.4 billion over the same period. However, the company could not ignore its eroding profits, posting the first quarterly loss in its history in the fourth quarter of 2008 driven largely by losses in its proprietary trading operations (Exhibit 6).

Meanwhile, Morgan Stanley, ironically created in 1938 when the passage of Glass-Steagall forced JP Morgan to divest its investment banking operations, found itself plagued by exposure to the widening credit crisis (Exhibit 7). By the fourth quarter of 2007, the firm had written down $10.3 billion in mortgage-related securities, trailing only Merrill, Citigroup, and UBS in write-downs. CEO John Mack called the results "embarrassing," and dismissed co-president Zoe Cruz, who had headed Morgan Stanley's institutional-securities business. In December 2007 the bank attempted to shore up its liquidity position by raising capital from a foreign wealth fund, joining Citigroup and UBS, who had sold $7.5 billion in equity to an Abu Dhabi fund and $11.5 billion in equity to a Singaporean fund, respectively. Morgan sold 9 percent coupon convertible preferred shares amounting to roughly 9.9 percent of the company to China Investment Corporation for $5 billion.[28]

After Lehman declared bankruptcy in September 2008, Morgan Stanley and Goldman Sachs found themselves under pressure from investors who felt that the credit crisis had revealed the

[26]"Will BofA Retreat From Investment Banking?" October 18, 2007, http://dealbook.blogs.nytimes.com/2007/10/18/will-bofa-retreat-from-investment-banking (accessed November 9, 2008).

[27]Joseph A. Giannone, "Goldman Earnings Fall By Half, Yet Beat Views," Reuters News, March 18, 2008, http://www.reuters.com/article/businessNews/idUSWNAS527620080318 (accessed November 9, 2008).

[28]John Spence, "Morgan Stanley Write-Downs Grow by $5.7 Billion," *MarketWatch*, December 19, 2007, http://www.marketwatch.com/news/story/morgan-stanley-sets-57-bln/story.aspx?guid=%7BA49D1DF8-A341-409C-9574-E035AF79EFC9%7D (accessed November 10, 2008).

**EXHIBIT 6**   Goldman Sachs's Financial Performance Since 1999

|  | Sales ($ in millions) | Total Net Income ($ in millions) | Net Margin (%) | EPS ($) |
|---|---|---|---|---|
| 1999 | 25,363 | 2,708 | 10.7 | 5.57 |
| 2000 | 33,000 | 3,067 | 9.3 | 6.00 |
| 2001 | 31,138 | 2,310 | 7.4 | 4.26 |
| 2002 | 22,854 | 2,114 | 9.3 | 4.03 |
| 2003 | 23,623 | 3,005 | 12.7 | 5.87 |
| 2004 | 29,839 | 4,553 | 15.3 | 8.92 |
| 2005 | 43,391 | 5,626 | 13.0 | 11.21 |
| 2006 | 69,353 | 9,537 | 13.8 | 19.69 |
| 2007 | 87,968 | 11,599 | 13.2 | 24.73 |

|  | Total Assets ($ in millions) | Current Liabilities ($ in millions) | Long-Term Debt ($ in millions) | Total Liabilities ($ in millions) | Shareholders' Equity ($ in millions) |
|---|---|---|---|---|---|
| 1999 | 271,443 | 240,346 | 20,952 | 261,298 | 10,145 |
| 2000 | 315,805 | 267,880 | 31,395 | 299,275 | 16,530 |
| 2001 | 343,234 | 293,987 | 31,016 | 325,003 | 18,231 |
| 2002 | 394,285 | 336,571 | 38,711 | 375,282 | 19,003 |
| 2003 | 461,281 | 382,167 | 57,482 | 439,649 | 21,632 |
| 2004 | 612,075 | 506,300 | 80,696 | 586,996 | 25,079 |
| 2005 | 806,811 | 678,802 | 100,007 | 778,809 | 28,002 |
| 2006 | 987,177 | 802,415 | 148,976 | 951,391 | 35,786 |
| 2007 | 1,317,270 | 1,076,996 | 197,474 | 1,274,470 | 42,800 |

untenability of their more than 20× leverage multiples. One week after Lehman's Chapter 11 filing, both firms announced that they would reorganize as bank holding companies. The move meant that the banks would for the first time become deposit-taking institutions regulated by the Federal Reserve, the FDIC, and either state or federal bank regulators, and would have to de-lever their balance sheets significantly. On September 23, Berkshire Hathaway announced a $5 billion purchase of perpetual preferred stock in Goldman (priced with a 10 percent dividend and warrants to purchase $5 billion of common stock at a strike price of $115). The following day, Goldman issued an additional $5 billion of equity in a public offering. Despite Goldman's lower reliance on repo lending (it had financed just 14.8 percent of its balance sheet with repos) and limited exposure to the mortgage-backed securities industry, the fall in prices of its marketable securities and the drought in M&A activity forced Goldman to announce layoffs of 3,200 employees.[29]

Goldman applied for a New York state bank charter, differentiating it from competitors such as Citigroup and Bank of America, who operated under a national bank charter. (Morgan Stanley applied for a national bank charter at the same time.) The firm also accepted $10 billion (as did Morgan Stanley) from the controversial $700 billion federal bailout passed in early October 2008, and Goldman Sachs also benefited from the bailout of AIG, which enabled the insurance company to make payments on debt held by Goldman. Morgan Stanley similarly tapped new funding with a $9 billion investment by Japan's Mitsubishi UFJ Financial Group in

---

[29]Prince of Wall Street, "Goldman's Contrarian Move."

**EXHIBIT 7   Morgan Stanley's Financial Performance Since 1999**

|  | Sales ($ in millions) | Total Net Income ($ in millions) | Net Margin (%) | EPS ($) |
|---|---|---|---|---|
| 1999 | 34,343 | 4,791 | 14.0 | 4.10 |
| 2000 | 44,593 | 5,484 | 12.3 | 4.73 |
| 2001 | 43,333 | 3,630 | 8.4 | 3.16 |
| 2002 | 32,449 | 3,086 | 9.5 | 2.70 |
| 2003 | 34,550 | 4,174 | 12.1 | 3.66 |
| 2004 | 39,017 | 4,634 | 11.9 | 4.15 |
| 2005 | 46,581 | 4,532 | 9.7 | 4.20 |
| 2006 | 70,151 | 6,335 | 9.0 | 5.99 |
| 2007 | 84,120 | 2,563 | 3.0 | 2.37 |

|  | Total Assets ($ in millions) | Current Liabilities ($ in millions) | Long-Term Debt ($ in millions) | Total Liabilities ($ in millions) | Shareholders' Equity ($ in millions) |
|---|---|---|---|---|---|
| 1999 | 385,240 | 349,953 | 29,004 | 378,957 | 6,283 |
| 2000 | 452,240 | 402,008 | 42,451 | 444,459 | 7,781 |
| 2001 | 521,249 | 461,912 | 50,878 | 512,790 | 8,459 |
| 2002 | 572,927 | 507,614 | 56,371 | 563,985 | 8,942 |
| 2003 | 659,560 | 577,976 | 68,410 | 646,386 | 13,174 |
| 2004 | 829,334 | 719,128 | 95,286 | 814,414 | 14,920 |
| 2005 | 996,600 | 869,341 | 110,465 | 979,806 | 16,794 |
| 2006 | 1,248,902 | 1,085,828 | 144,978 | 1,230,806 | 18,096 |
| 2007 | 1,227,254 | 1,014,140 | 190,624 | 1,204,764 | 22,490 |

common and perpetual noncumulative convertible preferred stock. Both firms announced plans to build out deposit-taking businesses, essentially making them commercial banks with diversified investment banking operations.

As 2008 came to a close, the landscape of the investment banking industry had dramatically changed. While investment banking clients would always require advisory work, underwriting services, and sales and trading services, the days of the 30× leveraged pure-play investment bank ended during a six month period when Bear Stearns collapsed into the arms of JP Morgan, Lehman Brothers filed for bankruptcy protection, Merrill Lynch merged into Bank of America, and Goldman Sachs and Morgan Stanley converted to bank holding companies. With the new-found prohibition on aggressive leverage and a regulation-induced reduction in risk-taking, the latter two firms would be challenged to deliver their previous return on equity and would likely come to resemble their chief remaining competitors: JP Morgan, Citigroup, Bank of America, Credit Suisse, Deutsche Bank, and UBS.

# Freeport-McMoRan: Financing an Acquisition

A November 19, 2006, press release announced Freeport-McMoRan Copper & Gold's (NYSE: FCX) acquisition of Phelps Dodge, creating the world's largest publicly traded copper company. FCX chief executive officer Richard Adkerson said, "This acquisition is financially compelling for FCX shareholders, who will benefit from significant cash flow accretion, lower cost of capital, and improved geographic and asset diversification. The new FCX will continue to invest in future growth opportunities with high rates of return and will aggressively seek to reduce debt incurred in the acquisition using the substantial free cash flow generated from the combined business."[1] The press release went on to note that "FCX has received financing commitments from JPMorgan and Merrill Lynch." This was the culmination of weeks of work "inside the wall" at the two investment banks. However, the public announcement was only the beginning of a new stream of work that would take place "outside the wall" in the sales and trading divisions at these firms.

## Metals Heating Up

At the time of the announced merger, FCX described itself as a company that "explores for, develops, mines, and processes ore containing copper, gold, and silver in Indonesia, and smelts and refines copper concentrates in Spain and Indonesia."[2] Phelps Dodge was described as "one of the world's leading producers of copper and molybdenum and is the largest producer of molybdenum-based chemicals and continuous-cast copper rod."[3] The merger of these two companies took place after an unprecedented run in the value of copper, based in part on the rapid growth in demand from China (see Exhibit 1), resulting in the world's largest publicly traded copper company.

These two merger candidates came together only after a tumultuous series of events in the mergers and acquisitions (M&A) landscape within the mining industry. Just months earlier, in June 2006, Phelps Dodge announced a three-way merger between itself and two Canadian mining companies, Inco and Falconbridge, for $56 billion.[4] At the time, this would have created the world's largest nickel producer and largest publicly traded copper producer. J. Steven Whisler, CEO of Phelps Dodge, made the following proclamation at the time of the announced merger:

---

[1] FCX company press release, November 19, 2006.

[2] Ibid.

[3] Ibid.

[4] Phelps Dodge company press release, June 26, 2006.

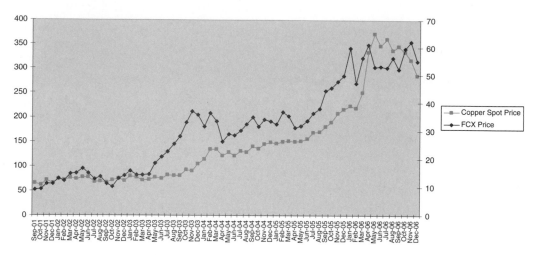

**EXHIBIT 1** Copper Spot Price vs. FCX Stock, September, 2001-December, 2006. *Source*: NYMEX COMEX data; FCX historical prices

*This transaction represents a unique opportunity in a rapidly consolidating industry to create a global leader based in North America—home of the world's deepest and most liquid capital markets. The combined company has one of the industry's most exciting portfolios of development projects, and the scale and management expertise to pursue their development successfully. The creation of this new company gives us the scale and diversification to manage cyclicality, stabilize earnings, and increase shareholder returns. At the same time, we are committed to maintaining an investment-grade credit rating throughout the business cycle.[5]*

The Phelps Dodge announcement came months into Falconbridge's implementation of a "poison pill" defense in an ongoing attempt to protect itself from a takeover by Swiss mining giant Xstrata, which had accumulated more than 20 percent of Falconbridge's stock.[6]

Eventually, the attempted combination between Phelps Dodge, Inco, and Falconbridge fell apart after Xstrata upped its bid for Falconbridge,[7] causing Falconbridge's board of directors to accept this higher bid and reject Phelps Dodge and Inco.[8]

As the events with Xstrata unfolded, Companhia Vale do Rio Doce (CVRD), a Brazilian mining company, made an unsolicited all-cash offer for Inco of C$86 per share; Phelps Dodge, on the other hand, had made a partial-equity bid of C$86.89. In spite of the lower price, analysts prophetically suggested that investors would favor the all-cash bid of CVRD at the time.[9] By early September Phelps Dodge and Inco had decided to go their separate ways, and CVRD soon claimed victory in acquiring Inco.[10] Having been left at the altar now twice, analysts predicted

---

[5]Ibid.

[6]"Falconbridge Protects Against 'Creeping Takeover' by Xstrata," *Metal Bulletin*, September 23, 2005.

[7]"Falconbridge Gets $52.50-Per-Share Offer from Xstrata," *Stockwatch*, May 17, 2006.

[8]"Falconbridge Yields to Xstrata," *Steel Business Briefing*, August 11, 2006.

[9]"In the Battle to Control Inco, CVRD Looks Ready to Rumble," *American Metal Market*, August 11, 2006.

[10]"Phelps Leaves CVRD as Sole Bidder for Inco," *Financial Times*, September 6, 2006.

that Phelps Dodge "could soon find itself transformed from a bidder to a target in the deal-making that has engulfed the global mining industry."[11]

Whisler attempted to reassure his investor base when his company announced that it was terminating its combination agreement with Inco:

> *We are very confident about the prospects of Phelps Dodge. The market fundamentals for copper and molybdenum are excellent, and at current prices we are generating significant amounts of cash. Throughout the past several months, management and the board have focused on our fundamental responsibilities to build long-term value for all our shareholders while managing our balance sheet prudently and maintaining investment-grade credit in this cyclical industry. While we regret the proposed three-way combination could not be completed on acceptable terms, the future of Phelps Dodge remains very bright.[12]*

## Enter Freeport-McMoRan

On November 19, 2006, FCX and Phelps Dodge signed a definitive merger agreement in which the acquirer, FCX, would purchase the larger Phelps Dodge for $25.9 billion in cash and stock. The joint press release announced the following transaction details:

> *FCX will acquire all of the outstanding common shares of Phelps Dodge for a combination of cash and common shares of FCX for a total consideration of $126.46 per Phelps Dodge share, based on the closing price of FCX stock on November 17, 2006. Each Phelps Dodge shareholder would receive $88.00 per share in cash plus 0.67 common shares of FCX. This represents a premium of 33 percent to Phelps Dodge's closing price on November 17, 2006, and 29 percent to its one-month average price at that date.*
>
> > *The cash portion of $18 billion represents approximately 70 percent of the total consideration. In addition, FCX would deliver a total of 137 million shares to Phelps Dodge shareholders, resulting in Phelps Dodge shareholders owning approximately 38 percent of the combined company on a fully diluted basis.*
> >
> > *The boards of directors of FCX and Phelps Dodge have each unanimously approved the terms of the agreement and have recommended that their shareholders approve the transaction. The transaction is subject to the approval of the shareholders of FCX and Phelps Dodge, receipt of regulatory approvals and customary closing conditions. The transaction is expected to close at the end of the first quarter of 2007. FCX has received financing commitments from JPMorgan and Merrill Lynch to fund the cash required to complete the transaction. After giving effect to the transaction, estimated pro forma total debt at December 31, 2006, would be approximately $17.6 billion, or approximately $15 billion net of cash.[13]*

The initial reaction to the merger announcement among Wall Street analysts was mixed (see Exhibit 2 and Exhibit 3 for stock price performance):

---

[11]Ibid.

[12]Phelps Dodge company press release, September 5, 2006.

[13]FCX company press release, November 19, 2006.

**EXHIBIT 2** Phelps Dodge Stock Performance, January 3, 2006–March 19, 2007. *Source*: Bloomberg

*In our view this transaction makes sense for both companies ... Freeport is basically a single mine company, with its only significant asset located in Indonesia (asset has a long life, but limited growth opportunities). Phelps Dodge has a geographically diverse operating base and also has a growth profile, targeting increased output of 20 percent by 2009 but a relatively short reserve life. Hence for Freeport, this deal spreads the company's operating risk and gives the company a growth profile. In our view this deal also highlights the scarcity of copper reserves globally, with one large producer acquiring another, instead of building large-scale copper mines.[14]*

\* \* \*

*There are several positives surrounding this transaction: (1) an improved cost position (vs. PD standalone); (2) long reserve life; (3) a more diversified geographic footprint; (4) an attractive growth profile; and (5) enhanced management depth. We do not see any anti-trust issues surrounding this transaction. For PD shareholders specifically— the 33 percent premium to Friday's close and departure of CEO Steven Whisler from the combined entity is the antidote we believe they were looking for—post the failed three-way merger attempt for two nickel producers earlier in the year. For FCX—we are surprised—we believed FCX was more of a seller than a buyer of assets.[15]*

\* \* \*

---

[14]Credit Suisse Equity Research, November 20, 2006.
[15]Bear Stearns Equity Research, November 20, 2006.

**EXHIBIT 3** FCX Stock Performance, January 3, 2006–March 19, 2007. *Source:* Bloomberg

> *We assign a one-third likelihood that Freeport acquires Phelps Dodge as announced. Two-thirds likelihood that Freeport collects the $750 million breakup fee. The deal appears very accretive to FCX and likely to attract higher bidder.*[16]

As the companies initially projected in their joint press release, the shareholders ultimately approved the merger on March 14, 2007, under the announced terms.[17] Of course, one of the worst kept secrets on Wall Street was that the smaller FCX still had a tremendous amount of work to do in financing the acquisition of Phelps Dodge. An initial step in this financing was the joint commitment by JPMorgan and Merrill Lynch to a combined $6 billion bridge loan prior to approval of the merger. FCX announced on March 15 the pricing of a total of $17.5 billion in debt financing for the Phelps Dodge acquisition, including $6 billion in high-yield senior notes offered in the public debt market (the bridge loan would be drawn down only if this public offering failed) and $10 billion in senior secured term loans. In addition, a $1.5 billion senior secured revolving credit facility was provided, which was to be undrawn at closing.[18] JPMorgan and Merrill Lynch jointly underwrote the note offerings and term loans and led the credit facility. Finally, on March 19, in conjunction with the closing of the Phelps Dodge acquisition, FCX announced a public offering of common stock and convertible preferred stock. The initial press release indicated an offering of "approximately 35 million shares of common stock" and

---

[16]Prudential Equity Research, November 21, 2006.

[17]FCX press release, March 14, 2007.

[18]FCX press release, March 15, 2007.

10 million shares of mandatory convertible preferred stock at $100.00 per share.[19] Total proceeds from these two equity-related transactions were expected to be approximately $5 billion. The market received these financings positively, marking up FCX nearly 3 percent on a day when the S&P 500 increased just over 1 percent. At least one Wall Street analyst portrayed the announcement as an expected positive:

> *Management clearly communicated its intention to do an equity transaction. Likewise, the size of the transaction is consistent with our expectations. While diluting existing shareholders is not a positive, we believe this equity deal is a prudent transaction in terms of reducing some of the financial risk. We estimate the combination of the equity transaction and free cash flow at current copper prices has the potential to reduce FCX's debt burden by $5 billion, or 31 percent of the $16 billion in debt taken on from this transaction, with the magnitude of debt reduction to translate into higher multiples over time.[20]*

FCX's two equity-related transactions (common stock and mandatory convertible preferred) were led by JPMorgan and Merrill Lynch as joint book-runners. The two firms equally shared fees and league table credit for these transactions. Each quarter, league tables ranking the major investment banks by underwriting proceeds from various categories (debt, equity, convertible bonds, etc.) are released. At the end of the first quarter of 2007 (1Q07), JPMorgan ranked first in U.S. convertibles, with a 23.9 percent market share and nearly $6 billion in proceeds from convertible issuance. Merrill Lynch ranked third in U.S. convertibles at the end of 1Q07 with nearly $4 billion, a 15.8 percent market share. For common stock underwriting at 1Q07, JPMorgan was first at just over $5.1 billion in underwriting proceeds, with a 16.2 percent market share; Merrill Lynch was second at over $4.3 billion, with a 13.7 percent market share.[21]

## Role of the Investment Banks

Throughout the flurry of activity centered around FCX, from merger advisory to debt and equity underwriting, there was a consistent theme: JPMorgan and Merrill Lynch were involved at nearly every step of the way. Typically, when a company needs advisory or financial assistance, it holds a "bake-off" between investment banks, where firms are invited to present their credentials, preliminary valuation, and view of investor demand. Companies will choose an investment bank (or banks) for a variety of reasons, but over time, they usually focus on existing relationships, in addition to factors such as execution capability, independent research function, and league table rankings. In the case of FCX, it had well-established ties to both JPMorgan and Merrill Lynch, and placed its trust in them for both M&A advisory and underwriting responsibilities.

Investment banks typically talk about two sides of a "Chinese wall" of information. Coverage, M&A, and capital markets teams within the investment banking function are responsible for all of the due diligence and valuation work. As a result, they are considered to be insiders working on the "private side" of the wall (or inside the wall) because of the sensitive information that they

---

[19]FCX press release, March 19, 2007.
[20]Credit Suisse Equity Research, March 19, 2007.
[21]Thomson Equity Capital Markets Review, First Quarter 2007.

receive. Generally, an investment bank's sales and trading group sits on the "public side" of this wall, working with investors and having access only to information that has been made publicly available. When a company issues a press release describing a merger and/or financing it is generally the first time that an individual in sales and trading will hear of it.

## Inside the Wall

Prior to the public announcements of the transactions surrounding the merger, the investment banking coverage teams at JPMorgan and Merrill Lynch were actively coordinating the entire process, from the acquisition to all aspects of the capital raising. The metals and mining industry coverage team at each bank was primarily responsible for knowing FCX's general needs and priorities. From there, each bank's M&A group was responsible for advising the company on merger valuation, mix of cash and stock, timing, and likely shareholder reaction. The leveraged finance group at each bank was responsible for the analysis behind making the bridge financing commitment to the company (which was never drawn down because the banks successfully placed high-yield notes with institutional investors). The bridge loan was particularly important to enable FCX to show committed financing to Phelps Dodge. The equity capital markets groups at JPMorgan and Merrill Lynch were responsible for all aspects of the equity offering: advising the company regarding the optimal structure, size, pricing and timing of the financing (the "origination" function), as well as working with colleagues in their firm's institutional equity sales area to determine potential investor interest (the "placement" function).

The investment banks and FCX needed to determine a permanent financing structure based on expected credit ratings. Essentially, FCX's management first had to decide on the optimal capital structure and acceptable equity dilution levels before selecting the best financing alternatives. Ratings advisory professionals who were part of the debt capital markets group at JPMorgan advised the company on the credit ratings process and the expected ratings outcomes based on the selected capital structure. All of the information about financing terms and conditions, as well as pricing, was fed back to each bank's M&A team, which assessed the impact to earnings per share (EPS), expected valuation, and likely investor reaction.

There are several forms of risk that investment banks must consider when advising clients and executing transactions. *Capital risk* is the financial risk associated with a bank's financing commitment in relation to an acquisition. If the bank commits to providing a loan, it undertakes considerable risk. Large banks mitigate this risk by syndicating up to 90 percent of these loans to a wider group of banks and money managers. However, banks are forced to keep the debt that they are unable to syndicate to others. During the first half of 2007, banks had committed more than $350 billion in loan commitments to facilitate acquisitions of companies by private equity firms. Because of severe dislocation in the mortgage-backed securities market starting in mid-2007, these loans became very difficult to syndicate, leaving huge unanticipated risk positions that resulted in billions of dollars in reported losses (see Exhibit 4). Banks set aside capital (usually cash invested in risk-free securities) commensurate with the risk they undertake in their underwriting and lending commitments. *Reputation risk* is less tangible, but no less important. This is the risk that comes from associating the investment banking firm with the company for which it is raising capital. Serious problems experienced by the company may have a residual effect on the investment bank's reputation.

■ ■ ■

## EXHIBIT 4 Banks on a Bridge Too Far? As Risk Rises in LBOs, Investors Start to Balk; Warning from Overseas

### By Robin Sidel, Valerie Bauerlein and Carrick Mollenkamp

The nation's largest financial institutions have spent the past year relying on robust capital markets to offset woes in their retail-banking operations. Now, that big revenue stream may be starting to dry up.

A sudden retrenchment in debt markets is likely to nip at profits at the big banks that have been financing the leveraged-buyout boom around the globe. The latest deal bonanza, in which private-equity firms buy public companies and load them up with debt, has created several new financing techniques that mint money for the banks, but can also leave them holding more risk.

For J.P. Morgan Chase & Co., Citigroup Inc. and Bank of America Corp., the biggest players in the leveraged-loan business, a slowdown in deal financings comes as they grapple with difficult issues. Among them: a tricky interest-rate environment that makes it less lucrative to make loans, a slowdown in mortgage and home-equity lending, and fierce competition to acquire deposits, even as banks are still struggling to assess the fallout from the turmoil in subprime housing.

Banks won't "lose money, but what will happen is that they won't make as much and earnings may decline," said Ganesh Rathnam, a banking analyst at Morningstar Inc. in Chicago.

As they have raced to finance leveraged buyouts, the banks have also steadily taken on more risk. Although much of it is typically parceled out to investors, the banks can be left holding the bag, as happened when investors balked at the U.S. Foodservice deal.

In the U.S., so-called covenant-lite deals accounted for about 26% of first-quarter deals versus 4.6% in European leveraged-loan issues. The pace began to sharply increase in Europe in March, according to Bank of America research. The "cov-lite" deals – where a bank's covenant protections are weakened – have been a result of the cheap financing, allowing borrowers to reduce financial covenants that typically require borrowers to meet financial hurdles on a quarterly basis, the report noted earlier this week.

In particular, regulators are expressing concern about "equity bridge loans" in which private-equity firms ask their banks to provide stop-gap financing for some deals. The loans, which carry high interest rates, last from three to 24 months and are repaid once the sale of below-investment-grade, or junk, bonds has occurred.

So far this year, banks have provided $33.38 billion in bridge loans to leveraged-buyout deals, more than double last year's $12.87 billion, according to Reuters Loan Pricing/DealScan. The volume is the highest since the LBO heyday 20 years ago, when $48.14 billion in bridge loans was issued in 1988.

Of the banks, Citigroup, Deutsche Bank AG and J.P. Morgan have arranged the most bridge loans for leveraged-buyout deals this year.

Regulators expect to take another look at guidance they issued in 2001 on leveraged lending to see if it still fits. At the time, banks kept most leveraged loans on their balance sheets, and regulators thus expected them to consider the borrower's ability to repay principal, not just interest. Banks now typically distribute their loans to institutional investors, so regulators say they may need to consider different criteria. It may be less important for a bank to consider the borrower's ability to amortize a loan, and more important to weigh the "reputational risk" that a loan it sold to investors goes bad, or "pipeline risk" – when adverse financing conditions force it to keep a loan on its balance sheet rather than distributing it.

A report this month by the Bank for International Settlements said, "The fact that banks are now increasingly providing bridge equity, along with bridge loans, to support the still growing number of corporate mergers and acquisitions is not a good sign." It went on to say: "A closely related concern is the possibility that banks have, either intentionally or inadvertently, retained a significant degree of credit risk on their books."

*Source*: Wall Street Journal, June 28, 2007

■ ■ ■

# Outside the Wall

Freeport announced its acquisition of Phelps Dodge in a formal press release that "hit the tape" (published on the news wire services) on November 19, 2006.

After the Phelps Dodge acquisition had been signed, the investment banks' focus soon shifted to syndicating out the bridge loan in order to raise the capital necessary to complete the transaction. Included in this process was negotiating with credit rating agencies to secure the highest possible ratings on the upcoming bond offerings. On February 28, 2007, S&P upgraded its debt rating on FCX's existing 2014 senior debt from B+ to BB+. It followed this with another upgrade to BBB- on April 4. Just two months after this, on June 7, it upgraded FCX's debt rating once again to BBB. Similarly, Moody's had placed the company on positive watch on November 20, 2006. It followed this up with an upgrade from B1 to Ba2 on February 26, 2007, and then to Baa3 on March 27. The credit upgrades resulted from both the more-than-$5 billion in equity capital raised through the common stock and convertible offering and the significant increase in cash flow that resulted from the merger (see Exhibit 5).[22]

After the completion of all debt-related transactions, FCX and Phelps Dodge finalized the acquisition. Once this was complete, it opened the door to the equity and equity-linked capital raising.

## Placing the Equity and Convertible Offerings

Institutional salespeople at investment banks are responsible for bringing investment opportunities to the analysts and portfolio managers of large asset managers such as mutual funds, hedge funds, pension funds, and some insurance companies. Their investment ideas come from a variety of sources, including research done by the firm's equity research analysts. The institutional asset managers do not pay investment banks for their investment ideas; rather, they pay commissions on the large trades that they execute. This process is part art and part science. Traditionally,

---

[22]Bloomberg.

**EXHIBIT 5**   Bond Ratings by Date and Rating Agency

| Date | Rating Agency | Upgrade |
|---|---|---|
| November 20, 2006 | Moody's | Positive outlook |
| February 26, 2007 | Moody's | B1 to Ba2 |
| February 28, 2007 | S&P | B+ to BB+ |
| March 27, 2007 | Moody's | Ba2 to Baa3 |
| April 4, 2007 | S&P | BB+ to BBB- |
| June 7, 2007 | S&P | BBB- to BBB |

*Source*: Bloomberg

institutional managers conduct a periodic vote to rank each investment bank and attempt to allocate commissions for the next period accordingly.

Shortly after FCX's intention to issue equity and convertible securities was announced, the JPMorgan institutional sales force heard a "teach-in" by the firm's metals and mining industry analyst. Because of JPMorgan's involvement as advisor to Freeport on the acquisition, their equity research analyst was restricted from providing an investment opinion on shares of FCX. However, he was allowed to provide the institutional sales force an overview of the equity and convertible offerings and their uses, as well as answer any related questions that salespeople had. After this presentation, the sales force had the opportunity to hear from FCX's management team regarding both the rationale for the Phelps Dodge acquisition as well as the method of financing chosen. Altogether, this session provided the sales team with enough information to be able to discuss the offerings in detail with their institutional asset manager clients.

The management team at FCX also participated in an investor "roadshow": a series of meetings with institutional investors to discuss the company's current financial position and business activities. For IPOs, roadshows typically last one or two weeks, providing the company a forum to tell its story to new investors. For secondary offerings (follow-on capital raisings from an existing public company) and convertibles, roadshows are considered optional, depending on how well the company is known. In this case, FCX had done a "non-deal" roadshow after the acquisition announcement, educating investors on the transaction, and so only a limited roadshow was scheduled for the equity and convertible financings.

The combined equity and convertible roadshow began on Tuesday, March 20, one day after the public announcement regarding closing of the acquisition. Salespeople from both JPMorgan and Merrill Lynch lined up a series of meetings in multiple cities over a three-day period and then joined a member of the investment banking team and several members of the company's management team on the roadshow. Because of the high demand for meetings and the limited time frame, sales force management had to work with the capital markets syndicate team to decide which investors to see. The decision to meet with investors depended on several factors, such as the size of the investor, quality of relationship with the company, and level of previous interest in it. Current share ownership was also an important consideration.

During this time, salespeople had a series of conversations with their institutional investor clients about the stock and convertible issues and provided feedback to the capital markets syndicate team, who kept track of investor concerns and overall sentiment about the issue. The syndicate team communicated any recurring issues that came up during the feedback process to company management. This feedback loop was particularly important for the price discovery process, as the syndicate team was responsible for establishing a price for the offering. The price discovery process is relatively transparent because the stock is already traded in the open market. However, the key question that remains is how much of a discount (if any) will be applied to the "last sale," or closing price of the stock on the day of pricing. Some investors put in limit orders, which dictate the highest price they would be willing to pay, while others are content with market orders, which indicate a willingness to pay the market-clearing price for the offering. This affects the final pricing decision because investment banks, as well as companies, are reluctant to shut out large and important investors who have submitted limit orders, even though market orders are always preferable.

For the convertible offering, price discovery focuses on the coupon and conversion premium relative to the underlying common stock. Similar to the common stock transaction, the equity capital markets syndicate maintains a book of investor demand and makes a pricing recommendation to the company that is designed to allow the security to trade up modestly. Demand for the convertible comprises approximately half convertible arbitrage hedge funds and half traditional mutual funds or dedicated convertible funds. In smaller transactions and for convertibles that do not have a mandatory conversion feature, allocations tend to be skewed toward convertible arbitrage funds. Convertible arbitrage funds attempt to purchase the convertible instrument while short-selling shares of the common stock in a manner to take advantage of inherent arbitrage opportunities. While companies might have concerns about a large pool of investors shorting their common stock, convertible arbitrage funds provide several advantages: (1) the incremental demand from convertible arbitrage funds allows companies to achieve better pricing in their convertible offerings (cheaper financing); and (2) the demand also ensures more trading liquidity in the convertible security, adding to the attractiveness for traditional long-only investors.

## Mandatory Convertible Preferred Shares

FCX's convertible instrument was designed to be converted mandatorily into a predetermined number of the company's common shares in three years. As a result, rating agencies assigned "equity content" of up to 90 percent to this convertible transaction (see Exhibit 6 and Exhibit 7). For a more traditional optionally converting convertible, rating agencies usually attribute no equity content and, in fact, assume the convertible is more like a bond unless and until it converts in the future into common shares (which will happen only if the investor determines that the value of the common shares the convertible can convert into exceeds the cash redemption value of the original security). The use of a mandatory convertible structure by FCX facilitated the rapid credit rating upgrades previously discussed. The issuance of common stock in conjunction with the convertible enabled convertible arbitrage hedge fund investors to more easily borrow and then short sell FCX common shares, which facilitated stronger demand for and resulted in better pricing of the convertible.

## FCX Post-Allocation

Shares of FCX closed on Thursday, March 22, 2007, at $61.91. On March 23, the company priced 47.15 million shares of stock at $61.25 per share (proceeds of approximately $2.9 billion), along with 28.75 million shares of 6¾ percent mandatory convertible preferred stock at $100.00

## EXHIBIT 6   Selections from SEC Filing for Convertible Preferred Offering, 3/23

**THE OFFERING**

| | |
|---|---|
| Issuer | Freeport-McMoRan Copper & Gold Inc. |
| Securities offered | 25,000,000 shares of $6\frac{3}{4}$% mandatory convertible preferred stock (28,750,000 shares if the underwriters exercise their overallotment option in full), which we refer to in this prospectus supplement as the "mandatory convertible preferred stock." |
| Initial offering price | $100.00 per share of mandatory convertible preferred stock. |
| Option to purchase additional shares of mandatory convertible preferred stock | To the extent the underwriters sell more than 25,000,000 shares of our mandatory convertible preferred stock, the underwriters have the option to purchase up to 3,750,000 additional shares of our mandatory convertible preferred stock from us at the initial offering price, less underwriting discounts and commissions, within 30 days from the date of this prospectus supplement. |
| Dividends | $6\frac{3}{4}$% per share on the liquidation preference thereof of $100.00 for each share of our mandatory convertible preferred stock per year. Dividends will accrue and cumulate from the date of issuance and, to the extent that we are legally permitted to pay dividends and our board of directors, or an authorized committee of our board of directors, declares a dividend payable, we will pay dividends in cash or, subject to certain limitations, in common stock on each dividend payment date. The expected dividend payable on the first dividend payment date is $2.30625 per share, and on each subsequent dividend payment date is expected to be $1.6875 per share. See "Description of mandatory convertible preferred stock—Dividends." |
| Dividend payment dates | February 1, May 1, August 1, and November 1 of each year prior to the mandatory conversion date (as defined below), and on the mandatory conversion date, commencing on August 1, 2007. |
| Redemption | Our mandatory convertible preferred stock is not redeemable. |
| Mandatory conversion date | May 1, 2010. |
| Mandatory conversion | On the mandatory conversion date, each share of our mandatory convertible preferred stock will automatically convert into shares of our common stock, based on the conversion rate as described below.<br><br>Holders of mandatory convertible preferred stock on the mandatory conversion date will have the right to receive the dividend due on such date (including any accrued, cumulated, and unpaid dividends on the mandatory convertible preferred stock as of the mandatory conversion date), whether or not declared (other than previously declared dividends on the mandatory convertible preferred stock payable to holders of record as of a prior date), to the extent we are legally permitted to pay such dividends at such time. |
| Conversion rate | The conversion rate for each share of our mandatory convertible preferred stock will not be more than 1.6327 shares of common stock and not less than 1.3605 shares of common stock, depending on the applicable market value of our common stock, as described below.<br><br>The "applicable market value" of our common stock is the average of the daily closing price per share of our common stock on each of the 20 consecutive trading days ending on the third trading day immediately preceding the mandatory conversion date.<br><br>The following table illustrates the conversion rate per share of our mandatory convertible preferred stock subject to certain anti-dilution |

adjustments described under "Description of mandatory convertible preferred stock—Anti-dilution adjustments."

| Applicable Market Value | Conversion Rate |
|---|---|
| Less than or equal to $61.25 | 1.6327 |
| Between $61.25 and $73.50 | $100.00 divided by the applicable market value |
| Equal to or greater than $73.50 | 1.3605 |

**Optional conversion**

At any time prior to May 1, 2010, you may elect to convert each of your shares of our mandatory convertible preferred stock at the minimum conversion rate of 1.3605 shares of common stock for each share of mandatory convertible preferred stock. This conversion rate is subject to certain adjustments as described under "Description of mandatory convertible preferred stock—Anti-dilution adjustments."

**Ranking**

The mandatory convertible preferred stock will rank with respect to dividend rights and rights upon our liquidation, winding up, or dissolution: senior to all of our common stock and to all of our other capital stock issued in the future unless the terms of that stock expressly provide that it ranks senior to, or on a parity with, the mandatory convertible preferred stock.

**Use of proceeds**

We intend to use the net proceeds from the offering to repay outstanding indebtedness under our Tranche A term loan facility and Tranche B term loan facility.

**Listing**

The mandatory convertible preferred stock has been approved for listing on the New York Stock Exchange.

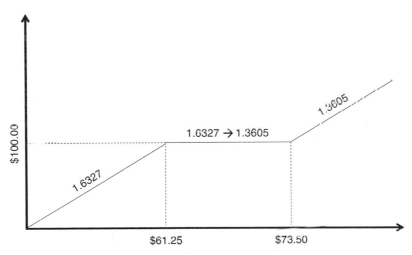

| Applicable Market Value | Conversion Rate |
|---|---|
| Less than or equal to $61.25 | 1.6327 |
| Between $61.25 and $73.50 | $100.00 divided by the applicable market value |
| Equal to or greater than $73.50 | 1.3605 |

As of the mandatory conversion date, for each $100 mandatory convertible preferred share purchased by investors, they will receive 1.6327 FCX shares if FCX share price is less than or equal to $61.25 on that date. If FCX share price is between $61.25 and $73.50, investors will receive between 1.6527 and 1.3605 FCX shares. If FCX share price is equal to or greater than $73.50, investors will receive 1.3605 FCX shares.

**EXHIBIT 7** Convertible Preferred Mechanics

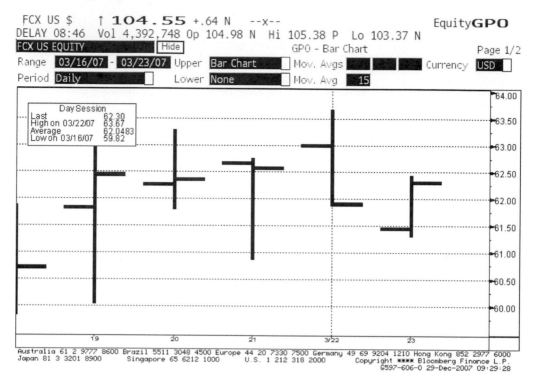

**EXHIBIT 8** FCX Stock Price, March 16, 2007–March 23, 2007. *Source*: Bloomberg

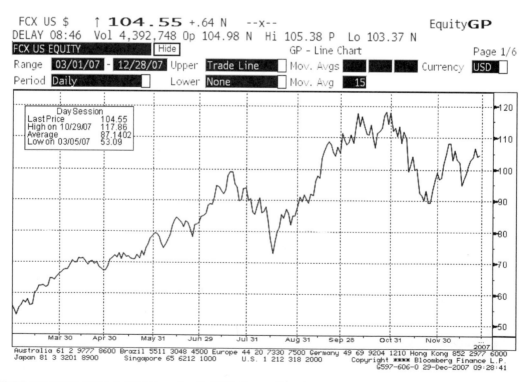

**EXHIBIT 9** FCX Equity, March 1, 2007–December 28, 2007. *Source*: Bloomberg

FCX $6\frac{3}{4}$ % $    ↓ **153.000** +.660 N    --x--    EXCH         Pfd   **GP**
Screen saved as D:\Documents and Settings\plr610\Desktop\preferred.bmp

| EP026611 PFD | Hide | | GP - Line Chart | | Page 1/6 |

Range 03/23/07 - 12/28/07 Upper Trade Line ☐ Mov. Avgs ▮▮ Currency USD ☐

Period Daily ☐ Lower None ☐ Mov. Avg 15

| | |
|---|---|
| Last Price | 153.000 |
| High on 10/10/07 | 171.440 |
| Average | 135.514 |
| Low on 03/23/07 | 101.800 |

Australia 61 2 9777 8600 Brazil 5511 3048 4500 Europe 44 20 7330 7500 Germany 49 69 9204 1210 Hong Kong 852 2977 6000
Japan 81 3 3201 8900    Singapore 65 6212 1000    U.S. 1 212 318 2000    Copyright **** Bloomberg Finance L.P.
G597-G06-0 29-Dec-2007 09:27:44

**EXHIBIT 10** FCX Convertible Preferred, March 23, 2007–December 14, 2007. *Source*: Bloomberg

per share (proceeds of approximately $2.9 billion). Net proceeds to FCX, after underwriting discount and expenses, totaled $5.6 billion.[23] By the end of trading on March 23, FCX shares closed up 39 cents from the prior close to $62.30, a nearly 2 percent gain from the transaction price (see Exhibit 8). By most accounts, this was a successful offering for both the company and investors. FCX was interested in the quality of the investor base. Generally, if a company has an opportunity to allocate newly issued shares to investors it believes will be long-term holders, it is willing to make some concession on price, which was the case with the FCX offering.

The convertible ended the trading day at 101.5, having been offered to investors at 100 (the "par" price). As was the case with the equity offering, FCX had an interest in making sure that it did not leave significant money on the table for the convertible transaction. At the same time, it wanted to ensure that both offerings—common shares and convertible—were placed with appropriate investors who were willing to take long-term positions (see Exhibit 9 and Exhibit 10 for post-transaction price action).

---

[23]FCX press release, March 28, 2007.

# The Best Deal Gillette Could Get?: Procter & Gamble's Acquisition of Gillette

January 27, 2005, was an extraordinary day for Gillette's James Kilts, the show-stopping turnaround expert known as the "Razor Boss of Boston." Kilts, along with Procter & Gamble chairman Alan Lafley, had just orchestrated a $57 billion acquisition of Gillette by P&G. The creation of the world's largest consumer products company would end Kilts's four-year tenure as CEO of Gillette and bring to a close Gillette's 104-year history as an independent corporate titan in the Boston area. The deal also capped a series of courtships between Gillette and other companies that had waxed and waned at various points throughout Kilts's stewardship of Gillette. But almost immediately after the transaction was announced, P&G and Gillette drew criticism from the media and the state of Massachusetts concerning the terms of the sale. Would this merger actually benefit shareholders, or was it principally a wealth creation vehicle for Kilts?

## A Dream Deal

Procter & Gamble was known for its consumer products like soap, shampoo, laundry detergent, and food and beverages, as well as products for health and beauty care.[1] The company owned a portfolio of approximately 150 brands—ranging from Ace bleach to Zest soap—including some of the world's most recognizable: Pampers, Tide, Folgers, Charmin, Crest, Olay, and Head & Shoulders.[2] Gillette was best known for its razor business, but the company controlled two other brands—Oral-B toothbrushes and Duracell batteries—that produced at least $1 billion in annual revenue (see Exhibit 1). Whereas P&G was particularly skilled in marketing to women,[3] Gillette's core customer segment was men (with the memorable marketing tagline "The Best a Man Can Get"). Gillette had expanded into female product lines with its Venus razor, and P&G also had several brands—Head & Shoulders dandruff shampoo among them—that targeted male customers, but the two companies were naturally stronger in distinct gender segments. They also performed better in different regions of the globe. Gillette understood how to operate successfully in India and Brazil, while P&G brought expertise in the Chinese market.[4]

---

[1] Naomi Aoki and Steve Bailey, "P&G to Buy Gillette for $55B Latest in String of Deals for Old-Line Hub Firms," *Boston Globe*, January 28, 2005.

[2] James F. Peltz, *"P&G-Gillette Union Could Hit Shoppers in Pocketbook,"* Los Angeles Times, *January 29, 2005.*

[3] Aoki and Bailey, *"P&G to Buy Gillette for $55B."*

[4] Steve Jordon, *"Billion-Dollar Brands Buffett Says 'Dream Deal' Should Make the Most of Magic in Household Names of Products Made by P&G and Gillette,"* Omaha World-Herald, *January 29, 2005.*

### 21 "Billion Dollar Brands"

| Baby & Family Care | Bounty, Charmin, Pampers |
|---|---|
| Beauty Care | Always, Olay, Pantene, Head & Shoulders, Wella |
| Fabric & Home Care | Ariel, Downy, Tide |
| Oral Care | Crest, Oral-B |
| Snacks & Beverages | Folgers, Pringles |
| Blades & Razors | Gillette, Mach 3 |
| Batteries | Duracell |
| Small Appliances | Braun |
| Pet Food | IAMS |
| Health Care | Actionel |

### An Unparalleled Portfolio and Consumer Proposition

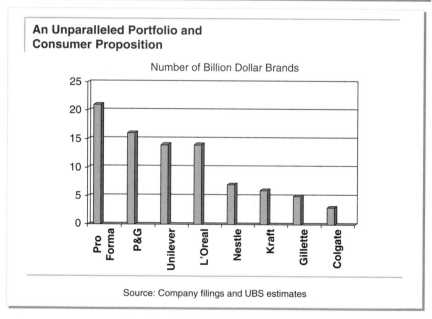

Number of Billion Dollar Brands

Source: Company filings and UBS estimates

**EXHIBIT 1** P&G's and Gillette's Billion Dollar Brands

Gillette was no stranger to overtures from both strategic and financial investors. The company had successfully defended itself against four takeover attempts in the late 1980s, three from Ronald Perelman and his cosmetics company Revlon, and one from Coniston Partners.[5] Yet the P&G proposal promised to be different. While some of the same key drivers (including an array of excellent brands) that had interested Perelman and Coniston likely drove P&G's interest in Gillette, the two companies also saw new opportunities that had not previously existed, including

---

[5]Steve Jordon, *"Buffett Calls It a 'Dream Deal',"* Omaha World-Herald, *January 28, 2005.*

the chance to combine complementary business lines and the ability to create an industry leader that could better negotiate with mass merchandisers.

A combined firm would capitalize on the core marketing competencies of both companies and be able to more effectively reach both male and female consumer segments worldwide. The combination would also enable the entities to better negotiate with large retailers like Wal-Mart and Target. Throughout the 1990s, as mass retailing increased in geographic scope and customer base, the retailers' reach had forced more consumer products group (CPG) companies to channel their sales through superstores. In 2003 Wal-Mart accounted for 13 percent of Gillette's sales, enough to be listed in accounting statements filed with the Securities and Exchange Commission (SEC) as a substantial business risk.[6] Preserving a Wal-Mart relationship was so important that many of the larger and more successful CPG firms had gone so far as to establish permanent offices in what had become known as Vendorville, a community of hundreds of CPG companies near Wal-Mart's headquarters in Arkansas. Wal-Mart's reach and market clout enabled it to negotiate significant pricing concessions from CPG firms. Its buyers were able to say to retailers: "If you'd like to reach our 138 million customers per week, here's the deal."[7] CPG companies therefore had to bow to ever-mounting price pressure from Wal-Mart and other large retailers. The acquisition of Gillette by P&G could counterbalance this pressure and allow the combined firm to better control pricing and product placement in superstores nationwide.

As early as 2002, Kilts had approached P&G about a possible merger, and he began courting P&G anew in late 2004 (see Exhibit 2 and Exhibit 3). On November 17, 2004, representatives of senior management from Gillette and P&G met with representatives from Merrill Lynch (representing P&G) and UBS and Goldman Sachs (representing Gillette) to discuss a

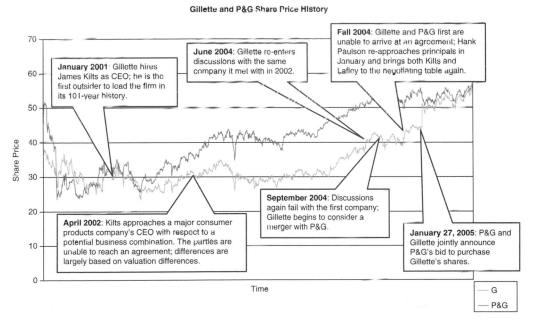

**EXHIBIT 2** Key Deal Dates Compared with Stock Price of P&G and Gillette

---

[6]Mike Hughlett and Becky Yerak, *"P&G, Gillette Deal a Matter of Clout; Combined, Firm Can Fight Retail Squeeze,"* Chicago Tribune, *January 29, 2005.*

[7]Greg Gatlin, *"Deal Is No Blue-Light Special for Wal-Mart,"* Boston Herald, *January 29, 2005.*

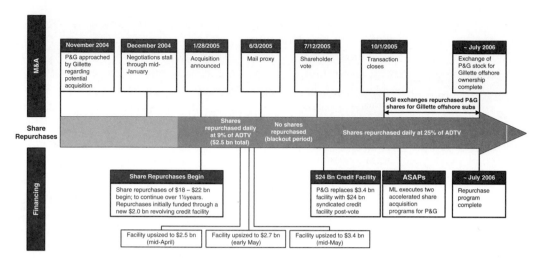

**EXHIBIT 3** Timeline of the Transaction

possible merger between the companies. The following day, Lafley met with McKinsey & Company consultants to receive their assessment of a combined firm. After receiving the blessing of both the bankers and the consultants, the two companies appeared close to completing a transaction. However, the deal fell apart in early December 2004, largely because Gillette's leadership believed that the valuation P&G had offered to Gillette shareholders (approximately $50 per share) was too low.

Yet hope remained that the two companies would be able to bridge the valuation divide. On January 4, 2005, Hank Paulson (board chairman and CEO of Goldman Sachs) called Lafley to remind him of the long-term strategic value of the merger and asked that P&G reconsider its offer. One week later, P&G's board of directors authorized Lafley to resume discussions with Gillette. Lafley then asked Rajat Gupta (former managing director of McKinsey & Company) to phone Kilts. The two met two days later, on January 13, 2005, to explore the possibility of reaching an agreement between the two companies.[8] Paulson and Gupta successfully bridged the gap between Lafley and Kilts. Instead of the original offer (0.915 P&G shares for every Gillette share), Lafley now offered 0.975 P&G shares for every Gillette share, which was accepted by Kilts and Gillette's board of directors.

## Deal Structure: An "All-Stock," 60/40, No-Collar Acquisition

A key concern of any acquisition involves how the consideration paid to complete the transaction will be structured. Acquisitions may be completed using one of three forms: all-cash, all-stock, or a hybrid of the two. Each option provides costs and benefits to both the buyer (acquiring company) and the target (purchased company). In an all-cash deal, the acquiring company typically pays the target company's shareholders a fixed price (per share) in cash. The benefit of this arrangement lies in its efficiency and transparency. Because companies are often acquired for a premium over their current stock price, a cash offer creates an immediately recognizable gain and allows shareholders to easily reallocate their newfound cash.

---

[8]Proxy Statement filed under Section 14A.

However, cash transactions have negative consequences as well. First, the target company's shareholders must pay taxes if there is a capital gain. Second, a cash payment requires the acquiring company to dip into its corporate coffers. This can adversely impact a company's bond rating and stock price, since credit rating services are wary of a firm greatly increasing its debt load or significantly reducing its cash resources.

Because of the negative tax and leverage consequences of all-cash deals, acquiring firms often provide the target company's shareholders with shares of the acquiring company instead. Yet all-stock deals also have drawbacks. For one, the target company's shareholders may not wish to hold the stock of the acquiring company. Doing so requires additional time and effort to analyze the financial health and future opportunities of the new firm. Second, the acquiring company may be concerned about diluting the value of its shares in the marketplace. Because both all-cash and all-stock transactions present problems, acquiring firms sometimes create a blended offer that contains elements of both cash and stock.

P&G's offer for Gillette, for example, was a modified all-stock deal (see Exhibit 4 and Exhibit 5). Under the terms of the agreement, P&G would issue 0.975 shares of its stock for each share of Gillette. This would avoid triggering a taxable event for Gillette's shareholders and would allow P&G to retain more of its cash. However, P&G also agreed to begin repurchasing $18–$22 billion of P&G stock over an eighteen-month period. This stock repurchase program sweetened the deal for Gillette shareholders. It provided them with a wholly tax-free transaction as well as an opportunity to continue to participate in the combined company if they wished or to sell stock back to P&G for cash.[9] P&G's share repurchases would result in reduced shareholder dilution. By the end of the eighteen-month buyback period, the transaction would be comprised of about 60 percent stock and 40 percent cash.[10]

## EXHIBIT 4 Transaction Summary

| | |
|---|---|
| Structure | 0.975 shares of P&G for each share of Gillette |
| Consideration | 100% stock acquisition |
| Implied offer price | $54.05, based on P&G closing price of $55.04 on January 26, 2005 (20.1% premium to Gillette share price of $45 on that date) |
| Tax treatment | Tax-free reorganization |
| Break-up fee | $1.9 billion |
| Closing | October 1, 2005 |
| Share repurchase | P&G to repurchase $18–$22 billion of P&G shares by June 2006 |
| Dilution | Expected to be dilutive in 2006, break even in 2007, and accretive in 2008 |
| Synergies | More than $1 billion of cost synergies expected to be achieved over a three-year period |
| Enterprise value | Approximately $57.2 billion, including $2.3 billion of Gillette net debt assumption |

[9]Ibid.

[10]Jordon, *"Buffett Calls It a 'Dream Deal'."*

■ ■ ■

## EXHIBIT 5 Terms and Overview of the Deal

| Rationale | Process |
|---|---|
| • Merger accomplished via an all-equity deal<br>• Transaction followed by $18–$22 bn share repurchase program over 12–18 months<br> ○ Equivalent to ~60–65% stock and ~35–40% debt-financed acquisition<br>• $18–$22 bn of debt in P&G International (PGI), along with all international subsidiaries of P&G and Gillette<br>• Transaction financed with portion of cash<br>• Simultaneous announcement of buyback to help support P&G stock price<br>• Offshore entities receive their fair share of the economic cost of the deal<br> ○ Future cash flow of PGI used to pay down offshore debt<br>• All international business aligned to facilitate business synergies and efficiencies | • PGI borrows and buys P&G shares<br>• Acquisition Co. (parent subsidiary) exchanges P&G shares for Gillette shares<br>• Periodically, PGI exchanges repurchased P&G shares for shares of Gillette offshore subsidiaries<br>• By ~July 2006 PGI will have borrowed $18–$22 bn, repurchased $18–$22 bn of P&G stock, and exchanged it all for international subsidiaries of Gillette<br>• Ongoing PGI debt will be supported by all international cash flows of the combined entities |

■ ■ ■

This buyback, however, could still impact P&G's credit standing with major rating agencies. Shortly after announcing the details of the acquisition and buyback programs, P&G was notified by Standard & Poor's, Moody's, and Fitch Ratings that "borrowings associated with [the] announced stock repurchase program have resulted in the re-examination and possible downgrading of its credit rating."[11] However, when P&G began issuing debt to complete the share buyback program in August 2005, it continued to enjoy the fourth-highest investment-grade credit ratings at both Moody's Investors Service (Aa3) and Standard & Poor's (AA–).[12]

Another notable aspect of the acquisition included the deal protections agreed to by both companies' boards of directors, including a breakup fee of $1.9 billion, or approximately 3 percent of the value of the transaction. Under this provision, if Gillette's board received and accepted a competing offer, the new acquirer would be required to pay $1.9 billion to P&G. Although the companies agreed to a breakup fee, they did not employ a collar on the 0.975

[11]Proxy Statement filed under Section 14A.

[12]Ed Leefeldt, "P&G Leads U.S. Borrowers with $24 Billion Stock-Buyback Loan," Bloomberg News, August 5, 2005.

P&G shares offered. A collar, common in many mergers and acquisitions, creates a ceiling and a floor on the value of the shares offered to complete the transaction. By creating a definitive price range, the collar assuages shareholders' (from both companies) fears regarding potential fluctuations in the acquiring company's share price while the transaction awaits shareholder approval (a process often three to six months in length). Since both companies would have received protection from a collar, it was surprising that it was not employed.

## Valuation of the Deal

Based on P&G's closing price on January 26, 2005, its offer of 0.975 P&G shares for every share of Gillette translated into an implied offer price of $54.05 per share. This price fell somewhere in the middle of a series of valuations prepared by investment bankers ranging from $43.25 to $61.90 (see Exhibit 6). A valuation based on public market reference points, including Gillette's 52-week trading range and a present value of Wall Street price targets, would have priced Gillette's stock at $43.25 to $45.00. A valuation analysis based on discounted cash flows was more favorable. One such valuation that incorporated only the cash flows from Gillette in its current form valued the shares at $47.10. A second valuation that took into account the potential cost savings resulting from the combination of Gillette and P&G valued the stock at $56.60. Cost savings were expected to be realized in purchasing, manufacturing, logistics, and administrative costs. A third valuation that incorporated total synergies (both cost savings and capitalizing on complementary strengths) valued the stock at $61.90 per share. This valuation included not only the cost savings, but also potential revenue synergy opportunities that a combined firm might realize, including the increased market power that a combined firm would wield in dealing with large retailing firms such as Wal-Mart. Finally, a sum-of-the-parts valuation established a price of $52.50 per share (see Exhibit 7).

The valuation of the proposed acquisition was also compared with recent acquisitions, both in the sector and across similarly sized companies, to ensure that the compensation paid

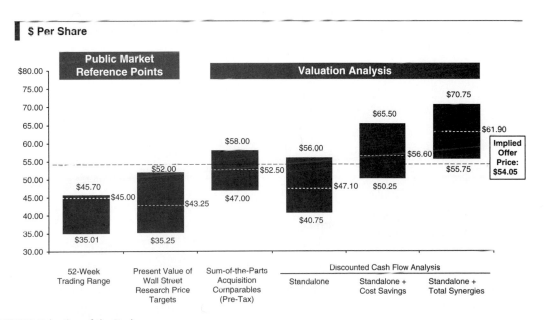

**EXHIBIT 6** Valuation of the Deal

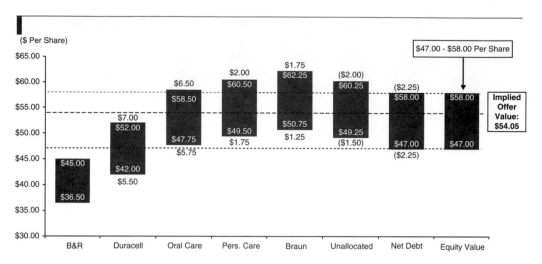

**EXHIBIT 7** Sum-of-the-Parts Valuation Note: Assumes approximately 1 billion Gillette shares.

## EXHIBIT 8 Comparison with Other Acquisitions

| Announcement Date | Acquiror | Target | Transaction Value ($ in billions) | Premium to Share Price | |
|---|---|---|---|---|---|
| | | | | 1 Day Prior | 1 Week Prior |
| 06/25/2000 | Philip Morris | Nabisco | 19.2 | 69.9% | 103.2% |
| 08/22/1994 | Johnson & Johnson | Neutrogena | 1.0 | 63.0% | 76.3% |
| 11/03/2004 | Constellation Brands | Robert Mondavi | 1.4 | 49.9% | 52.3% |
| 03/18/2003 | P&G | Wella | 7.0 | 44.5% | 47.3% |
| 10/23/2003 | Tchibo | Beiersdorf | 13.0 | 51.2% | 45.7% |
| 06/06/2000 | Unilever | Bestfoods | 23.7 | 44.4% | 39.9% |
| 12/04/2000 | PepsiCo | Quaker Oats | 15.1 | 22.2% | 24.0% |
| Average | | | | 49.3% | 55.5% |
| *At 0.975× exchange ratio:* | | | | | |
| 01/26/2005 | P&G | Gillette | 57.2 | 20.1% | 20.1% |

to Gillette's shareholders was in line with recent transactions (see Exhibit 8). The total transaction value at the implied offer price of $54.05 per share was $57.177 billion (see Exhibit 9).

## Key Stakeholders: Beantown, Wall Street, DC, and Main Street

The turbulence associated with an acquisition can cause a host of negative effects, and leaders navigating a company through an acquisition can face opposition from managers, employees,

■ ■ ■

# EXHIBIT 9 Transaction Values and Multiples

## Offer and Transaction Values

| | |
|---|---|
| P&G share price (01/26/2005) | $55.44 |
| Proposed exchange ratio | 0.975x |
| *Implied offer price per share* | $54.05 |
| Total Gillette shares & options outstanding | 1,068.379[a] |
| Gross offer value | $57,750[a] |
| Less: Option proceeds | (2,893)[a] |
| *Net offer value* | $54,857[a] |
| Plus: Net debt assumed | 2,321[a] |
| *Transaction value* | $57,177[a] |

[a]In millions.

## Offer Premiums

| | Stock Prices | Offer Price $54.05 |
|---|---|---|
| Current 01/26/2005 | $45.00 | 20.1% |
| 30-day average | $44.58 | 21.3% |
| 90-day average | $44.00 | 22.8% |

## Transaction Multiples

| | | Gillette Multiples | | |
|---|---|---|---|---|
| | Gillette Results | Market $45.00 | Offer Price $54.05 | P&G Market Multiples |
| *Revenues* | | | | |
| 12/2004A (LTM) | $10,366[a] | 4.6x | 5.5x | 3.0x |
| 06/2005E | $10,581[a] | 4.5 | 5.4 | 2.9 |
| *EBITDA* | | | | |
| 12/2004A (LTM) | $3,013[a] | 15.8x | 19.0x | 13.1x |
| 06/2005E | $3,149[a] | 15.1 | 18.2 | 12.4 |
| *P/E* | | | | |
| 06/2005E | $1.78 | 25.2x | 30.3x | 21.3x |
| 06/2006E | $2.01 | 22.4 | 26.9 | 19.3 |

[a]In millions.

■ ■ ■

politicians, shareholders, and regulators. Top management might be forced out as a result of the acquisition or asked to take lower-profile positions. Employees often fear the consequences of consolidation, including work force reductions mandated by cost-saving synergies (see Exhibit 10). Politicians, in turn, are concerned about the long-term social and economic impact that reduced employment can have on a community. Shareholders fear that the price brokered

---

**P&G / Gillette Transition**
**5 Guiding Principles to the Integration Process**

- 1. Maintain P&G and Gillette business momentum

- 2. Field the best team

- 3. Treat people with dignity/respect

- 4. Move quickly, making decisions promptly, objectively, and fairly

- 5. Communicate openly and proactively

4/29/2005

---

**Gillette – Procter & Gamble**

P&G wants to field the *best possible team* … with members from BOTH companies

- There will be job losses

- Losses are estimated at approximately 4% of the combined company's work force of 140,000

- Many will occur at the corporate office … but NO decisions have been made

- We've implemented special severance protection

  - ❑ Change of control measures
  - ❑ Fully vested stock option plan

---

**EXHIBIT 10** Gillette's Presentation to Its Employees

for their shares may not be adequate compensation. Finally, regulators evaluate every aspect of the transaction to determine whether the combined or separate entities have violated applicable state and federal laws, including antitrust laws. The approval of each of these stakeholder groups is essential, and managing the diverse interests of each group can be as challenging as managing the initial financial and strategic interests driving the acquisition.

## The Razor Boss of Boston: James Kilts, Gillette CEO

Former Nabisco executive James Kilts was a turnaround expert who had orchestrated the sale of Nabisco to Philip Morris in 2000. He was named CEO of Gillette in January 2001 and immediately set on a course to turn it around. Kilts succeeded in resurrecting the company's stagnant stock price by pursuing a policy of "slash and earn." Under this policy, he reduced overhead expenses and invested the savings in promoting the company's razors, blades, and batteries.[13]

---

[13]Greg Gatlin, "Boston Blockbuster; Hub Icon Gillette Sold in $56B Deal," Boston Herald, *January 28, 2005.*

The strategy performed remarkably well, and Gillette's stock rose 50 percent under Kilts's stewardship (see Exhibit 2). In total, it was estimated that he created about $20 billion in shareholder value.[14]

Gillette's board of directors' 2001 executive search effort had yielded a CEO who restored investor confidence in the company and crafted a strategy that would enhance the value of its well-known and respected brands. In its recruiting efforts, Gillette's board had offered Kilts an extensive executive compensation package customary for a capable leader with a "knack for rescuing ailing companies."[15] However, though investors had not balked at the structure of Kilts's package in 2001, interest in his compensation increased after the P&G transaction was announced in 2005.

Kilts's compensation package allowed him to realize impressive financial gains in the event that the company was sold. The package included stock options and rights and a one-time $12.6 million "change-of-control" payment.[16] Kilts was also compensated by P&G with options and restricted stock valued at $24 million. His total compensation package amounted to more than $164 million (see Exhibit 11). To some business leaders, this amount did not seem outlandish.[17] After all, the figure represented less than 1 percent of the total value that he had created during his tenure as Gillette's CEO. Yet Kilts took on fierce criticism from the Boston media and some political leaders, including Secretary of the Commonwealth of Massachusetts William Galvin and U.S. Congressman Barney Frank (D-Mass), when the acquisition was announced. Kilts, expressing frustration over this criticism, would refer to himself as Boston's piñata.[18] The moniker reflected his irritation at the negative press attention he received over a deal that he felt would

■ ■ ■

### EXHIBIT 11 Severance and Change in Control Benefits (Gillette's Officers)

| Name and Principal Position | Net Equity Award | All Other Payments and Benefits | Estimated Aggregate Dollar Value |
|---|---|---|---|
| James M. Kilts, Chairman, President and CEO | $125,260,167 | $39,272,025 | $164,532,192 |
| Edward F. DeGraan, Vice Chairman | 29,711,715 | 15,655,483 | 45,367,198 |
| Charles W. Cramb, Senior VP | 16,258,040 | 10,174,097 | 26,432,137 |
| Peter K. Hoffman, VP | 10,695,578 | 9,567,625 | 20,263,203 |
| Mark M. Leckie, VP | 9,426,564 | 7,528,840 | 16,955,404 |
| All other executive officers as a group (12) | 96,073,693 | 79,795,179 | 175,868,872 |

■ ■ ■

[14]Naomi Aoki, *"Kilts' Many Options,"* Boston Globe, *February 2, 2005.*

[15]Ibid.

[16]Ibid.

[17]Ibid., citing Shawn Kravetz, president of Boston money management firm Esplanade Capital.

[18]Jenn Abelson, *"'Boston's Pinata' Slams Media, Politicians for P&G Deal Attacks,"* Boston Globe, *September 9, 2005.*

provide many stakeholders with tangible benefits. In a press conference defending the acquisition and his compensation, he pointed out that Massachusetts would retain a key manufacturing plant located south of Boston, job losses would be less than 5 percent, and Gillette's razor business would continue to be run from the Boston area.

## The Rainmakers: Investment Bankers and Power Brokers

The investment bankers that had assisted in the transaction (Goldman, Merrill, and UBS) equally split a $90 million acquisition completion fee for their merger advisory services.[19] In addition, each investment bank provided its client a fairness opinion (see Exhibit 12). Fairness opinions are drafted by investment banks "to assure the directors of companies involved in a merger, acquisition, or other deal that its terms are fair to shareholders."[20] This can be problematic, however, because "the bank affirming the fairness of the transaction is often the same one that proposed the deal—and that stands to reap millions in fees if it goes through."[21] This was precisely the case in the P&G-Gillette transaction. Hank Paulson of Goldman Sachs had been directly responsible for bringing the two parties back to the negotiating table in January 2005. His firm netted a $30 million fee for assisting the companies with the transaction after rendering a fairness opinion in support of the transaction. Merrill Lynch and UBS also received fees of $30 million each after providing fairness opinions, putting them in the same position as Goldman Sachs.

The investment bankers and top management at Gillette and P&G faced substantial criticism for the consideration paid to the firms. However, Gillette spokesperson Eric Kraus advised those investigating the bankers' role in the transaction that "virtually no financial expert thinks the deal is anything but excellent for Gillette shareholders."[22] Though Kraus's statement reminded the investment community how much support the transaction enjoyed, it did not appease the investigating appetite of regulators in the United States and abroad.

## The Regulators: International, National, and Local

Mergers and acquisitions face scrutiny from regulators at multiple levels of government. For publicly traded companies, the regulatory process begins with the SEC. Each firm is required to disclose its plans to merge (or be acquired) in a series of forms. Form 8-K is filed whenever a publicly traded company has a material event and is often accompanied by Form 425, which is filed whenever a public company makes an important announcement. The net effect of filing both of these forms is that they put investors on notice as to a major decision reached by the board of directors.

Once the information concerning a proposed merger or acquisition is publicly available, regulators begin to scrutinize the transaction to ensure that economic and financial fairness is achieved. Often in a consolidation, two firms with similar business models are forced to divest assets (or entire business lines) in order to satisfy the antitrust and consumer-watchdog concerns voiced by federal regulators in the United States and by regulators at the European Commission (EC). In Europe, the EC is responsible for approving transactions between public companies and is charged with investigating the impact that a merger or acquisition would likely have on consumers and employees in Europe. As a result of the EC's investigation, "P&G offered to

---

[19]Brett Arends, "Gillette Shareholders OK P&G Takeover," *Boston Herald*, July 13, 2005.

[20]Gretchen Morgenson, "Mirror, Mirror, Who Is the Unfairest?" *New York Times*, May 29, 2005.

[21]Ibid.

[22]Ibid.

■ ■ ■

## EXHIBIT 12  Excerpts of Goldman Sachs's Fairness Opinion Sent to Gillette's Board of Directors

Ladies and Gentlemen:

You have requested our opinion as to the fairness from a financial point of view to the holders of the outstanding shares of common stock, par value $1.00 per share (the "Company Common Stock"), of The Gillette Company (the "Company") of the exchange ratio of 0.975 of a share of common stock, without par value (the "P&G Common Stock"), of The Procter & Gamble Company ("P&G") to be received for each Share (the "Exchange Ratio") pursuant to the Agreement and Plan of Merger, dated as of January 27, 2005 (the "Merger Agreement"), among P&G, Aquarium Acquisition Corp., a wholly owned subsidiary of P&G, and the Company.

\* \* \*

We have acted as financial advisor to the Company in connection with, and have participated in certain of the negotiations leading to, the transaction contemplated by the Merger Agreement (the "Transaction"). We expect to receive fees for our services in connection with the Transaction, substantially all of which are contingent upon consummation of the Transaction, and the Company has agreed to reimburse our expenses and indemnify us against certain liabilities arising out of our engagement.

\* \* \*

In connection with this opinion, we have reviewed, among other things, the Merger Agreement; certain publicly available business and financial information relating to the Company and P&G; certain financial estimates and forecasts relating to the business and financial prospects of the Company prepared by certain research analysts that were publicly available; certain internal financial information and other data relating to the business and financial prospects of the Company, including financial analyses and forecasts for the Company prepared by its management (the "Company Forecasts"), and certain cost savings and operating synergies projected by the managements of the Company and P&G to result from the Transaction (collectively, the "Synergies"), in each case provided to us by the management of the Company and not publicly available; and certain financial information and other data relating to the business of P&G provided to us by the managements of the Company and P&G and which were not publicly available, which information did not include forecasts for P&G. In such connection, we also have reviewed certain financial estimates and forecasts relating to the business and financial prospects of P&G prepared by certain research analysts that were publicly available, as adjusted and provided to us by the management of the Company following their discussions with the management of P&G as to public guidance expected to be given by P&G contemporaneously with the announcement of the Transaction (the "P&G Adjusted Street Forecasts"). We have held discussions with members of the senior management of the Company and P&G regarding their assessment of the strategic rationale for, and the potential benefits of, the Transaction and the past and current business operations, financial condition and future prospects of the Company and P&G (including as a result of the significant stock buyback being announced by P&G contemporaneously with the Transaction). In addition, we have reviewed the reported price and trading activity for the Company Common Stock and the P&G Common Stock,

*Continued*

■ ■ ■ ━━━━━━━━━━━━━━━━━━━━━━━━━━━━━━━━━━━━

## EXHIBIT 12   Excerpts of Goldman Sachs's Fairness Opinion Sent to Gillette's Board of Directors — Cont'd

compared certain publicly available financial and stock market information for the Company and P&G with similar financial and stock market information for certain other companies the securities of which are publicly traded, reviewed certain financial terms of certain recent publicly available business combinations in the consumer products industry specifically and in other industries generally, considered certain pro forma effects of the Transaction, and performed such other studies and analyses, and considered such other factors, as we considered appropriate.

　　　* * *

Our opinion is necessarily based on economic, monetary, market and other conditions as in effect on, and the information made available to us as of, the date hereof.

Based upon and subject to the foregoing, it is our opinion that, as of the date hereof, the Exchange Ratio pursuant to the Merger Agreement is fair from a financial point of view to the holders of the Company Common Stock.

Very truly yours,

GOLDMAN, SACHS & CO.

━━━━━━━━━━━━━━━━━━━━━━━━━━━━━━━━━━━━ ■ ■ ■

improve the conditions of its proposed disposals" to include not only its electronic toothbrush business in the UK, but also other brands elsewhere in Europe.[23]

In the United States, the Federal Trade Commission is responsible for investigating the possible effects of a merger or acquisition. The FTC derives its authority to investigate such transactions from the Clayton Act and the Federal Trade Commission Act. The Hart-Scott-Rodino Act requires prospective acquirers to notify the FTC of a potential transaction and allow thirty days for a review. While investigating P&G's acquisition of Gillette, the FTC found that there might be anticompetition problems within the at-home teeth whitening products, adult battery-powered toothbrushes, and men's antiperspirants/deodorants markets.[24] As a result of the FTC's ruling, the two companies began divesting themselves of business lines that might run afoul of anticompetition laws.[25] Gillette sold its Rembrandt teeth-whitening products to Johnson & Johnson and its Right Guard, Soft & Dri, and Dry Idea deodorant brands to Dial. P&G, for its part, sold its Crest SpinBrush line to Church & Dwight.

Companies intending to merge can also face scrutiny from state governments. The state of Massachusetts, under Secretary Galvin, attempted to subpoena records and information from Gillette to investigate whether the sale of Gillette ran contrary to Massachusetts laws. Under state law, it is the Secretary's duty to prohibit fraud "in connection with the offer, sale, or purchase of any security [and is] expected to prohibit fraud by any person who is paid for advising [another] as to the value of the securities or their purchase or sale."[26] Yet mergers and acquisitions are

---

[23]Tobias Buck and Jeremy Grant, *"EU Officials Back P&G/Gillette Merger,"* Financial Times, *July 15, 2005.*

[24]*In the Matter of the Procter & Gamble Co.,* Federal Trade Commission Docket No. C-4151 (2005).

[25]Jenn Abelson, "Gillette Selling Its Deodorants to Dial," *Boston Globe, February 21, 2006.*

[26]*Galvin v. Gillette,* 19 Mass. L. Rep. 291 (2005).

"expressly removed from the scope of the Uniform Securities Act,"[27] the law under which Galvin was attempting to subpoena Gillette. Therefore, a state court in Massachusetts determined that in spite of Galvin's concerns about the impact of the acquisition on employees and shareholders in Massachusetts, the state did not have the authority to further subpoena Gillette regarding its acquisition by P&G. The court left open the possibility that Galvin could subpoena the investment banking firms advising Gillette and P&G during the transaction, as the law did not exempt those firms. Hank Paulson of Goldman Sachs was ultimately subpoenaed by Galvin and gave testimony to state lawyers in June 2005. Though Galvin raised a series of questions about the deal and the fairness opinion, as of April 2006 he had not brought suit against Goldman Sachs or any other investment banks involved in the transaction.

## The White Squire from Omaha: Warren Buffett, Gillette Investor

To help deal with the scrutiny caused by the acquisition of Gillette, the company turned to Warren Buffett, one of its most notable brand investors. Buffett's involvement in the P&G-Gillette transaction stemmed from his longstanding investment in Gillette, dating back to the 1980s. Though Gillette had successfully fended off several hostile takeover attempts between 1986 and 1989, the defensive efforts it had employed had placed it in financial peril at the time. The firm was saddled with $1 billion in debt as a result of measures deployed defending against these takeover attempts, and remained a possible acquisition target.[28] But the company still had a series of strong brands, which attracted Buffett. In 1989 Buffett agreed to purchase $600 million of convertible securities that could later be converted into an 11 percent interest in Gillette stock. Buffett's purchase provided the cash infusion Gillette desperately needed to retire debt, and also placed a large number of shares in the hands of an investor friendly to Gillette's board. With such a large concentration of shares controlled by one friendly investor, Gillette was able to ensure that any attempt to take over the company would have to be approved by its new "white squire."[29] This became Gillette's "insurance policy" against any future corporate raiders.

Buffett had executed a well-timed entrance into what would become a booming industry. Consumer product firms were favored by investors throughout the 1990s, and Buffett saw his Gillette investment appreciate more than tenfold during that decade. However, the stock languished during the late 1990s, and investors lost patience with former Gillette CEOs Al Zeien and Michael Hawley. Buffett was reportedly instrumental in Hawley's removal and he initiated the search that led to the selection of James Kilts as Gillette's new CEO in 2001.

When Gillette again turned to Buffett for assistance in 2005, instead of asking him to invest additional funds in the company, Gillette sought his blessing of its sale to P&G. So powerful was Buffett's reputation throughout the investment community that Gillette's board of directors felt certain that his approval would assuage investors' fears and pave the way toward a quick approval of the deal. Buffett, who participated (via remote video) in the initial press conference announcing the agreement between P&G and Gillette, declared the transaction a "dream deal" that would "create the greatest consumer products company in the world."[30] Although Buffett already held 10 percent of Gillette's stock, he announced his intention to purchase more stock of both P&G and Gillette so that, after the acquisition, he would own 3.9 percent of P&G stock.

[27]Ibid.
[28]Steven Syre, "As Firm's Chief Shareholder, Buffett Likes What He Sees," Boston Globe, *January 29, 2005.*
[29]Ibid.
[30]Ibid.

His comments and commitments on the heels of the announcement seemed to calm investors in both companies.

## Conclusion

The complementary strengths of the two firms were clear, as was their motivation for combining. Though management was unable to secure the full cooperation of all stakeholders, it was able to successfully leverage the support of one of the world's most respected investors. Additionally, P&G made overtures to the Massachusetts community to reduce fears that the acquirer would lay off Gillette's employees at the company's state-of-the-art production facility near Boston. However, despite the key synergies, the complementary strengths, and the support of Warren Buffett, the deal still raised questions on Main Street, Wall Street, and in the offices of elected officials.

# A Tale of Two Hedge Funds: Magnetar and Peloton

*"It was the best of times, it was the worst of times . . ."*
—*Charles Dickens*

## What a Year

Magnetar Capital had returned 25 percent in 2007—only its third year in business. This return was achieved with significantly lower risk than the S&P 500. Investors were happy; assets under management were among the largest of any hedge fund manager and growing.

On the other hand, the team at Magnetar recognized that investors can have short memories. Magnetar needed to consistently generate new ideas in order to meet investor return objectives. Formerly well-respected hedge funds such as Peloton, Thornburg, and Carlyle Capital were closing at a record pace due to illiquidity. Even the world's largest banks were not immune to a crisis, as Bear Stearns and Lehman Brothers had proven. Magnetar's diversification, low leverage, and capital call restrictions offered additional stability, but could not in themselves be relied upon to produce future success.

Magnetar employed approximately two hundred of some of the smartest investment professionals in the world. It was the job of Alec Litowitz, chairman and chief investment officer, to provide guidance to his team, evaluate and prioritize (and allocate resources to) their ideas, and generate new ideas of his own. Although Litowitz preferred to limit exposure by separating risk capital across multiple businesses and trades, he knew that much of Magnetar's returns in 2007 had come from one brilliant trading strategy. This strategy was based on the view that certain tranches of CDOs (collateralized debt obligations) were systematically mispriced (see Exhibit 1). Magnetar made dozens of bets across multiple securities in order to capitalize on this observation. At the same time, the firm undertook comparatively little risk. According to the *Wall Street Journal*, "Mortgage analysts note that Magnetar's trading strategy wasn't all luck—it would have benefited whether the subprime market held up or collapsed."[1]

Recent turmoil in the markets had caused new mispricings—and therefore new investment opportunities. Magnetar would seek to locate and prioritize them.

---

[1]Serena Ng and Carrick Mollenkamp, "**A Fund Behind Astronomical Losses**," *Wall Street Journal*, January 14, 2008.

■ ■ ■  ━━━━━━━━━━━━━━━━━━━━━━━━━━━━━━━━━━

## EXHIBIT 1  A Fund Behind Astronomical Losses (Abridged)

The trading strategy of a little-known hedge fund run by an astronomy buff contributed to billions in losses on Wall Street, even as the fund itself profited from the subprime-mortgage crisis.

Even as it helped to spawn CDOs that would later wrack Wall Street with painful losses, Magnetar, which has around $9 billion in assets, itself made a tidy profit. Its funds returned 25 percent across a range of stock and debt strategies last year, thanks largely to the way it hedged these trades.

In this case, Magnetar swooped in on securities that it believed could become troubled but were paying big returns. CDOs are sliced based on risk, with the riskiest pieces having the highest yield but the greatest chance of losing value. Less-risky pieces have lower yields and some pieces were once considered so safe that they paid only a bit more than a U.S. Treasury bond.

Magnetar helped to spawn CDOs by buying the riskiest slices of the instruments, which paid returns of around 20 percent during good times, according to people familiar with its strategy. Back in 2006, when Magnetar began investing, these were the slices Wall Street found hardest to sell because they would be the first to lose money if subprime defaults rose. . . . Magnetar then hedged its holdings by betting against the less-risky slices of some of these same securities as well as other CDOs, according to people familiar with its strategy. While it lost money on many of the risky slices it bought, it made far more when its hedges paid off as the market collapsed in the second half of last year.

Magnetar hedged itself by buying credit default swaps that act as a form of protection—similar to an insurance policy—against losses on the CDOs. It isn't clear which CDOs it hedged against, but these swaps broadly soared in value when the CDOs dived last year.

Mortgage analysts note that Magnetar's trading strategy wasn't all luck—it would have benefited whether the subprime market held up or collapsed.

*Source*: Serena Ng and Carrick Mollenkamp, "**A Fund Behind Astronomical Losses**," *Wall Street Journal*, January 14, 2008

━━━━━━━━━━━━━━━━━━━━━━━━━━━━━━━━━━  ■ ■ ■

# What a Nightmare

An ocean away, Ron Beller was contemplating some very different issues than was Alec Litowitz. Beller's firm, Peloton Partners LLP (also founded in 2005), had been one of the top-performing hedge funds in 2007, returning in excess of 80 percent. In late January 2008 Beller accepted two prestigious awards at a black-tie EuroHedge ceremony. A month later, his firm was bankrupt (see Exhibit 2).

Beller shorted the U.S. housing market before the subprime crisis hit, and was paid handsomely for his bet. After the crisis began, however, he believed that panicking investors were throwing out the proverbial baby with the bath water. Beller felt that prices for highly rated mortgage securities were being unfairly punished, so he decided to go long AAA-rated securities backed by Alt-A mortgage loans (between prime and subprime). As was common at Peloton, he levered up the investments at an average of 9×.

## EXHIBIT 2  Peloton Flew High, Fell Fast (Abridged)

When hedge-fund chief Ron Beller's investments in U.S. mortgages turned against him, he got a rude awakening to Wall Street's unsentimental ways. Bankers who had vied for his business reeled in credit lines and seized the fund's assets. In a matter of days, Peloton Partners LLP, once one of the world's best-performing hedge-fund operators, lost some $17 billion. In its sheer speed, Peloton's demise offers an illustration of the delicate relationships upon which the financial industry is built, and the breakneck pace at which they have been unraveling.

There is a widespread weakness in the hedge-fund business: highflying managers sometimes fail to fully factor in broader risks, such as what happens when troubled banks pull back the borrowed money many funds need to make their investments. Peloton was particularly susceptible because it borrowed heavily to boost returns. For every dollar of client money, Peloton had borrowed at least another nine dollars to buy some bonds.

. . . In mid-February, Messrs. Beller's and Grant's investments took a hit when Swiss bank UBS AG said it had marked down the value of highly rated mortgage securities similar to those that Peloton held.

Peloton had $750 million in cash and believed its funding from banks was secure. That provided a level of comfort to Messrs. Beller and Grant that Peloton could cover banker demands, known as margin calls, to put up more collateral as the value of its investments fell.

But by Monday, Feb. 25, further sharp drops had left Peloton scraping for cash to meet margin calls from lenders, including UBS and Lehman Brothers Holdings Inc. When Peloton traders tried to sell securities to raise money, brokers were unwilling to bid, according to people familiar with the situation.

Mr. Beller and his team worked around the clock to assemble a rescue plan, persuading investors to provide a $600 million loan. But the financial lifeline, which included some twenty-five parties, depended on Peloton's banks agreeing to postpone certain margin calls. Some banks were reluctant to sign off on such an unusual deal at a time when they were dialing back risk amid the financial crisis. On Wednesday morning, Feb. 27, yet another sharp drop in Peloton's mortgage investments killed a rescue. Mr. Beller at one point collapsed on a couch in distress.

Mr. Beller and his team made one final effort to sell Peloton's portfolio, including to other hedge funds, working late into Wednesday night. By 4 a.m. Thursday morning, Mr. Beller threw in the towel and went home, exhausted.

The next day, lenders seized Peloton's assets, bringing a chaotic end to the fund. Mr. Beller later likened the situation to the final scene in Quentin Tarantino's movie "Reservoir Dogs," when several actors, guns trained on each other, simultaneously blow each other away.

---

*Source*: Carrick Mollenkamp and Gregory Zuckerman, "Peloton Flew High, Fell Fast; Winning Hedge Fund Lost on Bets as Credit Crunch Moved at Breakneck Speed," *Wall Street Journal*, May 12, 2008

The trade moved against Beller in a big way on February 14, 2008, when UBS disclosed that the bank owned $21.2 billion of high-rated Alt-A securities and the market speculated that UBS would need to sell those securities in a hurry.[2] Over the next two weeks, Alt-A backed AAA securities dropped by 10 to 15 percent. Beller did what any fund manager would do: he lined up additional funding from investors, liquidated positions where possible to raise cash, and tried to persuade his banks to delay their margin calls. Unfortunately, the banks were not providing any bids on his securities. Banks were also unwilling to delay margin calls at a time when they too were dealing with enormous losses from their own mortgage-related holdings. Investors, meanwhile, would only guarantee the new money if the banks agreed to delay the margin calls. It was a perfect storm. The firm ran out of liquidity, lost $17 billion, and was forced to close.

## Magnetar's Structured Finance Arbitrage Trade

Magnetar had made more than $1 billion in profit by noticing that the equity tranche of CDOs and CDO-derivative instruments were relatively mispriced. It took advantage of this anomaly by purchasing CDO equity and buying credit default swap (CDS) protection on tranches that were considered less risky.

Magnetar performed its own calculation of risk for each tranche of security and compared that with the return that the tranche offered. By conducting such an analysis, investors could find a glaring irregularity: two classes of securities had very similar risks but significantly different yields. More importantly, this mispricing was occurring across multiple ABS CDOs (see pages 4 and 5). Successful investors developed a long/short strategy to take advantage of the anomaly. Using this strategy, they could replicate the same basic trade many times across many securities. Further, they could put large sums of money to work while having little effect on market prices, undertaking little risk, and locking in a return that was nearly certain. This was the type of trade about which hedge funds dream.

Specifically, astute investors noticed that the equity and mezzanine tranches of ABS CDOs had very different yields. This did not seem to make sense. After all, an ABS CDO simply consisted of slim mezzanine tranches of multiple ABS notes, which were then packaged together and sold in different tranches. It was unlikely that holders of the mezzanine tranche would get paid off while the equity holders would not. Either both securities would be paid, or neither would be paid. Since the risk was similar, the yield should also be similar. Instead, due to illiquidity in the equity tranche and the market's misunderstanding of correlation across tranches, the yield of the equity tranche was often much higher than that of the mezzanine tranche.

Successful investors such as Magnetar capitalized on this observation by buying CDS protection on the mezzanine tranche and going long the equity tranche. In some cases, the market was so spooked by the equity tranche that few buyers existed and the entire CDO deal was at risk of not getting funded. As the *Wall Street Journal* reported, "In all, roughly $30 billion of these constellation CDOs were issued from mid-2006 to mid-2007, with Magnetar as their lynchpin investor."[3]

Magnetar did not need to form a view on absolute prices; it only needed to realize that the two tranches were *relatively* mispriced. Trades could be structured to generate cash on an ongoing basis because the current yields flowing in from the equity long positions were so much higher

---

[2]Jody Shenn, "Alt-A Mortgage Securities Tumble, Signaling Losses," Bloomberg News, February 28, 2008.
[3]Ng and Mollenkamp, **"Fund Behind Astronomical Losses."**

than the current yields being paid on the mezzanine short positions. Meanwhile, in the event of high defaults, the principal balance on the mezzanine shorts would be higher than that of the equity longs, so the strategy would have a large payoff if prices of the overall underlying collateral took a turn for the worse. The strategy would only lose money if the equity got wiped out while the mezzanine tranche stayed intact. Magnetar reasoned that the probability of this scenario was remote.

Rating agencies based their CDO credit ratings primarily on historical data, which showed that a nationwide housing downturn was unprecedented. However, astute investors recognized that this cycle was very different from the previous ones and therefore the historical data used by the agencies could not be relied upon as the sole predictor of future events. This recognition was the catalyst for Magnetar's trade on the pricing anomalies in the ABS CDO space. Its strategy was very different from the well-publicized bearish bet on housing established during 2007 by John Paulson of Paulson & Company, who personally made $3.7 billion when the market crashed.[4] Paulson took a position on the market, whereas Magnetar focused on locating relative pricing anomalies that should profit no matter what happened in the market. Strategies such as Magnetar's are consistent with the objectives of many hedge funds: to earn returns that are uncorrelated with the market.

## The 2007–2008 Financial Crisis

In the aftermath of the 2001 recession, concerns about deflation and the economy caused the Federal Reserve to bring interest rates to forty-year lows. These low interest rates were partially responsible for the housing bubble. Because they significantly lowered a borrower's monthly home payment, borrowers often bought larger houses than they could afford. "Teaser rates" would sometimes increase after a short initial period. Other loans were based on variable rates rather than the fixed rates of traditional home mortgages. Consumers often brushed aside fears that rates would increase because they believed the housing market could only increase in value. Millions of Americans became homeowners for the first time, as homeownership reached an all-time high of 70 percent.[5] Moreover, the housing boom was only one part of a broader increase in leverage across the economy that had been ongoing for thirty years (see Exhibit 3).

Beyond pure interest rate effects, however, lending practices became extremely loose. Lenders granted loans with no money down and no proof of income. These practices did not result from banks becoming more generous or consumers more creditworthy. Financial innovation was largely to blame, in the form of CDOs. Despite all the benefits CDOs offered, they created a principal-agent problem. Banks are the most capable entities for assessing a borrower's risk and determining a fair interest rate. However, when banks can securitize all of their loans within a few months and transfer most of the risk to someone else, their economic incentive changes. The new focus becomes making as many loans as possible in order to collect origination fees. The bankers who granted the original home loans were likely more concerned with their annual bonuses (which were based on fee income) than the ultimate performance of the loan.

While large investment banks originated some loans themselves, many home loans were originated by small regional banks, which then sold the loans to major investment banks. The investment banks then securitized the loans into CDOs, which were sold to investors. Still, the

---

[4]Andrew Clark, "The $3.7bn King of New York," *The Guardian*, April 19, 2008.

[5]Roger M. Showley, "Working Families See Little Hope For Homes," *San Diego Union-Tribune*, March 23, 2006, http://www.signonsandiego.com/news/business/20060323-9999-1b23owners.html.

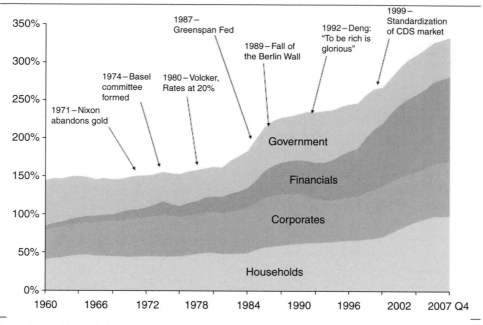

Source: Morgan Stanley, Federal Reserve
*Financials consists of government-sponsored enterprises, agency-and GSE-backed mortgage pools, and private financial institutions

**EXHIBIT 3** U.S. Credit Market Debt/GDP. *Source*: Neil McLeish (Morgan Stanley), "A Summer Rally, But Still a Bear Market," July 2008

investment banks held large inventories of loans and CDOs for three reasons. First, the securitization procedure took time, so loans in the process of being securitized were owned by banks temporarily. Second, banks held inventories because their trading divisions made markets in the security. Finally, when an investment bank created a CDO, it often kept a small "holdback" amount. These three forms of exposure led to investment banking losses of $300 billion between July 2007 and July 2008. Some predict the total will rise to $1 trillion before the carnage is over.[6]

## The CDO Market

A CDO is a general term that describes securities backed by a pool of fixed-income assets. These assets can be bank loans (CLOs), bonds (CBOs), residential mortgages (residential mortgage-backed securities, or RMBSs), and many others. A CDO is a subset of asset-backed securities (ABS), which is a general term for a security backed by assets such as mortgages, credit card receivables, auto loans, or other debt.

To create a CDO, a bank or other entity transfers the underlying assets ("the collateral") to a special purpose vehicle (SPV) that is a separate legal entity from the issuer. The SPV then issues securities backed with cash flows generated by assets in the collateral pool. This general process is called securitization. The securities are separated into tranches, which differ primarily in the priority of their rights to the cash flows coming from the asset pool. The senior tranche has first

---

[6]Peter Goodman, "Uncomfortable Answers to Questions on the Economy," *New York Times*, July 22, 2008.

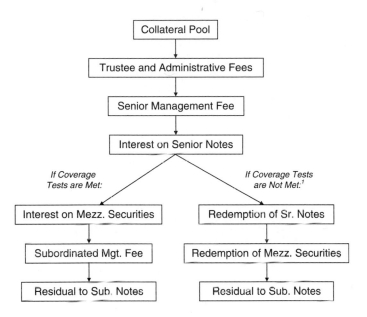

1) If coverage tests are not met, and to the extent not corrected with principal proceeds, the remaining interest proceeds will be used to redeem the most senior notes to bring the structure back into compliance with the coverage tests. Interest on the mezzanine securities may be deferred and compounded if cash flow is not available to pay current interest due.

**EXHIBIT 4** Interest Waterfall of a Sample CDO. *Source*: Sivan Mahadevan (Morgan Stanley), "Structured Credit Insights," April 30, 2008

priority, the mezzanine second, and the equity third. The allocation of cash flows to specific securities is called a "waterfall" (see Exhibits 4 and 5). A waterfall is specified in the CDO's indenture[7] and governs both principal and interest payments.

One may observe that the creation of a CDO is a complex and costly process. Professionals such as bankers, lawyers, rating agencies, accountants, trustees, fund managers, and insurers all charge considerable fees to create and manage a CDO. In other words, the cash coming from the collateral is greater than the sum of the cash paid to all security holders. Professional fees to create and manage the CDO make up the difference.

CDOs are designed to offer asset exposure precisely tailored to the risk that investors desire, and they provide liquidity because they trade daily on the secondary market. This liquidity enables, for example, a finance minister from the Chinese government to gain exposure to the U.S. mortgage market and to buy or sell that exposure at will. However, because CDOs are more complex securities than corporate bonds, they are designed to pay slightly higher interest rates than correspondingly rated corporate bonds.

CDOs enable a bank that specializes in making loans to homeowners to make more loans than its capital would otherwise allow, because the bank can sell its loans to a third party. The bank can therefore originate more loans and take in more origination fees. As a result, consumers have more access to capital, banks can make more loans, and investors

---

[7]An indenture is "the legal agreement between the firm issuing the bond and the bondholders, providing the specific terms of the loan agreement." http://www.financeglossary.net.

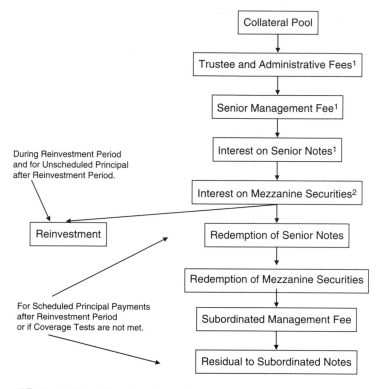

During Reinvestment Period and for Unscheduled Principal after Reinvestment Period.

For Scheduled Principal Payments after Reinvestment Period or if Coverage Tests are not met.

Collateral Pool

Trustee and Administrative Fees[1]

Senior Management Fee[1]

Interest on Senior Notes[1]

Interest on Mezzanine Securities[2]

Reinvestment

Redemption of Senior Notes

Redemption of Mezzanine Securities

Subordinated Management Fee

Residual to Subordinated Notes

1) To the extent not paid by interest proceeds.
2) To the extent senior note coverage tests are met and to the extent not already paid by interest proceeds. If coverage tests are not met, the remaining principal proceeds will be used to redeem the most senior notes to bring the structure back into compliance with the coverage tests.  Interest on the mezzanine securities may be deferred and compounded if cash flow is not available to pay current interest due.

**EXHIBIT 5** Principal Waterfall of a Sample CDO. *Source*: Sivan Mahadevan (Morgan Stanley), "Structured Credit Insights," April 30, 2008

a world away can not only access the consumer loan market but also invest with precisely the level of risk they desire.

The Structured Credit Handbook provides an explanation of investors' nearly insatiable appetite for CDOs:

> Demand for [fixed income] assets is heavily bifurcated, with the demand concentrated at the two ends of the safety spectrum . . . Prior to the securitization boom, the universe of fixed-income instruments issued tended to cluster around the BBB rating, offering neither complete safety nor sizzling returns. For example, the number of AA- and AAA-rated companies is quite small, as is debt issuance of companies rated B or lower. Structured credit technology has evolved essentially in order to match investors' demands with the available profile of fixed-income assets. By issuing CDOs from portfolios of bonds or loans rated A, BBB, or BB, financial intermediaries can create a larger pool of AAA-rated securities and a small unrated or low-rated bucket where almost all the risk is concentrated.[8]

---

[8] Arvind Rajan, Glen McDermott, and Ratul Roy, *The Structured Credit Handbook* (Hoboken, NJ: John Wiley & Sons, 2007), 2.

CDOs have been around for more than twenty years, but their popularity skyrocketed during the late 1990s. CDO issuance nearly doubled in 2005 and then again in 2006, when it topped $500 billion for the first time. "Structured finance" groups at large investment banks (the division responsible for issuing and managing CDOs) became one of the fastest-growing areas on Wall Street. These divisions, along with the investment banking trading desks that made markets in CDOs, contributed to highly successful results for the banking sector during the 2003–2007 boom. Many CDOs became quite liquid due to their size, investor breadth, and rating agency coverage.

## Rating Agencies

Rating agencies helped bring liquidity to the CDO market. They analyzed each tranche of a CDO and assigned ratings accordingly. Equity tranches were often unrated. The rating agencies had limited manpower and needed to gauge the risk on literally thousands of new CDO securities. The agencies also specialized in using historical models to predict risk. Although CDOs had been around for a long time, they did not exist in a significant number until recently. Historical models therefore couldn't possibly capture the full picture. Still, the underlying collateral could be assessed with a strong degree of confidence. After all, banks have been making home loans for hundreds of years. The rating agencies simply had to allocate risk to the appropriate tranche and understand how the loans in the collateral base were correlated with each other—an easy task in theory perhaps, but not in practice.

## Correlation

The most difficult part of valuing a CDO tranche is determining correlation. If loans are uncorrelated, defaults will occur evenly over time and asset diversification can solve most problems. For instance, a housing crisis in California will be isolated from one in New York, so the CDO simply needs to diversify the geographic makeup of its assets in order to offer stable returns. With low correlation, an AAA-rated senior tranche should be safe and the interest rate attached to this tranche should be close to the rate for AAA-rated corporate bonds, or even U.S. treasuries. High correlation, however, creates non-diversifiable risk, in which case the senior tranche has a reasonable likelihood of becoming impaired. Correlation does not affect the price of the CDO in total because the expected value of each individual loan remains the same. Correlation does, however, affect the relative price of each tranche: any increase in the yield of a senior tranche (to compensate for additional correlation) will be offset by a decrease in the yield of the junior tranches.[9]

If a security related to the housing market contained geographically diverse collateral, it was generally assumed to have low correlation. This is because there had not been a nationwide housing crisis in recent history and local downturns had been isolated. As the *Wall Street Journal* reported, "Upbeat mortgage specialists kept repeating that home prices never fall on a national basis or that the Fed could save the market by slashing interest rates."[10] Because of the market's confidence in this assumption, senior tranches typically received very high debt ratings—often AAA—and correspondingly paid low interest rates.

---

[9]Todd Buys, Karina Hirai, Wendy Kam, Charles Lalanne, and Kazuhiro Shibata, "Correlation of Risky Assets and the Effect on CDO Pricing in the Credit Crunch of 2007," student paper, Kellogg School of Management, June 5, 2008.

[10]Gregory Zuckerman, "Trader Made Billions on Subprime," *Wall Street Journal*, January 15, 2008.

**EXHIBIT 6**    LBO-Related Leveraged Loans

| Estimated new-issue backlog has declined since the start of the year | | | | |
|---|---|---|---|---|
| | Volumes in billions ($) | | | |
| | Total | Pro rata | Institutional Loans | Bonds |
| **Original Pipeline-June 2007** | **338.0** | | **227.4** | **110.6** |
| 2007 Completed Pipeline | 55.0 | | 33.0 | 22.0 |
| 2007 Cancelled | 51.0 | | 34.9 | 16.1 |
| **End of 2007 Pipeline** | **232.0** | | **159.5** | **72.5** |
| 2008 Completed Pipeline | 29.4 | | 17.3 | 12.1 |
| 2008 Estimated private sales | 15.0 | | 15.0 | |
| 2008 Cancelled/Uncertain | 35.0 | | 22.2 | 12.8 |
| Remaining Pipeline | 152.7 | 35.0 | 70.0 | 47.7 |
| **Remaining Pipeline excluding pro rata** | **117.7** | | | |
| **Hexion/Huntsman** | **11.9** | | **6.0** | **6.0** |
| **Pipeline excluding Huntsman** | **105.8** | **35.0** | **64.0** | **41.7** |

Note: All information is based on public news and analyst estimates

Source: JP Morgan

*Note*: This backlog tracks LBO-related leveraged loans on deals that have been underwritten by major investment banks but have not yet closed
*Source*: Peter Acciavatti (JP Morgan), "Midyear 2008 High Yield and Leveraged Loan Outlook and Strategy," June 28, 2008

# CDO Market Evolution

Although the market for new CDO origination was essentially dead by mid-2008, hedge funds considered whether it would resurface. After all, CDOs provided liquidity and unique access to risk that investors would continue to seek. It would take some time for banks to work through their existing backlog of underwritten but unsold new-issue leveraged loans, but they had made significant progress over the past year: the original backlog of $338 billion was now down to $105 billion (see Exhibit 6). Once this backlog was clear, would CDO origination slowly ramp up again? What strategies should hedge funds use to be ahead of the market?

    While some funds thought that the market for new CDO origination would soon return, others had doubts. Many CDO investors, especially hedge funds, relied on leverage to earn their targeted absolute returns. For instance, in 2006 and the first half of 2007, an investor might have purchased the senior tranche of a CDO even though it only yielded fifty basis points above the London Interbank Offered Rate (LIBOR). However, the investor would then have leveraged the investment 25× in order to earn a return commensurate with the equity tranche, or 1,250 basis points above LIBOR. Because of this practice, some investors feared that the CDO origination market would not return until investment banks provided their hedge fund clients with ample and cheap debt funding, as was the case before the summer of 2007—a practice that might not return for a considerable time.

# Bank Debt and the Cov-Lite Craze

The market for corporate bank debt was similar to the housing bubble in at least one respect: frothy credit markets and a push for financial innovation spawned lending practices that strayed

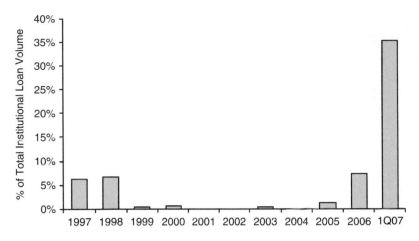

**EXHIBIT 7** Explosion in Covenant-Lite Loan Issuance. *Source*: Morgan Stanley, "Focusing on Recoveries," April 11, 2007

widely from historical norms. Fueled by the LBO (leveraged buyout) boom, covenant-lite corporate bank debt allowed companies to operate with no maintenance covenants[11] for leverage (debt/EBITDA) or interest coverage (EBITDA/cash interest) ratios. Sponsors (LBO firms) demanded loose terms by playing lenders against each other and by using their clout as enormous fee generators for the bank. By mid-2007 covenant-lite deals had ballooned and were increasingly considered the norm (see Exhibit 7). As in the residential mortgage market, securitization also played a major role.

Lenders knew they could pass off large portions of weak covenant-lite loans by syndicating them into CLOs (collateralized loan obligations). These CLOs were bought by third parties who often did not bother to do the same level of diligence as would a bank that intended to hold the loan to maturity. Investors often analyzed loan information at a summary level only, instead of reviewing each loan individually. This practice masked the problems of the worst loans, many of which were LBO-backed covenant-lite deals. Rating agencies often gave investors a false sense of security and helped them to justify performing scant due diligence. A study by Fitch indicates that covenant-lite loans were nearly 50 percent more prevalent in CLOs than in the market as a whole.[12]

Further complicating matters, PIK toggles enabled a company simply to add additional debt instead of paying interest in cash. "Equity cures" were also permitted, so in cases where a company did have maintenance covenants, a technical default could be "cured" by a small equity contribution that would be added to bank-defined EBITDA.[13] As the *Wall Street Journal* reported, "Bankers began marketing debt deals for companies that . . . didn't have comfortable cash flow.

---

[11]Maintenance covenants are specified in a loan indenture and measured quarterly on an LTM (last twelve months) basis. The leverage covenant typically specifies a certain ratio of debt to LTM EBITDA above which the company cannot go. The coverage covenant specifies a certain ratio of LTM EBITDA to LTM cash interest below which the company cannot go. Most bank loans contained covenants such as these before 2006 and the first half of 2007.

[12]Fitch Ratings, "CLOs More Concentrated in Shareholder-Friendly and Covenant-Light Loans," December 21, 2006.

[13]EBITDA (earnings before interest, taxes, depreciation, and amortization) is not a standardized term defined by generally accepted accounting principles (GAAP). However, it is a common measure of cash flow used by banks to determine whether a borrowing company is in compliance with its covenants. A common "maintenance" covenant states that total debt cannot exceed a specified multiple of the company's last twelve months of EBITDA.

There was Chrysler, burning cash rather than producing it. And there was First Data Corp., whose post-takeover cash flow would barely cover interest payments and capital spending."[14]

The downturn rippled throughout the financial industry starting in mid-2007. It put a premium on liquidity and drove down the prices of leveraged securities in general and leveraged bank loans in particular. Bank loans were hit particularly hard because of the large inventory held by investment banks, which needed to liquidate investment holdings in order to improve their balance sheets.

The bank loan market bottomed during February 2008 (see Exhibit 8), before coming back somewhat by the summer of 2008. Exhibit 9 shows that in order to justify bank debt valuations, an investor needed to assume that default rates would hit levels not seen since the Great Depression and stay there until maturity of the loans. With this in mind, some investors increased their exposure to the bank loan market. Non-traditional players such as private equity firms entered the market, often purchasing loans in large private transactions directly from banks rather than on the open market. The Blackstone Group reported that it achieved a 20 percent return on a $7.8 billion investment in leveraged loans that it made in Q2 2008.[15]

Instead of investing in the overall bank loan market, some hedge funds were more intrigued with covenant-lite loans. Although new cov-lite loans were unlikely to be brought to market, many existing cov-lite loans were heavily traded. Cov-lite loans, it was thought, would have limited near-term defaults because companies would keep operating until they ran out of cash. However, once those defaults ultimately occurred, the question is whether recovery rates would

**EXHIBIT 8** Bank Loan Prices During 2008. *Note:* LCDX 9 is a standardized, tradable tranche of the North American loan credit default swap index. *Source:* Markit LCDX Analytics, http://www.markit.com/information/products/category/indices/lcdx/analytics.html.

[14]Greg Ip and Jon Hilsenrath, "Debt Bomb: Inside the 'Subprime' Mortgage Debacle," *Wall Street Journal*, August 7, 2007.

[15]Pierre Paulden and Jason Kelly, "Blackstone Gains 20 Percent Buying $7.8 Billion of LBO Loans," *Bloomberg News*, August 6, 2008.

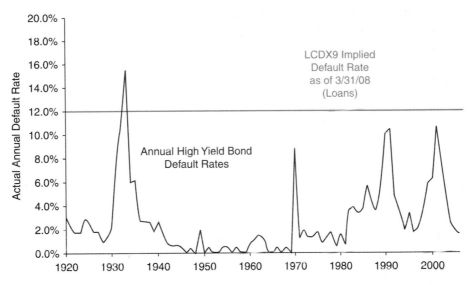

**EXHIBIT 9** Historical Annual Default Rates. *Source*: Kellogg student/faculty presentation by Ares Management, Spring 2008

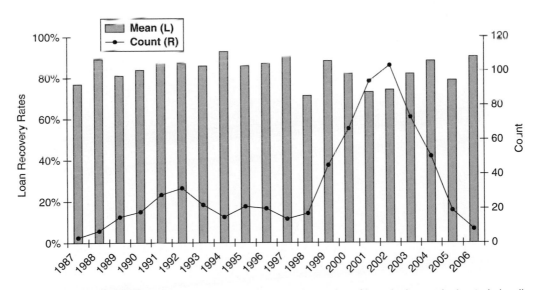

**EXHIBIT 10** Loan Recovery Rates by Default Year. *Note*: Count means the number of loans in the sample size. Includes all defaulted loans, not just those that were classified as leveraged loans when they were originated. *Source*: Emery, Cantor, Keisman, and Ou, (Moody's), "Moody's Ultimate Recovery Database," April 2007

be significantly lower than the historical average of 82 percent (see Exhibit 10). Since cov-lite loans did not exist in large numbers until 2005 and there have been no defaults of cov-lite loans in the past, it is difficult for investors to know what recovery rates to use in their valuations. Cov-lite loans trade at a discount to cov-heavy (traditional) loans, and this spread continues to widen (see Exhibit 11). Funds who bet that there would be a flight to quality away from cov-lite loans have profited handsomely. The exhibit also shows that, paradoxically, cov-lite loans have lower nominal coupons than cov-heavy loans. This is because lending practices were very loose during 2006 and the first half of 2007, when most of the cov-lite deals were originated.

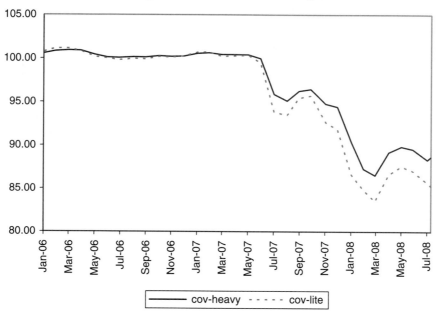

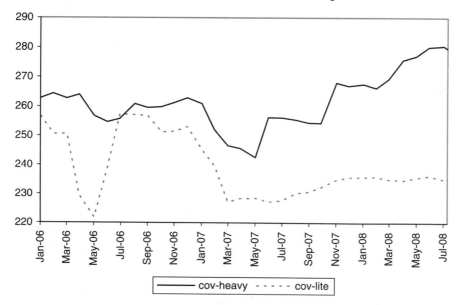

**EXHIBIT 11** *Source:* S&P LCD, August 11, 2008, author analysis

Although the spread widened, investors still profited by taking a position that the spread would widen further. As of August 11, 2008, B-rated cov-lite loans traded at prices 336 basis points below cov-heavy loans. To analyze whether the spread should widen even more, one must make assumptions about future default rates and recovery rates (see Exhibit 12).

Some funds believed that the best way to play cov-lite bank debt was through a relative value trade. One can look at the yields on secured cov-lite bank loans and compare them with the yields on unsecured bonds of the same company. If the two yields are close, a long secured bank loan/short unsecured bond trading opportunity may exist because bank debt will typically recover more than bonds in a bankruptcy. As companies become more risky, the spread between bonds and secured bank debt of the same company should widen (see Exhibit 13). In such capital structure arbitrage trades, investors are betting on the difference in recovery rates among various securities. Default rates will be identical because the two securities are issued by the same company.

Exhibit 13 includes all companies that have (1) first lien cov-lite bank debt, (2) unsecured bonds, (3) easily accessible prices, and (4) bank debt that will mature prior to bonds. Companies on the right side of the line represent long bank debt/short bond opportunities. This position is especially compelling for companies that also have low absolute interest rates (NRG Holdco and Hawker Beechcraft). Companies on the left side represent the reverse strategy. Investors could

**EXHIBIT 12   Default Rate and Recovery Rate Discount Necessary to Justify Cov-Lite Valuations**

| Difference in Recovery Rate | Annual Default Rate | | | | | |
| --- | --- | --- | --- | --- | --- | --- |
| | 3% | 4% | 5% | 6% | 7% | 8% |
| −5% | 244 | 264 | 283 | 303 | 323 | 343 |
| −10% | 303 | 343 | 383 | 423 | 463 | 503 |
| 15% | 363 | 423 | 483 | 543 | 603 | 663 |
| −20% | 423 | 503 | 583 | 663 | 743 | 822 |
| −25% | 483 | 583 | 683 | 783 | 882 | 982 |
| −30% | 543 | 663 | 783 | 902 | 1,022 | 1,142 |
| −35% | 603 | 743 | 882 | 1,022 | 1,162 | 1,302 |
| −40% | 663 | 822 | 982 | 1,142 | 1,302 | 1,461 |
| −45% | 723 | 902 | 1,082 | 1,262 | 1,441 | 1,621 |
| −50% | 783 | 982 | 1,182 | 1,381 | 1,581 | 1,781 |

Basis point discount from non-cov-lite loans.

Assumptions:   8% discount rate
　　　　　　　5-year loan life
　　　　　　　46 bp avg. coupon discount for cov-lite

*Note*: Shaded combinations of default rates and recovery rate differentials are above the current 336 bps average spread between cov-lite and cov-heavy loans, indicating that a wider spread is necessary to justify assumptions

*Source*: Stephen Carlson, "Covenant-Lite Bank Loans: What Will Be Their Implications in a Period of Significant Defaults, and Are Markets Correctly Pricing the Risk?" student paper, Kellogg School of Management, August 2008

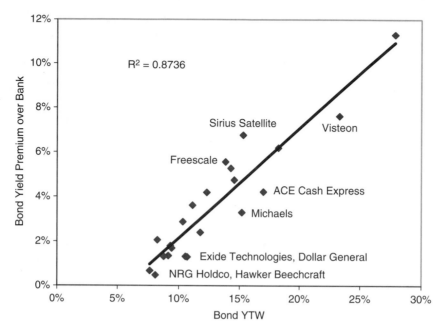

**EXHIBIT 13** Bank vs. Bond Yield Premium on Companies with Covenant-Lite Bank Debt. *Note:* YTW = Yield to Worst. The lowest potential yield that can be received on a bond without the issuer actually defaulting. The yield to worst is calculated by making worst-case scenario assumptions on the issue by calculating the returns that would be received if provisions, including prepayment, call or sinking fund, are used by the issuer. This metric is used to evaluate the worst-case scenario for yield to help investors manage risks and ensure that specific income requirements will still be met even in the worst scenarios. Yield to worst is calculated on all possible call dates. It is assumed that prepayment occurs if the bond has call or put provisions and the issuer can offer a lower coupon rate based on current market rates. If market rates are higher than the current yield of a bond, the yield to worst calculation will assume no prepayments are made, and yield to worst will equal the yield to maturity. The assumption is made that prevailing rates are static when making the calculation. The yield to worst will be the lowest of yield to maturity or yield to call (if the bond has prepayment provisions); yield to worst may be the same as yield to maturity but never higher. Definition from Investopedia, http://www.investopedia.com/terms/y/yieldtoworst.asp. *Source:* Stephen Carlson, "Covenant-Lite Bank Loans: What Will Be Their Implications in a Period of Significant Defaults, and Are Markets Correctly Pricing the Risk?" student paper, Kellogg School of Management, August 2008

also follow a related strategy by analyzing second-lien bank debt and unsecured bonds in the same company. In a bankruptcy, second-lien debt is paid off before unsecured bonds up to the point at which the collateral value is recovered (see Exhibit 14). After that point, second-lien debt has the same priority as other unsecured creditors. Therefore, in normal circumstances, second-lien debt should have a lower yield than unsecured bonds.

This anomaly and many others exist because large holders of bank debt (including many troubled banks that have large investment banking arms) have been forced to sell bank debt for regulatory or liquidity reasons. Bonds, on the other hand, are less frequently held by banks, so the bond market has consequently not experienced the same forced selling pressure that the secured bank debt market has seen. What can hedge funds do to exploit this opportunity? What are the risks they face if they make the wrong bet? How can they best set up trades to hedge their exposure? What is the catalyst that will bring the market back to normal levels? Hedge funds that can accurately answer these questions stand to gain handsomely.

## EXHIBIT 14 Leveraged Loans and Junk Bonds

### LOANS

The bank loans referenced in this case are leveraged loans. A bank loan is classified as leveraged if any of the following occur:[16]

- The company to whom the loan is being made has outstanding debt rated below investment grade, meaning below Baa3/BBB– from Moody's and S&P
- The company's debt/EBITDA ratio is 3.0 times or greater
- The loan bears a coupon of +125 bps or more over LIBOR

Leveraged loans generally grant lenders collateral in all (or most) assets of a company. In some leveraged loans, there is an agreement that separates lenders into two classes: first lien and second lien. These two classes agree on contractual subordination terms of the second lien to the first lien.

Some leveraged loans may have traditional, full covenants, whereas others may be covenant-lite.

### BONDS (JUNK)

(Junk) bonds are typically unsecured, and therefore have a lower claim on the assets of a company in a bankruptcy scenario. Although each bankruptcy is different and can have its own idiosyncrasies, bondholders in bankrupt companies typically receive much lower recovery rates than do holders of bank loans. The mean recovery rate for bank loans is 82 percent while the mean recovery rate for senior unsecured bonds (the most common type of bond) is 38 percent.[17]

---

[16]Timothy Aker (Prudential), "Leveraged Loans: Capturing Investor Attention," July 2006.

[17]Emery, Cantor, Keisman, and Ou (Moody's), "Moody's Ultimate Recovery Database," April 2007.

# Kmart, Sears, and ESL: How a Hedge Fund Became One of the World's Largest Retailers

## The Unusual Weekend

January 11, 2003, was the weirdest Saturday that Eddie Lampert could remember. Most Greenwich billionaires do not spend their weekends lying in bathtubs in cheap motels eating cold chicken. Unfortunately, the setting was not only odd; it was quite ominous. Lampert was fully clothed, blindfolded, and handcuffed.

The previous day, Lampert, 42, had sat in his office at ESL Investments, the multibillion-dollar hedge fund he controlled. The fund's clients included savvy institutions and famous names such as Michael Dell and David Geffen, but Lampert himself was the single largest investor. He had spent much of his time that Friday poring over documents related to Kmart's Chapter 11 bankruptcy. Lampert had access to experienced attorneys, bankers, and accountants who specialized in restructurings, but he insisted on personally understanding every detail of the complicated swap of defaulted debt for new equity. On first glance, Lampert thought he smelled a great opportunity that rival retailers and private equity shops were missing. He had already accumulated a sizeable amount of Kmart's defaulted debt for less than half of its face value. But before he really took the plunge and started buying larger amounts in the biggest trade of his career, he wanted to study the upside potential and downside protection in excruciating detail. After all, it was his reputation, and largely his money, on the line.

Lampert discovered within hours that money and reputation are not the most serious assets that one can have on the line, as he took an unexpected plunge of a different sort. When he left his low-rise Greenwich office building and walked to his car in the parking garage around 7:30 p.m., four men unknown to Lampert approached, and one suddenly drew a pistol. Lampert soon found himself locked in the trunk of a car that had been parked near his. Presumably, Kmart's bankruptcy was the last thing on his mind as he tried to determine which direction the vehicle was headed on Interstate 95. He would soon have to apply his considerable intelligence to negotiations of a different kind.

## Flash Forward: November 2004

Lampert had always been somewhat secretive and tried to avoid much press coverage for ESL Investments, but since talking his kidnappers into letting him go free in exchange for a small amount of money, he had become extremely tight-lipped. (Lampert never actually turned over the money, and his inept kidnappers later found themselves in police custody after using Lampert's credit card to order pizza.)

Despite Lampert's desire to stay out of the limelight, he was not the sort of person to turn down a compelling investment, even if it meant an explosion of press coverage. Since his kidnapping, Lampert had gone from being a talented manager of a hedge fund to also serving as chairman of Kmart Holdings, the new company that emerged from the bankruptcy of the venerable retailer. Then, on November 17, 2004, Lampert announced that he had reached an agreement with the board of Sears to acquire the famous company for approximately $11 billion in cash or Kmart stock. The financial community was surprised, and research reports from Wall Street analysts revealed a wide divergence of opinion on the wisdom of the combination. Lampert's preference for a low profile became hopeless as it became clear that, despite his day job managing a hedge fund that did not even have a Web site, he would soon be the chairman of the nation's third largest retailer. *BusinessWeek* featured Lampert in several major articles, following a cover story whose copy deadline apparently pre-dated the announcement of the acquisition by days if not hours. The title posed the flattering question: "The Next Warren Buffett?"[1]

## Case Focus

The idea of a hedge fund manager becoming chairman of Kmart and Sears was laughable just a decade ago. This case examines some of the notable and rapid changes in the capital markets over the last twenty years that have made such an idea a reality. In particular, the case explores the emergence of financial buyers (principally private equity funds and hedge funds) as strong competitors to strategic buyers (companies buying other companies in the same industry) in the mergers and acquisitions market. The case presents two key questions: First, as a strictly financial buyer, should ESL have acquired a controlling stake in Kmart's defaulted debt in 2002? Second, as a largely strategic buyer, should Kmart under ESL's control have acquired Sears (announced in November 2004 and consummated in March 2005)?

## The Rise and Fall of Kmart

Kmart was founded in 1899 as S. S. Kresge Company, and at various times in the last twenty years had owned Borders Books, Walden Book, The Sports Authority, and OfficeMax. After mismanaging its Internet efforts and finding itself unable to keep its supply chain as low-cost as rivals Wal-Mart and Target, Kmart by mid-2000 was suffering from stagnant same-store sales, comparatively low sales per square foot, and complaints from customers that the stores were disorganized and run-down. Wal-Mart and Kmart each had $32 billion in sales in 1990; since that time Kmart's sales had been essentially flat, while Wal-Mart's had grown to over $250 billion.[2] (See Exhibit 1 for sales comparisons.) One of the *Wall Street Journal*'s epitaphs for Kmart remarked on the decades-long role played by Wal-Mart in the demise:

> In the late 1970s, Wal-Mart's sales were 5 percent of Kmart's; it had 150 stores to Kmart's 1,000 or so, mostly in urban locations. Wal-Mart, meanwhile, invaded rural America, where it quietly perfected a format of using technology to reduce inventory,

---

[1] *BusinessWeek*, November 22, 2004.

[2] COMPUSTAT database.

*keep shelves stocked and offer the lowest prices. By the time it began meeting Kmart head on, Wal-Mart enjoyed a significant price advantage that a series of Kmart executives failed to overcome.*[3]

The recession of 2001, especially following the 9/11 attacks, hit Kmart very hard. CEO Charles Conaway instituted price cuts to match Wal-Mart on selected goods in early 2001 and then decided on a bold holiday season strategy: Kmart would dramatically cut its advertising budget and use the savings to match Wal-Mart's low prices on almost everything. The plan was executed; the results were disastrous. With reduced marketing, Kmart did not draw many new customers. Those that did come were surprised and gleeful at the reduced prices. In December 2001, with the stock trading below $5 per share (see Exhibit 2), Kmart sold millions of items

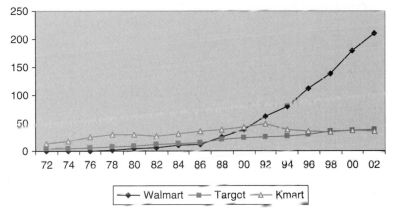

**EXHIBIT 1** Kmart, Target and Walmart Sales, 1972–2001 ($ in 2001 billions). *Sources:* COMPUSTAT database; Bureau of Labor Statistics, author's calculations.

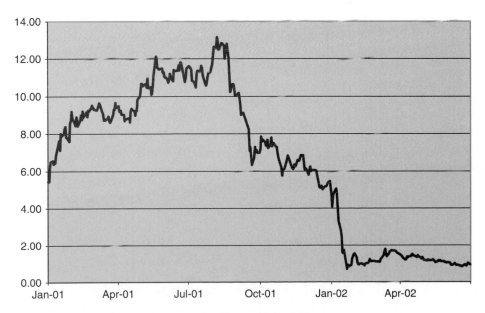

**EXHIBIT 2** Kmart Daily Closing Prices, January 2001–July 2002. *Source:* Bloomberg.

---

[3]"Kmart to Buy Sears for $11.5 Billion," *Wall Street Journal*, November 18, 2004.

below cost, and below the already marked-down value recorded as inventory on its balance sheet. As details on the scope of the holiday season losses were still emerging, Kmart faced a cash crunch, and after a vendor announced Kmart had fallen behind on payments, the 103-year-old company filed for Chapter 11 bankruptcy on January 22, 2002. In early March, the company fired Conaway and set ambitious plans to emerge from bankruptcy by July 2003.

Not long afterwards, hedge funds specializing in trading distressed debt started studying Kmart's assets, but none of them had the capital or the confidence to amass a controlling stake in the defaulted bonds. With the company in bankruptcy, shareholders had lost all of their investment. The question that remained was the value of Kmart's assets now belonging exclusively to its creditors, including bond holders. Clearly, the bonds would never be paid off at their face value, but holders would have a clear legal claim on assets, with each creditor's share depending on the number of bonds held and the level of seniority of the bond covenants.

## Bankruptcy and Inefficient Financial Markets

In most bankruptcy cases, bond holders receive either cash from sale of assets in the event of liquidation or equity in the new company that successfully emerges from bankruptcy. In either case, each step of the process generally requires both court approval and broad agreement among the bondholders. The complexities that arise from these procedures make it very difficult for mainstream investment managers who focus on traditional equity valuation and credit spread analysis to understand the risks and rewards sufficiently well to include defaulted debt in their portfolios. Furthermore, many pension fund and mutual fund managers are prohibited by the guidelines of their funds to own bankrupt assets, or in some cases to own any "junk" or "high-yield" securities, those bonds for which the ratings agencies Standard & Poor's and Moody's have signified the issuer has a higher probability of bankruptcy.

The difficulty of analyzing competing claims on assets, forging agreements with other bondholders, and satisfying a bankruptcy court gave rise to a small industry of bankruptcy specialists. Twenty years ago, such specialists were largely attorneys who found themselves in high demand when corporations considered snapping up assets at cheap prices following the bankruptcy of a competitor or a company that had a strong position in an adjacent market. Acquiring assets during a bankruptcy was seen as just one piece of a corporation's mergers and acquisitions strategy. Bankruptcy was considered an opportunistic time to acquire businesses that had strong synergies with existing, healthy lines. Since most companies in the same industry experienced the same business cycle, however, the timing of a rival's bankruptcy often found the industry's survivors in a weak position and unable or unwilling to commit cash to an acquisition. This timing mismatch encouraged financial buyer interest in bankruptcy-related activity.

## Financial Buyers vs. Strategic Buyers

Among Warren Buffett's many skills evident in the 1960s and 1970s was the ability to "keep his powder dry" and build up cash for deployment in a counter-cyclical manner in several different industries. Thus, when companies were either bankrupt or distressed, Buffett was often the only player who could commit cash on short notice to acquire cheap assets. In many cases, these assets did not have any synergies with Buffett's other holdings. In these instances, Buffett was a pure *financial* buyer, as opposed to a *strategic* buyer. Despite the fact that strategic buyers should theoretically have been willing to offer a higher price for the assets because of the synergies that would come from merging them with similar operations, those bidders found themselves without the ability to acquire at the moment when the assets were available at the most attractive price. On the other hand, pension funds, endowments, and mutual fund managers always had cash to deploy and theoretically should have been able to match Buffett on price, but these managers had neither the expertise, nor in many cases the flexibility, to acquire large, illiquid, and complex assets.

Eddie Lampert's transition from a hedge fund manager to the chairman of Kmart and acquirer of Sears was an example of a financial buyer who had also become a strategic buyer. In 2002, with cash positions under pressure and risk appetites very low, potential corporate buyers of Kmart's assets preferred to stay away from the bankruptcy proceedings, despite the many synergies that might have been available in combining Kmart with another big box retailer. ESL had large holdings in several public companies, but Lampert also had lots of cash on hand that could be deployed opportunistically, regardless of what part of the cycle the macro economy or the retail industry was in.

## Private Equity

Private equity is usually defined to include venture capital (VC) funds, leveraged buy-out (LBO) funds, and mezzanine funds. VC funds seek out small, early-stage companies that are generally several years away from having the size and track record to launch a successful public equity offering. VC funds thus pursue a portfolio of high-risk, high-reward investments, with the full understanding that the majority of their individual investments may fail. Mezzanine funds, a very small portion of the private equity market, typically provide subordinated debt financing to growth companies that require relatively small amounts of debt that is junior to senior debt.

LBO funds have a very different profile from VC funds in that they seek to acquire mature businesses that they can use as vehicles to produce an attractive medium-term return on investment. LBO shops have been able to produce attractive returns because of two market inefficiencies. First, despite many attempts to bring them together, the incentives of managers and shareholders have never been perfectly aligned in public companies. Shareholder activism takes an immense amount of energy and organization, and the more widely dispersed a company's ownership is, the more difficult it is for shareholders to make sure that managers are always acting in the best interest of the owners. Thus, publicly owned companies may in some cases not be managed as effectively as private companies. Or, to put it differently, managers may be maximizing something other than profit. For instance, managers may be maximizing employment, executive compensation and perks, or perhaps even political clout. By taking a public company private and either directly managing it or closely supervising its management, LBO funds believe they can return a company to its *raison d'être* by cutting costs and running the business for cash.

The second inefficiency that LBOs claim to address is that certain types of companies, even when well-managed, are perennially undervalued by the public equity markets. There are certain fixed costs associated with being a public company, including ongoing required reports to shareholders and disclosures to the Securities and Exchange Commission (SEC), National Association of Securities Dealers (NASD), New York Stock Exchange (NYSE), and other regulatory bodies. Such costs have increased dramatically due to more aggressive regulators and stock exchanges on top of new accounting demands following passage of the Sarbanes-Oxley bill in 2002.

These costs are borne disproportionately by shareholders in smaller companies. In addition, one LBO manager argues, "Many mid-cap companies have begun to feel orphaned by the public equity markets and have a difficult time attracting research coverage and investor interest."[4]

LBO funds have been notably active in the market for mergers and acquisitions (M&A) in recent years. During the recession of 2001 and its aftermath, traditional corporate strategic acquirers to a large degree shunned M&A as a potential avenue for growth and efficiency, and their shareholders for the most part seemed to approve of this newfound caution after the obvious excesses that characterized some of the acquisitions of the late 1990s. LBO funds, on the other hand, found themselves flush with cash during this period due to their increasing acceptance among institutional investors. The private equity industry had still not deployed the large amount of cash that had been raised during the period 1997–2000, and the decline in new LBO funds during 2001–2002 was much less dramatic than the overall slowdown in the M&A market. Overall, the amount of funds raised by private equity sponsors from 1999–2004 was comparable to the total amount raised by the industry in its entire history up to 1998. (See Exhibit 3.)

When an LBO fund seeks to take a public company private, or to acquire a large division of a public company that seeks a divestiture, the "buy-out" of the entity is generally done with an infusion of some equity from the fund's cash reserves, but that thin equity slice is stretched over a large asset with borrowed funds. By tapping the high-yield bond market, LBO funds are often able to leverage their equity infusion many times in order to complete large transactions with mostly borrowed money. By setting up separate legal entities, the LBO funds ensure that they cannot be held liable (beyond the loss of their equity investment) if companies under their control ultimately fail. High-yield bond investors are willing to lend money to these entities because they earn a high interest rate, the LBO funds have a good track record of managing businesses for

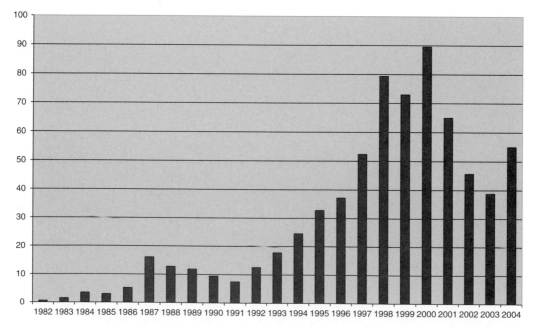

**EXHIBIT 3** U.S. Private Equity Annual Inflow of New Funds ($ in billions). *Source:* Venture Economics and *The Private Equity Analyst,* cited in Finnegan presentation.

---

[4]Paul Finnegan presentation at Kellogg Private Equity Conference, March 2005.

cash, and in the event of business failure and default the bondholders will at least recognize some value as they will become the new owners of the company's assets.

In addition to experiencing only a limited slowdown in new commitments of capital, LBO funds over the period 2001–2004 benefited from historically low interest rates. While the reduction of short-term and long-term rates from 2001–2003 was symptomatic of the general economic malaise that caused potential strategic buyers to retreat from M&A activity, it was beneficial for LBO shops because of their reliance on borrowing to fund acquisitions that cost many times their available cash. (See Exhibit 4 and Exhibit 5.) In effect, lowered interest rates meant that LBO funds operated in the M&A market with a much higher leverage multiplier.

## Hedge Funds

The line between some types of hedge funds and LBO funds blurred in the last few years, but most hedge fund strategies remained quite distinct from the LBO investing model. Many hedge funds could be thought of as unrestricted mutual funds. Regulators allowed hedge funds to operate outside the limitations of the Investment Company Act of 1940 as long as they did not market their services to, or accept money from, small or unsophisticated investors. In 2005 the SEC was planning new regulations for the industry (the scope of which remained unclear), but for many years hedge funds had been completely unregulated, except that they could accept funds only from large institutions or accredited individual investors who met a high standard of net worth. The regulatory philosophy regarding the hedge fund industry in the United States had essentially been that rich and sophisticated investors were free to have their money managed by whomever they wished and to choose any level of risk that suited their appetite. Small investors, on the other hand, were protected and well-served by the myriad of regulations that covered mutual fund managers.

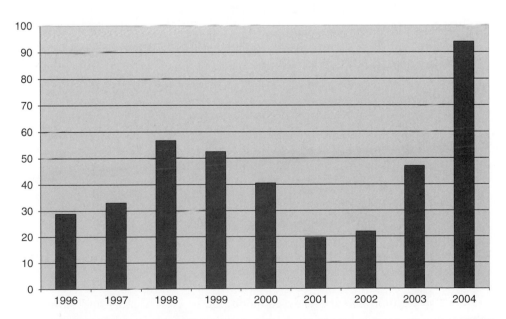

**EXHIBIT 4** Value of Completed LBO Transactions ($ in billions). *Source:* Standard & Poor's, cited in Finnegan presentation.

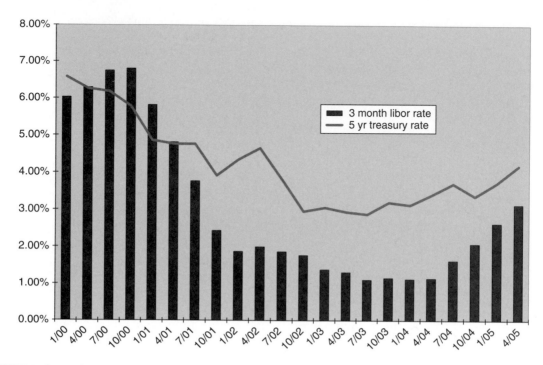

**EXHIBIT 5** Libor and Treasury Rates, 2000–2005. *Source:* Bloomberg.

The freedom of hedge fund managers from "long-only" decisions that face traditional managers has given rise to many different investing strategies that are unavailable to mutual funds. The most basic variation on an equity mutual fund is a "long-short" equity hedge fund, in which managers take long positions in stocks that they like and also take short positions in stocks that they feel will decline over the short- or medium-term. Most such funds hope to be market-neutral, which is to say that since they hold long and short exposures in roughly equal amounts, their returns over time will have limited correlation to the stock market at large. This suits the goals of many of such funds' investors since one of the reasons investors shift assets to hedge funds is because of their preference for absolute return rather than relative return. Long-short managers are expected to deliver a positive return every year, regardless of whether the stock market goes up or down.

The early years of the hedge fund industry, before institutional money starting pouring in since the early 1990s, was dominated by long-short and other hedging strategies, so the name "hedge fund" stuck even as it became a misnomer for many funds carrying that classification. It is important to note that the main distinction between hedge funds and mutual funds is not that all hedge funds are hedged, or that mutual funds cannot hedge any of their investments. In fact, some mutual funds are allowed to buy put options to protect (hedge) against some of their downside risk, or to sell covered call options to generate income in return for giving up some of the potential upside in their investments. The distinction between the two types of funds is simply whether or not they are open to the general public, and therefore whether they are subject to large amounts of regulation. Hedge funds' investing styles range from completely hedged, low-risk strategies that seek simply to generate returns of 6 to 8 percent in any market condition to unhedged, highly leveraged speculation on currencies, commodities, or even weather and natural disasters.

Hedge funds on average do not carry any more risk (as measured by standard deviation of returns over time) than the average equity mutual fund, but no mutual fund manager would be allowed to take the risks undertaken by the small minority of hedge funds that carry very high risk but offer very high potential rewards. For instance, in 1992 George Soros, head of the Quantum Fund, became known as "the man who broke the Bank of England" when he borrowed at least $10 billion to short the British pound while buying German marks, betting that Great Britain would eventually be forced to remove itself from the European Monetary System. When the size of his bets forced British officials to admit that their stated policies were unsustainable, the Quantum Fund made a quick profit of more than $1 billion. While such hedge fund trades capture headlines, they are not the norm for an industry in which most funds market themselves by pointing out that their historical returns exhibit less volatility than the stock market.

Hedge fund strategies that bear limited correlation to the broad stock and bond markets include convertible arbitrage, risk arbitrage, and distressed debt trading. Convertible arbitrage involves investing in corporate debt that is convertible into a company's stock and usually selling short common stock in the same company, trying to find an arbitrage between the value of two different securities issued by the same corporation, or else trying through constant readjustment of the position to realize the "volatility" or "optionality" value embedded in the convertible security. Risk arbitrage involves betting on whether announced mergers or acquisitions will be consummated as planned. By taking long positions in a target company and short positions in a would-be acquirer, a trader is taking the view that an acquisition will go ahead, because the spread in the price of the two company's common stock will reflect some possibility of the deal falling apart until it actually happens and the spread narrows to the exact terms laid out in the acquisition agreement. Traders realize that they cannot know for sure what will happen in the future, but they translate the spread in prices into the market's opinion of the implied probability of the deal going through. Then they can do their own estimation of the probability of deal success based on all of the available facts and potential complications such as shareholder proxy votes, anti-trust concerns, or even volatile personalities in the executive suites of the acquirer or the target. If, for example, the market believes there is a 70 percent chance of success, but the trader believes it is closer to 50 percent or to 90 percent, the trader will take a position to exploit the difference.

For many years, hedge funds active in the distressed arena tried to buy defaulted or near-default bonds and then resell them weeks or months later at a profit. While managers of such funds felt they had the expertise sufficient to risk capital in the complicated and esoteric world of bankruptcy, they were generally looking for exit strategies by reselling distressed bonds at a profit as a company moved to the later stages of restructuring. This stands in contrast to some current hedge fund investors who are attracted to restructurings because of the potential to acquire longer-term control over attractive assets. The blurring of the line between LBO and hedge funds began when hedge funds specializing in bankruptcy started hanging onto their distressed investments through the entire restructuring process, leaving them with substantial, and sometimes controlling, stakes in companies when upon emergence from bankruptcy bondholders' claims are transformed into equity in the new entity.

## ESL: The Hedge Fund That Could Not Be Categorized

ESL Investments, so named after the initials of its manager, Edward S. Lampert, had always been an atypical hedge fund in that it tended to buy big chunks of companies' common stock and then stick with its investments for a few years at a time. ESL for the most part did not pursue short-term trading strategies, and it also did not specialize in distressed debt. Instead, Lampert hewed closer to the line of Warren Buffett in acquiring substantial but noncontrolling stakes in public companies that he perceived could provide an attractive return. In some important respects, however, he differed from Buffett. First, Lampert tended to buy stakes in companies that were in worse shape than those Buffett favored. Buffett acquired unhealthy companies only if he was going to take full control and use the assets as springboards for other investments. As far as minority stakes in public companies went, Buffett bought stakes in such companies as Coca Cola and Gillette because he believed they had great management and excellent long-term prospects.

Two of Warren Buffett's most famous quotes show Lampert's deviation from the Buffett model. Buffett wrote that "it's far better to buy a wonderful company at a fair price than a fair company at a wonderful price." Buffett also said many times over the years that his "favorite holding period is forever." Lampert, since leaving a plum job working for Robert Rubin in risk arbitrage at Goldman Sachs, had shown himself very willing to take minority positions in fair companies selling at a discount in order to benefit from potential improvements in operating businesses. While certainly having a much longer holding period than most of his hedge fund peers, he had also shown no indication of preferring unlimited holding periods. Many of his investments had been in companies that were limping along, neither near death nor extremely successful, where management was able to respond with energy and action to his recommendations.

## 2002–2003 Decision: Should ESL Seek to Gain Control of Kmart during Bankruptcy?

ESL, as a hedge fund investing on behalf of its clients, should pursue a single goal: to maximize return on investments in any market condition without unacceptable levels of volatility. In 2002, ESL was a financial buyer seeking to earn high returns from a Kmart acquisition despite having no synergies with other investments.

For years before its bankruptcy filing, Kmart had been consistently beaten by competitors with much more advanced supply chain technologies (Wal-Mart) and superior marketing and store design (Target, Old Navy, and others). Attempts to compete despite a clearly inferior cost structure led to increasing leverage over time. Kmart's balance sheet was ill-equipped to handle the recession of 2001, and the problem was exacerbated by poor decisions on the part of management.

As Lampert and his associates at ESL pondered the risks and rewards of a big infusion of cash into such a troubled entity, they pored over its balance sheet. (See Exhibit 6.) The operating business was in shambles, but could a large reduction in debt and a new, energized management team make Kmart a viable operation? No one had delusions that Kmart could take Wal-Mart on head to head, but Kmart retained many assets, including one that was becoming increasingly difficult for Wal-Mart to find: real estate.

In studying the potential downside of an investment, the ESL team likely took comfort from the fact that if the operating business just could not be salvaged after an all-out effort, Kmart would still retain value even in liquidation because of its real estate holdings. Kmart owned some of its big-box retail locations, but most of them were on long-term below-market leases that could have considerable present value in the event that Kmart wanted to (or had to) sell the leases to other businesses. Later, in response to considerable speculation among Wall Street analysts that ESL just wanted to realize the inherent real estate value of Kmart or Sears and then look for an exit strategy, Lampert would remark that no "retailer should aspire to have its real estate be

## EXHIBIT 6 Kmart Balance Sheet, January 1999–January 2003 ($ in millions)

| | JAN 2003 | JAN 2002 | JAN 2001 | JAN 2000 | JAN 1999 |
|---|---|---|---|---|---|
| *ASSETS* | | | | | |
| Cash and short-term investments | 2,088.00 | 613.00 | 1,245.00 | 401.00 | 344.0 |
| Receivables | 301.00 | 473.00 | 0.00 | 0.00 | 0.00 |
| Inventories—total | 3,238.00 | 4,825.00 | 5,822.00 | 6,412.00 | 7,101.00 |
| Prepaid expense | 27.00 | 191.00 | 0.00 | 0.00 | 0.00 |
| Other current assets | 157.00 | 0.00 | 817.00 | 811.00 | 715.00 |
| Total current assets | 5,811.00 | 6,102.00 | 7,884.00 | 7,624.00 | 8,160.00 |
| Property, plant, and equipment—total (gross) | 159.00 | 10,896.00 | 12,309.00 | 11,942.00 | 11,554.00 |
| Depreciation, depletion, and amortization (accumulated) | 6.00 | 6,004.00 | 6,148.00 | 5,385.00 | 5,144.00 |
| Property, plant, and equipment—total (net) | 153.00 | 4,892.00 | 6,161.00 | 6,557.00 | 6,410.00 |
| Other assets | 120.00 | 244.00 | 253.00 | 449.00 | 534.00 |
| TOTAL ASSETS | 6,084.00 | 11,238.00 | 14,298.00 | 14,630.00 | 15,104.00 |
| *LIABILITIES* | | | | | |
| Debt—due in one year | 51.00 | 68.00 | 64.00 | 68.00 | 66.00 |
| Accounts payable | 820.00 | 1,287.00 | 103.00 | 2,288.00 | 2,204.00 |
| Income taxes payable | 37.00 | 42.00 | 40.00 | 73.00 | 249.00 |
| Accrued expense | 778.00 | 504.00 | 138.00 | 265.00 | 337.00 |
| Other current liabilities | 90.00 | 219.00 | 259.00 | 1,105.00 | 1,220.00 |
| Total current liabilities | 1,776.00 | 2,120.00 | 624.00 | 3,799.00 | 4,076.00 |
| Long-term debt—total | 477.00 | 1,269.00 | 2,076.00 | 2,011.00 | 3,759.00 |
| Deferred taxes | 0.00 | 0.00 | 0.00 | 0.00 | 0.00 |
| Investment tax credit | 0.00 | 0.00 | 0.00 | 0.00 | 0.00 |
| Other liabilities | 1,639.00 | 8,150.00 | 8,139.00 | 834.00 | 965.00 |
| *EQUITY* | | | | | |
| Common stock | 1.00 | 519.00 | 503.00 | 487.00 | 481.00 |
| Capital surplus | 1,943.00 | 1,922.00 | 1,695.00 | 1,578.00 | 1,555.00 |
| Retained earnings | 249.00 | (2,742.00) | 1,261.00 | 4,018.00 | 4,268.00 |
| Less: Treasury stock—total dollar amount | 1.00 | 0.00 | 0.00 | 0.00 | 0.00 |
| Total common equity | 2,192.00 | (301.00) | 3,459.00 | 6,083.00 | 6,304.00 |
| *Total stockholders' equity* | 2,192.00 | (301.00) | 3,459.00 | 6,083.00 | 6,304.00 |
| *Total liabilities and stockholders' equity* | 6,084.00 | AG 11,238.00 | TL 14,298.00 | TL 14,630.00 | 15,104.00 |
| *Common shares outstanding* | 89.59 | 519.12 | 503.30 | 486.51 | 481.38 |

*Source:* COMPUSTAT

worth more than its operating business"[5] and emphatically declare his commitment to making Kmart's retail operations strong and viable. But at the time of the decision to plunge into Kmart's defaulted debt, Lampert must have considered the effective "put option" that the real estate represented if things did not work out. In fact, some analysts later decided that the real estate holdings of Kmart alone were worth several times what ESL had paid to acquire control of the company in 2002–2003. For instance, in July 2004, Deutsche Bank released a twenty-five-page study of retailers' real estate holdings, which showed that Kmart's shares at that time, despite

---

[5]News conference, November 17, 2004. Transcript available in company's SEC filings at http://www.sec.gov.

having already quadrupled since emergence from bankruptcy, were still trading at a minimum 24 percent, and perhaps as high as 133 percent, discount to the net asset value of Kmart's real estate holdings including favorable long-term leases.[6] In other words, the analysts believed that even if Kmart were to send all its employees home and shut its doors to business, the company would still be worth much more than the equity market value of the company.

## Lampert's Kmart Play

Based on ESL's analysis of the situation, Lampert decided to plunge into the Kmart restructuring despite ESL's lack of experience in both bankruptcy proceedings and running businesses with majority control of a company's common stock. During the spring of 2002, ESL began quietly accumulating Kmart's defaulted bonds. Trading in distressed debt occurs through private, unpublished transactions, so the exact timing and size of Lampert's trades are unknown. Sometime during the summer of 2002, ESL informed Kmart, then operating under a bankruptcy trustee and a new CEO, that the fund had accumulated more than $1 billion in face value of the company's defaulted debt.[7] In September 2002 ESL was able to gain a voice in the restructuring process through a seat on the Financial Institutions Committee, a statutory body appointed by the bankruptcy court. Lampert pushed for the restructuring to move more quickly than it had been up to that time and argued that the company could emerge from Chapter 11 within a shorter time frame than the management team thought. UBS Investment Bank provided the following commentary:

> In early November, Mr. Lampert met with Kmart's then Chairman and CEO Jim Adamson to emphasize the importance of early emergence and to make clear his opinion that the process was moving too slowly; he specifically pressed Mr. Adamson to file a plan of reorganization by Thanksgiving. When the Company did not meet such a timetable, Mr. Lampert's attorney demanded Mr. Adamson's resignation.

With Lampert's support, Julian Day was appointed the new CEO of Kmart in January 2003, and the bankruptcy process starting moving at a faster pace. ESL continued to buy Kmart debt in privately negotiated transactions throughout the period. During final preparations for emergence from bankruptcy in March and April of 2003, many of Kmart's creditors, both banks and bond investors, made it clear that they would prefer to receive cash and end their involvement with Kmart, as opposed to receiving equity in the new company. ESL took advantage of the bank lenders' preference to cut their losses, buying many of their claims for approximately 40 percent of their face value. Holders of Kmart bonds likely received an even lower recovery value on sales to Lampert's fund. Ultimately, ESL controlled 51 percent of the new Kmart's equity when it emerged from bankruptcy, after debt was transformed into equity. Lampert became the company's chairman and was also able to nominate three additional directors to the board of directors of Kmart Holdings, whose new stock soon began trading on the NASDAQ National Market. As Lampert made several small sales of Kmart real estate leases to other retailers and managed the retail business for cash, the market realized that Kmart could be a viable business now that it was stripped of almost all of its debt. As a result, the stock started trading up dramatically. (See Exhibit 7.)

---

[6] *Gold in Them Thar Retailers*, Deutsche Bank, July 26, 2004.

[7] ESL's role during restructuring in 2002–2003 was largely out of the public eye. This account is consistent with recently published articles and also relies on a timeline created by UBS Investment Bank.

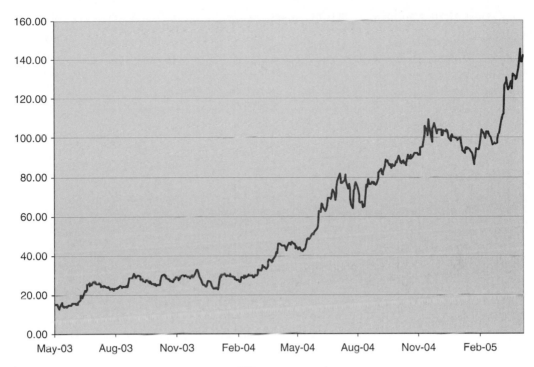

**EXHIBIT 7** Kmart Daily Closing Prices, May 2003–March 2005. *Source:* Bloomberg.

## November 2004 Decision: Should Kmart (under ESL's Control) Acquire Sears?

The Sears chain had been almost entirely based in malls for decades, but after seeing its sales growth eroded by stand-alone "big box" retailers during the 1990s, management in the last few years started experimenting with an "off-mall" concept called Sears Grand. After good results from the early phases of testing, Sears was ready in 2004 to expand the idea at a rapid clip. The chain found that much of the demographic that once constituted reliable consumers at its urban and close suburban mall locations had moved farther away from cities to far suburbs and rural areas. Lampert's desire to sell fifty Kmart locations coincided exactly with Sears management's desire to roll out the off-mall Sears Grand concept nationwide at a fast pace.

During 2002 Lampert had built a substantial minority position in Sears stock, in keeping with his history of acquiring minority stakes in underperforming companies. Owning nearly 10 percent of the company, he was familiar with its challenges, but also with the opportunities available if the chain could re-establish relationships with its traditional customer base by following them out to neighborhoods and communities without any large malls. After Kmart and Sears closed the deal for the transfer of fifty stores in September 2004, wheels must have begun turning in the heads of each chain's management. The deal seemed to create significant value for each counterparty, and Kmart, a struggling chain, still had 1,400 stores left, hundreds of them in the exact types of locations Sears hoped to target with Sears Grand. Sears's sales per square foot were $80 higher than Kmart's, so converting dozens of stores at a time in the right neighborhoods could provide tens of millions of dollars in additional value.

However, in making these new outlays of cash to acquire locations, Sears would clearly be taking a risk as it increased its leverage. (See Exhibit 8 and Exhibit 9.) It would also for the first time be entering the off-mall arena, thus exposing itself to Wal-Mart and Target. Kmart's bankruptcy had come about largely due to being overleveraged and competing with Wal-Mart during a recession, so the additional risk Sears was taking on even with just fifty new locations could not be taken lightly. To acquire additional Kmarts that would have higher operating value as Sears Grands would mean more borrowing.

With Lampert as chairman of Kmart and the second largest shareholder in Sears, and also having recently completed a real estate deal that both sides found to be highly advantageous, it is reasonable to suspect that Lampert stayed in close contact with the top management of Sears throughout September and October of 2004. When the question of combining the two companies was first raised is not known, but it is hard to imagine that Lampert himself was not considering the idea. Then, in the first week of November, a sudden and unexpected flurry of news provided a catalyst.

On November 5, 2004, to Lampert's and Sears's surprise, Vornado Realty Trust announced in a regulatory filing that it had acquired a 4.3 percent stake in Sears common stock. Vornado was a large real estate investor that had a reputation for buying cheap real estate assets. Sears stock jumped 23 percent on the news, as speculation swirled that Vornado might purchase the rest of the company at a premium in order to acquire its real estate. (Unlike Kmart, Sears actually owned most of it store locations.) (See Exhibit 10.)

Now came the moment of decision for Lampert and the Sears board of directors. Both controlled retailers that had struggled against Wal-Mart and whose real estate had been undervalued by the market for several years. But now the market had woken up rather suddenly to the real estate argument, and a decision had to be made. How would Sears respond if Vornado or other "vulture investors" made a bid for the company? Could either of the chains, each at one time

## EXHIBIT 8    Sears Income Statement ($ in millions)

|  | Dec 2003 | Dec 2002 | Dec 2001 |
|---|---|---|---|
| Sales | 41,124 | 41,366 | 40,990 |
| Cost of goods sold | 26,202 | 25,646 | 26,234 |
| Selling, general, and administrative expense | 10,951 | 11,510 | 10,758 |
| Operating income before depreciation | 3,971 | 4,210 | 3,998 |
| Depreciation and amortization | 909 | 875 | 863 |
| Interest expense | 1,027 | 1,148 | 1,426 |
| Nonoperating income (expense) and special items | 3,414 | 266 | −486 |
| Pretax income | 5,449 | 2,453 | 1,223 |
| Income taxes—total | 2,007 | 858 | 467 |
| Minority interest | 45 | 11 | 21 |
| Income before extraordinary items | 3,397 | 1,584 | 735 |
| Extraordinary items and discontinued operations | 0 | −208 | 0 |
| Net income (loss) | 3,397 | 1,376 | 735 |
| Earnings per share (primary)—excluding extraordinary items | 11.95 | 4.99 | 2.25 |
| Earnings per share (primary)—including extraordinary items | 11.95 | 4.34 | 2.25 |
| Common shares used to calculate primary EPS | 284.30 | 317.40 | 326.40 |
| Earnings per share (fully diluted)—excluding extraordinary items | 11.86 | 4.94 | 2.24 |
| Earnings per share (fully diluted)—including extraordinary Items | 11.86 | 4.29 | 2.24 |

Source: COMPUSTAT

## EXHIBIT 9    Sears Balance Sheet ($ in millions)

|  | Dec 2003 | Dec 2002 | Dec 2001 |
|---|---|---|---|
| *ASSETS* | | | |
| Cash and short-term investments | 9,057 | 1,962 | 1,064 |
| Receivables | 2,689 | 31,622 | 28,813 |
| Inventories—total | 5,335 | 5,115 | 4,912 |
| Other current assets | 1,115 | 1,284 | 1,316 |
| Total current assets | 18,196 | 39,983 | 36,105 |
| Property, plant, and equipment—total (gross) | 13,124 | 12,979 | 13,137 |
| Depreciation, depletion, and amortization (accumulated) | 6,336 | 6,069 | 6,313 |
| Property, plant, and equipment—total (net) | 6,788 | 6,910 | 6,824 |
| Intangibles | 1,653 | 1,648 | C |
| Deferred charges | 24 | 277 | C |
| Other assets | 1,062 | 1,591 | 1,388 |
| TOTAL ASSETS | 27,723 | 50,409 | 44,317 |
| *LIABILITIES* | | | |
| Debt—due in one year | 2,950 | 4,808 | 3,157 |
| Notes payable | 1,033 | 4,525 | 3,557 |
| Accounts payable | 3,106 | 7,485 | 7,176 |
| Income taxes payable | 1,867 | 0 | 0 |
| Accrued expense | 609 | C | C |
| Other current liabilities | 4,194 | 1,779 | 1,694 |
| Total current liabilities | 13,759 | 18,597 | 15,584 |
| Long-term debt—total | 4,218 | 21,304 | 18,921 |
| Deferred taxes | 0 | 0 | 0 |
| Investment tax credit | 0 | 0 | 0 |
| Other liabilities | 3,345 | 3,755 | 3,693 |
| *EQUITY* | | | |
| Common stock | 323 | 323 | 323 |
| Capital surplus | 3,493 | 3,463 | 3,437 |
| Retained earnings | 10,530 | 7,441 | 6,582 |
| Less: Treasury stock—total dollar amount | 7,945 | 4,474 | 4,223 |
| Total common equity | 6,401 | 6,753 | 6,119 |
| *Total stockholders' equity* | 6,401 | 6,753 | 6,119 |
| *Total liabilities and stockholders' equity* | 27,723 | 50,409 | 44,317 |
| *Common shares outstanding* | 230.38 | 316.73 | 320.4 |

*Source:* COMPUSTAT

the nation's largest retailer, succeed against competitors with lower cost structures and higher sales per square foot?

As a financial buyer, Lampert had not previously been interested in acquiring more than 10 to 15 percent of Sears. But now he found himself as a potential strategic buyer, and the timing of his decision was being forced by the emergence of a financial buyer (Vornado) that had much more experience than ESL did in real estate investments. (See Exhibit 11 and Exhibit 12.)

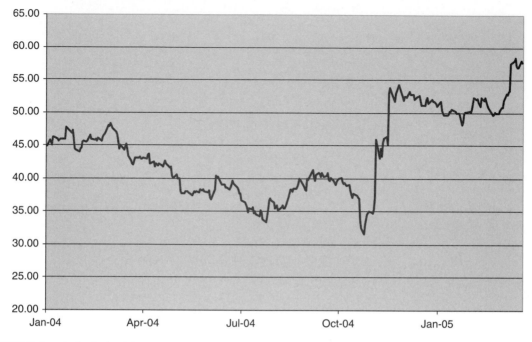

**EXHIBIT 10** Sears Daily Closing Prices, January 2004–March 2005. *Source:* Bloomberg.

■ ■ ■

**EXHIBIT 11** Selected Quotes from Edward S. Lampert, Chairman of Kmart Holdings, at Kmart-Sears Joint News Conference, November 17, 2004 (Emphasis Added)

"This truly is a historic day and something that we've been working on very diligently to make happen. *The combination of Kmart and Sears, as you can see, will jointly have roughly $55 billion in revenues, nearly 3,500 store locations consisting of roughly 1,500 Kmart locations and 870 or so Sears locations on the mall* ... The terms of the deal are that Kmart shares are going to be converted to 1 share of Sears Holdings Corporation, and the Sears shares will receive for 55 percent of the Sears a half a share of the combined company, and for 45 percent of the Sears share $50 in stock. There will be an election. Shareholders will have an opportunity to elect either stock or cash, and the stock portion of the merger will be tax-free to shareholders. *As part of the merger agreement, ESL and its affiliates, our affiliates, have elected to receive all stock in the merger, and we think that is something that is a very important sign of our confidence in the combined company* ...

"We are going to need really the best of us, but the best of both the Kmart team as well as the Sears team. I think that *there is going to be a lot of work to do in converting Kmart stores into Sears stores where appropriate, bringing Sears products into Kmart stores* ...

"Given the large ownership that we will have on the Board, we will be able, *similar to what Kmart has been able to do for the last couple of years, we will be able to manage the business strategically and for the long term without having to worry about figuring out how to make monthly same-store sales, hit a specific target, and without giving any type of quarterly earnings guidance* and then trying to manage the business to that guidance.

"In terms of the *strategic perspective* behind the merger, I think it is pretty obvious that *scale is very important to compete effectively ... we need to have a very low-cost structure in order to compete with our biggest competitors*. And I think that while we need to have a low-cost structure, it needs to be consistent with the reputation and quality of service that Sears has always provided and the type of service that we at Kmart aspire to achieve.

"*Clearly, the Kmart locations are very significant, 1,500 off-the-mall locations in high-traffic areas. Sears has the best offerings ... in hard lines, with Craftsman, Kenmore, DieHard.... The issue for Sears, however, has been with competitors opening hundreds of stores a year; the ability to actually be closer to the customer is something that Sears has started to move towards with the launching of the Sears Grand stores. But the time—the time and capital required to get there quickly—is both prohibitive and risky, and I think that the ability to take the Kmart store base and determine whether we want to convert those Kmart stores over to the Sears nameplate and to bring Sears products into the Kmart stores is a great opportunity.*

"The other factor with competitors opening so many stores and Sears not having been opening stores off the mall is *Sears has had to spend a significant amount of money, both in marketing and capital expenditures, just to stay even*. That same capital which has been running roughly, call it $900 million or $1 billion a year can now be really directed at very, very high return on investment opportunities, both in the conversion process as well as helping to upgrade, whether it is the fixtures or the appearance of the existing Kmart stores.

"From a Kmart perspective, in addition to the products, which is something that we've aspired to and we've been working towards and we did this really with the relaunch of our apparel brands; *we clearly need to find at Kmart points of differentiation with our major competitors*. This has been something that has been talked about. It has been talked about before the Company went into bankruptcy, when it was in bankruptcy and since it has emerged ...

"*The combined cost of goods sold of the two companies is roughly $40 billion*. We purchase roughly $40 billion of merchandise from around the world. And I think that the ability to sort of work together to really get best practices from both organizations and work with our supplier base to really help drive their business and help them save money, so that we can save money for our customers, is a big opportunity. In terms of SG&A of the two companies, *the combined SG&A is roughly $12 billion. And as you will see when we discuss the synergy opportunity, the opportunity both on the purchase of merchandise as well as the SG&A is fairly significant* when you think of those numbers ...

"*Sears stores in general are roughly $80 per square foot more productive than Kmart stores. And if you talk about roughly 100 million square feet of real estate that Kmart has, if we could ever achieve that level of productivity in the Kmart stores, either as Sears or as Kmart, you're talking about an $8 billion opportunity. So I think that the financial dimensions are very, very significant and they blend very well with the strategic dimensions.*

■ ■ ■ ────────────────────────────

**EXHIBIT 11**  Selected Quotes from Edward S. Lampert, Chairman of Kmart Holdings, at Kmart-Sears Joint News Conference, November 17, 2004 (Emphasis Added) — Cont'd

"Finally, I think that as a board and a management team, *we're going to have an ability and a willingness to monetize noncore and nonproductive assets.* We want to make sure that the businesses that we run are going to be able to produce real economic value for the shareholders over time, and at the same time I think we want to make sure that we stay focused on the biggest opportunities ...

"I think finally before I turn the podium over, *I don't think any retailer should aspire to have its real estate be worth more than its operating business. There's been a lot of speculation about real estate strategy, real estate value, and I think that there is some truth to the notion that there are certain retailers whose real estate is worth more than its operating business. I think while that may have been true at Kmart at one point in time, we've worked very, very hard to improve the profitability of each of our stores and to make those stores worth a lot more as an operating business than as real estate. The more money the store makes, the more valuable they are as operating businesses, and that's something that I think the combined company can do very, very well.*

"To the extent that we have stores that can't produce the type of profit that we're looking for, we would have to consider other alternatives. I think *well-run retailers over time should be able to earn a 10 percent EBITDA to sales ratio.* I think when you look at Home Depot, you look at Target, you look at The Gap, they all achieve that metric. And again, *that's not something we think that we're going to be able to do anytime soon, but that's something that we're going to work towards. We're going to work towards best-in-class financial metrics and best-in-class customer metrics.*"

*Source*: Press conference transcript, available in SEC filings at http://www.sec.gov.

──────────────────────────── ■ ■ ■

■ ■ ■ ────────────────────────────

**EXHIBIT 12**  Selected Quotes on Kmart Acquisition of Sears, November 17–19, 2004

*Tom Peters, management author:* "If you think they'll be able to take on Wal-Mart, I've got a nice bridge." (*Wall Street Journal*, 11/18/04)

*Burt Flickinger, retail consultant:* "This is cause for celebration for competitors." (*WSJ*)

*Emme P. Kozloff, Sanford Bernstein retail analyst:* "Wal-Mart is in a good position. It could take advantage of the inevitable disarray at Kmart over the next year to take market share. And it's always harder to get customers back that have defected." (*WSJ*)

*Michael B. Exstein and Shirley Lee, Credit Suisse First Boston retail analysts:* "In the near term, we do believe that the opportunities for cost savings and improvements are real, not to mention significant opportunities for the combined entity to monetize some of its real estate (i.e., overlapping/'nonstrategic' store locations). As a result, we believe Sears shares will continue to rally on today's news given these two points. In the longer term, however, we believe that the integration (such as systems and logistics) and execution challenges before the combined entity is [sic] enormous and far more complex than any combination attempted in the retail industry to date. Prior to today's announcement, many would consider Sears and Kmart to be the industry laggards with uncertain business models. It is not clear to us how the combination of such two [sic] retailers could work long term." (*CSFB Retail Industry Flash, 11/17/04*)

*Kozloff, McGranahan et al., Sanford Bernstein retail research team:* "The merger of Sears and Kmart has strong strategic rationale for two beleaguered retailers: real estate for Sears, brands for Kmart. Sears is currently trapped in a capital-consuming but obsolete on-mall real estate footprint. Kmart real estate helps level the playing field with other hard line players. However, the integration promises to be complex, difficult and lengthy; near-term risk is substantial and probability of success is mixed. Execution will be the key to making the merger work, and the track records of the two companies are not encouraging. The task of integrating supply chains, systems and two disparate cultures is enormous. We expect existing Kmart locations that have appropriate demographic trade areas to be candidates for conversion to the Sears 'mini-grand' format. Management sees 'several hundred' candidates over time, although the pace is likely to be measured and returns carefully monitored. Our demographic analysis suggests roughly 300 potential conversions over time. Potential synergies—revenue, purchasing and cost—are powerful (pegged by company at $500 million) and, if realized, will create value." (*Bernstein Research Weekly Notes, 11/19/04*)

---

*Source*:   http://www.sec.gov/Archives/edgar/data/319256/000095012304013859/y68947fe425.htm (accessed January 15, 2005).

# McDonald's, Wendy's, and Hedge Funds: Hamburger Hedging? Hedge Fund Activism and Impact on Corporate Governance

## Growing Hedge Fund Activism

Are hedge funds heroes or villains? Management of Blockbuster, Time Warner, Six Flags, Knight-Ridder, and Bally Total Fitness might prefer the "villain" appellation, but Enron, WorldCom, Tyco, and HealthSouth shareholders might view management as the real villains and hedge funds as vehicles to oust incompetent corporate managers before they run companies into the ground or steal them through fraudulent transactions. Could the pressure exerted by activist hedge funds on targeted companies result in increased share prices, management accountability, and better communication with shareholders? Or does it distract management from its primary goal of enhancing long-term shareholder value?

Hedge funds have been compared to the corporate raiders of the 1980s, who initiated hostile takeovers by using large amounts of debt to acquire target companies and then ousted management (and often thousands of employees as well). However, activist hedge funds typically use only their own equity to invest, without leveraging the target company, and generally work with existing management to effect change rather than dumping management and employees. And if hedge funds cannot engender support among the other major shareholders, they are usually forced to back down. Another difference between corporate raiders and hedge funds involves "greenmail"—forcing a company to buy out a large hostile shareholder at a premium price to escape unwanted attention. Raiders frequently initiate greenmail, but hedge funds never do.

Following corporate scandals at Enron and WorldCom, some observers believe activist hedge funds serve as catalysts for positive change at targeted underperforming companies. Even if hedge funds do not get everything they want, when they initiate an activist campaign target companies are frequently compelled to make changes that benefit all shareholders. Others think that, although hedge fund strategies may improve a company's share price in the short term, they may not always enhance the company's long-term viability. The evidence is mixed. Some studies suggest that target companies benefit from a more than 5 percent rise in share price after the campaign is initiated. Other studies propose that activism has little impact on share values and earnings in the long run. Only a small percentage of hedge fund assets are allocated to activist projects, but this activity is increasing and has been well publicized through proxy fights and "hostile 13-D" letters. When filed with the Securities and Exchange Commission (SEC), these letters become public vehicles for criticizing management in an effort to effect change (Exhibit 1).

■ ■ ■

## EXHIBIT 1 13-D Letters as a Public Vehicle

SEC Regulation 13-D requires every investor who acquires a beneficial ownership of more than 5 percent of a publicly traded security to file a holdings report with the SEC. The filing includes information on the investor's background and future plans. Since it warns of a changing shareholder base, it allows the target company to initiate potential defensive actions such as share repurchases, preferential share reallotments (poison pills), and announcements of strategic changes, acquisitions, and debt-loading if the target is concerned about a hostile action.

13-D filings and attached letters can also become a public vehicle for criticizing management. For example, Daniel Loeb, a hedge fund activist who managed a $3.5 billion fund called Third Point, was known for being rather blunt and abrupt in his 13-D filings and statements to management, earning him the nickname "Wall Street's Merchant of Venom."[18] In a 13-D letter to Star Gas's CEO, Loeb stated, "Do what you do best: Retreat to your waterfront mansion in the Hamptons."[19] To another CEO, Loeb stated, "I also have excellent news, which I would like to share with you and the board: After significant reflection regarding the time commitments and constraints that such a responsibility would entail, I have decided to volunteer to serve on the company's board of directors . . . ."[20] He told yet another CEO, "Since you ascended to your current role of Chief Value Destroyer, the shares have dropped over 45 percent . . . ."[21]

---

[18] Nichola Groom, "McDonald's Investors Unswayed by Activist Proposal," *Reuters*, January 19, 2006.
[19] James Altucher, "Activist Track: The Softer Side of Loeb," *TheStreet.com, Inc.*, August 23, 2005.
[20] Ibid.
[21] Ibid.

■ ■ ■

Assets under management by hedge funds exceeded $1 trillion in 2005, almost 3 percent of global financial assets. More than 8,000 hedge funds and approximately 1,750 fund of hedge funds shared these assets. Because hedge funds have been particularly active stock traders, they have accounted for up to 50 percent of daily New York Stock Exchange trading volume. Hedge fund assets have grown at an annual rate of 26 percent since 1990, with approximately 40 percent of total assets concentrated in the top fifty hedge funds. High net worth investors represent nearly 75 percent of the asset base, but starting in 2001 more than 50 percent of the growth in this industry has come from institutional investors, with further "institutionalization" expected to provide most of the future growth. In February 2006 the hedge fund industry was required, for the first time, to register with the SEC (Exhibit 2).

## A Tale of Two Activists: Carl Icahn and William Ackman

Well-known hedge fund activist Carl Icahn evolved from a feared corporate raider and green-mailer during the 1980s to a ubiquitous hedge fund manager with $2.5 billion in assets and a personal net worth of $8.5 billion. Icahn's image as a feared and disliked corporate raider has transformed in some quarters to a "white knight." He has pushed through corporate change at Fairmont Hotels, Blockbuster, Kerr-McGee, Hollywood Entertainment, Siebel Systems, RiteAid,

■ ■ ■

## EXHIBIT 2 SEC Hedge Fund Regulation

Historically, hedge funds were not required to register with the SEC and had minimal regulatory oversight. However, in February 2006 the SEC required hedge funds to register in an effort to deter or detect fraud at early stages. During 2005 the SEC had taken action against twenty hedge funds, a significant increase over previous years, with the most common violation related to misrepresentation of management experience and investment performance track record. On its Web site, the SEC advises investors to seek out a hedge fund's prospectus, valuation methodology of the fund's assets, impact on returns from both management and performance fees, limitations on redemption of shares (timing/lock-ups), management background, and asset allocation.

■ ■ ■

UnumProvident, and Time Warner. In late December 2005 he called Time Warner's sale of a 5 percent stake in its AOL division to Google a "disastrous decision," making a potential AOL merger with other companies, such as eBay, Yahoo, or Microsoft, difficult.[1] Icahn said, "This joint venture is short-sighted in nature and may preclude any consideration of a broader set of alternatives that would better maximize value and ensure a bright future for AOL."[2] In spite of these statements, he ultimately backed down from his threatened proxy battle to gain board seats as a prelude to breaking up the company, following Time Warner's agreement to boost its stock buyback effort and implement a $1 billion cost reduction program. The most likely reason he aborted this effort was lack of support from other significant institutional investors.

Icahn's activism initiatives have principally focused on threatening or initiating proxy fights (asking shareholders to vote on key initiatives he has advocated), pushing companies to distribute more cash to shareholders through dividends and share repurchases, and reducing CEO compensation. In regard to proxies, Icahn has said, "We need to ensure we have the best minds possible focused on business issues, and shareholders cannot trust that corporations being advised by management consultants and investment bankers, neither of which are compensated based on the results they achieve for businesses over time, are going to come up with the best decisions for the company."[3] Concerning CEO compensation, he has argued, "CEO comp eats into earnings, creates a cycle of invisible dilution and further waste of cash through share buybacks at any level to prevent dilution, and perhaps worst of all, stratifies the company, making the CEO a demi-god in the organization for, basically, being highly paid."[4]

Inherent in Icahn's activist behavior was the view that many corporations were sitting on too much cash. S&P 500 corporations held more than $615 billion in cash at the end of 2005, the most in more than twenty five years. This cash pile was equal to 40 percent of long-term debt, which was also the highest percentage in twenty five years. Icahn and other hedge fund activists wanted companies to pay out cash to shareholders through share repurchases (if the share price is weak) or through increased dividends. They also wanted companies to take on more risk by

---

[1] Verne Kopytoff, "Icahn Rips into AOL's $1 Billion Google Deal," *San Francisco Chronicle*, December 20, 2005.
[2] Ibid.
[3] Deborah Solomon, "Fighting for a Fair Share," *New York Times Magazine*, June 5, 2005.
[4] Ibid.

borrowing to increase leverage, creating pressure on management to become more efficient and accountable.

Another well-known activist, William Ackman, co-founded Gotham Partners in 1993 shortly after graduating from business school at the age of twenty-six. This fund, which made investments in both private equity and public markets, was liquidated nearly a decade later, before Ackman started Pershing Square Capital Management in early 2004. He launched Pershing with $10 million of his own capital and $50 million from a strategic investor. The Pershing fund was opened to new investors in early 2005, adding more than $200 million to the prior base. With net returns of 42 percent in 2004 and 40 percent in 2005, funds under management exceeded $1 billion from performance and additional investment in early 2006. Pershing took significant positions in both Sears and Kmart before their merger in the fall of 2004. It then drew substantial media attention in the latter half of 2005 after building equity positions through options in both McDonald's and Wendy's, prior to squaring off with each firm's management team regarding comprehensive restructuring and recapitalization plans. Ackman felt that neither company was managing its cash and other resources optimally, so he took large equity stakes believing he could then persuade management to make changes to enhance shareholder value. He explained, "It has become an environment in which boards of directors are more receptive as they are much more aware of potential for personal liability. Management is more willing to listen as mutual funds vote proxies for value-additive transactions and hedge funds are willing to take a much more active and influential role in corporate governance."[5]

## Pershing Square's Initial Involvement: Wendy's and McDonald's

### Wendy's

By mid-April 2005, Pershing Square had acquired nearly a 10 percent stake in Wendy's and encouraged the restaurant chain to spin off its Tim Hortons doughnut chain, enabling it to operate autonomously from Wendy's and to unlock shareholder value. At that point, Tim Hortons was Wendy's most significant growth driver, representing nearly 50 percent of overall operating profits. Many shareholders believed Wendy's stock price did not fully reflect the contribution of that unit until Pershing and others pressed for the spinoff. In his April 2005 earnings note, Lehman Brothers restaurant analyst Jeff Bernstein valued standalone Wendy's (excluding Tim Hortons) at a price/earnings (P/E) multiple of 14×, versus standalone Tim Hortons at a 24× P/E multiple. Wendy's stock rose 15 percent during the two-week period following Ackman's advocacy of a spinoff.

In mid-July Pershing submitted a detailed proposal to Wendy's management recommending not only the spinoff of Tim Hortons, but also the sale of a large portion of the company's restaurants to franchisees, a major share repurchase, and management avoidance of any large acquisitions. However, in spite of Ackman's 10 percent ownership of the company, Wendy's management refused to discuss these recommendations with him.

In late July Wendy's announced it would sell 15 to 18 percent of Tim Hortons in a tax-free spinoff during the first quarter of 2006, and also disclosed authorization for an additional $1 billion in stock repurchases, an increase in the company's dividend by 25 percent, the reduction of debt by $100 million, and a program to sell more than two hundred real estate sites, close sixty poorly performing stores, and sell hundreds of company-owned restaurants (reducing company ownership levels from 22 percent to as low as 15 percent).

---

[5]William Ackman, Pershing Square Capital Management, interview with the author, December 19, 2005.

While Pershing's activism appeared to have accelerated management's initiatives, Wendy's stated in its late-July strategic initiative press release, "The board of directors and management began in 2004 a thorough review of the company's operations and strategic plan with its long-term, independent financial advisor, Goldman Sachs. The resulting initiatives announced today are a comprehensive approach to manage the company for the future."[6] Despite this public statement, which ignored Ackman's efforts, many investors acknowledged that his vocal push motivated management to proactively restructure. From the initiation of Ackman's campaign for change at Wendy's starting in mid-April 2005 until early March 2006, Wendy's stock appreciated by 55 percent, from $39 to nearly $61.

## McDonald's

At the end of 2005, McDonald's was one the few major restaurant chains that owned large amounts of real estate. Most restaurant chains principally used operating leases and off-balance-sheet financing to support their restaurant businesses and limit their actual real estate ownership. With thousands of well-positioned real estate properties, McDonald's carried a significantly higher property value on its balance sheet than any competitor. At the end of 2005 the real estate carrying value was approximately $30 billion (property and equipment before accumulated depreciation and amortization), equal to almost two-thirds of the company's equity market value of $45.6 billion. McDonald's 2005 year-end balance sheet is shown in Exhibit 3.

McDonald's had benefited from its 90 percent ownership in Chipotle, a Mexican restaurant that posted double-digit revenue growth from 1998 to 2005. However, even with a strong performance from this business, as of January 2006 McDonald's share price had not broken out of the low- to mid-$30s price range that it had traded within since early 2001—well below its all-time high of $48 in late 1999. In order to unlock the value of Chipotle from the relatively weaker value of the parent company, McDonald's decided to spin off 20 percent of the subsidiary through an IPO offering.

Since 2003 McDonald's had not increased or altered its long-term annual targets for system-wide sales and revenue growth of 3 to 5 percent, operating income growth of 6 to 7 percent, and return on invested capital in the high teens. This led to analyst commentary and McDonald's management discussions regarding a range of strategic options to improve the business. Exhibit 4 through Exhibit 7 show McDonald's historical performance and relative valuation.

In the late 1990s, when Ackman's Gotham Partners fund held a small stake in McDonald's, he researched the topic of spinning off restaurants and real estate. In late September 2005 Ackman resumed his focus on McDonald's by acquiring call options on 4.9 percent of the company's stock (approximately $2 billion in value if options were exercised to acquire shares). After establishing this equity position, he met with McDonald's management and pushed for a recapitalization of the company. He indicated that the result of this recapitalization would be a share price increase of up to $15 per share, nearly a 50 percent boost to the stock price at that time.

Ackman viewed McDonald's as three separate entities (highlighted in Exhibit 8):

1. Franchising operation: representing nearly 75 percent of the 32,000 McDonald's restaurants
2. Restaurant operation: company restaurant ownership of remaining 25 percent ("McOpCo")
3. Real estate business: land ownership of roughly 37 percent of all restaurants and 59 percent of all buildings

---

[6]Wendy's press release, July 29, 2005.

# EXHIBIT 3 McDonald's Balance Sheet, 2005

| | December 31 | |
| --- | --- | --- |
| | **2005** | **2004** |
| ASSETS | | |
| *Current assets* | | |
| Cash and equivalents | $ 4,260.40 | $ 1,379.80 |
| Accounts and notes receivable | 795.90 | 745.50 |
| Inventories, at cost, not in excess of market | 147.00 | 147.50 |
| Prepaid expenses and other current assets | 646.40 | 585.00 |
| Total current assets | 5,849.70 | 2,857.80 |
| *Other assets* | | |
| Investments in and advances to affiliates | 1,035.40 | 1,109.90 |
| Goodwill, net | 1,950.70 | 1,828.30 |
| Miscellaneous | 1,245.00 | 1,338.40 |
| Total other assets | 4,231.10 | 4,276.60 |
| *Property and equipment* | | |
| Property and equipment, at cost | 29,897.20 | 30,507.80 |
| Accumulated depreciation and amortization | (9,989.20) | (9,804.70) |
| Net property and equipment | 19,908.00 | 20,703.10 |
| Total assets | 29,988.80 | 27,837.50 |
| LIABILITIES AND SHAREHOLDERS' EQUITY | | |
| *Current liabilities* | | |
| Notes payable | 544.00 | — |
| Accounts payable | 689.40 | 714.30 |
| Income taxes | 567.60 | 331.30 |
| Other taxes | 233.50 | 245.10 |
| Accrued interest | 158.50 | 179.40 |
| Accrued payroll and other liabilities | 1,184.60 | 1,188.20 |
| Current maturities of long-term debt | 658.70 | 862.20 |
| Total current liabilities | 4,036.30 | 3,520.50 |
| Long-term debt | 8,937.40 | 8,357.30 |
| Other long-term liabilities | 892.30 | 976.70 |
| Deferred income taxes | 976.70 | 781.50 |
| Shareholders' equity | | |
| Preferred stock, no par value; authorized—165.0 million shares; issued—none | | |
| Common stock, $0.01 par value; authorized—3.5 billion shares; issued—1,660.6 million shares | 16.60 | 16.60 |
| Additional paid-in capital | 2,797.60 | 2,186.00 |
| Unearned ESOP compensation | (77.40) | (82.80) |
| Retained earnings | 23,516.00 | 21,755.80 |
| Accumulated other comprehensive income (loss) | (733.10) | (96.00) |
| Common stock in treasury, at cost; 397.4 and 390.7 million shares | (10,373.60) | (9,578.10) |
| Total shareholders' equity | 15,146.10 | 14,201.50 |
| Total liabilities and shareholders' equity | 29,988.80 | 27,837.50 |

*Note*: Dollars in millions, except per share data. *Source*: McDonald's Corporation 10-K Filing.

**Revenue and EBITDA Performance**
**($ In Millions)**

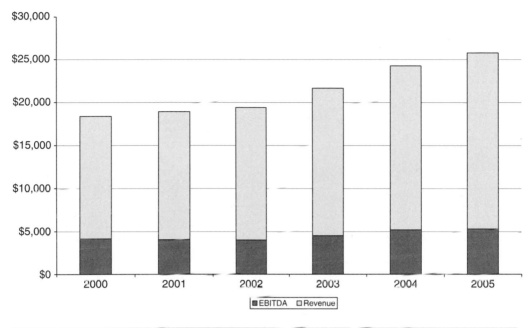

| | 2000 | 2001 | 2002 | 2003 | 2004 | 2005 |
|---|---|---|---|---|---|---|
| Same-store sales | 0.6% | −1.3% | −2.1% | 2.4% | 6.9% | 3.9% |
| EBITDA margin | 29.0% | 27.0% | 26.0% | 26.0% | 27.0% | 26.0% |

*Note:* 2005 EBITDA is an estimate since 2005 10-K has not been filed with depreciation and amortization results.

EXHIBIT 4 McDonald's Historical Revenue and EBITDA Performance

McDonald's franchising operation received fees equivalent to 4 percent of individual non-company-owned restaurant unit sales. The company's real estate business received annual rent payments of 9 to 10 percent, with higher rates outside the United States and in high-priced areas like New York City. Both franchise fees and rent payments provided stable cash flow, which amply supported the company's debt service requirements, share repurchase program, and capital improvement program.

Ackman's proposal to McDonald's recommended a large IPO of McOpCo (the company-owned restaurant operation), which historically underperformed the franchise system average returns by a nearly 2 percentage point margin.[7] Pershing's full proposal[8] included the following provisions:

Step 1. Initiate an IPO of 65 percent of McOpCo—which owned about 8,000 restaurants—raising $3.3 billion after taxes.

Step 2. Issue nearly $14.7 billion in debt secured against McDonald's real estate holdings.

Step 3. Use the IPO proceeds and debt proceeds to:

a. Refinance the existing debt of "pro forma" McDonald's, a newly organized company operating as a real estate business ("Prop Co") and a restaurant franchise business ("Fran Co") ($5 billion).

---

[7]Jeremy Grant, "Pershing Drops Push for McDonald's Shake-Up," *Financial Times*, January 25, 2006.

[8]Pershing Square Capital Management, "Presentation: A Value Menu for McDonald's," November 2005.

**McDonald's Stock Price**

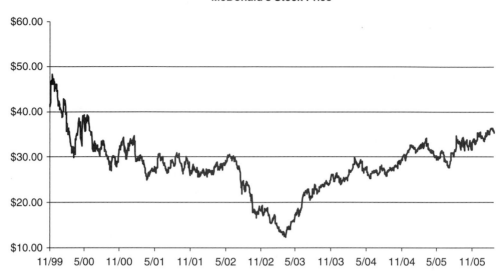

EXHIBIT 5 McDonald's Stock Price Performance Since All-Time High in November 1999

**McDonald's Relative Stock Price Performance**

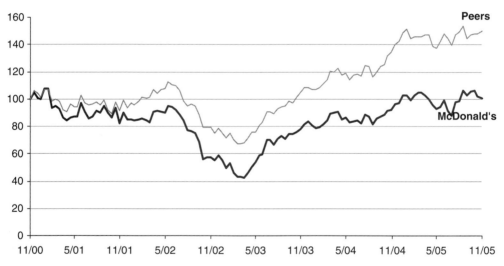

EXHIBIT 6 McDonald's Five-Year Relative Stock Price Performance vs. Peers

  b. Repurchase 316 million shares at an estimated $40 per share ($12.6 billion).

  c. Fund transaction costs and related fees ($300 million).

    Exhibit 9 through Exhibit 13 provide more details regarding Ackman's full proposal to McDonald's.

# McDonald's Management and Franchisees Respond

In late October 2005, after a Pershing team made its presentation to McDonald's management, Ackman had a follow-up meeting with the McDonald's board of directors. To help build his case,

**EV/EBITDA** (2006 Estimates in November 2005)

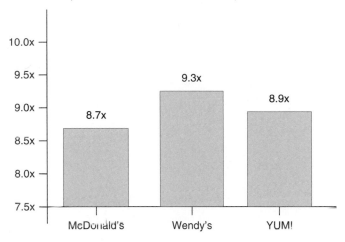

**P/E** (2006 Estimates in November 2005)

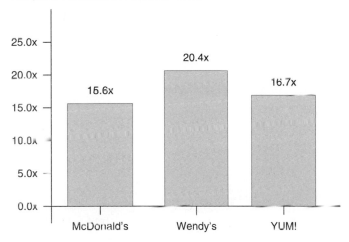

*Source:* Pershing Square Presentation, November 2005.

**EXHIBIT 7** McDonald's Relative Valuation Despite McDonald's strong real estate outlets, number-one market share position in the industry, and leading brand, McDonald's traded at a discount to peers (November 2005). *Source:* Pershing Square Capital Management, "Presentation: A Value Menu for McDonald's," November 2005.

he cited precedent transactions and suggested that a restructuring would attract new dividend/ income-focused investors and real estate investors. Two independent investment banking advisors for McDonald's reviewed the Pershing proposal in regard to valuation and credit impact, and the McDonald's management team analyzed friction costs (property tax revaluations, legal, financing structure) and governance/alignment issues. Although McDonald's advisors agreed with most of Pershing's views on the McOpCo IPO valuation, they disagreed with the suggestion that a recapitalization would create a new pro forma entity that would trade at a higher P/E multiple.

In November McDonald's CFO rejected Pershing's suggestions, stating, "The proposal is an exercise in financial engineering and does not take into account McDonald's unique business model. While we remain open to ideas, we simply will not jeopardize the long-term health of

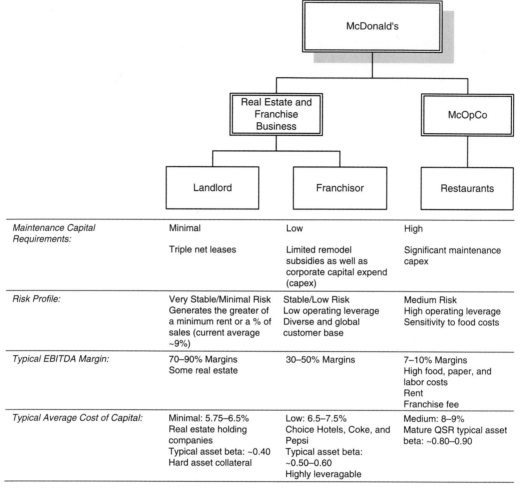

| | Landlord | Franchisor | Restaurants |
|---|---|---|---|
| *Maintenance Capital Requirements:* | Minimal<br><br>Triple net leases | Low<br><br>Limited remodel subsidies as well as corporate capital expend (capex) | High<br><br>Significant maintenance capex |
| *Risk Profile:* | Very Stable/Minimal Risk<br>Generates the greater of a minimum rent or a % of sales (current average ~9%) | Stable/Low Risk<br>Low operating leverage<br>Diverse and global customer base | Medium Risk<br>High operating leverage<br>Sensitivity to food costs |
| *Typical EBITDA Margin:* | 70–90% Margins<br>Some real estate | 30–50% Margins | 7–10% Margins<br>High food, paper, and labor costs<br>Rent<br>Franchise fee |
| *Typical Average Cost of Capital:* | Minimal: 5.75–6.5%<br>Real estate holding companies<br>Typical asset beta: ~0.40<br>Hard asset collateral | Low: 6.5–7.5%<br>Choice Hotels, Coke, and Pepsi<br>Typical asset beta: ~0.50–0.60<br>Highly leveragable | Medium: 8–9%<br>Mature QSR typical asset beta: ~0.80–0.90 |

*Notes:* Typical margins are illustrative of restaurant EBITDA margins and assume the payment of a market rent and franchisee fee similar to a franchisee.

Typical betas are Pershing approximations based on selected companies' Barra predictive betas. Average cost of capital estimates are illustrative estimates based on average asset betas.

*Source:* Pershing Square Presentation, November 2005.

**EXHIBIT 8** Pershing's View of McDonald's as Three Separate Entities

our company, nor our relationships with customers, franchisees, and suppliers."[9] Management also asserted that it was focusing on enhancing shareholder value by developing plans to sell more company-owned restaurants to franchisees in underperforming markets like the United Kingdom. McDonald's CEO reiterated that the company's "unmatchable" competitive advantage was its "three-legged stool": the company, its franchisees, and its suppliers. Exhibit 14 highlights McDonald's rejection rationale.

A large franchisee group regarded Pershing's proposal as "injurious" to restaurant owners.[10] The head of the national group of franchisees encouraged members to ignore Ackman's plan, stating in a letter distributed in late December, "While on the surface some of the ideas he is floating might seem to benefit us, we have serious concerns regarding the long-term impact of his approach and the

---

[9]Bethany McLean, "Taking on McDonald's," *Fortune*, November 15, 2005.

[10]Julie Jargon, "McD's, Ackman Lobby for Franchisee Backing," *Crain's Chicago Business*, December 1, 2005.

**STEP1: IPO OF 65% MCOPCO**

- IPO 65% of McOpCo
- IPO generates estimated $3.27 billion of after-tax proceeds
    - Assumes a 7x EV/FY 2006E EBITDA multiple
    - Assumes $1.35 billion of net debt allocated to McOpCo

**STEP 2: ISSUE DEBT AND PURSUE LEVERAGED SELF-TENDER**

- Issue $14.7 billion of financing secured against pro forma McDonald's ("PF McDonald's") real estate
- Debt financing and IPO proceeds used to:
    - Refinance all of the existing $5 billion of net debt at PF McDonald's
    - Repurchase 316 million shares at $40 per share
    - Pay $300 million in fees and transaction costs

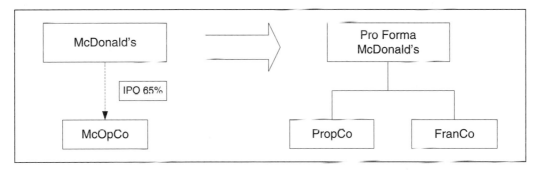

- At the time of IPO, McOpCo signs market lease and franchise agreements with PF McDonald's
- Resulting PF McDonald's is a world-class real estate and franchise business
    - McOpCo financials deconsolidated from PF McDonald's
- Leverage is placed only on PropCo
- FranCo is unlevered, maximizing its credit rating

*Source:* Pershing Square Presentation, November 2005.

**EXHIBIT 9** McOpCo IPO Process

unintended consequences that this might have for us and our system." McDonald's CFO characterized the plan as a "threat" to the company's relationship with franchisees that would lead to "unhealthy restaurant-level cash flow" and "loss of franchisee equity." McDonald's argued that franchisees were more comfortable knowing that corporate headquarters was not only a landlord but also a knowledgeable restaurant mentor.

Ackman believed that franchisees thought he wanted to sell the real estate their restaurants sat on, resulting in their having a new landlord. In fact, he wanted McDonald's to continue to be their landlord. Prior to unveiling a revised "franchisee-friendly" proposal, Ackman spoke with more than a dozen franchisees in an effort to earn their support to put more pressure on McDonald's management. He also suggested that dropping restrictions on the number of stores each franchisee could own would make franchisees more effective at running their stores because of economies of scale. Ackman pointed out that managers at company-owned stores lacked motivation without direct equity compensation, unlike franchisees. Finally, he reminded franchisees that a more profitable pricing structure would emerge as a result of reducing the number of company-owned stores because company stores did not have to pay 3 to 4 percent franchisee fees.

■ ■ ■

**EXHIBIT 10** Transaction Transformation Estimates

# Improves Operating and Financial Metrics at Every Level

- Significantly improves PF McDonald's EBITDA and free cash flow margins
- Enhances return on capital and overall capital allocation for PF McDonald's
- Improves ability of PF McDonald's to pay significant ongoing dividends

| | McDonald's Standalone FY 2006E | Pro Forma McDonald's FY 2006E | Typical Mature QSR |
|---|---|---|---|
| Revenue | $20,816 | $7,393 | |
| EBITDA | 5,594 | 4,464 | |
| EBITDA margin | 26.9% | 60.4% | 15–20% |
| EBITDA—Capex | 4,335 | 3,739 | |
| EBITDA—Capex margin | 20.8% | 50.6% | 7.5–12.5% |
| EBITDA—Maintenance capex | 4,651 | 4,025 | |
| EBITDA—Maintenance capex margin | 22.3% | 54.4% | 10–15% |
| FCF | 3,059 | 2,440 | |
| FCF margin | 14.7% | 33.0% | 5–10% |

*Note*: Capex projections are net of proceeds obtained from store closures. Dollars in millions.
*Source*: Pershing Square Presentation, November 2005.

■ ■ ■

## Rating Agency Concern

Credit rating agencies had significant concerns about Ackman's proposal. They felt that adding more debt to McDonald's in combination with a company-owned restaurant spinoff and a large share repurchase would result in ratings downgrades to just above high-yield/junk-bond status as a result of significant new debt service requirements. McDonald's had been rated A/Stable by Standard and Poor's and A2 by Moody's since 2003 for senior unsecured debt. A Standard & Poor's rating agency director stated, "If McDonald's leveraged up their balance sheet to do a share repurchase, their credit rating would be under great pressure. The lower the credit rating, the higher their interest rate becomes and the more expensive it becomes to finance expansion."[11] Many analysts believed that the massive amount of incremental debt recommended by Ackman's initial proposal would seriously erode earnings. An estimated 20 cents from every dollar operating profit would be used to service debt, leaving the company with less cash to invest in existing stores and for expansion.[12]

---

[11]Julie Jargon, "Ackman 101: Debt Could Squeeze Growth at McDonald's," *Crain's Chicago Business*, December 12, 2005.
[12]Ibid.

## EXHIBIT 11 Comparable Companies

PF McDonald's operating metrics are much closer to those of a typical real estate C corporation or a high-branded intellectual property business such as PepsiCo or Coca-Cola than they are of a typical QSR.

| | Pro Forma McDonald's | Typical Real Estate C Corp | High-Branded Intangible Property | | | Typical Mature QSR[a] |
|---|---|---|---|---|---|---|
| | | | Choice Hotels | PepsiCo | Coca-Cola | |
| 2005E operating metrics: | | | | | | |
| EBITDA margins | 60% | ~70–80% | 66% | 23% | 31% | ~15–20% |
| EBITDA—Capex margins | 50% | ~65–75% | 61% | 18% | 27% | ~7.5–12.5% |
| EPS growth | 9% | NA | 16% | 11% | 9% | ~10–12% |
| Trading multiples: | | | | | | |
| Adjusted enterprise value[b] | | | | | | |
| CY 2006E EBITDA | 13.0x | ~13x–16x | 15.1x | 12.3x | 12.6x | ~8.5x–9.5x |
| CY 2006E EBITDA—Capex | 15.5x | ~17x–20x | 16.0x | 15.5x | 14.2x | ~12x–15x |
| Price | | | | | | |
| CY 2006E EPS | 21.1x | NA | 24.3x | 20.1x | 18.8x | ~15x–19x |
| CY 2006E FCF[c] | 20.9x | ~20x–25x | 24.0x | 20.8x | 18.9x | ~16x–20x |
| Leverage multiples: | | | | | | |
| Net debt/EBITDA | 3.4x | ~5x–10x | 1.7x | 0.0x | NM | ~0.5x–1.8x |
| Total debt/enterprise value | 24% | ~35–60% | 11% | 4% | 4% | ~7.5–20% |

[a]Typical mature QSR based on YUM! Brands and Wendy's.
[b]Adjusted for unconsolidated assets.
[c]FCF denotes net income plus D&A less capex.
   *Notes*: Stock prices as of 11/11/2005. Projections based on Wall Street estimates. Assumes PF McDonald's price of ~$47.50.

# Unlocking McDonald's Real Estate Value

The Pershing team valued McDonald's total real estate, including leaseholds, at $46 billion, substantially higher than its recorded book value of $30 billion ($20 billion after depreciation and amortization). The $46 billion valuation was nearly equal to the company's enterprise value of $52 billion ($46 billion market capitalization at that time plus $6 billion net debt). This implied a substantial disconnect between how investors viewed McDonald's and how Ackman viewed it. The question was whether the market was ignoring most of the company's real estate value and even its brand value by focusing instead principally on earnings.

■ ■ ■

# EXHIBIT 12A  McOpCo Valuation Summary and Potential IPO Proceeds

McOpCo would likely be valued at $6.0–$7.1 billion of equity market value or 6.5×–7.5× EV/2006E EBITDA.

| McOpCo Financial Summary | FY 2006E | McOpCo Valuation Summary | Low | High |
|---|---|---|---|---|
| Company-operated revenues | $15,429 | EV/2006E EBITDA multiple range | 6.5x | 7.5x |
| Segment EBITDA, pre-G&A | 1,690 | McOpCo enterprise value | $7,343 | $8,472 |
| EBITDA margin, pre-G&A | 11.0% | Net debt (12/31/05) | 1,350 | 1,350 |
| Assumed G&A for McOpCo | 560 | Equity value of McOpCo | $5,993 | $7,122 |
| Assumed G&A as % of total G&A | 25.0% | Ending shares outstanding | 1,274 | 1,274 |
| EBITDA post-G&A | $1,130 | Price per share | $4.70 | $5.59 |
| EBITDA margins | 7.3% | Estimated after-tax IPO proceeds | $3,042 | $3,497 |
| Net income | $308 | | | |
| EPS | $0.24 | | | |

*Note*: Dollars in millions, except per share data. *Source*: Pershing Square Presentation, November 2005.

■ ■ ■

Vornado Realty Trust, which owned nearly 90 million square feet of office and retail space principally in the Northeast, had purchased a 4.3 percent stake in Sears prior to its merger with Kmart and had acquired a more-than-30 percent stake in Toys "R" Us at the time of its buyout. Both of these acquisitions were premised on the assumption that the equity market was undervaluing the real estate component of these retailers. In an early November 2005 filing with the SEC, Vornado indicated that it had acquired a 1.2 percent stake in McDonald's during the third quarter of 2005 and implied that it viewed that company's real estate undervalued. Vornado had used a combination of puts and calls to obtain its stake, transacted exclusively through private negotiations during the third quarter of 2005. It asserted that, although McDonald's carried $30 billion of real estate on its books, the true worth was not being adequately recognized by the market at current terms.[13] A popular and simple method of valuing real estate is to apply a capitalization rate (cap rate) to the net operating income of the property. While cap rates vary by market, property type (residential, commercial, industrial, etc.), and economic conditions, analysts believed a 7 percent cap rate was appropriate for McDonald's real estate portfolio. Using this cap rate resulted in a McDonald's total real estate value (land, buildings, and leaseholds) of nearly $64 billion prior to subtracting net rent (Exhibit 15).[14] Although Vornado did not disclose its exact valuation view, it might not have been very different from this level.

Vornado was focused on transferring all or most of McDonald's real estate assets into an REIT (real estate investment trust), which would be required to distribute almost all unpaid earnings and profits tied to real estate. Deutsche Bank estimated that an REIT distribution would be equal to $20 billion pre-tax—or a nearly-$16-per-share payout after taxes (equal to 45 percent of

---

[13]Nicholas Yulico, "McDonald's REIT Could Be a Sizzler," *TheStreet.com, Inc.*, November 9, 2005.

[14]Ibid. (Lou Taylor, Deutsche Bank equity research analyst.)

■ ■ ■

## EXHIBIT 12B  PF McDonald's Valuation Summary

Based on relevant publicly traded comparable companies, including several real estate holding C corporations, PF McDonald's should trade in the range of 12.5×–13.5× EV/ CY 2006E. This implies a 37 to 52 percent premium over the recent stock price of $33.

| PF McDonald's Summary Financials | FY 2006E | PF McDonald's Valuation | Low | High |
|---|---|---|---|---|
| Franchise revenue | $2,275 | EV/2006E EBITDA multiple range | 12.5x | 13.5x |
| Real estate revenue | 5,118 | Enterprise value | $55,799 | $60,263 |
| Total revenue | $7,393 | Less: Net debt (12/31/05E)[a] | 14,650 | 14,650 |
| | | Plus: Remaining stake in McOpCo[b] | 2,097 | 2,493 |
| Franchise EBITDA, pre-G&A | $2,275 | Equity value | $43,247 | $48,106 |
| Real estate EBITDA, pre-G&A | 3,869 | Ending shares outstanding (12/31/05E)[c] | 957.3 | 957.3 |
| Less: Allocated G&A | 1,680 | Price per share | $45 | $50 |
| Assumed G&A as % of total G&A | 75.0% | Premium to recent price[d] | 36.9% | 52.3% |
| Total EBITDA | $4,464 | Implied P/FY 2006 EPS multiple | 19.9x | 22.2x |
| EBITDA margins | 60.4% | Implied P/FY 2006 FCF multiple[e] | 19.8x | 21.9x |
| | | Implied FCF/dividend yield | 5.1% | 4.6% |
| Net income | 2,141 | Memo: share buyback: | | |
| EPS | $2.27 | Incremental debt issued | | $9,685 |
| | | Less transaction fees and expenses[f] | | ($300) |
| | | Approximate cash received from IPO, after tax | | $3,270 |
| | | Total funds available for repurchase | | $12,654 |
| | | # of shares repurchased (in millions) | | 316 |
| | | Average price of stock purchased | | $40 |

[a]Assumes $1.35 billion of net debt allocated to McOpCo and $5.0 billion of net debt allocated to PF McDonald's. In addition, assumes $9.7 billion of incremental leverage placed on PF McDonald's.
[b]Represents 35% of market equity value of McOpCo.
[c]Assumes incremental leverage and after-tax proceeds from McOpCo IPO (net of fees and expenses) are used to buy back approximately 316 million shares at an average price of $40.
[d]Assumes recent stock price of $33.
[e]P/FY 2006E FCF multiple adjusted for PF McDonald's 35% stake in McOpCo.
[f]Fees and expenses associated with the IPO and financing transactions.

*Note*: Dollars in millions, except per share data. *Source*: Pershing Square Presentation, November 2005.

■ ■ ■

McDonald's stock price in February 2006). An REIT is a publicly traded trust or corporation that pools capital from investors to buy or manage income properties and mortgages. REITs tend to trade with valuations reflecting broader market conditions and act as a liquid means of investing in real estate. They are generally not taxed on income, provided their dividend payout is at least 90 percent of taxable income and certain other provisions are also met. While a $20 billion special REIT dividend would attract attention and strong investor interest, a popular criticism of this

**Total Debt/2005E EBITDA[a]**

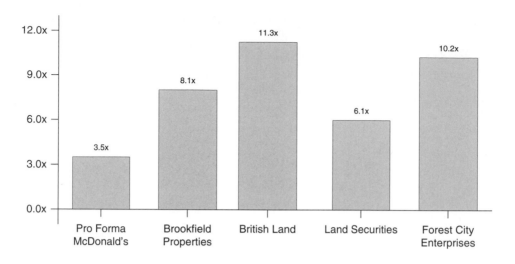

A review of large REITs indicates that these businesses support investment grade ratings with a debt-to-enterprise value of 36 percent on average, as compared to pro forma McDonald's, which would have a debt-to-enterprise value of 25 percent.

| Company Name | Total Debt/ Enterprise Value | Moody's Rating | Moody's Outlook | S&P Rating | S&P Outlook |
|---|---|---|---|---|---|
| Simon Property Group Inc. | 47.2% | Baa2 | Stable | BBB+ | Stable |
| Equity Office Properties Trust | 50.9% | Baa3 | Stable | BBB+ | Stable |
| | 37.4% | Baa3 | Stable | BBB+ | Stable |
| Vornado Realty Trust | 38.4% | Baa1 | Stable | BBB+ | Stable |
| Equity Residential | 31.5% | Baa1 | Stable | BBB+ | Stable |
| Prologis | 33.5% | Baa1 | Stable | BBB+ | Stable |
| Archstone-Smith Trust | 36.0% | NR | NR | BBB+ | Stable |
| Boston Properties Inc. | 25.2% | Baa1 | Stable | A– | Stable |
| Kimco Realty Corp. | 27.3% | Baa1 | Stable | BBB+ | Stable |
| AvalonBay Communities Inc. | | | | | |
| | | | | | |
| Median total debt/EV | 36% | | | | |
| Average total debt/EV | 36% | | | | |
| | | | | | |
| PF McDonald's total debt/EV | 25% | | | | |

*Notes:* Stock prices as of 11/11/2001.

PF McDonald's EV assumes valuation multiple of 13x EV/FY 2006 EBITDA.

Total debt includes preferred.

*Source:* Pershing Square Presentation, November 2005.

**EXHIBIT 13** Comparison of Pro Forma McDonald's with Real Estate Holding Corporations

new REIT formation was the likelihood of its involving significant costs from transfer taxes, property tax reassessment expenses, and capital gains taxes on particular properties. Moreover, loss of control and the future value of lease renewals tend to be top concerns for REIT transfers.

There were distinct differences in the proposals offered by Pershing and Vornado. Pershing argued that, since McDonald's company-operated restaurant business was very capital intensive and yielded low margins, part of McOpCo should be sold through an IPO. However, Pershing

■ ■ ■

**EXHIBIT 14** Rationale for McDonald's Rejection of Pershing's Proposals (2005 and 2006)

- Valuation potential short of proposal's forecasts, not taking into account unique model
- Alignment and conflict issues would surface between parent company and franchisees
- More leverage would result in negative rating agency decision to downgrade debt, possibly increasing borrowing rates up to 150 bps, which would impact franchisee borrowing costs
- Unlikely valuation multiple expansion potential
- High friction costs from IPO spinoff
- Possible higher rents and less income for franchisees
- Already returning value to shareholders via increased dividend and large share repurchases

■ ■ ■

would keep all of McDonald's real estate and use it as a vehicle for issuing collateralized debt to fund a large share repurchase. Vornado, on the other hand, was focused on spinning off McDonald's real estate assets into an REIT and did not advocate either an IPO of McOpCo or a share repurchase.

## Aftermath of McDonald's Rejection

In the week following management's rejection of Ackman's proposal, Pershing hosted a conference in November 2005 for McDonald's shareholders to discuss potential options for McDonald's. In his presentation, Ackman praised McDonald's management for its strong operational execution over the past two years, but indicated that the company should be doing more for its shareholders, maintaining pressure for change.

Lehman Brothers restaurant analyst Jeff Bernstein later explained, "Hedge funds were happy with Pershing's proposal to Wendy's and have reaped the benefits. Long-term holders are mixed about the impact, yet Wendy's stock was not doing well, so many should have been happy with the price appreciation. It made Wendy's further consider whatever they had previously contemplated. McDonald's has adopted and will continue to adopt certain aspects of Ackman's proposal. However, some of McDonald's stockholders are saying that Pershing and others should stop pressuring management since fundamentals are strong."[15]

In mid-January 2006, three months after his original proposal and two months after its rejection, and after speaking to more than a third of McDonald's largest investors, Ackman revised his plan based on the following key points:

- Sell off 20 percent of McOpCo, the company-operated franchises, in an IPO instead of the previous 65 percent target (tax-free benefit if stake sold is 20 percent or lower)

[15]Jeff Bernstein, Lehman Brothers restaurant equity research analyst, interview with the author, December 21, 2005.

| Property Value = Net Operating Income / Capitalization Rate ("Cap Rate") |

⬇

| Net Operating Income = ~$4.4 Billion (Derived from 2005 EBITDA of $5.3 Billion) |

⬇

| Property Value = $4.4 Billion / 7.0% Cap Rate |

⬇

| Property Value = ~$64 Billion (vs. Carrying Book Value of $29.7 Billion)[a] |

Although PF McDonald's would not be configured as an REIT and would not have the tax advantages of an REIT, it would have several superior credit characteristics:

- REITs are required to pay 90 percent of earnings through dividends, whereas PF McDonald's would have much more credit flexibility

- PF McDonald's would have significant brand value to support its cash flows and overall credit

[a]10-K filing for fourth quarter ending 12/31/2005. Net book value of $19.9 billion after depreciation and amortization.

The $64 billion of property value includes net rental income from franchises, which inflates property value and might not reflect true market value. Capitalization rate estimate provided by Deutsche Bank analyst Lou Taylor.

Source: Nicholas Yulico, "McDonald's REIT Could Be a Sizzler," The Street.com, Inc., November 9, 2005.

**EXHIBIT 15** McDonald's REIT Valuation Estimation

- Use the IPO funds along with existing cash balances to boost expansion of restaurants in China and Russia
- Triple the current dividend to $2, retire all unsecured debt, and repurchase more shares than currently targeted by the company
- Refranchise 1,000 stores in mature markets over the next two to three years (retire lower-performing franchisees and start new ones in replacement)
- Provide more disclosure around financial performance of company-owned stores

Basically, Ackman dropped the two most controversial parts of his previous proposal ($12.6 billion in share repurchases and $14.7 billion in new debt issuance backed by real estate), while reducing the percentage of the McOpCo IPO and increasing the company's dividend.

McDonald's quickly rejected Ackman's second proposal, asserting there was nothing "fundamentally new" about it. Ackman responded, "If something is not done to boost McDonald's share price, it could become the target of a leveraged buyout. With $50 billion in leverageable real estate and a robust commercial mortgage-backed securities market, McDonald's is going to be bought if it languishes at $30 per share."[16] He remained resolute in pushing for a McOpCo

---

[16]Christine Richard, "Pershing Sq Scraps Debt Issuance in McDonald's Plan," *Dow Jones Newswires*, January 18, 2006.

IPO to create a separate restaurant operating company, indicating that this would result in greater transparency and efficiency, and an expansion in the company's P/E multiple. Exhibit 16 highlights quotes and outside criticisms relating to hedge fund activism and Pershing Square's McDonald's proposal.

## The Truce

During a year-end earnings conference call in late January 2006, McDonald's CEO said, "The system is a bastion of credibility for a company that is, at its core, a franchising operation. Abandoning it or restructuring it—as hedge-fund activist William Ackman has proposed recently—is out of the question." However, notwithstanding this strong statement, the CEO announced that McDonald's would shift some underperforming stores to more profit-focused owners by selling nearly 1,500 company-owned stores in fifteen to twenty countries to "development license ownership" over the next three years, including 800 stores in the United Kingdom. The CEO also committed to providing better information comparing the performance of company-operated restaurants and franchised restaurants. The day following McDonald's agreement to sell underperforming company-owned restaurants and to provide better financial transparency, Ackman dropped his activist campaign, stating, "We are supporting McDonald's because they're doing the right thing. They've pretty much given us everything we wanted. The only thing we didn't get, which we felt would have given more instant value, would've been a true separation for McOpCo" (the IPO).[17] Exhibit 17 contrasts the cash payout differences between Pershing's two proposals and McDonald's management's final decision.

## Retrospective

In November 2005, when asked about the likelihood of Pershing's proposal actually being executed by McDonald's, Ackman responded, "I'm the most persistent person, especially when I believe I'm right. I don't think this will have to be taken to a proxy contest. It's an intellectual contest. We have the ability to share our ideas." Pershing's option on up to 4.9 percent of the company's stock represented the second largest shareholding in McDonald's after Dodge & Cox at 5.5 percent. The top ten stakeholders combined, excluding Pershing, accounted for 30 percent of outstanding shares. Vornado and Pershing combined represented slightly more than 6 percent of shares; however, their full level of backing by other investors, whether hedge or mutual funds, was not publicly determinable.

In December Ackman explained, "If businesses are undervalued and if there are simple things to do, the shareholder base becomes more perceptive. McDonald's had done nothing in five years and Wendy's had not done much prior to the summer. We convinced Wendy's to restructure and the stock is up $17 in the last few months since Pershing stepped in. McDonald's management was more willing to discuss our thoughts and we will see how that turns out."

Ackman went on, "We do our homework to find a deep discount between price paid and actual value. Our approach is to talk to management first without going public." Pershing considered only public companies because Ackman believed it took different skill sets to invest in private and public companies. He added, "Pershing focuses on high-quality businesses, and so if you are wrong on timing, you can still make up for it on attractive quality as the company

---

[17]Nicholas Yulico, "McDonald's Placates Pershing," *TheStreet.com, Inc.*, January 25, 2006.

### EXHIBIT 16   Pershing's Proposal—Outside Criticisms and Counterarguments

*Mr. Ackman is clearly passionate about the company and we respect that. We also appreciate his candor in acknowledging that his previous ideas presented publicly were not workable. But the fact is, with his latest presentation, he has not presented anything fundamentally new beyond what we've discussed with him previously and what we have evaluated. Ackman's proposal will not deliver the value already being created by our current strategy.*[22]

—Mary Kay Shaw, vice president of investor relations, McDonald's

*The typical hedge fund manager's idea of long-term planning is figuring out where to have dinner tonight. Their strategy is to buy stock in a company whose assets—such as real estate or cash—aren't reflected in the price of the stock, and browbeat management until they force the sale of those assets, with proceeds distributed to them and other shareholders. Then they grab their money, and move on to their next quarry.*[23]

—Dan Miller, *Chicago Sun-Times* (regarding Pershing/McDonald's)

*Ackman was off-base in arguing that McDonald's has been a "slacker." In fact, the company's U.S. operations are the envy of the industry. After all, franchisees want to see the company put their own skin in the game first.*[24]

—Peter Oakes and Scott Waltmann, Piper Jaffray analysts

*The company is going to get to these [earnings]* levels by themselves regardless of the push Ackman is putting on. In the end it's going to be a slow process . . . I'm OK with that as a shareholder because I think we get to the same place eventually.*[25]

—Herb Achey, U.S. Trust

*By creating a separate restaurant company, you may create some kind of diametrically opposing forces that in the long run could be detrimental, not beneficial, to shareholders.*[26]

—Scott Rothbort, LakeView Asset Management

*If McDonald's leveraged up their balance sheet to do a share repurchase, their credit rating would be under great pressure. The lower the credit rating, the higher their interest rate becomes and the more expensive it becomes to finance expansion.*[27]

—A Standard & Poor's Director

*We think the greatest long-term risk of a McOpCo spinoff is its potential damage to franchise-company relations. With its current ownership of 2,000 U.S. stores, McDonald's communicates to franchisees its focus on the bottom line and not just sales. Conversely, by not having any involvement in restaurant operations as the proposal suggests,*

---

[22] McDonald's press release, January 18, 2006.
[22] McDonald's press release, January 18, 2006.
[23] Dan Miller, "Greedy Mac Attack Bad for Business," *Chicago Sun-Times*, December 2, 2005.
[24] Nichola Groom, "McDonald's Investors Unswayed by Activist Proposal," *Reuters*, January 19, 2006.
[25] Ibid.
[26] Deepak Gopinath, "Hedge Fund Rabble-Rouser," *Bloomberg Markets*, October 2005.
[27] Jargon, "Ackman 101."

*McDonald's would likely tarnish the franchisees' trust of the company. Overall, spinoff would threaten the three-legged stool.*[28]

—Mark Wiltamuth & Dana Greenberg, Morgan Stanley

*On the surface, there is a lot of merit to the argument. Ackman's view is that the market is misvaluing the company and I'm inclined to agree with him. The guy has got very good arguments, and I think the company owes its shareholders a reasoned response.*[29]

—Leon Cooperman, Omega Advisors

---

[28] Mark Wiltamuth and Dana Greenberg, Morgan Stanley Equity Research North America, November 1, 2005.
[29] "McDonald's Rejects Shareholder Plan to Restructure," *Reuters*, January 18, 2006.

■ ■ ■

■ ■ ■

**EXHIBIT 17** Differences Between Pershing Square's Proposal and McDonald's Management's Plan ($ in billions)

| | Pershing Proposal (Sept. 2005) | Pershing Revised Proposal (Jan. 2006) | McDonald's Management's Plan |
|---|---|---|---|
| Dividends | Unspecified | $1.7 | $5–6 total dividends and share repurchases payout in 2006 and 2007[a] |
| Share repurchases | $12.6 | Unspecified | |
| IPO proceeds (post-tax) | $3.3 | $1.3 | None |
| Secured debt issue | $14.7 | None | None |
| Debt reduction | $5.0 | None | None |
| Transaction fees | $0.3 | Unspecified (less than $0.3) | Minor amount for refranchising |

[a]2005 payout was dividends of $850 million and repurchases of $1.2 billion ($2.05 billion total).

■ ■ ■

becomes more valuable with each day that passes." Wendy's stock was up 55 percent since Pershing first established its equity position; however, McDonald's stock was up only 20 percent. Ackman still believed that his original transformational strategic plan for McDonald's would push the share price to $45–50 per share, a 37 to 52 percent premium to the stock price at the time of his initial proposal.

Separately, two of the most anticipated IPOs of early 2006 included Chipotle (McDonald's stake) and Tim Hortons (Wendy's stake). The Chipotle IPO broke the five-year largest opening day gain record when it was launched during January 2006, doubling on the first day of the offering, and Tim Hortons IPO traded up 42 percent during its opening day in late March 2006.

# Porsche, Volkswagen, and CSX: Cars, Trains, and Derivatives

Family members knew something was very wrong when Adolf Merckle, who had guided the family holding company, VEM Vermögensverwaltung GmbH, through successful investments in dozens of firms in industries from pharmaceutical drugs to cement, left the house one afternoon in January 2009 and failed to return. That night their fears were confirmed when a German railway worker located Merckle's body near a commuter train line near his hometown of Blaubeuren, about a hundred miles west of Munich.

It was no secret that the financial crisis had taken a toll on Merckle's investments following his frank comments to the media in 2008. Merckle, known in Germany as a savvy investor, had lost hundreds of millions of Euros after being caught on the wrong side of a short squeeze of epic proportions. In a short squeeze, investors who are shorting a company's stock, or betting against the rise in its price, are forced into the market to buy back stock to cover their short position if the price unexpectedly increases. Merckle's misplaced bet against Volkswagen's stock had been one significant cost among several that eventually led to talks between the Merckle family and thirty creditors about the viability of VEM.

## Using Derivatives to Obtain Control Positions

### Volkswagen Equity Derivatives

Merckle's was not the only large bet against Volkswagen's stock. A number of hedge funds, including Greenlight Capital, SAC Capital, Glenview Capital, Tiger Asia, and Perry Capital, lost billions of Euros in a few hours based on their large short positions in Volkswagen's stock following the news on October 26, 2008, that Porsche AG had obtained a large long synthetic position in Volkswagen stock through cash-settled options. Porsche's news release that day showed it had a 74.1 percent equity position in Volkswagen, a combination of its known ownership of 42.6 percent of Volkswagen stock and cash-settled options on shares representing an additional 31.5 percent of the company. The funds and other investors quickly realized that, factoring in the non-borrowable 20 percent ownership held by the German state of Lower Saxony, just 5.9 percent of Volkswagen shares remained on the market for short sellers to buy in order to cover their short positions. In the next two days, this short squeeze produced a fivefold increase in Volkswagen's share price, as demand for shares from hedge funds exceeded the supply of borrowable shares. In addition, there was upside pressure on Volkswagen's share price because the company's stock was included in the DAX Index (a capitalization-weighted index), and as the share price increased, index funds were required to purchase more stock.

Porsche's effort to obtain majority control over Volkswagen through derivative contracts created one of the most dramatic runups in a large company's share price in history. The result of this shrewd strategy on the part of Porsche's CFO, Holger Härter, was gaining control over Volkswagen without allowing hedge funds and other third parties to drive the price upward. The consequence of this strategy was major losses at hedge funds that had shorted Volkswagen's stock.

## CSX Equity Derivatives

A similar situation had taken place overseas just a few months previously. During the summer of 2008 a court ruled that two UK-based hedge funds, the Children's Investment Fund Management (TCI) and 3G Capital Partners (3G), had been illegally plotting a bid for control of American railroad company CSX Corporation without disclosing their intentions. Another court ruled that TCI and 3G violated Securities and Exchange Commission (SEC) disclosure requirements by disguising their takeover intentions regarding CSX when they entered into equity derivatives called total return swaps (TRS) with multiple investment banks.[1] TRS are agreements in which one party makes interest payments based on a set rate—fixed or variable—while the other party makes payments based on the return of an underlying asset, which includes both the income it generates and any capital gains or losses. Regulation 13D requirements mandated that stock ownership of greater than 5 percent must be disclosed, but the hedge funds took the position that equity swaps did not give them beneficial control over shares and so there was no disclosure obligation. The ruling against the hedge funds moved equity swaps into new territory. Equity swaps are a form of "synthetic shares," which endow the holder with the economic benefits of share ownership without the voting rights.

However, it was not a total victory for CSX. Although the hedge funds had their hands slapped for the disclosure violations, they ultimately prevailed in obtaining seats on CSX's board. The court acknowledged it was too late to reverse the funds' actions, as it was prohibited from denying shareholders the right to vote for a new board of directors. Though the court battle carried on into the fall, a federal appeals judge ultimately granted TCI and 3G a total of four seats, replacing two CSX-backed directors with dissident nominees, including TCI's Christopher Hohn.[2]

While many U.S. companies had already expanded the definition of equity ownership to include anyone who held derivatives on a company's stock, this ruling forced the SEC to regulate the meaning of ownership more stringently under American law.

These two stories demonstrate the rapidly increasing importance of equity derivatives such as cash-settled options and equity swaps. Porsche and the hedge funds had used equity derivatives for similar control purposes but ended up with dramatically different results. Porsche's use of these instruments in its pursuit of ownership in Volkswagen resulted in a significant swing in market capitalization and huge losses for short-selling hedge funds, while TCI and 3G's pursuit of ownership in CSX resulted in legal wrangling and condemnation by a U.S. federal judge, as well as an increase in the hedge funds' control when they were granted seats on the company's board.

Comparing the two stories provides a framework for comprehending the uses of equity derivatives; assessing the growing regulatory, economic, and legal risks associated with these instruments; and learning valuable lessons regarding their use as a vehicle to achieve beneficial ownership of a company's stock. This analysis provokes the following questions: Should there always be public disclosure of equity derivatives? Should CEOs actively consider using derivative

---

[1] The court held that the two hedge funds had violated provisions of Section 13(d) of the Securities Exchange Act of 1934 and Rule 13d-3(b) by using cash-settled swap transactions in a way that, given the circumstances, improperly evaded disclosure obligations related to the formation of a group "beneficial owner."

[2] "CSX Accedes Seats to Dissidents," *Directorship*, September 17, 2008, http://www.directorship.com/csx-fills-board.

contracts? Are investment banks complicit, or just doing their jobs for clients, when they act as counterparties to derivative contracts? Are hedge funds playing fair in their use of equity derivatives? How can hedge funds get burned by equity derivatives? Should regulators make derivative disclosure requirements absolute?

# CSX Collides with TCI and 3G

## Background

CSX Corporation—a Jacksonville-based rail and transport conglomerate—was a descendant of Chessie Systems, which started in 1836 and owned such famous rail lines as the C&O and B&O railroads. CSX was the result of Chessie's 1980 merger with Seaboard Coast Line Industries (formed in 1958), and a flurry of mergers and divestments that cumulatively added line capacity in addition to terminal and switching operations. Through its coal business, CSX delivered about 1.9 million carloads of coal, coke, and iron ore to electric utilities and manufacturers in 2007. Almost 100 percent of revenue came from its rail and intermodal businesses.

CSX primarily operated in North American nerve centers via its principal operating company, CSX Transportation (CSXT), which delivered merchandise, coal, and automobiles via its approximately 21,000-route-mile rail network. CSXT was one of the largest railroads in the eastern United States, serving thousands of production and distribution facilities through track connections to more than 230 short-line and regional railroads in twenty-three states.[3] Michael Ward, CEO of CSX, was widely hailed as an innovator and leader in the transport segment, delivering returns far exceeding the S&P during the five years prior to the recent economic downturn. In addition, *Railway Age* named him Railroader of the Year in 2008.

Since 2003, when money manager Christopher Hohn founded the TCI hedge fund with $3 billion initially under management, TCI had taken public stances against management at Deutsche Börse, ABN Amro, and South Korean cigarette maker KT&G. Its activist approach paid off in 2005 when it led a successful movement to oust the leadership of German stock exchange operator Deutsche Börse. An activist strategy did not work in 2007, however, when the Japanese government forced TCI to unwind its position in the electric utility JPower on national security grounds. The forced sale resulted in a ¥12.5 billion ($127.3 million) loss for the fund.

Hohn first gained recognition as a money manager for hedge fund Perry Capital in London, where he had overseen European investments. Since starting TCI, he posted strong results, predominantly by one-off, large-scale trades in European and Asian equities. In 2006, when the S&P Hedge Fund Index rose just 3.9 percent, TCI's returns topped 40 percent and won the fund a top award from EuroHedge, a London newsletter that ranked Europe's best-performing hedge funds. Yet Hohn had some "rough edges," according to acolytes and detractors alike.[4] He was known for a demanding style, combative e-mails to target companies, and a staccato, bullying way of speech.

3G Capital had been co-founded in 2004 by Pavel Begun and Corey Bailey to be a long-term-oriented fund with no more than ten investment positions. The name derived from the three Gs in their firm-wide objective: to invest in good business, run by good management, and available at a good price.

---

[3]CSX Company Report, Datamonitor 2008.

[4]Laura Cohn, "A Little Fund With Big Demands," *BusinessWeek*, May 23, 2005, http://www.businessweek.com/magazine/content/05_21/b3934161_mz035.htm.

## TCI and 3G Take a Position

2007 ended with TCI and 3G actively calling for change at CSX, pushing for the railroad to improve performance by changing senior management, including separating the chairman and chief executive roles, both held by Michael Ward. They also sought to add five independent directors to its board and link management compensation to performance. In response, CSX stated that it was the only major railroad that already had 100 percent performance-based annual and long-term incentive plans.[5]

In February 2008 CSX wrote to TCI, calling the investor's interest in pushing change "not in good corporate governance, but in achieving effective control of the company." CSX had amended its bylaws to provide that a special meeting would be called only after the company received a written request from shareholders representing at least 15 percent of its voting power.

The following month CSX filed a lawsuit against TCI and 3G, alleging a violation of Regulation 13D of the Securities and Exchange Act, which requires disclosure for ownership positions greater than 5 percent of a target company. CSX had learned the hedge funds had initially entered into TRS with eight counterparties, which in aggregate gave TCI and 3G economic upside on a position of more than 14 percent of CSX's shares, with a notional value of more than $2.5 billion at the time. It was alleged that "most if not all" of the TRS counterparties accumulated an equivalent position in CSX shares to hedge these positions. See Exhibit 1 for a chronology of the lawsuit.

TCI and 3G, meanwhile, formed a group to nominate a slate of directors to stand for election at the CSX annual meeting in June 2008. Later in May, the two investors went on the offensive with CSX shareholders, writing that the funds had increased their position to a 21 percent interest in the company based on a $2.0 billion share holding (8.7 percent of CSX stock) combined with a notional value of $2.8 billion in TRS on the company's stock

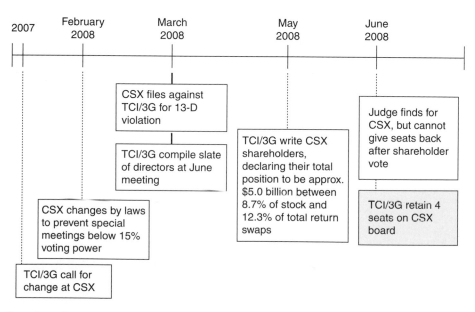

**EXHIBIT 1** Chronology of CSX Proxy Fight with TCI/3G

---

[5]Performance-based earnings excludes time-based stock options and restricted stock.

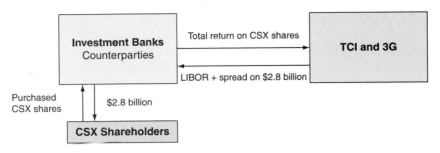

**EXHIBIT 2** CSX Transaction Diagram

(12.3 percent of CSX stock).[6] The funds' stated goal was to persuade shareholders to vote the slate of candidates proposed by the funds onto the company board at the next election and accept the funds' recommendations (which they said could help CSX achieve $2.2 billion in annual productivity gains within five years).[7]

In the CSX TRS, the underlying asset, or reference asset, was CSX common shares owned by the party receiving the set rate payment.[8] For the period of the transaction, the TRS receiver of reference asset returns had a synthetic long position in the market risk of the reference asset.

In the CSX TRS, TCI and 3G made interest payments to eight investment banks, which made payments back to the hedge funds based on the returns of CSX shares. A key benefit of the TRS for TCI and 3G was that they gained equity exposure to CSX without actually owning the shares that underlined the TRS. Hedge funds preferred these swaps because they got the benefit of a large exposure with a minimal cash outlay and, until the 2008 court ruling, without a legal requirement to disclose their position. See Exhibit 2 for a diagram of the CSX TRS.

## Porsche and Volkswagen: Brothers Reunited

Following on the American court ruling in 2008 that begrudgingly granted board seats to TCI and 3G, Porsche's strategic use of equity derivatives to gain ownership of Volkswagen was well-received in Germany. Of course, this warm perception was partially due to the long, interwoven history of the firms there.

Ferdinand Porsche was the creator of the VW Beetle in 1931 and founder of the luxury car manufacturer Porsche. The Porsche 64, the company's first product, was built with many of the same components as the Beetle. Ferdinand Porsche was also the grandfather to the board chairmen of both Porsche and Volkswagen.

Porsche primarily made a line of luxury automobiles, including the famous 911, Boxster, and more modern Cayenne SUV, among others. It produced approximately 100,000 cars a year.

Volkswagen, in contrast, made more than six million cars a year for major markets in Europe, the Americas, Asia/Pacific, and Africa. Its stable of brands ranged from the middle-market proprietary brand and family-oriented Scania to Audi, Lamborghini, and Bentley.

In recent years German politicians had begun publicly vilifying foreign investors (who had bought more than 5,000 German firms since 1990) and clamoring for more domestic ownership.

---

[6]Dan Slater, "Judge Kaplan Reprimands Hedge Funds in Takeover Battle with CSX," June 12, 2008, http://blogs.wsj.com/law/2008/06/12/judge-kaplan-reprimands-hedge-funds-in-takeover-battle-with-csx.

[7]Lisa LaMotta, "CSX Tells Activists To Get Off The Tracks," *Forbes.com*, May 20, 2008, http://www.forbes.com/equities/2008/05/20/csx-tci-update-markets-equities-cx_lal_0520markets41.html.

[8]Barron's Dictionary of Financial Terms.

In 2005 Porsche's CEO, Wendelin Wiedeking, announced the company's intention to purchase 20 percent of Volkswagen stock to support a "German solution" to the takeover dilemma, matching the 20 percent held by the state of Lower Saxony.[9] The company increased its holding to 30 percent in 2007, prompting German legislators to change securities laws, which put pressure on Porsche to make a tender offer. Its hand forced, Porsche publicly disclaimed its interest in majority control and offered the legal minimum for additional shares in Volkswagen, leading to a meager 0.6 percent increase in its ownership. See Exhibit 3 for a chronology of Porsche's position in Volkswagen.

Suddenly, Porsche changed course. Less than a year after its public refusal to ratchet up its ownership in Volkswagen, in March 2008 Porsche's board backed the CEO's goal to increase its net position in Volkswagen up to 50 percent. Between March and October, Wiedeking and other Porsche officials denied rumors that Porsche would take this position up to 75 percent.

On Friday, October 24, 2008, Volkswagen's share price closed at € 211.

On October 26, Porsche dropped a bombshell, disclosing in a news release that it had obtained 42.6 percent in Volkswagen equities and cash-settled options accounting for an additional 31.5 percent of the company. The news meant just 5.9 percent of Volkswagen equities remained in circulation after considering Lower Saxony's position of 20 percent, creating a perfect condition for a short squeeze.

By October 28, the price of Volkswagen shares exceeded € 1,000 ($1,125) in intraday trading, creating a total market capitalization of € 324 billion ($364 billion) and making it temporarily the most valuable company in the world (see Exhibit 4). By entering into option contracts with investment banks before the disclosure was made, Porsche made purchase of Volkswagen shares by others very difficult.

Many hedge funds had entered pairs trades involving Volkswagen stock prior to Porsche's disclosure. They were long Volkswagen preferred shares and short Volkswagen common shares. In addition, many funds were also long Porsche common stock and short Volkswagen common shares.

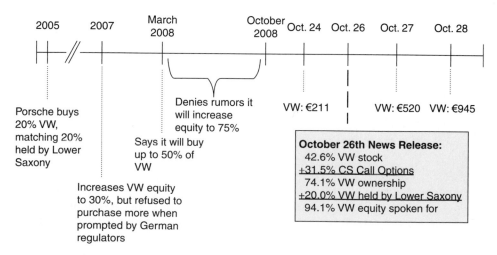

**EXHIBIT 3** Chronology of Porsche Position in Volkswagen

[9]Mike Esterl et al., "As Giant Rivals Stall, Porsche Engineers a Financial Windfall," *Wall Street Journal.com*, November 10, 2008, http://online.wsj.com/article/SB122610533132510217.html.

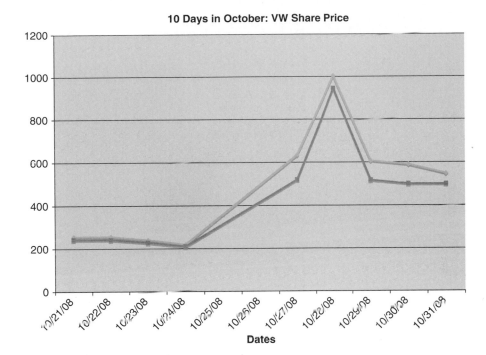

**EXHIBIT 4** Volkswagen's Share Price

The hedge funds found themselves in a short squeeze of epic proportions following Porsche's disclosure. To cover their short position, the funds scrambled to purchase Volkswagen shares, bidding up the share price to previously unimaginable levels. The upside share price pressure was exacerbated by index funds that purchased Volkswagen shares to maintain proper weighting in the DAX Index, as Volkswagen's share of the index grew with the rising share price. The result of this enormous demand was a fivefold increase in Volkswagen's share price and an estimated $15 billion loss for hedge funds that had entered into the pairs trades.

## Cash-Settled Options

Cash-settled options are option contracts in which settlement is completed by paying cash equal to the difference between the market value and the contractual value of the underlying security at the time of exercise or expiration. This compares to physically settled options in which actual physical delivery of the underlying security is required.

The cash-settled options on Volkswagen's stock into which Porsche entered were call spread options, which gave Porsche the right to receive a predetermined maximum cash payment if Volkswagen's share price increased during the option period. See Exhibits 5 and 6. The purchase of cash-settled options on Volkswagen stock by Porsche gave Porsche the right to receive a future payment of cash based on the amount by which Volkswagen's share price exceeded the options' lower strike price on the earlier of the date of exercise or maturity. The cash payment was limited by a cap determined prior to initiation, which was set at the higher strike price. The higher the cap, the higher the cost of the option premium. Investment banks hedged their cash payment

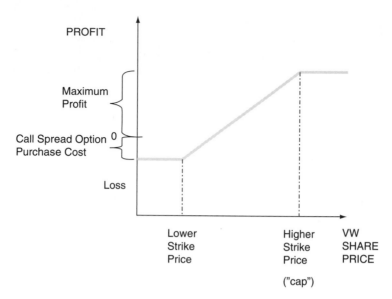

**EXHIBIT 5** Cash-Settled Options

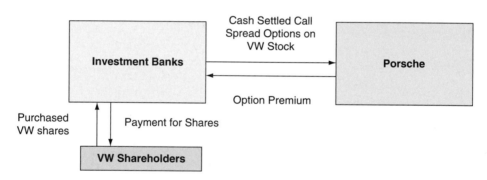

**EXHIBIT 6** Cash-Settled Options: Porsche and Investment Banks

exposure by buying a "delta" number of Volkswagen shares, depending on the probability of the shares exceeding the strike price.

Porsche began purchasing cash-settled options tied to Volkswagen stock in 2005, when the share price was less than € 100. If the price rose, Porsche could exercise the options and receive the difference between the lower strike price and the higher market price (creating a cap on the cash received). It could then use the cash to buy Volkswagen shares. Alternatively, Porsche could request that its investment banking counterparties deliver the shares to Porsche based on a value equal to the cash settlement value of the options when exercised (although the banks could decline to alter the contract in this way).

German law did not require an investor to disclose ownership of any size holding of cash-settled options, allowing Porsche to build a large stake in Volkswagen while keeping the rest of the market unaware of this activity.

Banks that were counterparties to Porsche hedged their exposure by holding actual Volkswagen shares, removing them from circulation.

## Stealth by Swaps

As with the hedge funds that entered into TRS in their bid for influence at CSX, Porsche's derivatives created a synthetic form of ownership. In both cases, counterparties to the derivatives contracts held common shares as a hedge while the paying party for the derivative contract assumed the economic risks and benefits of ownership. This form of silent acquisition via derivatives was becoming more common as both companies and investors attempted to create control positions in corporate shares while avoiding disclosure.

## Dilemma

In the aftermath of Porsche's effort to control Volkswagen, German politicians initially dismissed calls for a public inquiry into Porsche's strategic use of the cash-settled options to skirt disclosure. Their comments seconded the view of most Germans that this merger was destined to happen and that no sympathy for hedge funds and their mounting losses should be felt. Later, the German securities regulator Bundesanstalt für Finanzdienstleistungsaufsicht (BaFin) found "there was no evidence of wrongdoing."[10] Even if BaFin had found that Porsche broke its rules, it could have imposed fines of no more than € 200,000 for the nondisclosure and 1 million for violating the mandatory bid rule.

It appeared that Porsche's CEO had made a careful and smart calculation, assuming that the costs were far outweighed by the benefits of his strategy—much like TCI and 3G in their proxy fight for seats on the board at CSX.

That was before January 5, 2009, when Adolf Merckle threw himself in front of a German train, presumably distraught by the extreme losses his firm had suffered from its bearish bets on Volkswagen.

---

[10]Chris Reiter, "Porsche May Delay VW Stake Increase as Debts Mount," *Bloomberg.com*, March 31, 2009, http://www.bloomberg.com/apps/news?pid=newsarchive&sid=aI48e1cKDQog.

# The Toys "R" Us LBO

"I don't want to grow up, I'm a Toys 'R' Us kid" was the famous marketing slogan of Toys "R" Us (the "Company"), the world's leading specialty toy retailer for much of the 1980s and 1990s. Private equity industry veterans may have had a similar attitude regarding the maturation of their industry. In its infancy, the industry had consisted of relatively few firms and lucrative investing opportunities that far exceeded capital in the industry. By 2005, however, a record amount of capital had been committed to the industry and aggregate transaction values had reached a new high. The industry had become intensely competitive and the best investing opportunities were being chased by too much capital, making it difficult for investors to match historically lofty returns. While private equity executives would have preferred that the industry not grow up, they continued to find investment opportunities that provided compelling value to themselves and their limited partners.

In 2006 $252 billion of capital was committed to the private equity industry, compared to $90 billion in 2000—an absolute increase of 181 percent (Exhibit 1). As the amount of committed capital increased, so did the need for more investment opportunities. In 2006 there was more than $233 billion of aggregate transaction value in private equity deals, compared to $41 billion in 2000—an absolute increase of 475 percent (Exhibit 2). An increasing supply/demand imbalance led to an increase in the average purchase price multiple in leveraged buyouts (LBOs), which reached a record high of 8.6× EBITDA in 2006 (Exhibit 3).

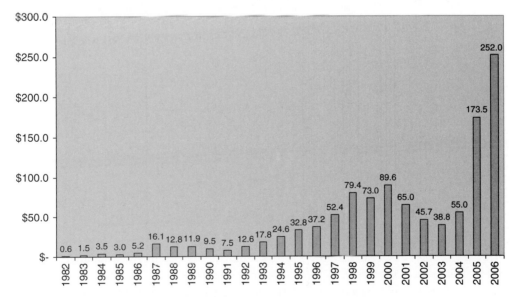

**EXHIBIT 1** U.S. Private Equity Committed Capital ($ in billions). *Source:* Standard & Poor's.

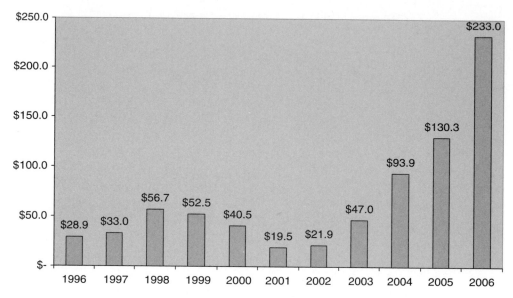

**EXHIBIT 2** Value of LBO Transactions ($ in billions). *Source*: Standard & Poor's.

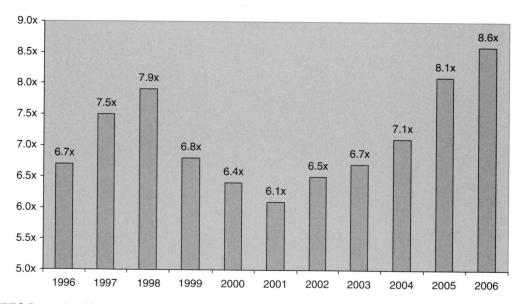

**EXHIBIT 3** Buyout Acquisition Multiple. *Source*: Standard & Poor's.

## Case Focus

This case simulates the experience of a private equity investor evaluating a potential investment. It requires the reader to: (1) determine the risks and merits of an investment in Toys "R" Us, (2) evaluate the spectrum of returns using multiple operating model scenarios, and (3) identify strategic actions that might be undertaken to improve the risk/return profile of the investment. The case discusses the participants in the Toys "R" Us LBO and emerging trends in the private equity industry.

# Emergence of Club Deals in a Maturing Industry

In the past, the largest private equity funds were able to minimize competition with smaller funds because of the distinct advantage their fund size provided. As of November 2004, the largest single private equity fund, raised for JP Morgan's Global 2001 Fund, was approximately $6.5 billion.[1] That amount would be greatly overshadowed by the capital raised by private equity firms just a few years later, however. As of January 2007, for example, both KKR and Blackstone had raised single private equity funds with approximately $16.0 billion of committed capital.[2] JP Morgan's Global 2001 Fund would not rank in the top ten largest funds raised as of January 2007.[3]

Historically, private equity firms preferred to complete acquisitions without other financial partners to ensure complete control over acquired companies. In an industry that required a precise strategy to create value, partnering issues (e.g., agreeing on strategic decisions, capital structure, and investment exits) could prove problematic. However, as the asset class grew and competition for traditional private equity transactions increased, private equity firms turned to club deals.

A club deal was an acquisition completed by two or more private equity firms that allowed them to acquire companies that were too large for one private equity firm to acquire. Many funds set concentration limits on the percentage of committed capital that could be invested in a single asset. Club deals expanded the universe of potential acquisitions by bringing together the capital of multiple firms, enabling very large acquisitions. By allowing large private equity firms to target companies beyond the reach of smaller private equity firms, club deals reduced competition and increased potential returns.

Although there was competition between consortia—for example, more than one club chasing an asset—this competition was below the level observed in the traditional small/middle private equity market. Chasing bigger assets through club deals allowed the largest funds to more efficiently allocate their time (the industry's most precious resource) as they put money to work.

Club deals offered the following advantages:

- Limited competition
- Allowed for greater deployment of capital
- Leveraged multiple sources of expertise while conducting due diligence and evaluating an investment
- Spread expenses incurred while evaluating the investment and reduced "busted" deal costs

Disadvantages included the following:

- Limited ability to control an investment—potential for strategic disagreements
- Interfered with limited partners' desire for risk diversification because they became owners of the same asset through participation in multiple funds
- Created potential regulatory issues regarding anticompetitive behavior

Specific charges included submitting separate bids to gauge a competitive price with an agreement to "club up" in the future and "clubbing up" at the beginning of a process to reduce the field of potential buyers. In October 2006 the Department of Justice began an inquiry into

---

[1]"The New Kings of Capitalism," *The Economist*, November 25, 2004.

[2]"The Uneasy Crown," *The Economist*, February 8, 2007.

[3]Ibid.

potential anticompetitive behavior by private equity firms. Justice Department officials sent letters requesting information on deals and auctions to Kohlberg, Kravis & Roberts, Silver Lake Partners, and other firms.[4]

According to *Buyouts* magazine, of the 845 private equity deals completed in 2005, 125 were club deals, meaning that private equity shops were teaming up nearly 15 percent of the time.[5] Recent high-profile club deals included SunGard Data Systems, Hertz Corporation, and HCA. Barring a major change in the regulatory environment or problems in existing club deals, club deal activity was likely to continue to increase.

## Dividends and Fees Paid to Private Equity Firms

Another trend that was gaining popularity in the private equity industry involved rapidly accessing the capital markets after closing a deal to raise cash to pay a large dividend to the private equity owners. Firms typically used the debt markets to finance these dividends, creating more highly levered, riskier companies. In some cases, dividends paid to private equity firms within one year of their original investment equaled the original equity commitment. In the Hertz LBO transaction, Clayton, Dubilier & Rice, Carlyle Group, and Merrill Lynch collected $1 billion in bank-funded dividends six months after buying rental car company Hertz for $15 billion.[6] About four months later, Hertz issued an IPO to pay off the debt and to fund an additional dividend, resulting in total dividends paid to the owners that equaled 54 percent of their original investment of $2.3 billion (still leaving them with 71 percent ownership).

Private equity funds also took cash out of their portfolio companies to pay large "advisory" fees to themselves. These fees exceeded $50 million on large transactions during the buyout phase and annual fees often continued throughout their ownership.

## U.S. Retail Toy Industry in 2005

In 2005 sales in the U.S. retail toy industry totaled $21.3 billion, down 4 percent from $22.1 billion in 2004.[7] While some categories—such as plush, vehicles, and games and puzzles—had large declines in sales in 2005, there was growth in certain subcategories. It is difficult to track consistent data across multiple sources as category and subcategory definitions varied. However, it is important to note that, in aggregate, dollar sales in the industry declined for a third consecutive year. See Exhibit 4 for growth by category.

Video game sales continued to outperform traditional toy sales in 2005 as younger children increasingly chose video games over traditional toys. In addition, the video game market benefited from the increased acceptance of video gaming among adults. In 2004 the average video game player was 29 years old.[8] Video game sales were expected to continue to outperform the traditional toy market.

After a period of robust growth in the 1990s, analysts and industry experts in 2005 were expecting 0 to 2 percent growth in the traditional toys and games market over the next three

---

[4]"Justice Department Probing Buyout Funds," *MSNBC.com*, October 10, 2006.

[5]Mark L. Mandel, "Wielding a Club," *New York Law Journal*, June 29, 2006.

[6]"Gluttons at the Gate," *BusinessWeek*, October 30, 2006.

[7]NPD Group Press Release, February 13, 2006.

[8]Citigroup Equity Research, "Toy Industry Outlook," September 22, 2004.

EXHIBIT 4    U.S. Retail Toy Industry ($ in billions)

| Category | 2004 ($) | 2005 ($) | Growth (%) |
|---|---|---|---|
| Action figures and accessories | 1.25 | 1.30 | 4.0 |
| Arts and crafts | 2.50 | 2.40 | −4.0 |
| Building sets | 0.60 | 0.70 | 16.0 |
| Dolls | 2.76 | 2.70 | −2.0 |
| Games/puzzles | 2.64 | 2.40 | −9.0 |
| Infant/preschool | 3.13 | 3.10 | −1.0 |
| Learning and exploration | 0.37 | 0.39 | 5.0 |
| Outdoor and sports toys | 2.78 | 2.70 | −3.0 |
| Plush | 1.53 | 1.30 | −15.0 |
| Vehicles | 1.96 | 1.80 | −8.0 |
| Other | 2.00 | 2.50 | 4.0 |
| Total traditional toys | 22.12 | 21.29 | −3.8 |
| Total video games | 9.91 | 10.50 | 6.0 |

*Source*: NPD Group Press Release, February 2006

EXHIBIT 5    Projected Population Growth (in millions)

| Age Cohort | 2005 | 2010E | Total Growth (%) | Implied CAGR (%) |
|---|---|---|---|---|
| Ages 5 and under | 20,311 | 21,426 | 5.5 | 1.1 |
| Ages 6–8 | 11,782 | 12,228 | 3.8 | 0.7 |
| Ages 9–12 | 15,744 | 15,986 | 1.5 | 0.3 |

*Source*: NPD Group, October 2006

to five years. This stabilization was based in part on a view that the worst of the price competition was behind the industry and continued consolidation should improve the competitive dynamic. In addition, favorable demographic trends were expected to help the industry. See Exhibit 5 for growth estimates by age cohort.

According to the NPD Group, the mass/discount channel continued to gain share from other toy retailers in 2005, accounting for 54 percent of total toy sales, while toy stores represented 20 percent (the vast majority of this was Toys "R" Us). Clearly the mass/discount channel—specifically Wal-Mart and Target—were growing at the expense of the specialty toy retailers (see Exhibit 6).[9] Toys "R" Us was the largest specialty toy retailer in the industry, and while it struggled in a difficult operating environment, it was better equipped to compete with the mass/discount channel than its peers. For example, two other leading specialty toy retailers, KB Toys and FAO Schwarz, filed for Chapter 11 protection in 2004. Online toy sales continued to increase as well, generating more than $1.3 billion in 2005, a 2.6 percent increase over the prior year, and accounting for approximately 6 percent of sales for the year.[10]

The retail toy industry was highly competitive. Competitors included discount and mass merchandisers, electronics retailers, national and regional chains, and local retailers. Competition

---

[9]JP Morgan Equity Research, "Toy Retailing: The Shakeout Goes On," May 5, 2003.
[10]NPD Group Press Release, February 13, 2006.

EXHIBIT 6   U.S. Toy Retail Market Share (%)

|                    | 2003 | 2005 |
|--------------------|------|------|
| Mass market share  | 48.6 | 54.0 |
| Toy stores         | 25.1 | 20.0 |

*Source*: NPD Group Press Release, February 2006, and Doug Desjardins, "Toy Market Still Full of Surprises," *DSN RetailingToday*, September 6, 2004

was principally based on price, store location, advertising and promotion, product selection, quality, and service. Advantages in financial resources, lower merchandise acquisition costs, and/or lower operating expenses were usually passed along to customers in an attempt to preserve or gain market share. Discount and mass merchandisers increasingly used aggressive pricing policies and enlarged toy-selling areas during the holiday season to build traffic for other store departments (e.g., toys were used as a loss leader).

Success in the retail toy industry depended on a company's ability to identify, originate, and define product trends, as well as anticipate, gauge, and react to changing consumer demands in a timely manner. If a retailer misjudged the market for products, it might have significant excess inventories for some products and missed opportunities for others. Sales of toys and other products depended upon discretionary consumer spending, which was affected by general economic conditions, consumer confidence, and other macroeconomic factors. A decline in consumer spending would, among other things, negatively impact sales across the toy industry and result in excess inventories, requiring discounting to move old inventory.

Electronics retailers became more relevant competitors in toy retailing by capitalizing on "age compression," the acceleration of the trend of younger children leaving traditional play categories for more sophisticated products such as cell phones, DVD players, CD players, MP3 devices, and other electronics products. The age compression pattern tended to decrease consumer demand for traditional toys or at least increase competition for purchases within the segment of 5- to 12-year-olds.

An article in *DSN Retailing Today*[11] examined the competitive environment in the industry during 2003–2004:

> Retailers can't afford a repeat of the 2003 holiday season when a slow economy and price wars between Wal-Mart and Target produced a nightmare scenario. Toys "R" Us reported a 5% decline in fourth quarter same-store sales, and KB Toys reported a 10% decline in sales in 2003.
>
> In the aftermath, Toys "R" Us closed its Kids "R" Us and Imaginarium divisions, and KB filed for Chapter 11 bankruptcy and closed nearly 500 stores. FAO Schwarz fared worst of all and liquidated its 89-store Zany Brainy chain and sold its flagship stores in New York City and Las Vegas.
> \* \* \*
> Toy industry analyst Chris Byrne doesn't expect the specialists to fare any better during the upcoming [2004] holiday season. "The business model for toy retail is really changing, and we could be seeing the end of the specialty toy store," said Byrne.

---

[11]Doug Desjardins, "Toy Market Still Full of Surprises," *DSN Retailing Today*, September 6, 2004.

EXHIBIT 7   European Traditional Toy Sale Market Share by Country (%)

| Country | 2004 | 2005 |
|---|---|---|
| UK | 22.8 | 24.0 |
| France | 19.6 | 19.6 |
| Germany | 18.1 | 17.0 |
| Italy | 8.0 | 7.9 |
| Spain | 6.3 | 6.5 |
| Poland | 2.0 | 2.0 |
| Hungary | 0.6 | 0.6 |
| Czech Republic | 0.5 | 0.5 |
| Others | 22.1 | 21.9 |
| Total | 100.0 | 100.0 |

*Source*: Toy Industries of Europe, Facts & Figures, July 2006

*He said the specialists are not being hurt just by mass merchants, noting that other chains are stealing away business in core categories, such as video games and action figures. "What we're seeing is more and more category specialists," said Byrne. "Places like Best Buy and GameStop have become great places to buy toys."*

## European Retail Toy Industry

In 2005 traditional toy sales in Europe (excluding video games) grew 3 percent to €13.3 billion from €12.9 billion.[12] The market had been stable over the previous few years, and in most European countries there was increased demand for infant/preschool toys, building sets, and action figures.[13] Analysts and industry experts expected European traditional toy sales to outpace sales in the United States. Including video games, growth was expected to be in the 3 to 6 percent range. Exhibit 7 shows market share by country in Europe.

While the industry drivers and demand trends in Europe were similar to those in the United States, the competitive landscape was different. On average, the specialty toy retailers had better market share across Europe than in the United States. Exhibit 8 shows distribution channel market share across Europe.

## Infant, Toddler, and Preschool Market

The U.S. market for infant, toddler, and preschool products was approximately $34 billion in 2005 and consisted primarily of the following segments: home furnishings and accessories ($8 billion), clothing ($17 billion), baby care supplies ($6 billion), and traditional toys ($3 billion).[14] Traditional toys in this market segment overlapped with sales in the broader traditional U.S. toy market. The mass/discount retailers and Babies "R" Us (the Company's specialty baby/juvenile stores) were the clear market share leaders in this segment, with the remaining market share

---

[12]Toy Industries of Europe, Facts & Figures, July 2006.

[13]Ibid.

[14]Data compiled from various packaged facts industry reports.

**EXHIBIT 8   Distribution Channel by Country (%)**

|  | France | Germany | Spain | Italy | UK | Europe |
|---|---|---|---|---|---|---|
| Toy specialist | 44.3 | 40.8 | 46.0 | 34.0 | 26.9 | 36.2 |
| Mass merchant/discount stores | 42.9 | 14.2 | 30.8 | 39.0 | 10.6 | 24.0 |
| General merchandise | 3.3 | 5.5 | 5.8 | 13.2 | 27.0 | 13.2 |
| Department stores | 1.9 | 15.7 | 11.8 | 7.6 | 3.3 | 6.5 |
| Mail order | 3.5 | 6.7 | 0.0 |  | 3.5 | 3.9 |
| Other | 4.1 | 17.1 | 5.6 | 6.2 | 28.7 | 16.2 |
| Total | 100.0 | 100.0 | 100.0 | 100.0 | 100.0 | 100.0 |

*Source*: Toy Industries of Europe, Facts & Figures, July 2006

distributed across a highly fragmented, specialty retailer base and department/grocery stores. This market had shown steady growth over the previous few years and analysts and industry experts estimated it would continue to grow at a 3 to 6 percent rate. Growth was expected to come from an anticipated increase in the infant population and increased spending per child.

This market segment had become more attractive to retailers as competition in the traditional toy market intensified, and it was insulated from age compression as it focused on very young children. In addition, it did not have the same price competition as the traditional toy market because retailers were better able to differentiate based on perceived product quality and shopping experience.

## Overview of Toys "R" Us

Toys "R" Us was a worldwide specialty retailer of toys, baby products, and children's apparel. As of January 29, 2005, it operated 1,499 retail stores worldwide.[15] These consisted of 898 locations in the United States, including 681 toy stores and 217 Babies "R" Us stores. Internationally, the Company operated, licensed, or franchised 601 stores (299 operated stores, two of which were Babies "R" Us, and 302 licensed or franchised stores, seven of which were Babies "R" Us). See Exhibit 9 for a breakdown of owned and leased stores. The Company also sold merchandise through its Internet sites.

The retail business began in 1948 when founder Charles Lazarus opened a baby furniture store, Children's Bargain Town, in Washington, D.C. The Company changed its name to Toys "R" Us in 1957. The first Babies "R" Us stores opened in 1996, expanding the Company's presence in the specialty baby/juvenile market. The Company was among the market share leaders in most of the largest markets in which its retail stores operated, including the United States, the United Kingdom, and Japan. See Exhibit 10 through Exhibit 13 for consolidated and segment financial results.

The Company's worldwide toy business was highly seasonal, with net sales and earnings highest in the fourth quarter, which included the all-important holiday sales of November and December. More than 40 percent of net sales from the Company's worldwide toy business and a substantial portion of its operating earnings and cash flows from operations were generated in the fourth quarter. See Exhibit 14 for quarterly results from the fiscal year ending January 29, 2005.

---

[15]Toys "R" Us FYE 2005 10-K Filing. Note all financial data related to the Company is from the 2005 10-K Filing.

## EXHIBIT 9    Toys "R" Us Property Summary

| | Owned | % of Total | Ground Lease | % of Total | Leased | % of Total | Total |
|---|---|---|---|---|---|---|---|
| Stores | | | | | | | |
| Toys "R" Us | 315 | *46.3* | 155 | *22.8* | 211 | *31.0* | 681 |
| International[a] | 80 | *26.8* | 23 | *7.7* | 196 | *65.6* | 299 |
| Babies "R" Us | 31 | *14.3* | 76 | *35.0* | 110 | *50.7* | 217 |
| Total | 426 | *35.6* | 254 | *21.2* | 517 | *43.2* | 1,197 |
| Distribution centers | | | | | | | |
| U.S. | 9 | *75.0* | 0 | *0.0* | 3 | *25.0* | 12 |
| International | 5 | *62.5* | 0 | *0.0* | 3 | *37.5* | 8 |
| Total | 14 | *70.0* | 0 | *0.0* | 6 | *30.0* | 20 |
| Operating stores and distribution centers | 440 | *36.2* | 254 | *20.9* | 523 | *43.0* | 1,217 |

[a]Excludes 302 licensed or franchised stores in international markets.
*Source*: Toys "R" Us FYE 2005 10-K Filing

## Toys "R" Us—United States

The Company sold toys, plush, games, bicycles, sporting goods, VHS and DVD movies, electronic and video games, small pools, books, educational and development products, clothing, infant and juvenile furniture, and electronics, as well as educational and entertainment computer software for children. Its toy stores offered approximately 8,000–10,000 distinct items year round, more than twice the number found in other discount or specialty stores selling toys. The Company sought to differentiate itself from competitors in several key areas, including product selection, product presentation, service, in-store experience, and marketing. This became increasingly important as discount retailers and other specialty retailers increased competition.

## Toys "R" Us—International

Toys "R" Us—International operated, licensed, and franchised toy stores in thirty foreign countries. These stores generally conformed to prototypical designs similar to those used by Toys "R" Us in the United States. As noted above, as of January 29, 2005, the Company operated 299 international stores, two of which were Babies "R" Us, and licensed or franchised 302 international stores, seven of which were Babies "R" Us. International added thirty-three new toy stores in calendar year 2004, including twenty-six licensed or franchised stores, and closed ten stores, including five licensed or franchised stores. The division intended to add forty-one new toy stores in 2005, including thirty-one licensed or franchised stores. As of January 29, 2005, Toys "R" Us—Japan, Ltd., a licensee of the Company, operated 153 stores, which were included in the 302 licensed or franchised international stores. The Company had a 48 percent ownership in the common stock of Toys "R" Us—Japan.

## Babies "R" Us

In 1996 the Company opened its first Babies "R" Us stores. The acquisition of Baby Superstore, Inc. in 1997 added seventy-six locations, and the continued expansion of this brand helped Babies "R" Us become the leader in the specialty baby/juvenile market. Babies "R" Us stores targeted

**EXHIBIT 10   Consolidated Financial Results ($ in millions, except per share data)**

| | For the Year Ended | | |
| --- | --- | --- | --- |
| | 2/1/2003 | 1/31/2004 | 1/29/2005 |
| Net sales | $11,305 | $11,320 | $11,100 |
| Growth | | 0.1% | −1.9% |
| Cost of sales | (7,799) | (7,646) | (7,506) |
| Gross margin | $3,506 | $3,674 | $3,594 |
| Growth | | 4.8% | −2.2% |
| Margin | 31.0% | 32.5% | 32.4% |
| SG&A | ($2,724) | ($3,026) | ($2,932) |
| Growth | | 11.1% | −3.1% |
| Margin | −24.1% | −26.7% | −26.4% |
| Reported EBITDA (pre-restructuring charges) | $782 | $648 | $662 |
| Growth | | −17.1% | 2.2% |
| Margin | 6.9% | 5.7% | 6.0% |
| D&A | ($339) | ($368) | ($354) |
| Restructuring and other charges | 0 | (63) | (4) |
| EBIT | $443 | $217 | $304 |
| Growth | | −51.0% | 40.1% |
| Margin | 3.9% | 1.9% | 2.7% |
| Interest expense | ($119) | ($142) | ($130) |
| Interest and other income | 9 | 18 | 19 |
| Pretax income | $333 | $93 | $193 |
| Growth | | −72.1% | 107.5% |
| Margin | 2.9% | 0.8% | 1.7% |
| Income tax (expense)/benefit | (120) | (30) | 59 |
| Net income | $213 | $63 | $252 |
| Growth | | −70.4% | 300.0% |
| Margin | 1.9% | 0.6% | 2.3% |
| Diluted EPS | $1.02 | $0.29 | $1.16 |
| Growth | | −71.6% | 300.0% |
| Adjusted consolidated EBITDA | | | |
| Reported EBITDA (pre-restructuring charges) | $782 | $648 | $662 |
| Add-back of one-time items in Toys "R" Us—U.S.[a] | 0 | 0 | 118 |
| Adjusted consolidated EBITDA | $782 | $648 | $780 |
| Growth | | −17.1% | 20.4% |
| Margin | 6.9% | 5.7% | 7.0% |

[a]EBITDA for FY 2005 adjusted by adding back $132 million in inventory markdowns and excluding $14 million related to a lawsuit settlement—$118 million net add-back in FY 2005.
*Source*: Toys "R" Us FYE 2005 10-K Filing

the prenatal and infant markets by offering juvenile furniture such as cribs, dressers, changing tables, and bedding. In addition, the Company provided baby gear such as play yards, booster seats, high chairs, strollers, car seats, toddler and infant plush toys, and nursing equipment. As of January 29, 2005, Babies "R" Us operated 217 specialty baby/juvenile retail locations, all in the United States. Based on demographic data used to determine which markets to enter, the

## EXHIBIT 11    Consolidated Balance Sheet ($ in millions)

| | For the Year Ended | |
|---|---|---|
| | 1/31/2004 | 1/29/2005 |
| ASSETS | | |
| Cash and cash equivalents | $1,432 | $1,250 |
| Short-term investments | 571 | 953 |
| Accounts and other receivables | 146 | 153 |
| Merchandise inventories | 2,094 | 1,884 |
| Net property assets held for sale | 163 | 7 |
| Current portion of derivative assets | 162 | 1 |
| Prepaid expenses and other current assets | 161 | 159 |
| Total current assets | $4,729 | $4,407 |
| Property, plant, and equipment | | |
| Real estate, net | $2,165 | $2,393 |
| Other, net | 2,274 | 1,946 |
| Total PP&E | $4,439 | $4,339 |
| Goodwill, net | 348 | 353 |
| Derivative assets | 77 | 43 |
| Deferred tax asset | 399 | 426 |
| Other assets | 273 | 200 |
| *Total assets* | $10,265 | $9,768 |
| LIABILITIES AND STOCKHOLDERS' EQUITY | | |
| Short-term borrowings | $0 | $0 |
| Accounts payable | 1,022 | 1,023 |
| Accrued expenses and other current liabilities | 866 | 881 |
| Income taxes payable | 319 | 245 |
| Current portion of long-term debt | 657 | 452 |
| Total current liabilities | $2,864 | $2,601 |
| Long-term debt | 2,349 | 1,860 |
| Deferred income taxes | 538 | 485 |
| Derivative liabilities | 26 | 16 |
| Deferred rent liability | 280 | 269 |
| Other liabilities | 225 | 212 |
| Minority interest in Toysrus.com | 9 | 0 |
| Total liabilities | $6,291 | $5,443 |
| Stockholders' equity | | |
| Common stock | $30 | $30 |
| Additional paid-in capital | 407 | 405 |
| Retained earnings | 5,308 | 5,560 |
| Accumulated other comprehensive loss | (64) | (7) |
| Restricted stock | 0 | (5) |
| Treasury shares, at cost | (1,707) | (1,658) |
| Total stockholders' equity | $3,974 | $4,325 |
| *Total liabilities and stockholders' equity* | $10,265 | $9,768 |

*Source*: Toys "R" Us FYE 2005 10-K Filing

## EXHIBIT 12   Consolidated Statement of Cash Flow ($ in millions)

| | For the Year Ended | | |
| --- | --- | --- | --- |
| | 2/1/2003 | 1/31/2004 | 1/29/2005 |
| CASH FLOWS FROM OPERATING ACTIVITIES | | | |
| Net earnings | $213 | $63 | $252 |
| Adjustments to reconcile net earnings to net cash from operating activities: | | | |
| Depreciation and amortization | $339 | $368 | $354 |
| Amortization of restricted stock | 0 | 0 | 7 |
| Deferred income taxes | 99 | 27 | (40) |
| Minority interest in Toysrus.com | (14) | (8) | (6) |
| Other non-cash items | (9) | 1 | 2 |
| Non-cash portion of restructuring and other charges | 0 | 63 | 4 |
| Changes in operating assets and liabilities: | | | |
| Accounts and other receivables | 8 | 62 | (5) |
| Merchandise inventories | (100) | 133 | 221 |
| Prepaid expenses and other operating assets | (118) | 28 | 76 |
| Accounts payable, accrued expenses, and other liabilities | 109 | 117 | (45) |
| Income taxes payable | 48 | (53) | (74) |
| *Net cash provided by operating activities* | $575 | $801 | $746 |
| CASH FLOWS FROM INVESTING ACTIVITIES | | | |
| Capital expenditures, net | ($395) | ($262) | ($269) |
| Proceeds from sale of fixed assets | 0 | 0 | 216 |
| Purchase of SB Toys, Inc. | 0 | 0 | (42) |
| Purchase of short-term investments and other | 0 | (572) | (382) |
| *Net cash used in investing activities* | ($395) | ($834) | ($477) |
| CASH FLOWS FROM FINANCING ACTIVITIES | | | |
| Short-term borrowings, net | $0 | $0 | $0 |
| Long-term borrowings | 548 | 792 | 0 |
| Long-term debt repayment | (141) | (370) | (503) |
| Decrease/(increase) in restricted cash | (60) | 60 | 0 |
| Proceeds from issuance of stock and contracts to purchase stock | 266 | 0 | 0 |
| Proceeds from exercise of stock options | 0 | 0 | 27 |
| *Net cash (used in)/provided by financing activities* | $613 | $482 | ($476) |
| Effect of exchange rate changes on cash and cash equivalents | ($53) | ($40) | $25 |
| CASH AND CASH EQUIVALENTS | | | |
| (Decrease)/increase during year | $740 | $409 | ($182) |
| Beginning of year | 283 | 1,023 | 1,432 |
| End of year | $1,023 | $1,432 | $1,250 |

*Source*: Toys "R" Us FYE 2005 10-K Filing

Company opened nineteen Babies "R" Us stores in calendar year 2004. As part of its long-range growth plan, it planned to continue expanding its Babies "R" Us store base in 2005.

## Toysrus.com

Toysrus.com sold merchandise to the public via the Internet at *www.toysrus.com*, *www.babiesrus.com*, *www.imaginarium.com*, *www.sportsrus.com*, and *www.personalizedbyrus.com*. The Company launched its e-commerce Web site in 1998. To improve customer service and order fulfillment, the Company entered into a strategic alliance with Amazon.com and launched a co-branded toy store in 2000.

EXHIBIT 13  Financial Performance by Segment ($ in millions)

| | For the Year Ended | | | | | | For the Year Ended | | |
|---|---|---|---|---|---|---|---|---|---|
| | 2/1/ 2003 | % of Total | 1/31/ 2004 | % of Total | 1/29/ 2005 | % of Total | 2/1/ 2003 | 1/31/ 2004 | 1/29/ 2005 |
| NET SALES BY SEGMENT | | | | | | | GROWTH BY SEGMENT (%) | | |
| Toys "R" Us—U.S. | $6,755 | 59.8 | $6,326 | 55.9 | $6,104 | 55.0 | | −6.4 | −3.5 |
| Toys "R" Us—International | 2,161 | 19.1 | 2,470 | 21.8 | 2,739 | 24.7 | | 14.3 | 10.9 |
| Babies "R" Us | 1,595 | 14.1 | 1,738 | 15.4 | 1,863 | 16.8 | | 9.0 | 7.2 |
| Toysrus.com | 340 | 3.0 | 371 | 3.3 | 366 | 3.3 | | 9.1 | −1.3 |
| Kids "R" Us | 454 | 4.0 | 415 | 3.7 | 28 | 0.3 | | −8.6 | −93.3 |
| Consolidated net sales | $11,305 | 100.0 | $11,320 | 100.0 | $11,100 | 100.0 | | 0.1 | −1.9 |
| OPERATING EARNINGS BY SEGMENT | | | | | | | MARGIN BY SEGMENT (%) | | |
| Toys "R" Us—U.S. | $256 | 49.4 | $70 | 20.4 | $4 | 0.9 | 3.8 | 1.1 | 0.1 |
| Toys "R" Us—International | 158 | 30.5 | 166 | 48.4 | 220 | 51.9 | 7.3 | 6.7 | 8.0 |
| Babies "R" Us | 169 | 32.6 | 192 | 56.0 | 224 | 52.8 | 10.6 | 11.0 | 12.0 |
| Toysrus.com | (37) | −7.1 | (18) | −5.2 | 1 | 0.2 | −10.9 | 4.9 | 0.3 |
| Kids "R" Us[a] | (28) | −5.4 | (67) | −19.5 | (25) | −5.9 | −6.2 | −16.1 | −89.3 |
| Segment operating earnings | $518 | 100.0 | $343 | 100.0 | $424 | 100.0 | 4.6 | 3.0 | 3.8 |
| Corporate/other expenses[b] | (75) | | (63) | | (116) | | | | |
| Restructuring charges | 0 | | (63) | | (4) | | | | |
| Reported operating earnings | $443 | | $217 | | $304 | | 3.9 | 1.9 | 2.7 |
| ADJUSTED EBITDA BY SEGMENT | | | | | | | MARGIN BY SEGMENT (%) | | |
| Toys "R" Us—U.S.[c] | $447 | 55.1 | $264 | 39.3 | $322 | 37.4 | 6.6 | 4.2 | 5.3 |
| Toys "R" Us—International | 210 | 25.9 | 227 | 33.8 | 295 | 34.3 | 9.7 | 9.2 | 10.8 |
| Babies "R" Us | 197 | 24.3 | 223 | 33.2 | 262 | 30.5 | 12.4 | 12.8 | 14.1 |
| Toysrus.com | (33) | −4.1 | (16) | −2.4 | 1 | 0.1 | −9.7 | −4.3 | 0.3 |
| Kids "R" Us[a] | (10) | −1.2 | (27) | −4.0 | (20) | −2.3 | −2.2 | −6.5 | −71.4 |
| Adjusted segment EBITDA | $811 | 100.0 | $671 | 100.0 | $860 | 100.0 | 7.2 | 5.9 | 7.7 |
| Corporate/other expenses[b] | (75) | | (63) | | (116) | | | | |
| Add-back: other D&A | 46 | | 40 | | 36 | | | | |
| Consolidated adjusted EBITDA | $782 | | $648 | | $780 | | 6.9 | 5.7 | 7.0 |

[a]Includes markdowns of $49 million and accelerated depreciation of $24 million in 2003 related to the closing of all stores.

[b]Includes corporate expenses, the operating results of Toy Box, and the equity in net earnings of Toys "R" Us—Japan. Increase in amount is due to our strategic review expenses and Sarbanes-Oxley Section 404 compliance totaling $29 million. In addition, we incurred charges of $8 million relating to our 2004 restructuring of the Company's corporate headquarters operations, and a $19 million increase in incentive compensation costs.

[c]EBITDA for FY 2005 adjusted by adding back $132 million in inventory markdowns and excluding $14 million related to a lawsuit settlement—$118 million net add-back in FY 2005.

Source: Toys "R" Us FYE 2005 10-K Filing

**EXHIBIT 14   Quarterly Financial Results ($ in millions)**

| | For the Quarter Ended | | | | | | | | FYE |
|---|---|---|---|---|---|---|---|---|---|
| | 5/1/ 2004 | % of Total | 7/31/ 2004 | % of Total | 10/30/ 2004 | % of Total | 1/29/ 2005 | % of Total | 1/29/ 2005 |
| Net sales | $2,058 | 18.5 | $2,022 | 18.2 | $2,214 | 19.9 | $4,806 | 43.3 | $11,100 |
| COGS | (1,330) | 17.7 | (1,441) | 19.2 | (1,475) | 19.7 | (3,260) | 43.4 | (7,506) |
| Gross margin | $728 | 20.3 | $581 | 16.2 | $739 | 20.6 | $1,546 | 43.0 | $3,594 |
| SG&A | (643) | 21.9 | (661) | 22.5 | (682) | 23.3 | (946) | 32.3 | (2,932) |
| D&A | (86) | 24.3 | (86) | 24.3 | (88) | 24.9 | (94) | 26.6 | (354) |
| Restructuring (charges)/ income | (14) | NM | (31) | NM | 26 | NM | 15 | NM | (4) |
| Operating earnings | ($15) | -4.9 | ($197) | -64.8 | ($5) | -1.6 | $521 | 171.4 | $304 |
| Reported EBITDA (includes one-time items) | $85 | 12.8 | ($80) | -12.1 | $57 | 8.6 | $600 | 90.6 | $662 |

*Note*: EBITDA is defined as operating earnings with an add-back of D&A and restructuring charges (does not exclude one-time items)

*Source*: Toys "R" Us FYE 2005 10-K Filing

# Challenging Times for Toys "R" Us

During 2003–2004, the Company's performance and prospects were hurt by developments in the retail toy industry. Discount and mass merchandisers with greater financial resources and lower operating expenses had reduced pricing and profit margins for other players in the retail toy industry, and the Company's toy sales had decreased because of changing consumer habits, including age compression. On November 17, 2003, the Company announced plans to close all 146 of the freestanding Kids "R" Us stores, with final closings completed by January 29, 2005.

The Company's consolidated net sales decreased 1.9 percent to $11.1 billion in fiscal year end (FYE) January 29, 2005, from $11.3 billion in FYE January 31, 2004, and $11.3 billion in FYE February 1, 2003. The decrease in net sales was primarily the result of declines in comparable store sales at the Toys "R" Us—U.S. division, which posted comparable store sales declines of 3.7 percent for FYE 2005, following comparable store sales decreases of 3.6 percent and 1.3 percent in FYE 2004 and FYE 2003, respectively (see Exhibit 15).

These decreases in net sales were partially offset by net sales increases in the Babies "R" Us division of 7.2 percent to $1.9 billion in FYE 2005, and net sales increases in the international division of 10.9 percent (these figures include the effect of currency translation) to $2.7 billion in FYE 2005, primarily due to the addition of nineteen Babies "R" Us stores in the United States and seven wholly owned international stores in 2004. In addition, comparable store sales at Babies "R" Us and international divisions showed favorable increases.

# Toys "R" Us Strategic Review and Sale

Facing both difficult industry trends and weak performance of U.S. toy stores during the 2003 holiday season, Toys "R" Us decided to conduct a strategic evaluation of its worldwide assets

EXHIBIT 15   Comparable Store Sales Performance (%)

|  | For the Year Ended | | |
|---|---|---|---|
|  | **2/1/2003** | **1/31/2004** | **1/29/2005** |
| Toys "R" Us—U.S. | −1.3 | −3.6 | −3.7 |
| Toys "R" Us—International | 5.9 | 2.1 | 0.6 |
| Babies "R" Us | 2.7 | 2.8 | 2.2 |

*Note*: This does not reflect sales from new store openings or store closings, comparable stores year over year.
*Source*: Toys "R" Us FYE 2005 10-K Filing

and operations. The Company retained Credit Suisse First Boston (CSFB) as its financial advisor. The Company and CSFB considered several alternatives, including:

- Maintaining status quo and refocusing management on reviving domestic performance at Toys "R" Us
- Unlocking value in a faster-growing asset by selling the global Toys "R" Us business or spinning off Babies "R" Us
- Pursuing the sale of consolidated Toys "R" Us

The Company and CSFB initially decided to separate the U.S. toy retailing business and Babies "R" Us by running a thorough sale process for its toy retailing business. However, participants in the auction determined it would be too difficult to uncouple the businesses. One participant said, "It would be like selling your kitchen to one buyer and your dining room to another."[16] With no compelling bids for any of the individual businesses after an extended period of time, pressure increased for Toys "R" Us to sell the portfolio of businesses together.

Ultimately, a consortium that included Cerberus, Goldman Sachs, and Kimco Realty Corp. submitted a bid for the entire business. Subsequently Kohlberg, Kravis & Roberts (KKR) teamed up with Bain Capital Partners and Vornado Realty Trust (Bain and Vornado initially joined to bid on the toy business) and submitted a rival bid. On March 17, 2005, the Company announced that it had reached a definitive agreement to sell the entire worldwide operations to the consortium of KKR, Bain Capital, and Vornado Realty Trust for $26.75 per share in a $6.7 billion transaction.[17] The acquisition price represented a 122.5 percent premium over the stock price on the day before the announcement of the strategic review on January 7, 2004, and a 62.9 percent over the stock price on August 10, 2004, the day before the Company announced it was seeking to divest its toy retailing business.

The $26.75 per share winning bid for Toys "R" Us represented an aggregate value of $6.7 billion, including all transaction fees. It is important to note that as part of the transaction, the consortium assumed the Company's existing debt and cash not used in the transaction. Exhibit 16 summarizes the sources and uses for the transaction. Based on adjusted EBITDA of $780 million during FYE January 29, 2005, Exhibit 17 shows the implied purchase price and leverage multiples (including all assumed debt and cash) for the Toys "R" Us transaction.

As part of this transaction, John H. Eyler, Jr. (chairman, CEO, and president of Toys "R" Us) and Christopher K. Kay (executive vice president and chief operations officer) were to leave

---

[16]"Toys 'R' Us Narrows Suitors to Four," *Wall Street Journal*, March 1, 2005.
[17]Toys "R" Us Company Press Release, March 17, 2005.

**EXHIBIT 16   Sources and Uses ($ in millions)**

| Sources | | Uses | |
|---|---|---|---|
| Cash on balance sheet | $956 | Purchase of common stock | $5,900 |
| Senior secured credit facility | 700 | Purchase of stock options and restricted stock | 227 |
| Unsecured bridge loan | 1,900 | Settlement of equity security interests | 114 |
| Secured European bridge loan | 1,000 | Purchase of all warrants | 17 |
| Mortgage loan agreements | 800 | Transaction fees | 362 |
| Sponsor equity | 1,300 | Severance and bonus payments | 36 |
| *Total* | $6,656 | *Total* | $6,656 |

**Summary of Fees**

| Summary of Fees | |
|---|---|
| Advisory fees and expenses | $78 |
| Financing fees | 135 |
| Sponsor fees | 81 |
| Other | 68 |
| *Total* | $362 |

*Note*: Senior secured credit facility has $2.0 billion of availability.
*Source*: Toys "R" Us, Form 10-Q, July 30, 2005

**EXHIBIT 17   Enterprise Value and Leverage Summary ($ in millions)**

| | Amount | Multiple of FYE 2005 Adj. EBITDA |
|---|---|---|
| Transaction proceeds (excl. fees) | $6,294 | |
| Approximate existing debt assumed by the consortium | 2,312 | |
| Remaining cash and short-term investments on balance sheet | (1,247) | |
| Enterprise value | $7,359 | 9.4x |
| Transaction fees | 362 | |
| *Total transaction value* | $7,721 | 9.9x |
| FYE 2005 adjusted EBITDA | $780 | |
| LEVERAGE ANALYSIS | | Cumul. Multiple |
| Approximate existing debt | $2,312 | 3.0x |
| $2 billion senior secured credit facility | 700 | 3.9x |
| Unsecured bridge loan | 1,900 | 6.3x |
| Secured European bridge loan | 1,000 | 7.6x |
| Mortgage loan agreements | 800 | 8.6x |
| Total | $6,712 | 8.6x |
| Remaining cash and short-term investments on balance sheet assumed by the consortium | (1,247) | |
| Net leverage | $5,465 | 7.0x |

*Note*: Assumes transaction closed on January 29, 2005 for simplicity.

the Company. The consortium appointed Richard L. Markee (a Company veteran) as interim CEO, with the expectation of filling out the management team over time. This was somewhat unusual, as financial sponsors typically preferred to back an in-place management team to lead a company through the initial period after an LBO. This action was particularly noteworthy given the pressures of operating a business in a difficult industry with a significant amount of new leverage.

Markee had served as president of Babies "R" Us since August 2004. Prior to that, he had been vice chairman of Toys "R" Us Inc., president of Toys "R" Us Domestic, president of Specialty Businesses and International Operations, president of Babies "R" Us, and chairman of Kids "R" Us.

## The Toys "R" Us Club

The Toys "R" Us Club featured two of the premier private equity firms in the world and a leading real estate investment trust (REIT). The two private equity firms—KKR and Bain Capital—had also partnered in several deals, including a $11.4 billion buyout of SunGard Data Systems, which had closed in August 2005. Including the Toys "R" Us deal, KKR had become the most active participant in club deals, having participated in ten announced club deals valued at $95.3 billion during the previous two years.[18]

The Toys "R" Us Club was particularly interesting because of the diverse core competencies of each member. KKR was known for structuring highly complex transactions with expert use of financial engineering, a skill that was of particular importance given the recent performance issues at Toys "R" Us. Bain Capital, while also skilled at financial engineering, had built a reputation for in-depth industry research capabilities, especially in retail. The consortium leveraged Bain Capital's resources to understand and analyze the nature of the industry downturn and to forecast the future viability of both the Company and the industry. The inclusion of Vornado highlighted the club's focus on understanding the value of the Company's real estate portfolio. While it historically had been rare for an REIT to be involved in a typical private equity deal, as private equity firms began to target companies with large real estate portfolios, there was an increased need for expertise in valuing real estate.

### KKR

Established in 1976 and led by co-founding members Henry Kravis and George Roberts, KKR had completed more than 140 transactions valued at approximately $215 billion[19] and created $68 billion of value from $26 billion of invested capital, a multiple of 2.5 times.[20] KKR historically had been involved with the highest-profile, largest transactions in the private equity industry, including those involving RJR Nabisco, SunGard Data Systems, and HCA.

### Bain Capital

Established in 1984, Bain Capital was one of the world's leading private investment firms with approximately $40 billion in assets under management. Since its inception, Bain Capital had completed more than 200 equity investments. The aggregate transaction value of these investments exceeded $17 billion.[21] Bain Capital had been founded by three ex-Bain & Company partners, Mitt Romney, T. Coleman Andrews, and Eric Kriss. Less than one year before its acquisition of

---

[18]"KKR Tops 'Club' Buyout Deals," *CNN Money.com*, October 17, 2006.

[19]KKR, http://www.kkr.com.

[20]Ibid.

[21]Bain Capital, http://www.baincapital.com.

Toys "R" Us, Bain Capital had completed the acquisition of another specialty retailer, the Canadian dollar store chain Dollarama.

## Vornado Realty Trust

Vornado Realty Trust was a fully integrated REIT. The firm was one of the largest owners and managers of real estate in the United States, with a portfolio of approximately 60 million square feet in its major platforms, primarily in the New York and Washington, D.C. metro areas.[22]

# The Assignment

Your private equity firm has been approached by KKR, Bain, and Vornado to join the consortium. You have been asked by a senior member of your firm to prepare a presentation that summarizes the Toys "R" Us investment opportunity. You should:

- Use the provided operating model template to develop assumptions that drive a base case operating model and analyze the returns for the investment group

  o Use the operating model to generate input for an LBO model, which will calculate relevant returns, financial data, and credit statistics
  o Focus on developing a reasonable set of projections on which to base your investment recommendation
  The presentation should include the following (a template has been included for guidance):

- Risks and merits of the transaction
- Summary of the industry dynamics, including the major issues and potential catalysts for improvements
- A list of key due diligence questions/requests you want to ask the Company
- Summary of the debt in the transaction: indicate whether you feel comfortable with the capital structure proposed by the consortium
- Downside case(s) that stress test the investment under various difficult operating outcomes: quantify the risk/return profile of the transaction and evaluate this profile
- Potential exit alternatives for this investment
- Recommendation whether or not to join the consortium

For the purpose of your evaluation assume that you are not able to change the consortium's proposed capital structure.

---

[22]Vornado Realty Trust, http://www.vno.com.

# Cerberus and the U.S. Auto Industry

## Introduction

In August 2005 General Motors Acceptance Corporation (GMAC) announced that it had entered into an agreement to sell a 60 percent equity interest in its commercial mortgage subsidiary, GMAC Commercial Holding Corp (GMACCH), to a high-profile investor group led by private equity giant Kohlberg Kravis Roberts & Co. (KKR). The KKR-led group later upped its ante in March of the following year, increasing its investment to almost $9 billion for a 78 percent stake in the mortgage business's equity. Less than two weeks after this announcement, Cerberus Capital Management—a multistrategy, $22 billion New York hedge fund led by manager Stephen Feinberg—made its own announcement, stealing KKR's headlines. With Citibank's private equity division and a large Japanese bank on board, Cerberus agreed to buy a 51 percent controlling interest of GMAC in a deal that would net the cash-starved General Motors (GM) $14 billion over three years.

In May 2007 Cerberus acquired 80.1 percent of Chrysler LLC from Daimler-Benz AG for about $7.8 billion. At the time, Cerberus was hailed as a hero—the private equity firm that saved the American car industry. But two years later Cerberus's dream had turned into a nightmare. Both GM and Chrysler declared bankruptcy, causing massive losses for Cerberus and the firm's co-investors, including the investment arm of Abu Dhabi, as well as hedge funds such as York Capital and Eaton Park.

## "What's Good for GM?"

### GM a Power

At his confirmation hearing as the newly appointed Secretary of Defense in 1953, Charles E. Wilson, former CEO and president of GM, is often misquoted as having boldly claimed, "What's good for GM is good for the country." (In response to a question about potential conflict of interest, Wilson had actually stated his belief that "what's good for the country is good for GM and vice versa.") The difference was semantic. At the midpoint of the century GM was a dominant force in the U.S. economy. Half a century ago "the only thing standing between [GM] and virtually limitless profits was the possibility of labor unrest,"[1] noted (ominously, as it were) historian David Halberstam. The first American corporation to boast profits of more than $1 billion (in 1955), GM was one of the largest employers in the world for much of the twentieth century, with automobile market share in the United States reaching 47.7 percent in 1978.

---

[1] David Halberstam, "The Fifties" (New York: History Channel: A&E Home Video, 1994).

## GM Hard Times

How times have changed. In 2006 GM reported sales of $207.3 billion, a 6.5 percent year-over-year increase. And while GM showed an improvement over 2005's operating loss of more than $10 billion, GM's operations remained in the red with losses of nearly $2 billion in 2006. Operating margins had fallen from 5.2 percent in 1995 to 1.7 percent in 2004 before the company announced the sizable annual loss from 2005 (see Exhibit 1 and Exhibit 2 for General Motors Balance Sheet and Income Statement). Its business had eroded over the previous decade under the weight of enormous employee liabilities, rapidly declining market share, and a deteriorating macroeconomic environment. In the first five months of 2006, GM's market share in the United States fell to 23.8 percent. February 2006 may have marked the low point, as the once-proud giant of American economic strength slashed its annual dividend from $20 to $10. Headlines involving GM over the preceding several years had invariably focused on restructuring-related manufacturing closings, layoffs, and divestitures. Pension, healthcare, and other employee benefit costs swelled along with the rapidly aging work force at the once-powerful corporation, causing deterioration in profitability. In addition, increased competition from foreign automakers, unsaddled with the labor agreements and pension obligations of their U.S. counterparts, significantly reduced GM's market power (see Exhibit 3: General Motors Two-Year Stock Chart).

## Effect on Suppliers

Labor and healthcare costs and rising raw material and transportation prices were also forcing many of GM's major suppliers into financial distress. Coupled with the lower production at GM and other major U.S. automakers as a result of restructuring, these ballooning cost structures had forced large U.S. suppliers, including Delphi Automotive (a former unit of GM and the largest U.S. auto parts supplier) and Dana Corporation, to file for bankruptcy protection. The implications to GM of its suppliers' distress were significant. Strapped for cash and in the midst of restructuring, the companies, most prominently Delphi, often found themselves asking for wage concessions from their workers. Labor stoppage, and thus production stoppage, at any of its suppliers would have dire consequences for GM. With protecting production its top priority, GM had spent billions of dollars subsidizing its suppliers through extended financing.

## CEO Wagoner's Tough Task Remaking Company

G. Richard Wagoner joined the GM treasurer's office in 1977 as an analyst before steadily climbing his way up the corporate ladder to become GM's chairman and CEO in May 2003. Wagoner had a reputation for success in making tough decisions, and his storied career had given him a true sense of purpose in turning around this once-great company. "I feel a tremendous sense of responsibility to the job that I have,"[2] he told the *Detroit Free Press* in a September 2006 interview, and given his history with the company it was hard not to believe him. However, soon after taking the job, Wagoner was faced with some of the toughest challenges in GM's history.

Rising oil prices; the failure of unparalleled incentives to meaningfully drive auto sales; bankruptcy of suppliers, including Delphi; and enormous, crippling, long-tailed liabilities all

---

[2]"Interview with Rick Wagoner," *Detroit Free Press*, September 10, 2006.

## EXHIBIT 1   General Motors Balance Sheet, 2004–2006 ($ in millions)

| | 2004 | 2005 | 2006 |
|---|---|---|---|
| ASSETS | | | |
| Cash and equivalents | 13,148 | 15,187 | 23,774 |
| Short-term investments | 6,655 | 1,416 | 138 |
| Accounts receivable | 6,713 | 7,758 | 8,216 |
| Inventory | 11,717 | 13,851 | 13,921 |
| Finance dividends, loans and leases, short-term | 220,712 | 203,821 | 0 |
| Finance dividends, other current assets | 26,390 | 19,436 | 349 |
| Deferred tax assets | 8,883 | 7,073 | 10,293 |
| Other current assets | 8,399 | 8,797 | 7,789 |
| Total current assets | 302,617 | 277,339 | 64,480 |
| PP&E | 76,575 | 80,020 | 85,374 |
| Accumulated depreciation | (39,405) | (41,554) | (43,440) |
| Net PP&E | 37,170 | 38,466 | 41,934 |
| Long-term investments | 7,126 | 3,726 | 1,969 |
| Goodwill | 600 | 757 | 799 |
| Other intangibles | 234 | 362 | 319 |
| Finance dividends, loans and leases, long-term | 1,763 | 1,873 | — |
| Finance dividends, other long-term assets | 73,939 | 93,747 | 21,774 |
| Deferred tax assets, long-term | 17,639 | 22,849 | 32,967 |
| Other long-term assets | 41,259 | 41,411 | 21,950 |
| Total assets | 482,347 | 480,530 | 186,192 |
| LIABILITIES | | | |
| Accounts payable | 24,257 | 26,182 | 26,931 |
| Accrued expenses | 46,202 | 42,665 | 35,225 |
| Short-term borrowings | 1,478 | 955 | 3,325 |
| Current portfolio, long-term debt | 584 | 564 | 2,341 |
| Finance dividend debt, current | 91,043 | 82,054 | 4,423 |
| Finance dividends, other current liabilities | 4,573 | 3,731 | 1,214 |
| Other current liabilities | 2,426 | 4,452 | — |
| Total current liabilities | 170,563 | 160,603 | 73,459 |
| Long-term debt | 30,460 | 31,014 | 33,067 |
| Minority interest | 397 | 1,039 | 1,190 |
| Finance dividend debt, noncurrent | 176,714 | 171,163 | 5,015 |
| Finance dividends, other noncurrent liabilities | 27,799 | 39,887 | 925 |
| Pension and other post-retirement benefits | 32,848 | 40,204 | 62,020 |
| Other noncurrent liabilities | 16,206 | 22,023 | 15,957 |
| Total liabilities | 454,987 | 465,933 | 191,633 |
| Common stock | 942 | 943 | 943 |
| APIC | 15,241 | 15,285 | 15,336 |
| Retained earnings | 14,062 | 2,361 | 406 |
| Treasury stock | — | — | — |
| Comprehensive income | (2,885) | (3,992) | (22,126) |
| Total common equity | 27,360 | 14,597 | (5,441) |
| Total liabilities and equity | 482,347 | 480,530 | 186,192 |

*Source*: Capital IQ

**EXHIBIT 2**   General Motors Income Statement, 2004–2006 ($ in millions, except per share data)

| | 2004 | 2005 | 2006 |
|---|---|---|---|
| Revenue | 161,545 | 158,221 | 172,927 |
| Finance dividend revenue | 31,972 | 34,383 | 34,422 |
| Gain (loss) on sale of investment | — | — | — |
| *Total revenue* | 193,517 | 192,604 | 207,349 |
| Cost of goods sold | 150,224 | 162,173 | 157,782 |
| Finance dividend operating expense | 17,991 | 17,875 | 1,350 |
| Interest expense—Finance division | 9,500 | 12,895 | 14,301 |
| *Gross profit* | 15,802 | (339) | 33,916 |
| SG&A | 11,863 | 13,222 | 25,081 |
| Other operating expenses | 273 | 497 | 500 |
| *Operating income* | 3,666 | (14,058) | 8,335 |
| Interest expense | (2,480) | (2,873) | (2,644) |
| Income (loss) from affiliates | 702 | 595 | 184 |
| Other nonoperating income | — | — | — |
| EBT excluding unusual items | 1,888 | (16,336) | 5,875 |
| *EBT including unusual items* | 1,888 | (16,336) | (15,461) |
| Income tax expense | (916) | (5,878) | (5,882) |
| Restructuring charges | | | (6,200) |
| Impairment of goodwill | | | (828) |
| Gain (loss) on sale of assets | | | (2,910) |
| Asset writedown | | | (700) |
| Earnings from continuing operations | 2,804 | (10,458) | (1,978) |
| Extraordinary item and accounting charge | — | (109) | — |
| *Net income* | 2,804 | (10,567) | (1,978) |
| *Basic EPS* | 4.96 | (18.70) | (3.50) |

*Source*: Capital IQ

conspired to drive GM's credit ratings into a downward spiral. This, in turn, created pressure on GMAC, the company's most successful business unit and its financing arm.

# Cerberus Capital Management to the Rescue … Maybe

While the automotive division suffered, GMAC boasted a healthy EBITDA of $20 billion and net income of $2.4 billion on $34 billion in sales in 2005. As a wholly owned subsidiary of GM since 1919, GMAC provided automotive and commercial financing, insurance and mortgage products and services, and real estate services. Despite being the crown jewel of GM, GMAC saw its credit rating downgraded to junk in the spring of 2005 as a result of its association with GM. Following the downgrade, widespread speculation began in the press and on Wall Street that a sale of all or part of the finance arm would be a centerpiece to GM's restructuring, under the assumption that a sale would potentially allow the finance company to obtain its own independent debt rating (presumably investment-grade). After all, GMAC was much more than an auto financing company; greater than 50 percent of its business focused on nonautomotive businesses. Spokeswoman

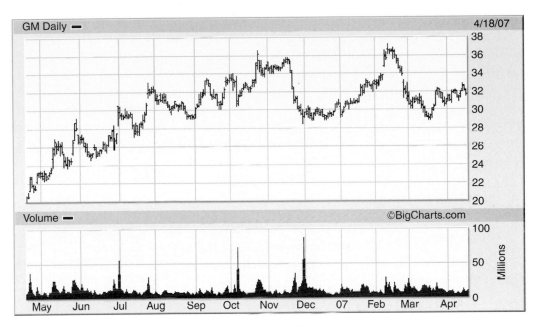

**EXHIBIT 3** General Motors Stock Chart, 5/2006–4/18/2007. *Source:* BigCharts.com

Toni Simonetti responded to speculation at the time, "We are exploring how we would attain a separate rating for GMAC. We would probably look at and evaluate any and all options that would lead to that."[3] Supporting analysts' predictions was the announcement of the sale by GMAC of 78 percent of its real estate finance unit to the KKR-led consortium. This sale, which accounted for about 11 percent of GMAC's 2005 net income, was seen as a precursor to the sale of the entire unit. In a press release following the deal, it was noted that "in conjunction with the equity sale, GMACCH will seek to obtain a standalone credit rating in order to enhance its ability to fund its operations on an ongoing basis."[4] Shortly thereafter, GM announced that it would be selling a 51 percent stake in the remaining parts of GMAC to a consortium led by Cerberus Capital Management that included Citigroup and Aozora Bank Ltd (a Japanese bank 62 percent owned by Cerberus).

## Cerberus—New Beast of the Investment Community

Cerberus Capital Management LP was a private, highly secretive investment firm located in New York with reportedly more than $22 billion under management. Led by founder and manager Stephen Feinberg, Cerberus grew from a fringe vulture fund in the early 1990s to a multistrategy behemoth that defied definition, as its business straddled private equity, venture capital, and hedge fund investing. Cerberus began its life as a distressed-debt shop with around

---

[3]"Will GM Part with GMAC?" CNNMoney.com, May 25, 2006, http://money.cnn.com/2005/05/25/news/fortune500/gm_gmac/index.htm.

[4]KKR press release, August 3, 2005.

$10 million under management. The firm quickly earned a reputation as a tough investment firm that, like its founder, shied away from the spotlight. It became increasingly difficult to remain below the radar as the firm's assets quickly grew into the billions in the late 1990s. Named after the three-headed dog that guarded the gates to Hades, the underworld in Greek mythology, by the end of 2006 Feinberg's investment company owned controlling stakes in forty-five diverse companies that boasted combined revenues in excess of $60 billion.[5] The firm's marketing materials claimed a 22 percent average annual return from 1998 to 2005. Among Cerberus's more successful investments were software firm SSA Global; communications services provider Teleglobe International Holdings; and Vanguard Car Rental USA, the parent of car rental brands National and Alamo.[6] The firm also had stakes in supermarket retailer Albertson's and Air Canada. Historically, Cerberus had taken a benign approach to the management of its portfolio companies, preferring friendly takeovers and deals that included the current stakeholders in the future strategic decision-making process. Though almost half the company's investments were in the manufacturing and services sectors, Cerberus's portfolio included stakes in companies from the healthcare, retail, financial services, and transportation industries as well (see Exhibit 4 for a breakdown of its operating professionals).

## The Deal and Its Details

In successfully winning the bidding for GMAC, Cerberus launched itself from a behind-the-scenes operator to a front-row participant by beating out a competing group led by KKR. In exchange for $14 billion in cash over three years, Cerberus would take control of more than $300 billion worth of leases, loans, mortgages, and insurance policies.[7] An excerpt from the press release discussed several terms of the deal (see Exhibit 5 for full press release):

*The $14 billion in cash that GM is to receive as part of the transaction includes $7.4 billion from the Cerberus-led consortium at closing and an estimated $2.7 billion*

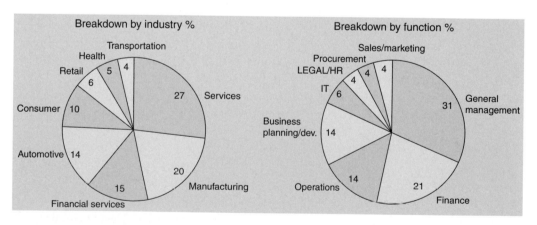

**EXHIBIT 4** Cerberus Operating Professionals. *Source*: Cerberus Capital Web site

---

[5]Charles Duhigg, "Can Private Equity Build a Public Face?" *New York Times*, December 24, 2006 and Cerberus Web site.

[6]"What's Bigger than Cisco, Coke or McDonald's?" *BusinessWeek Online*, October 3, 2005.

[7]"Cerberus to KKR: Eat Our Dust," *BusinessWeek Online*, April 24, 2006.

■ ■ ■

**EXHIBIT 5** GMAC Sale Press Release

For Release: April 2, 2006

# *GM Reaches Agreement to Sell Controlling Stake in GMAC*

## *Cerberus-Led Consortium to Buy 51 Percent of GMAC Equity*

### *GM to Receive $14 Billion in Cash Over Three-Year Period*

DETROIT—General Motors Corp. (NYSE: GM) today announced it has entered into a definitive agreement to sell a 51-percent controlling interest in General Motors Acceptance Corp. (GMAC) to a consortium of investors led by Cerberus Capital Management, L.P., a private investment firm, and including Citigroup Inc., and Aozora Bank Ltd. GM expects to receive approximately $14 billion in cash from this transaction over three years, including distributions from GMAC, with an estimated $10 billion by closing.

The transaction strengthens GMAC's ability to support GM's automotive operations, improves GMAC's access to cost-effective funding, provides significant liquidity to GM and allows GM to continue to participate in the profitability of GMAC over the long term through its 49-percent ownership stake.

"We look forward to working with Cerberus to maintain and grow GMAC's traditional strong performance and contribution to the GM family," said GM chairman and chief executive officer Rick Wagoner. "This agreement is another important milestone in the turnaround of General Motors. It creates a stronger GMAC while preserving the mutually beneficial relationship between GM and GMAC. At the same time, it provides significant liquidity to support our North American turnaround plan, finance future GM growth initiatives, strengthen our balance sheet and fund other corporate priorities.

"Over the last nine months we have been aggressively implementing our North American turnaround plan," Wagoner said. "We've made some big moves, such as the health-care agreement with the United Auto Workers union; the manufacturing capacity plan; changes to our salaried health-care and pension plans; an accelerated attrition plan for hourly employees; and a complete overhaul of our marketing strategy. These bold initiatives are designed to immediately improve our competitiveness and position GM for long-term success and today's transition is a further step in that direction."

The GM board of directors approved the sale in a special meeting on Sunday which followed extensive consideration of this transaction and alternative strategies over the past several months. Speaking for the GM board, presiding director George Fisher stated, "This transaction along with the other progress GM has been making on its turnaround plan, is an important milestone. While there is still much work to be done, the GM board has great confidence in Rick Wagoner, his management team and the plan they are implementing to restore the company to profitability."

The transaction is subject to a number of U.S. and international regulatory and other approvals. The companies expect to close the transaction in the fourth quarter of 2006.

*(Continued)*

■ ■ ■

## EXHIBIT 5 GMAC Sale Press Release — Cont'd

### GM to Receive $14 Billion in Cash

The $14 billion in cash that GM is to receive as part of the transaction includes $7.4 billion from the Cerberus-led consortium at closing and an estimated $2.7 billion cash distribution from GMAC related to the conversion of most of GMAC and its U.S. subsidiaries to limited liability companies. In addition, GM will retain about $20 billion of GMAC automotive lease and retail assets and associated funding with an estimated net book value of $4 billion that will monetize over three years.

GM also will receive dividends from GMAC equivalent to its earnings prior to closing, which largely will be used to fund the repayment of various intercompany loans from GMAC. As a result of these reductions, GMAC's unsecured exposure to GM is expected to be reduced to approximately $400 million and will be capped at $1.5 billion on an ongoing basis.

GM and the consortium will invest $1.9 billion of cash in new GMAC preferred equity—$1.4 billion to be issued to GM and $500 million to the Cerberus consortium. GM also will continue to receive its 49 percent share of common dividends and other value generated by GMAC.

GM will take a non-cash pre-tax charge to earnings of approximately $1.1 billion to $1.3 billion in the second quarter of 2006 associated with the sale of 51 percent of GMAC.

### Citigroup Providing $25 Billion Syndicated Funding Facility

Citigroup will arrange two syndicated asset-based funding facilities that total $25 billion which will support GMAC's ongoing business and enhance GMAC's already strong liquidity position. Citigroup has committed $12.5 billion in the aggregate to these two facilities. The funding facilities are in addition to Citigroup's initial equity investment in GMAC.

"Citigroup has a 90-year relationship with GM and this transaction represents both an opportunity to demonstrate our ongoing commitment to its long-term success as well as an attractive investment opportunity. We are pleased to be part of this unique and strong partnership, led by Cerberus," said Michael Klein, chief executive officer of the Global Banking Unit of Citigroup Corporate and Investment Banking.

The GMAC board of directors will have 13 members—six appointed by the consortium; four appointed by GM; and three independent members. GMAC will continue to be managed by its existing executive management.

GM expects that the introduction of a new controlling investor for GMAC, new equity capital at GMAC, and significantly reduced inter-company exposures to GM will provide GMAC with a solid foundation to improve its current credit rating. GM and GMAC expect that these actions will de-link the GMAC credit ratings from those of GM.

■ ■ ■

*cash distribution from GMAC related to the conversion of most of GMAC and its U.S. subsidiaries to limited liability companies. In addition, GM will retain about $20 billion of GMAC automotive lease and retail assets and associated funding with an estimated net book value of $4 billion that will monetize over three years.*

In addition, GM and the consortium agreed to invest $1.9 billion of cash in a new GMAC preferred equity ($1.4 billion from GM and the balance from the consortium). Because a large goal of the deal for both parties was a decrease in GMAC's unsecured exposure to GM, Citigroup provided GMAC with a new $25 billion syndicated asset-backed funding facility. GM planned to continue receiving a 49 percent share of common dividends and other value generated by GMAC. A pretax charge of approximately $1.2 billion was taken by GM in the second quarter of 2006 associated with the sale. Finally, GM retained an option, exercisable for ten years after closing, to reacquire GMAC's auto finance operations subject to certain conditions, including an investment-grade credit rating at GM. (The option is summarized in Exhibit 6 and the post-acquisition GMAC credit profile, revenue diversification, and bond spreads are provided in Exhibit 7.)

## Roadblocks and Hurdles

In addition to regular state and federal regulatory issues, additional hurdles delayed the deal's closing. In July 2006 GM cleared the first major hurdle to a sale when the Pension Benefit Guaranty Corporation (PBGC) said that it would not impose GM's pension liability on the buyer of GMAC. In a public filing with the Securities and Exchange Commission, GM announced that the PBGC had given assurance that Cerberus would not be held responsible for the automaker's pension obligations. The agency, through a spokesperson, stated its satisfaction that the sale of a majority stake in GMAC was not an attempt to evade pension liabilities.

A major motivating factor for Cerberus's investment in GMAC was the assumption that it would be able to transfer GMAC's industrial bank charter to the consortium. It was widely believed (and more or less confirmed by spokespeople from both parties) that a failure to transfer the charter by the end of 2006 would result in a potential deal-breaking roadblock. When the Federal Deposit Insurance Corporation announced a six-month moratorium on approving new applications for industrial banking charters in the summer of 2006 (largely in response to retailing giant Wal-Mart's application for its own private bank), it placed a potentially crippling barrier

■ ■ ■

## EXHIBIT 6  GM Call Option Summary

- GM call option term of ten years on global auto finance business
  - Does not include mortgage and insurance operations
- Can exercise if GM ratings are investment grade or are higher than GMAC's ratings
- Exercise price greater of:
  - Fair market value
  - 9.5 times the global auto finance business net income

*Source*: GMAC Financial Services Fixed Income Investor Presentation, December 1, 2006.

■ ■ ■

in front of the deal. In mid-November 2006, however, the FDIC voted to allow GM to transfer its charter to the Cerberus-led group, clearing a major condition for the deal.

Another hurdle was only partially overcome when, in late November 2006, rating services Fitch and Standard & Poor's both upgraded GMAC one notch, to BB+. S&P also removed GMAC from CreditWatch, where it had been since October 2005. At the same time, Moody's confirmed GMAC's unchanged rating at Ba1, leaving in place their negative rating outlook. Moody's noted that GM's call option on GMAC's automotive operations represented an upside ceiling on GMAC's rating. It acknowledged, however, that GMAC's negative rating outlook could improve to stable should the firm strengthen its liquidity profile. As a significant customer, GM would still have an effect on GMAC's future rating status, however, the agencies were explicit in stating that GMAC's rating was no longer directly linked to GM's rating. Although this was a positive development, GMAC's rating as of the end of 2006 was still substantially lower than the company had hoped.

## GM's Supplier Relationships

More so than almost any other industry in the United States, automakers' relationships with their suppliers have been fraught with difficulty and discontent on both sides for the better part of the past two decades. While the U.S. auto industry faced a perfect storm of adverse business conditions, suppliers felt an almost exponential flow-through effect. As Detroit's Big Three scrambled to reduce capacity, lay off workers, and cut costs, GM and the other auto manufacturers pushed for deeper and deeper price concessions from suppliers. As a result, major suppliers such as Dana Corporation, Collins & Aikman, and Delphi Automotive, were all forced into bankruptcy. The financial crisis for U.S. auto manufacturers revealed the downside of the symbiotic relationship between car makers and their suppliers; while many suppliers were dependent on GM for their existence, GM was equally dependent on its suppliers. GM's top priority was ensuring that

■ ■ ■ ━━━━━━━━━━━━━━━━━━━━━━━━━━━━━━━━━━━━━━━━━

**EXHIBIT 7** GMAC Credit Profile, Revenue Diversification, and Five-Year Bond Spreads

*Strengthened Credit Profile*

- New $2.1 billion (face) layer of preferred equity injected
- $1 billion GM equity contribution in March 2007
- Essentially all 2007–2008 "after-tax earnings" to be retained by GMAC
- All 2009–2011 after-tax profit distributions to Cerberus to be reinvested in GMAC as preferred equity
- Certain unsecured exposure to GM in the United States capped at $1.5 billion
- Eliminated potential risks related to GM pension liability
- Substantial committed funding facilities
  - $10 billion Citibank secured facility in place
  - New $6 billion wholesale bridge facility
- Improved access to unsecured funding at lower cost of borrowing

**Gross Revenue—Business Diversification**

- Notably strong growth in diversified revenues, with about 50 percent of revenue being contributed by mortgage and insurance operations

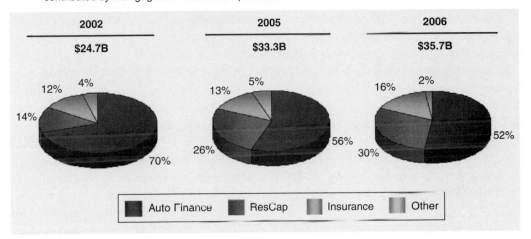

Gross revenue reflects gross financing revenues plus Insurance premiums and service revenue plus mortgage banking income plus investment income and other income. Gross revenue is not net of interest and discount expense and provision for credit losses.

**GMAC 5-Year Unsecured Bond Spreads**

- GMAC bond spreads have narrowed to the lowest level since early 2004

    ○ Market acknowledges credit de-linkage with GM

    ○ Nonetheless, GMAC 5-year spreads still 90 bps above those of the BBB– composite

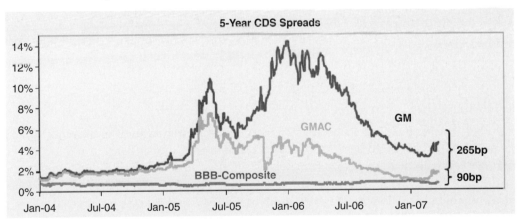

*Source:* GMAC Financial Services, 2007 Investor Forum

production did not stop, as a shutdown would lead to estimated weekly losses in the billions of dollars.[8] As such, its solution essentially was to throw money at the problem through subordinated loans and extended financing—anything to prevent production stoppage.

These bailouts and infusions of capital were an effective bandaid in keeping Big Three production going. However, the dynamics of raising financing changed as the trillion-dollar hedge fund industry became an important new source of cash for the industry. Private investment funds descended on the distressed supplier industry like never before, buying up debt and offering debt financing, including second-lien loans, to these beleaguered companies.

Second-lien loans offered hedge funds—who are "not necessarily driven by internal credit risk ratings"[9]—greater security than other forms of debt, with only slightly lower returns. With the same rights and covenants as a bank loan, this class of debt, as its name suggests, is second in line in terms of repayment priority.[10] Second-lien loans offered returns of about 10 to 15 percent compared to less-secured mezzanine debt rates in the mid- to high teens and traditional bank loans with substantially lower returns. Second liens are usually secured by either incremental dollars against the same collateral pool as first liens or, more often, by an alternative pool of collateral. In this second scenario, for example, should the first-lien loan be secured by working capital assets (receivables, inventory, etc.), the second-lien loan would use fixed assets (property, plant, and equipment) as collateral (see Exhibit 8).[11]

Hedge funds brought much needed funding to the auto suppliers, but they often also introduced disparate priorities to those of the suppliers' traditional providers of debt. With enormous capital behind them, funds such as Appaloosa Management, Davidson Kempner, and legendary buyout investors Carl Ichan and Wilbur Ross swooped into the troubled sector and threw their considerable weight around. Their approach to providing financing and their exposure to—and perspective on—troubled suppliers were often at odds with those of traditional lenders. David Tepper was one of the most active players through his hedge fund, Appaloosa Management. After investing nearly 10 percent in Delphi's equity immediately following its bankruptcy filing at the end of 2005, Appaloosa became an active player in the supplier's bankruptcy proceedings, leading an equity committee as a voice in the firm's restructuring.[12] The Appaloosa-led committee (partnered with several investors, including Cerberus) reached an agreement in December 2006 to invest $3.4 billion in Delphi and reorganize the company.[13]

## Cerberus Builds an Even Bigger Auto Stage

In May 2007 Cerberus added to its auto industry investment portfolio by agreeing to acquire 80.1 percent of Chrysler Holdings for about $7.8 billion from Daimler Benz, nearly a decade after the German company had paid approximately $36 billion for Chrysler. In this groundbreaking transaction Cerberus stood to gain not only a large, iconic auto manufacturer but also Chrysler Financial, enabling the potential combination of GMAC and Chrysler Financial. This gave Cerberus an approximately 11 percent market share in auto loans, more than double the market

---

[8]"GM Boosts Profit But Not Recovery," *Boston Globe*, October 25, 2006.

[9]"Capital Eyes: Completing the Capital Structure with a Second-Lien Loan," Bank of America e-newsletter, April 2003.

[10]Ibid.

[11]Ibid.

[12]Micheline Maynard, "Equity Firms to Invest up to $3.4 Billion in Delphi," *International Herald Tribune*, December 18, 2006.

[13]David Welch, "Bankruptcy Becomes Delphi," *BusinessWeek Online*, January 15, 2007.

**EXHIBIT 8   Second-Lien Loans at a Glance**

| Secondary Lien Loans | Asset-Based | Cash Flow-Based |
|---|---|---|
| Priority Structure | Secondary credit behind senior lenders. | Secondary credit behind senior lenders. |
| | Assets serve as collateral—such as accounts receivable, inventory, machinery, equipment, real estate, and intellectual property. | Financing is based on company's going concern value instead of asset liquidation values. |
| Term | 3–5 years. | 3–7 years. |
| Pricing | LIBOR plus 5–12%. | LIBOR plus 5–15%. |
| | Pricing is typically a function of asset quality and supportability of advance rates. | Pricing is typically a function of size, availability of credit ratings, and financial sponsor support. |
| | | Secondary market liquidity afforded to larger tranches ($50 million+) with acceptable risk ratings; minimum B3 (Moody's) or B– (S&P), and equity sponsor support will drive more competitive pricing. Increased leverage or weaker enterprise valuation will typically increase spreads. |
| Benefits | Additional source of financing, with no equity dilution or additional covenants. | Additional source of financing, with no equity dilution or additional covenants. |
| | Also offers flexibility in loan amortization schedule. | Also offers flexibility in loan amortization schedule. |

Source: GE Commercial Finance

share of Ford Motor Credit, the next largest auto lender. As a result, Cerberus expected to achieve the combined benefits of dominant market share and significant cost and operating synergies. Cerberus was now positioned to create even more meaningful future earnings from its original investment in GMAC.

## The Dream Becomes a Nightmare

After acquiring Chrysler, Cerberus piled about $20 billion of debt onto the company's balance sheet, mortgaging all available plants and property to secure this debt. When gasoline prices shot up to $4 a gallon in 2008, consumers started buying smaller cars and hybrids—unfortunately, Chrysler's model line was heavily skewed toward "gas-guzzling" trucks, SUVs, and minivans. At the same time, the subprime mortgage crisis worsened and credit tightened, making it harder for consumers to fund large purchases such as cars. In addition, Chrysler Financial had a difficult time borrowing to fund car loans, given the parent company's increasingly dire financial condition. By summer of that year, Cerberus's plan to turn Chrysler Financial into a highly profitable finance firm had unraveled. Banks forced the company to discontinue leases and loans to customers with marginal credit. This, in turn, negatively impacted Chrysler's ability to sell cars and trucks. During August 2008, Chrysler's sales dropped 35 percent. In September Lehman Brothers collapsed and Wall Street fell into turmoil. With customers staying away from dealerships, Chrysler slashed production, revenue plunged, and the company raked up huge losses every day.

By November, Chrysler's sales were in a free fall and Chrysler Financial practically stopped providing loans altogether, leaving dealers with no financing source. At this point, Cerberus came to the realization that an auto financing business was viable only if it is connected with a healthy car company. At the end of March 2009, the U.S. government gave Chrysler thirty days to finalize a deal to merge with Fiat, which required an agreement with the United Auto Workers (UAW) to achieve significant cost cutting. By the middle of April, the only major hurdle was the resolution of $6.9 billion in debt obligations. The U.S. Treasury offered $2.25 billion in cash in exchange for giving up the debt. However, the forty-five banks and hedge fund creditors refused to agree, throwing the company into bankruptcy court and destroying any remaining value for Cerberus and its partners.

The action by the banks and hedge funds angered President Obama, who stated that these creditors "decided to hold out for the prospect of an unjustified, taxpayer-funded bailout."[14] Rep. John Dingell, a Michigan Democrat, called the creditors "rogue hedge funds" and "vultures," who "will now be dealt with accordingly in court."[15] The bankruptcy court strategy by the Obama administration was to give the UAW's retiree health fund cash at more than 50 cents on the dollar and majority ownership of Chrysler, while limiting the cash payment to the bank and hedge fund creditors to $2 billion and not providing any equity ownership in Chrysler (even though the creditor claims exceeded the UAW claims prior to entering bankruptcy court). The creditors indicated their intention to argue in court that this outcome meant that the United States was overriding contract law, bankruptcy law, and constitutional protections against the seizure of private property.

In June 2009 GM followed Chrysler into bankruptcy court after a majority of its bondholders refused to exchange their $27 billion in debt for equity in the company. Prior to this event, GMAC's effort to survive included converting to a bank holding company as it accepted $7 billion in federal bailout funds and then changing the name of its online bank to Ally Bank, because this name "conveys the sense of a trusted partner,"[16] according to new chief marketing officer Sanjay Gupta. GM's bankruptcy weighed heavily on GMAC and forced GM and Cerberus to significantly reduce their combined ownership of the company, opening the door for majority ownership by the Treasury.

The original separation of GMAC from GM was intended to preserve, and eventually increase, GMAC's credit ratings so that it could borrow funds at a competitive rate. This effort ultimately proved unsuccessful, as did the effort to achieve scale and profitability by combining GMAC with Chrysler Financial. Cerberus's dream investment in the U.S auto industry turned into its worst nightmare.

---

[14]White House press release, "Remarks By the President on the Auto Industry," April 30, 2009, http://www .whitehouse.gov/the_press_office/remarks-by-the-president-on-the-Auto-Industry.

[15]Neil King Jr. and Jeffrey McCracken, "Chrysler Pushed Into Fiat's Arms," *Wall Street Journal.com*, May 1, 2009.

[16]Aparajita Saha-Bubna, "GMAC Will Change the Name of Its Bank," *Wall Street Journal.com*, May 15, 2009.

# Exhibit Sources

**List of sources and the exhibits/footnotes that reference them**
Note: An exhibit may have more than one source, in which case the exhibit is listed more than once.

(2003). *Implications of the Growth of Hedge Funds.* Staff Report to the United States Securities and Exchange Commission.
Ch11, footnote #1

*PEI 50 (2009).* Private Equity International.
20.11   20.12   20.13   20.14   20.15

(Jan 2009). *The Globalization of Alternative Investments Working Papers Volume 2: The Global Economic Impact of Private Equity Report 2009.* World Economic Forum.
18.1

Absolute Return Billion Dollar Club, March 2009 rankings
1.18   11.6

Analyst reports
18.9   18.11

Annual Report: Goldman Sachs
1.8   1.16

Annual Report: JPMorgan Chase
1.9

Asness, C., Krail, R., & Liew, J. (2001). Do Hedge Funds Hedge? *Journal of Portfolio Management, 28,* 6–19.
Ch11, footnote #2

Bank for International Settlements
7.5

Bankruptcy Abuse Prevention & Consumer Protection Act of 2005
2.7

Basile, D. (2006). Convertible bonds: Convertible arbitrage versus long-only strategies. *Morgan Stanley Investment Management Journal, 2*(1).
12.4

Capital IQ
18.17 18.18   Ch18, footnote #1

Castillo, J., & McAniff, P. (2007). *The Practitioner's Guide to Investment Banking, Mergers & Acquisitions, Corporate Finance.* Circinus Business Press.
4.6

Chan, Getmansky, Haas, & Lo, (2006). Do Hedge Funds Increase Systemic Risk? *Federal Reserve of Atlanta Economic Review, 4th Quarter.*
`Ch14, footnote #2

(2008). Committee on Taxation. Estimated Revenue Effects Of H.R. 6275, The 'Alternative Minimum Tax Relief Act Of 2008,' Scheduled For Markup By The Committee On Ways And Means On June 18, 2008" (JCX-51-08).
Ch14, footnote #3

Commodity Systems Inc.
1.5   9.4   11.8   11.12   11.16   16.8   20.5

Company press releases
8.1   18.7   18.8

Connor, G., Goldberg, L., & Korajczyk, R. *Portfolio Risk Analysis.* Princeton University Press, (forthcoming).
Ch11, footnote #3

Credit Suisse/Tremont
11.12

Dealogic
3.2   3.3   3.9   3.14   3.15   4.1   8.2   8.5   8.6   8.7   16.12   16.13   16.16   16.19   16.20

Deponte, K (2007, September). "Hung Bridge" Funds. *Probitas Partners.*
10.9

(2009). Deutsche Bank roadshow presentation from February 19–20.
1.4   10.2

Ferguson, R., & Laster, D. (2006). Hedge Funds and Systemic Risk. *Banque de France Financial Stability Review.*
Ch11, footnote #4

Fitch
3.6   7.3

Francis, J. C., Toy, W. W., & Gregg Whittaker, J. (1999). *The Handbook of Equity Derivatives.* John Wiley and Sons.
9.3   9.5   9.6   9.7

Gotham Consulting Partners LLC
20.7   20.8   20.9   20.10

Greenwood, R., & Schor, M. (2009). Investor Activism and Takeovers. *Journal of Financial Economics*, 92, 362–375.
Ch12, footnote #1

Grosvenor Capital Management
11.17   14.1

Hedge Fund Research, Inc.
11.3   11.4   11.8   12.2   13.3   15.1   15.3   15.4   15.5   15.6   15.7

Hennessee Group, LLC
11.5

Highbridge Capital Management, LLC
12.5

Ibbotson, R., & Chen, P. (2006). *The A,B,Cs of Hedge Funds: Alphas, Betas and Costs.*
Ch11, footnote #5

Institutional Investor
8.4

Morgan, J. P. (2004). US Fixed Income Markets 2005 Outlook.  Spreads data as of November 18.
5.5

Jenner & Block LLP
2.2

Kaplan, S. N., & Strömberg, P. (2009, Winter). Leveraged Buyouts and Private Equity. *Journal of Economic Perspectives*, 23(1), 129.
19.3

Mallon, P. C.
14.4

McDonald, R. L. (2006). *Derivatives Markets*. Prentice Hall.
9.1

McKinsey Global Institute: Farrell, D., et al. (2007). *The New Power Brokers: How Oil, Asia, Hedge Funds and Private Equity Are Shaping the Global Capital Markets*. McKinsey Global Institute.
11.1   11.11   11.14   11.5   11.7   12.1   14.3   16.6   16.7   18.21   18.22

McKinsey Global Institute: Farrell, D., et al. (2008). *The New Power Brokers: Gaining Clout in Turbulent Markets*. McKinsey Global Institute.
10.5   10.8

McKinsey Global Institute: Roxburgh, C., et al. (2009). *The New Power Brokers: How Oil, Asia, Hedge Funds and Private Equity Are Are Faring in the Financial Crisis*. McKinsey Global Institute.
10.4   10.6   10.7   11.10   11.2   11.9   14.2   15.2   16.1   16.22   16.23   16.6

Metrick, A., & Yasuda, A. (2009). The Economics of Private Equity Funds. *Review of Financial Studies, Forthcoming*, June 9.
16.2

Mitchell, M. L., & Pulvino, T. C. Characteristics of Risk and Return in Risk Arbitrage. *Journal of Finance, 56*, 2135–2176.
12.9

Moody's
3.67.3

Morgan Stanley
3.10    5.1    13.1    13.4    13.9    14.5    19.6    19.7

Stanley, M. (2009). *Industry and Regional Coverage*. Morgan Stanley. Web. 25 Aug.
1.11

Stanley, M. (2009). *Product Overview Services*. Morgan Stanley. Web. 25 Aug.
1.12

Morgan Stanley Financial Sponsors Group
16.13    16.14

Morningstar, Inc.
20.5

Morrison & Foerster LLP
2.3    2.4    14.4

MSCI Barra
8.3

NYT. (2007). DealBook, "Third Bear Stearns Fund Skids on Mortgages." *New York Times*.
11.15

Preqin
16.11

Press reports
15.11    16.9    16.15    18.3    18.7    18.8    18.10    18.16    18.17    20.17

Reuters Loan Pricing Corp.
10.9

S&P's Leveraged Lending Review
18.5    18.6    18.15    16.4    16.5

Schell, J. M. (1999). Private Equity Funds: Business Structure and Operations. *Law Journal Press*, 2–16.
19.4

SEC filings
1.2  1.3  1.4  1.5  5.9  5.10  6.1  6.2  10.2  10.3  10.9  13.5  15.9  15.10  15.12  16.10
18.4  18.9  18.14  18.15  18.18  18.19  18.20  20.2  20.3  20.4

Sir John Gieve, Deputy Governor, Bank of England. 17 Oct. 2006 speech on Hedge Funds and Financial Stability given at the HEDGE 2006 Conference.
Ch14, footnote #1

Slater, D. (2008). Judge Kaplan Reprimands Hedge Funds in Takeover Battle with CSX. *The Wall Street Journal*, June 12.
4.3

Sovereign Wealth Fund Institute
8.8

Standard & Poor's
3.6  7.1  7.2  7.3  16.12  16.13  16.17  16.18  16.19

The Carlyle Group. (2009, September 24). *Assets Under Management. The Carlyle Group.* Web.
20.16

Thomson Financial
18.2

Thomson Reuters; Morgan Stanley
18.23

BusinessWeek: Thornton, E., et al. (2005, October 3). What's Bigger Than Cisco, Coke or McDonald's? *BusinessWeek*, .
15.11

Training the Street, Inc.
17.1  17.2  17.4  17.5  17.6  19.2

Tunick, B. E. (2005). Google Goes Its Own Way: Novel Dutch auction had twists and turns all the way to IPO. *IDD*, 17 Jan.
3.11

U.S. Securities and Exchange Commission
2.1  2.5  2.6  2.8  2.9

Wachtell, L., Rosen, & Katz. (2009). *memo from Martin Lipton*, "Takeover Response Checklist and Dealing with Activist Hedge Funds".
13.2

World Federation of Exchanges
7.4

WSJ: Lattman, P. (2009). Lacking Leverage, Firms Embrace EBOs. *Wall Street Journal*.
20.1

WSJ: Moore, H. N. (2008). Bill Ackman Part II: Eight Easy Steps to Becoming a Short-Seller. *Wall Street Journal*.
13.8

WSJ: Zuckerman, G., & Strasburg, J. (2009). For Many Hedge Funds, No Escape. *Wall Street Journal*.
11.13

DPS
1.1   1.6   1.7   1.10   1.13   1.14   1.15   1.17   2.10   3.1   3.4   3.5   3.7   3.8   3.12   3.13   3.16   3.17   4.2   4.4   4.5   4.7   4.8   5.2   5.3   5.4   5.6   5.7   5.8   6.2   6.3   9.1   9.2   9.8   9.9   10.1   10.9   12.1   12.3   12.6   12.7   12.8   12.10   12.11   12.12   12.13   12.14   12.15   12.16   12.17   12.18   12.19   12.20   12.21   12.22   13.6   13.7   15.8   16.3   16.21   17.3   17.7   17.8   17.9   17.10   17.11   17.12   17.13   17.14   17.15   17.16   17.17   17.18   17.19   17.20   17.21   18.12   18.13   19.1   19.5   20.6

# Reading List

(2003). *Implications of the Growth of Hedge Funds*. Staff Report to the United States Securities and Exchange Commission. U.S. Securities and Exchange Commission.

(2008). *Estimated Revenue Effects Of H.R. 6275, The 'Alternative Minimum Tax Relief Act Of 2008,' Scheduled For Markup By The Committee On Ways And Means On June 18, 2008*. United States Congress Joint Committee on Taxation (JCX-51-08).

(2009). *PEI 50 2009*. Private Equity International.

(2009). The Globalization of Alternative Investments Working Papers Volume 2: The Global Economic Impact of Private Equity Report 2009. World Economic Forum.

Asness, C., Krail, R., & Liew, J. (2001). Do Hedge Funds Hedge? *Journal of Portfolio Management*, 28, 6–19.

Basile, D. (2006). Convertible bonds: Convertible arbitrage versus long-only strategies. *Morgan Stanley Investment Management Journal*, 2(1).

Brealey, R., Myers, S., & Allen, F. (2006). *Principles of Corporate Finance* (8th ed.). McGraw-Hill.

Biggs, B. (2006). *Hedge Hogging*. John Wiley & Sons, Inc.

Bookstaber, R. (2007). *A Demon of Our Own Design*. John Wiley & Sons, Inc.

Castillo, J., & McAniff, P. (2007). *The Practitioner's Guide to Investment Banking, Mergers & Acquisitions, Corporate Finance*. Circinus Business Press.

Chan, G., Haas, , & Lo, (2006). Do Hedge Funds Increase Systemic Risk? *Federal Reserve of Atlanta Economic Review*, 4th Quarter.

Connor, G., Goldberg, L., & Korajczyk, R. (forthcoming). *Portfolio Risk Analysis*. Princeton University Press.

Deponte, K. (2007). *"Hung Bridge" Funds*. Probitas Partners.

Ellis, C. D. (2008). *The Partnership: The Making of Goldman Sachs*. The Penguin Press.

Farrell, D., et al. (2007). *The New Power Brokers: How Oil, Asia, Hedge Funds and Private Equity Are Shaping the Global Capital Markets*. McKinsey Global Institute.

Farrell, D., et al. (2008). *The New Power Brokers: Gaining Clout in Turbulent Markets*. McKinsey Global Institute.

Ferguson, R., & Laster, D. (2006). Hedge Funds and Systemic Risk. *Banque de France Financial Stability Review*.

Flanagan, C. (2004). *J.P. Morgan US Fixed Income Markets 2005 Outlook*. J. P. Morgan Securities Inc.

Francis, J. C., Toy, W. W., & Gregg Whittaker, J. (1999). *The Handbook of Equity Derivatives* (Revised ed.). John Wiley & Sons.

Greenwood, R., & Schor, M. (2009). Investor Activism and Takeovers. *Journal of Financial Economics*, 92, 362–375.

Ibbotson, R., & Chen, P. (2006). The A,B,Cs of Hedge Funds: Alphas, Betas and Costs. *Yale ICF Working Paper*.

Kaplan, S. N., & Strömberg, P. (2009). Leveraged Buyouts and Private Equity. *Journal of Economic Perspectives*, 23(1), 129 Winter.

Koller, T., Goedhart, M., & Wessels, D. McKinsey & Company, Inc. (2005). *Valuation: Measuring and Managing the Value of Companies* (4th ed.). John Wiley & Sons.

Langley, M. (2006). *Tearing Down the Walls*. Free Press.

Lipton, M. (2009). *Takeover Response Checklist and Dealing with Activist Hedge Funds*. Wachtell, Lipton, Rosen & Katz Memo.

McDonald, R. L. (2006). *Derivatives Markets* (2nd ed.). Prentice Hall.

Metrick, A., & Yasuda, A. (Forthcoming) (2009). The Economics of Private Equity Funds. *Review of Financial Studies*.

Mitchell, M. L., & Pulvino, T. C. Characteristics of Risk and Return in Risk Arbitrage. *Journal of Finance*, 56, 2135–2176.

Roxburgh, C., et al. (2009). *The New Power Brokers: How Oil, Asia, Hedge Funds and Private Equity Are Are Faring in the Financial Crisis*. McKinsey Global Institute.

Schell, J. M. (1999). *Private Equity Funds: Business Structure and Operations* (pp. 2–18). Law Journal Press.

Sir Gieve, J. Deputy Governor, Bank of England. 17 Oct. 2006 speech on Hedge Funds and Financial Stability given at the HEDGE 2006 Conference.

# References

(2003). *Implications of the Growth of Hedge Funds*. Staff Report to the United States Securities and Exchange Commission. U.S. Securities and Exchange Commission.

(2008). *Estimated Revenue Effects Of H.R. 6275, The 'Alternative Minimum Tax Relief Act Of 2008,' Scheduled For Markup By The Committee On Ways And Means On June 18, 2008*. United States Congress Joint Committee on Taxation (JCX-51-08).

(2009). Goldman Sachs 2008 Annual Report.

(2009). JPMorgan Chase & Co. 2008 Annual Report.

(2009). *Fourth Annual Private Equity Survey*. Gotham Consulting Partners LLC.

(2009). *PEI 50 2009*. Private Equity International.

(2009). The Globalization of Alternative Investments Working Papers Volume 2: The Global Economic Impact of Private Equity Report 2009. World Economic Forum.

Asness, C., Krail, R., & Liew, J. (2001). Do Hedge Funds Hedge? *Journal of Portfolio Management*, 28, 6–19.

Bank for International Settlements

Basile, D. (2006). Convertible bonds: Convertible arbitrage versus long-only strategies. *Morgan Stanley Investment Management Journal*, 2(1).

Brealey, R., Myers, S., & Allen, F. (2006). *Principles of Corporate Finance* (8th ed.). McGraw-Hill.

Castillo, J., & McAniff, P. (2007). *The Practitioner's Guide to Investment Banking, Mergers & Acquisitions, Corporate Finance*. Circinus Business Press.

Chan, G., Haas, , & Lo, (2006). Do Hedge Funds Increase Systemic Risk? *Federal Reserve of Atlanta Economic Review*, 4th Quarter.

Connor, G., Goldberg, L., & Korajczyk, R. (forthcoming). *Portfolio Risk Analysis*. Princeton University Press.

Credit Suisse Tremont Index LLC.

DealBook. (2007). Third Bear Stearns Fund Skids on Mortgages. *New York Times*, 1 Aug.

Deponte, K. (2007). *"Hung Bridge" Funds*. Probitas Partners.

Farrell, D., et al. (2007). *The New Power Brokers: How Oil, Asia, Hedge Funds and Private Equity Are Shaping the Global Capital Markets*. McKinsey Global Institute.

Farrell, D., et al. (2008). *The New Power Brokers: Gaining Clout in Turbulent Markets*. McKinsey Global Institute.

Ferguson, R., & Laster, D. (2006). Hedge Funds and Systemic Risk. *Banque de France Financial Stability Review*.

Flanagan, C. (2004). *J. P. Morgan US Fixed Income Markets 2005 Outlook*. J. P. Morgan Securities Inc.

Francis, J. C., Toy, W. W., & Gregg Whittaker, J. (1999). *The Handbook of Equity Derivatives* (Revised ed.). John Wiley & Sons.

Greenwood, R., & Schor, M. (2009). Investor Activism and Takeovers. *Journal of Financial Economics*, 92, 362–375.

Grosvenor Capital Management.

Hedge Fund Research, Inc.

Hennessee Group, LLC.

Ibbotson, R., & Chen, P. (2006). *The A,B,Cs of Hedge Funds: Alphas, Betas and Costs. Yale ICF Working Paper.*

Kaplan, S. N., & Strömberg, P. (2009). Leveraged Buyouts and Private Equity. *Journal of Economic Perspectives, 23*(1), 129 Winter.

Koller, T., Goedhart, M., & Wessels, D. McKinsey & Company, Inc. (2005). *Valuation: Measuring and Managing the Value of Companies* (4th ed.). John Wiley & Sons.

Lattman, P. (2009). Lacking Leverage, Firms Embrace EBOs. *Wall Street Journal,* 12 Mar.

Lipton, M. (2009). *Takeover Response Checklist and Dealing with Activist Hedge Funds.* Wachtell, Lipton, Rosen & Katz Memo.

McDonald, R. L. (2006). *Derivatives Markets* (2nd ed.). Prentice Hall.

Metrick, A., & Yasuda, A. (Forthcoming) (2006). The Economics of Private Equity Funds. *Review of Financial Studies.*

Mitchell, M. L., & Pulvino, T. C. Characteristics of Risk and Return in Risk Arbitrage. *Journal of Finance,* 56, 2135–2176.

Moore, H. N. (2008). Bill Ackman Part II: Eight Easy Steps to Becoming a Short-Seller. *Wall Street Journal,* 12 Jun.

Roxburgh, C., et al. (2009). *The New Power Brokers: How Oil, Asia, Hedge Funds and Private Equity Are Are Faring in the Financial Crisis.* McKinsey Global Institute.

Schell, J. M. (1999). *Private Equity Funds: Business Structure and Operations* (pp. 2–18). Law Journal Press.

Sharpe, W. F. (1964). Capital Asset Prices: A Theory of Market Equilibrium Under Conditions of Risk. *Journal of Finance,* 19(3), 425–442.

Sir Gieve, J. Deputy Governor, Bank of England. 17 Oct. 2006 speech on Hedge Funds and Financial Stability given at the HEDGE 2006 Conference.

Slater, D. (2008). Judge Kaplan Reprimands Hedge Funds in Takeover Battle with CSX. *The Wall Street Journal,* 12 Jun.

S&P Leveraged Lending Review.

Thornton, E., et al. (2005). What's Bigger Than Cisco, Coke or McDonald's? *BusinessWeek,* 3 Oct.

Training the Street, Inc.

Tunick, B. E. (2005). Google Goes Its Own Way: Novel Dutch auction had twists and turns all the way to IPO. *IDD,* 17 Jan.

World Federation of Exchanges.

Zuckerman, G., & Strasburg, J. (2009). For Many Hedge Funds, No Escape. *Wall Street Journal,* 2 Jan.

# Index